PLAN, CONTRACT, AND BUILD YOUR OWN HOME

Richard M. Scutella
Dave Heberle

Illustrations by
Jay Marcinowski
and Jessica Heberle

Fifth Edition

New York   Chicago   San Francisco
Lisbon   London   Madrid   Mexico City
Milan   New Delhi   San Juan   Seoul
Singapore   Sydney   Toronto

Library of Congress Cataloging-in-Publication Data

Scutella, Richard M.
  How to plan, contract, and build your own home / Richard M. Scutella, Dave Heberle.—5th ed.
    p.   cm.
  ISBN 978-0-07-160330-0 (alk. paper)
  1. House construction—Amateurs' manuals. 2. Building—Superintendence—Amateurs'
manuals. 3. Contractors—Selection and appointment—Amateurs' manuals. I. Heberle, Dave.
II. Title.
  TH4815.S395   2010
  690'.837—dc22

                                                                  2010024315

1 2 3 4 5 6 7 8 9 0   DOC/DOC 1 6 5 4 3 2 1 0

ISBN 978-0-07-160330-0
MHID 0-07-160330-1

Sponsoring Editor: Joy Bramble
Editing Supervisor: Stephen M. Smith
Production Supervisor: Pamela A. Pelton
Acquisitions Coordinator: Michael Mulcahy
Project Manager: Patricia Wallenburg, TypeWriting
Copy Editor: James Madru
Proofreader: Teresa Barensfeld
Indexer: Judy Davis
Art Director, Cover: Jeff Weeks
Composition: TypeWriting

Printed and bound by RR Donnelley.

McGraw-Hill books are available at special quantity discounts to use as premiums and sales
promotions, or for use in corporate training programs. To contact a representative, please e-mail
us at bulksales@mcgraw-hill.com.

This book is printed on acid-free paper.

CONTENTS

DISCARDED

This book is, technically, the first "green" edition of *How to Plan, Contract, and Build Your Own Home*. However, it's presented as simply the fifth edition. Why? Because in the near future—nearer than you might think, but probably not within the life expectancy of the edition you are holding right now—"greenness" marketing factors in construction books will become passé, outdated, redundant, assumed, expected, and unnecessary. It's becoming plain to practically everyone that if a company doesn't already align itself with green building design, principles of sustainability, energy savings, and waste reduction, its service or products will be bumped aside by others that do.

Today, greenness is everywhere: on television and radio and in magazines, trade journals, books, and newspapers. It's in curricula from grade schools to graduate schools in small to large universities. It's literally permeating politics, rewriting municipal permit procedures and regulations. It's attracting a great deal of interest and money from all angles. There are high hopes of creating green jobs that by their very nature are difficult to outsource.

But is green building for *your* home construction project, and if so, at what level? What level of greenness is for you? The government, with its great resources (really *our* resources, recycled), sometimes seemingly unlimited, can afford to pay a premium for technologies that, once paid for, can supply alternative energy for a relatively low cost—as long as the developmental and capital expenses are not factored in. But your pockets may not be as deep.

Fortunately, there are many green design elements that can be included at minimal or reasonable cost. Passive-solar elements, for instance, or highly efficient heating and cooling systems, effective insulating materials, and many new construction techniques do not require excessive expenditures.

Then there's the question of *when* to go green. Do you wait for additional technological advances, perhaps for some revolutionary wind or solar or biomass fuel invention that creates affordability for all? When any new technology comes out, the same question is asked: Buy brand-new technology at expensive prices? Or wait until new and improved models become so available and inexpensive that almost anyone can afford them? Look at cell phones. When they first came out, you practically needed backpack straps to carry them; they were extremely costly and bulky, but they could make phone calls. Now, what self-respecting 13-year-old would be without his or her own cell phone—happily texting away, taking digital photos, playing video games, listening to music, all while downloading stuff from the Internet? Plus it fits in a shirt pocket. With green homes, you needn't wait any longer. They're available now, and they're affordable.

This fifth edition, while keeping true to its original intent as a practical guide to planning and building a new home, identifies additional green products and systems available for use within that process—many of which also can be used for retrofitting an existing dwelling, additions, and remodeling jobs. Each chapter has been restructured, where needed, to focus on green points.

Over 20 years have passed since the editors at McGraw-Hill received the manuscript for the first edition of this book. Back then, energy efficiency was not a topic to be dwelt on by most home builders or home buyers; the same with the second edition that came out in 1991. The third edition, published in 2000, received a general overhaul, with numerous chapter upgrades and many new sections. Still, there was no clamor for energy efficiencies. Manufacturers continued to get better at what they did, though—designing and making innovative home products. The fourth edition came out in 2005. Conditions at that time finally demanded a concentrated focus on energy conservation. To help ease the pain of rising energy prices, the fourth edition featured practical information on construction details that saved home owners energy and money. A few years after the fourth edition, drivers in the United States started paying four and five dollars for a gallon of unleaded gasoline. The cost of all fuels followed gasoline up and out of sight. The economy started doing somersaults, with portfolios and 401k's shrinking drastically and a housing market that deconstructed from one coast to the other. Mortgage loans became harder to get as credit tightened up once bank after bank disappeared or received bailouts.

Now this edition, the fifth, is thinking green. It adds newer cost-effective ways to include energy-saving components in a new home. They're discussed in practically every chapter.

As in the previous editions, the importance of quality materials and components will be reviewed throughout this book. Historically, most minimum building codes could be satisfied with economy-grade materials. *Economy grade* is a misleading term at best because materials in this class actually end up costing *more* than materials of high quality owing to the frequent maintenance and repairs needed and shorter life spans. This can mean early replacements, all at extra cost and inconvenience to the home owner. Unnecessary replacements are definitely not a green characteristic. Marginal products, because they're less durable, also can lead to a very annoying and even uncomfortable house. Unfortunately, marginal-quality materials are found not only in low-priced houses but also in many high-priced dwellings. Today's green construction materials and techniques are all about quality.

High-quality flooring, paneling, wiring, heating, and many other products cost only a little more, by and large, than the same products of marginal quality. Certainly, the installation costs are about the same in either case; an identical amount of labor is required to lay a new roof of the best or worst asphalt shingles. All things considered, studies indicate that the base price of a house built with high-quality green materials will run only about 8 to 10 percent more than an identical economy-grade, nongreen dwelling. But even those products, when put together incorrectly, will not result in an energy-efficient green dwelling. Never assume that just because high-quality green materials and products are selected the resulting home will be green and energy-efficient.

There's more to green construction than simply using green components. But it's not that much more. It's just understanding some simple but very important concepts and paying attention to construction details. You'll see throughout the following chapters that building green is within everyone's grasp. It doesn't need to be costly, but it can be if you want. Energy efficiency does not necessarily require a mysterious recipe of wind turbines and costly cutting-edge heating and cooling systems. There are plenty of other ways to build green using materials, products, and methods just a little bit beyond what has been employed traditionally within the home construction industry.

And whenever another green project has been completed, it's a great feeling—building responsibly and saving money on energy bills.

ABOUT THE AUTHORS

Richard M. Scutella has written several books on new construction, home buying, home maintenance, and safety, including McGraw-Hill's *Homebuyer's Checklist*, Second Edition, and is the co-author of the first four editions of this book. He has designed and supervised the construction of many new homes.

Dave Heberle is the author of McGraw-Hill's *Construction Safety Manual* and the co-author of the first four editions of this book. A former environmental and safety consultant, he currently manages investment real estate.

The Green Home

The four chapters of Part 1 introduce the green movement and green home and present a number of energy-efficient home-building systems, strategies, and steps. Since there is no singularly best way to acquire or build green, a person's or family's individual projects are best custom tailored to satisfy particular needs and goals obtainable through available resources. Some green home construction or remodeling plans require intensive investments in research and design, involving do-it-yourself skills or learning as you go. Other green road maps rely on experienced contractors and subcontractors who bring already-designed and professionally installed components and building systems into play, and trade greater initial outlays for quicker completion times. The best plan for you will likely be formulated after pertinent questions are carefully considered, such as: Do you have plenty of free time? Or will you be on a strict timetable? Do you have construction or building trade skills and experience? Is your budget tight? Can experienced friends or relatives assist or help show you the way? As Part 1 explains, there are many ways to approach and plan green construction and remodeling projects.

Researching green construction, especially now, can be fascinating. Consider supplementing your efforts with green building information from additional media streams. Do-it-yourself television networks and shows are currently concentrating on energy-efficient building products, techniques, and systems. It's difficult to find a major newspaper or magazine without articles or columns on how to build or remodel green. Visiting open houses and speaking with real estate agents and builders will likely call attention to useful variations of products or design features you may decide to employ later. It also helps to attend functions offered by local or regional green building organizations, including tours of commercial and residential projects. Electric, natural gas, and other utility companies have a stake in reducing dependency on their products and are often mandated to help customers use less energy—these energy companies can be willing partners in helping you plan green projects. Keep abreast of current information resources so you can supplement the following four chapters with available local and regional planning resources.

The Green Movement

What exactly is a green home? Simply put, it's a durable dwelling built from a high percentage of sustainable natural resources that requires as little energy as possible and provides its occupants with a healthy environment, including comfort, convenience, and security.

Some people consider the average green construction project to be lots of cutting-edge, high-tech equipment powered by expensive, complex solar- or wind-generating systems that spin electric meters backward and enable home owners to thumb their noses at electric and natural gas companies. Nothing could be further from the truth, not yet, anyway. Other people think that typical green construction is a collection of signature green products such as bamboo, rammed earth, adobe, recycled siding and roofing, and switchgrass-pellet-fueled central heating systems. Nope, not that either. You could build a leaky home with 100 percent green materials and products, and the end result would not be a green home.

Practically speaking, for all home builders except those with bottomless pockets and the desire to create architectural wonders, green construction means two words: *energy efficiency*. Everything about green construction, in some way, revolves around energy efficiency: in reduced energy demands or needs, in greater durability plus extended material and product lifespans, in resource efficiency, in sustainable energy, in reclaimed or recycled resources, in less waste and pollution, and in healthier inside natural air quality at zero or very little mechanical conditioning effort. Green construction is within the means of anyone who has the ability to build a new home or, for that matter, who can undertake the smallest or largest remodeling project. Green construction is here, right now, and waiting for you.

The term *green construction* currently has meaning. As mentioned in the Preface, at some point in the future, the word *green* likely will drop out of the picture because eventually all new home building will be assumed to be green. Owing to our changing needs, the conservation of resources and energy is becoming the rule rather than a desired exception. It's similar to the term *lead-free paint.* Not too long ago, most paints contained lead. Lead in paint helped to increase the coating's durability and ease of coverage. Unfortunately, it also caused serious health damage. Companies therefore developed water- and oil-based paints that contained no lead and proudly advertised them as "lead-free." These days, walk into a home-improvement store and ask for lead-free paint and the sales attendant probably won't know what you're talking about. Why ask for a product without an ingredient that's no longer being included anyway? And the same with asbestos-free insulation: you needn't specify because it's not offered for sale anymore. Although government regulations have disallowed its availability, the open market would have done the same thing. People would have stopped buying it when its health issues became known. Like lead-free paint or asbestos-free insulation, green construction eventually will no longer be a meaningful term.

Because we're so early in the modern green revolution, get used to seeing the word *green* for a while. Building science, inventors, designers, and manufacturers have been making huge advances in green-related fields, with products coming out every day that help to build more efficiently while reducing reliance on fuel- and power-consumption needs. Gradually, these new, efficient materials will be replacing inefficient, traditional materials, methods, and technology used in past decades. This is how the home-building industry will advance. Certain components, such as low-flush toilets, will continue to be regulated until they become part of building codes and regulations. To differentiate their product lines, manufacturers will continue to design, build, and offer for sale components that are more energy efficient that those offered by their competitors. Home builders will want to use those products—especially if they're also comparable in cost to old models—because home buyers will demand them.

WHY GREEN?

Why is this happening? Some people would like to point to altruistic reasons—that people have finally realized what can happen to the planet if we don't change our wasteful ways. This is partly true. But other reasons likely come into play with most home owners and home builders. The drive for energy efficiency has never been stronger or more immediate. The increasing cost of energy has created a tremendous market for efficient design, construction systems, and products at all building levels, from skyscrapers to hospitals, schools, churches, retail malls, government buildings, gas stations, restaurants, and houses. Who in this day and age, could imagine building a home that *won't* be energy efficient? Even individuals living in the most neutral, not-too-hot, not-too-cold climates are installing Energy Star appliances to save water and electricity wherever they can.

SURVEY YOUR AREA

On the other hand, even though green construction has been getting a lot of attention, we're certainly not there yet. Wherever you live, take a drive through the surrounding neighborhood or area, and look at the housing. Chances are, whether you're passing by single-family homes within large suburban subdivisions or multifamily townhouse or apartment buildings, rural farmhouses, or city high-rises and dwellings in between or on top of retail or commercial businesses, you're driving by buildings that are collectively wasting enormous amounts of energy, water, and residential construction resources. Try to spot some solar panels on roofs or a small windmill, either of which could be generating supplemental supplies of electric current. Or can you see a water-heating system or two that also would be installed on a rooftop, with its low-tech tube or panel heat collectors that simply absorb heat from the sun and use it constructively inside the home?

Unless you're driving past some of the very tiny proportion of homes that have already-installed sustainable-energy systems, it's not very likely that you'll see any. For all the talk of green home construction, for all the promotion, publicity, advertising, and media coverage sustainability has received, there's not much of it that's happened yet—at least that can be seen by a casual drive-by. One obvious reason is that most housing units inhabited at the present time were designed and constructed years ago, at a time when green building features were not all that important to people.

GREEN HOUSING HISTORY

Certainly, the concept of green housing is not new; it's been around as long as humans have. At first, there was only green, at least regarding what we now call *natural*, *sustainable*, and *passive-solar features*. Centuries-old communities lived in caves and adobe cliff dwellings that faced south, with generous openings that enabled low-angled winter sunshine to heat and illuminate primitive floor plans within while blistering summer rays were blocked from above by rock overhangs at the entrances. Ancient Roman baths had window openings facing the same direction to help conserve warm water. Early civilizations learned how to use the sun and the wind to help heat, cool, and ventilate their homes and developed effective methods for capturing rainwater and snowmelt.

Before the advent of electricity, people used basic fuels for elementary power needs. Wood, coal, and various fats and oils were commonly burned for warmth and light for centuries in open campfires, fireplaces, stoves, and lanterns with varying degrees of efficiency. Some space-heating appliance designs, especially in

Eastern Europe, made with intricate firebrick passages, were incredibly efficient at absorbing heat from ferociously hot fires built with split tar-pine logs harvested in Polish and Russian forests. The relatively small amounts of pollution from these localized combustion sources were dispersed by winds and later filtered and kept in check by the abundance of trees and vegetation across the land. During those times, natural resources—water, wood, coal, oil, land, and wildlife— seemed in unlimited supply.

After the industrial revolution and the beginning of modern manufacturing processes, things started heading away from green construction and lifestyles. In fact, between then and the 1960s, natural resources were harvested and used in tremendously wasteful ways. Forests were cut and cleared for lumber to build with and land to build on. Oil wells were drilled just anywhere, while manufacturing processes spewed pollution into the atmosphere and discarded solid wastes on land and in the sea. Homes were constructed at a rapid pace, and urban sprawl began. Largely thanks to the automobile, people moved away from cities— not to farm but to live in the country just for the experience. Fuels and energy supplies were bountiful and cheap and were used with abandon. Waste could be found everywhere.

A decade or so later, people were wondering where their next gallon of gasoline was coming from. Prices of fuels and energy skyrocketed, and horror stories of countries and populations left high and dry amid mixed-up, ineffective energy plans for coal, nuclear, and crude oil strategies persisted. At the same time, environmental activists cranked up their justifiable criticism of the polluting and land-wasting processes used by energy companies and manufacturers to access the planet's dwindling natural resources. This point of view had been gaining steam slowly since the early 1960s, after Rachel Carson's book *Silent Spring* was published, detailing the devastating effects that pesticides had on the environment. These energy- and natural resources–related crises collectively sent politicians, scientists, economists, and Fortune 500 corporations back to their drawing boards to search for solutions.

Meanwhile, the Department of Energy (DOE), to help stave off the oil-embargo energy crises in the 1970s and early 1980s, literally invented a whole litany of passive-solar design guidelines for homes and other buildings. The design methods and features the DOE came up with were and continue to be extremely energy efficient. Then, unfortunately (as it now seems), the energy crises ended, inexpensive energy access returned, and many people either ignored or forgot what was briefly being learned about conserving resources. The few individuals who had taken note, though, decided to continue building homes heated with passive-solar features and even tried to take things a few steps further. Since practically every home site has some kind of southern exposure, these individuals realized that the sun might as well be tapped for all the free warmth and energy it could supply. But they often earnestly planned for *too much* southern exposure and built homes with entire south sides and roofs of glass that worked wonderfully during winter but had the uncomfortable result of "cooking" the occupants all summer long from relentless overhead sunshine. Word of these "hothouses" spread and discouraged other passive-solar design dwellings from being built. These passive-solar design problems have since been solved with physics—simply by increasing the amount of insulation in walls and attic floors and decreasing the proportion of southern windows to exterior wall space to between 8 and 12 percent of total southern room interior floor coverage. During fall and winter, that same window configuration allows the desired amount of low-angled sunshine to warm the home's interior—the sun's heat is usually captured in high-mass stone, tile, or concrete floors and interior walls—and the insulation keeps that warmth from leaving too quickly at night. Summer sunshine is prevented from directly entering from high in the sky, being blocked or reflected away to avoid unwanted heat gain.

While passive-solar dwellings were being experimented with, other types of homes briefly flirted with energy-efficient designs, including A-frames, geodesic domes, tree houses, houses made of glass bottles and rubber tires, and even all-underground "earth" houses. These homes had their place on the covers of alternative back-to-the-land magazines, but they never quite caught on, mostly because the home builders were fairly set in their way of constructing stick-built homes, one at a time, in the same manner their grandfathers and fathers had done, decade after decade.

Once the energy crises of the 1970s and early 1980s passed, so did much of the public's attention to passive-solar design, even though passive solar was able to reduce the heating and cooling costs of the homes in which it was used by up to 50 percent. Looking back to the 1970s and 1980s, the preoccupation with passive-solar design, while beneficial in the long run, overshadowed a number of other factors that contributed to fuel shortages and higher energy prices. Just switching from traditional energy sources to solar failed to address the overall problem of consumption. We were using too much fuel and energy to heat with and to operate electrical appliances. Leaky buildings allowed heat to escape practically as fast as it was being produced, and a considerable amount of electricity was wasted powering products that had been grossly overengineered. Neither the systems that produced the heat or electricity nor the homes that the heat was supposed to remain in nor the products run by electricity were anywhere near efficient. Since it was just too expensive to create sustainable-energy solutions at that time, stakeholders had to look elsewhere for solutions.

People and organizations started to worry about the future of energy in their countries and in their world. They found that they shared concerns with others—with environmentalists and those who had been talking about resources conservation for years. It was a given that country and world expansion was not about to be stopped. So maybe it could be done in a more controlled, less harmful way.

Discussions spurred various studies, and soon people were becoming somewhat familiar with such terms as *acid rain*, *ozone*, *oil spills*, *greenhouse gases*, *carbon credits*, and so on. Again, unusual-looking (and sounding) homes started being constructed, such as those built from straw bales or rammed earth. Steel framing became commonplace with commercial buildings and large residential projects. Remember the A-frames? And the geodesic homes in the wilderness? People at different times have tried numerous building methods and home shapes. They've built underground, on stilts, in trees, spanning streams, and on the sides of sheer rock cliffs. Name the location, and someone has the engineering and construction skills to build a home there. But usually those dwellings far outside the norm cost considerably more than average—so much more, in fact, that most people could not afford such experimental or "pushing-the-envelope" housing.

By the 1990s and early 2000s, residential building entered a transitional phase, headed toward green construction guidelines and standards. On the one hand, largely for the sake of convenience and standardization, and partially supported by lower energy prices, good economic times, and rising stock markets, home buyers and builders had drifted back to building larger dwellings and automatically installing larger (yet, at that time, more efficient) heating and air-conditioning systems. For sure, those units had been improved as heating, cooling, and ventilating technology advanced. Then, owing to flipflopping energy prices, new, energy-efficient products again started being introduced for exterior wall systems, roofing systems, and thermal envelope construction. Product after product became available to home designers and contractors, including expandable foam insulations, building wraps, reflective coatings, and a host of improved fire-resistant materials. Furnaces, boilers, geothermal heat pumps, tankless water heaters, solar panels, small wind turbines, and a tremendous cast of supporting green materials and products started to enter the market. The days of a few decades ago, when new houses were not being well sealed, are now gone forever.

GREEN HOUSING NOW

Now that green construction once again has moved to the forefront—owing to yet another bout of increased energy prices—passive-solar design and sustainable-energy systems are getting the attention they deserve. Even if energy prices once again become suppressed, people are finally realizing that the end of plentiful fossil fuel access is in sight, and preparations must be made for alternate power systems. There are just too many organizations, government agencies, and manufacturing and service companies gearing up to green construction and lifestyles to step backward again.

The good news is that green construction, even though still in its relatively early days, is rapidly becoming mainstream and soon will be likely to completely transform or replace old construction traditions that have persisted for decades.

Both the small and large builders have seen the light and are becoming involved with various green construction organizations or are having their buildings certified in testing programs and building systems such as the DOE's Energy Star Homes or the U.S. Green Building Council's Leadership in Energy and Environmental Design (LEED) for Homes standards, the National Association of Home Builders (NAHB) *Model Green Home Building Guidelines* or *National Green Building Standard*, or other similar programs.

Give the manufacturers a little room to compete, and they'll develop and make the products that people want to buy. This is capitalism at its best. Along with infrastructure improvements that government agencies and municipalities are bound to make, manufacturers will continue to work toward making incredibly efficient materials and products available for home builders to include in affordable houses that will require less energy to operate.

GREEN MOTIVATIONS

The motivations for people to build green homes and live green lifestyles are many. Individuals feel helpless that they must pay higher and higher gas and energy prices. They're frustrated seeing Middle East empires exporting oil and practically blackmailing others to pay higher prices for it. Our country's energy dependence rubs people the wrong way and colors our behavior within world society. People doubt our motivations. They also associate terrorism with our links to oil-producing countries. There's a greater realization today of how the use of fossil fuels contributes to pollution and greenhouse gases. Al Gore's movie and numerous media efforts are bandying about, posing global warming arguments, and predicting how our children will be living in a polluted world. Eventually, the oil supply will run out, and we can't wait around for millions of years while more of it is being made. After we squeeze the last drops out of the ground or from beneath the seas, then what?

With China, India, and other emerging countries rapidly industrializing to catch up with the modern manufacturing world, how long can carbon-based fuels last? Energy efficiency is critical now in order to postpone the inevitable day when other sources of fuel and power will be needed to support our descendants' lifestyles. How long before huge quantities of sulfur and carbon dioxide and carbon monoxide coursing through our atmosphere cause irreparable damage?

GREEN HELP

To be an active participant in today's green revolution, you certainly don't have to figure out things for yourself. A number of awfully smart individuals and groups have been experimenting with and studying green construction methods, materials, systems, and products for decades. The Internet is full of green resources, by material and product categories and topics. Private and public groups and organizations have been publishing materials on green construction for years. The media climbed aboard a few years ago and routinely feature do-it-yourself television programs, dedicated magazines, trade and hardbound books, videos, and DVD sets on almost every aspect of green construction.

Green construction standards and guidelines from the large programs already mentioned are all excellent to review when planning your own green home-building project, and they present wide ranges of suggestions and ideas. Little by little, some municipalities are taking certain elements from these guidelines and writing them into their own local programs. There are similar guidelines in other countries throughout the world and have been for years—European countries recognized their need to develop sustainability and conservation guidelines and regulations long ago and also have guidelines available through the Internet.

Other easily accessible organizations focus on product types and determine whether particular products are either responsibly made or energy efficient. For example, the Forest Stewardship Council (FSC) is an international nonprofit organization that does extensive research into forests and wood products and certifies that those products are managed according to responsible guidelines. Such products as wood flooring, roofing, dimensional lumber, beams and timbers, engineered boards, fiber, and most other wood-based materials and components that receive an FSC certification stamp have been followed from forest through harvesting, manufacture, and distribution to make sure that they have come from sustainable and renewable sources. The FCS Web site and thousands of similar sites contain almost limitless information about green materials, products, and building systems and can lead you to topics that you never imagined were out there.

YOUR ROLE IN THE GREEN MOVEMENT

For the most part, right now, most existing homes still rely on the exact same system that got us into trouble in the first place. Take a look at where you currently get your fuel or power for heating, for cooling, for lighting, and for other household tasks. What kind of furnace heats your spaces? How old is it? What's the level of insulation in your home? How are the windows and doors? Do you have Energy Star appliances and light fixtures? Or not? We, as a nation and world, have a long way to go before we're living in a green culture. But it's got to begin somewhere for everyone. It's already started for designers, manufacturers, builders, governments, a host of well-intentioned organizations, and a select segment of home owners. Now we, the rest of us citizens—the renters, the home owners, the young and old—must get on board. How would your residence stack up against typical green construction guidelines? Against the LEED standards or the NAHB plan?

On the other hand, if you have a new opportunity to build, buy, or remodel, what will you do? The smart money is that you'll pay attention to green guidelines and build as green and as energy efficient as you can. Instead of getting overwhelmed by "that next new green high-tech product" or the latest and greatest new innovations, decide for yourself how green you want to be, and do the best you can. Work within your budget and time constraints. As long as you think things through; take advantage of passive-solar design; create an efficient thermal envelope; use lots of the right insulation; get good windows and efficient plumbing, heating, cooling, ventilation, lighting, and electric systems; and landscape for energy efficiency, you'll do fine.

Anyway, you'll want to—because now that green is back, it's here to stay.

Green Home Construction Programs and Systems

In the United States alone, knowledgeable estimates of the total number of different (yet similar) green home construction systems, guidelines, and standards that are competing for marketplace attention range beyond several hundred. That's a lot of programs. These carefully prepared sets of green building guidelines or standards may be directed at either local or national audiences, but most of them—even the local ones—generally can be accessed online. A tremendous amount of information is out there, for the asking, about green home construction programs and systems. A basic Google search will result in the available lineup. They all come with varying degrees of complexity and options and are either self-certifying or require third-party testing and verification. Many dovetail with other programs for support. Why reinvent the energy-efficient wheel? Some offer suggested guidelines, whereas others supply prescriptive standards with prerequisites that must be adhered to and proven in order for a project eventually to be awarded a certified green level status. Although most of the programs are actually aimed at production builders, the information also can be helpful to individuals planning to build or remodel.

Most of the programs revolve around action checklists pertaining to important home construction steps and building features installed in a home that's designed and at least partially completed to green guidelines. The individual action steps are assigned numerical point values. The more checklist points followed and completed, the greater are the cumulative efficiency results of the dwelling, and the darker is its shade of green. All the items deal with—in one way or another—energy-efficient construction techniques, materials, and products; healthy indoor environments; water-efficient products and processes; renewable-energy features; waste reduction and recycling during the construction process; and sustainable site planning and land-development practices. Some of the checklist actions are mandatory, whereas others may be optional. The entire project can achieve one of several levels of green rating depending on the total number of points secured, with each successively higher level being more energy efficient and difficult to attain than the preceding one. The programs themselves continue to be fine-tuned as new green products come onto the market and efficiency expectations rise. Informal competitions exist among product manufacturers by category—with window manufacturers, for instance—attempting to come out with models with R-values and other efficiency characteristics that are a little better than those of the current leader. Almost as quickly as these industry advances come about, they're reflected in the green construction programs.

Because homes built in different climate locations have different requirements, green building guidelines and standards typically make necessary adjustments for the particular climate type in which the home is being constructed. Since an energy-efficient home constructed in Bangor, Maine, would not likely be as energy efficient if it were built in Laredo, Texas, there really is no all-in-one "standard" for energy-efficient homes for all occasions. Instead, any green dwelling must be either specifically designed for regional weather characteristics or, on a smaller scale, at least "tweaked" for whatever weather pattern is most predominate, such as for a hot and dry, a hot and humid, a cold and dry, or a cold and hot climate. The Energy Star program, as well as other green home programs, generally makes allowances for including climate-effective energy-saving techniques within design and construction plans. Similar allowances are also included in many of the other programs as well.

The highest levels of green achievement usually require third-party performance verification or simply proof to an impartial third party that the green construction steps were done and the efficiency results are what's expected. Third-party verification most often involves extra cost, which can be weighed or justified against any benefits of receiving certification, such as becoming qualified to apply for homeowner lower-cost energy-efficient mortgages, tax credits, grants, and other related incentives. Another advantage to third-party efficiency performance verification is the assurance and peace of mind that home owners receive, knowing they've received what they planned and paid for. The same inspections and tests also confirm the degree of quality that went into the construction and identify possible mistakes and shortcomings so that the contractors can remedy them.

This chapter discusses—in brief and general terms—some of the most widely used and written about green home programs or systems: The Department of Energy's Energy Star program, the National Association of Home Builders (NAHB) *Model Green Home Building Guidelines* and *National Green Building Standard*, and the U.S. Green Building Council's LEED for Homes program. There are many other programs available locally, nationally, and internationally. Some have been developed for local climate conditions. Most offer variations of the same green concepts that are highlighted throughout the media, educational institutions, manufacturing industries, and government agencies. If there's one thing for sure, it is that all these green organizations are evolving at a rapid pace. One set of green guidelines is soon likely to morph into the next version as materials and products become more energy efficient and environmentally friendly. Critics have already said that over 200 different green building guidelines and standards are too many, and such a wide range of programs is not in itself sustainable. Eventually, there likely will be some consolidation and shaking out. For now, however, there are lots of programs to choose from, and as a class, they're good. Most of the programs can be reviewed online. Some, having local connections, can refer you to individual users for firsthand commentary. And depending on your intentions, you should be able to find at least several programs to satisfy your green construction or remodeling goals. If you're determined to use such a ready-made program, review the checklists, match up the level of verification you need for certification, compare the costs of each, and select the best one for your own project.

THE ENERGY STAR PROGRAM

You can yell at the U.S. government all you want, for a lot of things, but not for the Department of Energy's Energy Star program. This is one terrific, user-friendly operation. It's a multipart resource that is free and mostly available online at www.energystar.gov.

Overall, the Energy Star program started out by developing standards for energy-efficient computers and other consumer products and rating product models. It was initiated by the U.S. Environmental Protection Agency (EPA) in 1992, during the Clinton administration, to help reduce energy consumption and power-plant greenhouse gas emissions. The handling of the first product line—computers and peripherals—set a pattern that continues today, where the most efficient available models in a product category are voluntary identified and labeled with power requirements and average fuel/power operating usage so that consumers can compare product life-cycle costs of competing appliance models. By doing so, consumers eventually can reap the rewards of more energy-efficient products coming to market as manufacturers try to qualify for favorable Energy Star ratings. By 1996, the Department of Energy (DOE) had come on board, and the constantly evolving program was greatly expanded to include the evaluation of heating and cooling systems and new homes. Since then, Energy Star has taken on categories for water heaters, insulation, lighting, windows, doors, skylights, home air sealing, roofing, office equipment, home electronics, and most large and small appliances. It actively promotes the use of energy-efficient products such as light-emitting diode (LED) lighting and power management systems for home electronic equipment and has become an integral part of many other green home construction guideline and standards systems.

Beyond energy efficiency, Energy Star also offers an indoor air package label. After receiving the Energy Star for New Homes qualification, additional design and construction features to control moisture, chemical exposure, radon, pests, ventilation, and filtration may be included to help protect the occupants from mold, chemicals, combustion gases, and other airborne pollutants. Although the Energy Star label indicates that a product or home is near the top of its class in energy efficiency, it does not necessarily mean that other products without the label must be energy laggards. There are certainly appliances and homes built by small companies or manufactured in different countries that are remarkably energy efficient. They may be rated by other systems, or they may not be rated at all yet. Ultimately, it's still up to the consumer to sort through and research products and product ratings. Luckily, with all the attention currently given to energy efficiency, this is getting easier all the time.

ENERGY STAR–QUALIFIED NEW HOMES

The EPA has always kept its green home construction guidelines fairly simple. The original intent of Energy Star green homes was to improve the way that homes and home-building sites use energy, water, and materials to reduce impacts on human health and the environment. As the program itself says, "Building a green home means making environmentally preferable and sustainable decisions throughout the building process—decisions that will minimize the environmental impact of the home while it is being built and over the many years it will be lived in." Certainly, we need energy-efficient homes because much of the energy that powers our households comes from the burning of fossil fuels in power plants, which contributes to smog, acid rain, greenhouse gases, and risks of global warming. The less energy used, the less air pollution is generated.

A home that qualifies for the Energy Star label is a home that uses at least 15 percent less energy (and often up to 30 percent or more less energy) than other homes built to modern average new-construction standards. A typical home among the large number of dwellings constructed in the United States between 1975 and 1985—following the 1973 oil embargo, when there was a renewed awareness of energy use in households—served as an early baseline standard for energy-efficiency comparisons by the EPA and consisted of about

- 1,500 square feet of conditioned floor area
- 14 percent window-to-floor-area ratio
- 20 percent heating/cooling duct leakage to the outside
- Three bedrooms
- "Stick-built" construction using wooden studs, joists, and rafters
- Batt insulation in walls and blown-in insulation in attics

As home-building standards evolved, a later baseline home became a "standard" residential dwelling built to the 2004 International Residential Code (IRC). As practically everything does within green construction products and design, that standard also may be subject to revision in the near future as the "average" home changes. Simply put, Energy Star–certified homes are a lot more efficient than most homes constructed outside the program.

To achieve energy efficiency, Energy Star relies on simple, effective green guidelines and features in each Energy Star home that are arranged within major categories, including the following:

- *A complete insulation package.* What's the use of having high-efficiency heating and cooling equipment if the air conditioned by those systems is strongly influenced by outdoor temperatures—which is exactly what happens when insulation is lacking. The correct types and amounts of insulation, carefully installed in walls, roofs, attics, and floors, as well as around plumbing pipes, water heater storage tanks, and ductwork that runs through attics or crawlspaces, help to prevent conditioned air from being affected by outdoor temperatures and heated or cooled water from unintentional heat gain or loss. The attic is the easiest place to get the biggest savings with insulation. Insulating crawlspace ceilings or walls, as well as basement walls, also can make a big impact on comfort—as long as moisture protection is also taken care of. Even though a garage door may not be heated or cooled, air infiltration and heat or cold transfer can make a difference in a home's energy efficiency.

- *High-performance windows, doors, and skylights.* Energy Star is a great place to start for the lowdown on windows and doors. Multipaned, coated glazing, engineered-frame-construction high-performance windows, correctly sized, placed, and installed, save large amounts of energy throughout the year by reducing unwanted heat gain and loss when appropriate. They also protect against damaging ultraviolet sunlight that can break down and discolor flooring, wall coverings, and furnishings. They keep a home cooler in summer and warmer in winter. Energy Star units can save 15 percent or more on home energy bills. Compare makes and models, and review simplified discussions on how energy-efficient units are manufactured, installed, and operated.

- *Tight construction and ducts.* No matter how well a home is insulated or how high-performing the windows are, a home won't be energy efficient if it's loosely built and leaks air. If inside air leaks outdoors as fast as it gets heated by a boiler or furnace or cooled by central air conditioning, what's the point? Insulation and high-efficiency equipment alone cannot keep up with constant air leakage. The solution involves both effective equipment and especially correct installation methods. Ductwork that delivers conditioned air also needs to be sealed so that furnaces and air-conditioning compressors needn't work overtime. Leaking ducts can decrease the overall efficiency of heating and cooling systems by as much as 20 percent. Duct mastic and metal-backed tape can seal those leaks far more efficiently than simple duct tape that eventually dries out and cracks. Energy Star explains and presents graphics on the importance of tight envelope planning and construction.

■ *Efficient heating and cooling equipment.* Because the heating and cooling systems in a home demand the most power, it's difficult to have an energy-efficient home without high-performance heating and cooling equipment. These units need to be carefully selected, sized, and installed to provide proper temperature, humidity, and ventilation control and are critical to maintaining a healthy, comfortable indoor environment. An Energy Star–qualified programmable thermostat permits four or more different temperature settings to be selected, which allows occupants to choose a different temperature for different times of the day or night. Water-heating systems are also critical to achieving overall energy efficiency. These systems lend themselves nicely to sustainably powered systems such as solar water heating and supplemental electricity generating, and small wind turbines are also available for use in certain residential situations.

■ *Efficient products.* There are tens of thousands of consumer products that Energy Star has rated and qualified as energy-efficient leaders in their categories. The big, bright yellow and black energy labels prepared with information approved by the DOE and applied by the manufacturers provide a wealth of information for consumers. Labels on efficient lighting, appliances, and heating and cooling units are especially beneficial when buyers are comparison planning and shopping.

■ *Third-party verification.* Independent home energy raters are available to assist Energy Star builder partners with selecting the most appropriate energy-saving features and products for a particular building project. After the project has been completed, the home energy raters conduct on-site inspections and tests to verify the energy efficiency of features and products such as insulation, air tightness, and duct-sealing functions. Special diagnostic tools are usually brought on-site. A blower door tester consists of a variable-speed fan mounted in an outer doorframe and used to pressurize and depressurize a house to measure air leakage. A duct blower performs a similar function for heating and cooling ductwork. Manometers measure pressure difference between two locations; flow hoods measure the amount of air flowing through a register. Infrared video or still cameras register still images or video that show surface heat variations that can be used to help detect heat losses (or gains) and air leakage in buildings. Numerous other physical tests can determine if contractors have followed through with agreed-on plans, such as whether promised components actually were installed and if proper depths of insulation are present. Energy Star standards for home energy ratings, protocols for inspections, and guidelines for testing are maintained by the Residential Energy Services Network (RESNET).

One potentially difficult aspect of green construction, recognized early in the "green revolution," can be the additional time and expense involved when the design, planning, and construction are done on a custom basis, especially for the first time by home buyers, designers, builders, and craftspersons. To encourage potential new home owners to find an easier path to a more practical, plentiful supply of new home plans and already-constructed homes to select from (without having to design each home from scratch), Energy Star has developed a green-rated program through which home builders may become Energy Star "partners" by signing a partnership agreement stating their intent to actively build new Energy Star–qualified homes according to the Energy Star guidelines.

The Energy Star program has a major advantage in its consumer-driven approach of reviewing, testing, and certifying the most energy-efficient models within many classes of products, as well as identifying and encouraging the best approach to building practices. A further example of how relevant Energy Star energy performance ratings have become is their incorporation into many other existing green building standards and programs, such as the NAHB *Model Green Home Building Guidelines* and *National Green Building Standard* and the LEED programs.

While other green building programs focus primarily on the dwelling and its contents and how the home performs against energy-efficiency parameters, the Energy Star program enables the project to be planned green from the very start and provides support before the first shovel is turned by assisting in the certification of green builders and aiding the project by helping to line up certified green builders as general contractors.

Energy Star is an excellent program. In fact, many of the other green building programs depend on and refer to product information developed by the Energy Star rating system. The bright yellow labels created through the DOE showing the annual cost of operation have been very well received. They're almost impossible to miss in large and small appliance and home-improvement stores all over the Unites States and elsewhere.

Still, some criticism of the program has occurred after studies indicated that certain product ratings had been issued following somewhat generous assumptions on how various models were used, allegedly resulting in Energy Star labels being awarded to models not as energy efficient as they were presumed to be.

Another issue includes the inadvertent exclusion of appliances and products manufactured by small and international companies that, although their models may be very energy efficient, are just not included in the rating system. A third criticism focused on the possibility that manufacturers have been sacrificing durability, expected service life, and practical use capabilities of a product to achieve energy efficiency. For example, electronics used to control the functions of an appliance may be too delicately assembled to stand up to strenuous daily handling of the product. Even if the product is energy efficient, if it breaks down and needs to be replaced often enough—contributing to landfill pollution—its energy efficiency may be for naught, and additional natural resources will have to be used to construct its replacement. A refrigerator, to achieve a higher capacity insulation value, might have to cut down on the number of cubic inches of freezer storage space offered. Energy Star likely will address such concerns in future editions. It can be noted that any program as extensive as Energy Star occasionally will receive a brickbat or two. A few negative barbs should not detract from the rest of the program's important work on promoting energy-efficient products, equipment, new homes, and remodeling efforts for the betterment of consumers everywhere.

MODEL GREEN HOME BUILDING GUIDELINES AND *NATIONAL GREEN BUILDING STANDARD*

The NAHB *Model Green Home Building Guidelines* and *National Green Building Standard* programs were developed through and largely driven by the home-builders' industry. The NAHB first organized in 1942, during World War II, at an unsettling time in home-building history when building materials were being strictly rationed owing to the war effort. Resulting from the combination of two home-building groups—the National Home Builders Association and the Home Builders' Institute of America—the joining was billed as "the voice of the housing industry." In the few decades after the war, a tremendous housing boom paralleled that of the arrival of the baby boomers and spurred the need for thousands of new home builders across the country to keep up with the demand for literally millions of new single-family homes.

Throughout the 1960s, 1970s, and 1980s, the association set out to assist its members by educating them in marketing and business skills while performing practical home-building research to improve construction methods and product selection. The NAHB grew to almost 200,000 members and was instrumental in developing various builder promotional efforts. Events such as business-to-business and business-to-consumer trade and home shows, cable television programs, and print advertising campaigns spread the word about the association's agenda. The development of numerous building trade and product manufacturing Web sites immediately opened up instant nonstop avenues for building news and product communications and supplied access to global information sources and marketplaces.

A Green Building Subcommittee was formed in 1998, and with considerable member input, the first edition of the NAHB *Model Green Home Building Guidelines* was published in 2005 as the first national rating system for green single-family dwellings. Certifications at various levels are still available. The guidelines were prepared to assist mainstream home builders with ways they could bolster their construction plans and skills by using environmentally friendly designs and features. It provided an effective template for home-builder associations to form new green building programs in their own areas; each program and each green home would not have to be planned from scratch. Instead, builders simply select from a generous offering of specific green items and features while "building" their program or dwellings. The organization's helpful Web site is at www.nahbgreen.org, where you can access tools to find participating builders or local programs and get further information about the certification process, the guidelines checklist, and a green scoring calculator. The same site also features, at this writing, a detailed look at how the NAHB's green home building rating system compares with another popular national rating system.

In 2007, the NAHB partnered with the International Code Council (ICC) to form a national green building standard that the American National Standards Institute (ANSI) would soon recognize as the ANSI ICC 700-2008, *National Green Building Standard*, which is similar to the NAHB *Model Green Home Building Guidelines* but contains more mandatory items and requires higher levels of energy efficiency and environmental features. This program is available for single- and multifamily dwellings, as well as for residential remodeling and land development projects. Unlike the *Model Green Home Building Guidelines*, which can be accessed as a free download from the Web site, the *National Green Building Standard* is available for sale in book form through the same Web site.

The NAHB's programs cover most of the same green construction categories that similar green building guidelines and standards systems address. Builders can plan to achieve basic, entry-level green projects or more challenging, highly efficient construction of top-level, sustainable green dwellings that can yield energy savings of even 30 to 60 percent beyond that of regular baseline homes. Categories in the programs include

- *Lot design, preparation, and development.* This encompasses site selection, establishing green goals with a planning and development team, and readying the site for construction. Green concerns such as storm-water management, landscaping for passive-solar, and plans for conserving trees, native vegetation, and other natural resources on the site are all available for point awards. The site selection should minimize environmental impact. Points are awarded for selecting infill, grayfield, or brownfield sites that tend not to have recreational, agricultural, or wildlife uses. Restoration of those often avoided sites is also encouraged. As in each category, there's also a checklist line for innovative options—meaning available options that go one or more steps beyond the usual, such as the construction of shared driveways.

■ *Resource efficiency.* This involves reducing the quantity of materials used and waste produced. This can be accomplished by creating efficient floor plans and by making the best use of available material sizes (e.g., lumber, panels, windows, and beams) so that fewer cuts and leftovers result. Resource efficiency also can be achieved through building with panelized wall, floor, and roof systems in a modular fashion. Energy-efficient panels not only save time and energy but also virtually eliminate wasted materials. The use of quality materials is also encouraged to enhance durability and reduce maintenance tasks. The longer a home's systems will last, the less often they'll have to be replaced. Other options encouraged in this category include the use of reclaimed, recycled, recycled-content, or renewable materials. When waste materials are generated by the construction, the disposal plan must as much as possible specify means of recycling instead of landfilling. Innovative options may include the use of locally manufactured materials and products and the use of a demonstrable life-cycle assessment tool to identify the most environmentally green materials and products chosen and used in the project.

■ *Energy efficiency.* This is one of the most important categories in the program. It involves developing a comprehensive strategy and plan by coordinating multiple systems that together will result in a home that requires less energy to heat and cool. If there's one category where third-party input is best put to use, this is it. Sizing space-heating and -cooling equipment and evaluating site-specific requirements related to the availability of systems and fuel types are complex tasks best left to professionals who specialize in doing so for a living. To prove that the building meets minimum energy-efficiency requirements, third-party calculations, inspections, or objective verifications are mandatory. Related features include an airtight building envelope; energy-efficient heating, cooling, and ventilation equipment and systems; efficient lighting and household appliances; sealed and insulated duct and delivery systems; and efficient water-heating setups.

Passive-solar design and features are encouraged and awarded points, as are the inclusion of renewable-energy source systems for heating, cooling, and electrical generation. Innovative options may include extra-step items such as drain water heat-recovery systems, renewable-energy features and systems, and lighting occupancy sensors. Points may be awarded for infrastructure equipment installations that are ready for future additions of solar collectors or photovoltaic cells on an unshaded roof area. Additional points can be secured by arranging third-party tests and verification of energy-related features and favorable results of blower-door tests. Expectations are for various degrees of energy efficiency beyond that of a normal home ranging from at least 15 percent through 30 or 40 percent and even higher as ascending rating levels are achieved. Verification of this category must be performed by a competent third-party (someone outside the builder's company) tester/inspector.

■ *Water efficiency.* The program addresses both indoor and outdoor water usage. Points are awarded for the inclusion of Energy Star water-conserving appliances such as "low usage" dishwashers and clothes washers. Other inside low-flow features include toilets, urinals, shower heads, faucet aerators, faucet controls, and efficient water heater positioning. Outdoor features include landscape drip irrigation systems and rainwater collection systems. Innovative options may involve the design and use of graywater systems and composting toilets.

■ *Indoor environmental quality.* This is accomplished by reducing the potential sources of pollutants inside the home. Effective ventilation equipment and systems can ensure adequate changes of fresh for stale air. Points are awarded for direct-vent, sealed combustion equipment; for tightly sealed doors and air barriers between the garage and living area; and for ensuring that furniture, cabinets, flooring, or other substrates produce no or very low formaldehyde emissions. Individual room vent fans in the kitchen and bathrooms can exhaust cooking smoke, fumes, and moisture. Wall coverings, flooring, and furnishings using low volatile organic compounds (VOCs) will prevent dangerous off-gasing indoors. Reliance on preventive measures can help to manage rainwater and snowmelt. Radon testing and elimination systems and other contaminant testing equipment can also improve occupant safety and are rewarded by the point system as well.

■ *Operation, maintenance, and home-owner education.* This can be prepared for the new owners and conveyed by final inspection walk-throughs and with binders or folders packed full of equipment serial numbers, model numbers, manufacturer and distributor representative phone numbers, operating manuals, warranties, and maintenance checklists. Available options to be discussed include home recycling equipment and systems and the setup of a composting collection container and outdoor composting bin. In some cases, the impact of occupant behavior on energy efficiencies also can be reviewed with the idea that certain tasks, when identified, can save considerable amounts of water (e.g., temporarily turning off the water when soaping up in the shower or while brushing one's teeth or establishing a set pattern of controlling heating and cooling systems by using multiple programmable thermostats to yield conditioned air only where and when needed).

■ *Global impact.* This category refers to the manufacturers and companies involved in producing some of the green materials, products, and equipment used in a home's construction. It shifts the emphasis to the manufacturers' and service suppliers' own operations. Are those businesses run in an environmentally responsible manner? Are their standard operations and practices in line with sustainable goals? Are you able to purchase nonpolluting products such as low- or no-VOC indoor paints and sealants? Are the companies setting good examples of environmental stewardship in their daily operations, and are they known for doing so?

Ascending totals of best-green-practices scores are required to reach recognized levels of green home construction and energy-efficiency performance. Further refinements and improvements in the program resulted in the current *National Green Building Standard* to which NAHB members build. There are numerous optional ways to accumulate points within the seven basic categories, and such flexibility has been a strength of the program to member builders. By employing multiple green features, a home's energy-efficiency levels can quickly surpass those of Energy Star's baseline for certification, so an NAHB green home can achieve almost any green performance level within reach.

An advantage of the basic NAHB *Model Green Home Building Guidelines* is that it usually doesn't cost much to certify a home. What's required instead of more expensive and intensive third-party comprehensive testing and inspection is voluntary supporting data and proof of green guidelines construction materials, products, and features. Some kind of document needs to back up every point awarded on the way to whatever program building level is attempted. If any of the documentation looks suspicious or is lacking, an audit may be scheduled to investigate the entire project and could result in cancellation of the rating level if necessary. On the other hand, verification for upper-level certifications in the *National Green Building Standard* is more intensive and more costly.

Another advantage of the NAHB programs for builders and home buyers is that often most of the work and most of the planning of the material, product, and features selection can be done up-front by the builder and planning team. The builder's intention is to design, build, and market an energy-efficient, green dwelling. On the other hand, if a buyer becomes involved early in a building project, he or she can have as much input as agreed on by the builder and will find a generous array of options to pursue. As with most of the green building programs, the home can be designed and constructed as green as the builder and owner want.

THE LEED FOR HOMES GREEN BUILDING RATING SYSTEM

The U.S. Green Building Council (USGBC) is a national nonprofit group that consists of a coalition of over 13,500 building industry organizations and includes numerous individual leaders and representatives from a wide range of backgrounds. The council's main purpose is to promote environmentally responsible design, construction, and operation of commercial, industrial, institutional, and residential buildings so that those structures are cost-effective, healthy places to live and work. By educating and encouraging manufacturers, builders, political leaders, and organizations across public and private strata to participate in responsible planning and development, the council is determined to make an ever-improving difference in the world. Its flagship accomplishment, LEED, stands for Leadership in Energy and Environmental Design, a green building rating system first introduced in March 2000 for new commercial construction, and it has since grown to include specialized versions for homes, schools, neighborhood development, commercial interiors, high-performance building operations and maintenance, and core and shell development.

LEED for Homes, which was launched in February 2008, measures green home-building performance based on key categories: innovation and design, location and linkages, sustainable sites, water efficiency, energy and atmosphere, materials and resources, indoor environmental quality, and awareness and education. Within each of these areas, projects earn points toward certification with the inclusion of both mandatory and optional energy-efficient and environmentally friendly features.

The Web site at www.usgbc.org/LEED/homes has a download for the LEED for Homes rating system and checklist. These documents are an easy way to familiarize yourself with the program so that you can decide if you want to partner up with a builder through which your project can be designed, planned, built, and registered. The Web site will help your builder to find and connect with the LEED for Homes provider of choice. Reference guides and instructor-led workshops are also available to help builders prepare for LEED participation. A preliminary walkthrough of the checklist will give you a good idea of how LEED for Homes applies to your project. LEED is a flexible system, so you'll need to choose which credits are aligned with your project's green goals. Your plans should include which level of LEED certification—certified, silver, gold, or platinum—you wish to achieve. After construction, the provider also will help the builder arrange for and complete a home energy rating by a qualified Home Energy Rating System (HERS) rater and other on-site inspections of green features required to verify that construction has gone as planned—a requisite for LEED certification. The USGBC will review the third-party-verified data and application materials submitted through the provider and make sure that it meets all requirements before certifying the home or project for the final, appropriate level of green building achievement.

This voluntary home-building certification program evaluates homes in the following areas:

- *Home size adjuster.* By using a sliding scale based on a home's square footage, the LEED checklist encourages building smaller versus building large. This sliding scale employs a ratio of bedroom numbers to overall usable square footage. A negative "adjuster number" lowers the threshold total point numbers for each award level, making certification easier to reach, whereas a home that's larger than average for the number of bedrooms it contains receives a positive adjuster that, when added to the neutral certification baseline, will make each level more difficult to attain. In other words, larger than average homes require more resource consumption and energy to operate, so they need more energy-efficient features per square foot of space to achieve comparable levels of green. The square footage refers to all the directly conditioned space within the home's thermal boundary, calculated to the exterior wall. This includes all normal living spaces and service areas such as garages, utility rooms, closets, entries, crawl spaces, attics, and basements that are within the thermal boundary—except those that are separated from primary living spaces by isolated, weather-stripped doors and neither heated nor cooled directly. In mild climates, where normal living spaces in a home are not heated or cooled, this includes all spaces normally used as living areas and accessory spaces such as closets, utility rooms, and entry foyers. Since larger homes use more materials and energy than smaller homes do over their useful life cycles, the adjustment compensates for those factors by making it easier or harder to reach LEED for Homes certification.

- *Innovative design process.* These three words say a lot. Instead of the same basic homes that have been constructed in the same way for about the last 50 years or so, today we've got design methods, tools, and materials that are resulting in superior energy- and resource-efficient dwellings. So why not design, plan, and build them? The overall green design effort done in this way can achieve an integrated and cost-effective project. To do so, though, requires the combined experience and expertise of individuals familiar with green construction. A project team is assembled, and a preliminary rating goal is decided on, after which the team decides on appropriate design steps and features to include in the project in ongoing monthly meetings. Decisions are made on who will do what and what major systems will be included. It's an early-stage road map of how the overall process will unfold. Team members include at least one professionally credentialed LEED for Homes representative, as well as individuals representing appropriate expertise in building science, mechanical or energy engineering, sustainable design or green building, land-use planning or landscape architecture, and architecture or residential building design. Topics include passive-solar orientation, durability planning, and third-party verification of such.

■ *Location and linkages.* Location and linkages refer to where the home is located and how occupants access the places they need to go on a daily basis, such as work, school, shopping, banking, recreation, and the like. They also involve how a home is sited, encouraging placement on nonsensitive land having already-installed infrastructure, community resources, and mass transit to reduce reliance on individual vehicle use. Close access to open space such as public parks, state game lands, or bodies of water for the enjoyment of wildlife and nature activities is important, and points are awarded for that. Instead of selecting a lot in a rural area where no other development has occurred, points are awarded for building on the edge of an already developed site, on an infill lot that's almost surrounded by development, or on predeveloped ground. LEED's intention is to discourage development on agricultural, recreational, or pristine virgin ground.

■ *Sustainable sites.* This section awards points for handling the site in an environmentally friendly manner, minimizing long-term damage to the land. It includes establishing erosion controls during construction, such as stockpiling and protecting topsoil; controlling and preventing rainwater and snowmelt from eroding the site during construction; and protecting on-site streams, ponds, and wetlands from damage or pollutants and returning the land to something similar to what it was before construction occurred. Permanent erosion controls also receive points. Landscaping with natural, native plants is a hugely positive feature; no invasive plants can be used. Grass plantings must be drought-tolerant, and turf should not be used in densely shaded areas or on sloped ground. Mulch or soil amendments can help to reduce erosion and water loss. Grass should be limited to reduce the amount of watering required. The use of drought-tolerant plants and reduced overall irrigation demand is encouraged. Local heat-island effects should be minimized by avoiding large areas of black asphalt and using white concrete instead and installing light-colored foliage and other materials that have reflective surfaces. Permeable pavers enable water to drain between them to reduce runoff to storm sewers. Surface water management is important. Rainwater from roof runoff should be managed, such as with a vegetated roof cover or gutter diversion system. Trees and shrubs can be designed for erosion control. Features can be designed near the foundation walls to avoid having to use poisons to control termites and other potential pests. Compact home positioning can conserve as much of the site as possible from disturbance.

■ *Water efficiency.* This can include, if zoning and building codes allow, graywater and rainwater capture systems. Reusing rainwater and snowmelt is encouraged. Rainwater harvesting can be accomplished for nonpotable water uses such as irrigation, car washing, and possibly for operating toilets. If municipal recycled water is available, that also can be used for outdoor applications. Reduced overall irrigation demand can include designing landscape by using drought-tolerant plants and native vegetation and trees, mulch, and groundcover—and minimal amounts of grass turf. Indoor water opportunities for reduced usage include high-efficiency and ultra-high-efficiency fixtures and fittings such as low-flow toilets, dual-flush toilets and urinals, and low-flow shower heads and faucets. Practical savings of water can be up to 50 percent of total usage.

■ *Energy and atmosphere.* This is the most complex and far-reaching section; it's also the most technologically intensive. Nowhere can energy efficiency and savings be reflected as directly as in space-heating and -cooling and water-heating systems. Included in this section are options for insulation, windows, air infiltration, duct-sealing efforts, space heating and cooling, hot water, lighting, major appliances, renewable-energy systems, and refrigerant management. Included in the calculations for points are a number of Energy Star features and checklists as well. There's a lot of potential in this section, and the expertise needed is considerable. Depending on the certification level achieved, home owners can expect between 30 and 70 percent energy bill reductions.

■ *Materials and resources.* Materials and resources cover the home's framing systems, environmentally friendly products, and waste management. Points are awarded for advanced framing techniques, for structural insulated panels (SIPs), and for certain types of trusses. The same goes for locally produced materials, Forest Stewardship Council (FSC)–certified wood products, recycled-content materials, low-VOC coatings and substrates, and similar green materials and products. Site waste management includes best practices for construction waste management planning and waste reduction (except for land-clearing and demolition waste from a previous structure). This can be done by using detailed framing plans and exact specifications integrating standard-size products. By following checklist options, construction waste can be lessened by 50 percent or more, on average.

■ *Indoor environmental quality.* This is another section best accomplished with expert help. Exhaust and ventilation systems need to be carefully selected, sized, and installed and must be integrated with accompanying heating and cooling equipment. Included in this section are environmental features that filter, exhaust, or vent and control various contaminants, including radon, carbon monoxide, particulates, smoke, fumes, vehicle emissions, and even moisture. Energy Star indoor air package equipment may be included with related installations.

■ *Awareness and education.* Awareness and education points are awarded for home-owner educational materials and training. This includes the preparation of a maintenance and repair resource that will enable occupants to inspect, maintain, and keep systems in efficient working order throughout the useful life of the home. Site walk-throughs and demonstrations also assist home owners with firsthand knowledge of systems they may never have used before. Basic identification and operations training is especially helpful with space-heating and -cooling equipment; mechanical ventilation units; renewable-energy systems; and irrigation-, graywater-, or rainwater-capturing setups. Public awareness training through open houses, Web sites, or newspaper articles highlights the green construction and LEED features to help promote of energy-efficient homes to the community.

CHOOSING A GREEN CONSTRUCTION GUIDELINE OR STANDARD PROGRAM

After reading and considering any number of green building guideline systems, including those briefly discussed in this chapter, it can quickly become difficult to differentiate one from another. Really, they're all heading in the same direction. They're about building homes that weigh easy on the environment and on home builders' pocketbooks. They're about energy efficiency and conserving natural resources. They're about technological advances resulting in building materials, products, and equipment that can squeeze out and hold in every possible heat-producing calorie from our dwindling fossil fuels. And they're about harnessing plentiful supplies of sustainable basic nonpolluting power sources such as wind, solar, and water. They highlight materials such as bamboo, cork, switchgrass, responsibly managed lumber, products from Energy Star and other efficient appliance lineups, fluorescent and LED lighting, structural insulated panels, concrete insulated forms, geothermal heat pumps, and a wide variety of heat exchangers and other equipment that will heat water or make electricity from pure, free sunshine.

Since selecting materials, products, and features for your project can be incredibly detailed and complex, especially when you're attempting to qualify for one of the upper-tier green construction rating levels, this is another reason to assemble a planning team consisting of members already experienced in working with green construction systems. A lot of steps can be taken, such as determining which prerequisites and credits will be planned. Which ones will require specifications? There's the need to research products and systems in advance and figure out the costs. Who will install the major pieces of equipment? The plan needs to be fairly solid but should be able to be "tweaked" midstream if unforeseen problems arise or better product alternatives are found. Again, considerable coordination is needed for tying the dwelling's systems together, and the design requirements need to be specific enough to enable the builder to purchase supplies and components and put them together in a timely manner.

One strategy puts your top three or four programs side by side and selects what you feel to be the best of them. Go through the rest of the chapters in this book, and pick out features and ideas that appeal to you. For now, realize what your reasons are for green building and what your goals are. Then identify the program that you feel will do the most for your situation. If a formal certification is important to you and you agree with paying a little more for third-party verification, select a system known for strict third-party verification. It may depend somewhat on local resources—the experiences of others and what programs are available locally. Do you have to import experts and contractors from elsewhere? Or is green support and experience to be found locally?

How do those desired features play into the guidelines and standards of the program(s) being considered? Certainly, you can drill down to whatever level of detail you want; there are entire books focusing on each individual chapter of this book, as well as on sections or specific options in LEED and other program requirements. Be realistic and practical. Can you obtain and afford the materials and products you want? Does your contractor know how to install what you're planning? Has there been enough professional input from early design meetings? Consider the need to plan ongoing photographic documentation and construction photos. What verification procedures will the builder have to go through, and what expense will those add to the project? What rating level is sought? Is testing for indoor air quality part of the plan? Is there enough time in advance to locate and include salvaged or refurbished products? Have recycled-content materials been considered? What about aspects such as certified wood, low-VOC-emitting materials, construction waste management, and site disturbance?

The decision to use one of the green construction rating guidelines or standards should be taken seriously. Many local and state governments, utility companies, and other agencies across the country offer rebates, tax breaks, and miscellaneous incentives for new construction and remodeling projects tied into achieving nationally recognized green building rating levels.

FUTURE GREEN BUILDING SYSTEM EXPECTATIONS

Certain high-profile programs currently have strong national promotional and advertising campaigns and actively recruit participants and customers through publications, educational systems, conferences, and endorsements. Various chapter groups and partners throughout the building industry—within public and private sectors—are reaching out to involve other groups within their own networks.

All these systems are probably heading toward a period where some consolidation or survival of the fittest will be likely. Perhaps some systems or programs will be swallowed up by others. Eventually, the large number of current programs probably will not be sustainable. Indeed, duplication of effort may be considered wasteful.

Some green experts predict that the LEED for Homes program eventually will gain a majority of acceptance, aided by Energy Star and the NAHB programs, backed by the building industry, and will continue to be developed and commonly used as well. From a consumer-driven perspective, having an element of choice between home-building programs is generally a good thing because fair and friendly competition tends to stimulate advances in materials, products, and building methods.

Conventional thought is that for "affordable" housing, money usually will go farther on green construction when less third-party verification must be arranged in addition to the building costs, especially when smaller "custom-home" builders are doing the construction. Since most promotional efforts are aimed at production builders—builders who repeatedly construct the same or similar variations of floor plans—it costs them considerably less per home to certify their dwellings owing to uniformity of materials, products, methods, and floor plans. A custom, one-of-a-kind home simply will cost more to verify and certify. Some people will pay and can afford extra for custom certification of their projects. Your decision will depend on your situation, goals, and resources.

Other individuals may be able to educate themselves and contract their own dwellings using green materials and building methods. Most people, however, neither have the time nor could arrange for such a lengthy period of financing needed to cover the piecemealing together of a home. Far more home owners arrive at new-construction home ownership through the services of a general contractor, one of the builder types mentioned later in this book, in Chapter 35, on selecting a contractor.

Green Construction Strategies

After familiarizing yourself with some of the green construction programs and reviewing the various guidelines, standards, and options, the next step is to consider establishing your own strategy—for new construction or remodeling. There are many strategies—and combinations of strategies—that can be taken to arrive at a green home that will suit your needs. This chapter presents some of the more popular and more effective strategies, beginning with the simplest.

STRATEGY 1: REMODEL, FOR NOW

Yes, this book focuses on new construction, but some individuals, after reading what's involved in building a new home, may decide to stay where they are for a while. In this case, remodeling strategies can include several options worth pursuing, depending on what you plan to do with your existing home. If you want to sell your home within a relatively short time period, you may see things differently. Remodeling allows you to acquire a green home without the material investment of tons of wood, concrete, and other building materials. If your house is structurally solid and can meet most of your needs, remodeling is a reasonable alternative to building new. On the other hand, if your home is old and lacking adequate insulation, a sturdy roof and walls, energy-efficient windows, and modern plumbing and electrical services, plus water-saving fixtures, or is plagued with environmental issues such as mold, dry rot, asbestos, substandard water quality, or a combination of such, you may want to start from scratch.

Another way to approach the question of "Remodeling or new construction?" is to review how well your current home satisfies your living needs. Is there enough space to house yourself, your family, and your belongings? Or can you shrink those needs by recognizing that a son or daughter will be going out on his or her own in a year or two, and can you get rid of maybe half the belongings you've been storing—unused—for years, including racks and racks of too-small clothes and box after box of old books, papers, and who knows what else? Maybe you won't need a larger home? Is noise an issue? Once insulation is added to thin, hollow walls, sounds may no longer be a problem. Is the dining room too small for your family's Thanksgiving dinner? Once a year, then, arrange the family gathering at a restaurant or club banquet room instead of planning a special addition for one meal a year. Are you tired of being in the dark? Some older homes had numerous nooks, crannies, and even whole interior spaces untouched by natural lighting. Consider new windows, sun tubes, skylights, and any of the thousands of modern fixtures and pinpoint illumination controls now available. Draft, temperature, and humidity issues also can be taken care of with caulk, trim, insulation, and new heating and cooling equipment.

There can be definite benefits to remodeling:

■ When the whole picture is considered, remodeling an older house avoids using large amounts of raw materials otherwise required by the construction of a new home.

■ Remodeling involves far less work than building new and usually far less construction costs. Most older homes have attics and basements that may be converted to living space.

■ Money saved by not building new can be put toward remodeling energy-efficient features, nicer finishes, and better-quality furnishings and appliances into an existing home.

Another way of looking at remodeling is financially. If the home in question is already one of the most valuable houses in the neighborhood, then no matter how much remodeling is done, those upgrades probably won't result in a reasonable payback. The remodeled home may sell quicker than it otherwise might have sold but probably won't fully recapture the total remodeling costs. On average, experts say that money spent on remodeling should increase the value of home by 1½ times that amount. Spend $20,000 to get $30,000 in appreciated value. That formula likely will not hold true, though, if the home has already been overbuilt for the neighborhood, with a market value approaching the neighborhood's upper limit. Real estate professionals note that some room additions bring more value than others. For maximum remodeling bang for the buck, bedrooms, kitchen upgrades, and bathrooms (full or half) of the right number, size, and design typically will offer the greatest remodeling payback potential.

Now, on to the strategies for new green construction.

STRATEGY 2: FIND AN ALREADY-CONSTRUCTED OR ABOUT-TO-BE-BUILT NEW GREEN HOME

This is a home that is planned by a contractor who is actively marketing his or her green construction skills. If you don't have much time available and are looking for a home anyway, this can be an excellent choice. Reviewing the chapters in this book will assist by familiarizing you with the basics of green-built homes. If you can find one already constructed to a set of green guidelines or a program such as Energy Star or LEED for Homes or advertised as designed and built based on the National Association of Home Builders (NAHB) *Model Green Home Building Guidelines* or *National Green Building Standard*, so much the better. Just realize that you'll likely have few choices or options to make with the building details— maybe flooring options—and certainly can do nothing about where that particular home is located. But you could get an excellent deal if the builder wants to move on to other projects and agrees to take a reasonable or minimal profit. Builders trying to make a name for themselves see green home construction as an ideal means of differentiating themselves from established builders who may be reluctantly changing their ways while being tugged along by the green construction wave. In addition, green developments and communities are springing up in various forward-thinking places. Real estate brokers and agents will know where such developments exist, and local county planning departments usually know about such minicommunities long before the first building site is excavated.

STRATEGY 3: CONTRACT A SPECIFIC ALREADY-PLANNED GREEN DWELLING

This is done through a major home-building company that markets and builds from a menu of green homes. Some large home-building companies, even if they're not located near where you want the house to be, will agree to build one of their proven green models where you want it. At the very least, they will supply and put together enough of the house to a point where local contractors can finish it off after the foundation; shell; heating, ventilation, and air-conditioning (HVAC) systems; sustainable energy; and other systems are in place. This can take much of the upfront planning time out of the loop.

STRATEGY 4: BUILD A "CONVENTIONAL" NEW HOME AS ENERGY EFFICIENTLY AS POSSIBLE

This is the path taken most often. Because there's a shortage of good builders who are currently immersed in green construction techniques, people are starting to insist that an established, well-known builder who has been constructing sound, proven homes pay special attention to building basic green construction features into a project. Instead of planning cutting-edge sustainable energy production with top-end solar photovoltaic (PV) and wind turbine systems, think how to conserve and lessen your need for fuels and energy. Think thermal envelope and insulation. Think conservation of resources. The idea is to build a home with quality materials and components and concentrate on energy efficiency, thereby getting the greatest return for your investment while still keeping within green building guidelines. Regardless of the location, plan an exceptionally airtight building envelope with plenty of insulation, top-grade windows, and plenty of natural and efficient electrical lighting, and splurge on energy-efficient mechanical ventilation, heating, air-conditioning (if needed), and plumbing systems.

In general, use high-quality system components that will last a long time and provide reliable use. Design on the small, compact side, using shared living spaces for multiple activities instead of single-purpose rooms. Ideally, the builder is experienced in building green and/or in the Energy Star for New Homes program or LEED for Homes program. If this option is not available yet in your location, an established, reliable builder simply can use as many green building materials and components as practical in the home's design—as long as they effectively increase efficiency or decrease reliance on fossil fuel sources. You don't need to sink a lot of money into items such as expensive countertops or fancy fixtures. Keep to the basic energy-efficient materials and products. And you don't necessarily need the latest technology for everything. Include water- and energy-saving fixtures and appliances. The main building systems must be efficient—the heating, cooling, and ventilation system; the plumbing system; and the electric and lighting systems. Outfit the home with numerous energy-saving features, the total sum of which will add up to major operating savings. Pay attention to components such as door thresholds, adding sheltered foyers or storm-door installations to entrances and using prevailing breezes for ventilation. Research the building materials. If planned from the beginning, this kind of green construction can be accomplished for as little as 5 percent more than the cost of conventional average-quality building materials and components.

STRATEGY 5: IN ADDITION TO STRATEGY 4, ADD INEXPENSIVE GREEN DESIGN CHARACTERISTICS

Employ deliberate orienting of the home to the sun and prevailing winds, and include natural ventilation and passive-solar features for supplemental space and water heating. This, too, costs very little or nothing—when life-cycle costs are considered—and the payback is considerable. Let the sun and wind be your friends and help to provide you with free heat, light, and natural ventilation. To make the most use of this strategy, it also must be included from the beginning of your planning and building process.

STRATEGY 6: INCLUDE RELATIVELY LOW-COST SPECIAL GREEN COMPONENTS

This goes along with the preceding two strategies. Use such special components as heat-recovery systems; insulating concrete forms (ICFs) for foundations and exterior walls; premanufactured structural insulated panels (SIPs) for floor, wall, or roof sections; roof knee trusses; rainwater-capturing systems; native plant landscaping; advanced framing techniques; sun tempering; and light tubes.

STRATEGY 7: DESIGN AND INCLUDE BEEFED-UP ROOF FRAMING, WIRING, PLUMBING, AND OTHER INFRASTRUCTURE FOR FUTURE INSTALLATIONS OF WATER HEATING OR MODULAR RENEWABLE-ENERGY COMPONENTS

Add these to the green features employed in strategies 5 and 6 in order to be able to heat water or add or convert power, heating, and cooling systems to active solar or wind power generation later.

STRATEGY 8: INCLUDE, IN ADDITION TO THE ENERGY-SAVING HVAC SYSTEMS, ON-SITE RENEWABLE-ENERGY SOURCES TO SUPPLEMENT YOUR HOME'S ENERGY NEEDS

These include solar, wind, biomass, and geothermal systems. Substantially sized systems that truly can reduce the amount of energy you purchase will require considerable research and collective planning with the help of specialized professionals, but once the systems are in place, there's very little maintenance involved. For smaller systems or trial systems that can be expanded later, fewer investment dollars will be needed. Some individuals begin with, say, water-heating solar systems before adding solar PV modules. Since many sustainable-energy systems are modular, upgrades can be made when additional money or funding programs become available. Another green construction step is to make conscious decisions to use as many green construction materials as possible on the basis of their intrinsic green characteristics—even if they are intrinsically not as durable or cost-effective.

STRATEGY 9: BUILD TO A GREEN CERTIFICATION PROGRAM

These include programs such as those offered by the NAHB, Energy Star, LEED for Homes, or one of the many excellent regional green-building certification programs that have evolved over recent years. This typically will require a design team and professionals thoroughly familiar with building green and the certification standards involved. Additional upfront costs will be involved, but the proper planning could mean savings in materials and operating costs resulting in more home for the money over a 6-year or greater life cycle. More effort is needed to design for the specific site, size, and type of home. But the benefits of complying to the system's guidelines are positive characteristics. It typically would mean going beyond local building code efficiency requirements, resulting in more energy saved over the years, greater comfort, higher resale value, and so on, including all the benefits of a darker green construction. Keep in mind, however, that you still can have this without making the effort and spending the money on getting the certification. In a sense, though, it would be like getting a college education without receiving the corresponding degree. You still have whatever knowledge you paid for, but not the diploma. Some people don't need the diploma—they will do what they want to with the knowledge. Others need the diploma to get on with their careers. Professionals tend to need the diploma. How many dentists, physicians, accountants, or attorneys are practicing without the benefit of a diploma?

STRATEGY 10: DESIGN FOR THE MOST TECHNOLOGICALLY ADVANCED GREEN CONSTRUCTION POSSIBLE

This is accomplished by using innovative green materials, methods, and design at every construction stage. Aim for a net-zero-energy home or one that produces as much energy as it uses. By producing enough on-site renewable power to match your energy needs, none will need to be purchased. This also will require a team of supporting professionals. Such a green-built home might include a wind turbine and PV solar panels and batteries to store electricity. This may not be justified for purely financial reasons, but if funds are available and you want a very green dwelling, the satisfaction of showing others that it can be accomplished and the pleasure of avoiding future rising heating, cooling, and electricity costs may be too tempting. Typically, a high-end, high-cost house that may be able to exist apart from the grid usually means avoiding major electric appliances of any kind and using other fuels for tasks such as space heating, water heating, and drying clothes. It simply doesn't make much sense to invest in additional solar panels or wind turbine capacity to satisfy power demands that can be handled through nonelectrical means—unless, of course, you make a conscious decision to do so and have the financial means to expand your generating ability to take care of all your home's power needs, even if those power needs do not involve rigorous energy-conservation equipment and behaviors.

STRATEGY 11: DESIGN TO PRODUCE MORE THAN ENOUGH ON-SITE RENEWABLE ENERGY

This is done so that you operate consistently in the black, with an ability to provide or sell excess power into the grid. This requires professionals, the cooperation of local power utilities, the right zoning and building codes, a suitable location, and probably lots of money, even if government tax credits, grants, and subsidies are available. From the get-go, expect a high-cost, high-end project.

Now, other circumstances can come into play here. If the home will be built in a place that enjoys a very moderate climate—neither too hot, nor too cold, nor too humid—then, naturally, less power for HVAC will be required, and smaller or less efficient heating and cooling systems may be sufficient. Therefore, designing for heating and cooling efficiency is less intensive, and components such as windows, insulation systems, and framing needn't be so expensive. However, electricity is still needed for lighting and appliances.

The strategies are also somewhat dependent on your location needs. Where must you live? Green-building communities are springing up across the country. These communities follow green guidelines and offer green infrastructure that nicely complements individual homes that are planned and built within their boundaries.

Modular homes have their own green versions—built in tightly controlled factory conditions to exacting specifications. They greatly reduce waste and the overall construction time period from start to finish and in some cases offer custom green features.

Can you afford any of the latter strategies? They may cost quite a bit more on the surface, but when their effects are considered, you may be able to save or eliminate something else by going with green components that in the long run save on other maintenance or operating costs.

You may qualify for various government subsidies, grants, or tax breaks. "Energy-efficient" mortgage loans may be available for homes built to certain green certification standards or programs—and proven to test out as being as energy efficient as planned. Money can be saved with less construction waste— and hence fewer overall materials bought. Landfill costs have risen dramatically in the past decade, as have the transportation costs for moving good materials in and waste materials out. Advance framing techniques require less wood or steel— expensive products and more inexpensive insulation. And the more efficient your building envelope is—your framing shell, windows, doors, and insulation—the simpler and smaller your heating and cooling system needs will be.

In every case, it makes sense to do everything you can after meeting your general and special living needs to minimize your home's heating and cooling requirements. The less heating and cooling you must provide, the less energy and cost they take. After reducing those energy needs, follow up with installation of heating and cooling systems that have high operating efficiencies. Next, work on ways to reduce electrical consumption for powering lighting, appliances, and various HVAC and other systems. A large portion of electricity avoidance can come from how the home is used and how the systems are controlled and used by the occupants. Reducing water usage is another measure of good green construction that can be done by installing Energy Star fixtures and developing conserving habits. Not wasting heat already provided, through various recovery systems, is also desirable. Such measures all lead to using less fuel and energy and getting more out of the energy used.

Other ways to save money and still build green are to build close to existing utilities so that construction costs are not inflated by numerous lengthy hookups. Ask any contractor about the convenience and cost avoidance of running power, gas, sewer, and water lines from the street instead of bringing those same lines from a distance.

In short, you can build as green as you want and as you can afford, but by far the most payback can be had with strategies 2, 3, and 4.

Earlier editions of this book suggested that someone interested in planning their new home would be best off by first deciding on what house to build and then on what building site to construct it on. In that way, a person would be certain that he or she would purchase a site that fit the type of home best arrived at that would suit his or her needs. For example, if someone were set on a split-level dwelling, he or she would best look for a sloping lot rather than a flat site. Or if a two-story house with an attached garage were desired, a rather level lot would well serve the building. This still can be done, but if you are looking to build green and want to take advantage of orientation to the sun, prevailing winds, and certain topographic characteristics, it might be tough to find your ideal site—one that's available for sale, is the right size, in the right area, and has the right topography or configuration.

When building green, the lot or building site becomes far more important than it has been traditionally. Years ago, most people didn't think too much about which side of the street they wanted to be on.

Does it matter if you build LEED-certified? Are there implied or very real advantages? You need to weigh the original investment versus the expected and realized financial savings, comfort realized, and other benefits that are important to you, both tangible and intangible. If you sleep better and hold your head higher knowing that you've gone beyond the expected in minimizing your environmental footprint, it may be worth the extra cost and financial resources. If, however, you believe that your compromises still result in the best possible project you could complete at the time, so be it. Let it go. In a way, you are like the person who is always waiting for the next upgraded computer, rationalizing that it doesn't make sense to purchase just yet, and who loses out on all the benefits from having any computer along the way. There are untold product revisions, improvements, and developments in the pipeline yet to come. You've got to drop anchor somewhere and get on board, or you'll be left standing by the wayside.

The difference between being certified or not can merely be the process of documentation—and that will not make your home any more energy efficient—unless the contractors have been telling you something and have not been performing as they said. It is difficult to appreciate the level of insulation or the airtightness of a home unless tests are included with the performance. Such tests could be arranged anyway, and you could do everything as if you were going for the certification—but just not do the final paperwork and related costs—but then you might think that since everything has been done except the formality of certification, why not just finish it? It could matter with energy-efficient financing or grants along the way or in ways that you haven't even figured on just yet. It may help to sell the house someday or may help bring a higher price.

Must you forego a refrigerator with an automatic ice dispenser because someone advises you to get a refrigerator without one given that the ice dispenser takes more electricity to run? There will be inevitable tradeoffs to consider. Do you want to go Spartan for the good of the world? Or do you want to split the difference in some manner by building a green home that makes sense to you and results in a home that you'd consider green enough? Since almost every green component and system is voluntary at this time, it's still your choice.

Planning Your Green Home's Design and Construction

Depending on the strategy you select, here are some of the steps that need to be considered and taken when you plan your new home:

1. *Research, research, research.* Have you ever heard the statement regarding real estate: "Location, location, location"? Even though it's still somewhat applicable today, and the location you select ultimately will affect your ability to place a green-built home on your building site, many other factors also will greatly influence the success of your project. You can only appreciate the number of building materials, products, systems, and design options from which you have to select by doing the research. Get a feel for the difference between traditional home building that occurred decades ago—with its loosely constructed and poorly insulated frames, hardly any attention to ventilation and moisture control, and preoccupation with "bigger is better"—and what's occurring today with designers and builders who are building to green construction guidelines. Understanding the differences will greatly assist you in planning and design and help you screen out inefficient components and old-building thinking and replace those antiquated features with much more modern energy- and resource-efficient ones.

2. *Assemble a support team of knowledgeable professionals.* After familiarizing yourself with the basics of today's green-building guidelines and standards and with the green materials and products available in today's marketplace, you're ready to start assembling a support team of knowledgeable individuals with whom you can meet at the beginning of and throughout the process. This can be an informal group of individuals who have varying degrees of knowledge in fields related to land development and home construction and

can include lending representatives, real estate brokers and agents, home designers, general contractors, home builders, interior designers, architects, energy engineers, civil engineers, landscape designers, excavation contractors, sustainable-energy generating system providers, and green materials or product representatives. The assistance that can be provided by a few rather informal meetings with experienced professionals cannot be understated. This doesn't mean that your team needs to have dozens of members—only four or five members representing the most important aspects of your project may make a huge difference in how efficiently and smoothly things go. Some of the green-building guidelines or standards programs insist that such a team is established as a prerequisite to certification. It's that important.

3. *Decide on your strategy.* From the start, have a strategy. If it changes when you're partway into the process, realize it, and restructure. Just be aware of what your own project guidelines are. Recognize that practically every green feature is an option, and you have the ability to try to get it exactly as you want it—if you take the time and make the effort. Refer to Chapter 3.

4. *Decide on the approximate size of your home.* How many rooms do you need? How many bedrooms? How many baths? Visit open houses. Do a pros and cons checklist on your present home. Is it way too small for your daily living activities? Is it too large? You needn't design your floor plan yet because it should depend somewhat on the building site you line up. But you should have a definite idea of how much living, dining, bathing, utility, storage, outdoor add-to space (such as porches or patios), and garage space you need or definitely want. In addition, are any special-purpose rooms or spaces required?

5. *Research the costs of new construction in your area and the costs of borrowing money, if needed.* Share the basics of what you're planning with several lenders and real estate agents, and attempt to get preapproval for a new-construction load up to a specific amount—the maximum you plan on spending. Realize how such a monthly payment will affect your monthly budget. If you plan on having money to purchase a building site or a general down payment, identify the source and amount of those funds. Determine, based on the size of the home you want, a general price range for the entire project. Contact green-building distributors, and survey the organizations that may supply grants, rebates, tax credits, and low-interest loans for sustainability or energy-efficiency components such as Energy Star heating or cooling systems, windows, lighting, and insulation. Don't figure on receiving "free" or subsidized money, but consider what that could mean to the project if it comes through. Additional books are available on energy-efficient wall systems, roofing systems, heating and cooling systems, windows, and sustainable electricity generation.

Consider that new groups and contacts are coming online. The Internet perhaps will be your most often used resource. Use it to verify and further explore the topics you discover in book stores or on do-it-yourself television channels. DVDs are being prepared by manufacturers, architectural societies, and numerous government and private green-building organizations. Join some, and receive their trade journals. Keep notes and file folders. Talk with people. Identify individuals who are quoted in the newspaper or on television locally or within a few hundred miles. This research may sound like a lot of work, but it's interesting and not all that difficult to understand. Moreover, it will pay off. Most people do not do much research and consequently are satisfied with less efficient and less green homes. Identify people to approach to be part of your design team if your strategy demands that, especially if your design will involve sustainable energy or major passive-solar design. Identify the builders from which you will select one. See Chapter 35 on selecting a builder.

6. *Do some more research on green construction components and materials.* Reading this book is a good start, but you'll need more exposure to green-built homes and the products and components of which they are made. Make a point to visit green homes, even if they aren't local. Real estate agents can be a tremendous help, as can sustainable building organizations that frequently sponsor tours of green homes in their locations. Other leads include utility companies and manufacturers and distributors of products such as heating and cooling equipment, insulation, and various building products associated with green construction. Narrow down some of the main building products to consider. Think of the large "wear" interior surfaces and components, such as flooring, wall coverings, countertops, cabinets, window treatments, and other furnishings. Make sure that they don't clash with the heating system. Refer to Chapter 2 concerning green products.

7. *Start trying to find reclaimed or recycled products and building materials.* Review Chapter 10 on reclaimed and recycled products. Field trips to local or area "deconstruction" operations and yards can be worth the time for items such as hardwood doors, flooring, steel beams and supports, stone, brick, exterior siding details, staircases, mantels, bathroom vanities, stone countertops, and even lighting fixtures such as chandeliers that can be refinished. Old wood beams and barn siding sometimes can be located by driving through the countryside looking for fallen and wind-blown barns. After a brief meeting and careful inspection with the owner, an offer may be considered and accepted—usually with you having to arrange for the complete deconstruction and removal, with the usable pieces to be salvaged and the unusable ones disposed of. Old stained-glass windows, though not energy efficient, may add the perfect focal point when installed between rooms on

interior walls. These trips may help you to locate some unique pieces—beams or reclaimed components that could become centerpieces or key structural members of a staircase, a room divider, a ceiling support, or a kitchen island base—something to give a memorable design feature to the home.

8. *Search for a building site.* See Chapters 31 through 33 on areas, building sites, and orientation. Narrow your search, and make a selection after reviewing your general intent with your potential builders. Be aware of the type of home that will be able to be placed on the building site you have in mind. Ask yourself if the match will be acceptable. If you are planning any unusual building designs or any sustainable-energy systems, make sure that the zoning and local ordinances support such installations. If in doubt, speak directly with zoning officials, who may be able to provide a copy of written regulations or interpretations. Make sure that the builder also agrees to follow through on the needed permits and that no further questions or concerns remain. If you plan to tie into the local electrical grid, check with the solar or wind system distributor or installation company for details of what needs to be accomplished before installation begins. Start thinking about where the home could be positioned on the site and how it could be oriented. Keep in mind the travel of the sun and how that might affect the dwelling's layout.

9. *Decide on your house type and style.* Now that you know the general size and the location and configuration of the building site, it is time to decide on the type and style of house. If it can be constructed with "traditional" framing methods, you'll know that any of your potential builders will be able to build it. If you decide on any other framing method, from steel to structural insulated panels (SIPs) or similar specialized systems, you'll need to find potential contractors who are experienced with those systems. Consider how the type of home—single-story, two-story, split-level, or other—will fit on the building site you have chosen. Do you want a detached garage? Are there any special features that you must have, such as an office above the garage or an in-ground swimming pool? Do you see an acceptable building orientation that will allow you to take advantage of passive-solar design? Review your ideas with the potential builders.

10. *Rough out the floor plans for traffic zoning and planning, and take another look at the size of the house you're planning.* Does everything still fit within your own price-range estimates? Do your floor plans follow the sun's travel so that a maximum amount of natural light and solar energy enters key rooms and spaces at key times during the day?

11. *Review your main and supplemental fuel and energy options.* Is there natural gas at the site? Do most of the neighbors heat with propane or oil? Are there any sustainable-energy projects in the area? Wind turbines? Solar photo-

voltaic (PV) systems? Since you have already surveyed zoning and building ordinances and codes to determine what is possible, now you need to start arriving at the heating, cooling, ventilation, and electrical systems you want.

12. *List the main types of important building components, products, and furnishings you specifically want.* These include such things as windows; light tubes; skylights; doors; exterior siding; roofing; floor coverings; lighting fixtures; insulation; wall coverings and trim; kitchen appliances; bathroom and plumbing fixtures; and heating, cooling, and ventilation systems. You should have ballpark prices for these items and materials, realizing that they're only order of magnitude numbers and that the builder you select will have to arrive at exact pricing in the final quotes and bids.

13. *Armed with your basic plans and product list, approach your potential builders, and work out a bid package on which the builders will bid.* At this point, you're still looking for builder input on how to put all your requests together into the most energy-efficient home within your budget. Review the status of current financing options and programs offering low-cost loans, grants, tax rebates, and incentives.

14. *Select the builder you feel will provide the best possible home for your situation.* Inform the other builders of your decision. Review your contractor's building schedule, and read Chapters 36 and 37 on working with your contractor and setting up your maintenance program.

15. *Supply your lender with a package of drawings and specification listings, and finalize your preapproved financing.*

16. *Discuss the excavation plans for following through with the placement and orientation of your home.* What methods is the contractor going to use to minimize the disturbance to the site beyond what's absolutely required for the footer and foundation, as well as the landscaping? Make arrangements for a photographic record to be taken at the major building steps to be placed in the final inspection and maintenance binder.

17. *Keep a regular eye on the construction process to make sure that the contractor and subcontractors are performing what they had planned and what had been captured in the building agreement.*

18. *Pay attention to contractors' management of materials at the site.* See that the generation of waste is minimized and that what waste is generated is separated and either recycled or disposed of in a responsible way.

19. *If performance testing is required, arrange to be present for tests such as blower-door tests, insulation inspections, air monitoring, and other tests.* If a certification is in process, ensure that the proper paperwork is filled out

while all subcontractors and others involved are still within calling distance. Have test results added to the final inspection and educational binder the contractor is preparing.

20. *Do a final walk-through and receive the warranty, maintenance, and operating binder for all the working systems and building components and products.* Make sure that you know how to operate and maintain any special components or systems, such as those included for solar water heating, rainwater capturing, PV solar systems, or wind turbines.

21. *Set up a simple system to track your utility usage.* There are measuring devices and meters available to help measure fuel and energy use and to see how your bills relate to the operation of various appliances and fixtures, especially electric, water, and sewer charges. Line up your expected energy usage data so that you have an idea of what to expect for water, sewer, electricity, natural gas, oil, and propane. Understand how your sewer relates to your water usage. Keep track of rainstorms and how the surface water drains or runs off your property—remember, you want it to percolate down into the ground, not run off, so that it eventually goes into a river or lake or a place where it will not have to get treated as sewage, especially the water that may run off from a driveway or hard surfaces or even from the roof.

22. *Start a new section in your binder where you can start making notes for your next home construction project.* Do this knowing that you can take your time and collect information and data that may help you with analyzing what you have and its pros and cons.

REMODELING NOTES

Depending on where you live while you're deciding on or planning to build a new home and how far away that home's construction may be in the future, you may be able to practice green remodeling with your present home. There are a number of considerations to review before deciding if and what to do.

First, you need to know your present home's estimated market value—what a willing buyer likely would pay for your home in the home's present condition. This is a dollar amount usually expressed in a general price range set somewhat by average home values in the neighborhood you're in. Any competent real estate agent can arrive at a price by doing a simple market analysis—comparing your house with similar houses in your neighborhood and like neighborhoods and reviewing what comparable homes recently sold for and are presently being offered for sale at. Next, ask yourself (and the real estate agent) if there are obvious remodeling improvements that would increase the value of your home within its present value range. If, by undertaking remodeling projects, your home would end up becoming overimproved, you may not be able to receive enough from a buyer to cover your remodeling costs. In that case, it doesn't make sense to sink money into remodeling, even if the remodeling would be green.

On the other hand, if your home is presently toward the lower end of the neighborhood expected home-value range, and remodeling in general will increase its market value, by all means remodel. In this case, remodeling green not only will add valuo but it also will yield sales features to make the home easier to sell. Remodeling your current home by adding green features is a wonderful way to put research into action and ultimately may help with your new home's design.

What to Build

To arrive at the best-possible home for yourself, first take a step back—away from houses and house construction in general—and review some basic concepts about what a home can and should contain. Here, you want to think green *and* you want to make sure that you plan for your own personal needs. To just blindly build green could be doing yourself a disservice. You want to select a dwelling that best satisfies your needs and build that as greenly as possible. You need to think about the pros and cons of the various house styles and types available and how you can arrive at a floor plan that will most favorably suit your present and future needs. You should realize that features can be built into a new house at minor cost that will permit efficient and convenient inner conversion of living space years later, when living conditions change or evolve. And you also should be mildly familiar with typical house construction plans, prints, and drawings.

Think durability, even if you aren't planning to stay in the house for a particularly long time. The difference in cost is somewhat marginal for better-grade materials and components largely because the installation costs typically are the same whether the components are low or high grade. Good, clean, simple design also facilitates durability because if all the parts work together as a system, there is less occupant and environmental stress within the dwelling. Heating and cooling systems that have to strain to keep up with the loss of conditioned air and water will wear out sooner. Inferior roofing and siding materials will degrade and need to be replaced quicker. Moisture trapped within walls and insulation owing to improper installation or deficient products or amounts of products will decompose the wall structure and efficiency from within. Low-grade windows will allow too much radiation and sun into the living areas. Always check and compare the prices of the various components and be aware of your options. You know that as soon as this book rolls off the presses, manufacturers will be coming out with more efficient products and building materials that satisfy one or more of green construction features. This is how manufacturers will be positioning themselves, how they will differentiate themselves from their competition.

It will be up to you to pay attention to trends via online research by visiting plumbing and contractor supply houses and keeping up with the latest affordable technology. You needn't always put in the most current technology, but try to be aware of it in case it's affordable and sensible to include at the outset. And sometimes there will be choices to make. Do you go with materials that are extremely durable—or other, less durable ones that may be manufactured in ways that are less green?

Another consideration is to design as if you had someone in the family who must get around in a wheelchair or walker. If you haven't looked lately, our overall population is getting older in a hurry. This means that you may need to plan on features for handicapped accessibility, especially with entranceways, bathrooms, kitchens, and laundry rooms. Called *universal design*, it's a way to enable you and other family members—perhaps a parent or two—to comfortably get around inside and out—so that daily living can still go on in the home, and alternative housing does not have to come into play. Relatively minor design features can enable you to retire in your new, green home without making construction alterations later.

It used to be enough to arrive at your "ideal" house on your own, with the help of books or articles, before approaching builders, who will naturally, even with good intentions, lead you toward house types they prefer or think that you should prefer. However, if you already have a building site picked out and your brother-in-law happens to be a builder, so be it. Still, read the chapters about what to build. If your initial plans (or those of your brother-in-law) are correct, then you'll be able to proceed full of confidence. On the other hand, if you discover that a different type of house would be better for you, don't let anyone tell you otherwise. Now that green construction, in some shade—light to dark—comes into play, the rules are changing. It makes sense to get some help while you are developing your plans.

Don't be one of the thousands of home buyers who are just on the receiving end of a new house, passively accepting whatever happens along. Let there be conscious reasons for what you end up with.

A House Divided

The modern house consists of at least six main types of areas:

- *Living and recreational space.* In any one dwelling, this can include a living room, family room, den, library, office, music room, sunroom, or other rooms and niches planned for entertainment, relaxation, hobbies, study, or even working at home.

- *Food-preparation space.* The kitchen ranks number one here, followed by additional food storage areas such as nearby walk-in pantries and "satellite" serving platforms, bars, and grills conveniently located in family rooms and other living and recreational spaces.

- *Dining space.* Depending on the floor plan, this can be a separate formal dining room adjacent to the kitchen or an open dining area having the kitchen on one side and the living room or family room on the other. Or, when economy is desired, a portion of the actual kitchen itself can be reserved for a dining table or booth.

- *Bathing and washing space.* This means bathrooms, both full and half, plus toilets, hand sinks, showers, saunas, and indoor hot tubs.

- *Sleeping and dressing space.* This means bedrooms, dressing nooks, and related storage areas.

- *Service and storage space.* Everything else in a house fits in here: basement, attic, stairs, hallways, laundry rooms, and garages.

LIVING AND RECREATIONAL SPACE

We've come a long way since our primitive ancestors stalked through forests in search of daily sustenance. Indeed, prehistoric life was tough. There were no plumbers, no cable televisions, and no supermarkets, doctors, or economists. Instead, you had one continuous struggle against the elements, with little time to do anything but attempt to satisfy the most basic of needs. And even if the typical primitive *had* the time, he or she still wouldn't have known how to put a formal living room to good use.

Okay, so they did have dens—in the strictest sense of the word (Fig. 5.1). Back then, a shelter was just that—a few walls against which to huddle. There was a roof for protection from rain, sleet, and snow, under which early humans could hunker down, relatively safe from predators.

Even though our primitive forerunners had the protection of rough shelters, they were still lucky just to make it through their teens in one piece. In fact, as late as the early 1900s, the expected American life span was only 46 years for men and 49 years for women. That didn't leave much free time for recreation.

Thanks to revolutionary medical and pharmaceutical advances, look how long people are living today. Consider also, especially during the latter half of the twentieth century, how work weeks have grown shorter and family sizes smaller. Automobiles, trucks, and aircraft have given us mobility and have sped up the

FIGURE 5.1

A primitive den.

delivery of time-saving conveniences to our doors. New leisure time has created a demand that greater attention be paid to the living and recreational space in modern dwellings.

Simply put, a house's living and recreational rooms should contain enough space to satisfy the needs of its occupants. This means enough space for general and specific leisure activities such as entertaining friends, watching television, listening to music, practicing musical instruments, gaming, reading, studying, writing, bookkeeping, children's play, and plain old relaxing—all in comfort and, if need be, privacy.

Living and recreational rooms also must be adequate in size to hold sufficient furniture for comfortable seating. At the same time, they should be large enough to permit the rearrangement of major pieces of furniture into a variety of positions while still maintaining good traffic circulation within the room.

Depending on a dwelling's size and floor plan, living and recreational space may be planned as a number of individual rooms or may be distilled into a single all-purpose area.

The Living Room

If one all-purpose room is all you desire or all you can afford at the outset, that room probably should be the living room. At one time referred to as a *parlor*, the living room was designed originally to entertain guests in a formal fashion. The living room should be a quiet place for reading and conversation. It should be close to the front door, next to the dining space, and away from sleeping areas. There also should be a closet outside the living room, near the front door, for coats, hats, boots, and other items. There are two main types of living rooms: traditional and open.

A traditional living room is a room placed away from the kitchen and other work or recreational rooms in the house. This out-of-the-way placement allows at least two separate entertainment centers (including the kitchen in a smaller house) so that more than one family member can plan activities with outside friends at the same time without infringing on each other's privacy. The traditional living room usually is situated at a dead-end location to minimize unwanted interruptions and through traffic. Doors can be considered for additional privacy.

As mentioned earlier, if the house you plan will not accommodate other recreational rooms beyond a living room, then consider that your living room will have to be used for whatever leisure-time activities you enjoy. When a single room must serve a variety of functions, a more open type of room is often the most practical choice. In fact, owing to the overall reduction in square footage in houses in recent years for cost reasons, open planning is becoming increasingly important because it lends the impression of maximum space for the money. In fact, it does give you more square footage of usable space because there are fewer walls to take up space. Open planning serves well in the more contemporary and expensive plans and in households having few or no children, where privacy is not as important as it would be to a large family. However, a danger in open-type rooms is that spaces must be carefully planned so that they don't appear jumbled and haphazardly thrown together.

The Family Room

A second recreational room that has grown popular in the past few decades is the family room. Instead of wearing out the living room furnishings, informal activities such as children's play, listening to music, and lounging on sofas while watching television can be pursued comfortably in a more casual environment.

A home that contains both a living room and a family room typically will have the main television set placed in the family room. And like it or not, television has become a mainstay in most modern households. On average, the tube is on for over 7 hours per day, 365 days per year in every household that has one. In addition, DVD players are practically as common as toasters.

Because people want the television where groups of family members and guests can watch it comfortably, it has a definite impact on interior decoration. This means that a wall or corner is effectively removed from the placement of seating and other furniture. Thus, when the room is sized and laid out, television placement should be taken into account—preferably some spot where the glaring sun will not interfere with viewing.

If you plan to have a separate family room in addition to a living room, consider locating it next to the kitchen, where only a few steps will separate food and drink from leisure-time activities and where a parent can work in the kitchen while still supervising children at play.

Another desirable feature for a family room is outdoors access, commonly provided by sliding glass doors that lead to a patio, terrace, or deck. Although some people add doors to the family room to seclude it from the rest of the house, most active families prefer an open-type plan that allows easy movement to and from the kitchen and that fosters efficient communications between the two areas.

Fireplaces

Whether you decide on one living room/family room combination or multiple living and recreational rooms, one feature to consider—even in warmer climates—is an energy-efficient fireplace. When planned from the beginning, one or more fireplaces can be integrated in the house in such a manner as to save space, materials, and money. For instance, if the back of a fireplace is located inside the garage, you can reduce the number of expensive finishing bricks or stones normally needed to construct an outside-wall chimney. Not only that, but instead of dissipating heat outside through an outer chimney wall, some heat will radiate into the garage, where it will do some good. The ash cleanout door can be built so that it opens at a convenient height within the garage, where messy ashes can be removed and disposed of in one efficient step. No more trudging across carpets or climbing stairs.

If you plan to put a fireplace in a first-floor living or family room, consider two other points: First, if your house will have a basement, do you plan on doing much socializing there? If so, you might want to include a second fireplace. Then an economical way would be to align both fireplaces one right over the other. Second, owing to their very nature, fireplaces demand comfortable seating around them and require freedom from internal traffic and other interference. Therefore, a door next to a fireplace is poor design. Anyone entering or exiting the room through such an access becomes an immediate intruder, an interruption to the conversation group. A door near a fireplace also prevents the placement of furniture on that side of the hearth, creating wasted space that, in turn, will effectively shrink the amount of usable space in the large living or family room down to that of a much smaller area.

Windows and Glass Doors

An important feature common to all living and recreational rooms is windows and glass sliding doors. While you should make sure that living and recreational rooms are bright and cheerful from natural light and plenty of ventilation, too much glass—especially sliding glass doors and floor-to-ceiling windows—can pose a number of irritating problems:

1. If too much wall space consists of glass, there might be no place to arrange furniture unless you decide to block off some of the glass with a piece of furniture such as a sofa or plush chair.

2. If you deliberately decide to place furniture in front of glass, consider how the furniture will look from outside, too.

3. Remember that too many glass walls will severely restrict possibilities for hanging pictures and other decorative works of art.

4. When you entertain in glass-lined living or recreational rooms, large panes of glass can be distracting. During the day, people find themselves gazing out the windows instead of paying attention to the conversation, and at night, huge panes of blackened glass make certain individuals uncomfortable: They feel that they're being watched from the outside.

The inclination to overuse glass is especially strong on sites having dramatic views, where the owners are naturally moved toward taking full advantage of those views. In this situation, you must be careful not to get carried away. Instead, strike a happy balance between beautiful views and functional rooms.

Along the same lines, in most settings (except in rural locations, where a house is tucked back from the main road), avoid an oversized picture window in the front of the house. Such a window invariably gets covered with drapes or blinds anyway, for privacy. When it's not covered, the residents feel like goldfish in a bowl. And typically, all that can be seen through the front window is passing traffic. Large picture windows are far more productive when they are placed at the side or back of the house, facing a private patio, terrace, yard, or other more intimate and less "public" views.

Built-Ins

To make for a more aesthetically pleasing appearance, it's wise to include sufficient built-ins for living and recreational rooms, especially to accommodate the items you want to store there. Books, records, mementos, knickknacks, card tables, and even fireplace wood are a few common objects to keep in mind.

Built-in bookcases and shelves are installed most efficiently when the carpenters and woodwork stainers are putting up the rest of the house trim.

Patios

Another recreational space to consider when planning a new house is a patio. Because it can easily become an important part of your home living experience, a patio deserves the same careful thought that goes into the arrangement of your interior living and recreational areas.

When pinching dollars, settle first for the foundation and concrete slab, and plan to add a roof, privacy screen, and other conveniences later. Location is a major factor for enjoyment of an open or screened-in patio or deck. Remember that an open concrete patio can get as hot as a city street when it bakes in the sun.

Other Living and Recreational Rooms

Rooms sometimes built into a house are a library, den or study, and a music or other hobby room. There are darkrooms for amateur photographers, billiard rooms for would-be Mosconis, sewing rooms, trophy rooms, and rooms designed specifically for personal computers and video games. These are special areas in a house that, depending on the interests of you and your family, can greatly enhance the total living experience.

HOME OFFICES AND WORK SPACES

Anyone paying attention to today's demographics, social structures, and modern career paths will acknowledge that the days of family breadwinners starting out and finishing their careers with the same company have changed. As large corporations continue to redefine their own identities and technological advances gain powerful influences over manufacturing techniques and products, more people are finding themselves working out of their own homes or work locations. This is one specialized room that is bucking the trend toward shared spaces in homes that are gradually being built smaller.

Magazines for entrepreneurs are flourishing. The large "office" superstores are selling business supplies not just to small, medium, and large companies but to millions of small-business owners who are working a "regular" job during the day and then operating a janitorial service at night, or servicing furnaces on weekends, or buying and fixing up small income properties. Many individuals, realizing how tenuous their "regular" jobs are and wishing to expand a part-time avocation into a full time career, carve out some space for themselves in a loft above the garage, a corner of the basement, a spare bedroom, or a study—or even a small desk in the kitchen.

In truth, a home office can be many things. It can occupy a corner of the dining room or be housed in the basement, a converted garage, a spare bedroom, or even an attic. The nature of the business is what typically dictates how large or elaborate the office may be. Ask yourself questions. Will you be working alone, or will you eventually need employees? Do you need space for a showcase for your product or service? If customers or clients need to access the office, then it probably should be located and configured to give a favorable professional appearance.

Do you have special tools or supplies that require considerable storage or must be kept away from curious children? What about the electrical requirements? Computers, fax machines, copy machines, printers, and modems all need to be plugged in somewhere. Consider dedicated circuits and surge protectors for your office equipment—so that other household appliances such as washing machines, refrigerators, coffee pots, and the like won't create internal power drains and surges that could affect your electronic equipment or the information stored within. The surge protectors also will supply some margin of safety from power surges that come from outside the home, too. Storms or power blackouts can affect the way electricity is transmitted to your system. These changes or spikes in voltage can cause major damage.

Other considerations include lighting requirements—certainly, a productive office needs more light than that found in typical bedrooms or spare rooms. Ventilation, air-conditioning, and efficient heating are also critical to the comfort and well-being of office occupants. Sound insulation is necessary in households with active family members.

SPECIAL-PURPOSE ROOMS

The conventional office may not be the only type of work-related space needed. Some individuals have hobbies they desire to turn into second incomes or eventually full-time careers. In such cases, special design components can be planned into a spare bedroom, a garage, a basement, or an attic. Remember, owing to overall size considerations, the green home tends to accomplish numerous activities within smaller spaces, which implies that a single room or space may host a variety of activities as needed simply by being set up with portable equipment or furnishings.

For example, consider how a photography darkroom could be designed into basement or laundry spaces. Or a sewing room, complete with natural and artificial lighting, plus space for cutting, fitting, pressing, and storing fabrics and completed items, could be part of a family room. As more of the baby boomers retire, they are looking for second or third careers involving activities such as painting, sculpture, and various crafts. For the artist, this might mean a quiet, well-lit, and well-ventilated attic loft.

Maybe it's a room used for appreciating music or films or an indoor greenhouse. A cellar space for wine making; a second kitchen for recipe testing, canning, and cookbook writing; a room for showing collectibles; or even a padded room for coaching youngsters wrestling are more examples of planning space for special activities. Consider that an extra bedroom may, with a little preplanning, function as a special-purpose room for as many years as you wish—before being converted back into a bedroom when the house needs another conventional sleeping room or must be sold. Other special-purpose areas likewise can be deconstructed into plain attic, basement, or garage spaces if and when necessary. Avoid building in extra space and room for activities that may run their course in relatively short spans of time.

FOOD-PREPARATION SPACE

For the bachelor who scratches his head in bewilderment while attempting to boil water for instant coffee, a kitchen complete with the appliances of his dreams might consist of a frost-free refrigerator, a microwave oven, a double-slotted toaster, and the plainest of sinks. Others, individuals who fancy themselves a step or two below award-winning French chefs, need wide expanses of counter space, double ovens, microwaves, electric grills and barbecues, three-tubbed stainless steel sinks, boxes of hand appliances, and piles of pots, pans, and multipurpose utensils.

Food is always being highlighted by the media. Sales of cookbooks and culinary magazines have reached huge proportions. Talk shows serve up celebrity cooks. Medical studies stress how a healthy diet can ward off heart disease, stress, and even cancer. And there's no denying that everyone has to eat. It's not something we can elect to pass up.

In any household, the primary food-preparation area is the kitchen.

Kitchen Size

The overall size of your kitchen should depend on the following points:

1. The size of your family and the number of individuals in your family who like to cook. Usually, the bigger the family, the bigger is the kitchen. And don't exclude the children. Psychologists say that youngsters, especially

teenagers, should be encouraged to learn how to cook and that culinary creativity helps a child's overall development.

2. Do family members and many friends and guests tend to congregate in the kitchen? Then make the kitchen large enough to accommodate plenty of seating space.

3. Do you approve of or insist on having meals other than breakfast in the kitchen? If you prefer nightly suppers in the kitchen, then you'd better plan an eat-in kitchen arrangement with space for a table and chairs. If only breakfast will be served there, then a bar at which three or four people can sit comfortably is likely to be all the eating space you'll need.

4. What are your shopping habits? If you prefer to go long periods of time between shopping, you'll need ample storage space for canned or packaged goods, as well as a roomy refrigerator and probably a separate freezer. Additional base and wall cabinets might be necessary, and an extralarge food pantry is a must. On the other hand, if your total food and beverage inventory at any one time is likely to consist of a six-pack of beer, a quart of buttermilk, and a few frozen TV dinners, you can get by with a lot less kitchen.

5. You might want to install a small built-in desk in the kitchen for making out shopping lists, menus, recipes, phone messages, and financial records. Or taking this a step further, consider an equipment desk with a computer, printer, and storage files for keeping in touch with children and your cooking while "working" on the Internet and accomplishing desk work. Many dandy recipes are available via the Internet, which will work out handily from this location. A broom closet keeps long and bulky brooms, mops, sweepers, and ironing boards out of sight in case your house doesn't include a first-floor laundry or utility room.

6. While it's true that a family's kitchen should be a direct reflection of how much that family likes to cook—why have a big kitchen if you spend most of your time in fast-food restaurants?—it also should be an indication of what kinds of cooking are preferred. A lot of baking encourages the installation of double ovens. In fact, if you have the room, consider leaving space in the form of cupboards for a second oven just in case a future potential buyer of your house finds a double oven to be an attractive feature. If you do a lot of entertaining, plan for an indoor grill or barbecue. If fancy presentations are important to you, select any of the other truly marvelous food-preparation aids available. Even simple items such as brackets and shelves for condiments and spices and bookshelves for cookbooks should be carefully planned in advance so that enough space is allowed. These built-ins might seem minor, but if you just ignore their placement until everything else is completed, you'll be hard-pressed to accommodate them neatly. Finishing

touches are often what separates the attractive, efficient kitchen from one that's awkward to work in and always appears cluttered.

Kitchen Functions

No matter what overall size your kitchen is, it still should

1. *Provide adequate working space.* Any kitchen can be thought of as a combination of three work areas (Fig. 5.2). The first is food preparation, which includes counter space; utensil storage drawers and cabinets; and places to store cutters, knives, food processors, chopping boards, glassware, cups, and plates. The second is food cooking, which includes the range, oven, counter space, and storage areas for pots, pans, cooking utensils, seasonings, ingredients, and other cooking supplies. The third is food cleaning, which includes single- or double-basin sinks, counter space, dishwasher, trash facilities, and perhaps a garbage disposal.

   Even the smallest kitchens should be set up so that the items stored at each work area are used for corresponding activities. For instance, the groceries should be stored near the refrigerator so that the sandwich maker has easy access to the peanut butter, jelly, bread, and milk without walking all over the kitchen. Likewise, cooking utensils and aids are best kept by the stove. Cleaning supplies and pot scrubbers should be stored within reach of the sink.

2. *Provide sufficient counter space.* Counter space at both sides of the sink is crucial. At least 3 linear feet of counter should be installed between the sink and the refrigerator so that you can remove food from storage and put it away with ease and can cut and chop foods or roll out dough. The counter space between the sink and the refrigerator is often called the mix center. Near the sink, you need one place to stage dirty cookware and dishes before you rinse and wash them and another to let them dry off after washing. Sink counter space is still a requirement even if you plan to have an automatic dishwasher.

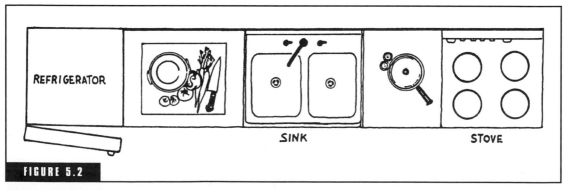

FIGURE 5.2

A kitchen work area.

The range or cooking center also should have counter space on both sides so that you can place prepared foods in one place before cooking and afterward in another while cooked foods are cooling. People frequently don't allow enough counter space here, and family cooks are sorry later on.

Beyond these areas, there should be enough additional counter space to accommodate all your favorite items and appliances, such as a mixer, blender, food processor, toaster, crockpot, microwave oven, electric sharpener, can opener, bread box, and even a telephone.

3. *Provide ample storage space.* In the kitchen, enough storage space can mean the difference between a food-preparation area that's easy to organize, easy to work in, and easy to keep clean and an area that's difficult to work in and always a mess. Neatness and cleanliness count heavily toward a cook's efficiency and enjoyment of his or her work. And it's a proven fact that substantial psychological stress occurs to people who occupy cluttered areas.

Here are a few points to keep in mind when planning your kitchen storage:

- All kitchens should contain cabinets beneath the sink to hold items such as soaps, cleaning utensils, washcloths, and drying towels. If you desire, a garbage disposal can make short work of most food waste and scraps, and an automatic dishwasher can be installed under one side of the sink counter to take care of dirty dishes, pots, pans, glasses, and utensils.

- There should be a good supply of cabinets and drawers around the food-preparation area for utensils, cutters, chopping boards, and glassware. The range and cooking center also requires cabinet space on both sides for pots, pans, dishes, trays, casserole dishes, strainers, and dozens of miscellaneous items.

- A pantry is a helpful addition for storing food, beverages, liquors, a stool, and even a small sweeper for quick cleanup (Fig. 5.3).

- After making sure that you have sufficient base and wall cabinets, drawers, and pantry space, give careful consideration to the size of your refrigerator and freezer units. Analyze your shopping habits again, and plan to purchase large enough refrigerators and freezers so that you won't find yourself short of storage space for cold and frozen foods. Do you like to hunt and fish? Is one of your hobbies picking farm-fresh fruits and vegetables? Do you raise your own bumper crops or prefer to buy meats in bulk?

- Have an efficient layout. There are four widely accepted arrangements of the three kitchen work centers: the U shape, the L shape, the parallel wall, and the one wall.

FIGURE 5.3

A pantry.

THE **U** SHAPE

With this plan, the sink is usually placed in the center leg of a U-shaped counter, between the food-storage and cooking centers. The work triangle consists of three relatively short and equal-length distances. This, plus the fact that no through traffic interferes with the triangle, is what makes the U-shape plan the most efficient and desirable arrangement for many kitchens. It's compact, step-saving, and keeps the cook out of the limelight (Fig. 5.4).

THE **L** SHAPE

This arrangement fits well on two adjacent walls and provides a good location for dining or laundry space on the opposite side of the room. It's not as convenient as the U shape, but it's the next best thing. This plan can be converted into a U shape by the addition of an island or peninsula section of counter and cabinet to work with (Fig. 5.5).

THE PARALLEL WALL

This arrangement has one work center on one wall and the others along an opposite wall. If your house seems to demand a parallel wall or "corridor" style of kitchen, take precautions to prevent kitchen traffic from interfering with the work triangle. Try to locate doors so that people won't naturally cut through the kitchen when entering or departing through a back or side door. For the sake of whatever

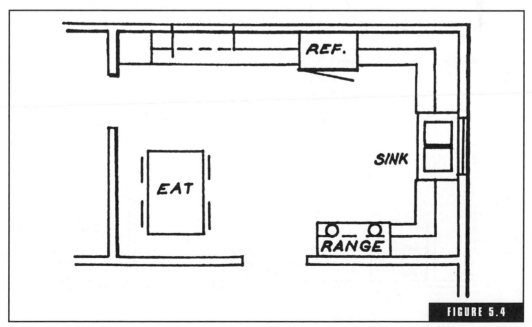

FIGURE 5.4

A U-shaped kitchen.

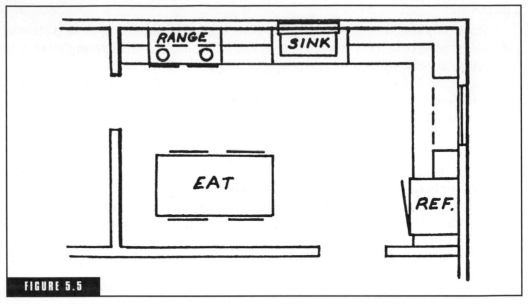

FIGURE 5.5

An L-shaped kitchen.

traffic you end up with, this corridor between the two walls should be a minimum of 4 feet wide between facing appliances and equipment. This lets two people easily pass each other while working. Avoid placing the refrigerator or oven where their open doors will block off a frequently used passageway. Otherwise, a work-triangle arrangement that is almost as efficient as that of a U shape can be constructed using this plan (Fig. 5.6).

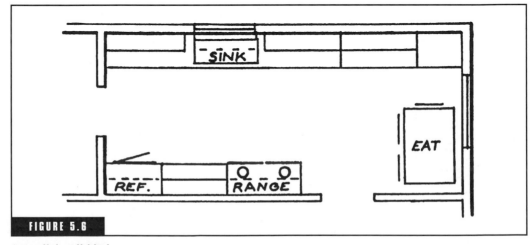

FIGURE 5.6

A parallel-wall kitchen.

THE ONE WALL

One-wall kitchens are best suited to small houses where space is extremely tight. At best, cabinet and counter space is minimal, and you have no choice but to live with relatively long kitchen traffic patterns. However, if the distance from one end of the cabinetry to the other is close to 10 feet, some degree of efficiency can be realized through carefully laid out appliances, even when a true work triangle is lacking (Fig. 5.7).

The same traffic precautions that apply to a parallel-wall kitchen also pertain to a one-wall plan.

Any kitchen arrangement can be further improved on or detracted from by placement of windows and doors. Effective lighting over the sink and main work surfaces is essential. Whenever possible, place a window that opens easily over the sink, for light, ventilation, keeping an eye on children, and even to provide a view to make washing dishes more palatable. Naturally, an electric light is still needed for night work at the sink.

Doors should encourage traffic to go around the kitchen work area instead of through it. This minimizes interruption of the cook and the possibility of spilling hot foods on innocent bystanders. The work area also should be out of the way to individuals who enter and exit the house from the rear or side and should not be directly adjacent to kitchen tables and chairs.

Other points to think about when planning the kitchen include

1. Someone will be spending a lot of time in the kitchen. Try to arrange the nicest views available through the windows or sliding doors.

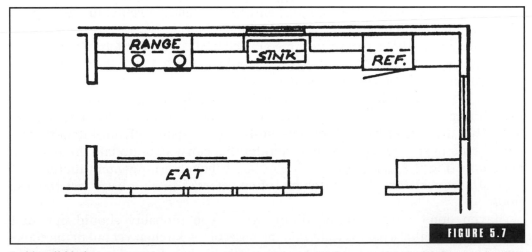

FIGURE 5.7

A sidewall kitchen.

2. There should be an exhaust fan or range hood with a built-in fan directly over the range. You need a way to expel cooking smoke, fumes, and odors to keep your kitchen fresh.

3. Plan for plenty of electrical outlets along the kitchen walls and counters. It's frustrating not to have enough outlets for the standard complement of kitchen appliances.

4. Be aware that because a kitchen is considered the heart of any household, it's best situated in a central location, close to dining areas and family entrances near the garage so that groceries can be easily carried into the house. If you plan a family room, consider having it adjoin the kitchen along one wall to facilitate traffic, communication, and even the ability to spread out if ever you throw a sizable party.

DINING SPACE

People have all kinds of theories on what dining should be. Some individuals prefer to dine on the run and aren't particular about what they eat, where they eat, or even how the food tastes. To them, eating is merely a necessary fact of life, a biological requirement.

Others enjoy taking the time and effort either to prepare or seek out gourmet-style meals. Good meals to them are to be savored slowly in the company of others in carefully structured atmospheres at home or in fine restaurants.

A typical household leans toward a happy median between the "fast-food" meal and the candlelit dinner. This is why there are often two dining areas in a typical home—one for quick breakfasts, lunches, and children's meals and another for more formal dining, which, though used less frequently, still plays an important role in holiday celebrations and special family events. In any event, a dining room should have direct access to the kitchen.

In many households, a third dining area consists of an outdoor patio or deck with a gas grill. All three areas, however, should be located near the kitchen food-preparation site for greatest convenience.

You have several basic choices to make when deciding on informal or formal dining space: Quick, easy meals and snacks can be served either at an attractive utilitarian bar, which is simply an extension of the kitchen work counter, an overhanging portion of counter that can accommodate three or four bar stools (Fig. 5.8), or a table/chairs or booth/bench arrangement included as part of an extension of the kitchen—often referred to as a breakfast room or *nook*.

If you don't want a formal dining room, you probably should opt for a table/chairs set that's placed right into the heart of the kitchen yet out of the cook's way. This arrangement is referred to as an *eat-in kitchen*. Formal meals still can be

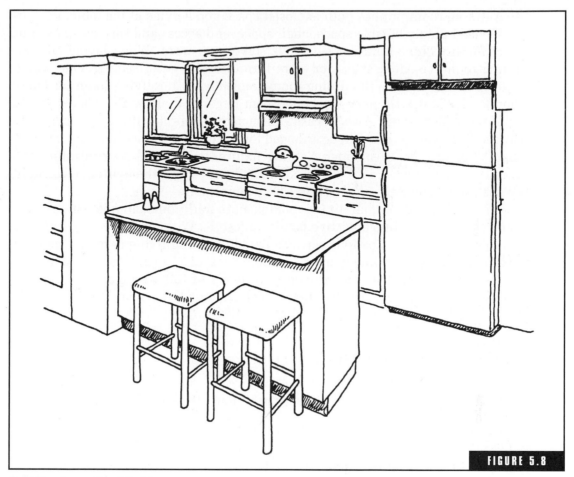

An eating bar, or breakfast bar.

served in an eat-in kitchen when special attention is given to items such as appropriate lighting, ventilation, and mood music.

The kind of kitchen dining space you prefer also depends on whether you plan to use the table, booth, or bar for other purposes. Certainly, you can hardly play cards at a breakfast bar.

If you want more than a breakfast bar or eat-in kitchen and you have the space and resources, then go with a formal dining room, too. This can be footage borrowed from a living or family room, often delineated by special interior decorations or furnishings such as vinyl flooring, wall coverings, or a chair rail. Or it could be a separate room of its own.

For ultimate privacy, doors can be installed to completely close off the dining room from the kitchen and living or family room. This can come in handy for special events such as birthday or graduation celebrations.

A dining room implies both enclosed space and service at the table. For this, you'll need plenty of table space, chair space, and access and serving space, plus room for any china hutch or side-table server you want. When laying out your dining room, consider space for extra furniture and guest seating. One way to achieve this is to have the dining room connected to the living room (or family room) area. This will make the home seem larger and allow for relaxed seating before and after dinner. Also, in case you need to expand the dining room table for extra seating, furniture could be arranged for temporary dining-table expansion. A chandelier or other suspended lighting fixture, preferably one controlled by a dimmer switch, makes a lot of sense. The ability to lower the lighting level, at little cost, will provide a relaxing and classy atmosphere.

While a separate formal dining room is more traditional, an open-style dining room can fit nicely into an active family's lifestyle. Without the walls of a formal dining room, communications between the kitchen and living or family room are greatly improved. And given to the additional cost of a separate dining room, plus the overall reduction in square footage in many of today's modern houses, the open-style dining room situated directly between the kitchen and living or family room is becoming increasingly popular.

BATHING AND WASHING SPACE

Three questions must be addressed when you consider the bathing, washing, and comfort facilities you want in your new house: Have you planned for enough bathrooms? Are the bathrooms large enough? And are the bathrooms conveniently located?

Are There Enough Bathrooms?

We've come a long way since the days of an outhouse behind every barn. Today, even a house having just one full bathroom is considered old-fashioned.

It's tempting to trade away the relatively high cost of bathroom construction and the space bathrooms require for more living and work space. As it is, though, to ensure a good market value for your house, you should seriously consider at least two bathrooms and possibly more if you have a large family.

Bathrooms come in both full and half sizes. A full bath includes a toilet, hand sink, bathtub, and/or shower (Fig. 5.9). Most modern premolded units combine a bathtub and shower in the same piece. A half bath consists of a toilet and hand sink (Fig. 5.10).

To begin with, one full bathroom should be designated for general use, close to the bedrooms. It should be accessible from most areas of the house and should not be reached by traveling through other rooms. A second bath, often directly adjacent to or back-to-back with the main bath so that plumbing fixtures can be

FIGURE 5.9

A full bath.

shared, is usually located next to the master bedroom. A third bath, or at least a half bath, can be a great convenience, especially when positioned near the living room, family room, and kitchen.

With the exception of single-level ranch houses, it is definitely a plus to locate a bathroom on each living level. This results in time and energy savings over the short and long term. If there's one thing that can make a house feel too small, it's standing in line in the morning, waiting to use the only bathroom.

A half bath.

Are the Bathrooms Large Enough?

All bathrooms should be large enough for ease of movement, proper traffic flow, and plenty of storage. Individuals who frequently get dirty at work or at play need roomy bathrooms with easy-to-clean surfaces. So do families with lots of children. People who depend on their appearances, such as models, airline attendants, politicians, salespeople, businesspeople, and others, also might prefer more spacious personal care areas with generous vanities, wide mirrors, and plusher appointments.

No matter what size full and half bathrooms you decide on, all the required fixtures and accessories should be provided and sensibly located.

- Built-in storage for towels, soap, toilet paper and tissues, shampoo, and other personal aids should be included.

- A roomy vanity and medicine cabinet rounds out the basic storage.

- Many clever and attractive shelving arrangements consisting of materials from woven reeds to glass and chrome can be custom installed into otherwise unusable space.

- A laundry hamper or built-in laundry chute will save many steps and will help to keep bathrooms neat and uncluttered.

- When no window space is available, a ventilation fan unit can be installed to ensure a turnover of fresh air and prevent stuffiness. If a window is used, though, the bathtub should not be placed beneath it. Sufficient lighting is important, and so is a heat vent.

Are the Bathrooms Conveniently Located?

In addition to being located near the bedrooms, bathrooms also should be planned near the main-floor living and working areas. If your family often engages in outdoor activities, at least one half bathroom should be placed near the outside access. That same half bath then can be used by guests and family members who congregate in the living or family room and by individuals coming from the kitchen and dining areas. This half bath is a real step saver, especially in a sprawling single-story ranch home. And remember, people—especially guests—should be able to use the bathrooms without being seen by everyone else.

The nearer to other plumbing lines you can locate the bathrooms, the better. Placing two baths back to back saves on the installation labor and material costs and takes up a minimum of space. So does situating rooms containing plumbing fixtures as close as possible and practical to where the sewer and water lines enter the house—this effectively reduces the length of indoor service piping and allows for fixtures to be drained and vented with a single stack.

SLEEPING AND DRESSING SPACE

We spend practically a third of our lives in bedrooms. When examining how bedrooms will fit into your new house, six factors should be given careful attention: size, layout, windows, closets, noise, and the importance of having a master bedroom.

Size

There should be a rhyme and reason for bedroom sizes. Look at each one separately. Will it be for children or adults? Do you want bunk beds or queen- and king-sized versions? Will a spare bedroom also serve as a sewing room? Are you planning a master bedroom complete with its own bath? In addition to providing space for beds, bedrooms should be able to comfortably accommodate a small desk, a dresser, and other clothes storage areas. Children's bedrooms should have suitable space for doing homework and for a desk, computer, computer stand, and printer. They also should contain storage shelves and sufficient closet space. There also should be enough room for dressing and personal care and ample window space to provide sufficient air and natural lighting.

Layout

There are no tricks to designing functional bedrooms, but a frequent mistake is to have a poor bed location in relation to the bedroom's traffic pattern. Because bedrooms usually have at least several doors—the entrance door from a hallway, closet doors in various arrangements, and possibly a door to a private bathroom, dressing room, or even an adjoining child's nursery—these entranceways make continuous wall space for furniture, including the bed, hard to find.

Typical bedroom traffic patterns are from the main bedroom door to the bathroom, clothes closet, or dresser in that order of frequency. If you have to walk around the end of the bed to reach any of these places, you'll have an awkward traffic pattern. When laying out each bedroom, make sure that there's a place to locate the bed or beds that won't result in the creation of obstacle courses.

An unused "secondary" bedroom is ideal for guests. If you expect frequent visitors, consider equipping such a bedroom with an attached bath for privacy. Try to have the heating and cooling for this bedroom zoned for energy savings.

Windows

Bedroom windows, like most other windows, have two primary functions: to provide light and ventilation. Windows are helpful both in cool climates, where they let the sun in to illuminate and heat bedrooms (although windows also can be mediums of rapid heat loss when the sun is absent), and in warm climates, where windows on opposite walls provide refreshing cross-ventilation breezes. At the same time, heavy-duty window shades or coverings can be used during the day to keep out the hot sun. In unusual circumstances, when only inside walls enclose a bedroom, the need for cross-ventilation can be negated by the installation of central air conditioning.

When considering the style, efficiency, and placement of bedroom windows, think about the possibility of drafts during cold weather, especially at the head of a bed placed near a window. On the other hand, such drafts can become cooling breezes that are welcome on hot summer evenings. Weigh the pros and cons, and remember that certain types of windows positioned over the head of a bed might be difficult to open or even reach.

After deciding on the types of windows you want, make sure they'll provide adequate safety, including an escape route in case of a fire. In a child's bedroom, you won't want windows so low that you'll have to worry about children falling out of them. If the windows are too high off the floor or too small, though, then the kids can't reach or escape from them during an emergency. All sleeping areas should have at least one easy-to-open window with an opening of not less than 7 square feet. Check local building code requirements for window opening width and height, as well as the sill height above the floor. All window locks should be able to be unlatched quickly so that a child or adult needing to exit for a fire is not delayed.

Closets

Closet space is vital to any bedroom. Without closets, orderly clothes storage becomes impossible. In fact, even individuals living in houses with an abundance of storage space always seem to want more closet room as the years go by and possessions keep accumulating.

To head off what could be an eventual problem, plan generous closets that make the most of their space. Consider going with a split-design version: half of it open all the way up so that dresses, raincoats, and other long garments can be hung and the other half consisting of two double-decked pole and shelf arrangements for shorter garments. Small items can be placed on shelves installed in what otherwise would have been wasted space within conventional closets. Many people are surprised when they learn how much a scientifically designed closet can neatly hold (Figs. 5.11 and 5.12).

For sheer convenience, there should be an inside light in every closet, not one operated by a pull string. Install an electrical switch either inside or outside the closet doors. Pull strings and chains have a way of getting tucked up on a shelf as something is being put away, and then they become difficult to find in the dark. Don't use a bare light bulb without some kind of glass cover. There's a danger of fire if the bulb is not at least 18 inches from the edge of the nearest shelf or from the closest item of clothing. A better alternative is to install recessed lighting in all closets.

FIGURE 5.11

An example of an efficiently laid out closet.

FIGURE 5.12

Another example of an efficiently laid out closet.

Finally, if you choose not to store extra replacement linens in a bedroom closet, see that storage for them is available in a different closet located close to the bedrooms, perhaps in a hallway.

Noise

As a rule, bedrooms should be placed together in a part of the house that's protected from outside vehicle noise from nearby streets. As much as possible, they also should be secluded from living, entertainment, and working space noise inside the house. Some dwellings lend themselves to a clear-cut separation of sleeping space: Two-story homes, for example, usually reserve the second floor for bedrooms. This clustering of bedrooms, generally near bathroom facilities, makes parental supervision easier and ensures a quiet sleeping area.

The Master Bedroom

The term *master bedroom* sounds like a throwback to medieval times, when the master and mistress of the house lived out their lives in luxury, catered to hand and foot by indentured servants. Today, a master bedroom is one common luxury item that many home owners still enjoy. But it's not a necessity. A master bedroom offers convenience and privacy, often includes a half or full bath, and typically is large enough to permit several alternative furniture arrangements. Include enough uninterrupted wall space for a queen- or king-sized bed.

As mentioned earlier, the clothes closet should be roomy. Two separate closets—"hers" and "his"—are ideal. The closets should have a minimum depth of 24 inches. The poles should have a height of between 5 and 6 feet and should be at least 12 inches from the closet rear wall. If hanging poles are to be double stacked, the top pole should be installed at least 6 feet high. It's also a good idea to sound-proof the wall between the master bath and master bedroom for the late-sleeping/early-rising couple.

SERVICE AND STORAGE SPACE

There's nothing glamorous about service and storage space. You can have spectacular living rooms for talk-of-the-town entertaining, modern kitchens that grace the covers of architectural magazines, luxurious master bedrooms, and spacious whirlpool and sauna bathrooms for pampering yourself. But who can get excited about hallways or stairs? Or laundry and utility rooms? Usually the home owners who have ill-planned ones.

Certainly these behind-the-scene features cannot be excluded from the typical house. Storage areas are also necessary accompaniments to the more popular parts of every dwelling. They include closets, small storage nooks and crannies, and garages, basements, and attics.

Hallways

There's something disconcerting about a main entrance that opens directly into your living room. Instead, look for a center hallway plan that offers access to any part of the house without leading you conspicuously through living and entertainment areas. On the other hand, excessive hallway footage, along with its special walls, means costly wasted space. To limit the space used by an entrance hall, make the entry a part of a corner of your living room but still keep it "separate" by installing a different flooring and by breaking up the ceiling line directly above the change of flooring.

Instead of completely writing off necessary hallway space as practically useless except as a pathway between rooms, consider the wall surfaces as potential showcases for artwork and photos. Strategically located lighting fixtures also will help to support an individual decorating effort. Where needed, specify 42-inch-wide hallways when possible. They make carrying large pieces of furniture safer and easier.

Stairways

This kind of house space has had its ups and downs over the years. Wrongly positioned, stairways—like hallways—can rob otherwise useful living and working space from any floor plan. To avoid this wasted effort, stairways should be constructed one on top of another whenever possible.

Even though you've probably heard a lot of nice things about the spiral stairway, don't believe all of them. Although this setup, which takes approximately 4 by 4 feet of floor space, is the most compact arrangement you can have, it's also the most expensive, inconvenient, and dangerous. The novelty quickly wears off. Ask anyone who has had to raise children around a spiral.

The most economical and convenient choice is a standard straight stairway, taking up about 8 by 3 feet of floor space. An altered version of the straight stairway that can be very acceptable is the landing stairway, consisting of a half flight of stairs that leads to a rectangular landing and then another half flight to the next floor level. The landing stairway takes up about 7 by 7 feet of floor space. It adds an extra touch to a room at a cost that is higher than that of a straight stairway but without the hazards of the spiral stairway.

When planning a basement, consider the practical advantages gained by an outside stairway. Bulky items can be carried from the back or side yard to the basement, and vice versa. This also increases the likelihood that you'll use your basement for storage instead of just dropping everything in the garage.

Laundry and Utility Rooms

Mention "laundry room" as a topic of conversation to anyone and you'll likely receive a polite nod and a yawn. Most home buyers tend to overlook the importance of both laundry and utility rooms because these areas simply don't have the pizzazz potential of other parts of a house. This is unfortunate. Haphazardly planned laundry and utility rooms are usually tucked somewhere out of the way, with little consideration for convenience.

There are two kinds of utility rooms: those with laundry facilities and those without. Utility rooms without laundry facilities can be located practically anywhere toward the outer reaches of the central living and work areas of the house. Utility rooms having laundry facilities must be positioned more carefully and can be located successfully in a number of places within a house.

The basement is one locale. This can be an economical place, although over the years you'll have to contend with constant stair climbing. If you decide on the basement as your laundry/utility area, give serious thought to a direct outside basement access (Fig. 5.13). A door to the yard lets you hang clothes outside during nice weather. It also lets you enter from the outdoors in wet or dirty clothes that can be changed right in the laundry area. Then you simply wash up at the laundry tub and proceed through the house. A clothes chute from the upstairs levels to the basement laundry basket can be another step saver.

A garage or carport is another locale. In warm-climate locations, people often choose to put their utility room either in the garage/carport or in an adjoining space called a *mud room*—so named because of its outdoors accessibility. There are no steps to climb (or very few), and with a laundry tub, you can enjoy all the conveniences found in a basement utility room having direct access to the outside. If there's a second story in the house, a laundry chute can be arranged to drop clothes straight into a garage or carport or mud room hamper.

The first floor of the house is yet another alternative. There are two types of in-house laundry rooms that can be positioned on the first floor of any house. First, there's a laundry room that's a full-size room that is a little smaller than the average bedroom but large enough to hold a washer, dryer, stationary tub, ironing board, soap, bleach, cleansers, a sewing machine and supplies, and, if enough

FIGURE 5.13

Outside basement stairs.

space is available, a working surface for sorting clothes before and after washing, drying, and ironing (Fig. 5.14). There also should be a clothes closet with floor space for storing dirty laundry out of sight. The closet should have shelves for laundry sprays, softeners, measuring cups, and scrub brushes. Consider having the clothes rod go only three-quarters of the way across the closet so that one-quarter of the vertical space can be reserved for shelves affixed from top to bottom.

The second type of first-floor in-house laundry room is a laundry center that's installed entirely within a closet (Fig. 5.15). This is a more economical route than the full-size room. Although you don't have as much space or versatility, you do have the basic necessities for washing clothes in a first-floor location. The closet in question need be only as deep and as wide as required to accommodate a washer, dryer, and stationary tub. A shelf across the top of the appliances can hold laundry baskets, soap, and other items. You might have room to stand up an ironing board, too. If not, just place it in a kitchen broom closet. A screen or folding louvered door should be installed to conceal the laundry center when no one is using it. This setup is clean, simple, and convenient.

When possible, try to have one of the first-floor laundry arrangements. They're usually the best alternatives and have the most conveniences.

Once you decide on the size and type of first-floor laundry you want, a number of other things must be considered when you're planning its location.

FIGURE 5.14

A full laundry room.

1. If it's situated near an outside door, you'll save wear and tear on carpeting. Someone walking into the house after playing football in the rain, jogging, or fishing can easily change clothes and clean up before trooping through the rest of the house. An outside access also makes it easier to hang clothes in the yard.

2. The nearer the kitchen, the better. Clothes washing can be made much more palatable when done in between other tasks. If the laundry is close to the kitchen, you can move from one area to the other with ease and accomplish more work in a shorter time span.

FIGURE 5.15

A laundry center closet.

3. If you plan your house so that the main bath and bedrooms are on the same floor as the kitchen, consider locating the laundry between the main bath/bedrooms and kitchen. Again, being near the kitchen will allow you to move easily between those work areas. Being near the main bathroom will save steps when collecting soiled clothing. And being near the bedrooms will make it simpler to put away clean clothes. If you plan a two-story house with the main bath and bedrooms on the second floor, try to include a clothes chute that will convey soiled clothes straight into the laundry room collection hamper.

4. It's nice to have a window in the laundry for the daytime sun. If you can't arrange one owing to your layout (e.g., if you have room for only a hallway closet–type laundry center), then make sure that you plan for adequate lighting. Working in the dark causes eyestrain and general fatigue.

5. The ideal laundry room should provide storage space to accommodate the following:

   ■ Soiled clothes. Preferably more than one container so that clothes can be sorted as they accumulate.

   ■ Detergents, bleach, sprays, iron, and related supplies. Be sure they are out of children's reach.

   ■ Space/shelves for folded clean clothes. Preferably a section for each family member.

   ■ If the room is large enough, an ironing board and sewing machine.

■ A place to hang clothes, especially permanent press items.

6. If you have enough room, a conventional standup ironing board will do fine. However, even if space isn't a factor, one arrangement to consider is a built-in ironing board (Fig. 5.16) that hides or folds into a wall when not in use. These ironing boards are usually strong and durable and between 40 and 48 inches in length. The units can be recessed into a wall or simply attached to it. The foldout ironing board is especially handy when you have to press one or two garments in a hurry. Ironing centers can be purchased with a variety of features, including

■ Unfinished wood cabinet doors, allowing you to stain, paint, or paper them to match a room's decor. A fully mirrored door is another alternative.

■ Storage shelves. In some, there's a special shelf for an iron to rest on, and it's constructed so that you can put the iron away immediately after use, with no cooling required. Other shelves are arranged to hold spray starch, water bottles, hangers, and similar items.

■ Automatic iron shutoffs. These devices will turn off your iron if you forget. A timer is set when you begin to iron for up to 60 minutes. If you're

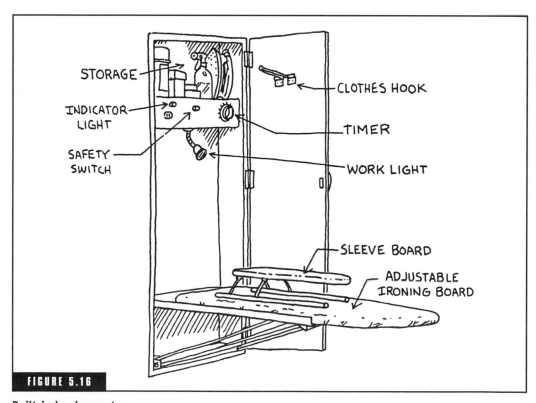

FIGURE 5.16

Built-in ironing center.

called away and cannot return before the 60 minutes are up, a red light will come on, and the iron will be turned off automatically. You simply reset the timer when you return. Look for a unit with a safety switch that turns off the electricity to the ironing center when the ironing board is put into its storage position.

- Adjustable work lights. A built-in work light that swivels up, down, and sideways to provide illumination exactly where you need it is a plus.

- Hanger hooks for just-ironed garments. The hook folds flat against the door when not in use.

- Swivel units. Some ironing centers have ironing boards that can swivel a full 180 degrees to face whatever direction you wish. This adds greater installation flexibility. An unusual room design or the location of furniture in the room usually can be accommodated by swiveling the board one way or another.

- Optional sleeve boards. This affords about a 4-inch clearance between the board and base, allowing room for maneuvering and arranging garments while ironing. These boards are great for ironing sleeves, pant legs, pleated garments, and baby clothes.

7. Double-stacked clothes washer/dryer arrangements can be used when space is at a premium. Improved design has resulted in narrower units that can be located in places previous models could not. A number of excellent 24-by-24-inch stackable washers and dryers are available. If you can live with the smaller capacities, they can be placed in a closet 30 inches wide by 30 inches deep. Necessary sprays, spot cleaners, and detergents can be kept in the same closet or in a nearby cabinet. One company makes a standard-capacity washer/dryer unit that can be placed side by side separately or double-stacked. This is an ideal option if you need large-capacity washing but still want to save space by stacking. The nice thing about double-stacking is that the clothes washing and drying machines actually can be located in a space that is comparable in size to an entrance hall closet.

8. A stationary sink located near the clothes washer will save a lot of steps. It's handy for a variety of tasks:

- Prewashing before machine washing

- Spraying spot remover on garments

- Soaking items

- Drying items

- Filling pails with water

■ Cleaning and spraying houseplants

■ Cleaning and rinsing off large items such as boots

Stationary sinks come in a variety of materials, including plastic, fiberglass, steel, and stainless steel. You'll find the plastic models to be extremely efficient and economical.

9. Clothes chutes and hampers can be an important part of the laundry center. The use of a clothes chute will save labor and time in getting the dirty clothes to the washer. Simplifying this task will encourage everyone to dispose of the items to be washed properly instead of leaving them all over the house.

   In addition to keeping the dirty clothes out of sight, hampers can be an attractive addition to the hallway or bathroom decor. Their style and shape can vary from a rectangular floor model to a bookcase-style stand-up model with adjustable shelves, an overhead cabinet, and a tip-out hamper on the bottom.

   The most popular hampers are made of machine-washable fabrics such as cotton and polyester, supported by a hardwood or brass-plated steel frame. Hand-woven rattan or willow strips are also very serviceable. If space permits, two separate hampers can be used, one for whites and one for colors.

10. One drawback to laundry centers can be the tangle of hoses and electrical cords that surround washing machines and dryers. A washing machine outlet box groups together all the water connections, drains, and electrical outlets for both machines into one neat, compact unit that can be almost hidden from view, recessed into a wall. Made of molded ABS plastic, the device meets safety standards and is available in a cream color that blends with any laundry decor. The unit should also have a contoured bottom for overflow drainage.

11. To prevent mold and mildew from forming inside closets, make sure that the clothes are dry before storing them. To help this happen, closets can be outfitted with louvered doors to provide air circulation.

As you can see, a number of arrangements are available to accommodate your laundry center. Some are more convenient than others. No matter where you locate it, here are a few additional considerations:

■ Make sure that there is an outside dryer vent. Otherwise, moisture from the clothes dryer will cause an uncomfortable environment that's tough on laundry machines and other appliances, tough on the house (moisture causes mold and mildew, will soften plasterboard, and will rust metal), and even tough on people (it's hard on the lungs).

■ If you're concerned with the possibility of overflowing wash or rinse water, have a drain installed beneath the washer. With a first-floor laundry not set up over concrete, consider vinyl flooring so that spills can be efficiently mopped up without leaving a mess.

Garages

People who have never had a garage don't realize what they're missing. They say that their cars have always been out in the weather, and but for a little inconvenience during winter, who needs a garage anyway? Once they move to a place that has a garage—even a small detached garage—they'll never go without one again. It's nice to get into a dry car after an all-evening snowstorm. It's nice to be able to pull out of the garage in the morning and drive past the neighbors who are stamping their feet and swearing while they scrape sheets of ice from their windshields. And by the same token, in the South or Southwest, it's nice to climb into a car that hasn't been roasting all day in the sun. Persistent sunlight fades paint, rots fabric, and cracks vinyl.

It's also nice to have storage space outside the house for seasonal items that can go 6 months of the year out of sight secured on garage rafters. It's nice to be able to lock up your cars, bicycles, golf clubs, tools, and spare tires in a garage.

When determining the size of your garage, consider how many vehicles you have (or plan to acquire), as well as the quantity of other items you want to store there. A roomy garage can serve many purposes other than being a car barn. Will you need additional room for workshop or hobby areas? You'll find a garage useful for storing canned foods, holding garage sales, and even as a handy play area for children when it's raining. When designing your garage,

1. Insist on at least one floor drain. If the garage will be connected to the house, there should be a drain under each car space. Contour the concrete floor to the drains so that the surface can be cleaned easily. Without the drains, dirt, mud, and slush inevitably will get tracked into the house.

2. If the garage is built under the same roofline as the rest of the house, it will simplify construction efforts and costs. The property assessment also likely will be lower with that kind of arrangement, which will, in turn, minimize real estate taxes.

3. A garage should conform to the slope of the lot. If necessary, side-sloping lots can be accommodated by lowering the garage to meet the natural lot line, but this increases the number of steps needed from garage to living area and in so doing takes away from some of the garage's usable space. On the other hand, if the garage is located higher on the same side-sloping lot, the driveway and garage floor will have to be built up substantially. This will be discussed further in Chapter 15 on garages.

4. In warm-climate locations, the garage is sometimes used to house the furnace, air conditioner, water heater, and laundry equipment. Whatever items you plan

on installing, make sure that your garage will be large enough to carry out your designs. If you place any equipment having natural gas pilot lights in a garage, precautions must be taken, especially if flammable liquids are stored there.

5. If the back of your fireplace will protrude into the garage, that must be taken into account. As mentioned earlier, such a setup will save on chimney finishing bricks, and excess heat will be radiated into the garage instead of being lost directly outside.

6. If there's enough room on the lot, consider having a three-car garage. After all, the garage is one of the least expensive parts of a house. In addition to the parent's vehicles, a son or daughter often will use the third space.

Basements

The decision to have or not have a basement is often influenced by the regional custom of the area in which you're building. Most houses in cold-climate locations will have basements. In areas having exceptionally high groundwater tables (e.g., swampy places) or not experiencing freezing temperatures during winter, however, houses do not need and sometimes should not have basements. In general, though, there are a number of advantages to a basement:

1. A basement will provide handy storage space for household materials and outdoor equipment, especially when an outside access door is installed.

2. It's an ideal out-of-the-way place to put your water heater and furnace. Both these appliances are simple to service and repair in a basement.

3. A house with a basement is usually easier to protect from wood-destroying insects such as carpenter ants and termites.

4. In a basement, water pipes are less likely to freeze, and wiring and all piping installed beneath the house are easy to get at for repairs and modifications.

5. A basement offers economical potential for future living expansion. A family room, bedroom, sauna, bathroom, workshop, darkroom, or other hobby and game room can be neatly situated in a basement. Consider a 9-foot-high basement for easier finishing later.

Some people, even though they live in areas where a basement is traditionally included with the typical house, have strong feelings that such a feature is a waste of both money and space. They consider basements as dark, dank areas suitable for merely storage and the housing of a furnace and water heater. Here are some frequently mentioned drawbacks to having a basement:

1. The necessary stairway encroaches on usable space both in the basement and on the floor above.

2. There's no doubt that basements *can* be dark, gloomy, wet, and clammy.

3. There's an expense for waterproofing and establishing proper draining around the foundation.

4. There's also the cost of basement flooring, finished walls if desired—plus heat, wiring, and lighting.

5. If the money spent on the basement could be used elsewhere, you could substantially add on to your upstairs living levels.

6. Unlike the rest of the house, the typical basement has little natural light or ventilation.

Attics

Here's a house feature that appears to be nearing extinction, going the same way as the covered sitdown front porch. Years ago, when two- and three-story houses were crammed together along big-city streets like upright dominoes, attics were included with every dwelling.

They held (and still do) old chests and cardboard boxes loaded with Christmas decorations, clothes, toys, school papers, books, antiques, and other mementos. Attics have always been cluttered, dusty repositories of family memorabilia—mostly because there was little other space built anywhere else into the house for storage. If you happen to decide on an attic, remember:

1. Although the attic opening should be located in a concealed, out-of-the-way area, it should be easily accessible when you have to use it. A good place to put a pull-down stairway unit is inside a utility room or spare bedroom closet.

2. The attic opening should at least be 23 by 54 inches. Don't settle for anything less than a drop-down staircase or ladder arrangement, especially when the attic opening is situated in the garage.

3. If possible, allow for ample attic height and headroom to enable you to move around without constantly stooping over.

4. Some individuals believe that they can store items across the attic floor joists without laying down flooring. Don't fall for this trap. Never settle for a completely unfloored attic. The more you lay down, the better.

5. Provide lighting and an electric outlet in the attic. Attics are generally dark inside. It's an inconvenience having to always carry a flashlight up there or to string an extension cord every time you want to use a vacuum cleaner, light, or power tool.

6. Provide ventilation in the attic to alleviate harmful heat and moisture buildup during summer.

7. If a pull-down stairway is not selected, don't settle for a flimsy piece of wood pulled over the attic access doorway. Instead, consider specifying a custom-made steel access door with frame, built on hinges for ease of use. This type of door will not warp, has an excellent fire rating, can be purchased with recessed hinges and catches, and is fully insulated.

Storage Space

A sufficient amount of storage space will make a home a much more pleasant place to live in. While some individuals catalog everything they own and are able to find the most obscure item at a moment's notice, others are so disorganized that they routinely lose anything from their Christmas decorations to last year's swimsuits.

The relatively recent reduction in the overall square footage of houses has wreaked havoc with storage space and thus has increased the importance that properly designed storage space can have for you. Efficient storage in bedrooms and kitchens is especially critical. Here are a few points to consider when planning your overall storage space:

1. Place a clothes closet near the main entrance.

2. Have a linen closet near the bedrooms and main bathroom to hold sheets, pillow cases, towels, washcloths, comforters, and other bulky whites.

3. Try to place a clothes closet near the garage or side entrance.

4. Locate a pantry closet in the kitchen for holding canned foods, beverages, liquor, and lots of other kitchen items.

5. Make sure that your "live" storage—for items used day in and day out—is very accessible. Live storage requires drawers, shelves, closets, and at times, chests. Each storage area should be thought out in advance for particular needs and sized accordingly. And each should be located in the proper place.

6. Your "dead" storage—for things you use only infrequently during the year, such as lawn furniture and snow tires—can be put in out-of-the-way locations. Find dead storage in the most inaccessible spots, in places such as attics, basements, and garages. Use boxes and chests to store smaller items.

It only stands to reason that as far as possible, your house should provide you with whatever you need for safety, comfort, enjoyment, and privacy. For individuals having particular interests requiring special adaptations, facilities such as the following may be desired: a sauna, steam bath, hot tub, greenhouse, elaborate garden, fountain, swimming pool, place for animals, patio/garden living room, or various outdoor work and hobby areas.

No matter which areas are most important to you, make sure that you at least consider each of the six main types of spaces under roof. In this way, you can make intelligent decisions when custom designing your house, realizing the tradeoff effects that having too much or too little of any particular space are likely to have once you move in.

A house ultimately expresses the unique personalities, goals, and lifestyles of its inhabitants. Thus a totally satisfying residence will provide you with deep-seated feelings of personal achievement and will remain a source of continuous pride.

▶▶▶▶▶ POINTS TO PONDER

1. Consider that a modern house consists of six main types of space: living and recreational, food preparation, dining, bathing and washing, sleeping and dressing, and service and storage space.

2. Carefully review and question your need for *both* a living room and a family room. Having both is no longer as necessary or traditional as it was in past years.

3. To make for a more aesthetically pleasing appearance, it's wise to include sufficient built-ins for living and recreational rooms, such as bookcases and shelves to exactly match the wood trim that's being installed throughout the home.

4. Plan in advance for special needs such as a photographic darkroom, library, den, billiard room, exercise room, or home office. They can be special areas that, depending on your interests, can greatly enhance the total living experience.

5. If you've ever heard the saying, "I hardly ever cook, so that's why I like such a small kitchen," don't believe it. The importance of counter space and storage space in a kitchen cannot be stressed enough. Consider the value of an open connection between the kitchen and family room. You can visit with family members, relatives, and guests while preparing or cleaning up food and refreshments.

6. To keep extremely messy teenagers and other so-inclined family members out of the nice bathrooms, consider a "knockaround" bathroom installed in the basement for such individuals to shower in, put makeup on, and toss their dirty clothes (if there's a basement laundry) directly near the washing machine.

7. Many home builders never understand how important closets are to bedrooms. Make them larger than you think they should be. And put lights and sturdy shelves in them.

8. Go for a larger garage than you think you'll need. If you've got enough room on the lot and you can make it fit with the overall house plan, a three-car garage may not cost much more, proportionally, than a two-car garage.

9. A well-planned attic can add inexpensive storage (and sometimes expandable) space to certain types of homes, especially when properly insulated, floored, and wired.

10. Keep in mind the value of a first-floor laundry. It will save you time and energy when conveniently located.

11. It doesn't cost much extra to run plenty of communications lines and outlets to rooms you eventually may turn into offices, such as third or fourth bedrooms. It's a lot simpler to hide the wiring in the walls while the place is under construction instead of drilling and fishing wires at a later date.

12. Although certain rooms can double as family rooms and offices simultaneously, consider that the Internal Revenue Service has strict rules for what an "office" is and may not allow deductions for a multipurpose space. Check with a tax consultant or attorney.

13. See that computers, fax machines, printers, and similar electronic components have electrical surge protection.

14. Try to store seldom-used materials in a place other than the office. Individuals are typically far more productive if they work in clean, uncluttered surroundings.

15. One drawback to many computer hutches, desks, and combination office units is that they lack clear desk space. Sure, there are all kinds of nooks, shelves, and drawers and a pullout keyboard drawer, but there's hardly enough room to place an open reference book or even enough desk space to make out checks to pay bills. Plan open desk space for any office, and you'll be glad you did.

16. Plan as much window space as possible for an office—with appropriate window treatments.

17. Make sure that the flooring matches the work or activities. For instance, artists may favor wood or vinyl that resists paint, glue, and ink spills. A section of family room may be covered with vinyl, composite, or tile, with a number of throw rugs for casual lounging and furniture placement, leaving the artist's corner with the more durable, easy-to-clean flooring.

18. Plan some noise-blocking control for an office, not necessarily soundproofing, but something to blunt television, play, or conversation sounds. This could mean a divider made from a bookcase, partial block glass wall, heating appliance, or portable units.

19. Set up a television/DVD player, if desired, for business and relaxation use.

20. Combine some sort of exercise equipment or small exercise area in the office (if it's not overwhelming, it won't encroach on the overall office use).

House Styles and Types

Your ideal house, a dwelling that's both handsome and practical, is much more than simply a collection of great rooms. Certainly, a well-designed house that offers plenty of living security, enjoyment, and pride of ownership should feature memorable individual rooms. But that's not enough.

To work as a single unit, rooms should be arranged to match your living requirements and lifestyle as closely as possible. Now, to add energy efficiency in a major way, the basic shape of the dwelling will have a huge impact on efficiency possibilities.

When it comes to green homes, is there any particular configuration or shape your house should take? As in most discussions about green construction, more than one perspective exists. The shape you choose for your house certainly will help to define the entire project. But is one particular shape a knockdown winner when it comes to green home building?

Not really. Almost any home type can be constructed using green building principles. While a square home might be intrinsically more resource and energy efficient because there is the smallest possible ratio of exterior wall coverage to interior square footage, looking at a single dimension or characteristic never tells the whole story. A longer rectangular home actually may be more energy efficient, even with more exterior wall space, if passive-solar design is included in one of the south-facing longer sides.

But the square home, usually with two or more stories, if no other conditions are considered, is probably the easiest with which to achieve energy and resource efficiency. Proportional to its volume, its environmental footprint is minimized, there's less roof area exposed to sun and elements, it will conserve heated and cooled air the easiest, and it results in more square feet of living space given the amount of building materials used.

Even with these apparent advantages, a square home is still not a slam dunk all the time. There are too many other factors involved in the decision-making process. A square, boxy house typically does best on a relatively flat building site. It won't work well on a side-to-side, back-to-front, or front-to-back construction site. And it won't work if a member of the family uses a wheelchair. There are reasons other than greenness for constructing a home. A person's or family's living requirements, the geographic area, the weather, and the possible orientations on the site also must be considered when deciding on a house type.

Depending on where the house is to be built, a low-to-the-ground single-story ranch may be the best house type to take advantage of passive heating features, natural ventilation, and the desire for multiple decks, patios, and sunrooms.

Your home should contain the correct amount of space to suit you and your family or future family. It shouldn't be too small or too large.

The best way to go about putting a house together in your mind is also the most logical. First, decide on the amount of space you want roofed over. Once that's established, you can go on to the style and type of house that will best lend itself to your objectively arrived at space requirements and your subjectively arrived at preferences for appearance and setting. Naturally, both advantages and disadvantages exist for all the various types of houses, and these characteristics will be pointed out later in this chapter.

Somewhere in the back of your thoughts, while considering space requirements and house types, keep in tune with your financial parameters. If money or income is a major problem, pay particular attention to Chapter 8 on planning for future expansion.

Traditional housing types and styles in your area are there for a reason, having evolved over the years from being constructed with local materials and shapes that best fit into their surroundings—lots of stucco, adobe, rammed earth, and flat tile roofs in the Southwest, for example. Solar designs are seen in the Southeast and on the West Coast, and single-story, squat homes are seen across the windy Great Plains, along with some earthen-berm construction aimed at survival in windstorms. Stone and brick multilevel and multifamily townhouses are seen up north and in the Northeast.

When deciding how much space will be roofed over

1. Arrive at the number of rooms you want. The six types of spaces were discussed in Chapter 5. Figure out your ideal number of rooms—what they are and their sizes—and then, just to be safe, also determine the minimum number of rooms you can get along with.

2. Determine a dollar-per-square-foot cost, and decide how much you can afford or wish to spend. Consider how much of a down payment you can come up with, plus the cost of current mortgage rates in your area. To arrive at how much you can expect to pay per square foot of house space, attend new-construction open houses for homes that are built with similar materials and workmanship to what you'd consider acceptable. When at an open house, ask what the going price for the house is excluding the lot, and then divide those total dollars by the amount of square feet the house has. Square footage means the livable area of the house. It doesn't include the garage, basement, or attic. What you can spend on a home mortgage is usually governed by ratios of indebtedness to income that are conservatively set by banks and savings and loan institutions.

3. Decide on the style of architecture you'd prefer. Some styles are innately larger than others. Some styles are low key, whereas others literally exude a certain social status. Your choice is likely to be influenced by climate, geographic location, personal taste, finances, and the dwellings already built in the area or neighborhood you decide on.

4. The last consideration, and a consideration more important than style, is the *type* of house you want: a single-story, one-and-one-half-story, two-story, split-foyer, or multilevel house.

HOUSE STYLES

Style is a broad concern that ultimately will affect your choice of house. It most commonly indicates the decorative features of the exterior and to some degree the interior. An overview of the various house architectural styles reveals that individual styles are best suited to their own particular climates and locations. They're frequently constructed of local or native materials, with exteriors and even appropriate colors that complement their surroundings.

When looking at particular styles, you will find that early American, Cape Cod, colonial, Georgian colonial, and southern colonial are all styles that have withstood the whims of change. The first two are compact, informal houses that are well suited to the northern sectors of the United States. The Georgian and southern colonial styles are larger and more formal. The Georgian is adaptable to both the northern climates and the milder climates, and the southern colonial—actually a form of Georgian—is especially suited to the warm and humid climate of southeastern regions. Meanwhile, the mission or adobe style is particularly good in the hot, dry climate of the Southwest; in the warm, wet areas of the Southeast, adobe would not withstand a single rainy season. The adobe style is a prime example of how house styles often incorporate local materials of a particular region.

A popular and far-reaching style that has been evolving over recent years is the contemporary. This style is suited to the theory that "anything goes" and has few rules to follow or break. Contemporary houses can be simple, basic, and inexpensive. Or they can be extremely liberal in their composition, consisting of any of a variety of singularly dominant characteristics from long, sweeping rooflines to a half-dozen levels juxtaposed over one the other. Contemporaries can be full of big open spaces and constructed with huge panes of glass, hand-hewn stones, posts, and beams and modern, brightly colored manufactured materials. Innovative features such as passive-solar heating, central courtyards or greenhouses, interior balconies, and spacious wood decks are frequently part of the contemporary plan.

But contemporary houses are not for everyone. They can mean skilled engineering, expensive plans and drawings, tricky construction, costly materials, and high utility bills from heating cathedral ceilings and similar extravagant spaces.

Although individual construction styles may vary greatly from one another, they all must answer to certain design guidelines. No matter which style you lean toward, consider the following points in regard to your own house plans:

1. Think about the design of your house in relation to the complexity of construction. If the house makes a turn anywhere—for example, L shaped or U shaped rather than running in a straight line—you introduce construction complications. A gable roof, which is simply two sloped surfaces meeting at a high point called a *ridge*, is economical and comparatively easy to build *until* you choose to turn a corner with it; then the junction forms a V-shaped indentation, and the affected rafters require compound angle fitting, a construction technique that takes much more time and skill. Instead of laying down simple angles where all the rafters are positioned in the same fashion, boards must be measured and cut individually to multiple lengths and angles.

   Another suggestion that will keep construction costs lower is to build the outside walls free from a lot of ins, outs, jigs, and jogs (Fig. 6.1). Most houses look better anyway if they don't have a number of rooflines joined together. Otherwise, a house will appear cluttered and haphazardly designed. In general, a simple square or rectangular plan gives you more house for the money.

2. A few additional comments about the roof and roofline should be made here: A continuous roofline gives an impression of greater size than a roofline broken up into several different planes. A roof should extend or overhang past the outer walls 2 to 4 feet. Not only does this lend a handsome and distinctive appearance to the house, but it also helps to protect windows and outer walls from snow, rain, and sun. Another plus is that it keeps water away from the foundation and basement. A substantial overhang is a feature largely ignored by many builders. It shouldn't be excluded. For the relatively small cost of an overhanging roof, there are too many benefits to go without one.

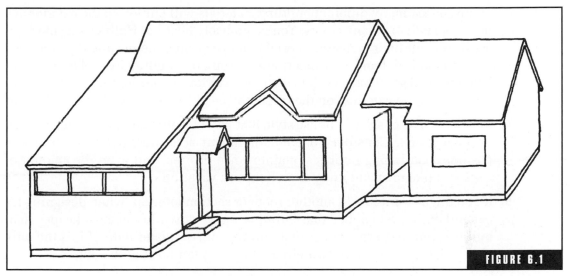

FIGURE 6.1

A house cluttered with many ins, outs, jigs, and jogs.

A roof over the main entranceway will shield you from the elements while you're fumbling for your house key or will keep your visitors out of the rain while they're waiting for you to answer the door. It also provides a nice spot for you to sit on a patio or lawn chair in comfortable shade during the summer.

3. Remember that good proportions are one of the first rules of a good-looking house. The exterior of your house should not have more than two (at *most*, four) sizes of matching windows, apart from glass sliding doors. At the same time, the doors should not be of abnormal size or located in odd places. To arrive at a satisfactory scale and proportion of doors and windows, compare what's already been installed on existing houses in neighborhoods in which you'd feel comfortable. Get a feeling for the styles of windows and doors you prefer.

The tops and bottoms of all equal-sized windows should line up, conforming to one long horizontal line across the house. Smaller windows should line up with the tops or bottoms of larger windows. When the tops of exterior doors also line up with window tops, things will look even better.

The exterior should not consist of more than two or at the very most three kinds of siding materials so that the whole appearance works toward a single theme. If a wide variety of materials is present, the house will not be pleasing to the eye, *and* the exterior likely will end up costing more than necessary and will be difficult to maintain properly. Never mix more than three materials such as aluminum siding, wood siding, bricks and stone, or glass. Each will compete with the others, resulting in an extremely "busy" and disconcerting effect.

Just as too many different building materials will clutter up the exterior of a house, so will too many colors. You've probably heard of Hollywood entertainers who paint their mansions a bright orange or obscene purple. If you merely want a practical, handsome exterior that won't draw curiosity seekers and will help ensure a good resale value, then the exterior of your house should be consistent with the exteriors on the rest of the neighborhood dwellings.

4. It makes sense to select a house style that will closely match the living pattern of your family. Consider your entertainment activities, hobbies, children's pastimes, gardening interests, maintenance desires, and even the amount of time you like to spend away from home on vacation.

5. If you might want to add another room or section later on, when designing for expandability, remember that building up or down is always cheaper than building out. Also remember that building out at a later date, if it is the only alternative, will be more cost efficient if you plan for it at the outset.

House Types

House *type* denotes the number and arrangement of a dwelling's living levels. The basic types of houses are the single-story ranch, the Cape Cod or one-and-one-half-story house, the two-story house, the split-foyer house, and the multilevel house.

Again, an important consideration that will affect your choice of house type is your lifestyle. You want the house that best fits your needs and meets your ideas of personal acceptance and preference, as well as something that fits the setting you desire.

Some family activities that will affect the type of house you want include

- *Entertaining.* Card playing, informal and formal dinners, outdoor barbecues, large cocktail parties, teenage parties, and other pursuits all present different requirements.

- *Privacy.* Families and individual members differ in their desire and need for privacy.

- *Hobbies.* These can present special problems related to space, storage, and noise levels. For example, a drummer needs a different kind of space than a stamp collector. The woodworker needs room for bulky tools and materials and will be a major generator of noise.

The Single-Story Ranch

This type of house (Fig. 6.2) can be constructed in a wide variety of sizes, shapes, and designs. It can be built over a full or partial basement or a crawl space or on a concrete slab foundation (Fig. 6.3).

FIGURE 6.2

A ranch home.

Before the advantages and disadvantages of the ranch are discussed, here are some general guidelines applicable to all single-story plans:

- The single-story plan should provide access from both the front main entrance and a rear or side entrance into the house without routing people directly through the center of the living room or kitchen work area.

- The living room should not be used as a corridor at the expense of carpeting and furnishings but instead should provide the privacy for which it was

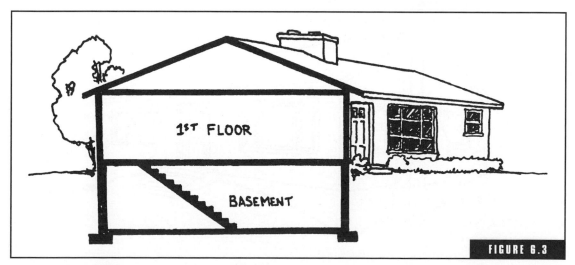

1ST FLOOR

BASEMENT

FIGURE 6.3

A ranch home cutaway.

intended. An entry foyer should distribute traffic so that visitors don't have to step directly into the living room. This prevents congested cross-traffic and interruptions.

■ The kitchen, laundry, family room, and any busy work center of the house should be accessible from an outdoor patio or deck if one is included in your plan.

■ The master bedroom suite should be assured of privacy by its remoteness from the family room, kitchen area, and outdoor living space.

■ If you choose to go with a ranch house, don't try to match it to a lot with a substantial forward slope. Ranches look best if they appear to be hugging the ground; a forward-sloping lot requires an exposed foundation in the front, which detracts from the low look of a ranch (Fig. 6.4). Single-story houses ideally are suited to flat lots or sites that gently slope to the sides or rear, particularly if the plans call for a walkout from a basement or lower living area. This is also a way of economically increasing the amount of living space because the lower level is an extension of the foundation.

ADVANTAGES

1. Single-story houses offer the greatest livability for all members of the household regardless of age. Major rooms are located on a single level (unless a

FIGURE 6.4

A ranch home on a forward-sloping lot.

basement has been expanded into living space). The overwhelming advantage of this house is its suitability to families having senior citizens or young children. There are no second-story stairs to climb up or tumble down.

2. Single-story houses can be made very relaxing and informal through the use of outdoor space. They offer the most convenience for indoor/outdoor living, with plenty of possibilities for porches, patios, terraces, planters, and gardens that can be built adjacent to and integral with any room.

3. Single-story houses can have spacious basements. You might be one of those persons who thinks that if you're going to have a cellar, it might as well be a large one. After all, basements are good for storage, workshops, heating appliances; billiards, Ping-Pong, and other sports and hobbies; future expansion of living space; and laundry facilities if you can't have your laundry on the first floor.

4. As a rule, ranch houses are easy to build. They're close to the ground. You needn't resort to double-length ladders and scaffolding to reach much of the structure, as you have to with two-story houses and Cape Cods, for instance.

5. Because there are fewer living levels, heating and cooling systems don't have to negotiate additional floors and ceilings once the main living level is taken care of. The same is true with the plumbing system. There is much less maneuvering of ducts, pipes, and electrical wiring in a single-story house.

6. A single-story house is the easiest to keep clean after it's built. Not having to climb stairs is a big time-saver. In a ranch, you don't have to worry about keeping cleaning equipment on more than one floor.

7. A single-story house is easy to expand even if no preparations were made at the time of original construction. You can simply convert part of the basement into living area, or you can add on an exterior wing. Of course, if you know in advance that you will want additional space later (as discussed in Chapter 7), you can make provisions in the walls where the expansion will be.

8. With a single-story house, you can consider a contemporary-looking sloped ceiling that follows the pitch of the roof so that ceiling joists are not required and a feeling of spaciousness is created. Insulation and ceiling materials are applied directly to the rafters. This is a common building practice in the South, but it also can be used—with today's energy-efficient insulation—in the North as well.

9. When designed with trussed rafters, a ranch can benefit from the popular open planning, in which living, dining, kitchen, and family alcove sections are designed as part of one interconnected space. Because structural partitions are not needed except for privacy, areas can be arranged by furniture

placements, room dividers, folding partitions, and even projecting or free-standing fireplaces.

10. A one-story house is much easier to inspect and maintain owing to its proximity to the ground. The roof pitch is usually very low, so it's not difficult to climb onto, walk on, or repair the roof. The outside walls, if constructed of painted materials, are simple to touch up or repaint, and it's easy to perform other routine housekeeping tasks such as washing windows and cleaning out gutters.

DISADVANTAGES

1. Single-story houses have been described as being typically informal owing to the reduced amount of privacy found between their walls. The single-floor layout increases the importance of effective interior zoning—for the careful placement of physical buffers between the living, working, and sleeping areas. The need for such buffers (along with an aversion to stair climbing) may be greater in a family that includes very old or very young members who need more rest than other family members.

2. Some people just don't feel comfortable sleeping on a first-floor level for reasons of privacy and security.

3. Ranch houses cost more to build per square foot than other house types because of their high ratio of foundation and roof to living space.

4. It's difficult and expensive to build upward on a ranch.

5. Single-story houses usually require relatively wide lots and might be difficult to locate on the smaller parcels found in many neighborhoods.

6. Heating and cooling costs tend to be higher per square foot in ranches because all the ceilings and floors are essentially exterior surfaces. Exterior surfaces allow heat to leak out during winter and coolness to escape during summer. On multilevel houses, at least some ceilings and floors are interior surfaces.

7. Although it's easy enough when you have room to spread out on a building site, expanding a single-story house can be expensive and difficult on smaller parcels where the house already has been situated on the lot based on zoning restrictions. Local restrictions may prohibit expanding any closer to lot sides and setbacks.

The Cape Cod

This traditional design (Fig. 6.5) derived its nickname from the place where it was first built. Originally a testament to pure function, it resembled a simple Monopoly-style square house capped with a broad, low-slung roof all constructed

FIGURE 6.5

A one-and-one-half-story home.

around and over a massive stone chimney that stood erect through the dead center of the house.

Such a monumental chimney served several purposes. First, since the entire house had been built up around the chimney, each room had its own fireplace—either for cooking or for warmth—and all fireplaces conveniently shared the same chimney. Second, the chimney also helped to give the house stability against fierce Atlantic gales and shifting seacoast sands.

Most of the original Cape Cods were 38 by 29 feet or smaller. They had low ceilings, rarely over 7 feet high. This was about the largest space that could be heated with wood. The entrance was centered at the front of the house, directly opposite a central stairway that led to the second floor. The second floor started at the roofline and was often supplemented with "eye" dormers for additional room, light, and ventilation. Thus resulting dormitory-style rooms were popular for storage and for children's bedrooms.

On the first floor, the front of the house consisted of two large rooms, one on each side of the central stairway. A large "colonial" kitchen took up the entire rear of the dwelling and was flush against the massive all-purpose fireplace hearth. The bathroom was out back. Way out back.

The Cape Cod's windows were small and shuttered to keep out windblown sand and hail and driving January snows. The small panes, or "lites," making up each window were used because of the limitations of the glass-blowing industry in those days. Large panes were difficult to make true and clear.

The entire house usually faced squarely south to take advantage of every available ray of winter sunshine, plus, cleverly enough, to enable occupants to tell time: When the sun's rays came straight through the front window, hitting a marker on the floor in such a way, the people inside knew it was high noon.

As decades passed, and long after the original reasons for the Cape Cod design had ceased to exist, the one-and-one-half-story house again found supporters during the Great Depression of the 1930s. Home builders liked them because Cape Cods were compact, thrifty houses to construct, especially when the huge fireplaces were left out. Cape Cods had another resurgence after World War II, when builders mass-produced row after row of them. And the houses are still popular today in larger, more luxurious versions.

Here are a few general guidelines for the one-and-one-half-story house:

- It can be built over a full or partial basement or a crawl space or on a concrete slab foundation.

- Although the Cape Cod typically still has a front center entrance, it's also a good idea to have a rear access as well.

- As with the ranch, an entrance foyer should distribute traffic so that visitors don't step directly into the living room from the outside.

- In a Cape Cod, the master bedroom is often located on the first floor, with the other bedrooms upstairs. Whether on the first or second floor, the master bedroom should be assured of privacy.

- Even if the second story will not be finished off initially, make provisions for future expansion (Fig. 6.6). Have the ceiling/roof area insulated instead of the second floor (more on this in Chapter 7).

ADVANTAGES

1. A Cape Cod is an economical house to build, with a low cost per square foot of living area. It requires proportionally less materials and labor to construct than other types, and because of its relatively small basement foundation and roof, a larger amount of living space can be had for a smaller financial outlay.

2. Its two living levels allow distinct zoning for privacy.

3. The Cape Cod is known for its low heating and energy costs owing to its efficient shape.

4. It can be constructed on a small lot.

5. The completed Cape Cod needs fewer furnishings and less interior decoration and takes less time to clean and maintain than other house types.

6. Its low roofline makes it fairly simple to build and maintain but not as simple as a ranch.

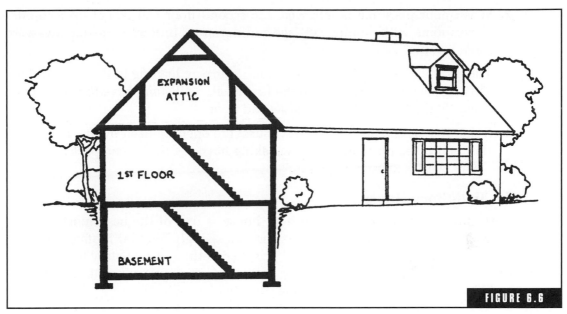

FIGURE 6.6

A one-and-one-half-story home cutaway.

7. The second story can be left unfinished and initially used for attic storage. Later, if more living space is needed, the area then can be employed for practical expansion. This is an economical approach to the problem of insufficient funds. You can initially run heat and air-conditioning pipes and ducts, plumbing pipes, and electrical lines to the second floor and then cap them off there. For air circulation, you can install louvered ventilators at each end of the attic from the start. In short, a design like the Cape Cod offers a great "finish it later" potential. This is good for young starters or newlyweds who at first need only a minimum of space but want more later on as the family grows. Then, when the children eventually leave home, the second floor can be converted into an income unit or merely sealed off and used for storage.

8. Here, one person's advantage can be another's disadvantage. Many people contend that climbing stairs in a Cape Cod or other house having stairs is good exercise to help keep them fit.

DISADVANTAGES

1. Upstairs rooms beneath the roof tend to be hot during summer and cold during winter unless special care is taken when insulating and installing heating and air-conditioning systems.

2. When poor planning is followed, the second floor can be cut up into odd-sized rooms with sloping ceilings and dormer windows—causing awkward room layouts.

3. There's the need to provide space for a stairway leading to the second floor. This is space taken away from the first level. And stairs have to be ascended every time you want to visit the second floor.

4. If there's a basement beneath the house, the opening used by the downstairs stairwell takes up more space, wreaking havoc with the compact first floor, where every square foot counts.

The Two-Story House

All things considered, the two-story house is one of the best, most efficient designs available (Fig. 6.7). It has become increasingly popular for families looking for a spacious yet economical and private dwelling. A two-story house can be built over a full or partial basement or a crawl space or on a concrete slab foundation (Fig. 6.8). Some general guidelines to consider include

- Once again, through the use of an entry foyer, access should be provided to all parts of the house from the main entrance. The entry foyer is usually the best place to start the upstairs stairway so that those entering the house can go straight to the second floor if they choose.

- As in the other house types, the living room should not be a traffic runway.

FIGURE 6.7

A two-story house.

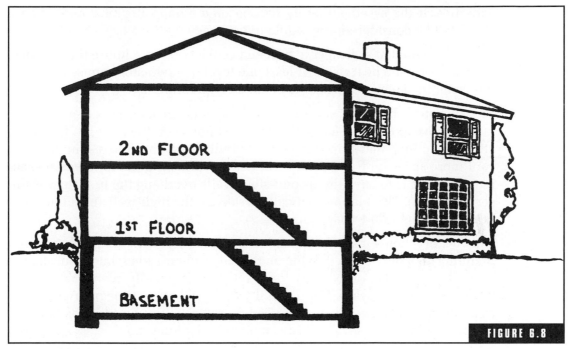

FIGURE 6.8

A two-story house cutaway.

- A rear entrance should be provided (or a side entrance), with direct access to the kitchen, laundry, family room, and all other working and living areas of the house.

- The upstairs bedrooms should be planned so that you don't have to walk through one bedroom to reach another.

ADVANTAGES

1. There's natural zoning between the upstairs and downstairs. The upstairs serves as an effective buffer between the sleeping areas and the downstairs living and work spaces.

2. Certain individuals prefer the feelings of privacy, security, and comfort brought about when their bedrooms are located on a second story, well above ground level.

3. Building up as opposed to out is cheaper per square foot. A two-level square house with a given amount of floor space requires only half as much foundation and roof as it would if constructed as a single-level dwelling. Building down means a basement. One justification for a basement is its value as living area. But here the term *living* area is broadly used to cover basement recreation rooms, workshops, hobby areas, and similar spaces planned for special

activities. If the basement likely will become a depository for junk, then it shouldn't be considered as possible living space.

4. Size being equal, it's cheaper to heat and cool a two-story house than a ranch. Cool air falls, and heat rises. At least one level in a two-story house reaps certain benefits, no matter what the outside temperature is.

5. The two-story house is adaptable to small lots. In fact, no other common house type can match it for getting the most house on the least lot. It's a good choice on either high-priced land or a tight little parcel. And a simple way to gain more space on the second level without affecting the foundation space requirements is to have the second-story walls overhang the first-story walls, garrison-style. This also aesthetically breaks up the high-wall appearance you otherwise might find unappealing.

6. A two-story house can be expanded successfully without much advance planning. A family room or wing on the side can be added, but at substantial cost. Owing to its compactness on a lot, there's usually plenty of room to build an attached garage. Naturally, if you decide at the time of original construction that someday you will need more space, by building expandable features into the house, you'll save money in the long run.

7. Physical fitness buffs will swear that a two-story house improves the cardio-vascular system because occupants are forced to exercise by climbing up and down stairs.

DISADVANTAGES

1. Having to go up and down stairs frequently makes housekeeping tougher and puts a strain on the parents of young children and the elderly.

2. It puts restrictions on a family that likes to spend a lot of time outdoors. Although the downstairs can be designed for easy access to the backyard, you might find the times needed to trudge upstairs to retrieve something from a bedroom will amount to a noticeable inconvenience.

3. Unless the attic of a two-story house is ventilated properly, the upstairs bedrooms will get uncomfortably hot during summer.

4. Without an elaborate network of wood decks and patios, the upstairs bedrooms are usually shut off from direct access to the outdoors and are not easy to escape from in case of fire or other emergencies.

5. Although the per-square-foot cost of a two-story house is much lower than that of a single-story house, extra footage must be provided in the two-story house to compensate for the space lost to the second-floor stairway. In addition, the upstairs stairway limits the flexibility of the overall design.

6. Long ladders are needed to reach the roof, gutters, and second-story windows.

The Split-Foyer House

A split-foyer house (Fig. 6.9) is essentially a raised single-story house with the basement or lower level lifted halfway out of the ground and joined to an entry foyer. The lower level is usually finished off into part of the house's living quarters. An identifying characteristic of the split-foyer house is that the entry foyer is always located about halfway between the two living levels. In other words, once you step into a split-foyer house, you have to go either up or down (usually a half flight of stairs) to reach a living level (Fig. 6.10). Split-foyer houses have also been called, rightly and wrongly, *midlevel houses*, *raised-level houses*, and *raised ranches*. As with the other house types, there are general points to keep in mind when designing a split-foyer house:

■ Split-foyer houses are meant to be constructed on lots having front-to-back or back-to-front slopes. It's silly to place them on dead-level ground. Take a drive through practically any middle-class suburb. You'll notice that the worst-looking split-foyer houses—the "no design" kind—have all been erected on flat lots. Built so, they appear ungainly and awkward. Instead, they should be closely fitted onto sloping parcels so that a natural marriage between the house and land results.

■ The two levels of a split-foyer house provide distinct zoning to help separate working and living activities. Further, room functions can be planned in a variety of ways. On a front-to-back downward sloping lot, the rear entrance is likely to be located in the upper living area, even if it means the

FIGURE 6.9

A split-foyer home.

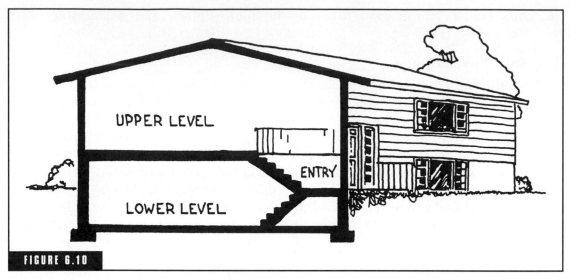

UPPER LEVEL

ENTRY

LOWER LEVEL

FIGURE 6.10

A split-foyer home cutaway.

construction of an outside wood deck or concrete patio with steps to the ground.

- A split-foyer house's entry, like the other entry setups, must direct traffic through a hall or foyer arrangement to upstairs and downstairs rooms without marching visitors through the center of other rooms along the way. The rear entrance also should permit easy travel to the kitchen, laundry, and remaining areas.

- The arrangement of living areas can vary greatly in split-foyer houses. Some plans have all the bedrooms on one floor, with the working and living spaces on the other level. Some plans combine living and sleeping areas on both floors. The garage can be included in the lower level or attached to the side of the house with its own entry. In any layout, the bedrooms—especially the master bedroom—should be assured privacy from the rest of the house.

ADVANTAGES

1. This design offers easy entry from the outside to either interior level.

2. The entrance foyer midway between the upper and lower levels has direct access to at least one bath, thus reducing traffic near the main living areas.

3. Properly designed, a split-foyer house can look handsome and large, with only a short stairway from either level to the outdoors.

4. The split-foyer house can provide automatic interior zoning, with the sleeping area on one level and the working and living areas on the other.

5. Greater window depth is allowed in the lower level, which yields improved lighting and ventilation. In turn, this helps the area normally referred to as the basement become more desirable for recreation rooms, baths, and bedrooms.

6. The split-foyer house uses its floor area to the maximum. It has a lower per-square-foot cost than a single-story ranch.

7. The simple floor plan and relatively compact design of this house result in construction convenience and savings.

8. With proper attention to correct insulation and careful positioning of heating and cooling systems, the split-foyer house is easier to make energy efficient than a house that has many projections and corners or one that is spread out.

9. Most split-foyer houses are suitable for small lots.

10. The minimal foundation and roof areas help to reduce construction costs.

11. When the upper living area faces downhill, you enjoy the full advantage of a view with height.

12. Again, with this design, a physical fitness buff will proclaim that exercise on the stairs helps to strengthen the heart.

DISADVANTAGES

1. There's the inconvenience of frequent stair climbing.

2. Even though this house can be energy efficient, because the stairway is more open than that of a two-story house, for instance, heat quickly rises to the upper level. If proper insulation, heating, and cooling steps are not taken, the lower level tends to be cold during winter. Special wall insulation below ground level is necessary, and a well-designed heating/cooling system is a must. Rooms over the garage also can be chilly if not well insulated. And during summer, without enough insulation, rooms on the upper level will tend to be on the warm side.

3. The open stairway also reduces the effect of the zoning, not visually, but because it allows odors and noise to move freely from floor to floor.

4. The split-foyer house, owing to its structure and design, is not easily expandable at a later date.

5. Because the lower level of a split-foyer house is usually designed for living areas, there's not much room to have a basement workshop or storage facilities.

The Split-Level or Multilevel House

These houses (Figs. 6.11 and 6.12) are essentially split in half vertically with two or more levels so that the upper level is only half as high as the ground level. A typical layout for this design has the kitchen, dining room, and living room on one level (the ground level) and with the bedrooms on another level a half story higher. The ground level may be over a full basement or over a crawl space in warm-climate regions, with the upper half story over a garage that's on a grade. Here are some general guidelines to keep in mind when planning a multilevel or split-level house:

- Split-level houses ideally are suited for side-sloping lots on hilly terrain where the bottom level faces and opens toward the downhill side and the upstairs level opens toward the uphill side (Fig. 6.13). A split-level house placed on a flat lot will look awkward and will not be a very functional dwelling.

- Arrangements of living areas vary in split-level houses. It's best to have the living facilities on one of the upper levels and the sleeping rooms on

FIGURE 6.11

A multilevel home.

FIGURE 6.12

A split-level home.

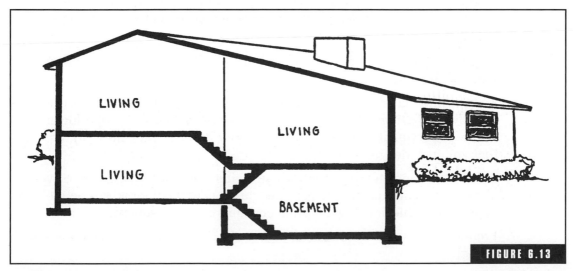

FIGURE 6.13

A split-level home cutaway.

another level for noise breakup and privacy zoning. As with other types of homes, the bedrooms, especially the master bedroom, should be carefully located for privacy.

■ The main entrance may be either on the upper or lower grade, as determined by the slope of the building site relative to the street.

■ Matching a split-level house to a side-sloping lot allows close to a full height exposure on both sides of the dwelling, making each side fully accessible to the outdoors.

■ As with other house types, it's a good idea to have a front and rear entrance in a split-level house, even though these entrances may be located on different levels. In any event, the living and working centers of the home, including the kitchen and laundry, should be easily accessible from either entrance.

■ An entry foyer should distribute traffic via a hallway to the rooms on its own level and to the stairs leading to other levels.

■ Consider that the basement is usually the best place to put the heating system, storage space, and perhaps a workshop, if desired.

ADVANTAGES

1. This style of house adapts well to lots with side slopes.

2. A split-level house has many of the same advantages as a split-foyer house. It produces automatic interior zoning. The sleeping area can be on one level and the working and living areas on other levels.

3. A split-level house can offer easy entry from the outdoors to any interior level. On a side-sloping lot, you will have at least two main floors with access straight to the outside.

4. When designed properly, a good split-level house will look handsome and large, with only a short stairway from one level to the other.

5. There can be greater window depths in the lower level, which will provide improved lighting and ventilation for possible expansion of the lower level into a recreational room, bedrooms, or any other living and working space that you may desire.

6. If the areas beneath the upper level are being used for living space or even for a garage, this means that at least three-quarters of the floor area is actively put to good use, thus making the price per square foot reasonably low.

7. Frequent short bursts of stair climbing are considered a plus by the health conscious.

8. When the upper level faces downhill, there's the scenic advantage of a view with height.

9. With the ability to have access from the outside on at least two levels, there should be no problem locating a bathroom near each entrance.

DISADVANTAGES

1. Split-level room arrangements can be jumbled and disjointed if care is not taken during the initial planning stage. You could end up with a house that requires you to climb steps no matter where you want to go or what you want to do.

2. The heating and cooling requirements of split-level houses can be very demanding. The lowest level tends to be cold during winter and needs special wall insulation for any area below ground. A well-designed heating/cooling system is a must. Rooms constructed over a garage tend to be chilly, and the rooms in the upper level are frequently too warm in the summer unless proper precautions are taken. This is largely due to the number of open stairways present, similar to those in a split-foyer house.

3. The open stairways reduce the zoning effect by letting odors and sounds travel freely from one level to another.

4. Because the split-level house has so many different levels, it can be tough to build. This runs up the cost per square foot, especially if substantial bulldozing of the lot is needed for the foundation and landscaping or if retaining walls must be constructed.

5. Another drawback to split-level houses is that they're often difficult to expand owing to limitations of the lot and also because tampering with the original plan easily can harm the dwelling's appearance. Too many jogs and angles in the rooflines or exterior walls make them look cluttered and unplanned, as if put together piecemeal.

6. The split-level house is a poor choice for individuals who prefer large basements for woodworking shops or want surplus storage space and footage to eventually turn into a basement recreational room.

7. With the two sections of the side-to-side split-level framed under two distinct rooflines, the builder must skillfully integrate the two sections in an artistic manner to avoid the appearance of two separate houses joined together to make a single dwelling.

ALTERNATE HOUSING

In this discussion, *alternate housing* refers to homes that are constructed differently from typical modern dwellings found in standard subdivisions across the country. Some dwellings, though, owing to local building materials and climates, can be considered "alternate" in one location but not in another (an adobe home in Michigan, for example, would be neither normal nor serviceable).

Special care is needed when planning alternate housing:

1. Allow plenty of time for the construction. Special materials must be obtained. Financing and building permits must be secured from institutions that may not be familiar with "different" methods of construction.

2. A builder experienced in the kind of construction techniques needed for you might be difficult to find.

3. You'll need good, complete budget estimates.

4. Site selection is usually crucial to the overall success of the completed home. Little things can mean a lot. Water tables, prevailing winds, orientation, and topography are all very important.

Steel-Framed Construction

Although steel-framed construction is not really a "type" of housing, the use of steel instead of wood framing members varies far enough from traditional construction methods to be mentioned here. Indeed, to some individuals, steel-framed dwellings sound just as alternative as *underground housing*. To others, they're a logical extension of modern architecture. After all, steel framing has been employed successfully in industrial and commercial buildings for decades.

ADVANTAGES

1. Steel is strong and relatively light for its weight. Steel studs and other framing components with outer dimensions equal to wood members are considerably lower in bulk and greater in strength. Steel members provide increased protection against high winds, hailstorms, heavy snows, hurricanes, earthquakes, and other weather extremes. Owing to steel's positive methods of attachment to the foundation, it's less likely that the home will separate from the foundation during an earthquake, hurricane, or other cataclysmic event.

   Because of steel's high strength-to-weight ratio, and depending on the design, studs can be placed farther apart instead of using standard 16-inch wood stud centers (Fig. 6.14). This permits greater lengths of uninterrupted wall insulation with fewer thermal breaks in between. Other advantages to steel's high strength-to-weight ratio include successful home design and

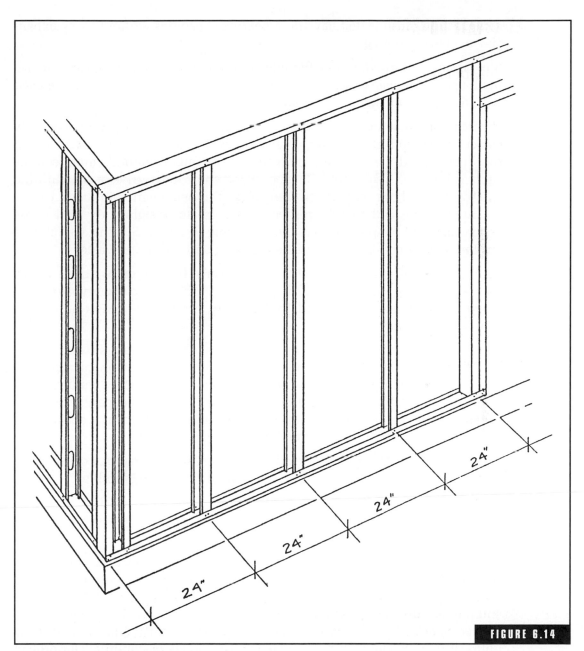

FIGURE 6.14

Twenty-four-inch steel stud centers.

construction on soils that have poor bearing capacities without using expensive oversized footings.

2. Steel framing allows for more flexible design with larger open spaces, including longer floor spans and higher walls. Light steel-framed walls can be used with dwellings of almost any shape.

3. Uniform manufacturing tolerances maintain a consistently dimensionally correct steel product. This translates into level floors, flat walls, and straight rooflines. Wood members are more likely to contain natural imperfections such as knots or weak spots. Cheaper wood studs may arrive at the building site twisted and can continue to warp even after being nailed in place. Unstable lumber can add to building costs and create unsightly drywall stress cracks and nail "pop outs" that are frustrating to repair. Steel is available in cut-to-length pieces to reduce in-field cutting and minimize waste.

4. Steel won't rot, splinter, crack, or readily warp, buckle, or twist. It's not as affected by moisture. Other building products, including paper, gypsum, and wood components, are affected by humidity, groundwater, and additional sources of moisture.

5. Steel framing members can be ordered to exact lengths and specifications, and they're available on the market in a wide variety of precut standard shapes and sizes. Custom shapes are also available. No high premiums must be paid for extralong steel framing members, as must be paid for wood, because steel is, of course, manufactured to length, whereas not all logs can be sawn into extralong boards and beams.

6. Steel resists termites and other wood-destroying insects that can cause wood roofs to sag, floors to slope, and main beams and posts to crumble.

7. Steel is not combustible. Although it can be ruined in a hot fire, it will not burn like wood and does not help fuel a home fire. This can result in lower fire insurance premiums for some policyholders.

8. Screw-attached metal framing members eliminate squeaks and "nail pops," which occur frequently with wood. Screws and bolts won't loosen or pull out under stress like nails can. Steel framing can be manufactured with openings and punch-outs spaced at regular intervals, allowing utility components such as electrical and plumbing lines to be roughed in easily instead of drilling holes through wooden framing members. Grommets or conduits can protect the wiring from the sharp edges of the punch-outs (Fig. 6.15).

9. Steel framing provides square walls and doors that aren't affected by moisture and don't stick. Such strongly built houses are also much less likely to settle over the years.

10. Steel framing components, especially studs, are resilient. This means that they help the walls absorb sound. When combined with sound-attenuating insulation, they provide quiet bedrooms and other living spaces.

11. Steel framing also helps to achieve good indoor air quality because no pesticides or other chemical treatments are used, nor are resin adhesives present, as they may be with wood.

12. Because steel framing allows for larger open spans (up to about 60 feet without interior support walls), a home can be designed with very few interior load-bearing partitions. Later on, additional nonbearing walls can be added, removed, altered, or even relocated without major disruptions to the home's structure.

13. What about lightning? Wouldn't a steel-framed home attract direct hits, like a lightning rod? The steel, if struck, would actually provide many conductive paths directly to ground, where electrical energy would dis-

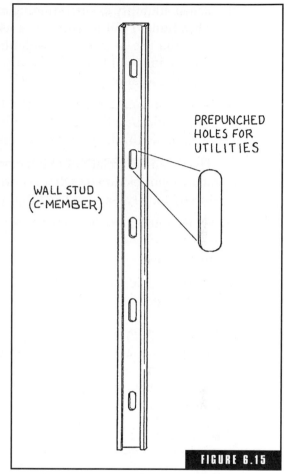

WALL STUD (C-MEMBER)

PREPUNCHED HOLES FOR UTILITIES

FIGURE 6.15

Steel framing with punch-outs.

perse with no greater chance of explosions, fires, or personal injury than with a dwelling made from wood framing.

14. What about radio-wave interference? The steel framing shouldn't interfere with radio, TV, or phone reception or garage door openers because the waves still can pass through the spaces between the studs.

15. What about fastening pictures on walls or other fixtures onto wall studs? No problem. Simply use metal screws instead of nails.

DISADVANTAGES

There aren't many drawbacks to the steel framing members and panels themselves, but what has been perceived as limiting factors to construction with steel framing are as follows:

1. The availability of steel framing members at building supply centers is some-what limited but is improving as various contractors are becoming familiar with the use of steel in residential dwellings. More and more lumberyards and commercial building supply warehouses are adding steel framing product lines as alternatives to wood.

2. Numerous builders are reluctant to switch from wood to steel simply because that would be a departure from long-standing building techniques they have been using throughout their entire careers.

3. There can be a relatively high cost to ship steel framing members from out-of-state manufacturers, whereas wood is much more likely to be "manufactured" locally—and subject to lower transportation costs.

4. A perception exists among many individuals that wood is a warm, natural, renewable resource and steel is "cold" and manufactured mainly for commercial use.

5. Some people fear that steel will rust, be an electrical hazard, and result in dwellings that look like commercial buildings.

STEEL-FRAMED-CONSTRUCTION BASICS

Entire books are available on steel-framed construction, and manufacturers offer videos, plans, written instructions, courses, and guidebooks on their products. Some basic points and characteristics of steel construction offered by the various steel kit, component, and package manufacturers include the following:

- Steel frame houses appear, inside and out, like wood frame construction. Once they're finished, the steel framing is not apparent.

- Steel component manufacture is typically cold-formed steel in shape, size, and function that mirrors dimensional lumber. The framing components are essentially used in four types of "sections": floor-joist systems, exterior and load-bearing walls, non-load-bearing partition walls, and roof rafter and support systems.

- Steel components such as studs, joists, and rafters are stamped into a squared C shape, called *structural-C*, *C-members*, or simply *C*. The C configuration is made of the cross-sectional configuration consisting of a web, flange, and lip. The web is the part of a C-member that connects the two flanges (Fig. 6.16). Web stiffeners are additional pieces attached to the web to strengthen the web against buckling or crimping (Fig. 6.17). The flange is the part that is perpendicular to the web, and the lip is the part of the C-member that extends from the flange at the open end. The lip increases the strength characteristics of the member and acts as a stiffener to the flange (see Fig. 6.16). C-studs, precut or site cut, are used in structural and nonstructural walls. Channel-type wall studs are designed so that facing materials can be screw-attached quickly (Fig. 6.18). Studs made for load-bearing walls are heavier, typically 20- to 16-gauge steel (*gauge* is a unit of measurement to describe the nominal thickness of steel—the lower the gauge, the greater is the thickness). The studs can be ordered in sizes up to 8 inches in depth. Deeper studs are used in plumbing walls and other special situations. Larger C-members such as 2 × 6s, 2 × 8s, and 2 × 10s are

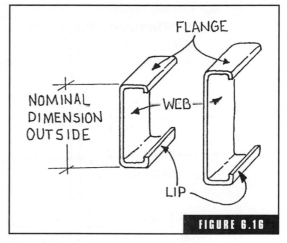

FIGURE 6.16

C-member.

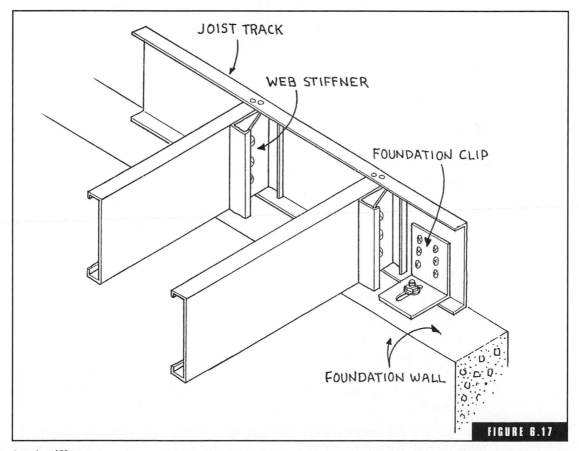

FIGURE 6.17

A web stiffener.

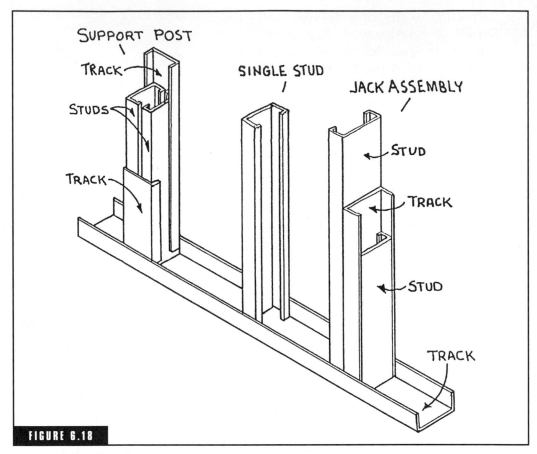

FIGURE 6.18

Channel-type wall studs.

also made of heavier steel and are used as floor joists, headers, and in some cases, rafters. When extra strength is needed, C-members are joined together to form heavier components. Studs are paired or assembled with tracks to create support posts and jack-stud assemblies. Deeper C-members are joined back to back or flange to flange where heavier beams and headers are required (see Fig. 6.18).

■ U-shaped channels or tracks are used for rim joists and wall plates and built-up assemblies of C-members (Fig. 6.19). The track has a web and flanges but no lip. When used as wall plates, vertical studs fit inside the tracks, and the flanges are fastened together (see Fig. 6.19). Clip angles are L-shaped short pieces of metal, usually with a 90-degree bend, used for connections (Fig. 6.20).

■ Zinc-coated galvanized steel protects against rust, as does the "red iron" with its red oxide coating.

- A home builder can purchase the steel framing components or a complete house package with windows, doors, roof, utilities, and more. All the steel framing members are predrilled, color coded, and numbered according to the purchase plans so that they bolt together almost like a life-size erector set. Most builders use screw guns and self-tapping screws and sometimes glue to fasten just about any material to steel framing.

- A steel-framed house typically is built over a conventional poured-concrete slab, foundation, or block basement featuring anchor bolts poured in concrete and sticking up for anchoring (Fig. 6.21). Subsequently, each I-beam framing assembly is securely bolted in place.

- Manufacturer kits often include flexible floor plans with clear-span interiors and options such as raised or vaulted ceilings and decks.

- Steel framing members usually are numbered and marked for specific kits and plans. Framing assemblies bolt together and then can be tilted up onto the foundation, each bolted to the anchor plates. For ranch homes, the assemblies are often light enough to be handled by several workers without special lifting equipment. Some designs use individual roof trusses, and others combine the roof framing members with the wall framing sections.

- To help compensate for the thermal conductivity of steel, builders

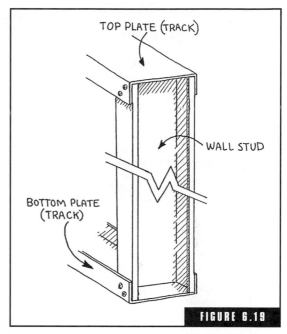

FIGURE 6.19

U-shaped channel.

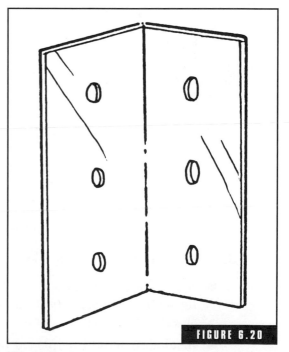

FIGURE 6.20

Clip angle.

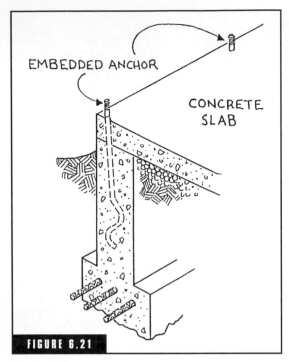

EMBEDDED ANCHOR

CONCRETE SLAB

FIGURE 6.21

Anchor bolts.

include a nonconducting buffer between the exterior siding and the steel studs—most generally a high-density foam board instead of plywood or fiberboard.

- It's possible to erect insulation vertically and hold it in place with Z-furring channels. The channels typically hold insulation blankets, polystyrene insulation, gypsum panels, or other rigid insulation (Fig. 6.22).

- A typical steel framing roof system is a purloin system that bolts to the top of the main-frame rafters. They provide excellent strength and will not sag or weaken over standard lifetimes.

- An excellent option when selecting steel framing is to use prebuilt panels or assemblies—walls, floors, and other components that have been prefabricated. Panels come in handy, especially when there is a repetition of panel types and dimensions. Panels can be erected quickly on site and even can be put into place during freezing weather. Because the assemblies are constructed by experienced crews and preinspected, they greatly reduce on-site wasted materials.

- Steel can't do it all. Even when a home is framed with steel, floor decking and roof sheathing are likely to be plywood or oriented-strand board. The wood backing, sheathing, and decking are also screwed into place, as are wood window and door frames. Casings and trim then can be nailed to these wood components in traditional fashion.

- If you decide to help engineer your own steel framing, consider that most steel suppliers offer in-house engineering at reduced rates.

STEEL FRAMING INSPECTION POINTERS

- Screws should be about ⅜ to ½ inch longer than the thickness of the connected materials. At least three exposed threads should extend through the steel to ensure a good connection.

- Insulation should be placed between all studs in exterior walls, between structural members and door and window frames on all four sides, in small spaces between window and door framing members, behind outlet boxes in exterior walls, against second-floor header joists and edge joists, between the top plate and subfloor of two-story and split-level dwellings, between ceiling joists of unheated garages or porches when the rooms above are used for living areas, between ceiling joists below unheated attics, below stairways to unheated attic spaces, in knee walls of heated attics, on basement walls when those spaces are used for living areas, around the inside perimeter of a concrete-slab floor in heated spaces, and in other logical spaces that, owing to the building's design, would need insulation.

■ Check that the places where framing members meet are flat or square, as they should be, with no uneven surfaces, odd projections, or extrawide seams or gaps.

Solar Houses

If anything was ever thought to be the answer to the heating fuel crisis, it has been (and continues to be) the sun. Just the thought of all that free energy has sent environmentalists scurrying to bookstores and libraries for information and plans on how to construct solar devices. Located just a tad over 90 million miles away from our planet, the sun is ultimately the single source of practically all the energy we've ever used.

There are two main types of solar heat- and energy-producing systems: passive and active. *Passive systems* include design features such as windows, skylights, and greenhouses coupled with materials that will absorb or collect and store heat so that the heat can be returned gradually to the home's living areas. *Active systems* feature more advanced methods of storing and distributing the sun's heat and energy.

In a nutshell, solar systems include about five variations, the first two being passive and the latter three active:

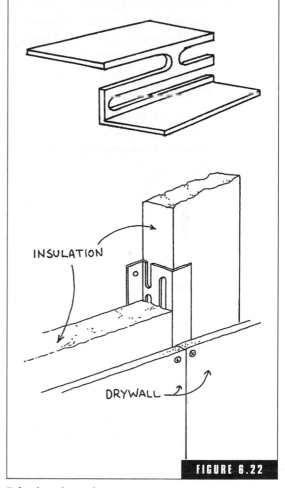

FIGURE 6.22

Z-furring channels.

INSULATION

DRYWALL

1. *Solar windows.* Even in the coldest climates, the south side of a building is warmed by the sun, especially on clear, cloudless days. Windows positioned on the south side of a home are the collectors that let the inside surfaces absorb heat. Depending on the heat-absorbing materials (i.e., floors, furniture, air, and so on), the heat is radiated back into the living spaces quickly or slowly.

2. *Building materials/components designed for heat collection and storage.* These could be a masonry or stone wall or floor or a water container of some type—something that would hold heat for a long time and radiate it back into the living spaces at a slow rate, even after the sun has set.

3. *Active collectors with storage and distribution.* These are what you'd probably recognize as solar panels positioned on the roof or side of a building. Heat is drawn from the collector by circulating air or liquid through the collector and is transferred to a storage device. The stored heat then is sent throughout the building in air ducts or piping and radiators.

4. *Active systems that power other heating and cooling equipment.* The only difference from the previous system is that the collected heat here is used to power a secondary heating or cooling system rather than being distributed directly throughout the dwelling.

5. *Photovoltaic (PV) cells.* These devices convert the sun's energy to electricity, which, in turn, can provide heat as well as plain old electrical energy for a variety of other uses.

Almost every home possesses some sort of passive energy features. Many can be designed into the building plans at surprisingly little cost. Full-fledged active solar heating, though, is another story. It can be quite expensive, especially when the services of a knowledgeable architect are required. Naturally, site planning is also a critical consideration when arranging for solar heating.

Wind-Powered Houses

Rarely are wind-powered homes entirely powered by wind. Instead, the available wind machines or "windmills" are designed to supplement energy usage.

Underground Houses

In the mid-nineteenth century, settlers throughout the Midwestern prairies had little selection of building materials. Owing to the lack of forests, little else was available but the sod of the earth. Early sod homes offered poor protection from the elements. They were dark, damp, and drafty. By itself, soil is an inadequate insulator. The walls of a typical sod dwelling possessed an R-factor of between 1 and 2, about the equivalent of a thin piece of plywood.

Today, what we know as underground dwellings also use soil and sod in their construction. The main difference is that they're finely engineered to give their occupants the following benefits:

- They conserve a site's surface space. They're no longer built *on* the surface of the ground. Instead, they're tucked into the site, beneath part of the surface.

- They provide the owner with low energy consumption. At least several sides, often three, are heavily banked with soil. This cavelike effect more easily maintains a constant temperature, summer and winter.

- They offer excellent privacy and quiet acoustics. Not much sound can penetrate from outside in or vice versa.

- Modern designs provide stable, durable construction, unlike the old sod homes that easily eroded in the face of prairie storms and winds.

- They're constructed needing low maintenance.

On the other hand, underground homes do not enjoy good reputations with individuals unfamiliar with their construction. People recall the cramped underground bomb shelters popular in the 1950s or imagine themselves emerging on a bright sunny morning from a dark, cellar-like space, eyes squinting like a mole's.

Legitimate concerns are for an underground dwelling's ventilation, waterproofing, and roof construction. In poorly engineered underground homes, these could pose major problems.

Log Houses

This easily recognized home can be built in practically any size, style, and floor plan. It's fairly inexpensive because it uses less framing in its construction than is required of more typically modern dwellings. Log homes can be either custom-built or of the kit type. A kit log house is usually the lowest-cost option because the manufacturer supplies only what is necessary, with everything cut to size and little waste. Directions are simple and the construction time quick, although inclement weather can be a major factor here, as in most construction schedules.

One limiting factor, however, is where the log home can be built. It looks out of place in a modern subdivision. Much of its charm comes from it being located on an agricultural or wooded site.

Pole-Frame Houses

Frequently featured in architectural magazines, pole-frame homes feature a rather strong, easy, cost-effective technique of construction, that of pressure-treated poles embedded in the earth 4 to 6 feet deep instead of the standard concrete foundation. When firmly anchored in the subsoil, pole-frame homes can be constructed safely in areas unsuitable for standard foundations, including extremely swampy, rocky, uneven, or even potentially seismic terrains. This can be so because the wood pole foundation for a pole-frame house also serves as the major framing members of the dwelling.

Pole frame dwellings also fit nicely into the most modern, exclusive neighborhoods and subdivisions. Their exteriors can be clad with modern sidings and frequently feature passive-solar components because fewer load-bearing walls are required with pole/beam construction.

Some building codes, however, have not caught up with pole-frame construction, and in certain places it could be difficult to talk savings and loan institutions and building inspectors into approving the plans. In addition, few contractors are familiar with this type of construction, so accurate cost and time estimates may be more difficult to come by in your location.

Prefabricated or Manufactured Houses

Prefabricated houses include all factory-built dwellings. For our purposes, we'll exclude motor homes and mobile homes and move on to the three remaining "prefabs": the shell home, the modular or sectional home, and the panelized home. Each type is available in a mind-boggling range of plans, cost, and quality.

SHELL HOUSES

These homes consist of little but the exterior shell: walls, rough flooring, and a roof. The idea is to put up a weather-tight outside shell of the home so that the inside can be finished off at leisure by the owner, who frequently, for better or for worse, chooses to do much of the work himself or herself.

MODULAR OR SECTIONAL HOUSES

These homes are completely built in the factory and are simply placed or assembled on a waiting foundation. Wiring and plumbing are already included in the sections or walls. These kinds of homes can be ready to be occupied within a few days of delivery.

PRECUT AND PANELIZED HOUSES

Precut homes are assembled on the building site out of materials that have been precisely cut and packaged at the factory. There's very little waste, but there's also a need for strict security at the building site to prevent theft of parts—of boards or key framing members that might disappear, as they sometimes do, from conventional stick-built sites, where they aren't missed as much. Panelized homes consist of wall sections built on a factory assembly line. Unlike the walls for modular or sectional houses, these walls must be finished off at the building site, frequently by a contractor who must be hired to erect them.

Considerations when comparing prefabricated houses include

- Will the finished product be what you expect? Take a look at several homes that have already been erected, and speak with their occupants. Prefab manufacturers, at least some of them, have wooed customers with all sorts of free giveaway gimmicks, extras, and other high-pressure sales tactics. Remember that reputable outfits will offer sound value and reliable customer follow-up services.

- Supposedly, the cost of prefabs should be less than the cost of stick-built houses because the factories use large quantities of the same materials with less expensive labor and less waste. Depending on the distance from the factory, those savings could be offset by transportation costs to get the finished product to your site.

- Popular designs include the A-frame, the ski chalet, and to a lesser extent, the geodesic dome and other multisided dwellings. These designs are frequently built as second homes, with their uniquely "different" floor plans affording their owners dramatic relief from everyday conventional dwellings.

Plenty of literature is available on prefabricated housing. Manufacturers offer brochures, reports, and sales materials, and many annual publications and monthly magazines are devoted to listing, discussing, and rating the various prefabs currently on the market.

▶▶▶▶▶ POINTS TO PONDER

1. Think about your lifestyle and how you presently live it or how you want to change it. Then decide on the amount of space you'll need under your roof.

2. Review and weigh the advantages and disadvantages of the various home types discussed in this chapter.

3. Decide on the type and style of house that will best lend itself to your objectively arrived at space requirements and your subjectively arrived at preferences for appearance and setting.

4. Seek additional advice from real estate professionals, who may urge you to plan more than you need to guarantee increased value or sales prospects if the home must be sold eventually.

5. All things considered, the two-story house is one of the best, most efficient designs available. But it does have stairs from one living space to another.

6. Single-story ranch homes offer the greatest livability for all members of a household regardless of age.

7. Cape Cod or one-and-one-half story homes are economical to build, heat, cool, and expand their living space from an unfinished second floor at a later date.

8. Split-foyer and split- or multilevel dwellings are best constructed on lots having front-to-back or back-to-front or side-to-side slopes.

9. Don't be afraid to consider alternate construction methods and materials, including steel framing, solar-power assistance, kit homes, pole framing, log homes, and prefabricated or manufactured homes. There even could be a manufacturer's incentive available for you to be the first in your area to showcase certain dwelling models.

10. If you decide on alternate housing, pay particular attention to choosing a contractor who has had experience with building the type of home with the type of construction materials and methods required by your plans.

Traffic Planning and Zoning

From a green perspective, traffic planning and zoning within the home should follow along with the home's orientation—its placement regarding geographic features and directions mostly dealing with the sun's travel and the direction of the prevailing winds but also tempered by what's on either side of the home and in front and behind. This is discussed in Part 4 in Chapters 32 and 33 and is one of those instances where you need to consider what's in more than one chapter at a time. In addition, more than just green construction design features now must be considered.

After you've reviewed the preceding chapters, you should be ready to begin sketching the general layout and design of your house. As you do, give careful consideration to the overall traffic plan and interior zoning best suited to your own particular situation.

First, look at the space in a typical house from another angle. What about the place you're living in now? Chances are that you can (or you wish you could) identify three kinds of spaces by function. Excluding storage areas, there's *private space*, or areas needed for sleeping, dressing, bathing, and studying. There's *social space*, or areas for being with others, entertaining, relaxing, and recreating. And there's *transitional space*, or places, depending on the circumstances, where either private or social activities can occur. To discuss interior zoning in relation to these areas, we must study traffic that enters and exits the house, traffic that moves within the house itself, and room-to-room relationships.

Design for how you live. Don't add a lot of formal space if you lead a casual lifestyle. Many people are finding that formal living or dining rooms and grand foyers don't fit the way they live today. It's your home—live in it the way that suits you.

TRAFFIC ENTERING AND EXITING THE HOUSE

Service Access

This might sound snobbish, but there should be a definite entrance to be used by service and repair people and individuals delivering items they have to carry into the house. Such an entry should be wide, direct, and as close to the service areas as possible. The kitchen, laundry, basement, and utility rooms should be the prime considerations here because these areas are the places most frequented by service people and vendors.

This entrance should be a logical alternative to protect the living room from unwanted intrusions by casual visitors such as messengers, salespersons, or unexpected visitors for whom a proper reception has not been prepared, such as your clergyman or parents-in-law. Ideally, this access, or a sidewalk that leads to it, should be visible and obvious from the front of your house so that people who have never been to your place can determine which entrance to use by themselves. Otherwise, a small, tasteful sign can be strategically placed at a sidewalk that leads to a side or rear entrance.

The most important idea of a service access is to reduce cross-traffic through the living areas of the house whenever possible. Why invite a meter reader or other service provider to pass through your dining room while en route to the basement? It's wise to eliminate as much of this type of cross-traffic as you can.

Guest Access

This entrance traditionally is for friends and guests of the family. It is the main front door, the entrance that usually faces the front street. It should be easily accessible from the driveway and the front street and from all rooms inside the house so that occupants are able to answer the door quickly when someone arrives.

This entrance should provide guests with exterior shelter from the elements while they're waiting at the door and should have a place to remove coats, a closet to hang them up in, and an area in which visitors can adjust to the surroundings (e.g., entrance hall, foyer, vestibule, or gallery).

It should provide efficient access to the parts of the house that guests are most likely to frequent. This includes the living room, dining room, recreational or party room, an office, a patio, and bathrooms—each family's pattern of living will determine the need for guest accessibility. In addition, this access should give a pleasant impression to visitors, as well as a sampling of the quality and character of the house.

Day-to-Day Indoor/Outdoor Movement

Children need a good access to repeatedly go in and out while playing. Because very young children need almost constant supervision, a back door to their play yard may be a necessity. Excessive running through the house can be minimized further by locating toilet facilities near the door most often used by children.

Guests invited for outdoor activities usually enter the house by the front door and then proceed to the location of the activity. This path should be fairly direct and avoid, if possible, passing through a room.

Because the outdoor living areas are likely to be the setting for picnics, barbecues, and similar events, the exits should be located near the kitchen. Here again, the availability of bathroom facilities for adult outdoor activities (in addition to the convenience for children) comes into play.

Removal of waste materials should involve a minimum of travel through the inside of the house. Containers for staging garbage and trash usually are located near the service areas, screened from public view.

If you have a basement planned, consider an outside door for the convenience of children who are playing downstairs. This lets them run straight outside without tracking through the rest of the house. And it's a great energy and time saver if your laundry equipment is situated in the basement, where you can quickly walk outdoors to hang up wet clothes in nice weather. Also, when you're working outside in the yard, you can enter the basement, change clothes, and get cleaned up. It's nice to be able to bring large items in through the basement door instead of carrying them through the house and down the basement stairs. This means a lot when transporting clothes washers and dryers, freezers, pool tables, and other large objects. A direct basement access also will be a time saver when you store outdoor equipment such as screens, storm windows, garden tools, and lawn mowers in the cellar.

In addition to the main front entrance, a separate side or rear access usually serves as the family entrance for grocery shopping, for children going to and coming from school, for family members taking out the laundry from a first-floor utility area, and for other informal activities.

General Guidelines for Entries

For safety's sake, install a peephole or window in your front and rear doors so that you can see who is ringing or knocking.

Again, it's not a good idea to have a front door that opens directly into the living room. A main entrance center hall or foyer should both shield you and your visitors from an inrush of wind, snow, or rain and keep your living room privacy intact. Although the main entrance should lead to the living room area, it shouldn't encourage people to pass through the living room on their way to the rest of the house. If so, it causes interruptions, wear and tear on the carpet, and other inconveniences. A good floor plan will provide access to all main living areas through hallways or foyers rather than directing traffic from one main room to another. This also means that you should provide the ability, even in open-style plans, for direct access to the kitchen and bedrooms without intruding on living room activities. Thus children can come and go without interrupting a conversation you are having with guests in the living room.

The access from the front door to the kitchen should be easy and direct because this path is used frequently. There should be a convenient sheltered entrance to the kitchen from the garage, carport, or driveway so that groceries can be brought into the house and put away without a lot of effort and fuss.

You'll want good guest circulation with the ability to move the guests from the front door to the coat closet, bathroom, and living room. A coat closet is essential near the front and side/rear entrance not only for guests but also for family members.

The remaining components of traffic planning and zoning in a house deal with internal movement and room-to-room relationships.

INTERNAL MOVEMENT

Here are five points to consider when developing your floor plan:

1. The living, sleeping, and work areas should be somewhat separate from each other, yet they should be positioned properly in relation to each other and to additional factors such as orientation to the street, the sun, and even to scenic views. It's important to weigh your feelings toward "bedrooms" versus "work and play noise" or "entertaining guests" versus "bothering sleeping children." In other words, how much of a buffer zone between the bedrooms and the rest of the house do you think you'll need?

   A two-story house contains natural zoning, with the kitchen and living rooms on the first floor—a full story below the bedrooms. In a single-story house, the living and sleeping areas generally should be located at opposite ends of the house, neatly connected by the kitchen and utility room.

2. Try to separate quiet rooms from noisy ones by distance. Keep bedrooms as far away as possible from the living, food preparation, and utility areas. Isolate study rooms from play areas, hobby rooms, party rooms, and workshops. Adequate sound-absorbing features become particularly important in moderate-sized houses with open kitchens, combined living and dining room areas, and all-purpose family rooms, as well as in children's play areas and adult workshops.

3. In the interest of silence, though, don't get carried away. Make sure that no key area is completely isolated (laundry rooms and bathrooms especially), and also see that there's a safe place for children to play while you're entertaining in the living room.

4. In houses where stairs are necessary, the head of the stairs should be centrally located. This not only minimizes the need for halls, but it also frees exterior

walls for windows and adds natural lighting and inexpensive ventilation. In two-story houses, the stairway to the basement is often positioned beneath the stairs to the second floor. The problem with this setup is one of arranging your plan so that the head of the basement stairs is located near the service or rear/side door so that items can come and go from the basement in an efficient manner. If so, it's more convenient, say, to save clothes drying energy by simply walking upstairs and outdoors to hang damp clothes on a line in the backyard.

5. For ease of internal movement, many people favor an open plan. Open planning attempts to achieve a feeling of spaciousness; the interior of a house is made to appear larger than it really is through the elimination of solid walls between activity centers and by substituting partial walls, screens, or open room dividers. This supports recent green construction trends toward smaller home designs.

A small dining room will appear larger if no solid wall stands between it and the living room. The uninterrupted expanse of ceiling visually increases the appearance of the dining room, and it has the same effect in the living room. The two rooms "borrow" space from each other.

Similarly, a kitchen will appear larger if it opens to a family room or dining space. This can be accomplished by using a breakfast bar to separate the two spaces. The open feeling is not lost even if you opt for a cabinet over the bar. Space between the bar and cabinet and the cabinet and the ceiling, as well as the absence of a door between the two areas, will be sufficient to retain the openness.

Of course, there are disadvantages to the open plan: a lack of privacy, conflicting activities that can be distracting, and incorrectly grouped furniture that might "float" without unifying walls.

ROOM-TO-ROOM RELATIONSHIPS

Although you might have already read about some of these points in the first two chapters, many are so important that they bear repeating. A main consideration to keep in mind is that your traffic patterns should not take people through the middle of several rooms (or even one room) while en route to another.

The Kitchen

This is considered to be the most important room in a house. Certainly it's the heart of a house, a place used by the entire family for a variety of activities. It's most often placed adjacent to both dining and living rooms and close to a patio or deck where a barbecue can be located. If you have a first-floor family room, this, too, should be within easy reach of the kitchen so that the dishes used for snacking are not far from the sink.

The kitchen should be centrally located to have "control" over the entire house. Here are other considerations:

- It should be easily accessible to the front door so that guests can be received and to the family entrance at the rear or side so that a car can be unloaded and deliveries accepted.

- From the kitchen, you should be able to keep an eye on children playing either inside or out.

- The basement stairs should be close by, especially if you have any food storage down there or if your laundry is in the cellar.

- Having a bathroom within a few steps of the kitchen saves a lot of time.

- Consider that an open area from the kitchen to the dining or family rooms allows for free conversation and visiting while you're cleaning up or preparing something to eat. An island or peninsula, while still "open," can help to separate the kitchen from a family room to keep curious hands away from hot pots, pans, and other kitchen hazards.

- Think twice about a kitchen that steps down into a family room. It may be harmless to household members who are used to this arrangement, but it could result in children and guests unfamiliar with such a step taking spills through the years ahead.

- Ideally, a kitchen has no more than two doors, one to the dining area or front of the house and one to the service/family entrance or garage. Within the house, there should be alternate ways to reach those areas without going through the kitchen. If there are three or more doors in the kitchen, they should be located in one passageway that doesn't break up the kitchen work traffic.

- After the kitchen's location is decided on, appliances should be arranged so that distances between the central cooking area (range), the preparation and cleaning area (the sink), and the food storage area (the refrigerator and pantry) are no more than 7 feet each (Fig. 7.1).

- If possible, the kitchen should have at least one, and preferably two, outside walls in which to place windows. An open kitchen room arrangement and windows facing the backyard enable parents to keep an eye on their children during meal preparation and cleanup. Window screens will enable greasy fumes and cooking odors to be removed. Windows also serve as pleasant distractions for the busy cook by providing scenic and interesting views when available.

- Although the kitchen should have a convenient central location, watch out for any traffic patterns that route individuals from the living room to the bedrooms by passing directly through the kitchen or dining areas.

The Laundry Area

This feature is usually placed in one of four areas within the house:

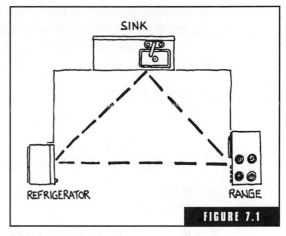

SINK

REFRIGERATOR

RANGE

FIGURE 7.1

A kitchen work triangle.

1. *In or next to the kitchen.* This allows much of the required housework to be done in the same general vicinity without wasted motions.

2. *In the basement.* But this forces you to constantly go up and down stairs when doing the wash, and if you don't have a direct outdoor access from the basement, it makes hanging up clothes in the yard cumbersome.

3. *Near the bedrooms.* This makes it handy for changing your soiled clothes and putting away clean garments.

4. In warmer climates where basements aren't included in many houses, a popular place to put the laundry is in a mud room attached to part of the garage or in a breezeway.

No matter where the laundry room is, you'll need easy access to the outdoors; you'll need space for a clothes washer and dryer, soaps, and cleansers; and you'll need enough room nearby to set up an ironing board.

The Utility Area

This is where the furnace, air-conditioning unit, water heater, and possibly a humidifier are set up. From the standpoints of maintenance, efficiency of operation, and cost of installation, this area should be somewhat centrally located in a basement but not out in the middle of the cellar floor. It should be close to a wall to avoid breaking up a large portion of otherwise usable space. Although the furnace, water heater, and related appliances typically are located in the basement, when there is no basement, they're placed in a mud room or garage or integrated into their own area right inside the house.

Again, in the basement, the furnace, water heater, heating and air-conditioning ducts, humidifier, main electrical box, central vacuum unit, plumbing pipes, water filters/conditioners, main water supply isolation valve, water fixture isolation valves, sump pump, burglar alarm panels, staircases, clothes washer and dryer and laundry sink/tub, freezer, storage shelves, and related appliances should be positioned out of the way or at least where you want them—in case you decide to finish off part of the space later. Yet the equipment needing preventive maintenance and eventual repairs should be laid out in a manner to allow easy access. At least one window should be large enough for an emergency exit—if no outside basement doors are planned.

Bathroom Facilities

Here are some considerations:

- Avoid having bathrooms visible from other rooms, especially from the living room or head of the stairs.

- Be certain that guests can get to a bathroom easily without being under direct observation from the living room.

- Position at least one bathroom near the bedrooms.

- A bathroom should be simple to get to from the rear or side entrance for children playing or adults entertaining outdoors.

Bedrooms

Bedrooms should be placed together in one part of the house, protected from outside noises as much as possible, and also convenient to bathrooms. This makes parental supervision easier and simplifies the problem of maintaining a quiet sleeping area.

- Don't situate bedrooms one after another in a series requiring passage through each other.

- When dressing, people should be able to move between the bedrooms and the main bathroom without being seen from the living areas.

- There should be a buffer zone between the living and sleeping areas so that parents can entertain while children sleep. The placement of bathrooms, hallways, closets, bookshelves, utility rooms, fireplaces, and other interior masonry walls can serve as sound barriers between the various quiet rooms and the noise-producing ones. Avoid closet walls that have only a thin plywood or fiberboard backing as the barrier between two rooms.

The Dining Area

The dining area should be adjacent to the food preparation space. For quick meals, many people use a bar that is part of the kitchen work counter. Others rely on a table in the kitchen or position a table in the family or breakfast room. Still others choose to have a separate formal dining room next to the kitchen.

The Living Room

The living room should be near the main front entrance. It is used for such activities as reading, visiting, and entertaining guests. If your house won't have a separate family room, you can use the living room for watching television and listening to music. In any case, this room should be at a dead-end location to discourage unnecessary traffic from interrupting conversations and other activities.

Storage Areas

As mentioned earlier, storage is a vital consideration when planning your home. Keep in mind the following points:

- There should be ample storage in all rooms of a house.
- Each bedroom should have its own closet(s).
- It is convenient to have storage space in bathrooms either under the sink or in a separate closet.
- The hallway leading to the bedrooms should have a linen closet for clean sheets, pillowcases, blankets, and other bedding and bathroom linens.
- Plan closets near all the entrance doors: front door, side door, and rear door. These closets are needed to keep guest and family member coats, hats, boots, umbrellas, and similar personal clothing and care items.
- If there's no formal laundry area, consider a laundry closet near the kitchen or bedrooms.
- In the kitchen, a pantry closet for storing canned foods and appliances is a true plus.
- A broom closet in the kitchen is needed to store dust mops, brooms, sweepers, ironing boards, and other unwieldy items.

GENERAL GUIDELINES

Make sure that the size and arrangement of your rooms allow for flexibility of living arrangements. Check that your house plan has enough windows to provide plenty of natural lighting and cross-ventilation yet that the windows will not severely limit the wall space for your furniture and decorations.

REMODELING NOTES

This is another topic that may require thinking outside the box. Knowing what you will soon understand about how the floor plan should best revolve around the sun's travel and how the correct window exposure can make such a major difference

✔✔✔✔✔ COMMON MISTAKES CHECKLIST

Before you go to Chapter 8 on size planning and future expansion, here's a checklist of things people often overlook or fall for.

___ No separate entranceway or foyer to receive visitors

___ No window or peephole in the front and rear doors, so the occupants can't see who's knocking or ringing the doorbell

___ No roof overhang or similar protection over the front door

___ An isolated carport or garage with no sheltered direct access from the car to the house

___ No direct access route from the driveway, carport, or garage to the kitchen

___ No direct route from the back or side yard to a bathroom so that children can come in and out with a minimum of bother

___ Gas, electric, and water meters located inside the house or in the garage or basement (If this is the case, move them outside to eliminate the need for meter readers to clomp through the house every other month.)

___ A fishbowl picture window in the front of the house that exposes you to every passerby

___ Accident-inviting basement doors that open inward toward the cellar steps

___ Walls so cut up by windows and doors that furniture placement is extremely limited (Plan ahead to accommodate your furnishings. Is there sufficient wall space? Develop a sense of scale and dimensions as you evaluate room sizes and window and door locations. The height of the window sills is important. Desks, bureaus, chests, dressers, and buffets all require wall space. If the window sills are high enough, some of the furniture can be placed beneath windows. Many major furniture pieces are between 30 and 32 inches high.)

___ Windows in children's rooms that are too low for safety, too high to see out from, and too small or difficult to escape from in case of a fire

___ A hard-to-open double-hung window over the kitchen sink (This is a big pain in the neck. An easy-to-crank casement window is best here, and a sliding window is second best.)

___ A window over the bathtub (This can cause problems. It can result in cold drafts as well as rotted window sills from condensation.)

___ Bathrooms located directly in the line of sight from living areas or directly in view from the top of the stairs so that everyone knows when others are using the bathrooms (This makes for embarrassing situations.)

✔✔✔✔✔ COMMON MISTAKES CHECKLIST *(continued)*

___ Having only one bathroom (This is especially tough in two-story and split-level houses.)

___ No light switches at every room entrance/exit

___ No lights or electrical outlets on a porch, patio, or terrace

___ No lighting outside to illuminate the approach to the front entrance

___ Noisy light switches that go off and on like pistol shots (Silent switches cost only a little more.)

___ Child-trap closets that can't be opened from the inside

___ Small closets that are hardly large enough for half your wardrobe (Also watch out for narrow closet doors that keep much of the closet out of easy reach unless you happen to use a fishing rod. Be careful of basketball-player shelves that are too high for a person of normal height and clothes poles fastened so low that dresses and trousers can't hang without hitting the floor.)

___ A house for which there is no room for expansion (Sometimes, given how the dwelling is placed on the lot, or because of building or zoning restrictions or construction methods, a house simply cannot be expanded. Try to avoid this situation.)

___ Rooms that are too small to be practical (There's competition among builders and developers to get the largest number of rooms in a given square footage at the lowest price. Be careful. A dining room is too small if you cannot walk around the table and chairs.)

___ A floor plan that provides poor circulation in and out of the house and from one room to another

___ No interior zoning (The living, working, and sleeping areas are all jumbled together, each infringing on the other's integrity.)

___ No consideration to the number of floor levels (One, one-and-one-half, two, or multilevels that offer the most advantages and greatest living conveniences to your family.)

___ A house interior that's dark and drab from a lack of ample window placements (Strategic windows and glass sliding doors can go a long way toward making your house bright, cheerful, and attractive. But don't overdo them; hang onto your privacy as well.)

___ A kitchen that's situated at one end of the house, not centrally located

(continued on next page)

✔✔✔✔✔ **COMMON MISTAKES CHECKLIST** *(continued)*

__ A poorly designed kitchen—an inefficient work triangle, skimpy counter space and storage, no place to eat in comfort, and a lack of outdoor access (If any room of the house deserves the most attention to detail, it's the kitchen.)

__ Inadequate storage space throughout the house (This might not become apparent for a few years, but when it does, that lack of space will be most frustrating. Make sure that the closets are large enough for storing household items, linen, and laundry, as well as personal possessions—seasonal and routine items.)

with heating and cooling comfort, would there be a way, working with the structure you have, to modify room uses to closely parallel ideal orientation and exposure? It may be possible to retune, with creative non-bearing-wall removals or additions, what rooms and spaces are used for. Are there single-use hallways or foyers that add little to the floor plan? Are there small rooms that could be opened up to share spaces so that you have larger, more open multiuse rooms? Can old-fashioned spaces be made more modern with minimal effort? A good carpenter/contractor could briefly review the possibilities. Can a garage be used for indoor living spaces and a detached garage be erected elsewhere on the lot? Is there a place to create an outside exit from a half-exposed basement and indoor living spaces with improved ventilation? Look at your home with open eyes. Are there potential living spaces in an attic or basement? Although the home may have been constructed 70 or 80 years ago, there are a lot more options now, thanks to modern materials; prefabricated wall, roof, and floor panels; and improved building techniques.

▶▶▶▶▶ **POINTS TO PONDER**

1. The living, sleeping, and work areas should be as separate from each other as possible. Quiet rooms can be separated from noisy ones by distance. For example, in a single-story home, the living and sleeping areas generally should be located at opposite ends of the dwelling, neatly connected by a kitchen and utility room.

2. "Open" planning encourages easy movement from one area to another and gives a feeling of spaciousness.

3. Adequate sound-absorbing features in ceilings, floors, and walls become particularly important in moderate-sized houses with open kitchens, combined living and dining rooms, and all-purpose family rooms.

4. There should be enough windows in your floor plan to allow for plenty of

natural lighting and cross-ventilation yet not too much glass to severely limit furniture and decorative item placements.

5. Bathrooms should be positioned so that their entrance doors are as private as possible.

6. There should be a direct route from the back or side yard to a bathroom so that children and adults can come in with a minimum of bother.

7. The kitchen should be centrally located whenever possible—not at one end of the house.

8. There should be a direct access from the driveway, carport, or garage to the kitchen.

9. An outside entrance/exit from the basement can be a great labor- and time-saving feature.

10. In houses where stairs are necessary, the head of the stairs should be as centrally located as possible to reduce the need for hallways and to free exterior walls for windows for natural lighting and efficient ventilation.

Size Planning

You've got to hand it to the Leadership in Energy and Environmental Design (LEED) for Homes rating system—it takes a stand on a very personal subject when it comes to new home construction—size planning. People typically don't like to be told (or to be even gently advised about) how much of something they can or cannot have. Before the green movement, home size was an issue ruled largely by how much a home owner could afford or wanted, and planning for enough space under the roof to eventually satisfy even unforeseen events and conditions was normal. Recently married, and maybe four children are in the cards . . . eventually? Then plan and include five bedrooms and three baths right off the bat. Need to take over the extended family's traditional Thanksgiving dinner celebration a few years from now? How about an oversized formal dining room just for that occasion? And since you're going to have a huge upstairs anyway—for all those bedrooms and baths—in addition to that big formal dining room, you've got to put something else underneath to fill in the rest of the first floor. What about an eat-in kitchen, a family room, and a formal living room accessed by a big single-use foyer and hallway—Hey, you had to use the space somehow. Many individuals still opt to build a far larger house that they actually need, just to have the spaces ready in case they actually need future expansion someday. It's probably more prudent to start with a smaller floor plan and design various features that will lend themselves to simpler construction if the need for expansion ever comes about. Certainly, the smaller the home's footprint, the less land will be disturbed, and if more space is needed, consider building or expanding up instead of out. Unless, of course, you *need* to build out to take advantage of passive-solar design. Or you can't climb stairs. Or any of a dozen other reasons. Again, this is just another instance of realizing that the greenest option may not always be the absolutely best option for a certain situation.

Getting back to why homes had been increasing in size until recently, there was resale value to think about. You *had* to have room for a fireplace because every other home in that price range had one or two, and—unless in an area mostly populated by retirees—even if you weren't planning to have children, you "had" to have at least three bedrooms, preferably four, to maintain optimal resale value. No matter the additional material and resources required, and no matter the increased continuing costs of heating, cooling, cleaning, and maintaining that "extra" seldom-used space.

The pregreen way of looking at size planning was to ensure that a new house would be large enough initially for an owner's every possible current and expected future need or at least to plan for and include the infrastructure or components that would enable future expansion with minimal construction disturbance and cost. This followed the trend of ever-greater house size, and the typical American home's square footage increased from 1,000 square feet in 1950 to about 1,500 square feet by 1970. By 2001, it had topped 2,300 square feet and continued to nearly 2,400 in recent years. As we made and had more money to spend, we spent greater amounts of it on larger houses. This, however, was not without consequences. Likely owing to the green construction movement, it appears that average new home size has peaked and is expected to drop slowly as the benefits of reducing overall home size are realized.

Certainly, in the decades favoring larger home size, conventional logic failed to identify and continued to ignore demographic and other factors such as shrinking household family size and pressure to build larger houses for status symbols and for greater resale values, all in the face of increasing fuel and maintenance costs, worn-out public utility systems, and dwindling buildable land supplies. How many single men, women, or empty-nesters are currently rattling around in huge four-bedroom, three-bath two-story houses? Also, just how many of those special-use rooms stand the test of time. Many individuals go through phases of interest for which a special room would be nice for a while, but once interest is lost in the activity, the room's purpose also ceases. A billiard or pool room or an exercise room comes to mind. Why not go to a pool hall or billiards/bowling alley to play occasionally? How many exercise machines across the country are sitting idle, cross-trainers and treadmills being used for clothes hangers instead of workouts? Instead, put a small barroom pool table into one end of the basement or family room, or if you must have a machine, get one or two portable ones that you can set up and take down with minimal trouble. In this way, the same room or space can be used for multiple activities without the extra cost of heating or cooling several single-use rooms at the same time. Figure out in advance how you can use the same space in a smaller home for multiple purposes.

Another way to gain more space out of less framing is to take advantage of an expandable attic; any way to expand without increasing the size of the shell or building envelope is generally a resource- and energy-saving way to go. Also, minimize the amount of "transient" space on each floor plan. For example, if the only reason a hallway or large foyer exists is to access one room from another, why not try to design the rooms so that they blend into one another, thereby gaining space previously used for mere transport. It's far more efficient to design usable space or to include additional storage—storage that could well be located along outside walls as an additional buffer to inside conditioned spaces. Storage space is sometimes added as an afterthought. Instead, make it part of the overall plan. Take advantage of garage space, basement space, and attic space for additional storage, but make certain that you don't bury the storage by filling the spaces with rarely or never used items.

The late comedian George Carlin had a hilarious routine that poked fun at all the belongings people accumulate and drag around with them from home to home, further implying that houses got so big because everyone had lots of "stuff" to store in them. In a way, this is true. Think of attics, basements, garages, and spare rooms that are so full of miscellaneous out-of-style and ill-fitting clothes, old books, and rarely used items that those spaces can't be used for anything else—including what they were originally intended for, such as parking a car.

A less recognized reason for stressing larger, higher-resale homes was that quality could easily be sacrificed for quantity. The thought was that since someone was only going to live in a place for a few years, why not build larger, simpler, with less expensive components? Now people are thinking about durability and good design, and they're thinking green. Another vote for smaller size is that real estate taxes are often based in part on a home's square footage, so taxes rise proportionally with a larger home, resulting in a yearly cost that keeps on costing. More furniture and furnishings are also needed to outfit a larger home—an additional expense seldom thought about when the floor plans are being laid out.

How do you make things feel or seem larger than they really are? By using interior walls to build furnishings, storage cabinets, shelves, and such into—you not only take advantage of nonbearing walls and walls that need not be chock-full of insulation, but you also save on space that otherwise would be taken up by placing cabinets and shelving alongside instead of within those walls. Built-in units, however, must not violate the thermal envelope, as they used to, for example, when clothes drawers were built into second-floor dormer bedrooms and stored their contents within unheated attic space without any attempt to insulate around them. This is especially important for storage purposes. Otherwise, in a smaller dwelling, where will you put things out of sight? There's not that much "out of sight" available, and there certainly aren't a lot of spare bedrooms.

With a smaller home, there's not much sense filling it full of interior walls—those walls will take up valuable floor space while adding very little in livability. This is why open floor plans are more practical and will lend a feeling of spaciousness inside. Why build a small formal dining room when a combination kitchen and dining area will be far more practical? If those areas lead directly into a living or family room, so much the better. Lots of connections to the outdoors—through a variety of windows, sliding and garden doors, sun rooms with walk-out patios or decks, and even solar tubes—also will make the home seem larger than it is. Good landscaping practices can further stretch out the living areas into which the decks and patios open. The judicious use of mirrors can even add an optical illusion of depth to a room or space. Light-colored furnishings, counters, paints and wallpapers, and other wall and floor coverings can further add to the feeling of spaciousness. Also consider what types of structural components will be used to construct floors, walls, and ceilings. Do you really need to cover them? Or could they be worked into the finished design in much the same way that commercial buildings use dramatic metal and wooden beams, cables, glass, and masonry. In all cases, think quality instead of quantity.

Along with a smaller size home, give some thought to acoustics, especially between sleeping areas and bathrooms and the living spaces. This means paying attention to insulating for sound absorption within interior walls and doors wherever privacy is desired. The use of interior windows can help to separate spaces while still allowing see-through views or for the passage of light when visual privacy is also a concern.

Again, you want a home that's large enough for your basic needs but not necessarily large enough for infrequent needs that may appear only for a small percentage of whatever time you'll spend at home. One good thing about starting smaller is that you may accommodate your living habits to the smaller dwelling and find that it's better for you, and then you may no longer even feel the need to expand.

With all this talk of smaller homes, you might wonder exactly how large *is* a smaller home? The informal consensus of today's home designers seems to be between 800 and 1,400 square feet, with the average small home coming in at about 1,100 square feet. For a home this small, built with green construction methods and materials appropriate for the climate it's in, an expensive heating and cooling system probably is not necessary because the dwelling will not require much energy or fuel to heat or cool. In fact, such a home may be ventilated and heated with a combination of a localized kitchen, bathroom, and other fans; high-efficiency airtight natural gas or wood pellet stoves (more than one might be needed) or fireplace inserts; simple electric-resistance baseboard or radiator units; and several well-placed heat exchangers to capture exhaust heat before it leaves. The electric demand will not be much, and a relatively small solar photovoltaic (PV) electricity-generating system may satisfy those needs and can be expanded at a later date, if required. This means that a whole-house heating and cooling distribution system may not be needed.

A note of caution: Such a small home serviced by individual space heaters should not include unvented heating appliances because they're too dangerous.

Tightly built homes without air leakage or natural drafts may be overwhelmed with lethal gases and fumes from malfunctioning appliances or incomplete combustion and backdrafting. Instead, all space heaters and combustion appliances should be of sealed-combustion design so that the air needed for burning comes directly from outside, and the exhausted fumes and gases are ultimately transported outdoors as well.

Before you begin drawing your final plans and layouts, within the best of your ability, try to determine how large your house should be and whether you can realistically afford it just yet. If your dream house is financially out of reach, face the facts. You'll have to decide exactly what's necessary and what can be scaled down, completely eliminated, or added on at a later date. If you elect future expansion as the best option, then plan for that expansion long before your new house is begun.

To start you out on the right track, this chapter covers two important subjects:

1. How to arrive at the correctly sized house to suit your present and future needs

2. How to prepare your house for future change or expansion

DECIDING ON THE SIZE OF YOUR HOUSE

The size of a house is generally expressed, as mentioned earlier, in total square footage of finished floor area. This is the key figure used today for determining building value.

Often, a higher-priced house offers more square footage for the money or more value in space per dollar than that offered by an inexpensive dwelling. Thus smaller, less expensive houses are frequently more costly per square foot. Of course, this also depends on special items and options built into each home, but all things equal, smaller houses tend to be more expensive per square foot of living space. Don't, however, build more house than you need simply to drive down the overall cost per square foot of living space. That would be like purchasing clothes that are too large for you because you get more material for the same price.

This is true because smaller houses incur overhead costs comparable with those of larger houses, and in smaller dwellings, those same overhead costs must be spread out over a lesser amount of square footage. In a sense, it's like buying groceries in bulk. The smaller packages usually cost more per ounce or per pound than their larger-sized counterparts. On the other hand, smaller homes generally use less energy to heat and cool, plus there are fewer square feet to maintain and keep clean.

To get a handle on how the costs in a typical house and lot are broken out, those expenses can be separated into three relatively equal categories (Fig. 8.1): One-third of the costs result from the land and improvements to that land. Improvements can

A breakdown of house/lot costs.

include a water well, septic system, utility connections, landscaping, a driveway and sidewalk, and even road construction, if needed. Another one-third of the costs go to the house structure from foundation to roof, including the house shell and entire framework. The remaining one-third of the costs come from the vital organs of the house, which include the plumbing, heating, and electrical systems and the kitchen and bathrooms.

If you study this division of costs, it becomes evident that when the first and last categories remain fairly constant in price, you can add considerably to the size of the house by increasing the dimensions of the basic structure at a substantially reduced cost per square foot of living space.

Here are some pointers to weigh when size planning:

1. When considering the overall size of your house, the number of bedrooms can be used as an acceptable guide. Until recently, at least three bedrooms were recommended even if you had no children or were planning no children in the future. A two-bedroom house for the most part used to be more difficult to sell because fewer people were looking for them, and the argument went that you could always turn a spare bedroom into a study, sewing room, or game area. Thus a three-bedroom home was marketable to families looking for either two or three bedrooms. More recently, families, pairs, and singles are seriously considering smaller homes as part of the green movement, as well as for financial reasons.

2. To economize on materials and labor, view the space inside your house in terms of actual requirements. Determine what each individual room will be used for, and then decide on its size and shape. You might realize that certain "appendage" rooms such as large walk-in closets are a waste for you.

3. When designing and planning rooms, consider your present dwelling. Are the rooms there too small? Or too large? Think about rooms in other houses you've been in. Focus on ones that are close to what you want. If you can, measure the ideal rooms to leave no doubt in your mind. And don't leave out the work area in the kitchen that will have to accommodate appliances, cabinets, and closet space.

4. The housing requirements of a typical family change about every 5 years as time marches on. You might want to keep that in mind while laying out the size and shape of your new house. How do you fit into the following typical household scenario?

   ■ Using a young couple just starting out together as the initial family unit, all their living requirements could be contained in a small dwelling, from a one-bedroom kitchenette/bath apartment to a two-bedroom house.

   ■ In between 5 and 10 years, with the addition of one or two children, the needs go up to at least two and possibly three bedrooms, larger living spaces, and more storage.

   ■ In between 10 and 15 years, the typical family, if three children are present by then, needs more sleeping space, a second bath, and more living and storage area.

   ■ From 15 to 25 years, this 10-year span while the children are maturing is likely to be stable unless the wage earner's business requires a change of locale or allows an upgrading of living standard.

   ■ At 25 through 40 years, during each 5-year period it's likely that one child will fly the nest—for marriage or at least for college or career.

   ■ Over 40 years, the family is once again down to two people, and large amounts of space can become a hindrance rather than a help.

Planning for Future Expansion

For any of a variety of reasons, you might not be able or willing to start out with the size house you'd like to have eventually. If you want to avoid jumping from house to house every few years as your housing needs increase, consider the following:

1. Initially plan a house that can be expanded easily or its inside walls reconfigured at a later date.

2. Review the house design you want in relation to the ease or complexity of making additions. Allow space and structure adaptability to add a garage, foyer, family room, bedrooms, second bath, or whatever it may be that you didn't build initially into your house.

3. When more space is required of a single-story ranch or two-story house, the construction of an addition to the rear or side of the house may be the best (but not the cheapest) answer. In both types of houses, it's a good idea to begin with dwellings that are able to accept additions without having their overall architectural character ruined by those additions. Consider how roof slopes, window types, exterior finishes, dormers, and similar features will be affected by the modifications you're planning. Also pay close attention to

property-line construction setbacks so that they won't rule out your ability to expand in other ways at some future date.

4. If your expansion plans call for knocking out a wall or walls later to enlarge part of your house, plan for that *before* the house is completed. Leave plumbing out of the walls that will be removed. Support the ceiling above or floor independently of the affected walls. Build the framework for the new entrance right into the wall so that all you need to do is knock out the rest of the wall when the time is right. Electricity is not a problem; light switches and outlets are moved easily.

5. When working with large unfinished places that eventually will be rendered into living areas, place doors and windows in such a way that easy-to-install partitions can be erected to turn big, open spaces into several individual rooms, as desired.

6. Although it might not be the way for you, there's no doubt that building up or down is cheaper than building out.

When Expanding Upward

If you start out with a Cape Cod, a two-story house, or even a ranch that has unfinished upper levels or attics, there are a number of technical points to be addressed when planning the initial structure. To permit maximum expansion without resorting to exterior modifications, the roof slope must be steep enough (or a gently sloped roof raised up enough) to provide adequate head room for new living areas. For example, on a house having a width of 24 feet or more, make sure that your roof slope—if the roof is not stepped up or raised up substantially—has a minimum of 9 inches of height for every 12 inches of travel or run toward the peak. Also make certain that the floor joists of the unfinished floor or attic are large enough to carry typical floor loads (Fig. 8.2).

Whatever your plan, you'll have to comply with local building codes that usually require one-half of a room's ceiling area to have a minimum floor-to-ceiling height of 7½ feet. Thus, if your attic space has windows at the gable ends, sufficient head room, and properly sized floor joists, the construction of one or more rooms is a relatively simple and inexpensive project, with no need for exterior remodeling. Extensions of existing heat, air-conditioning, and return-air ducts that had already been installed to and capped off at the area to be finished and activation of the already rough plumbing and wiring should result in a satisfactory expansion of your existing house at a nominal cost.

To attain increased floor area and more wall space for windows, dormers are recommended. Two types of dormers may be used: the shed dormer and the window, gable, or "eye" dormer (Fig. 8.3).

The shed dormer is the most practical because it adds a great deal of floor and wall space and is relatively simple to construct. However, because it's not as

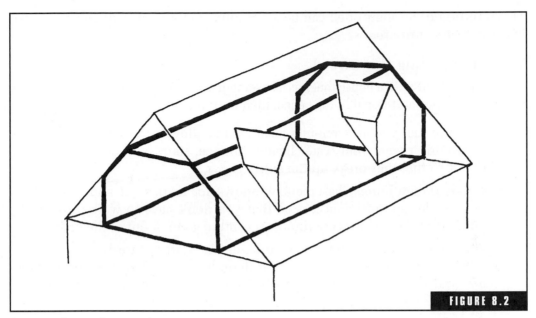

FIGURE 8.2

Cutaway of an attic expansion.

pleasant to look at as the window dormer, it's generally built at the rear of the house. A window or "eye" dormer offers less space, but it's still a major improvement over nothing. The illumination, ventilation, and increased floor space it brings can transfer an otherwise little-used space into a cozy bedroom or study.

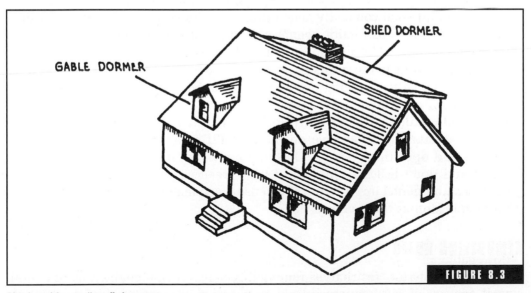

SHED DORMER

GABLE DORMER

FIGURE 8.3

Shed, gable, or "eye" dormers.

This addition of dormers often can be accomplished without removing the existing structure's entire roof.

When Expanding Downward

If you start out with a house that has a basement, and you plan on eventually using that basement for additional living space, then keep the following points in mind:

1. Make sure that you have enough clear area to allow for basement expansion. You wouldn't want your water heater, furnace, stairs, and other items to be laid out so that they break up the entire cellar.

2. Use larger-than-normal basement windows for extra light and ventilation, and consider an outside access so that you don't have to walk through the main part of the house every time you want to go in or out of the cellar.

3. If you plan to add a bathroom to your basement in the future, be sure to locate the sewer drain pipes below the cellar floor. If the sewer pipes enter the basement midway up the wall, you're in for extra expense and inconvenience when you have to add a pump system to push the refuse upward.

You'll usually find that interior expansion is more economical than exterior expansion. But exterior expansion provides extra space without sacrificing attic storage or basement areas. No matter which direction you plan to expand in—whether it be up, down, or out—make sure that your furnace/air-conditioning systems will have the capacity to handle the extra load. All in all, a small increase in effort in the initial planning, plus a little additional cost, can make an enormous difference in the ease and expense of expansion at a later date.

Just make sure that you really need the space before carrying out an expansion.

In short, green construction wants you to resist the urge—for whatever reason—to build larger. Instead, build as small as you comfortably can—but large enough to suit your living needs or with the flexibility to modify your spaces to expand and adjust to changing needs. A great benefit of building smaller is that you can include higher-quality components, such as hardwood floors instead of carpet, ceramic tile instead of vinyl flooring, top-grade windows, and expensive heating systems. What you save on bulk, you'll be able to spend on high-end materials and operating systems. On the other hand, if you need a large house, build it and don't feel bad. Just build it as green as you can. Yes, it will have greater environmental impacts, but if you use green materials and design, you will be able to minimize those effects.

REMODELING NOTES

Although interior "restrictive" remodeling may not change the home's overall square footage, it can temporarily reduce the size of areas serviced by heating, cooling, and ventilation. An upstairs or other section of a home's living area, if planned correctly, can be effectively "shut down" during the coldest (or warmest) two or three months of a year—thus saving on heating or air-conditioning costs. This can be achieved in all but the most open of home types and is especially effective when working with a two-story, multistory, or sprawling ranch-style home. Remodels can include re-sectioning of the home to exclude upper floors or other sections by blocking off areas—and, when appropriate plumbing, heat-delivery, and other temporary shutoffs are planned, sleeping arrangements even can be shifted temporarily to lower or first-level floors still being heated and ventilated. Sunrooms can be closed off at night with insulated shades and opened back up in the day to admit low-angled sunshine. Again, think outside the box. "Temporary" remodeling in order to save energy also should include such obvious features as programmable thermostats. By going smaller during peak heating and cooling months and modifying behaviors somewhat, extra energy savings can be achieved. Home owners even have resorted to the use of portable interior dividers that can be repositioned to expand or contract a bedroom's size by "moving" the narrowest wall accordingly. Small portable heaters also can come into play, but it's generally more effective to employ efficiencies afforded by the main heating and cooling systems.

▶▶▶▶▶ POINTS TO PONDER

1. As a rule, because smaller houses incur overhead costs comparable with those of larger dwellings, a larger home built on the same lot with the same quality of construction likely would cost less per square foot of living space than would a smaller house.

2. When considering the size of your house, the number of bedrooms can be used as a general guideline. At least three bedrooms are recommended even if you have no children or are planning no children in the future because—unless you're in an area heavily populated by retirees—two-bedroom homes are more difficult to sell.

3. Consider your present residence. Are the rooms there too small? Or too large? Measure ideal rooms to leave no doubt in your mind as to how large they are.

4. The housing requirements of a typical family change about every 5 years as time marches on. Consider your family's maturation and living needs as you lay out the size and shape of your new home.

5. If you're unable or unwilling to start out with the size home you'd eventually like to have, consider initially planning and building a house that can be expanded easily later.

6. If expansion plans call for knocking out walls later to enlarge part of the house, plan for this *before* the home is completed. Leave plumbing out of the walls that will be removed. Support the ceiling or floor above independently of the affected walls. Build the framework for the new entrance right into the wall so that all you need to do is knock out the rest of the wall when the time is right.

7. When working with large unfinished spaces that eventually will be rendered into living areas, place doors and windows in such a way that easy-to-install partitions can be erected to turn those big, open spaces into several individual rooms, as desired.

8. Dormers are excellent ways to increase floor area and provide more wall space for windows.

9. When expanding upward with a Cape Cod, a two-story, or even a ranch house that has unfinished upper levels or attics, the roof slope must be steep enough—or a gently sloped roof raised up enough—to provide adequate head room for new living areas. And make sure that the floor joists of the unfinished floor or attic are large enough to carry typical floor loads.

10. When expanding downward into a basement, make sure that the basement is high enough (9 feet is not too high) that the heating/cooling equipment and stairs are laid out so that they won't break up the entire cellar, that larger-than-normal basement windows are used for extra light and ventilation, that an outside access is considered, and that there's a logical place to install a bathroom.

Prints and Drawings

Now that previous chapters have touched on many of the major options involved when a house is planned, such as dwelling styles, types, floor plans, individual rooms, and sundry accessories, you can see how inefficient it is to just go to a builder and describe what you want in vague generalities.

WHY YOU SHOULD HELP TO CREATE THE PLANS

To walk into a skilled contractor's office and hint merely at what you think you need and then let the builder charge ahead and build it using his or her own discretion is in a sense like going into a clothing store and—without even browsing through the racks—telling a salesperson who knows neither your size nor your taste in clothes to please select an entire suit of clothes, right down to the shoes, that you'll be sure to like. The salesperson would be astonished. No one ever leaves that many decisions up to a total stranger, however knowledgeable about clothes the salesperson might be. Naturally, the salesperson would start asking questions, inquiring what *type* of clothes? Sports, leisure, business, or social? What *size* slacks do you take? Made of which materials, in what colors? For winter or fair-weather use? And what price range are you looking in?

To take the analogy a step further, what about the purchase of an automobile? A new car is a major expenditure to most of us. You decide what style, type, and size vehicle is best suited to your needs, desires, and pocketbook. Few people will stroll into a dealer's showroom and request a "four-door sedan," and fewer yet will ask a salesperson simply to suggest something out of the blue. Try it some time and see what happens. It's human nature for a salesperson to try to convince you to purchase whatever is being pushed at the time by the dealer. And sales-people are good at that. This is why they're in sales.

Builders are a different breed. Builders are accustomed to dealing with people who walk in cold, having only a foggy idea of what they want, especially now that another layer—that of green construction features—is in play. By far most builders will play fair with their customers and will try to help a potential home owner arrive at a suitable house design. Some, however, especially during times when plenty of work is available, become irritated by customers who come expecting counseling services to help plan an entire dwelling from scratch. These builders instead may strongly suggest a stock plan—a house they're thoroughly familiar with, perhaps one they've built within the past few months with a few green features thrown in at the last minute.

Other builders, when faced with an undecided client, will ask dozens of questions, such as, "How large do you want the bedrooms?" and "What size garage?" Neither will the answers to these types of questions change the builder's tact very much. A plan put together from your answers to simple, leading questions is probably also going to resemble one of the most recent dwellings the builder just completed. But you can't entirely fault builders for this. Somewhere along the line, each general contractor is going to have to know how much material to order and how to build the house. How else can he or she bid the job? To know how much material to order and how to build the house, the builder is going to need a set of plans—a set of blueprints and drawings to use as a guide. And just as a cook needs to follow a recipe in the kitchen to duplicate a favorite dish, so does a builder need prints and drawings to follow in the field to build the appropriate house. If you are determined to develop a specific plan designed with input that requires green strategies and components, the builder will have to buy into that plan or lose the work.

If you're still not convinced that you should participate fully in the creation of the prints and drawings by making many of the optional construction decisions yourself, then consider that the builder wants you to be pleased with the finished product, but rarely does that concern go too far past the technical level. Do you really think it will register on a contractor if you say, "Gee, you should have made the family room 2 feet longer so that we could fit our overstuffed sofa in front of the fireplace"? What else can he say except, "I'm sorry. It was working on the plans you approved." To mention that the basement has heaved up and is full of water—now *that* will register. But if you later realize that the walls contain less insulation than is recommended by Energy Star standards, if the prints, drawings, and contract all include the lesser amount, you've got little to back your complaints. Today's reputable builders almost always will correct deficiencies centering on the actual construction—the carrying out of original agreed-on plans. However, if you chastise a contractor after he or she erects the house because he or she should have known that the garage should have been located on the other side of the dwelling to act as a shield against prevailing winter winds, your efforts will likely fall on deaf ears.

FINAL SET OF PLANS

Most builders employ or have access to someone who can take the rough conceptual drawings that you prepare and, after arriving at a general consensus with the builder, will return simple drawings for you to review. After an agreement is reached (it might take any number of back-and-forth drawing revisions to actually reach an agreement), the drawings will then be turned into professional plans—specific drawings and specifications (or specs). The drawings and specifications include, in as much detail as possible, how the dwelling is to be constructed and where. This set of written and drawn instructions can be used for estimating, materials ordering, financing, and construction. The draftsperson or designer will frequently have suggestions on dimension sizes that may take full advantage of stock sizes of building components to help reduce costs and wasted materials in a similar way that an architect would design a home.

How many drawings does a typical house require? Depending on the size and complexity of construction, five to eight prints or drawings on paper about 24 by 36 inches in size should convey the required views. Although computerized drawings also may be available for you, a larger working-scale drawing available on oversize print paper is easier to see details on, make notes on, and grasp entire views without scrolling every which way on a computer screen. Generally, the more detail included on the drawings, the better—to a certain point. Too many details or repetitive views can balloon the cost of the drawings needlessly. The average set of drawings and specification lists usually contain the site plan with exterior elevations, floor plans, wall sections, major construction details, lists of materials, plumbing, electrical, and lighting fixtures, and appliances. Together they function as a graphic set of instructions on how the home should be built and of what it will be constructed.

No matter where you get them, your final set of prints and drawings should in some way address the following items.

Floor Plans

There should be one blueprint for each floor. These are working drawings that show overall dimensions, room and hallway sizes, locations and sizes of doors and windows, locations of interior partitions and wall thicknesses, and locations of electrical switches, plugs, appliances, plumbing fixtures, water supply, drains, and other information needed to complete the house (Fig. 9.1). Do the floor plans reflect your green strategy? Ask the builder such questions as what steps were taken to make sure that the dimensions take into account standard building material sizes so that wasted half- or three-quarter-length sheets won't result and what

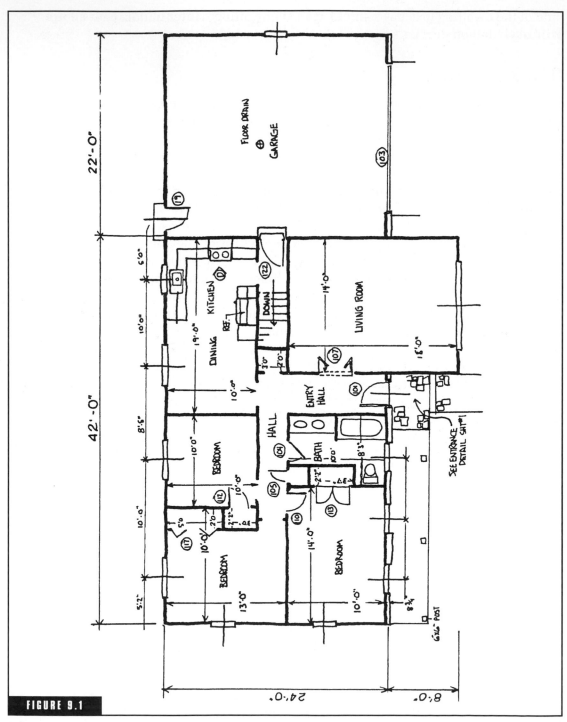

FIGURE 9.1

A floor plan.

percentage of supplies will be manufactured and/or purchased within a certain surrounding geographic area? What's the percentage of window area, and where are the windows located?

Lot or Site Plan

The lot or site plan shows the original contour of the land, the proposed finished contour, original trees and the ones which will be left standing, the location of the water well and septic tank if applicable, the driveway, electrical service, and the placement or orientation of the house on the building site (Fig. 9.2). Note

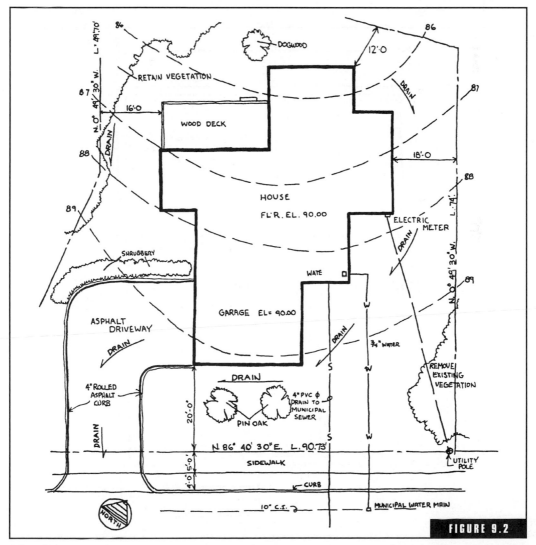

FIGURE 9.2

A lot plan.

whether there are any wetlands, specialized desirable vegetation to be saved, and how advantage can be taken of passive-solar exposures, prevailing breezes for natural ventilation, and topographic features that might have an impact on energy efficiencies. Is the proposed footprint as small as possible?

Foundation Plan

The foundation plan shows the height of the sill (where the house frame rests on the foundation or top of the basement) above grade, the chimney location, the extent of excavation and grading required, and the locations of water and sewer hookups and easements (Fig. 9.3).

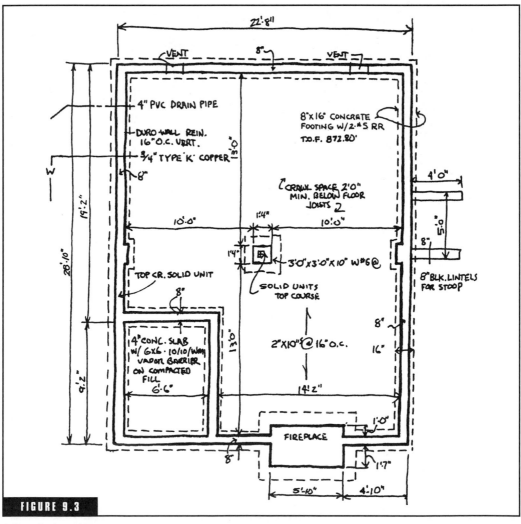

FIGURE 9.3

A foundation plan.

Elevation Drawing

The elevation drawing depicts the lines of the house from its four or more sides from north, south, east, and west. Do the exterior elevations follow your green strategy? Are windows, doors, vents, wall configurations, overhangs, and other features sized correctly and positioned at heights and places that will enable effective natural ventilation, lighting, views, and solar gain if needed? You might need a front, rear, and two-side views depending on the complexity of the house. Exterior material types also should be indicated here (Fig. 9.4).

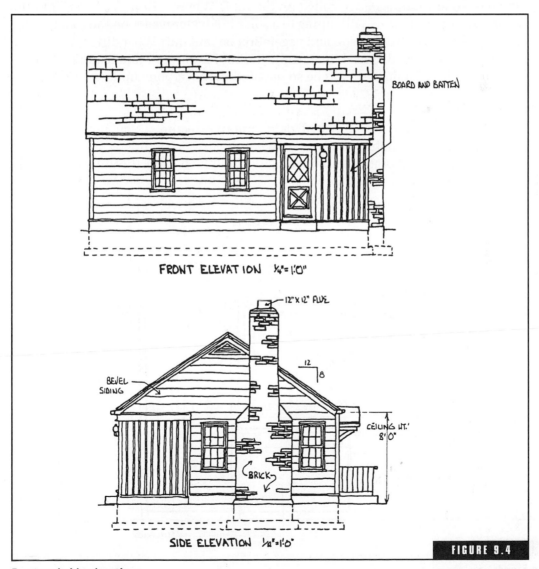

FRONT ELEVATION ¼"=1'0"

SIDE ELEVATION ⅛"=1'0"

FIGURE 9.4

Front and side elevations.

Exterior Wall Sections

These are often side views or cutaways showing how the all-important exterior walls will be built. Understand the insulation, air-infiltration, and moisture-prevention strategies. Ask the builder how he or she will be verifying the R-value of the exterior walls.

Special Construction Features

Details of special green components or systems should be shown. For example, how will solar modules be installed on the roof? Where will they be tied into the electric service, and how will piping to a solar hot water heater on the roof be run? How would a green roof of soil and vegetation be laid out? What different features will be included in advanced floor, wall, and roof framing? Main features that differ from traditional ones should be so detailed that everyone understands them.

Interior Sketch

If the interior has any unusual or distinctive features, you might want an artist's renditions to help you visualize what the interior will look like. An example would be an elaborate bathroom or special kitchen cabinet setups (Fig. 9.5).

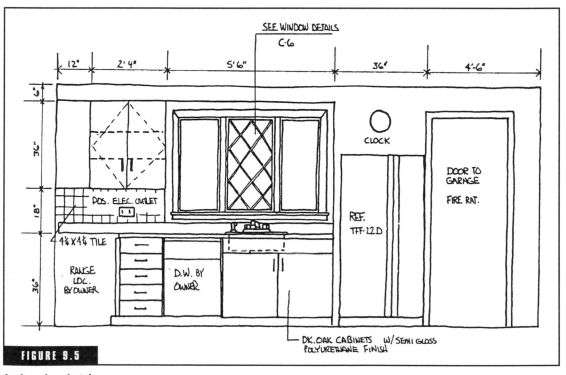

FIGURE 9.5

An interior sketch.

Perspective Sketch

This sketch shows what the completed house will look like from the outside, including landscaping, if desired.

Specifications

There also should be written narrative specifications for the materials and components to be used and the techniques that will be used with them. This specification listing should include the green building materials that you and your builder have already agreed would be included in the house. The builder also should understand that any substitutions need to be discussed with you or your design team before they are made.

Finally, you should request at least four and possibly five complete sets of plans—one for the builder, one for the lending institution, one for the local building department, one for yourself, and just in case, one extra set for your records.

PREPARING YOUR PLANS

There are a number of ways that you can rough out or complete the plans you'll need before going to contractors and soliciting bids.

1. Have an architect do the plans for you, with your help.
2. Purchase a set of stock plans through a mail-order company.
3. Prepare them yourself with help from books, magazines, and friends.
4. Use packaged planning kits.
5. Employ a personal computer and special home designing software.

Architects

The truly great houses in the world have practically all been designed by architects. Indeed, architects are wonderful at custom engineering houses that require complex construction techniques or unique materials. If you've got a building site in the middle of a swamp or on a ledge of solid rock, an architect will be able to figure out how to build on it. And given to the nature of their business, they stay abreast of the latest energy-saving techniques and other technical innovations. Whether an architect is right for you depends on the complexity of your design and building site, and your bank account. Like any professionals, architects are well compensated for their efforts. They can be invaluable for green construction projects, especially when their cost is amortized over the life of the dwelling, considering that an effective green home will have a continuous payback in reduced energy costs, increased comfort, long periods between material and component replacements, and low maintenance expenses.

Stock Plans

If you'd prefer not to draw your own initial plans, and hiring an architect is out of the question, consider stock prints and drawings that have already been prepared by green building professionals and are available through the Internet and mail-order companies. Even if you can't find exactly what you want, plans always can be modified to some extent by your builder/architect. Remember that care must be taken because major changes can cause structural problems—especially when altering a foundation to match a lot or when changing load-bearing walls.

One advantage to using stock plans is simple economy. They're inexpensive themselves, and their dimensioning of rooms and spaces for suitable structural members is done with a minimum amount of waste by using standard lumber and other building materials. This is so because stock plans are prepared by experienced home design experts who have accumulated a broad range of planning ideas over a considerable length of time. Some are licensed practicing architects.

Do-It-Yourself

To help you commit your ideas to paper, there's a wonderful invention available at nominal cost: graph paper. Graph paper is an ideal medium for expressing room sizes and relationships in a floor plan. A good scale to work with is ¼ inch equals 1 linear foot. You'll also need a roll-up steel or plastic tape measure at least 25 feet long, plus some home design books and magazines that will give you average dimensions and proportions of various features in houses such as hallway widths, door heights, and wall thicknesses. Many of these dimensions can be found within this book.

Once you finish your plans the best way you know how, the builder can use his or her knowledge of construction materials to point out where adding a few feet here or taking away a few inches there can result in substantial savings. If plywood sheets come in 4- by 8-foot sheets (and they do), it would be silly to spec out a room that would require coverage by 10 sheets of 4½- by 8-foot sheets. This would result in sizable waste.

Builder/architects can take your estimates and customize them—still keeping your plan's original integrity—to dimensions that lend themselves to standard building material sizes in order to reduce waste and give you more for your money. Builder/architects have a realistic feel for how to stretch materials to the maximum. They'll be able to take your rough drawings and show you where you can pick up efficiencies and where you could use substantially less material—perhaps merely by altering a particular dimension in some minor way.

Packaged Planning Kits

If you'd like to explore a simpler method of creating your own house plans, packaged planning kits are available from a number of companies and publishers.

They consist of scaled grid sheets or boards and appropriately sized furniture; construction parts such as windows, doors, and walls; and even landscaping trees and shrubs. They're simple to use, and they can help to plan how much furniture your house will need and where it should go.

The kits come with instructions, and most are designed at a ¼-inch scale. They can help you to reduce the cost of professional drawings; the designer can do the drawings a lot faster if he or she just copies from your layout.

Most kits are manufactured in two-dimensional (2D) style, but some offer three-dimensional (3D) planning—a great help if you have a difficult time conceptualizing and visualizing whether a room design you are planning would fit the space allotted. The 3D kits tend to be twice the scale of the others to give you a better grasp of the cardboard, plastic, or foam furniture replicas. These lifelike objects include plumbing fixtures, televisions, stereos, sofas, toilets, and even pianos. Some kits use decals and plastic or cardboard printed in 3D style. Other kits supply foam furniture that you can paint or even upholster to try out color schemes. If you don't use computers, these kits can be very helpful.

Computer-Assisted Plans

For the ultimate in home design at your fingertips, turn to the personal computer. Architects have been using computer-assisted design (CAD) graphics and engineering packages for years, but now that the personal computer has become so affordable and easy to use, it's certainly an interesting option for you.

Software is available to help you draw your own designs on a monitor or computer screen. And computer screens are great to work with because they're so easy to change, with no harm done if you make a mistake. With some programs, you can look at the drawings in 3D; you can rotate them right on the screen to see all angles of a room or the entire floor plan. You can save the drawings on disks and print them out on a printer whenever you need a copy.

The details on these programs are incredible—down to the patterns of wallpaper. You can ask for overhead and side views, and you can even fast-forward a newly planted landscaping scheme to see how it will look years in the future, when fully grown.

These accurate designs can help to reduce the effort and cost of having professionals complete your set of plans.

BEFORE APPROACHING THE BUILDER

It's important that your own plans are as detailed as possible before you meet with contractors; otherwise, you'll be at a disadvantage in terms of the bids. In order to protect themselves against work that is not clearly spelled out, they might pad their bids. At the same time, some could attempt to make you do without items that you are taking for granted and that are not specified initially.

REMODELING NOTES

If you've never had the original set of prints and drawings of your existing home, and you plan to remodel part of it, try to prepare "before" and "after" drawings to go by. Unless they can be prepared informally, an experienced draftsperson may be enlisted for reasonable cost. At the very least, document with a digital camera and have the images printed and stored as a future record of what's in the walls, below the floors, or above the ceilings. Add the modifications to your collection of drawings if you have them, and they should be relatively simple to modify and record dates, money spent, equipment manufacturers, and warranties and add to your packet of maintenance information, servicing contacts, equipment manufacturers, product information, and operating booklets.

▶▶▶▶▶ POINTS TO PONDER

1. Unless you have absolutely no opinion about what you're going to be living in, at the very least, provide some active input into the planning of your new home.

2. An ideal set of home plans includes floor plans, a lot plan, a foundation plan, an elevation drawing, an interior sketch, and a perspective or outside sketch with landscaping, if desired.

3. There are different ways to complete new house plans. You could use an architect; purchase a set of stock plans through a mail-order company; prepare the plans yourself with help from books, magazines, the Internet, and friends; use a packaged planning kit; or employ a personal computer with home-designing software.

4. Architects can be great assets or expensive planners. Depending on their abilities, they can be either expensive or can literally pay for themselves by figuring how to scale back on heating systems or construction components by adding more passive-solar and other green features.

5. Stock plans are good—and they can be modified to some extent by your builder/architect. They're usually quite economical because they're prepared by experienced home-design experts who have accumulated a broad range of planning ideas over a considerable length of time.

6. Do-it-yourself plans are entirely possible. Don't be afraid to try. A good builder can take your drawings and have a complete set of technically correct plans made, adding efficiencies when drawing from his or her knowledge of available construction material dimensions.

7. Packaged planning kits are available in two and three dimensions for a simple way of creating house plans. They can help you to reduce the cost of professional drawings because the designer can do the drawing a lot faster if he or she just copies from your layout.

8. If you're computer literate, some excellent software programs are available to walk you through numerous home-design scenarios and can print out a variety of overhead, side, and even landscaped views.

9. It's important that your plans are as detailed as possible before meeting with the contractors. Do your homework in advance. Make all the decisions you can beforehand.

10. Remain open, however, to good suggestions offered by builders. Don't be reluctant to modify your plans in the face of new information that would better suit your purposes.

How to Build It

If you never even lift a hammer throughout the entire construction process, it still pays to know how a house can and should be put together. How else could you make educated decisions about the building specifications that are so crucial to a dwelling's quality of construction and overall durability, safety, and comfort? Often the difference between mediocre and excellent construction involves a ridiculously small materials cost. Knowing construction methods and materials also will assist in your dealings with whichever contractor you choose.

While it's not necessary to be able to recite good specifications from memory, it's important that you have a sense of how the contractor should go about fulfilling his or her obligations. Chapters 10 through 30 cover how to decide on the greenest materials and products, plus what should happen from foundation to rooftop and point out essential decisions that need to be made and should be made with your input.

Green Materials and Products

Whether you are considering new construction or remodeling, green materials, components, and products should be an integral part of any plan. But what makes a material green? A series of questions in this chapter can help to prepare you to sift through an enormous range of products to arrive at practical and effective green options for your situation. The most important characteristic of any green material or product is probably its ability to renew or sustain itself (alone or with help) through a natural or benign process that does no harm to air, water, or land—which is a practical definition for sustainability.

Ask and seek answers to the following questions to help determine a material's or product's greenness.

WHAT IS IT (THE MATERIAL OR PRODUCT) MADE OF?

Is it sustainable? Or is it a material that will be irreversibly depleted as used? The greenest materials are sustainable and include products made from rapidly renewable or otherwise sustainable ingredients such as bamboo, silk, wool, Forest Stewardship Council (FSC)–managed wood, or materials that are so abundant they'll never run out, such as clay, steel, glass, stone, brick, tile, aluminum, and others. On the other hand, materials and products derived from fossil fuels, particularly crude oil, are not sustainable—they'll eventually run out—even though some fossil fuels may be relatively abundant for now, such as coal and natural gas. Of course, many materials and products are made of numerous ingredients, some of which may be sustainable, whereas others may not be.

HOW IS IT MADE?

Is the growing, gathering, or manufacturing process the material or product comes from wasteful and/or energy-intensive? Unless you're already familiar with basic manufacturing processes and the specific processes a company uses, it will likely take some research to find out how everyday materials are either harvested or made. Or you can rely on a third-party opinion from experts in the material's or product's field. For example, pieces of 2×6 lumber can be of the same species, same dimensions, and same age and weight. Yet one could have been sawed and processed from a forest that was clear-cut and left fallow or bulldozed over and not replanted or cared for in any way, whereas another virtually identical piece may have come from an FSC-certified stand of trees that had been managed responsibly—which means managed to ensure continuity of the forest so that harvested trees are replaced by saplings planted elsewhere in the tract. In this case, the FSC certification stamp does a lot of the work for you.

WHAT IS THE MATERIAL'S OR PRODUCT'S EMBODIED ENERGY?

How much energy goes into preparing or making the finished material or product? If the process is energy-intensive, then the resulting material or product by itself may not be very green. An example of this is the generation of electricity by burning coal. Very little of the energy embodied in coal or other fossil fuels burned to make steam that generates electricity is carried over to the electricity itself. Most is lost in the form of heat that's wasted during combustion and throughout the generation, transmission, and delivery processes. But low-tech combustion processes are not the only wasteful methods used to produce energy products. A recognized "green" complaint about computer or solar silicon chips and solar components is that far too much energy is used during the silicon's manufacture. Spending a lot of energy on products being developed to conserve energy seems somewhat ironic.

The amount of energy required to produce a building material or product is often called *embodied energy*. It can include energy spent on everything from harvesting the raw material, transporting it, manufacturing the product, taking it to market, and delivering it to the home site. Although the embodied energy of a particular product rarely can be found in product literature or reviews, once you understand the chain of manufacturing processes used to make a certain material or product, you can get a good order-of-magnitude idea of the energy inputs involved.

WHAT'S THE PACKAGING LIKE?

Some products come in elaborate packaging that, in turn, also must be manufactured. In fact, certain packaging designs can require more manufacturing energy consumption that the product itself does. What happens to the packaging after the product is put to use? Some may be recycled, but much of it—mostly plastic—may never find its way back to a recycler. The more biodegradable the packaging, the greener is the arrangement. Sure, the packaging must be sturdy enough to prevent handling or transportation damage, but some products—light bulbs come to mind—are so difficult to get open that you need industrial scissors to cut through the thick clear plastic. Building products, too, can be shipped and sold in heavy-duty packaging, including such products as paint, spackle, plaster, sealant, and other items sold in plastic buckets and containers. If those containers, still holding partial amounts of product, are sent directly to municipal landfills because they aren't accepted in that condition by local recycling programs, the products are definitely not as green as they otherwise could be if their containers were recycled properly. Packaging is meant to protect products while they are being handled or stored and to prevent materials from drying out, accidentally dispersing, rusting, or oxidizing—sometimes outdoors—and in general to facilitate handling, transport, and storage. The big question is, Can those packaging containers be cleaned out and recycled effectively so that they won't be thrown away with regularity?

IS THE MATERIAL OR PRODUCT CERTIFIED FOR GREEN CHARACTERISTICS BY A RECOGNIZED STANDARD-SETTING OR RATING ORGANIZATION?

Many products have certifications or follow standards from standard-setting or rating organizations that can be trusted to be accurate. The status of a green product is often reflected in what's known as an *eco-label*, which verifies a material's or product's green attributes. For example, in addition to the FSC and the American Forest and Paper Association's Sustainable Forestry Initiative for wood and wood-fiber products, there's the Green Seal logo, which concentrates on environmentally friendly paints, household cleaners, paper products, and similar supplies. Another trusted group issues the Greenguard Indoor Air Quality Certified logo approval for adhesives, appliances, ceiling, flooring, insulation, paint, and wall-covering products having low chemical emissions when used indoors. Scientific Certification Systems has a certification program for evaluating similar environmentally benign products and services that include recycled content and biodegradable abilities of many finishing products such as cabinets, flooring, wall coverings, paints, doors, sealants, and adhesives. Among other tests, these organizations often see for themselves whether manufacturer claims are true or not, performing investigations that help consumers to make choices that otherwise could be very confusing. Cradle-to-Cradle is yet another organization that concentrates on a product's entire life cycle to identify the most environmentally friendly products available.

The Soil Association's Organic Standard seal certifies that a product—including textiles, food, lumber, and landscape and garden products—has been manufactured organically, without the use of pesticides and other harmful chemicals. For carpeting choices, call on the Carpet and Rug Institute's Green Label and Green Label+ programs that identify carpeting having very low chemical and volatile organic compound (VOC) emissions. Other trusted groups having product certifications include Blue Angel and Gut of Germany, Environmental Choice of Canada, Nordic Swan of Scandinavia, and Eco-Labeling of the European Union. For overall energy- or water-consumption labels, a number of excellent organizations, including Energy Star and, in Europe, Energy Labels, lead the pack. These organizations certainly are not the only ones consumers can turn to. There are many private and semiprivate and public groups that have made it their business to keep manufacturers honest by identifying strong proponents of green products and services, as well as pointing out companies that say they make green products but really don't.

Another excellent source for determining if materials or products are green is the *GreenSpec Directory*, published by the BuildingGreen folks.

ARE THERE ANY SAFETY, HEALTH, OR ENVIRONMENTAL ISSUES WITH THE MATERIALS OR PRODUCTS?

This question also can concern any pollution and waste by-products resulting from the manufacturing process. Of prime importance is any harmful effect a material could have on indoor air quality, Does the product off-gas during application? We know that VOCs are substances that can be emitted into the air from materials containing solvents and other active chemical compounds and that these materials can pose health hazards to people and pets that live among them. These harmful ingredients historically have been present in oil-based paints, thinners, lacquers, urethanes, and other finishes, as well as in assorted hardboard products such as plywood, particleboard, and numerous substrates used in the manufacture of cabinetry and countertops, furniture, floors, wall and roof sheathing, and many other similar products. Some materials are especially problematic when they are being applied. As they dry, organic solvents "evaporate" into the surrounding air, which sends particles airborne that can easily be breathed by occupants. The rate of off-gassing varies considerably, with some products slowly emitting their VOCs for weeks, months, and even years after application or installation.

Formaldehyde, a known carcinogen, has for a long time been used as a part of manufacturing processes owing to its ability to retard the growth of mold, fungi, bacteria, and other undesirable organisms that otherwise could attack and break down ingredients in many building products. Especially present in glues and adhesives, paints, and liquid coating products, formaldehyde still can be found with regularity in new building materials, including many of the pressed-wood, particleboard, and substrates mentioned in the preceding paragraph. Sometimes it also may be found in fiberglass and other insulations.

Of course, other ingredients "no longer used" because they have been identified long ago as cancer-causing agents include lead used in plumbing and paint products; polychlorinated biphenyls (PCBs) used in electrical transformers and other power equipment; and water-contaminating mercury found in old thermostats, switches, and other heating and cooling controls—and once in a while in a wall thermometer or in a first-aid kit from the 1850s (responsibly get rid of anything with mercury in it without delay). Asbestos is another dangerous material now controlled, but for years it was used as an important ingredient in pipe and wall insulation. In the first sentence of this paragraph, "no longer used" is in quotes because try as the building materials regulators do, once in a while products are manufactured in countries that do not have strict environmental and health oversight. For example, recently, a huge influx of drywall made in such a country entered the American marketplace, and the drywall had ingredients that enabled mold to grow after installation.

Environmentally, the manufacturing process can pose problems, with amounts of heat, waste, and pollution given off that either must be dealt with right away or will have a cumulative effect on the air, ground, or waters in the area. Highly regulated processes often have scrubbers and processes that moderate these issues, and creative ways of recycling for environmental and financial reasons are being used more often in today's sensitive marketplace where green now can be used as a promotional characteristic of a product and can help to differentiate one product from another. There seems to be a race going on to see if products can be advertised as acceptable to be used for the Leadership in Energy and Environmental Design (LEED) for Homes program or other certification points.

HOW LONG SHOULD THE MATERIAL OR PRODUCT LAST?

What is its expected useful life? A telltale sign can be the warranty it comes with. They're something to consider, especially when they involve components of systems that are integrally built into the home—that would be difficult and expensive to replace in the future. Think of the expense and inconvenience of replacing in-floor heating systems, or insulation throughout the walls, or a foundation wall, or a plumbing system? Here, think of life-cycle costs, and combine this question with the next question about maintenance and replenishable supplies needed. A classic example is an electric-resistance heating system. The unit, along with its transmission and distribution components, is relatively inexpensive, simple, and easy to install and maintain, and the efficiency of the electricity used is high—unfortunately, though, the cost of purchased electricity is high and getting higher all the time.

Product durability is an important feature that not only affects operating costs but also directly affects the amount of materials that need to be landfilled. Carpeting comes to mind. Consider the useful life of wall-to-wall carpeting. If under hard use and in environments where soil, ultraviolet rays, and moisture are all present, wall-to-wall carpeting and its padding may need frequent replacement. There's not much hope of recycling many types of carpeting, so it is tossed into landfills, where its nylon and other fibers will resist degrading for many, many years. On the other hand, in more carefully managed environments, carpeting can last many years if kept clean and dry, such as in bedrooms and more lightly used interior living spaces. In addition, carpets are available that are made of sisal and other vegetable or grass matter or wool or naturally grown cottons. Typically, the greener the product, the more biodegradable it is. Unlike nylon, polypropylene, and other plastic-made carpets, those made of natural fibers are entirely biodegradable and will not plug up landfills for long periods of time.

HOW MUCH DOES IT COST?

This practical question dovetails with the preceding question. What's the total life-cycle cost to the home owner? This equals the sum of the money spent to purchase, install, and use whatever material, component, or product is being discussed divided by the number of years in service. When these factors are all considered, you can see how quickly a better grade of product can become the most cost-effective one as well, even though the initial investment may be higher. How quickly that investment of a few thousand dollars more for a 94 percent high-efficiency forced-air gas furnace will pay for itself rather than a standard 80 or 85 percent efficient furnace of similar design. You need to think about how much replenishable supplies are needed (in this case, natural gas) to keep the unit or system running at realistic levels. The same goes for appliances, such as storage-tank-type water heaters. The length of the warranty is often a good indicator of a product's durability.

Of all the questions, this one may be the most difficult to come to grips with when less green materials can supply longer useful lives than can green versions of the same type of product. A classic case is vinyl flooring versus linoleum flooring for the same application. Higher-quality vinyl floorings simply will stand up better to hard wear than will the better grades of linoleum. This is due to the wear-resistant characteristics of each product. Linoleum is probably the greener overall choice, but it may not last as long as some vinyl flooring would.

WHERE DOES THE MATERIAL OR PRODUCT COME FROM?

Where do the raw materials come from, and where are they processed and used in the product's manufacture? What you are after here is how far must the material or product has to be transported to reach your building site? Then the costs—

financial as well as expense of energy—must be considered. This is another question that can be confusing. When was the last time you saw bamboo growing in your neighborhood? Bamboo is a material that is being touted as the all-around sustainable green material "poster child." Yet rarely a living commercial-grade stalk of it can be found within thousands of miles of where much of it is used. Of course, bamboo generally is quite light in weight and doesn't take a lot of fuel to move, but in certain products, such as flooring or countertops, it does have some weight and requires a considerable amount of energy to be sent long distances.

The heavier the material, the greater is the need to find local sources if green construction purchasing or sourcing guidelines are to be satisfied. Consider a stone fireplace mantelpiece. A piece of sandstone quarried from a hundred miles away would require far less energy to transport to your building site than would a piece of granite quarried in Germany. There are typically local sources for materials such as concrete and asphalt, as well as products such as doors, windows, and landscape supplies. Large-scale home-improvement stores often carry competing local and long-distance products from far-away countries that have traveled thousands of miles to get near your door. You can do a little online research to see what products you can get from your local or regional area, or simply ask at a store where the products you're interested in come from. Manufacturer associations and product organizations have directories, and craftspeople often know what's available. You may be surprised to learn how many products are within a few hour's drive—their advertising budgets often do not promote locally, so you may never have heard about them previously. Large company purchasing agents also can be of help. Try to ferret out local suppliers as much as possible. The LEED for Homes guidelines award points for purchasing locally made materials and products.

HOW DOES THE MANUFACTURER STACK UP AGAINST GREEN OR SUSTAINABLE GUIDELINES?

Is the manufacturer involved with the green movement? Do the product lines have any sustainable offerings, and are energy-efficient processes and materials replacing less green materials and products? Does the manufacturer certify any products as to their performance when it comes to energy efficiency or healthy product characteristics? How long has the manufacturer been in business? Is the company recognized worldwide, nationally, or locally? Do the products have a history that can be researched. Are there any reviews available? Does the manufacturer publish data on the product's performance? Is there somewhere you can see the product working or at least installed? Is sustainability a part of the manufacturer's company policy, mission statement, and culture? Can the company point to energy-efficient and pollution- and waste-free manufacturing processes? What does the company do with its by-products and waste materials? How does the company treat and compensate its workers and suppliers? Is the company a good corporate citizen and neighbor? Does it protect air and water quality? Does it plant trees or buy carbon credits to help offset what it uses of natural resources?

COULD RECLAIMED MATERIALS OR PRODUCTS BE PURCHASED INSTEAD OF NEW ONES?

Reclaimed materials and products are materials and items that had been used previously for the same purposes that you will be using them for in your new home. For example, fireplace mantels, stairway railings, paneling, bricks, tiles, beams, decorative windows, interior doors and trim, stamped metal ceilings, cabinet and drawer handles and pull knobs, lighting fixtures (chandeliers and fixtures that can be rewired safely with modern insides and wiring), and many other products and components can be reclaimed from previous buildings and installed in your home-building project.

ARE THERE ANY RECYCLED-CONTENT GREEN MATERIALS OR PRODUCTS THAT CAN BE PURCHASED NEW?

There are many recycled-content materials and products in the marketplace now, and more are being designed all the time. In fact, it's getting difficult to find companies that don't offer some sort of recycled line, from rebuilt and refurbished electronics, appliances, and heating and cooling equipment to specially manufactured building materials and furnishings. For example, wall finishes include recycled-content wallpapers, panels, drywall, plaster, and even paint. Countertops and tiles contain recycled glass and tile shards. Metal and tile roofing materials contain recycled content, as do driveway and patio materials. Bricks are easily cleaned of mortar and reused. Large, old hand-hewn beams can make excellent decorative and structural (if professionally certified as strong enough for their application) framing members.

CAN THE MATERIALS OR PRODUCTS EVENTUALLY BE DECONSTRUCTED AND USED AGAIN?

Is the material or product durable enough to last 50 years or more? Or will it find a new home in a landfill?

IS THE MATERIAL, PRODUCT, OR COMPLETED HOME GREEN ENOUGH?

This is the end question for you. How green must your home be? By now, you've probably heard the term *shades of green*. The darker the shade, the greener is the material, product, or system. There is no right answer here. Your project should be as green as you determine it should be to suit your situation, to satisfy your needs, and to keep within your budget.

DOES USING PRACTICALLY ALL GREEN BUILDING MATERIALS AND PRODUCTS GUARANTEE A GREEN DWELLING?

It's easy to get caught up in the selection of individual green materials and components to the point where putting them all together becomes a mere afterthought. Unfortunately, the sum of many green materials and products may not result in the greenest of homes. The house may not be energy efficient. If it leaks air or moisture, no matter how green the components are, it will waste energy. The house could be much larger than needed. It could be 50 or 60 miles from work, requiring 3 or 4 hours of driving per day.

THINGS TO LOOK OUT FOR

Greenwashing

Greenwashing means advertising or promotional claims that either say or imply that a material, product, or component has one or more green characteristics and therefore is a green product that should be purchased and used. This can be like calling the bubonic plague "100 percent natural." There may be truth to the statement that the plague is a "naturally" occurring disease, but that certainly doesn't make it a beneficial condition. Crude oil is also a product of nature, in its natural state. So are all the fossil fuels. Some products advertised as green cannot live up to those claims when all their manufacturing and operational factors are considered. Electric resistant heat is practically 100 percent efficient—if you count the use of the electricity after it's generated by a coal-fired power plant.

As more and more companies are jumping on the green bandwagon, they're trying to align themselves and their products with green claims. Unfounded or false claims of green characteristics or benefits can be summed up by the term *greenwashing*. Some products are not green because they have hidden tradeoffs—they play up a green feature while hiding or conveniently not mentioning manufacturing or other characteristics that are definitely not green, such as "green" cleaning products that contain corn-based ethanol, which is an extremely expensive and inefficiently produced product. Other green claims may be little more than general statements that cannot be proven.

The trick is sometimes to avoid having to exchange product performance for product greenness. At what point does the importance of the greenness of a material or product surpass that product's ability to perform durably or otherwise? These characteristics must be carefully weighed. Ideally, if performance can be enhanced or achieved through the product's sustainability, you have a win-win situation. But do you go for a win-win result at any cost? Then, at what point does achieving greenness become too expensive? If you elect to do it even if it is expensive, you can be an example to others and may have followers.

How Much of a Good Product Do You Really Need?

Until only a few years ago, when the "stronger is better" philosophy ruled home-building circles, a lot of overbuilding was done. Contractors routinely impressed their customers by building extra sturdiness into the framing by using additional lumber and fasteners and extra supports beneath floors and roofs. They constructed huge basements, patios, and wooden decks. Kitchens contained commercial-sized appliances. Big quality seemed to rule, especially for those who could afford it. Now, green guidelines say to use fewer materials period. Build smaller. Scale back on square footage, on the size of appliances, and on the number of bathrooms and specialty rooms. Share spaces. Use building materials that double as structure and finished surfaces. Instead of large, go with durability and quality. Wood framing traditionally has been overbuilt. The advantages of advanced framing methods are now clear: They make room for more insulation, they allow for shorter pieces of lumber and engineered wood products that are straighter and stronger, they make good use of trusses, and they avoid wood-on-wood corners and blocking that frequently has resulted in moisture-trapping problems.

Cheap Knockoffs

One bamboo flooring panel can be responsibly made from a tight-grained, durable bamboo species put together with no-VOC binders and adhesives, whereas a similar version of flooring can be assembled with high-solvent adhesives and formaldehyde and made from a fast-growing bamboo species that does not have enough strength for flooring. In other words, just because a floor is made of bamboo doesn't make it a long-lasting green material.

DECIDE ON GREEN MATERIALS AND PRODUCTS FOR YOUR PROJECT(S)

How green should you go? Avoid comparing your situation with those featured in the latest and greatest architectural magazines and television shows. Those often achieve greenness at any cost. Be realistic, and simply go as green as you want to.

Consider your needs and your financial resources. Review what's available. Take advantage of green incentives whenever possible, such as tax credits, rebates, and grants. Educate yourself on opportunities to acquire local green materials and products. Be aware of and watch out for sources of reclaimed and recycled materials. Pay attention to others who are building green, both locally and within larger cities in the surrounding area. Research the Internet and the latest books and articles on green construction, energy-efficient products, and green lifestyles. Call manufacturers directly and ask for referrals—to satisfied customers with whom you can speak.

Regarding energy-efficient materials and products, it really is a green revolution out there, right now. Start taking advantage of it.

Footers and Foundations

No house will be solid enough to reach its full life expectancy unless it's carefully constructed on adequate footers and foundations. See Chapter 13 on wall framing for additional information on foundation and basement walls.

FOOTERS

A *footer*, as the name implies, is that lowest part of a house on which the rest of the dwelling is placed. And like anyone's foot, if it's not firmly planted on the ground, proper posture or position of the rest of the body (or, in this case, the house) becomes difficult if not impossible to maintain. A house footer serves to firmly situate the building onto and into the ground. And because it plays such a basic and critical role, it's important to make sure that the footer is done correctly. Footers are largely inaccessible once covered and landscaped over, and if they are constructed ineptly, major problems will result in huge expenses and inconveniences to home owners.

Few people realize exactly what a house sits on and how the house is joined to the earth. There are right and wrong ways to construct a footer; the main idea is to evenly spread or distribute the weight of the house over a large enough area of soil that settling or moving will never occur. The chief enemies are gravity and time. Downward pressure that's not evenly supported from below ultimately will result in cracked floors and foundations and telltale symptoms such as doors that will not close, cracks in plaster, and worst of all, an obvious tilting of the house.

Construction Guidelines

Consider the following when planning your footer:

1. It must be built on virgin soil if conventional building practices are to be followed. Sure, some houses are constructed on swampland—but they require extra engineering, expense, and effort. The standard-type house should rest on solid ground. This means that you should shy away from a building lot that has been filled in and graded to bring its surface up to a respectable level.

   Consider arranging for a soil test hole to be dug where the basement will be. It will identify soil types and may detect the presence of water or boulders below grade. Digging the test hole also will help get more accurate prices on excavation, foundation, and drainage work, plus it will prevent major surprises and possible delays.

2. If you find that the land consists of recently filled loose soil and you still desire to build on it, several options exist. You can have the soil compacted through mechanical means. Contractors can use a heavy-duty tamper that hammers the soil down, as well as a huge roller that passes back and forth over the surface, compacting as it moves. Together these machines press the soil until the proper "load level," or ability to support weight, is reached that's similar to that of virgin earth (undisturbed ground).

   If the depth of uncompacted soil is too great to be efficiently compacted, and a deep cellar might lend itself to the house's structure, you could excavate and remove the disturbed ground until you hit virgin soil, and then build from there.

   A last and most radical alternative could apply if virgin ground is entirely too far below grade to fix by either compacting or excavating. Here the solution is to architecturally design a one-of-a-kind footer of the floating nature to adequately support the house you plan. In most cases, though, the expense is too great to bother with. It is better to find a more suitable site.

   Either of the first two options also will cost more than an ideal lot, but they're necessary if you are to prevent the house from shifting and being subject to the difficult-to-correct ailments described earlier. Unless concrete is poured onto undisturbed or properly compacted soil, its weight, when coupled with that of the foundation and the rest of the house, will slowly press down the loose soil below. This will result in cracks, heaving, and tilting that naturally will disturb the framework of the rest of the house. Suddenly the windows won't go up as easily, the doors will no longer fit their frames, and plaster walls will crack—all indicating that stressful pressures are at work that will probably brand the house as shoddily constructed.

3. The frost line must be taken into account. The earth is an insulator, and in northern sections, some of the top ground freezes and offers protection to the unfrozen soil below. The *frost line* is an imaginary undulating plane located

at some depth below the surface or the average depth of ground that can be expected to freeze during winter, year after year. In the northern parts of the United States, for instance, the frost line ranges from about 2 to 5 feet below typical ground level. If a footer is not placed below that frost line, the alternate expansion and contraction of the earth above the frost line might cause the footer to move—to heave upward or list downward, causing cracks to occur in rigid concrete footers and foundations, with their accompanying ill-effects. In general, national building codes recommend that footers should be located at least 12 inches below the frost line (Fig. 11.1).

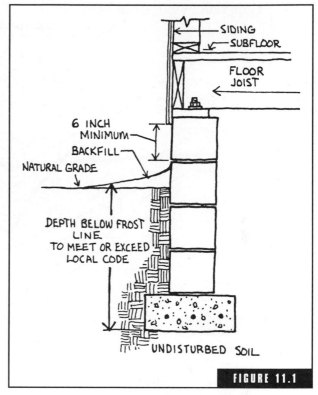

FIGURE 11.1

A footer and foundation below the frost line.

4. The type and condition of the soil also must be taken into consideration. For example, it's an unwise practice to build on organic-type soils such as peat. They haven't the proper load-bearing strength to support the weight of a house. Groundwater content likewise influences the ability of the soil to support weight and greatly affects the installation of proper drainage to prevent water from seeping into lower levels. Be careful not to build over a spot where a large tree root system still exists. The roots will slowly disintegrate, leaving voids that will undermine the footer and lower-level floor. Major tree roots should be removed and the holes left by them filled in and compacted.

5. Naturally, the contour of the building site and the distribution of the house's weight can have a major effect on the footer's construction demands. A two-story dwelling with one floor directly above the other, even if it weighs the same as a multilevel that's spaced out over more area of ground, will distribute its weight in a different manner—thus the need for a different footer than that for a multilevel home. In many cases, footers must be custom designed for lots having substantial slopes. *Steps* are commonly included to compensate for grade differences (Fig. 11.2). When preparing for a block foundation, as a general rule, the depth of each step should be in a multiple of 8 inches,

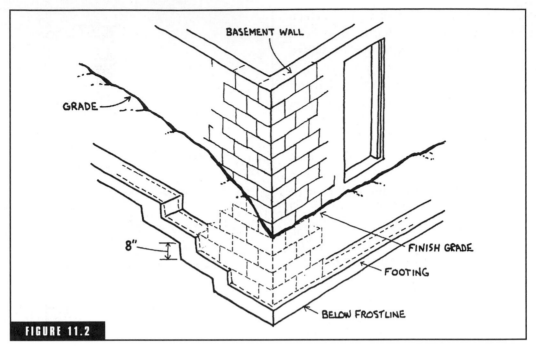

FIGURE 11.2

A step footer.

which happens to be the height of the standard concrete building block. This helps to build uniformity into the foundation so that you won't end up having to add a half-course of block somewhere along the top of the foundation with the accompanying waste and bother.

6. When a full basement is specified for a house, there should be an excavation of proper width, length, and depth to accommodate the foundation walls, piers and support columns, pilasters, entry ways, fireplaces, chimney stack, basement floor, garage, patio, and porches and an adequate drainage systems (Fig. 11.3).

7. Pour separate footers wherever steel-support columns will be located (concrete columns that support the house's main steel beam or beams). This helps to relieve downward pressure and will help to prevent the basement floor from cracking. A footer for a pier, post, or column should be square and should have a pin or fasteners to securely anchor the post bottom. Check local building codes.

8. A bed of gravel must be laid under and around the planned footer and foundation wall, no matter which type of footer is used (Fig. 11.4).

9. Footers for single-story and one-and-one-half-story houses should be at least 8 inches thick and 16 inches wide; for a two-story dwelling, they should be

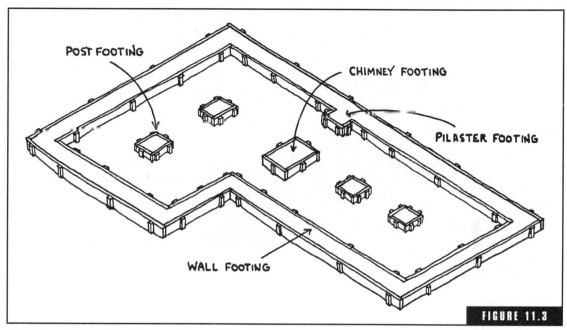

POST FOOTING

CHIMNEY FOOTING

PILASTER FOOTING

WALL FOOTING

FIGURE 11.3

A straight footer and wall, post, pilaster, and chimney footers.

12 inches thick and 24 inches wide. Larger footers are needed for homes constructed on unstable earth or on filled land. In general, a rule of thumb is that footers should be at least as deep as the foundation wall is thick and twice as wide (Fig. 11.5). With concrete slab construction, contractors often simply increase the thickness of the slab under the load-bearing walls instead of pouring separate footers. The width of the footer and foundation walls should be increased when brick or stone veneer is used on the exterior of the house. A single-story-home footer may go from 8 by 16 to 12 by 24 inches with foundation walls 12 inches thick. The contractor's engineer and local building code should determine the proper footer size and foundation wall thicknesses. In all cases, the footer must meet the local building code minimum specifications. When the footer excavation takes place, make sure that it's not dug too deep. You don't want the excavators to back-

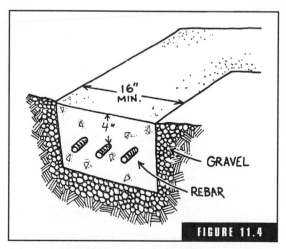

16" MIN.

4"

GRAVEL

REBAR

FIGURE 11.4

A footer with gravel and rebar.

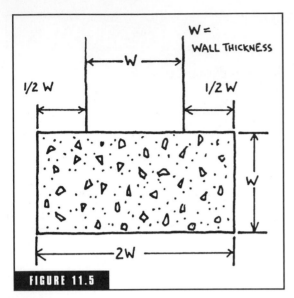

FIGURE 11.5

Footer design.

fill fresh soil before the footer and basement floor are poured. It is critical to pour both onto virgin soil.

10. As mentioned previously, if the earth on a potential building site is unstable, you would do best to avoid such a lot in favor of another with virgin soil. If you decide to build on a filled lot anyway, have a structural engineer design the footer. He or she may have to go extra lengths to compensate for soil weaknesses.

11. The concrete used in footers should have a strength of at least 4,000 pounds per square inch or more. The footer strength also must meet local building code requirements.

12. Reinforce a footer for extra strength. This applies to all footers, including those for fireplaces and support columns or piers. In normal situations, embed at least three steel reinforcement rebars lengthwise throughout the footer (Fig. 11.6). Typically, steel rebar should be at least ⅝ inch thick and elevated from the ground during and after the concrete pouring through the use of "foundation chairs" concreted right in about every 6 feet. Thicker steel rebar may be required depending on the application and on local building codes. The bars usually are situated so that they will be covered by a minimum of 3 inches of concrete at all points. Overlaps should occur wherever the bars meet, and those overlaps should be wired together. The use of 20-foot or longer rebar rods will minimize the number of overlaps necessary. The overlaps should occur in straight runs, never at corners, and parallel runs of rebar should have staggered overlaps so that two or three overlaps will not occur at the same point in a run. The rods should be bent and continued in single pieces around corners. The local building code may specify rod and overlap dimensions. Vertical support rods for the foundation walls also should be placed in the footer before the footer is poured so that the rods are securely anchored.

13. If you're going to have solid poured concrete foundation walls, consider placing a 2-inch keyway in the footer. Once the footer is poured and setting up, a 2-inch keyway can be formed into its top to allow the solid poured concrete wall to have a solid water resistant connection with the footer.

14. Allow concrete used for footers 2 days to set to gain most of its strength before anything is done on top of it. Make sure that footers are level, with no visible cracks.

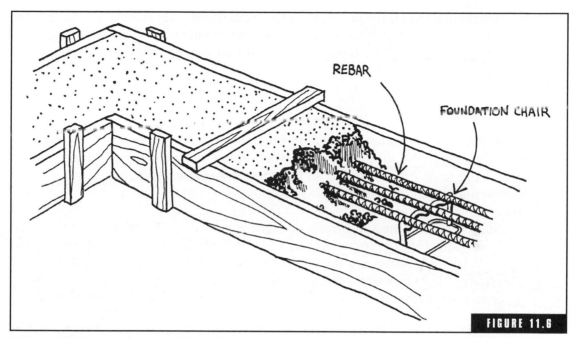

REBAR

FOUNDATION CHAIR

FIGURE 11.6

Footer reinforcement—rebar on "chairs."

15. Depending on the type of foundation your house requires, there are a number of items that might have to be prepared while the footer is being installed. These include drains and sewers, as well as water, gas, electric, and phone lines. If the necessary holes or trenches are dug for these items while the backhoe/shovel is present for excavating the footer and basement, they can be completed at less cost. The backhoe/shovel won't have to come back a second time, nor will the contractor need costly labor to dig them by hand.

16. Special attention to the sewer or septic lines prior to pouring the footer will prevent basic sewage problems. If your house will be connected to a street sewer, this connection should be made at the excavation/footer/foundation stage of construction. The sewer usually runs under a wall footer and basement floor to the main stack location. If a septic system will be used, the same sanitary sewer pipe installation must be made from the septic tank location to the stack. In any case, you don't want to end up with your house sewer discharge line below the line it needs to be hooked up to.

17. Last, make sure that the contractor grades and stones the driveway while the footer is going in—before construction of the foundation and the rest of the house begins. An early graded and stoned drive where the finished driveway will go is convenient for receiving material deliveries and simply for getting onto and off the site in bad weather. It also will encourage the heavy cement trucks needed for the footer, foundation, and basement floor to pack down the gravel and earth driveway long before the finished driveway will be poured or asphalted. All the heavy equipment and delivery traffic will result in a stronger driveway base.

FOUNDATIONS

To put it in simple terms, the *foundation* of a house is what sets directly above the concrete footer and below the wood-frame living levels. Another way of describing most foundations is to call them *basement walls*. In houses without basements, a slab foundation also incorporates the dwelling's footer in one continuous piece of concrete.

The foundation must be strong enough, whatever its construction, to support the house sills (heavy horizontal timbers or planks attached to the upper part of the foundation to serve as a starting point for the house walls) and other related members of the house structure, as required.

From a structural standpoint, the foundation performs several key functions:

- It supports the weight of the house and any other vertical loads, such as snow.

- It stabilizes the house against horizontal forces such as wind.

- It acts as a retaining wall against the earth fill around the house.

- In some cases, a basement might be needed to act as a barrier to moisture or heat loss.

No matter which foundation type you must have or elect to have, some general points apply. All foundations, whether slab-type, crawl spaces, basements, or any other, should extend above the final grade enough so that wood members of the house are some distance above the soil. That distance might be regulated by local building codes. However, keep in mind as the specs of your foundation are laid out that if local building codes are being used as a guide, they'll help, but they still could fall short of what many people would consider optimal construction. Local specs lay down minimum rules for safety and health, but that's about all. In other words, you might want to go a few steps beyond what they recommend. In this case, it's better to position the top of your foundation slightly higher, away from the ground level, for added protection against moisture and insects.

When excavating is necessary—and that's likely for any of the foundation types you will consider—have the valuable topsoil scraped off and saved. It should be pushed into a pile and kept out of the way until the house is completed and the landscaping is roughly finished so that you can spread the topsoil around to provide a fertile base in which to plant grass seed or to lay sod. Don't let the topsoil become "lost" amid the rest of the soil that's excavated and used to fill in around the foundation.

Slab Foundations

The slab foundation, as mentioned earlier, generally involves a combination of footer and foundation in a single slab of concrete (Fig. 11.7). They're popular wherever basements are impractical or impossible to have, in certain parts of the Southwest and South, for instance, or in areas with high groundwater levels.

The *floating* slab is unique in that the finished concrete floor, foundation walls, and footers are reinforced together with steel mesh and metal rods and poured as one integral mass over a bed of gravel (Fig. 11.8). The entire slab thus

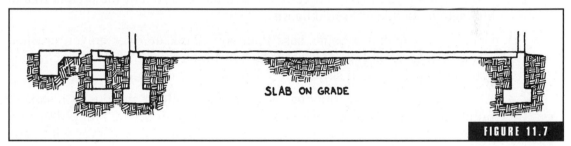

SLAB ON GRADE

FIGURE 11.7

Slab foundations.

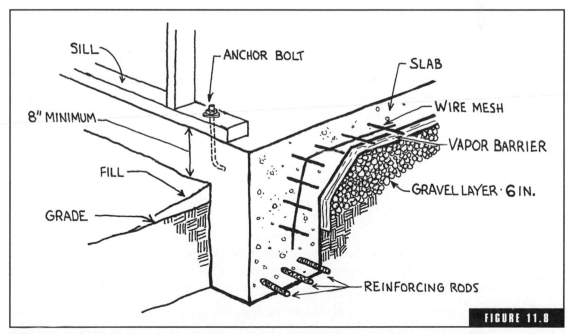

SILL

ANCHOR BOLT

SLAB

WIRE MESH

8" MINIMUM

VAPOR BARRIER

FILL

GRAVEL LAYER · 6 IN.

GRADE

REINFORCING RODS

FIGURE 11.8

A floating slab foundation.

floats on top of the ground while functioning as the floor of the house. However, the depth of the concrete should not be equal throughout its overall area: The slab must be thicker beneath support walls if the footer is considered part of the slab.

In cases where the terrain is not relatively flat, a footer must be poured separately from the slab and terraced or stepped down. Then a foundation, usually of concrete block, is constructed to a certain level so that a concrete slab floor can be poured. A slab foundation can be very trouble-free and economical when built in adherence to the following construction points:

1. The site must be properly graded and compacted and the footing trenches dug.

2. If the slab will be placed directly on soil, make sure that the area is free of biodegradable tree roots and debris.

3. Granular fill makes a better base than soil. Bank or river gravel, crushed stone, or slag can be used in sizes from ⅜ to 1 inch thick. A 6- to 12-inch-thick granular bed of fill will suffice.

4. At this stage, all the following underground utilities should be installed: plumbing, drains, sewers, heating service lines and ducts, radiant pipes, electrical work, and any other public or private utilities. Steel sleeves with foam insulation inside should be placed over all water and sewer pipes where those pipes protrude from a concrete slab, allowing the pipes to "give" if a slight adjustment is needed when the connection is made. Remember that if your house will have a slab foundation, you're going to end up with one continuous slab of concrete. If anything is done wrong and is not corrected after the concrete is poured and before it dries, just think of the trouble and expense you'd have to go through to simply get at the problem, let alone fix it. Take precautions to see that the utilities are all accounted for and installed in a safe and correct fashion.

    When run beneath a concrete floor, water lines should be laid in trenches deep enough to prevent freezing (below the frost line). Pressure-check the plumbing for leaks before the concrete is poured. The water should be turned on with all faucets and shut-offs closed to make sure that there are no leaking seams, cracks, or holes through which concrete could seep to solidify and plug water or drainage lines.

    Make sure that copper pipe is wrapped in a rubber or plastic tape wherever it will come in contact with concrete. An undesirable chemical reaction occurs when bare copper meets concrete. This is another simple precaution that can save a lot of time, expense, and inconvenience at some later date.

5. The subgrade for the slab should be dressed up or smoothed out in preparation for the concrete pour. Whether the subgrade is gravel or slag, it must be

thoroughly compacted. It should end up higher than the surrounding grade so that water will drain away from the house and so that the top of the slab is comfortably higher than ground level.

6. At this stage, a vapor barrier is placed over the subbase to stop the movement of liquid water and water vapor into the slab. Among materials used as successful vapor barriers are heavy-duty sheets of roofing material, polyethylene plastic, and construction paper. They act as both an insulation and moisture control, holding dampness in the ground rather than permitting it to penetrate cracks that could form in the slab foundation.

7. The slab now should be reinforced with steel rods. Although the steel reinforcement will not ensure the prevention of cracks, it might reduce the magnitude of cracks that otherwise would occur. For best results, the steel is placed horizontally through the middle of the slab and held in position until the concrete dries. A common practice of placing the reinforcement rods on the subbase and then pulling it up to the center of the slab with a rake or hook should not be permitted. It's virtually impossible to accurately control the location of the rods or wire fabric with this method. Instead, steel bridging or "chairs" can be anchored into the subbase. The "chairs" will stick up to about the midpoint of the slab and will hold the reinforcement correctly when the concrete is poured. Naturally, the "chairs" will be concreted right into the slab, along with the reinforcing steel.

8. In addition to steel rods, welded wire fabric or mesh is required for slab foundations. Again, this material makes the concrete less likely to break loose from itself. Wire joints should be overlapped and wired together according to your building code unless the entire job can be done with a single piece.

9. In an application where a foundation is required to hold up a concrete slab (with the interior filled with bank gravel to support the slab), then the top block—if it's a concrete block foundation—or the top ledge—if it's a poured foundation—should be a header or shoe block form in which a portion of the block/concrete has been cut/left out to provide a base for the concrete slab to be fastened to or supported on (Fig. 11.9). Vertical reinforcement rods also should come up from the foundation walls and be bent into the slab. This will help to hold the walls to the floor slab. More about this type of construction can be found in the crawl space/basement section of this chapter.

10. Before the concrete is poured, a means by which the house sill—the wooden horizontal planks that support the main upper structure of the house—can be secured to the foundation must be arranged. Anchor bolts can be positioned about every 3 feet around the perimeter of the slab so that they'll be embedded in the slab when the slab dries and cures. Check the local building code for the proper size and spacing of anchors.

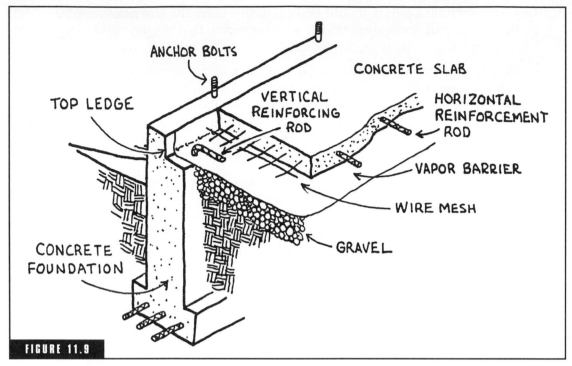

FIGURE 11.9

A foundation that supports a concrete slab.

11. When the slab is framed and ready to be poured, it should hold the top of the floor about 8 inches above the ground, and the surrounding grade should be sloped away from the foundation to keep water running away from the house. If an elevated floor slab is used, it should be a minimum of 4 inches thick at any part.

12. If a smooth finish is desired, specify that the concrete should be troweled by hand or by power-driven machine. A textured finish can be obtained by dragging a broom across the surface before the concrete is fully set.

ADVANTAGES

1. Slab foundations are very economical to build, especially when compared with crawl space or full basement foundations. Most slab foundations take much less labor and time to construct.

2. They're worm- and rot-proof.

3. They can't catch fire.

4. They're basically wear-proof and certainly are more secure than any other kind except solid rock.

5. They can store heat from the earth and are naturals for use in a passive-solar heating system.

6. They require little insulation from the elements.

7. As foundations, slabs are outstanding because they simultaneously act as one gigantic footer. Consequently, they impose the lowest soil loading per square foot of all foundations.

8. They experience less problems from ground moisture—there's no leaky basement from a slab.

9. The slab is more adaptable to filled or unstable soils, where conventional foundations might settle unevenly and crack.

10. The slab-on-grade foundation eliminates the need to frame a floor on the first level.

11. They are not affected by underneath drafts.

12. Vinyl flooring and wall-to-wall carpeting can be installed directly onto the top surface of a slab.

DISADVANTAGES

1. If a problem occurs with a utility that's concreted into or positioned beneath a slab, it's extremely expensive and troublesome to access the malfunction, to make repairs, and to restore the foundation to the way it was.

2. Slab foundations can be used efficiently only on relatively flat lots. They require substantial site work when employed on uneven ground, whereas a crawl space or basement foundation readily adapts to hilly terrain.

3. Floors constructed over a crawl space or basement foundation are easier on the feet and legs.

4. Plastic and other moisture barriers must be punctured for pipes and electrical wires to pass through, thus allowing some underground dampness to rest against the bottom of the slab.

5. Because the slab is mostly below ground, no ventilation reaches its lower surfaces. The slab tends to adjust to room temperature very slowly and instead follows fluctuations in ground temperatures whenever they occur.

Concrete and Block Wall Foundations

Many houses built today sit on foundation walls that form either a crawl space under the house, a partial basement, or a full basement. These types of foundations are more common in northern locations, where deep frost lines are encountered, but they are also found, conditions permitting, in the South. They're constructed of either solid poured concrete or concrete blocks, and if either has the edge over the other, it's concrete blocks. Both foundations not only will support a dwelling, but they'll also protect it from water, frost, and insects while providing (when desired) a basement to be used for storage or expanded living space.

If proper foundation construction is not followed, the result will be a below-standard foundation and possibly a house that tilts, floors that sag, walls that crack and leak, doors that won't fit their jambs, and windows that won't open or close—all the same defects that also can be attributed to a poorly executed footer.

Although crawl spaces are frequently left with soil or gravel floors, both the solid concrete and the block wall foundation floors should be poured with concrete to provide cleanliness, to prevent moisture and insect encroachment, and to supply a useful floor for storage or additional living areas.

The *National Building Code* requires a foundation to start at least 1 foot below the frost line. Local building codes can tell you how deep the frost line is in your area. Should bedrock (solid rock) be encountered before the prescribed depth is reached, digging can stop because bedrock will not move no matter what happens or how cold it gets. Even if you build where there's never freezing temperatures, still see that the foundation is situated at least 1 foot below grade (ground level) to ensure a firm and level base for the framing structure.

Crawl Space Foundations

These foundations are cheaper to construct than basements, and they are acceptable when the storage, utility, and living spaces otherwise found in basements are neither needed nor desired (Fig. 11.10).

ADVANTAGES

1. A crawl space foundation is cheaper to construct than a partial or full basement.

2. Because a crawl space is relatively low to the ground, there's not much risk of cracked walls.

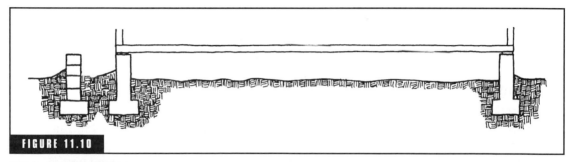

FIGURE 11.10

Crawl space foundations.

3. The crawl space foundation takes considerably less time to build, thus speeding up the overall construction time of the house.

4. A crawl space provides ventilation below the first floor, separating the living areas from contact with the ground and letting the floor follow suit with the temperatures maintained by the living spaces (unlike a slab, which is more affected by ground temperatures).

DISADVANTAGES

1. A crawl space foundation is practically useless for storage or living space (for humans).

2. A crawl space can't accommodate large or tall appliances, such as water heaters or furnaces.

3. Crawl spaces will attract a variety of small furry creatures (notably rabbits, squirrels, chipmunks, skunks, possums, and mice).

4. Water or sewer lines that run through crawl spaces must be insulated extra well to prevent the pipes from freezing.

Partial and Full Basement Foundations

There's a convincing argument that since the house will be placed over a footer anyway, you might as well put the potential space below the regular living level to good use, too (Fig. 11.11).

ADVANTAGES

1. The functional living areas of the house always can be expanded into a basement's lower level. A recreation room can be installed there at a minimal cost.

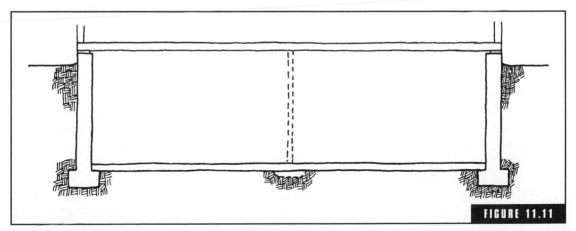

FIGURE 11.11

A basement foundation.

2. The partial or full basement can easily accommodate a water heater, furnace, and other major appliances such as freezers, washing machines, and clothes dryers.

3. A basement can include a separate entranceway into the house on the lowest level.

4. These foundations provide considerable storage and workbench areas.

5. Like a crawl space, a basement also insulates the main living areas from the ground.

DISADVANTAGES

1. Basement foundations are more expensive to construct.

2. Because of their height, the walls of a basement foundation are more likely to crack and develop problems.

3. A basement foundation at times can be virtually out of the question in areas where the water table is high.

4. Basement foundations take a relatively long time to construct and string out the entire house-building process.

FOUNDATION CONSTRUCTION

Once you decide on the type of foundation that you think best fits your requirements or is intrinsically suited to the house you are planning, then you must decide how that foundation should be constructed. Three options are concrete block, poured concrete, and precast concrete walls. All can be used to provide crawl space foundations (usually built up from a footer having walls 18 to 24 inches above ground level) or basement foundations that are typically 7 feet high on the inside.

Concrete Block Construction

You probably already know what concrete blocks are. They're rather rough-feeling, heavy, gray, and have several rectangular holes running through their insides vertically (Fig. 11.12). When installed, they're laid one course or row on top of another, staggered so that their vertical joints don't coincide with each other. The staggering of joints makes for a stronger interlocking bond. At the same time, the center rectangular holes are large enough to overlap so that the courses can be tied together with reinforcement rods that are inserted vertically and then filled with wet concrete.

On a foundation, the concrete blocks begin at the footer and are laid to form the desired height of the house foundation or basement. On houses using brick exterior finishes, the brick also may start with the footer and follow the house blocks right up. This will help to support the brick veneer and strengthen the entire foundation. An alternative for brick exteriors is to go with a wider foundation block that provides a ledge at the outer top of the foundation walls on which the brick can be conveniently laid.

ADVANTAGES

1. Concrete block walls permit a stop-and-go schedule during construction.

2. Concrete block walls are easier to repair than poured concrete walls.

3. Concrete block construction is often preferred by builders costing out the foundation job because block construction eliminates the need for concrete forms.

4. Concrete block walls absorb sound better than solid poured walls.

DISADVANTAGES

1. Concrete block walls are strong, but not as strong nor as impenetrable as solid poured concrete walls.

2. A concrete block wall is more likely to develop small cracks that can allow air infiltration, moisture, and even insects inside the foundation.

Solid Poured Concrete Construction

Solid poured concrete foundations, even though not as common as block foundations, are desirable in a number of situations.

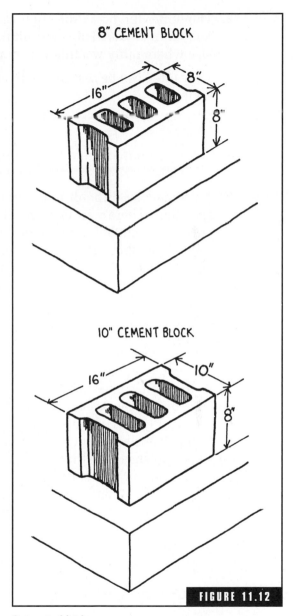

FIGURE 11.12

Concrete blocks.

ADVANTAGES

1. Solid poured concrete foundations have a slight advantage in strength and load-carrying capacity over block wall construction.

2. They offer the best protection against air infiltration, moisture, and insects. They're also less likely to result in wet basements. This can be a major advantage where rainy weather is common.

3. They often can be cast integrally with the footer at a substantial time and cost savings.

DISADVANTAGES

1. Solid poured concrete foundations can be more expensive than block construction.

2. It's somewhat difficult to be sure that you'll get as good a mix of cement as specified. There's an element of risk involved. This means, again, dealing only with reputable contractors for the concrete. Established builders will do so, but vanishing or marginal builders might not. A defective mix might not be detected until the house is up and the contractors are long gone. By then it will be a nightmare to correct major flaws or problems.

Precast Concrete Construction

Precast concrete stud wall construction provides an interesting alternative to concrete or block masonry construction. Precast walls are strong and capable of being installed efficiently as both foundation walls and walls above grade.

Precast wall panels are built with steel-reinforced concrete studs (typically about 7½ by 2 inches), 1-inch rigid insulation board, and rebar-reinforced top and bottom bond (footer) beams, along with a concrete facing about 2 inches thick. The bond beams and concrete facing are cast in one continuous pour. Studs are connected by encapsulating vertical rebars plus galvanized hooks and pins that protrude from the top, bottom, and back of each stud. The galvanized pins protruding from the studs secure an approximately 2-inch-thick face pour. Pressure-treated furring strips are preattached to the inner face of each stud. This construction provides a base for the home owner to finish the basement without having to add any additional studding. Holes are cast into each stud to accommodate wiring and small-diameter plumbing (Fig. 11.13).

PRECAST CONSTRUCTION POINTS

1. Custom-made panels are made to support door and window openings.

2. All precast panels and each individual concrete stud should include vertical rebar reinforcement. This gives considerable tensile strength to the entire structure.

3. The rebar-reinforced top bond beam typically has a perforation about every 24 inches to enable the secure bolting of a sill plate to the top of the wall. The

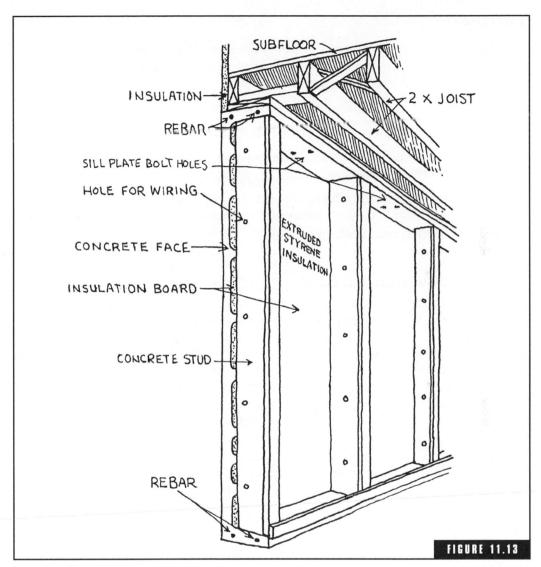

SUBFLOOR

INSULATION

2 X JOIST

REBAR

SILL PLATE BOLT HOLES

HOLE FOR WIRING

CONCRETE FACE

EXTRUDED STYRENE INSULATION

INSULATION BOARD

CONCRETE STUD

REBAR

FIGURE 11.13

Precast wall panel.

beam also provides strength and helps to distribute the weight of the home equally.

4. Insulation built into the wall supplies an insulating value of about R-5. The wall's cavity, about 7½ inches deep, permits a thick blanket of insulation to be applied. Combined with the 1-inch-thick polystyrene panels between the concrete studs and the concrete skin, these components can yield an effective cumulative rating approaching R-24.

ADVANTAGES

1. The panels come with ready-to-finish interior walls. A treated wood nailer is factory installed to the inside of the reinforced concrete studs, ready for the application of a vapor barrier and wall board.

2. The panels resist moisture, mold, and mildew well.

3. The insulation panels also provide a thermal break and vapor barrier.

4. Precast panels can be installed in almost any weather. There's no danger of the concrete freezing before it cures or curing too quickly from excessive heat.

5. These panels save time when being finished in a basement because there's no need for additional framing to support the insulation batts, vapor barrier, and drywall, which can be attached directly to the furring strips with no loss of space.

Foundation Construction Points

Here's a collection of various construction specs and procedures used in proper concrete block, poured concrete, and some precast concrete foundations:

1. The minimum thickness for any home in the most ideal situations requiring minimum loadings is 8 inches. However, 10 inches is preferable and safer. The minimum thickness should be increased to 10 inches if the walls will be subjected to any lateral pressures, such as large snowdrifts, if the walls are more than 7 feet below grade, if the walls are longer than 20 feet, or if the house is going to carry a heavier than normal load. This can be the case if you elect a two-story home or if you plan on having considerably heavy furniture and items such as a grand piano, pool table, waterbeds, or exercise equipment. For extradeep basements, use 12-inch concrete block. As the block size increases, so should the footer.

2. Before the foundation floor is concreted, all necessary plumbing and sewer pipes should be installed. Make sure that all pipe cleanouts are present in the foundation walls and floor. Once the rough (underground) plumbing is situated in the foundation, the plumbing inspector may wish to check that the drainage system, when full of water, will hold up without leaking, check for proper pipe slope or fall, check the cleanouts, or inspect the piping for proper sizing.

3. Once the foundation walls are up, the floor of the crawl space, basement, or garage should be filled with 6 to 12 inches of ¾-inch stone, with 3- to 4-inch drainpipes running through the stone. The stone (or gravel) should be compacted as it's put down. Over the drainpipe and stone, a plastic vapor barrier should be placed to seal out dampness. This is especially important if the

foundation is a crawl space. A concrete floor at least 4 inches thick will hold the water and dampness down into the ground, and the drainpipe will direct the water to a sump hole. Should the sump hole ever fill up, a sump pump can be installed to pump out the water and pipe it away from the house.

4. If concrete block is used, the first layer of blocks against the footer should be special drain blocks with grooved or weep holes along their bottoms. This will prevent a buildup of water pressure against the walls. Instead, the water will flow into the 6-inch gravel bed beneath the concrete floor. The drainpipe running through the gravel will convey the water to the sump hole.

5. Along the outside of the foundation, 4-inch rigid plastic pipe having openings or perforations along the top should be placed end-to-end on a gravel base along the footer, pitched toward the spot where the water will be piped away from the house. This pipe should be lower than the basement floor and not simply resting on the footer. With this setup, water flowing against the wall of a home has a place to go. These drainage pipes need to be continuously sloped toward the discharge end; otherwise, sediment might build up at a low point and completely block the line. If the soil is full of clay or silt, consider installing a soil-filtering fabric to protect the stone and drain piping from becoming plugged with sediment washed down from the backfill. The water table should be maintained no higher than the elevation of the pipe under the entire basement or crawl space so that water pressure is held at a minimum. This perimeter drainage pipe system should be covered with approximately 12 inches of ¾-inch stone.

6. On some lots, there is no place to discharge the house drain pipe from the foundation to daylight. In this situation, footer drains can be run inside to the basement sump hole.

7. A sump pump or pumps should be installed in the foundation floor when necessary (Fig. 11.14). Some foundations, either crawl space or basement types, may never need one, whereas others may have to employ one year-round. If, after checking with contractors and neighbors experienced with installing and using sump pumps in homes built within the neighborhood your project is in, you determine that drainage and water table conditions require frequent activation of the pumps, especially during spring, fall, and winter months, consider planning a multi-pump system to prevent basement flooding. Many building codes have been making it mandatory to include a sump hole so that a pump can be added later, if needed. For the most part, sump pumps are set up so that if water backs up to a certain level and threatens to flood the cellar, the pump will automatically kick in and pump out the water into an outside drainage line that will carry it away from the house. For the installation of a single-pump system, the sump hole itself should be 24 inches in diameter or

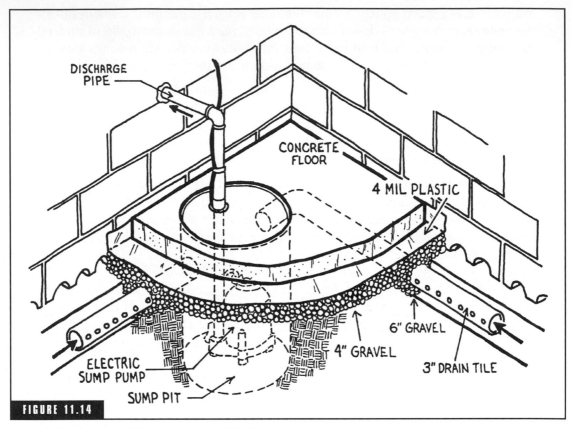

DISCHARGE PIPE

CONCRETE FLOOR

4 MIL PLASTIC

6" GRAVEL

4" GRAVEL

3" DRAIN TILE

ELECTRIC SUMP PUMP

SUMP PIT

FIGURE 11.14

A foundation interior with sump pump and drainage.

20 inches square and should extend at least 30 inches below the bottom of the basement or crawl space floor. The sump hole should be covered to prevent people and pets from stepping into it and moisture from escaping it into the basement. For a multi-pump system, the sump hole should be at least 30 inches wide, to accommodate three separate pumps (a main pump and two back-up pumps). Anyone with a single pump system can probably attest that when a single pump fails, it fails without warning, usually at a most inopportune time. To avoid single-pump failure and flooding, consider planning a three-pump system—for minor cost—during construction. The additional backup units are inexpensive insurance against flooding and will add resale value and features to the home. While an experienced plumber may have his or her own ideas of how best to install one main and two backup sump pumps, one example of how to arrange the three-pump system is:

■ Plan two electric sump pumps at offset heights, and one battery backup sump pump installed to activate during a power failure.

- The first electric sump pump at the bottom of the pit should rest on a single stackable pump stand designed to fit in the bottom of the pit, raised enough from the sump hole floor to keep silt and sediment washing in from blocking the water inlet flow at the pump's bottom. The battery backup pump should be placed on another stand next to the first electric unit, which should engage during a power outage.

- The second electric sump should be placed on top of the two stackable pump units, positioned to engage if the first electric pump cannot keep up with sump water flows.

- All three pumps should have their own discharge lines and check valves.

8. One aspect of the foundation that deserves special attention is waterproofing. Damage owing to water and moisture is among the most serious causes of home deterioration. Water and moisture cause wood rot, unsightly paint peeling, mildew, rusted appliances, and other maladies. They can even affect the health of the occupants. To prevent damp and wet basements, good waterproofing techniques, proper drainage, vapor barriers, correctly graded lots, appropriate landscaping and positioning of shrubs and trees, generous roof overhangs, and plenty of gutters and downspouts are necessary. Reducing basement moisture will minimize the operating time of a dehumidifier (if you have one).

9. If you're going to have a basement, have the septic disposal system line or the sewer line located below the basement floor, if possible. Otherwise, wastewater and solids generated in the basement have to be pumped up to the level of the main lines for disposal. If the disposal lines cannot be lowered, the simplest solution is often to completely avoid any sanitary drains in the basement (this means no toilets, wash basins, showers, or laundry equipment). Then the house sewer or septic lines can be suspended beneath the first-floor joists and run through openings cut in the foundation walls. The same thing can be done with a crawl space foundation, if necessary, as long as precautions are taken to prevent the lines from freezing.

FOUNDATION REINFORCEMENT

Reinforcement of a foundation's floor and walls is a critical part of the house-building process that can be easily slighted by marginal builders. Most home buyers don't realize what's involved and depend solely on the recommendations of contractors, who can, at times, underemphasize the specs that are needed for a sturdy foundation.

When a contractor underemphasizes the specs needed for a sturdy foundation as a cost-cutting philosophy, this can lead to big problems later, at the home

WATERPROOFING

Wet and damp basements can be more than just uncomfortable. Unchecked moisture allows mold and fungi to flourish, which can cause allergic reactions in people and pets and can result in peeling paint, rotting wood, and warped drywall or damage to other wall, floor, and ceiling components.

With either a basement or slab foundation, in addition to applying ½ inch of parging masonry (or cement) on the outside surface of basement walls, followed by two coats of a bituminous tar sealant, make sure that good drainage is achieved around the entire dwelling. Grading or sloping the soil away from the home's perimeter is essential to controlling roof and outside wall water runoff effectively. As a rule of thumb, the soil should slope downward at least 6 vertical inches in the first 10 horizontal feet of travel from the foundation wall or outer vertical surface of the slab.

Some of the best drainage systems direct water that comes near the foundation down toward the level of the home's footing, where clay, concrete, or plastic drainage tiles or pipes collect and convey the water away from the dwelling or collect and discharge the water through a sump pump. For drainage lines to work efficiently, they must be installed securely in beds of porous material—usually washed gravel. To achieve good drainage at window wells, the washed gravel should continue from the bottom of the wells to the foundation drainage tile. The window well should be wider than the window and frame and deep enough for at least two inches of washed gravel to be placed at the bottom of the well—while staying below the lower portion of the window's frame. It's important to prevent any chance of water getting up to any part of the window's frame.

To address the "open" nature of window wells, galvanized steel window wells are available to hold back the earth, and sturdy grating should be fitted at the well's top to prevent someone from stepping into the well. Plastic covers also can be placed over the top of window wells to keep out rain and snow.

Downspouts that carry rainwater away from roof gutters should be connected to a mostly horizontal (slightly sloped) length of pipe that carries the water several feet away from the foundation. If a sidewalk is in the way, drain tile can be used to run the water beneath the walk to open ground or a catch basin, depending on the landscaping serviced. If a downspout empties into a catch basin and then into a drain pipe, the catch basin should be positioned far enough away from the foundation so that runoff during a heavy rain will not overshoot it and yet close enough to catch the slower flow during a light rain. The water also can be conveyed to a bubbler or "dry well," where the water is allowed simply to drain off or dissipate into the surrounding ground. Bubblers or dry wells never should be located within the drip line of large trees—where the soil could become saturated for long periods of time and could allow the tree to fall over (roots and all) in high winds.

On flat or level building sites where there's no room for or possibility of establishing surface drainage slopes, a "trunk and arm" drainage system can help to handle water runoff (Fig. 11.15). Such a drainage system consists of a perforated drain tile (usually 6 inches in diameter) that acts as the trunk and runs parallel to the home's foundation, and solid drain tiles (usually 4 inches in diameter), which act as the arms, attached to the trunk with T-connectors. The arm tiles run perpendicular to the trunk, spaced about 10 feet apart from each other, and slope underground to dry wells filled with washed gravel, where the surface runoff water can collect and slowly dissipate into the surrounding earth.

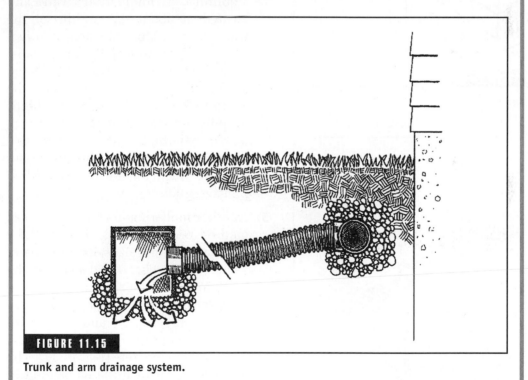

FIGURE 11.15

Trunk and arm drainage system.

owner's expense. Here are some guidelines for the reinforcement of foundation floors and walls:

1. A concrete floor should be strengthened with reinforcement rebar. The rebar should be elevated to the middle of the floor's thickness on steel bridges or "chairs" set so that they're positioned evenly across the floor with ends over-

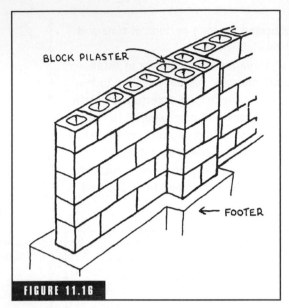

FIGURE 11.16

Foundation block pilaster.

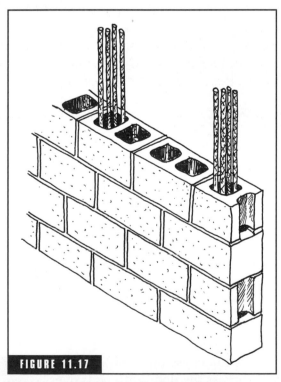

FIGURE 11.17

Vertical concrete block wall reinforcement.

lapped before the concrete is poured. If welded wire fabric is used along with the rebar, its joints should overlap. Material overlap should meet local building code standards.

2. If a foundation has long walls or walls subjected to above-average stresses, they can be strengthened with pilasters (Fig. 11.16). A *pilaster* is a vertical block or concrete column poured or constructed adjacent to or adjoining a foundation wall and located at about the middle of the wall's length. More pilasters are often needed along unusually long walls. By having thicker walls at selected points, this extra support lessens the overall stress on the walls and helps to prevent cracking. Steel rebar at least ⅝ inch thick, with four rebars to a set, should be installed in and extend the full height of the concrete-filled pilaster voids.

3. Another modern and commonly used method of reinforcing the walls of a foundation is to place long pieces of ⅝-inch-thick rebar the length of the wall, in sets of four, through the rectangular openings of every other concrete block vertically and then to fill in those reinforced holes or "cores" solidly with concrete (Fig. 11.17). The same rebar also can be embedded in the footing pour as a tie from wall to base, especially when high walls must withstand considerable pressures from slopes, water, or backfilling. All house foundations should have either the pilasters or the reinforcement rebar for vertical support. For a stronger foundation wall, use both

pilasters and vertical reinforcement rebar throughout the walls.

4. For horizontal support, reinforcement wire should be placed in the mortar bed joint of every other course of blocks (Fig. 11.18).

5. Block walls that are quickly erected and backfilled require bracing within the crawl space or basement for temporary support until the concrete and mortar dries to make sure that the structure is tightly knit before stresses are applied. Leave temporary wood supports up in the basement as long as possible, especially during and after backfilling takes place.

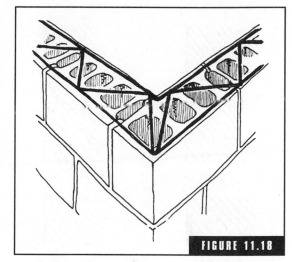

Horizontal concrete block wall reinforcement.

6. Load-bearing foundation walls should not be joined or tied together with a masonry bond unless the walls join at a corner. Instead, steel tie bars vertically spaced not farther than 4 feet apart (check the local building code) will form a strong bond (Fig. 11.19). If the walls are concrete block, strips of lath or steel mesh can be laid across the common joints in alternate layers or courses (Fig. 11.20). If a nonbearing wall will be constructed at a later date, ties should be incorporated into the first wall and left half exposed so that

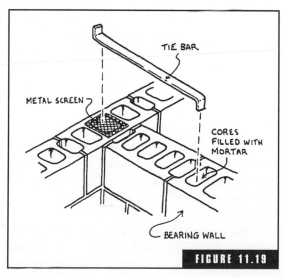

A steel tie bar.

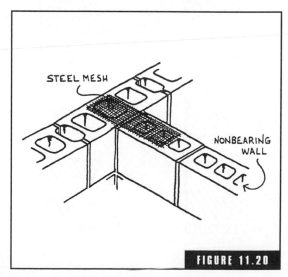

Steel mesh reinforcement.

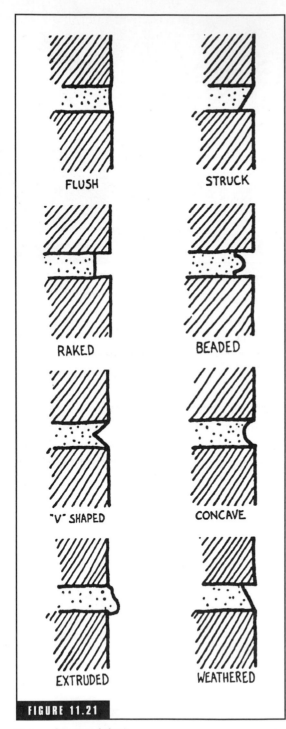

FLUSH

STRUCK

RAKED

BEADED

"V" SHAPED

CONCAVE

EXTRUDED

WEATHERED

FIGURE 11.21

Types of mortar joints.

they'll be available when needed for the second adjoining wall.

Masonry Joints

If you are using brick or block for foundation walls, you have an option to select any of the following mortar joint types that would best go with your style of construction: flush, struck, V, concave, raked, beaded, extruded, and weathered (Fig. 11.21). The V and concave versions are the most popular because they look neat and do not form a miniledge that could accumulate water. Beneath the grade, or ground level, where appearance does not count, the joints typically are left flush.

Concrete Forms

If you're using poured concrete walls, make sure that you realize that the quality of the concrete forms directly affects the finished appearance of the walls. Concrete forms must be tight, smooth, defect-free, properly aligned, and well-braced to resist the lateral pressures created by the poured concrete.

FOUNDATION FLOOR SUBBASES AND FLOORS

The floor subbase should consist of a compacted layer of ¾-inch stone 4 inches thick. Plastic sheathing that comes in 4- or 6-mil thicknesses or other suitable vapor barrier materials are placed over the subbase to form an effective insulating moisture barrier before the floor concrete is poured.

The concrete floor should be a minimum of 4 inches thick, with welded wire mesh and rebar running through it for strength, and the concrete should be sloped to the floor drains. If you desire a smooth finish on the basement floor, it will be necessary to specify that you want the concrete steel troweled. Should you desire a textured finish, it can be obtained by having brooms dragged across the surface before the concrete is set.

FOUNDATION WALL TOPS

On top of all foundation walls, anchor bolts (Figs. 11.22 and 11.23) should be installed or partially embedded at approximately 3-foot intervals (check the local building code), with protruding bolt lengths long enough to securely fasten the sill plates (wooden planks that join the upper framing structure to the foundation).

Have foundation walls constructed of concrete block capped with a course of solid masonry blocks that will act as an insect barrier and help to distribute the

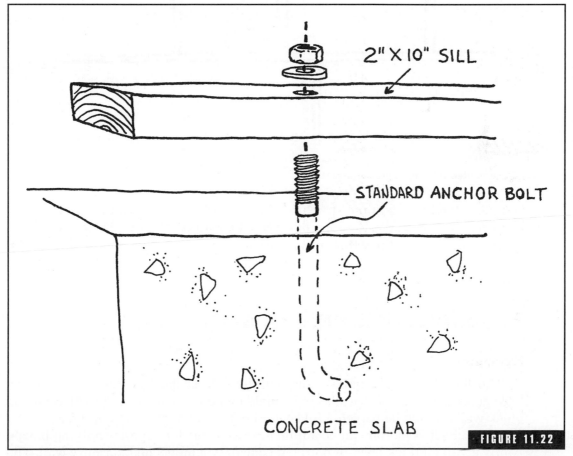

2" X 10" SILL

STANDARD ANCHOR BOLT

CONCRETE SLAB

FIGURE 11.22

Anchor bolt in a poured concrete wall.

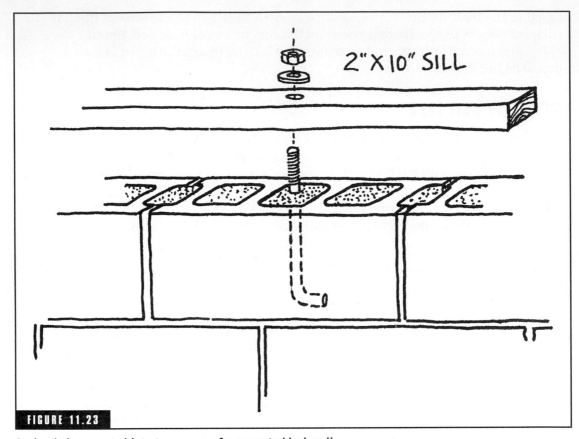

2" X 10" SILL

FIGURE 11.23

Anchor bolt cemented into top course of a concrete block wall.

weight of the house's upper structure. When solid blocks are not used, the cores, or rectangular holes, in the top course can be solidly filled with mortar or concrete. To do this, a strip of thin metal lath must be placed in the mortar joint under the top course. The strip, which is just wide enough to cover the block cavities, forms a base for the concrete that fills the top-course cavities.

WALL COVERINGS AND INSULATION FOR THE FOUNDATION

Exterior

The foundation will be less susceptible to frost damage, moisture transfer, leakage, and insects if the walls are insulated on the outside (Fig. 11.24). Concrete block walls should be pargeted (plastered) with ½ inch of cement mortar.

The ½ inch of mortar can be applied in two coats for superior holding power. Apply a ¼-inch-thick layer of portland cement to a moistened masonry wall. The first coating should be put on roughly and allowed to dry for 24 hours. When ready for the second coating, the first coat should be moistened, and then the second ¼-inch coating can be smoothed over the first and kept moist for about 48 hours while it hardens.

For any foundation wall, request two coats of tar or bituminous waterproofing material to be troweled on. Troweled tar is the best, but brushed- or sprayed-on waterproofing is better than nothing. If local weather conditions are severe, protection can be further improved with a layer of sheet polyethylene or asphalt-impregnated membrane. Make sure that there are no sharp surfaces that could tear or damage the membrane when it is applied. Remove any large rocks or roots from the backfill so that the membrane won't be damaged during backfilling.

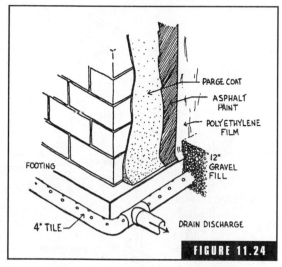

Cutaway of the exterior of a foundation wall.

Insulation inside the blocks can be accomplished by installing rigid foam insulation inserts that are friction fit into conventional block holes before the block is laid to increase R-values. Block holes that will be filled with concrete are skipped. This type of insulation is out of view and protected from the elements (Fig. 11.25).

Exterior insulation can be installed using extruded polystyrene rigid foam that's 1½ or 2 inches thick tongue and groove for a good seal. It will provide good thermal protection and moisture resistance above and below grade. The joints should be taped with a product from the manufacturer. The manufacturer also will supply installation instructions. For rigid board applications, make sure the board material is covered with weatherproof facing, since below-grade exterior insulation may provide a path for termites. Local building codes will often specify if the material being planned is acceptable. At least a 6-inch gap between the insulation and any wood foundation component should be left for a termite inspection view. When rigid board insulation extends above ground, it should be protected by covering it with stucco or another suitable

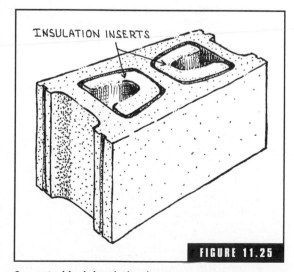

Concrete block insulation inserts.

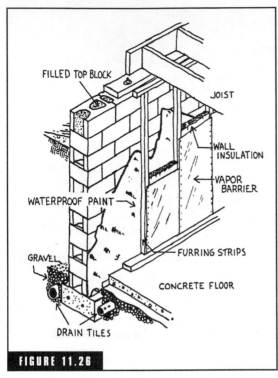

FIGURE 11.26

Cutaway of the interior of a foundation wall.

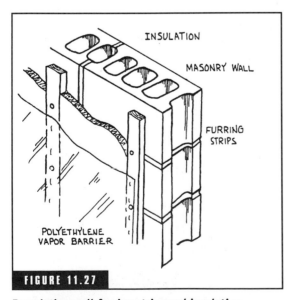

FIGURE 11.27

Foundation wall furring strips and insulation.

material. Above-grade foundation wall exteriors also can be protected with stucco or treated plywood.

Interior

To reduce heat loss, to prevent moisture and water leakage, and to further prevent the possibility of insect penetration, foundation interior walls can be insulated and covered.

A thick waterproofing white paint that's brushed onto the interior surface will reduce moisture penetration and discourage insects from infiltrating interior walls (Fig. 11.26). Foundation wall interiors can be insulated by first putting up furring strips and then applying blanket insulation in the usual way (Fig. 11.27).

FLOOR SUPPORT BEAMS OR GIRDERS

To support the house, one or more girders (load-bearing beams that help to support the first-floor joists) as determined by the contractor's structural engineer should be installed. Steel I beams make the most reliable girders, but wood girders constructed of planks joined together by bolts or nails are also used (Fig. 11.28). Steel I beams are rather consistent in quality. The wood girders will vary in quality depending on the quality of their individual component planks. Girders either rest in pockets formed in the tops of the foundation walls or on top of corresponding masonry pilasters. In any event, the steel girder tops generally are made flush with the top of the wooden sill with wood planking that's laid along the top of the entire steel beam (Fig. 11.29).

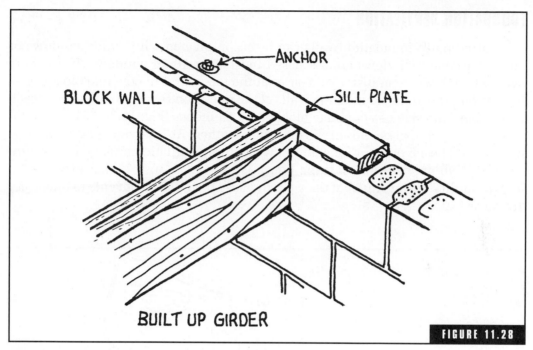

Wood girder.

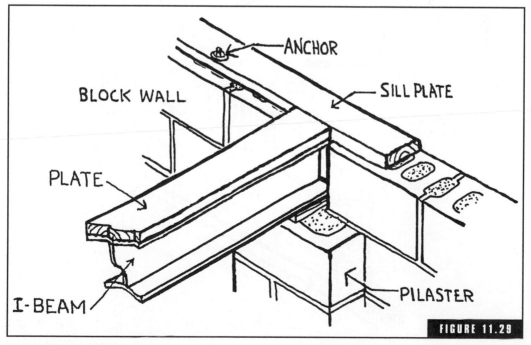

A steel I-beam girder.

FOUNDATION VENTILATION

Ventilation in foundation walls can be accomplished with either windows or vents. Basement windows are discussed in Chapter 18 on windows. If vents are decided on, have them installed near or at the top course of concrete blocks or as high as possible in the foundation walls at the rate of one every 50 linear feet, each being about the size of a concrete block: 8 by 16 inches (Fig. 11.30). They should be the type that can be closed during cold weather. At least one vent should be positioned at each corner of the house, with cross-ventilation arranged for a minimum of two opposite sides. If the house is located in an area that experiences high humidity during much of the year, increase the number of vents to one every 15 linear feet.

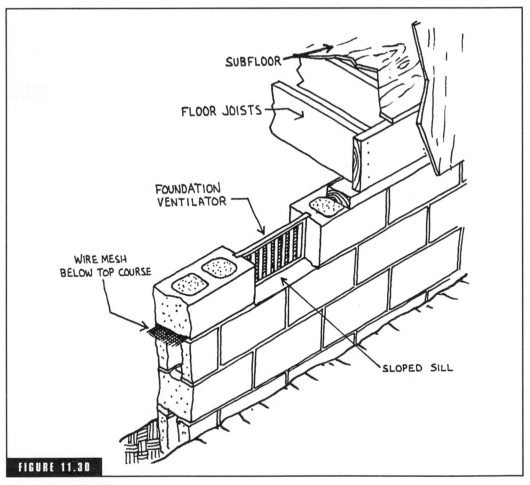

SUBFLOOR

FLOOR JOISTS

FOUNDATION
VENTILATOR

WIRE MESH
BELOW TOP COURSE

SLOPED SILL

FIGURE 11.30

Foundation wall vents.

On a crawl space foundation, in addition to vents, there should be at least one access door of not less than 32 by 36 inches. If it's a large crawl space of 2,000 square feet or more or an unusual shape, more than one access door should be included. Confirm this with local building code.

BACKFILLING

Once the foundation work has been completed and before backfilling occurs, you should make a formal inspection. Backfilling is simply the pushing back of excavated soil around the house to fill in the construction ditches. Backfilling should occur only after the first floor is framed and the walls are framed up so that the added weight of the structure will stiffen the walls and make them less likely to bulge from the pressure of the backfilled soil.

To avoid subjecting a "green" foundation that isn't fully cured to pressures that could damage it, plank or timber bracing should be installed inside the crawl space or basement that support the walls at about 12-foot intervals. The house's central longitudinal support beam or girder, plus the first-floor joists and floor decking, also should be erected to help strengthen the foundation walls before backfilling takes place. As a general rule, backfill height from footer to grade should not exceed about 7 feet.

The waterproofing must be protected during the backfilling because rocks and other hard materials in the backfill could scratch and penetrate the waterproofing and allow moisture seepage. If the soil that will be pushed back contains large rocks, the contractor should apply 4- by 8-foot or 4- by 10-foot sheets of impregnated sheathing or equal material for protection. The final grade must slope away from the foundation.

POLE AND PIER FOUNDATIONS

A less frequently used foundation is the pole and pier arrangement (Fig. 11.33). It's a good setup for small homes built in steep terrain or for vacation homes and cottages. Poles or piers are firmly implanted into solid ground so that they're stationary (frequently cemented right into the ground), and then the frame of the house is constructed on top of them. For this type of foundation, concrete tubes (concrete-filled cardboard cylinders) and telephone poles are very popular.

ADVANTAGES

1. A post and pier foundation lends itself to steep terrain, where there is considerable variation in the height of the piers and where a regular masonry foundation is impractical.

2. Grading isn't required. There's a minimum of site preparation involved.

STORM SHELTERS

Sometimes referred to as *tornado shelters*, these units typically are set within the ground and temporarily protect household members who may seek shelter during major storms. A good time to have one installed, of course, is when the home's foundation is being constructed and the backhoe or other piece of heavy equipment is already there anyway to excavate.

The most popular types of storm shelters are manufactured out of fiberglass—a forgiving material that withstands considerable movement and settling of earth; resists corrosion, mold, and mildew; and is very durable (Fig. 11.31). Units are available that seat up to 10 adults. These shelters often are anchored at the bottom of excavations in poured concrete foundations that hold the units below ground level. To provide enough air for the inhabitants to breathe, storm shelters need multiple ducts and vents that rise far enough above the ground to prevent surface water and runoff from entering. The vent openings also should be covered with insect screens.

Outside doors should be low profile to permit simple landscaping and to avoid tornado or hurricane winds from affecting the unit.

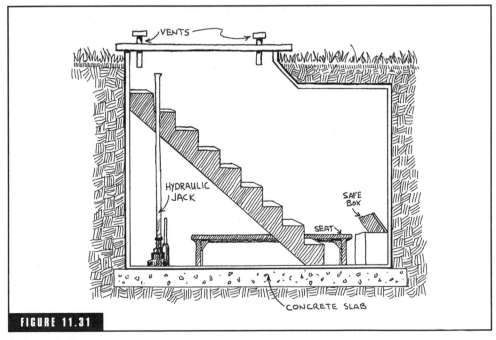

FIGURE 11.31

A storm shelter.

Some of the more important features found in storm shelters include the following:

- *Prewiring for a television and phone.* This would allow shelter users to stay in contact with what's in the news or what's going on outside and to phone for help in case problems occur.
- *A safe or storage box to hold valuables.*
- *Skid-resistant steps with handrails.*
- *A lifting jack inside the unit.* This is necessary in case the doors become blocked by a downed tree branch, for instance.
- *A carpeted floor.*

Other alternatives for tornado- or hurricane-resistant home protection for situations where major rain and flooding is not an issue include *in-residence shelters,* which employ more conventional construction methods to encase an interior room of a house with concrete or steel and to then bolt the reinforced room to the foundation. Such rooms can have practical uses as well—as closets, storage areas, or even photographic darkrooms.

SAFETY»NOTE

With any storm shelter, make sure that a number of relatives, friends, and/or neighbors know of its existence, and get them to agree to come looking for you following a major storm if you don't check in with them immediately afterward.

ROOT CELLARS

A root cellar may sound a bit old fashioned, but for households fond of gardening, farming, and cooking, a root cellar can be an interesting and useful addition. Root cellars are still standard fare in Europe and many other parts of the world—small- to medium-sized rooms or portions of cellars carved out of or built into the earth. Their name has evolved from two of their characteristics: First, root cellars have been used for centuries to store root vegetables such as potatoes, carrots, parsnips, turnips, and onions (as well as canned and pickled foods) that keep longer in dark, cool places, and second, the roots of trees and live plants often grew directly into the root cellar over the years.

The perfect time to build a root cellar is when the excavation and foundation are under way. Because a root cellar needs to be shaded from sunlight, the basement provides the best location, where it will help to resist temperature swings and has a natural ability to keep stored items cool. One way is to take a corner of the basement—a northern corner, if possible—with the greatest exposure to cold outer walls (concrete or concrete block) and frame in a rectangular room (large enough to suit your needs) with insulated studded walls. Another way—if the home will have a concrete porch or patio that rests on top of a full foundation wall—is to simply build the root cellar within that part of the foundation wall. It's typically a large enough area and will need only one insulated wall and door to enclose.

A third option is a root cellar that has three sides carved out of the soil, again, so that only one insulated wall and door separate the space from the rest of the basement. Any enclosing wall (or walls) should use 2- by 6-inch studs with fiberglass or rigid foam insulation. The ceiling needs to be insulated as well. Protect both sides of insulation from moisture in the air with polyethylene air-vapor barriers. The ceiling needs the same barriers running up and around each joist, above the insulation and below the insulation, too. A finish layer of drywall can be placed over the insulation and air-vapor barriers to protect against punctures. For access, an insulated steel door will do a good job here with a tight seal around its edges and extra rigid foam insulation bolted to the inside of the door with large, flat washers. Because the door needn't be fancy, contractors often suggest making it out of 2 × 2s, 2 × 4s, and plywood. Wood doors, however, likely will warp over the long haul and lose their temperature-tight seal.

A root cellar also must be ventilated. A small louvered metal vent the size of a concrete block works well. The louvers can be adjusted or closed as needed throughout the year.

Last, make sure that the contractor builds and installs whatever shelving you need to maximize storage space (Fig. 11.32).

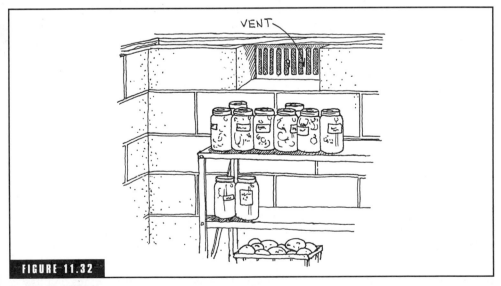

FIGURE 11.32

Root cellar shelving.

3. This is an inexpensive foundation that is easy to build.

4. There's plenty of natural ventilation between the ground and the living levels.

DISADVANTAGES

1. With the underside floor surface fully exposed to the elements, in cold climates the floor must be exceptionally well insulated.

2. This type of foundation allows wind and small creatures to get beneath the building.

3. Such a foundation is practically useless for any kind of storage or future expansion.

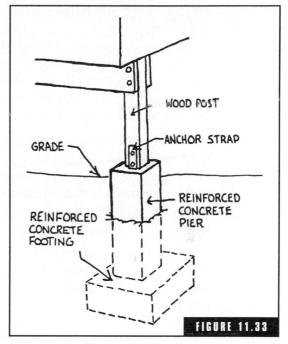

A post and pier foundation.

MISCELLANEOUS ITEMS

1. In locations with large populations of termites or carpenter ants, consult a qualified pest-control company to provide appropriate treatment. The company should provide a guarantee on its work that covers repairs if insects reinfest the treated areas.

2. Specify if you want windows in your foundation: their size and make, how many, and their location if in a full or partial basement.

3. Specify if you want a rear or side outdoor entrance to the basement. Use concrete or steel lintels for door openings. Precast lintels are simple to install because they're made to match the height and width of concrete blocks. They should be long enough to overlap (per building code) on the bearing block. Another method involves forming and pouring a lintel on the site, using wood forms and reinforcement rods.

   The outside stairwells should begin at a point lower than the basement floor to prevent water from entering the house. A 6-inch sill protecting the basement door is standard. Or a built-up curb could be constructed as a partial remedy. A decision also should be made as to whether you want the stairwell opening covered by steel doors.

4. Don't let the contractors confuse the topsoil that was pushed to the side when the construction first began with the soil that was excavated for the foundation.

The topsoil should only be used for finished-site grading, not as backfill around the foundation.

Trees you want saved should be marked with bright ribbons or spray paint so that the contractor won't damage or knock them down. The agreement should specify that all scrap tree stumps and brush must be pulled out and hauled away. If you get your builder to agree up front, hardwood trees that need to be removed could be cut up and piled for firewood.

5. It's not a common request, but poured concrete walls and floors can be colored by the addition (when the wet concrete is being mixed) of mineral pigments sold by ready-mix concrete and block producers, lumberyards, and building materials dealers. Reds, greens, yellows, browns, grays, and other colors are available.

6. If you're going to have a full basement and you plan to put in a recreational room eventually, try to locate it as closely as possible to the basement stairs. Opt for larger windows than normal so that the room will have adequate light and ventilation during the day. Check building code requirements related to any partitions you plan to install around the furnace and water heater; you might have to meet clearance and surfacing requirements.

   Avoid placing partitions, present or future, too close to plumbing-heating-electrical elements such as sump pumps, water meters, shutoff valves, and waste cleanouts. Give them an extra inch or two of clearance to permit quick access in case of trouble.

   When possible, plan a workshop area close to an outside access and also near an unexcavated sheltered area where a crawl space can be used for lumber and storage of other long materials.

   The typical cellar wall should be 11 courses high (88 inches). However, if any rooms on the floor above it will be sunken, consider an extra course (12 courses total) in case you someday decide to finish off the basement. If you go the extra block, you'll still be able to have a normal ceiling height when finished.

   All basements should have at least one water drain in the floor, and cellars larger than 900 square feet should have two drains. The floor should taper toward the drains, and the drains should transport water to the house's sump hole or exit drain.

   The local building code and the contractor's engineer should specify properly sized steel beams, girders, and vertical columns.

7. Consult a licensed radon mitigation company to check for radon or the likelihood of radon's presence where you are building, in order to include the installation of a simple radon mitigation system during construction. See Chapter 30 for additional information about radon.

REMODELING NOTES

This part of the home does not typically include remodeling projects but rather repairs or additions. The need for repairs can come from groundwater issues, where drainage systems that carry groundwater and rainwater away from the dwelling must be renewed, or from gradual deterioration of below-ground wall or foundation structural components. In such cases, the services of professional masons and other construction experts should be enlisted. Excavation or partial excavation generally is required, and the digging of trenches or holes is an activity left for experienced contractors with the right equipment.

▶▶▶▶▶ POINTS TO PONDER

1. The main goal of a footer is to evenly spread or distribute the weight of a house over a large enough area of soil so that settling or moving of the dwelling never occurs.

2. If the building site you select consists of recently filled loose soil, the loose soil must be either excavated out, compacted by mechanical means, or built on by custom engineering and construction of a footer for the exact home you are building.

3. The frost line always must be taken into account when constructing footers and foundations. If a footer is not placed below the frost line, the alternate expansion and contraction of the earth above the frost line might cause the footer to move—to heave upward or list downward—causing cracks in rigid concrete footers and foundations, with their accompanying ill-effects.

4. The type and condition of the soil must be taken into account; check it by having a soil test hole dug. Organic types of soils (such as peat), groundwater content, and large tree root systems all can interfere with traditional concrete footers and foundations.

5. Paying special attention to the sewer or septic lines prior to pouring a footer will help to prevent basic sewage and drainage problems.

6. Concrete foundations should extend above the final grade enough so that wood members of the house are some distance above the soil for protection against moisture and insects.

7. Concrete block or panel or poured concrete foundation walls enclosing a basement should be a minimum of 7 feet high from the basement floor; consider up to 9 feet if you know that you'll be finishing off parts of the basement later.

8. Achieving efficient outside drainage around a home's foundation is absolutely critical to prevent basements from developing moisture and leaks. So are good waterproofing techniques, vapor barriers, correctly graded lots, appropriate landscaping and positioning of shrubs and trees, generous roof overhangs, and plenty of gutters and downspouts.

9. Don't allow the contractors to confuse the topsoil that was pushed to the side when the excavation first began with the soil that was excavated for the foundation. The topsoil should only be used for finished-site grading, not as backfill around the foundation.

10. Consider the addition of a root cellar and/or storm shelter to be excavated at the same time that your home's footer and foundation are being installed.

Floor Framing

The wood frame of a house has been compared to the skeleton in a human body, in that it forms the shape and size and provides the strength of the dwelling. Even with a brick house (in today's modern construction, this usually means brick veneer), the framing actually supports the brick, not the reverse, as many people think. It's critical that the framing be erected correctly; it's not an area in which to compromise to reduce costs. Any errors discovered after the framing is complete are likely to be expensive to correct.

As a rule, the sills, girders, floor joists, and subflooring are the first members of the wood-framed structure placed on the foundation walls. These are followed by the outside wall studding and corner posts. Homes built on concrete slabs, of course, follow a different pattern, where the top surface of the concrete is likely the actual walking surface of the first floor. Insulation in floor framing will be especially important for floors constructed over unheated crawl spaces or as unheated attic floors. Here, structural insulated panels (SIPs), prefabricated panels that are moved into place with cranes and installation crews, do an excellent job of floor framing complete with insulation. See the section on SIPs in Chapter 13 on wall framing. It's difficult to think of floor, wall, or roof framing independently of each other because together they form a complete framing system. But there are enough differences for each to have its own brief chapter.

LUMBER

Traditionally, lumber used for floor framing has been air- or kiln-dried and of no. 2 grade or better. Regular lumber, while seasoning after it's nailed in place, can shrink away from the shank of a nail, reducing friction between the nail and the surrounding wood and causing *nail popping*, the protrusion of heads of nails from lumber that previously had been nailed flat. Remember to use Forest Stewardship Council (FSC)–certified wood or other responsibly managed and harvested lumber products.

Besides an increase in strength and nail-holding power, air- or kiln-dried lumber holds screws and glue better and results in superior adherence of paints and preservatives. It's also a better thermal insulator than regular lumber and is less likely to be attacked by fungi or insects. Only environmentally safe pressure-treated lumber should be used for framing members that are exposed to moisture. This wood typically is labeled or stamped for either "aboveground" use, or "ground contact" use, which means any wood that is either buried or comes within a foot or so of the ground.

SILL PLATES

The *sill* or *sill plate* is the timber (usually made of 2- by 10-foot wood planks) that's secured to the top of the foundation walls to form a link between the foundation and the home's upper structure. Some sill plates are laid in a bed of wet mortar. Most, however, are installed in the following manner: Anchor bolts are partially embedded in the concrete foundation wall tops, and then a resilient waterproof layer of sealant (similar to felt or Styrofoam) is pushed over the protruding bolts down onto the top surface of the foundation walls. The sill plate, having holes drilled in it to correspond with each anchor bolt, is then placed over the bolts onto the fiberglass layer, pressing the fiberglass flat against the top of the foundation walls. The sill plate is secured along the foundation top with sturdy lock washers and nuts tightened onto each anchor bolt (Fig. 12.1).

SUPPORT BEAMS OR GIRDERS AND POSTS

As mentioned in Chapter 11, floor joists that traverse long spans between foundation walls must be supported by longitudinal beams or girders. These structural members can be steel I beams (the best alternative) or wood planks nailed or bolted together, as determined by the

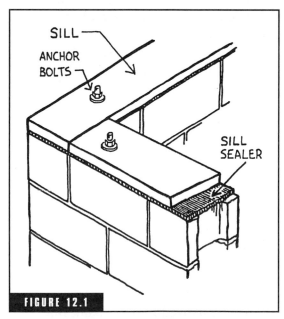

FIGURE 12.1

Securing and sealing the sill plate.

contractor's engineer. The ends of these longitudinal beams or girders rest either on pockets (rebar/poured concrete reinforced) in the foundation walls or on concrete block or poured pilasters. The girders should bear or rest on each foundation wall. The top surface of a longitudinal beam or girder must be made level with the top surface of the foundation wall via a wood plank secured on top.

Vertical posts of steel support the beams or girders through the interior of the span (Fig. 12.2). To prevent sinking, the vertical posts should be located over piers (concrete-filled holes about 18 inches across and 8 inches deep) set in a gravel floor or beneath a concrete floor so that the weight the posts support will be distributed over a broad area.

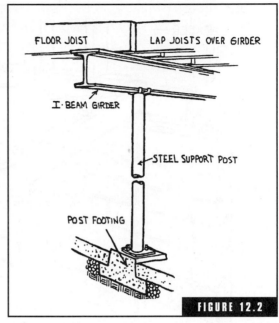

FIGURE 12.2

A vertical support post.

FLOOR JOISTS

Floor joists are horizontal structural planks placed on edge against a house's sill plate in an orderly fashion to distribute the weight of the wood framing to girders and sills and to provide a base for floor decking. Joist ends rest both on the sill plates and on interior longitudinal girders of steel or wood (Fig. 12.3). The joists should be of sufficient strength, stiffness, and number to support the floor loads over the area spanned with no perceivable deflection or "give" that could result in cracked plaster or pulled-apart drywall seams.

In good construction, joists are placed either 12 or 16 inches on center and are made of planks 2 by 10 inches or 2 by 12 inches. Planks running around outside wall perimeters that floor joists are fastened to are called *headers* (Fig. 12.4). A bead of caulk should be run between the edge of the sill plate and the top of the foundation wall. Caulking also should be installed along the top and bottom of the header before insulation is put in place and also run around holes for electrical, water, and gas lines. When advanced framing methods are employed by home designers and engineers, the use of stiffer pieces of engineered or composite wood could require less material for the same load-bearing capacity of a floor.

Sill plates and headers should be caulked. A caulk bead should be run between the edge of the sill plate and the top of the foundation wall, along the top and bottom of the header before insulation is put in place, and around holes or knockouts for electrical, water, gas, and other lines.

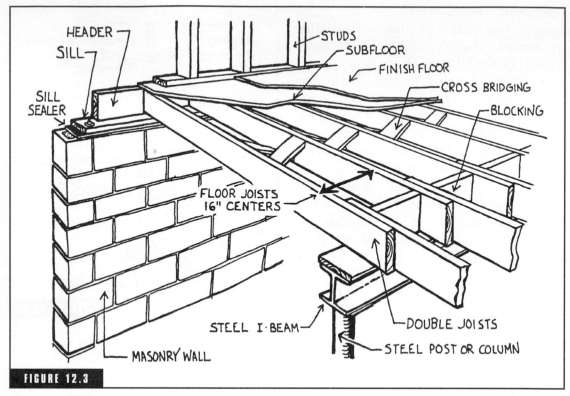

FIGURE 12.3

Floor joists support.

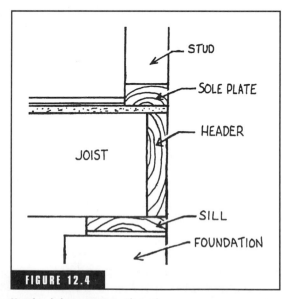

FIGURE 12.4

Header-joists construction view.

Double-thickness floor joists—two planks fastened together—should be used in certain situations, for example, wherever the first- or second-floor walls run parallel to the floor joists. This also will occur at openings around a stairway (Fig. 12.5), near a fireplace chimney, or at any major change in joist direction, such as where partitions are built to provide clearance for hot-air ducts and returns, under cast-iron bathtubs, or to provide additional support where joists cross a girder (Fig. 12.6).

When choosing the floor joist material, ask your builder about engineered wood I-beam floor joists. Engineered wood I beams are made with a top and bottom

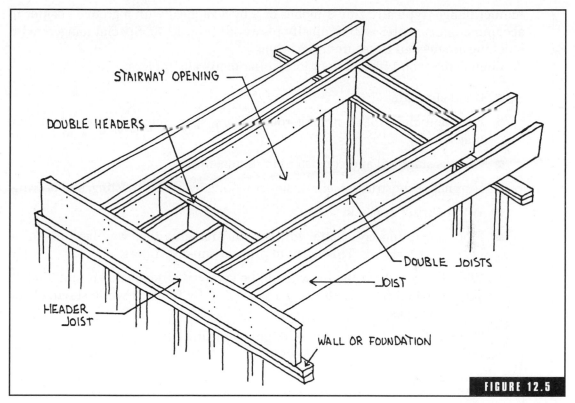

Framing a stairway opening.

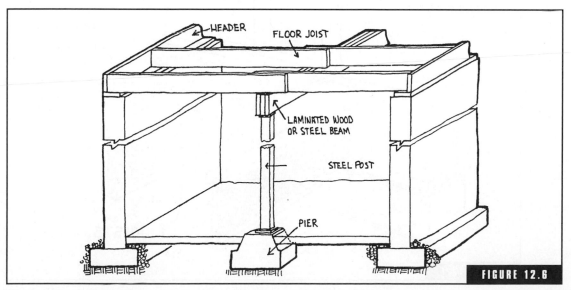

Double thicknesses of floor joists.

lumber flange (typically 2 by 3 inches or 2 by 4 inches) with a grooved center to accommodate a center web (typically plywood) (Fig. 12.7). Special hangers with blocking are needed to secure these beams.

Engineered wood I-beam floor joists offer many advantages:

- Good strength.

- Excellent clear spans on large rooms. They span longer distances than regular wood.

- Always standard and consistent in dimension.

- Laminated construction eliminates crowning, warping, twisting, and bowing.

- Won't shrink or crack.

- Floor sheathing lays flatter initially and remains that way because these beams don't shrink. This helps to prevent squeaky floors.

- Wide flanges allow the plywood to be screwed straight down (not angled, such as when trying to hit half a piece of 2-by lumber) while staying back from the edges.

- There is more bearing surface for glue and support.

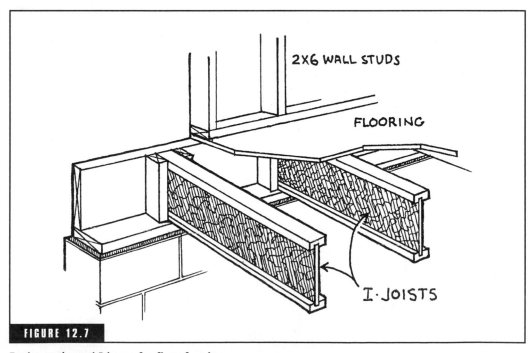

FIGURE 12.7

Engineered wood I beam for floor framing.

- Typically lighter than dimensional lumber.
- Can come with predrilled knockouts for wire and plumbing.

HEADERS

Again, a floor-framing header is a wood plank that the floor joists are nailed perpendicular against on two opposite sides of the house and parallel against on the other sides. It's erected vertically on its long edge, resting on the sill plate along the exterior of the foundation walls. Many contractors also use the term *rim joists* when referring to the floor header joists.

FLOOR DECKING

A number of structural materials, mostly wood or composition wood products, are used to cover floor joists and to construct the first-floor platform on which all subsequent house framing rests. These are mainly walls that are bearing units for the upper floors and the roof structure and walls that form interior partitions. The most popular materials are plywood, hardwood boards, and particleboard. Thicknesses of the floor should range from 1⅛-inch to even thicker. Remember to consider what you're going to have as furnishings. For example, if a room is expected to include a complete set of Olympic weights with a variety of exercise benches and machines, it likely will require a thicker floor.

Plywood is one of the strongest and most convenient floor materials available. It not only makes an effective floor, but it also serves as a strong structural tie between the floor joists and wood beams or girders.

Hardwood boards are available in many sizes and thicknesses. They are often used as floor coverings and alone over the joists as the main floor structure as well.

Particleboard is popular because of its low cost and lack of sheet curvature (it's stiff and straight). When used with an underlayer of plywood, what results is a thick, sturdy floor. If you use a two-layer floor with particleboard as your second layer, do not leave this material exposed to the weather. It will absorb moisture and swell up.

An excellent all-around floor construction consists first of ⅝-inch-thick (or thicker) plywood sheets glued and screwed to the floor joists. The glue helps to eliminate squeaks and nail popping and increases the stiffness of the plywood-to-beam bond from 10 to 90 percent. In fact, the adhesion of mastic-type glue is so strong that plywood and joists tend to behave like integral T-beam units. Screwing the flooring to the joists is superior to nailing. Screws have proven to be most efficient; they'll help to prevent springiness, uplift, horizontal shifting, warpage, and nail popping. When used along with glue, they'll provide a trouble-free floor.

The plywood and other sheet materials always should be attached so that the joints don't line up in a regular fashion (Fig. 12.8). On the first layer of flooring, it's best to arrange the plywood sheets so that their lengths run at right angles to the joists for maximum strength. Once the 4- by 8-foot sheets of plywood are laid down, they should be covered with 15-pound asphalt-saturated felt paper. Then a second structural layer of particleboard (⅝-inch) sheets can be fastened to the plywood—again staggered so that none of the seams coincide (Fig. 12.9). If additional strength is desired, the second layer can also be plywood sheets (⅝-inch). In either case, the result will be a sturdy, quiet floor.

When you select plywood, make sure that the contractor uses a good CDX grade, one that contains exterior glue lines on both sides. This grade of plywood, made with an exterior-type glue that is waterproof, will stand up to prolonged exposure to the elements during construction. The bottom plywood layer is first screwed down with an automatic screw gun; it should then be screwed along the vital joints—where one piece of plywood faces another—to prevent squeaking. Gaps of 1⁄16 inch or more, depending on the humidity levels in your area, should be

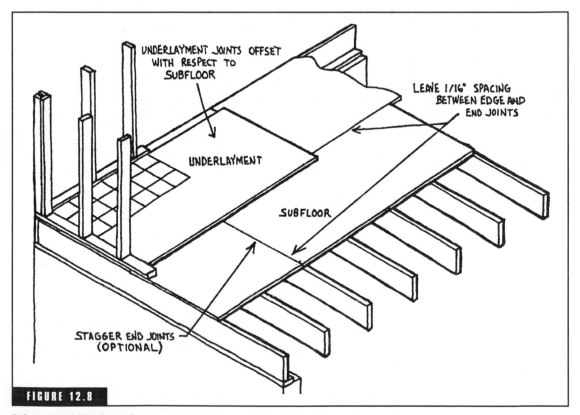

FIGURE 12.8

Joints should be irregular.

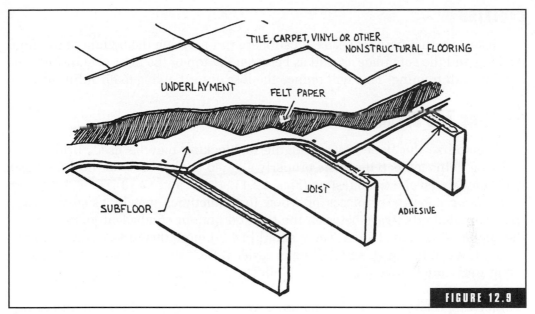

FIGURE 12.9

Covering the floor joists.

left between the sheet edges and end joints in all plywood layers. Plywood expands when it absorbs moisture and will buckle if it doesn't have enough room. Higher-humidity areas may require more of a gap for expansion. Even correctly installed single-layer floors will squeak and give if the sheets are too thin. Use 1⅛-inch-thick tongue-and-groove plywood if you're going with a single layer. Plywood used for single-layer construction should have an approved American Plywood Association (APA) stamp on it or be of equal quality (Fig. 12.10).

Formerly known as the *American Plywood Association*—APA now refers to the *Engineered Wood Association*'s trademark. This association's member mills produce about 75 percent of the structural wood panel products made in North America.

In any event, plywood subflooring always should end directly over a joist. The subflooring stabilizes the joists and keeps them from twisting or buckling.

FIGURE 12.10

Plywood tongue-and-groove sheets.

CAULKING

Make sure that parallel beads of caulk are run between the bottom of the floor decking and the sole plate as well as between the top of the floor decking and the outside wall framing. This will reduce the loss of heat owing to air infiltration.

BRIDGING AND BLOCKING

To stabilize the floor joists, bridging or blocking may be used. Bridging or blocking helps to keep the joists properly aligned so that the floor decking has a continuously level base to rest on (Figs. 12.11, 12.12, and 12.13).

Bridging consists of pieces of wood (or sometimes metal), usually 1 by 3 inches, nailed crossways between the top and bottom of adjacent joists at about the center of each joist span. There should be no more than 8 feet between individual rows of bridging, and nailing is easier if the bridging is slightly staggered along individual rows (Fig. 12.14). Solid bridging should be used under load-bearing partitions for support.

Blocking refers to 2- by 10-inch or 2- by 12-inch wood blocks fit and nailed firmly between joists at the center of each joist span. Again, there should be no more than 8 feet between individual rows of blocks.

Blocking not only holds the joists parallel and plumb but also will act as a firestop that will retard the horizontal spread of flames. In homes where bridging is used to support the floor joists, a row of blocking also can be installed for fire protection.

FIGURE 12.11

Cross-bridging of floor joists.

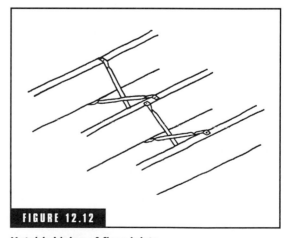

FIGURE 12.12

Metal bridging of floor joists.

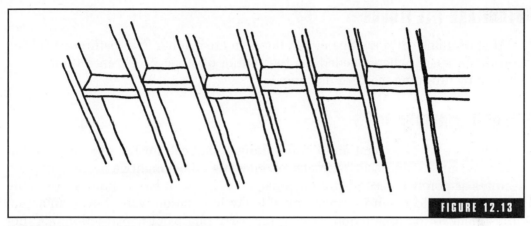

FIGURE 12.13

Solid bridging or blocking of floor joists.

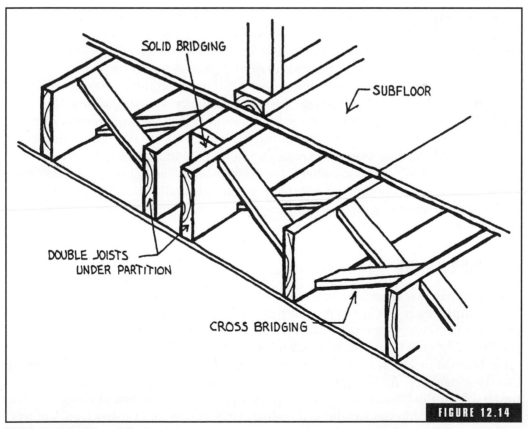

SOLID BRIDGING

SUBFLOOR

DOUBLE JOISTS
UNDER PARTITION

CROSS BRIDGING

FIGURE 12.14

Staggered bridging.

STONE AND TILE FLOORS

If your plans call for stone or tile floors in areas other than bathrooms, allow additional space where needed for the setting of stone or tile in a thin bed of cement by dropping the floor decking.

FLOOR EXTENSIONS

Give careful consideration to house designs that call for floor extensions that protrude outside the basic perimeter of the walls. They might be needed for such features as porches, second-story overhangs or decks, or bay windows. A sizable protrusion could require supports outside the foundation wall or even an actual adjustment to the foundation. During the early phases of construction, all subcontractors, including plumbers, electricians, and heating, ventilation, and air-conditioning (HVAC) crews, should be instructed to keep the spaces between floor joists as clear as possible to allow for a continuous insulation layer.

TERMITE CONTROL

Termites frequently enter a housing structure near the first-floor level. It's best to consult a qualified pest-control company to make sure that the necessary treatment is provided. The best companies give a lifetime guarantee on their work that will cover repairs if insect damage results eventually. Construction design precautions include, on a hollow-block foundation, filling the top courses of block with concrete and installing a metal termite shield along the foundation wall. Such a shield must be made of noncorroding metal and must be installed so that no gaps exist along seams or where the shield is attached. This continuous strip of thin metal, attached between the foundation and sill plate, should extend at least 2 inches out and 2 inches down from the foundation wall, bent downward at a 45-degree angle.

FLOOR INSULATION

The usual procedure for installing an effective vapor barrier is to place 15-pound building paper between the first and second layers of floor decking (if there are two layers) or else between the only layer of structural floor decking and the floor covering (Fig. 12.15). In addition, if required by your climate and house type, blanket or batt insulation can be installed between the floor joists beneath the floor decking. An integral vapor barrier also should be situated against the underside of the floor decking. This will prevent the movement of moisture from the living area into the insulation. During early phases of construction, contractors (especially plumbing, electrical, and heating/cooling) should be instructed

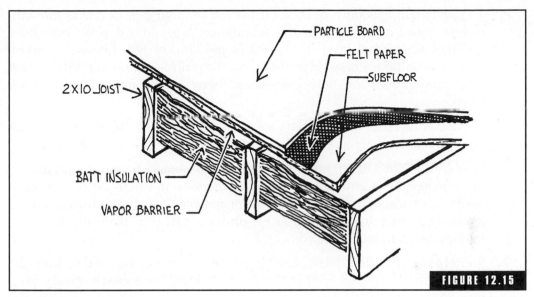

Floor insulation cutaway.

and reminded to keep spaces between the floor joists as clear as possible to allow room for as continuous a level of insulation as possible.

Insulation from noise can be an important feature in a home. An example of a soundproof type of floor, starting at the top, consists of a layer of carpet, the carpet pad, a ⅝-inch plywood top floor deck, a layer of 15-pound felt paper, a ⅝-inch plywood bottom floor deck, 8-inch-thick fiberglass batt insulation with a vapor barrier at the top against the warm side of the structure, and, finally, a layer of ½-inch fire-resistant gypsum board nailed to special resilient channels attached to the joists.

▶ ▶ ▶ ▶ ▶ POINTS TO PONDER

1. Lumber should be air- or kiln-dried no. 2 grade or better. It's already seasoned, it won't shrink as much as regular lumber will, it holds screws and glue better, it provides increased thermal insulating values, it holds paint and preservatives better, and it is less likely to be attacked by fungi and insects.

2. Only pressure-treated or exterior-grade lumber should be used for framing members that will be exposed to moisture.

3. Sill plates must be fastened to the foundation in a positive way, typically with anchor bolts that are partially embedded in the concrete foundation wall tops.

4. To prevent air, moisture, or insect intrusion through gaps or cracks that otherwise could exist between the foundation top and sill plate bottom, a resilient waterproof layer of sealant (some kind of felt, fiberglass, Styrofoam, or similar material) is pushed over the protruding anchor bolts so that it is sandwiched and tightly squeezed between the foundation and sill plate.

5. In good construction, floor joists are placed either 12 or 16 inches on center and are made of planks a minimum of 2 by 10 inches or 2 by 12 inches.

6. Double-thickness floor joists—two planks fastened together—should be used where extra strength is needed: wherever the first- or second-floor walls run parallel to the floor joists, for instance, or at openings around a stairway, near a fireplace chimney, under a cast-iron bathtub, or at any major change in joist direction.

7. To help stabilize floor joists, bridging or blocking may be used to keep the joists properly aligned so that the floor decking has a continuously level base to rest on.

8. Give careful consideration to house designs that call for floor extensions that protrude outside the basic perimeter of the walls. They might be needed for porches, second-story overhangs, decks, or bay windows. A sizable protrusion could require supports outside the foundation wall or even an actual adjustment to the foundation.

9. If you live in termite country, consult a professional exterminator, and arrange whatever precautionary work that's needed. Construction precautions may include filling in the top two courses of foundation blocks with concrete and installing a noncorrosive metal termite shield that extends at least 2 inches out and 2 inches down at a 45-degree angle from the foundation wall.

10. Insulation from noise can be an important feature in a home, especially in single-story dwellings with basement recreational rooms.

Wall Framing

The wall frame is the next logical part of the house to erect after the first-floor decking is attached to the foundation. Wall framing performs three basic tasks. First, it supports the home's upper floors, ceilings, and roof. Second, it acts as a base on which outside and inside coverings can be fastened. Third, it provides space for and conceals essential wiring, pipes, heating ducts, and insulation. In its most general sense, wall framing also includes room partitions that are constructed within the outer perimeter of a dwelling.

Naturally, a house consists of both exterior and interior walls. The exterior walls—or wall systems include framing members or structure, insulation, and anything else running through the walls, plus inner wall coverings and outer surface or siding materials—make up much of the home's thermal envelope, separating outside air from inside conditioned air. As such, exterior walls usually receive the most attention because they protect the home from the elements and provide security and safety from the outside world. Interior walls, though, are also important, even though they may not contain insulation (unless soundproofed) and do not have to face the elements. They still must separate the floor plan into meaningful areas and spaces, providing effective traffic flow patterns as well as individual areas and rooms to optimize heating, cooling, and ventilation system performance.

TYPES OF WALL FRAMING

The main goals in wall framing are to increase energy efficiency while using green products and minimizing waste. Remember that you should check the local building code if you plan to use some of the more recently developed wall constructions.

Stick or Platform Framing

In platform framing, each floor is built piece by piece, separately, one on top of the other, with the first floor providing a work platform for the second level, and so on (Fig. 13.1). The first floor can be either a concrete slab or a wood deck that is constructed atop a foundation wall. The second platform is either the second floor of a two- or more-story house or the attic floor of a single-story dwelling. The roof is similarly framed with individual wood rafters, one piece at a time, or with premanufactured trusses. Years ago, most homes were built primarily with 2 × 4 lumber. Today 2 × 6s are becoming standard for outside walls because they enable more insulation to be placed within the wall cavity.

Although many green improvements have been made in wood framing techniques, the traditional *stick-framed*, or platform-framed, method still accounts for most homes constructed today. One reason is because many of today's small builders have been building the exact same framing for decades and are reluctant to change, except for using 2 × 6s instead of 2 × 4s. Wood continues to lead the way because it remains one of the most renewable materials for home framing. It doesn't take much effort to grow, harvest, and render into usable 2 × 4s or 2 × 6s. It's durable and strong, if kept dry. It's clean and does not affect indoor air quality, and it's relatively inexpensive. One drawback to wood framing is that it takes up space within the outer walls. This is a negative characteristic because it's not a very effective insulator. Wherever the wood is, it takes the place of insulation. As contrary as it sounds, beefed-up, extrastrengthened wood-framed exterior walls are a hindrance when it comes to wall insulation values. Thus the less wood (while maintaining a thick cavity), the more room there is for insulation.

Balloon Framing

In balloon framing, the studs or vertical members of the exterior walls are continuous from the sill plate of the first floor to the top plate of the second floor. These long studs are more expensive than the studs used to frame single-floor levels, and the labor to erect the longer studs, owing to the scaffolding required, is more costly (Fig. 13.2).

Post-and-Beam or Timber Framing

Post-and-beam or timber wall framing uses long, thick structural members—often rough-hewn posts and beams. This is the same type of framing used hundreds of years ago, before modern dimensional lumber became standard. Fewer framing pieces are required, and those pieces must span lengthy open spaces. Wooden planks used for the floors and roof are left exposed. In fact, they supply the sole support over long spans in both, being nailed or otherwise attached to wood beams with mortise and tenon or dovetail joints, held together with exact fits and wooden pegs. Consequently, post-and-beam framing doesn't employ joists

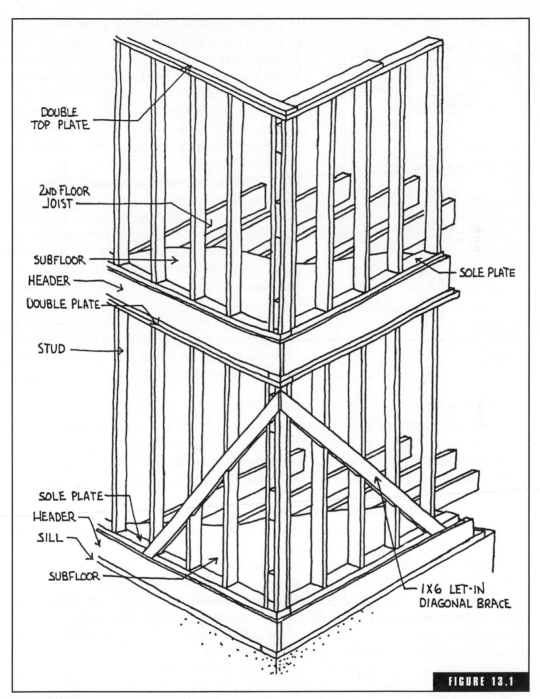

DOUBLE
TOP PLATE

2ND FLOOR
JOIST

SUBFLOOR

HEADER

DOUBLE PLATE

STUD

SOLE PLATE

SOLE PLATE

HEADER

SILL

SUBFLOOR

1X6 LET-IN
DIAGONAL BRACE

FIGURE 13.1

Platform framing.

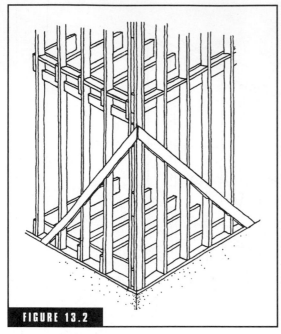

FIGURE 13.2

Balloon framing.

for the floors or ceiling. In some cases, the old is merged with the new when modern structural insulated panels (SIPs) are used for the roof. This type of construction typically is completed by experienced carpenters, craftspeople who know how to erect the exposed beams and airy ceilings desired in wide-open rooms and floor plans (Fig. 13.3).

Timber framing requires a lot of the best parts of mature trees, and because this is so, though employing a natural material, post-and-beam framing is not considered the greenest framing method by some environmentalists. It is a way, however, to show off the beauty of naturally finished wood in a home. To make post-and-beam framing as green as possible, try to locate reclaimed timbers, dead-wood timbers, or at the very least Forest Stewardship Council (FSC)–certified logs.

Pole Framing

In certain situations, this uncommon type of framing has an advantage over studded wall framing in that long wooden poles, if properly pressure treated, can be embedded deep in the ground to provide a total bracing effect for the walls against the force of strong winds (Fig. 13.4).

Advanced or Engineered Framing

This collection of recently developed framing variations helps to maximize energy efficiency and reduce lumber framing waste. Over the years, more attention had been paid to making wood framing extrastrong so that walls and rooflines will stay straight and true. It didn't cost much to add extra framing members—more than were actually needed—and overall wall insulation values suffered. Advanced framing uses the minimal amount of lumber instead, so there's less wood and more room for insulation. One caveat with advanced framing is that the framing crews must be experienced with it.

Some features of advanced framing techniques include

- Walls with 24-inch spacing instead of the traditional 16-inch spacing
- Box headers instead of large-dimension standard headers and no headers in non-bearing-wall openings

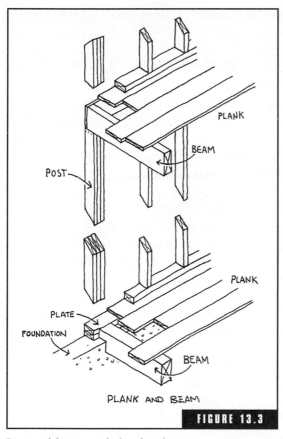

Post-and-beam or timber framing.

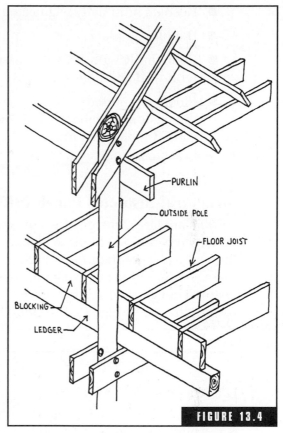

Pole framing.

- Header hangers instead of jack studs (In this way, the header can be insulated.)

- Window and door openings coordinated with stud layouts

- Single studs at rough openings to make room for more insulation

- Two-stud framing corners instead of three- or four-stud corners, making room for more insulation

- Lumber made of finger-jointed construction using shorter pieces of wood glued together into conventional stud lengths rather than single, long solid wood studs

- Instead of a wood-framed first floor, a concrete slab

- An outer layer of insulated sheathing that also helps to stabilize and further insulate the walls instead of plywood or oriented strandboard

- Headers minimally engineered to size instead of "one size (large) fits all"

- Double top plate

- Roofs built with SIPs or trusses instead of stick lumber (Trusses line up with wall and floor framing.)

- Floors supported with engineered wood structural beams instead of solid dimensional lumber (These engineered beams are straighter and stiffer than solid dimensional lumber. They often consist of laminated, glued timber, I joists made of wood, and oriented strandboard, all made with FSC-certified wood and without formaldehyde binders and adhesives.)

Structural Insulated Panels (SIPs)

SIPs are large, energy-efficient, prefabricated insulated wall, floor, or roof sections that can be set in place quickly by experienced crews and cranes. SIPs take the place of more traditional stick framing and typically are made of a thick middle layer of rigid foam insulation fastened between two panels of oriented strandboard. They're modular in nature and fit together with splines and grooves that form tight seals (Fig. 13.5). Windows, doors, and other components requiring

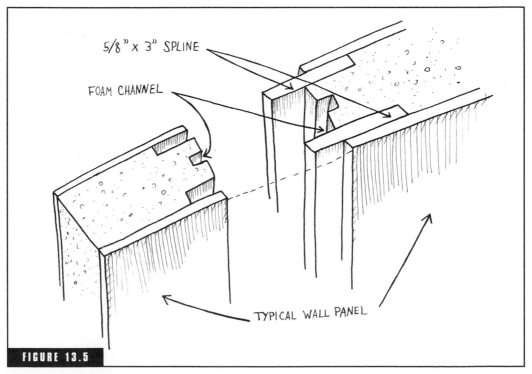

FIGURE 13.5

SIP wall panels.

penetrations in outside walls can be installed by rough-cutting holes and attaching pieces of dimensional lumber to affix window and door frames. The panels come with built-in slots or chases that electrical wiring can be run through for switches and receptacles.

Autoclaved Aerated Concrete (AAC) Blocks

These blocks, when built into strong, durable sections, supply ready-made walls that take the place of wood framing, insulation, vapor barrier, and inside drywall. The concrete mixture of which the blocks are made contains aluminum powder that's mixed with cement, sand, lime, and water. The blocks are "baked" in an autoclave, where the reaction of these heated materials produces a huge volume of tiny air bubbles having considerable insulating qualities. The blocks typically are 8 or 12 inches thick, 8 inches high, and 24 inches long. They can be customized—cut and pieced together using saws at the site—and laid up just like regular concrete blocks. Walls built from these AAC products have fairly good insulating values and reduced air infiltration rates. The blocks are relatively light—considerably lighter than regular concrete blocks. Naturally, the crews putting these walls up must be thoroughly familiar with their construction techniques.

Insulated Concrete Forms (ICFs)

Insulated concrete forms take the place of concrete walls that traditionally are poured between erected-on-site wood forms. After the concrete solidifies and dries, the forms are removed and typically discarded. IFCs are built using rigid foam (often expanded polystyrene) insulation panels instead of wood forms. When the concrete hardens, the rigid foam "forms" are left in place as wall insulation and soundproofing. Exterior and interior wall coverings (exterior siding above grade and drywall or other wall coverings on the inside) are then affixed to complete the wall. These blocks can be used to construct foundation walls or above-grade house walls.

Steel Framing

Steel framing techniques were discussed in Chapter 6 on house styles and types. Remember that owing to the poor insulation qualities of steel framing, if it's used for both inside and outside walls, with outer walls, in addition to within-the-wall insulation, a thick rigid layer of foam insulation panels should cover the outside wall framing to reduce the bridging effect of the steel. A second option is to use steel for interior walls and wood for the outer walls. Another green feature is the use of steel studs with recycled content. For a professional job, steel framing should be installed only by crews experienced with steel framing techniques.

STUDDED WALLS

By far studded walls support most of the floors, ceilings, and roofs of modern dwellings. This conventional wall framing consists of a combination of header, studding, and top plate, which should be doubled (Fig. 13.6).

Exterior Studded Walls

Because most walls are still being framed by traditional stick wood framing, the following discussion reviews those framing points.

The header for the exterior walls runs on and along the top outer edge of the sill plate and against the perimeter of the first-floor joists and decking. It should possess greater width than individual wall studs—usually 2 by 10 inches. Specify the quality of all framing lumber to be kiln-dried (KD) no. 2 BTR SPF or better grade and a species appropriate for the span, spacing, and load.

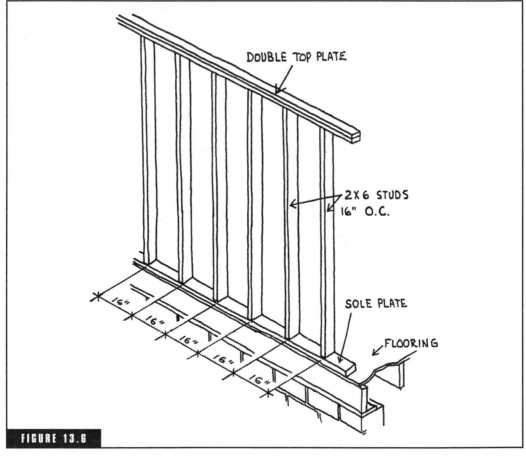

FIGURE 13.6

A studded wall frame with double top plate.

Many contractors will suggest the use of 2- by 4-inch studs in the wall framing. Don't be swayed by a builder who advocates such construction. By going with 2- by 6-inch studded walls, you'll end up with stronger walls that will accommodate thicker blankets of insulation—that will, in turn, yield greater energy efficiency for a proportionally small increase in construction costs.

Though overengineered, having the wall studs spaced 16 inches on center did provide a sturdy base for exterior and interior wall coverings to be attached to. A double-width top plate of 2- by 6-inch lumber typically held the top of the walls together. Again, today's proponents of advanced framing consider these features to be somewhat overengineered.

Interior Studded Walls, or Partitions

Conventional interior wall framing consists, as does the exterior wall, of a combination of sill plate, studding, and top plate (often doubled) to receive the weight of the ceiling joists. The sill plate generally runs across the floor decking, parallel or perpendicular to the floor joists, depending on the direction of the partition. The ceiling joists typically are positioned directly over the applicable supporting studs.

The partition tops also should be capped with two pieces of 2-inch-thick boards that are lapped or tied into exterior walls wherever they intersect.

If your house is a one-and-one-half-story or two-story design, it will require the installation of one or more load-bearing partitions before the structural framing work is completed. Later, interior partitioning consists of fitting the other various room and intersecting partitions to load-bearing partitions and exterior walls.

In a conventionally framed two-story home, the load-bearing first-floor partition should be placed directly over the main longitudinal support beam or girder that rests on the foundation walls. Load-bearing partitions on a second floor likewise should be positioned over corresponding members on the first floor so that weight will bear down on the main girder(s) beneath the first floor.

Remember, owing to their size and shape, combination bathtub/shower units must be installed during the wall partition and framing activity (Fig. 13.7). Select the models and colors well in advance so that

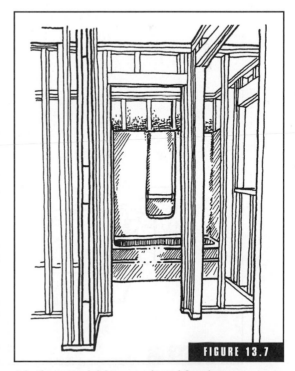

FIGURE 13.7

A bathroom tub/shower unit and framing.

they can be ordered and received in time for the plumbers to erect them when the framing crew is ready.

Corners

The corners of wall frames need extra support because they must provide stability to both intersecting walls. They involve the assembly of "posts" with insulation and corner bracing for strength, also with insulation (Fig. 13.8). Advanced framing calls for less lumber here, too.

Posts

The posts are block assemblies of 2- by 6-inch planks with blocking used at corners of wall frames and where interior partitions abut an outer perimeter wall. They should be constructed to provide a good nailing surface for exterior and interior wall coverings, and because they're hollow, they must be filled with fiberglass or other insulation so that heat is not wasted through the thermal break they'd otherwise create (Fig. 13.9). The insides of posts must be insulated as they're being put together. It can't be done later, when the posts are covered over.

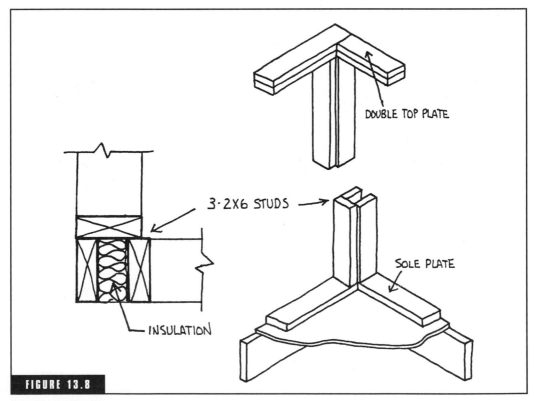

FIGURE 13.8

Exterior corner post construction.

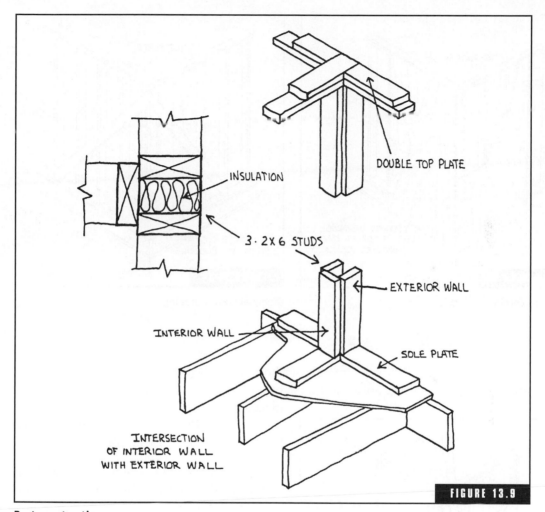

INSULATION

DOUBLE TOP PLATE

3 · 2 X 6 STUDS

EXTERIOR WALL

INTERIOR WALL

SOLE PLATE

INTERSECTION
OF INTERIOR WALL
WITH EXTERIOR WALL

FIGURE 13.9

Post construction.

Corner Bracing

If plywood at least ½ inch thick is used as the outer sheathing on the wall frame corners, depending on where you live (i.e., a location where strong winds and storms are common), other bracing may not be necessary (Fig. 13.10). However, if the outer sheathing is a material that's not very strong, such as particleboard, additional bracing will be needed. An effective corner brace to specify is the diagonal support that's "let into," or inset into, the outer corner studs (Fig. 13.11). This type of bracing is achieved with either 1- by 4-inch or 1- by 6-inch boards that fit snugly in notches cut at appropriate angles at the proper height of each wall stud crossed. The inset boards on both sides of a corner rise to meet each other in the shape of a triangle (Figs. 13.12 and 13.13).

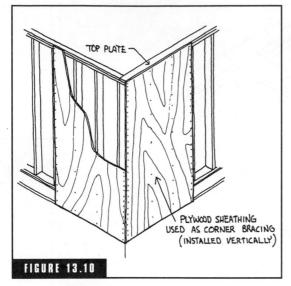

FIGURE 13.10

Plywood corner bracing.

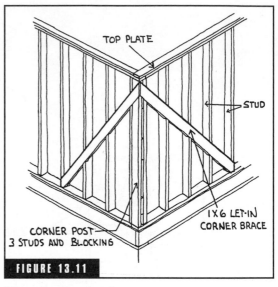

FIGURE 13.11

Diagonal corner bracing.

OPENINGS IN WALL FRAMING

Remember that it's the outer walls of a home that protect the occupants from winds and inclement weather, noise, and unsightly views. Openings should be strategically placed as well as being soundly framed. Here are some pointers to consider when planning the openings in your wall frames:

1. It's important to know far in advance of the wall framing, the size, type, and brand of each window and door you want so that the rough opening dimensions can be secured from the manufacturers and passed along to the carpenters who will be erecting the wall framing.

2. In good construction, board cuts and joints should be accurate and tight at the junction of the roof rafters and the ridge board, at the headers of windows and doors, and at all intersections. Cuts and joints that result in large, obvious gaps create weaknesses in the framing that you should not accept.

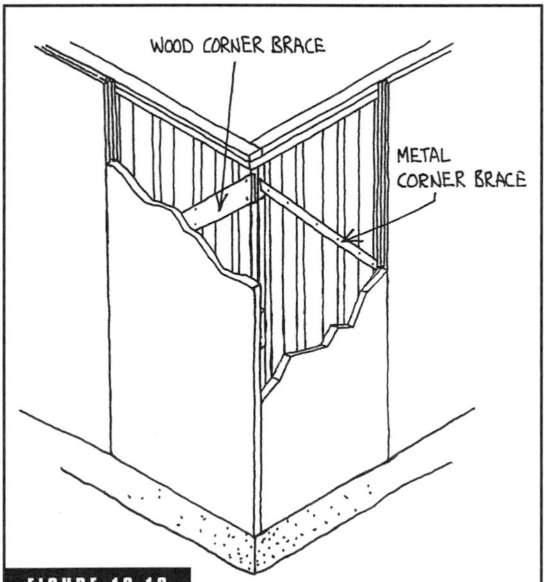

FIGURE 13.12

Corner bracing.

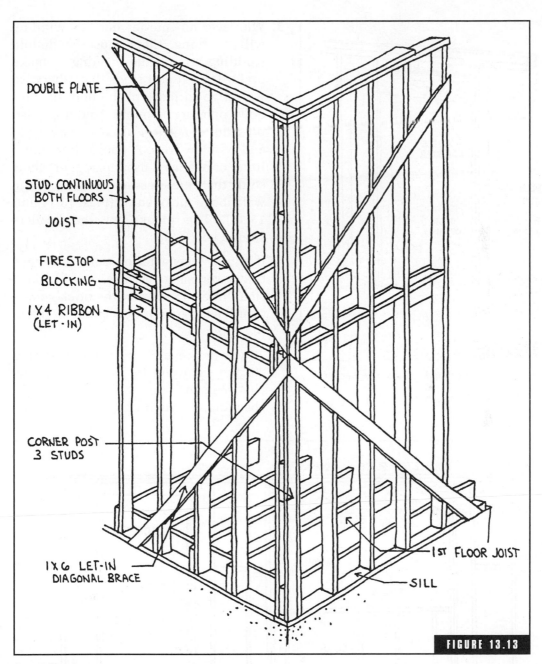

DOUBLE PLATE

STUD·CONTINUOUS
BOTH FLOORS

JOIST

FIRESTOP

BLOCKING

I X 4 RIBBON
(LET·IN)

CORNER POST
3 STUDS

I X 6 LET-IN
DIAGONAL BRACE

1ST FLOOR JOIST

SILL

FIGURE 13.13

Corner bracing.

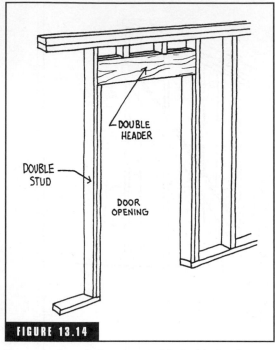

FIGURE 13.14

Door-opening reinforcement with double header.

3. Wherever an interior door or window will be hung, there must be double studding around the opening to make up for the support studs that otherwise would go in place of the door or window opening. Double studding also presents a needed place to nail door and window trim. A double horizontal lintel or header is used to support short studs that reinforce the top plate of the wall above the opening (Figs. 13.14 and 13.15). The planks for the headers should be 2 × 10s.

4. If any of your exterior walls will have brick veneer coverings, you'll need steel lintels to support the brick veneer over the tops of window and door openings (Fig. 13.16).

5. If you desire, blocking can be installed to the right and left of each window between the studs to provide a solid backing to which curtain rods can be

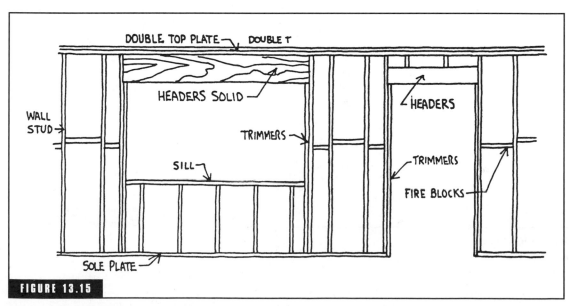

FIGURE 13.15

Door and window reinforcement.

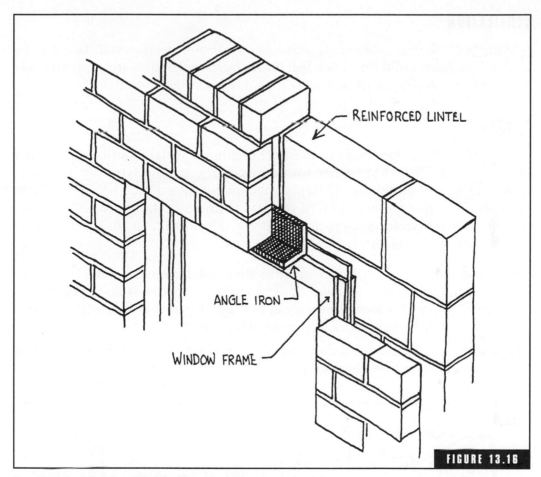

REINFORCED LINTEL

ANGLE IRON

WINDOW FRAME

FIGURE 13.16

Masonry/steel lintel reinforcement over window.

mounted. Anywhere you plan to hang heavy or often-used objects such as large pictures, trophies, or hanging bookcases, arrange for blocking between the studs to take the weight. Keep this in mind in the bathroom for fastening towel racks, soap dishes, and toothbrush holders to the wall.

6. If your bathrooms call for any flush-mounted medicine cabinets in which the storage portion of the cabinet is recessed into the wall, additional framing must be installed to accept them. Select the cabinets well in advance so that you'll have the correct dimensions of the rough openings to give to the framing crew.

7. Make sure that the framing crew remembers to install nailers to which drywall or plaster lathing can be attached, especially in odd corners and spaces where regular framing isn't used.

VENTILATION

Plan the openings—especially window openings—for cross-ventilation as far as possible. Good airflow occurs when the air inlets and outlets are approximately the same size. A better airflow results from a larger outlet than inlet.

SHEATHING

One of the last operations of the wall framing is installation of the exterior sheathing that's attached to the wall studs. Six materials typically are used, mostly in 4- by 8-foot sheets: CDX plywood, particleboard, fiberboard insulating sheathing, exterior gypsum board (if you plan to use stucco), rigid foam insulating sheathing, and Styrofoam insulating sheathing (Figs. 13.17, 13.18, and 13.19).

Exterior sheathing performs four functions:

1. It braces the structure. Plywood is the strongest, most rigid of the six materials, followed by particleboard. If plywood is used, at least on the corners, it may eliminate the need for diagonal bracing. Diagonal boards with plywood corners will provide superior structural bracing.

2. For best results, the sheathings should be applied vertically in 4- by 8-foot or longer sheets with edge and center nailing.

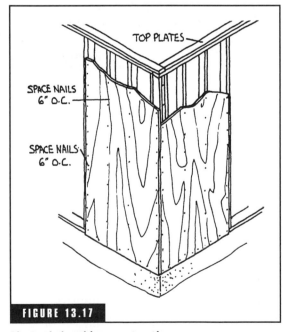

FIGURE 13.17

Plywood sheathing construction.

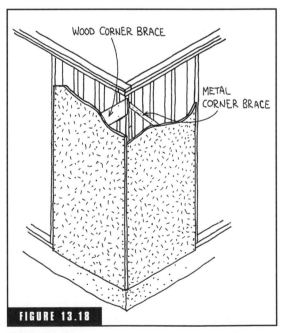

FIGURE 13.18

Particleboard.

3. It provides insulation. If insulation, not strength, is the main concern, rigid foam and Styrofoam board are the winners here. They can be purchased with tongue-and-groove edges to provide a tight fit to reduce air infiltration.

4. Sheathing provides a weathertight base for the exterior siding. Plywood and particleboard sheathings are a strong base for exterior siding. Make sure that the sheathing you choose will provide the needed base for the exterior siding you have selected. Be aware that there are two types of plywood: exterior and interior grade. Definitely, only exterior-grade plywood should be used for the outside of a house. Exterior CDX plywood is made with high-quality veneers and is bonded with waterproof glue. It offers the best durability, and its glue won't weaken with age or with long exposure to foul weather.

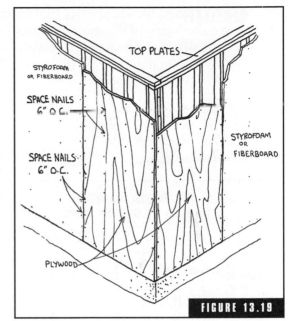

FIGURE 13.19

Styrofoam or fiberboard.

Last, with rigid foam or Styrofoam sheathing, review with the manufacturer and your contractor where an additional vapor barrier may be needed. Besides a vapor barrier applied to the inside of wall studs to prevent movement of moisture from living areas into insulation, a vapor barrier also may be needed on the outside of wall studs. If where you live rigid foam or Styrofoam traps any moisture inside an exterior wall, it will condense as it reaches its dewpoint and create water. The water will soak the insulation and rot the sill plates over time.

NAILS

As minor as they might seem, nails are what hold much of a house together. Only galvanized nails should be used on exposed materials, both inside and out. Unless the house is roofed over immediately, a sudden downpour could cause regular steel nails to rust and streak the surfaces in just one night.

If your walls will have studs with 24-inch on center (o.c.) placements instead of 16-inch o.c. as recommended, nailers will have to be installed so that drywall or plaster lathing can be attached securely. Nailers are small 2- by 4-inch or 2- by 6-inch blocks attached perpendicular to the studs in between pairs of studs. The nailers also will give extra support and stiffness to the walls and will act as a fire-block to discourage flames from spreading throughout a wall.

It's a good idea to specify that exterior wall sheathing be applied by hand nailing only. Some of the more fragile sheathings such as polyurethane board can be torn easily and damaged by power nailing equipment.

For optimal efficiency, nails should be spaced 6 inches o.c.

ENERGY

Energy is of great interest no matter which part of a house is being discussed. But here, with the exterior walls, insulation takes on a special importance. Naturally, you want to reduce the consumption of energy for heating and cooling and to increase the level of comfort in the home by muffling the effects of the elements. This is another reason why openings should be planned carefully to prevent unwanted heat loss or heat gain and to allow for natural ventilation and heat gain when desired.

The major obstacles to well-insulated, sealed walls are doors, windows, and electrical outlets. Again, eliminating as many potential problems as possible in the design stage is the first and most logical step. Place wall switches and outlets on interior walls when possible, and use as few windows, glass sliders, and doors as practical. Have reasons for everything that goes into the exterior walls. When you can, incorporate features that must be inset into a wall within interior walls, where the interruption of insulation is not a factor.

Because wall insulation is so important, the use of 2- by 6-inch studs is stressed over and over. Old-fashioned 2- by 4-inch studs were fine in their day, when energy was inexpensive, but only 3½ inches of fiberglass batt or blanket insulation will fit into such walls. With 2 × 6 studs, 5½ inches of the same kind of insulation can be laid (Fig. 13.20). This makes a big difference in energy use.

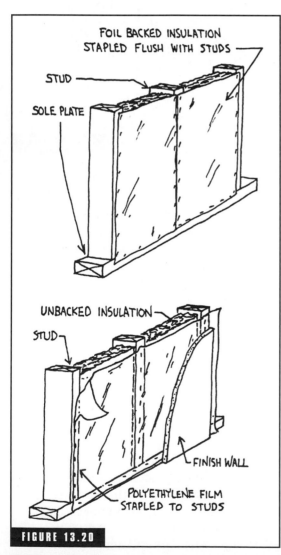

FOIL BACKED INSULATION STAPLED FLUSH WITH STUDS

STUD

SOLE PLATE

UNBACKED INSULATION

STUD

FINISH WALL

POLYETHYLENE FILM STAPLED TO STUDS

FIGURE 13.20

Wall insulation views.

SOUND INSULATION

There are two ways to arrange effective sound insulation for interior walls. The first employs staggered 2- by 4-inch studs erected on a 2- by 6-inch plate. The studs should be positioned 16 inches o.c. Because the studs are staggered, this technique eliminates the touching of drywall or plaster on both sides of the wall by any single stud, thus reducing the wall sound transmission capabilities. The air voids between the studs are "woven" with 3½-inch fiberglass blanket or batt insulation, which will further deaden noise transmission.

In the second procedure, interior walls are constructed with 2- by 6-inch studs and 5½- or 6-inch batt or blanket insulation. The additional wall thickness makes up for sound transmission deficiencies.

VAPOR BARRIERS

In addition to being insulated, living areas should also be sealed with a moisture-proof layer or vapor barrier that's applied to the inside of the wall studs to prevent the movement of moisture from the living areas into the insulation. Insulation will lose some of its thermal qualities if it becomes damp or wet, and if the moisture within the living spaces is retained within the house, the occupants will still feel comfortable with less heat owing to the inside humidity. Consult the local building code for guidance on specific vapor barrier requirements. Depending on your climate, whether it's hot, humid, or dry, vapor barrier needs vary.

There are several methods for applying a vapor barrier to exterior walls: Install insulating batts or blankets faced with vapor barrier backings such as treated kraft paper or aluminum foil. The vapor barrier always should be placed closest to the living area that's heated. If unfaced batts or blankets are used, a vapor barrier or polyethylene film not less than 3 mils thick (or an equivalent) should be applied.

If you decide to have loose-blown insulation, establish a vapor barrier by stapling or nailing polyethylene sheet material to the interior of the wall studs. You also can install aluminum foil–backed drywall before the insulation is blown between the studding.

BEFORE THE WALLS ARE CLOSED

Before the walls are closed up, the following items should be completed, if applicable:

- Sink drains
- Vents
- Water supply for sinks

- Cold water for toilets
- Water for showers and tubs
- Hot water for a dishwasher
- Hot and cold water for a clothes washer
- Gas lines
- Appliance vents
- Built-in vacuum system
- Electric wires and doorbell
- Intercom system
- Internet connections
- Phone lines
- Alarm systems
- Heating and cooling ducts
- Wall insulation
- Plumbing installed

> **≡INSPECTION**
>
> **WALL FRAMING**
>
> After the wall framing is complete, check the following:
>
> - Vertical walls are plumb.
> - Opposite walls of rooms are parallel.
> - Horizontal members (joists, headers, and subfloors) are level.
> - Exterior sheathing is not damaged or punctured.

>>>>>> POINTS TO PONDER

1. Again, if you're using wood, use only air- or kiln-dried no. 2 grade or better framing lumber. You don't need the warping and shrinking that could result from unseasoned lumber.

2. Don't be swayed by a builder who suggests the use of 2- by 4-inch wood studs in the wall framing to save a few dollars. By using 2- by 6-inch studded walls, you'll end up with stronger walls that will accommodate thicker blankets of insulation.

3. Conventional wood studding should be spaced 16 inches o.c. to provide a sturdy base to which exterior and interior wall coverings may be attached.

4. Consider advance wood framing techniques to save on lumber while increasing energy efficiency. An example is using 2- by 6-inch studded walls with 24-inch spacing.

5. Use double-width or double-thick top plates of 2- by 6-inch lumber to hold the tops of the walls together.

6. In a conventionally framed two-story home, load-bearing first-floor partition(s) should be placed directly over the main longitudinal support beam(s) or girder(s) that rest on the foundation.

7. Remember, owing to their size and shape, combination bathtub/shower units must be installed during the wall partition and framing activity or you won't be able to simply carry them into place later—they're too big.

8. Corners of wall frames need extra support because they must provide stability to both intersecting walls.

9. In addition to being insulated, living areas also should be sealed with a moisture-proof layer or vapor barrier that's applied to the inside of the wall studs to prevent the movement of moisture from the living areas into the insulation.

10. Sound insulation is important for establishing privacy between bedrooms, bathrooms, and other living areas.

11. While wall framing is still exposed or open, make sure that as much of the plumbing, electrical system, communications system, doorbells, security alarm system, certain types of insulation, central vacuum system, and heating and air-conditioning components, plus various vents, drains, built-ins, window and door openings, and other applicable items, are completed.

Roof Framing

There's no getting out from under it: The roof of a house is often all there is between you and the sky. And as such, the roof will protect you from such inconveniences as snow, sleet, hail, rain, sun rays, wind, dust and dirt, acid rain, insects and animals, moonlight, and noise. It will, when constructed and insulated properly, keep cool air in the house during summer and warm air outside. Then, conversely, during winter, the roof keeps cold air at bay and warm air inside.

The typical roof also serves, however infrequently, as a platform for contractors to walk on when they're performing maintenance and repairs—to renew the flashing on a chimney, for instance, or to dislodge a stubborn bird's nest from a false fluc.

A roof must be securely fastened to the rest of the house, not merely "tacked onto" the upper level. It has to be able to resist updrafts of wind that otherwise would yank a roof right off.

The roof and ceiling frame of a home's upper level needs to be sturdy enough to support whatever covering or options are planned, including heavy tiles or slates, solar panels, and skylights. If a large slope of the roof faces south, you may want to prepare for the eventual installation of solar panels. Many solar module or panel racks are fastened directly into trusses or rafters, with lines of conduit and insulated pipes leading into the home's utility spaces below. For greater energy efficiency, raised-heel trusses are preferred over standard-type trusses so that insulation installed along the roof's perimeter does not have to be squeezed or narrowed. At the same time, however, it should be noted that any irregularities or impediments to simple rooflines provide opportunities for water or moisture to seep through the roofing. This includes chimneys, vents, roof lights, and anywhere the roof has a valley or dormer where one roofline intersects another.

Other practical considerations to be made with the roof frame are the size and shape of the area between the upper level's ceiling and the rooftop, commonly known as the *attic space*. In certain types of houses, this space can be constructed in a variety of ways. It tends to follow patterns dictated by the shape of the rest of the house, tempered by basic aesthetics. Although it should be in correct proportion to the surrounding architectural components, certain decisions must be made regarding roof pitch, materials, and construction techniques.

The roof overhang—the part of the roof that protrudes beyond the exterior walls—protects the exterior sheathing or siding, windows, and doors from the elements, especially rain and sun. A wide overhang will block the sun on summer days when the sun rises high overhead and then will let the sun's rays enter during winter, when the sun travels a much lower route in the sky.

ROOF STYLES

Six styles of roofs account for the lion's share of roofs, old and new: gable, gambrel, hip, mansard, flat, and single-pitch or shed. The first three are the most widely used (Fig. 14.1). Keep in mind that the following styles are not restrictive of each other. A single dwelling can and often will have a combination of several roof styles.

The Gable Roof

The *gable* roof is the single most popular roof style built today. It consists of two usually equal-sloped roof planes that meet at a topmost ridge. In fact, it's the ridgeline running the entire length of the house, or at least on the parts of the house having that style of roof, that most characterizes the gable style. The gable also means the upper triangular area formed on each end of such a roof. Gable or shed dormers are frequently added to plain gable roofs to break monotonous lines or for the practical purpose of providing natural light, air, and additional space to make an attic area more useful.

The Gambrel Roof

In general, the *gambrel roof* is a gable roof having two separate roof slopes on each side of the topmost ridge, the flatter or least sloped of the two being above the level of any dormer windows. An advantage this roof has over the gable roof is that it increases the usable attic space, and when dormer windows are installed, it's almost equivalent to having a second story.

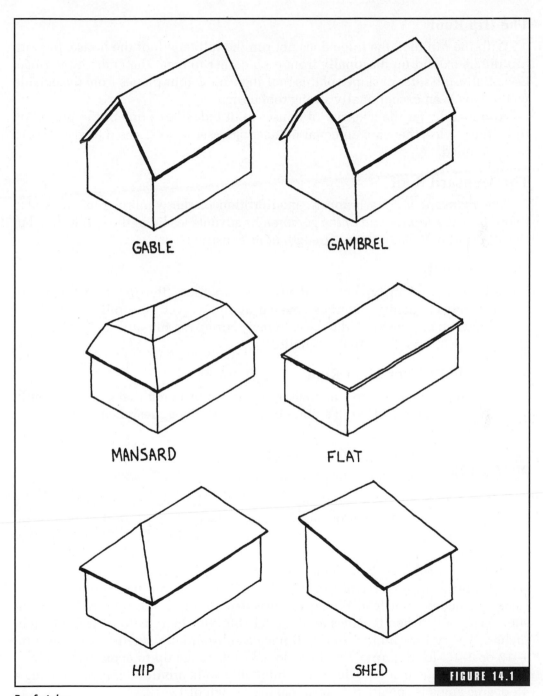

GABLE

GAMBREL

MANSARD

FLAT

HIP

SHED

FIGURE 14.1

Roof styles.

The Hip Roof

With the *hip roof*, the ridge does not run the full length of the house. Instead, hip rafters extend up diagonally from each corner to meet the ends of the ridge. Essentially, the sides or slopes of this roof angle up in four planes from the outside walls. This is an exceptionally strong roof design.

Although by far the majority of houses built today have one of the preceding three roof styles, there are an equal number of lesser-used styles that also should be mentioned.

The Mansard Roof

The *mansard* is a variation or modification of the gambrel roof. It is also referred to as a *hip version of the gambrel*. Its advantages lie in the space added to the attic and in the additional strength of its construction.

The Flat Roof

Not often used in typical residential construction, the *flat roof* frequently employs rubber roofing materials covered by fine gravel. Naturally, such a roof would have to be constructed to be extremely strong for any building located in a climate expecting substantial snowfalls.

The Single-Pitch or Shed Roof

This simple style features a single roof surface or plane that's usually gently sloped in a single direction. It's not a bad roof, but its appearance is rather dull and uninspiring.

ROOF PITCH

When describing a roof's configuration, *pitch* is the measure of its steepness or the degree of slope the roof or part of the roof has. It's expressed in two corresponding numbers: a value of rise per a value of run (Fig. 14.2). *Rise* means just what it says—a vertical distance. *Run* addresses the horizontal travel it takes to reach a given rise. A 4–12 pitch means that there are 4 units or measures of rise for each 12 units or measures of run (Fig. 14.3). This ratio can be expressed just as easily in inches or in feet. Whatever measures are used, the ratio remains constant. Generally, when it comes to roof pitch, builders tend to do their thinking in inches. A very low-pitched roof will have a substantially smaller rise than run: 1–12 or 2–12, for example. Medium-sloped roofs range up to about 6–12—about the steepest slope that a novice can comfortably walk around on. A roof having a 45-degree angle is considered steep, having a pitch of 12–12.

The pitch of a house roof is influenced by a variety of factors, including expected snowfall, the heaviness or lightness of the construction materials, how much storage or living space you want beneath the roof, how much insulation is planned, and, of course, how the house should look so that it's architecturally balanced. Different climate conditions and different house types will call for different roof pitches. Here are the main character-istics of a low-pitched roof:

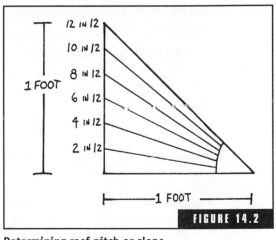

FIGURE 14.2

Determining roof pitch or slope.

1. It will shed water well in warm climates and will, if built soundly, retain snow for added insulation in colder climates.

2. The area directly under the roof will consistently be a wider, more open space, providing extra room with pleasantly sloped ceilings.

3. The low pitch will make both interior and exterior maintenance safer and less expensive.

4. Since its initial construction requires less material owing to its minimal surface area, it's also less costly to build than a steeply pitched roof.

To balance out our roof picture, here are some characteristics of a steeply pitched roof, from 6–12 to 12–12 and above:

1. A steeply pitched roof sheds just about everything in a hurry. Rain races off its surface, and snow is less likely to accumulate there. A steeply pitched roof rarely leaks. It doesn't give the moisture a chance to penetrate.

2. Although certain individuals can benefit from lofty storage spaces provided within a steeply pitched roof, care must be taken to avoid ending up with inaccessible, unpleasant attic rooms. Let no one sway you into believing that

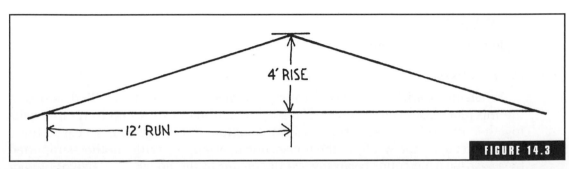

FIGURE 14.3

A pitch of 4–12.

every inch of an attic constructed beneath steeply sloped roof planes can be efficiently used.

3. A steep pitch makes maintenance and repair the tasks of professionals, especially when the exterior must be accessed. This means inconvenience and high expenses for both.

4. Since more surface area is involved, a steeply pitched roof requires more materials at an initially larger cost outlay.

5. Steeply pitched roofs are good for placing solar collectors on in cold and warm climate locations.

Keep in mind that the pitch of your roof might limit or even dictate what roofing materials you can use. Wood and asphalt shingles, wood shakes, and tile or slate can require a pitch of 4–12 or steeper. Roofs sloped less than 4–12 are uncommon and might need to be covered with an industrial-type roof of rubber or tar and fine gravel.

BUILDING METHODS

There are two common methods of constructing roofs and one relatively new method.

■ The *stick-built system* uses individually erected rafters, ridge boards, ceiling joists, and collar beams assembled on the job.

■ The *prefabricated truss system* is a newer method in which trusses are made to your roof's specifications by a fabricating company that specializes in this work.

■ The use of structural insulated panels (SIPs) similar to the ones used for floors and walls can result in a labor- and materials-efficient, durable, and energy-efficient roof. Their simple building assembly should be accomplished by crews experienced with SIP construction techniques.

Stick-Built Roofs

Figure 14.4 shows an example of a stick-built roof.

CEILING JOISTS

When all exterior and interior walls are framed, plumbed, and nailed, and after the top plate has been fastened in place, the ceiling joists go up to tie the walls together and to form a structural base for erection of the roof. In most cases, these joists must span the width of the house, one overlapping with another, supported by a load-bearing collar beam toward the center of the house. The size of lumber

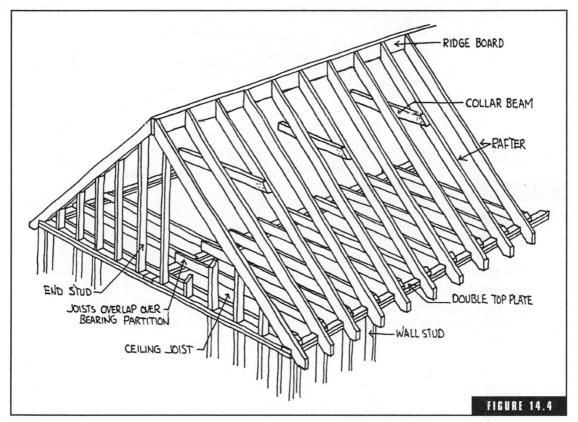

A stick-built roof.

to use for joists is determined by the distance to span, the type of wood used, and the load that will have to be supported above. The dimensions of the lumber used for ceiling joists should be specified in the plans. Do not settle for anything less than 2- by 6-inch planks.

In a two-story home, the ceiling joists at the second level become floor joists for the attic, and it's reasonable to ensure that they must be as sturdy as those used below and constructed in a similar fashion. The spacing of the ceiling joists may vary, but, as with studs, 16 inches on center (o.c.) has been considered standard good construction. The doubled top plate of the wall frame supplies sufficient strength. It makes sense to locate joists over the wall stud positions (Figs. 14.5 and 14.6). Install wood blocking between ceiling joists where bracing is needed for ceiling lights and fans.

Ceiling joists serve several purposes: They resist the outward thrust imposed on the walls by the roof rafters, they provide nailing surfaces for the ceiling and the upstairs or attic flooring, and they support any weight placed on the upper floor. Because of their place in the framing scheme, joists must be nailed securely

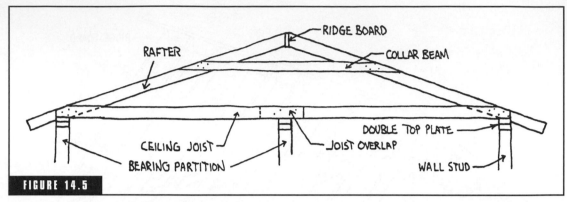

FIGURE 14.5

A stick-built roof construction view.

to the top plate of every wall that their ends rest on and to every load-bearing partition wall they cross or join on.

Note that ceiling joists are not used with houses having truss framing. The bottoms of the trusses, normally constructed of 2 × 4s or 2 × 6s, become the ceiling joists.

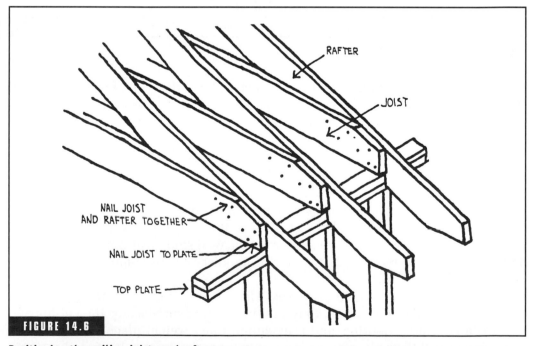

FIGURE 14.6

Positioning the ceiling joists and rafters.

RAFTERS

Rafters are wood planks or boards that span the distances from the top of the exterior walls to the roof ridgeline or peak to form the skeletal structure to which the roof deck is fastened. The size of the rafters varies with the distance they must span and the steepness or pitch of the roof. It's often computed by referring to tables that show the load-bearing capacities and deflection qualities of various woods and boards. When sizing your rafters, many variables go into selecting the proper dimensions, such as length of span, spacing of structural members, wood species, and lumber grade, plus expected wind forces and snowfall. Depending on the conditions, your rafters may need to be 2 × 8s, 2 × 10s, or even larger.

When selecting roof rafter joists, ask your builder about using engineered wood I-beam roof rafter joists. Engineered wood I beams are made with a top and bottom lumber flange with a grooved center to accommodate a center web (typically plywood) (Fig. 14.7). Special hangers with blocking are needed to secure these beams.

Engineered wood I-beam roof rafter joists offer many advantages:

- Good strength
- Excellent clear span on large rooms (They span longer distances than regular wood.)

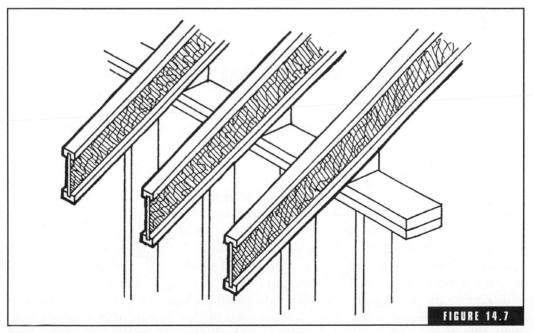

FIGURE 14.7

Engineered wood I-beam roof rafter joists.

- Always standard and consistent in dimension
- Laminated construction that eliminates crowning, warping, twisting, and bowing
- Won't shrink or crack
- Roof sheathing that lies flatter initially and remains that way because these beams don't shrink
- Wide flanges that allow the plywood to be screwed straight down (not angled as when trying to hit half a 2-by lumber) while staying back from the edges
- More bearing surface for glue and support
- Typically lighter than dimensional lumber

The rafters should be spaced in the same manner as ceiling joists are erected, and then each rafter can be tied or nailed to a companion joist as well as to the plate.

ADVANTAGES

1. Dormer expansions are relatively simple to make with rafter framing. If you think that you might want to expand into an attic, it's a must to use rafters instead of prefabricated trusses. And if expansion is likely, then increase the size of your floor joists.

2. The rafter or stick design is also the better choice when adding dormers because it's much easier to tailor the roof to accept the dormer framing.

3. Rafter-built roofs allow you to have cathedral ceilings.

DISADVANTAGES

The main disadvantage of rafter roof framing is that load-bearing interior walls must be relied on for support.

Truss-Built Roofs

Roof trusses, unlike ceiling joists used with rafters, span the entire width of a structure (Fig. 14.8). They are triangular with wood interior bridging (W-shaped) for strength. Mathematically, the principle that gives what appear to be flimsy components the strength to span such long distances is the inherent rigidity of the triangle. Trusses simply rest on and are fastened to opposite exterior walls. Unless advanced truss framing methods are employed, "normal" truss loads call for individual truss units spaced 16 inches o.c. to avoid the risk of a sagging roof deck.

Conventional practice for insulating attics is to blow loose-fill insulation—typically fiberglass, rock wool, or cellulose—onto the topside of the ceiling between

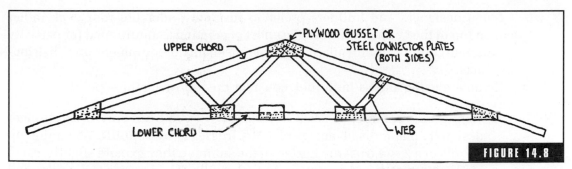

Truss-built construction.

and over the joists. R-38 is recommended, although some of the colder regions calls for R-49. Achieving R-38 with low-density loose-fill insulation generally requires material to be 12 or 13 inches deep. This depth covers the joists, disconnecting the thermal bridge the joists represent.

Around the roof perimeter, however, where the rafter falls to meet the joist (known as the *heel*), insulation effectiveness can be compromised in several ways. First, the available depth for insulation tapers off, in some cases to as little as 3½ inches in roofs using trusses constructed from 2 × 4 lumber. Second, air blowing up from soffit vents can "wash" the insulation away from the perimeter. The first problem is addressed by using a raised-heel truss (Fig. 14.9). By adding a vertical spacer at the truss heel, this design ensures that full-depth insulation covers all the way to the outer edge of the exterior wall. The second problem is addressed by using cardboard baffles fixed between the rafters for the first few feet above the heel to separate the ventilation air from the insulation. Note that raised-heel roof trusses can cost more than conventional roof trusses, and because the exterior wall is extended, additional sheathing and siding will be needed. Long-term energy savings will easily offset the initial cost.

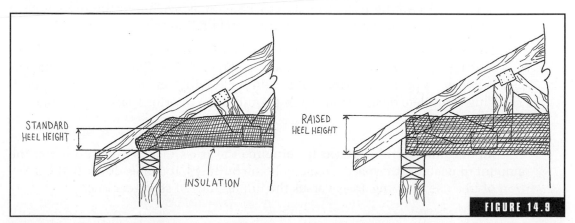

Standard versus raised-heel truss.

Some designers and builders prefer to insulate under the roof deck rather than on top of the ceiling. This has the effect of creating a conditioned (or partially conditioned) attic, a useful place to locate mechanical equipment and distribution ducts.

If you are using a truss-built roof, consider the following three points:

- While some contractors use 2 × 4 trusses, a 2 × 6 truss provides a stronger design. A major disadvantage of 2 × 4 trusses is truss uplift. When the top chords of a 2 × 4 truss are heated in the summer, they expand slightly, causing the bottom chord to bow up in the middle. The interior ceiling drywall or plasterboard is attached to these chords and is pulled upward, separating corners and cracking the joints. If 2 × 4 trusses are being used, consider requesting 2 × 6 bottom chords to help resist bowing.

- Trusses limit attic space as a result of their cross member supports. To alleviate the space loss, ask your contractor if W trusses will support the roof load. W trusses have the inner cross member angled to provide more attic space.

- Make sure that wood blocking is installed between trusses where bracing is needed for ceiling lights and fans.

Advantages

1. Ceiling joists aren't needed in the attic.

2. Trusses are built using smaller dimensional lumber than is used by the stick-built rafter system.

3. Despite the small lumber, the truss design still provides adequate strength to the roof.

4. Savings in framing costs usually can be realized owing to the reduction in materials and labor involved with truss installation.

5. The greatest advantage of a trussed roof is that it eliminates the need for load-bearing interior walls. Trusses are engineered to span entire distances between opposite exterior walls without relying on intermediate support. Thus complete design freedom in planning the interior space is possible.

Disadvantages

The diagonal members used to reinforce the truss design greatly restrict the amount of usable attic space. To many home builders, it comes down to the question of free use of living areas versus the importance of storage space.

THE ROOF DECK

The roof deck is what gets fastened to the exterior of the rafters and what the finished roofing shingles, shakes, tiles, or other materials are fastened to (Fig. 14.10). It consists of a structural sheathing and a moisture-resistant underlayment.

Roof Sheathings

Most roof sheathing is done with plywood sheets in thicknesses suitable to properly strengthen the rafters and to correctly prepare for whatever roof covering will be used. Here are some construction points to remember about plywood sheathing:

1. The type of plywood to specify is CDX. This comes with a clear (C) or smooth side to be seen and a rough side (D) to be hidden. The X means that it's all held together with exterior-type glue.

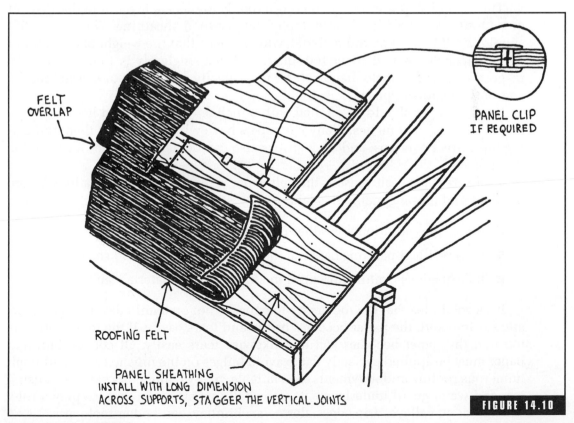

FELT
OVERLAP

PANEL CLIP
IF REQUIRED

ROOFING FELT

PANEL SHEATHING
INSTALL WITH LONG DIMENSION
ACROSS SUPPORTS, STAGGER THE VERTICAL JOINTS

FIGURE 14.10

A cutaway of a roof deck.

2. The plywood thickness for roof sheathings should be at least ⅝ inch and preferably ¾ inch. Review your local building requirements. The added thickness of ¾ inch gives superior resistance to high winds and affords better penetration for shingle nails. Plywood roof sheathing is strongly supported on 16-inch o.c. roof framing, with metal H clips fastened between the edges of the plywood sheets to reduce the potential of the sheathing to sag and to give extra support between the framing rafters or trusses.

3. For the greatest overall strength, the 4- by 8-foot or larger sheets of plywood should be laid crossways to the rafters or trusses—similar to their use over floor joists—to tie the greatest number of framing members together as possible with a single sheet.

4. The joints should also be staggered by at least one rafter or truss so that there is no continuous joint line from a cornice to the roof ridge board. No adjoining panels should abut over the same rafter or truss.

Roof Underlayments

The second step toward completing a roof is to place a layer of underlayment or saturated roofing felt paper on top of the plywood sheathing. The roofing felt should be a 15- or 30-pound material, which means that the weight of the amount of felt paper that would cover 100 square feet in a single ply is 15 or 30 pounds, respectively. The shingle manufacturer may specify which felt to use so that the warranty remains in place.

Roofing paper should be applied with 6-inch end overlaps and head overlaps along the edges of 3 inches. Many felt papers have white stripes on them indicating the correct overlaps, and such stripes also can be helpful guides for coursing the shingles.

There are three basic reasons that felt paper is placed over the sheathing before the final roof topping material is laid:

- It provides additional weather protection for the roof.

- It's a resilient padding between the shingles and the wood sheathing.

- It keeps the sheathing dry until the final roofing material can be applied.

It's a good idea that the roofers try to paper a roof on a mild day. If the temperature is too cold, the paper becomes brittle and tears easily. If the temperature is too hot, the paper becomes soft and likewise tears easily. Of course, building paper must be applied perfectly flat to avoid bulges on the finished roof. Although numerous roofing underlayments are available, many contractors have been using ice- and water-guard underlayments, especially where water and ice play a role, such as along valleys, drip edges, dormers, chimneys, and other roof parts.

VENTILATION

When closing a car door from the inside, have you ever experienced pressure in your ears because the car is practically airtight, and there's barely any means for the air to escape? Or how about storing fresh mushrooms in an airtight plastic bag? Any cook knows that to do so invites spoilage: If air cannot freely circulate around the mushrooms to remove "expired" moisture, then that moisture will quickly condense onto the mushrooms and cause them to deteriorate, even if they're kept cold.

The same principle holds true with houses, especially when it comes to roofs. A house/roof combination that's too "airtight" is unhealthy. Moisture that's given off from a variety of our appliances and fixtures such as toilets, showers, clothes washers and dryers, dishwashers, cooking surfaces, and even our own breathing—not to mention periods of high-humidity weather—becomes an agent that will, if not removed, rot wood, wreak havoc with insulation, and even go right through to the underlayment of a roof and affect asphalt or wood shingle roofing materials themselves—all from within. Materials stored in moist environments also will tend to be ruined by mildew over the long haul.

Thus an airtight, self-contained roof/house combination is not only undesirable but is also downright dangerous to have. Many old houses were constructed without vents. Instead, the owners relied on large double-hung windows and screens positioned at the gable ends, opening them for a cross breeze. This worked fine until the windows rotted or "froze" shut and couldn't be opened or were closed during rainstorms and times of high humidity. This is why you'll find so many old houses with rotting wood roofs and musty-smelling attics that are extremely hot in the summer and freezing in the winter.

Hot air accumulates in the attic as heated air rises from the home's living areas while the sun's rays superheat the roof. Trapped hot air in an unventilated or improperly ventilated attic will defeat the best efforts of air conditioning, insulation, and even shade trees to help keep a home cooler during summer. On the other hand, effective attic ventilation reduces heat buildup, helps to keep the living quarters comfortable, cuts cooling costs, extends shingle life by keeping the roof cooler during hot weather, helps to reduce moisture buildup that encourages mildew growth and rot on the roof's framing members and sheathing, and also minimizes the buildup of ice dams on the roof and gutters during winter.

Nowadays, all good builders realize that attic or roof vents are necessities, and the builders supply one or a combination of several vent types to let the house breathe and rid itself of unwanted moisture. Consider, too, that roof ventilation also allows heat that rises to the upper reaches of the roof interior to escape and does the same for dangerous gases or fumes that could collect there in the event of an accident or emergency.

How much ventilation is needed? Your builder should have a good feel for this. It can be affected by the direction of prevailing winds, the amount of shelter from the sun, or even the positions of neighboring buildings or parts of the house itself. Some rooflines can channel wind toward a certain part of the roof, whereas others might hinder particular airflows from having the desired effects. Roof ventilation is especially important to houses exposed to continuous sunshine and equipped with air-conditioning.

Proper ventilation helps to remove warm, moist air from the attic, making your home more comfortable and helping to reduce cooling costs in the summer and prevent ice dams in winter. An effective year-round ventilation system provides continuous airflow through the attic, with air entering via soffit vents and exiting at ridge, gable, turbine, or roof vents as well as roof fans.

The following are five popular types of vents that can be used on new houses (Fig. 14.11) along with window and roof fans.

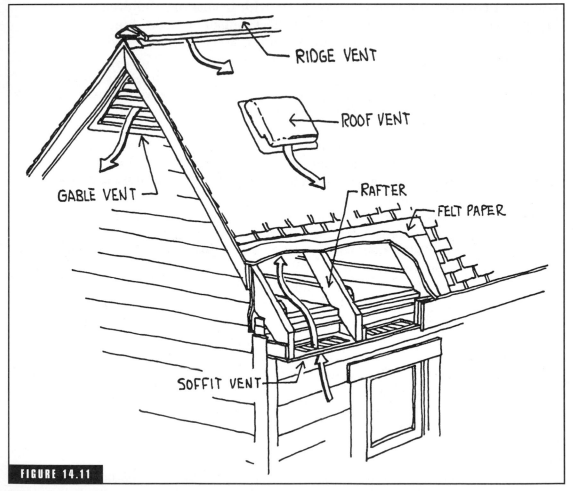

FIGURE 14.11

Types of roof ventilators.

Ridge Vents

Because the ridge line is the highest part of a roof, it offers an efficient location for a ventilator. A ridge vent typically consists of a long channel or "crack" covered by an upside-down gutter-like vent running along the roof ridge that permits air to escape from the house and prevents rain from entering. A ridge vent will vent your entire peak, working with the wind to siphon moist, hot air out of the attic spaces and protecting your roof and keeping your house more comfortable.

Ridge vents should be durable and weather-resistant. They typically come in metal or plastic. When choosing yours, make sure that it offers the following qualities:

- Rain- and snowproof (prevents both from entering)
- Rated to withstand high winds (in excess of 100 mi/h) and blizzard conditions
- Bug- and insectproof
- Resists denting and cracking
- Warpproof
- Unibody construction, rugged and durable, with no pieces to come loose
- Crushproof design
- Rustproof
- Design that allows for expansion and contraction during temperature extremes
- Allows shingles to be attached on its top so that it blends in with the roof

Gable Vents

Gable vents are the most widely used roofing vents (Fig. 14.12). These are the triangular slatted arrangements you'll notice on practically every house that has

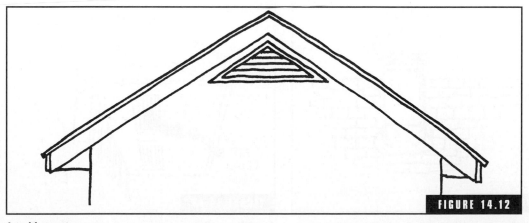

FIGURE 14.12

A gable vent.

gable ends. Frequently made of galvanized metal, gable vents do a good job of getting rid of heat because they are located close to the roof ridge. Depending on the location of the house, a cross-breeze will sometimes result.

Roof Turbines

Turbine vents help to get rid of heat and moisture. Roof turbines and fans are galvanized or aluminum vent units fastened to a side of a roof, on one of the slopes, positioned to act like a wind-powered turbine or fan when the wind blows and like a free vent when the air is still (Fig. 14.13). The turbine vent uses a series of specially shaped vanes to catch the wind and provide the rotary motion to pull hot and humid air from the attic. They can be electrically powered to assist in removing hot air during summer to augment an air-conditioning system so that it doesn't become overloaded. Look for a turbine vent with sturdy rust-free construction (typically aluminum) that has permanently lubricated upper and lower bearings rated to operate from as little as a breeze of 1 mile per hour through regular winds and able to withstand the strongest winds expected in your location.

Roof Vent

Roof vents are galvanized or aluminum vents that fasten to the side of a roof, on one of the slopes, that allow the attic air to vent out. The quantity used will depend on the size of your roof.

Soffit Vents

Soffit ventilators are similar to gable vents, except that they're positioned at the eave or soffit areas of the roof (Fig. 14.14). Install a continuous pattern of

FIGURE 14.13

A roof turbine vent.

FIGURE 14.14

A soffit ventilator.

soffit ventilation under the eaves to allow fresh, cooler air to enter the attic. Fresh air flows in through the soffit openings into the attic, and then stale air is expelled through the gable vents, roof vents, ridge vents, turbines, or fans.

Make sure that your contractor does not block the soffit vent spaces between rafters just above the exterior walls, where baffles should be installed to allow air to move past the insulation. Without ventilation baffles, effective airflow up and out the ridge vents may be hindered.

And finally, because air will be drawn into the soffit vents, the vents should include a fine-screen mesh to prevent insects from entering. Of course, soffit vents should be made of nonrusting materials, such as aluminum or plastic.

Window Fans

When any or all of the preceding vents do not provide enough air circulation, an attic window fan might be necessary to draw out hot air and rid the attic of unwanted moisture. If you plan to install an attic ventilation window fan, make sure that the builder includes large enough gable or other vents to permit the passage of enough air so that the fan can operate efficiently.

Roof Fans

Roof fans, also referred to as *attic fans*, traditionally have been electric ventilators that mount on a side of the roof and can quickly exhaust heat and humidity from the attic (Fig. 14.15). The fan motor typically is activated and shut down by a built-in thermostat that monitors the attic temperature. When the air rises above a set temperature, the fan comes on; when it falls below that temperature, the fan shuts down. A manual shutdown switch normally is placed in the hallway to allow turning the fan off. These units continue to be very popular in homes. They lower the attic temperature, save on air-conditioning, and make a home more comfortable.

Given the situation—a roof fan is needed most when the sun is shining during times of hot weather—it's an ideal candidate for solar power. An energy-efficient solar fan provides an excellent way to vent an attic or garage by using the sun's rays to exhaust heated air (Fig. 14.16). Its energy source is free and plentiful, with no electrical wiring or complicated controls to attach.

These relatively inexpensive fans operate fastest during the hottest parts of the day and then at lower speeds during early morning or late afternoon when inside air is cooler and needs less circulation. Since sunshine access by the roof-mounted solar

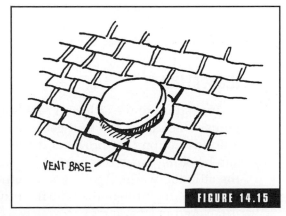

VENT BASE

FIGURE 14.15

A roof fan.

FIGURE 14.16

A solar-powered roof fan.

fan is so important, the units work best when facing south or southwest.

Consider these points when shopping for solar fans:

- Solar fans should be able to be set to come on at one temperature and turn themselves off at another lower temperature.

- The fan design should accomplish positive venting by creating negative air pressure that will draw heated air, including moisture, out from beneath the roof.

- A baffle system should enable heated air to exhaust but keep rain and snow from entering.

- The unit should provide ventilation even later in the day or at night if temperatures within the space remain elevated. This can be accomplished with a rechargeable backup battery charged by excess energy generated during the day by the solar cell. When fully charged, the battery should have the capability to operate the vent for nearly 3 days' worth of dark or cloudy weather conditions.

- A heavy-gauge screen should be attached around the top edge of the inside housing to keep out insects, birds, and other critters.

Chimney Vents

Although they have little to do with attic airflows, chimney vents also pass through the attic and roof or are positioned directly adjacent to them. Especially if it's a manufactured metal chimney that has a built-in airspace, the vent should be located at least 2 inches away from any nearby wood frame. The top of the chimney should clear the roof ridge by 3 feet.

INSULATION

Insulation of the attic and roof is a task that must not be taken lightly. In cold-climate locations, the heat generated by a furnace or fireplace rises, and it's the attic insulation that prevents it from escaping. In warm climates, heat from the sun beaming down on the roof tends to make the rooms that are directly beneath the attic too warm. Again, it's the attic and roof insulation that will prevent heat from passing through the attic floor into the living areas. Attic and roof insulation is covered in Chapter 25.

▶▶▶▶▶ **POINTS TO PONDER**

1. The roof overhang—the part of the roof that protrudes beyond the exterior walls—protects the exterior sheathing or siding, windows, and doors from the elements, especially rain and sun.

2. A wide roof overhang will block the sun on summer days, when the sun rises high overhead, and will let the sun rays enter during winter, when the sun travels a much lower route in the sky. This means that a wide overhang is usually preferred over a narrow one.

3. Simpler roofs, with fewer angles, valleys, and intersections, typically are less expensive roofs owing to simplicity of installation.

4. Stick-built roofing systems use individually erected rafters, ridge boards, ceiling joists, and collar beams assembled piecemeal on the job site.

5. Stick-built roofs allow for simpler dormer expansions and cathedral ceilings.

6. Using engineered wood in the roof framing can lessen twisting, which helps to enable window and door frames to stay true and aligned—further resulting in better energy efficiency.

7. Prefabricated truss systems employ trusses made to your specifications by a fabricating company that specializes in this work. They're simpler to erect on site than stick-built systems.

8. Include a complete ventilation system with soffit vents that allow outside air to enter and higher-level vents (ridge, gable, turbine, roof) or fans to provide air an exit.

9. If an attic is desired, trusses will not work as well as stick-built roofs because the truss components take up most of the otherwise usable attic space.

10. An airtight, self-contained roof/house combination is not only undesirable but is also dangerous to have. Attic and roof vents are absolute necessities.

11. Remember that the steeper the roof pitch, the more dangerous it is to be accessed for maintenance and repairs.

Roof Exterior Finishing

The exterior roof covering is an important milestone in the house construction process because it brings the job's progress to the point of being closed in against the weather or, in the terminology of many builders, *under roof*. The reasons for reaching this stage as quickly as possible are to protect the already completed construction from extensive damage owing to hail, rain, snow, and exposure to ultraviolet light and to provide cover and enclosure so that further construction can proceed despite inclement weather.

As with any exterior roofing component that offers protection from the weather, the installation is critical to performance. The surface layer of roofing—the shingles or outer roofing material—is the first layer of defense against rain, hail, sunlight, and wind, but it must work in tandem with the waterproofing membrane below and often benefits from a thin ventilation space between them both so that moisture doesn't build up and so that excessive heat won't readily transfer through the roofing and roof framing into the home.

ROOFING MATERIAL SELECTION

Good reasons exist as to why you should explore the various types of roofing materials available for your house. Indeed, your selection may be influenced by the following:

1. *The desire for fire protection.* At one time, the combustibility of a house's roofing material substantially influenced the fire insurance rate charged. Certainly, if you're miles away from the nearest hydrant, you might want to think twice about wood shakes or shingles. This can be a huge issue in places that

periodically experience seasonal draughts and high winds. Nonflammability can be a critical factor in your roofing selection.

2. *The effect that weather elements have in the area in which you live.* Certain roofing materials hold up better in certain climates than others.

3. *The life expectancy of the roofing.* The price of the labor needed to replace a roof is high. Therefore, it's important to pick out a roofing material that will last. Don't make the mistake of selecting a material that will need replacing in less than 10, 20, or even 30 years. A quality product should last for 40 to 50 years of normal use. Proportionally, for the value received, a higher-quality roof won't cost much more—especially when amortized over its useful life. Also saved is the cost and environmental impact of disposing of the deteriorated roofing one or more times.

4. *It should be relatively maintenance-free.* Although wood usually is considered a renewable resource, consider the amount of care and refinishing it will need periodically. Many of the other roofing types are practically carefree when it comes to maintenance.

5. *The type of house and how the house is positioned on the lot.* If large expanses of sloping roof will be visible from the ground, try to choose a material that will contribute to the overall attractiveness of the home. Too often an owner will select expensive siding materials only to downgrade the building's appearance with a cheap roof. Instead, give careful attention to your roof, and use materials that add color, patterns, or textures as desired.

6. *Include as many green features as possible.* More and more roofing components are being made with versions containing recycled content. This goes for metal, asphalt, rubber-based, and other products. Ask the builder or roofing contractor what's available along those recycled lines. Also make sure that the roofing itself will not leach any harmful chemicals or pollutants with its runoff. You certainly don't want to be capturing toxic rainwater and snowmelt and using it elsewhere on your property.

TYPES OF ROOFING

There are basically six types of roofing that cover about 95 percent of the residential roofs: asphalt shingles, fiberglass shingles, wood shingles and shakes, slate shingles, tile shingles, and metal shingles.

Asphalt Shingles

By far, asphalt shingles (Figs. 15.1 and 15.2) are the most common roofing material in both warm and cold climates. Sometimes they're also referred to as *composition shingles.*

These durable shingles, depending on their weight, have a life expectancy of 15 to 50 years. They're made of a heavy paper known as felt that is coated with hot liquid asphalt and then covered with fine rock granules.

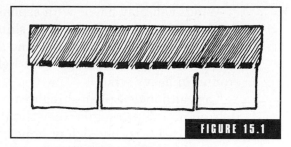

FIGURE 15.1

An asphalt three-tab shingle.

Asphalt shingles are manufactured in many different colors by many different companies. The heavier shingles are more expensive and have greater texture and longer life. They also take more time and effort to put up, and most roofers will charge a higher rate for applying them.

There are many different kinds of asphalt shingles. The heavier the shingle, the longer is its life expectancy. Besides being more durable, premium shingles are offered in better colors, colors that do not fade as quickly as the less expensive models do. Heavier shingles are also less susceptible to wind damage than lighter shingles because of their heavier, stiffer construction. Even if you live in a severe windstorm or hurricane area and decide to use the heavier asphalt shingles, though, they should have self-sealing tabs so that curling doesn't result.

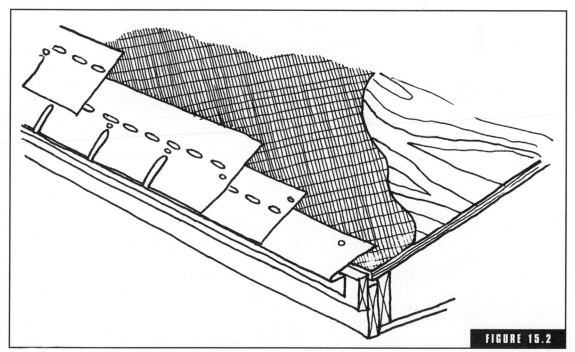

FIGURE 15.2

Asphalt shingle installation.

Winds can play havoc with asphalt and other shingles. To prevent such damage from occurring, choose only shingles with self-sealing tabs, and opt for the interlocking types that have tabs and slots used to hook each shingle together with the adjacent ones. Consider that light shingles have a tendency to get blown around in heavy wind.

Last, although asphalt shingles are the most popular selection for roofing materials on new construction, they should be used warily on roofs having pitches of less than 3–12. With very low slopes, water seepage can occur under the shingles, especially during times of high winds.

Fiberglass Shingles

These shingles are similar in appearance to the asphalt variety but are lighter in weight, more resistant to fire, and more durable. Ask your insurance agent about the possibility of reduced premiums for your home owner's policy if you elect to go with fiberglass shingles. As with the asphalt type, the heavier fiberglass shingles are more durable. Stick with self-sealing or interlocking shingles for protection against wind and curling. Along with asphalt shingles, fiberglass shingles should not be used with a pitch of less than 3–12 unless a properly installed special underlayment is laid first. Fiberglass is a popular choice because of its favorable combination of appearance, price, and durability. It's also lighter in weight.

SHINGLE
(SAWN)

SHAKE
(HANDSPLIT)

FIGURE 15.3

A wood shake and shingle.

Wood Shakes and Shingles

Wood shakes and shingles are available in several species of wood, with red and white cedars being the most popular, followed by cypress, redwood, and yellow pine (Fig. 15.3). The term *shingle* means that the wood has been sawn, usually from the solid heartwood of mature trees, whereas *shake* indicates that the same wood has been split. The shake is usually thicker and has a more rustic appearance. Yellow pine shingles are typically treated with preservatives.

Supply and labor costs to install wood shakes or shingles can be four to five times that of installing standard asphalt or fiberglass shingles. Home owners, though, consider wood shakes and shingles a step up in quality and beauty.

"Hand split" wood shakes and shingles have been popular for quite a while in the western United States but did not reach the Midwest and East in appreciable numbers until the late 1960s. Their increasing popularity is attributed to their textures, deep shadow tones, longevity, weather resistance, and compatibility with colonial, modern, and contemporary house styles. Make sure that you select only Forest Stewardship Council (FSC)–certified lines to keep within acceptable green guidelines.

The main drawbacks to wood shakes and shingles, in addition to their cost, is their flammable nature, their maintenance requirements, and that they come from the kinds of mature trees that are becoming scarcer across the world. If you still would like to have the look but want to avoid actual wood, rubber-plastic look-alike shakes and shingles are available. They're durable and maintenance-free substitutes.

Slate Shingles

Slate is one of the finest natural roofing materials available and one of the most expensive (Fig. 15.4). Certainly it's one of the most durable shingles with which you can cover a roof. But it also can weigh over 3,000 pounds per square (compared with 200 to 450 pounds for wood), so a slate roof frame must be designed strong enough to support such an ambitious load.

Roofs made of slate shingles can add considerably to the value of a house. Pieces of slate are available in smooth commercial grades or rough quarry runs and in different colors and variegated shades depending on where they come from. They make a beautiful roof and, if cut from a good mineral bed, will last 100

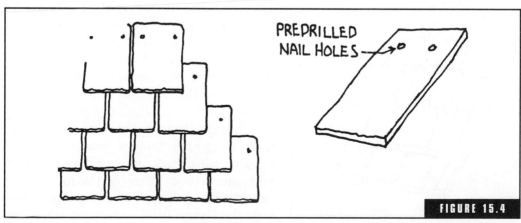

FIGURE 15.4

Slate shingles.

years and more (unless there's a lot of acid rain in the area). They're fully recyclable, can be reclaimed from old homes and industrial buildings, and cause no safety or environmental issues from their manufacture or use.

It's unfortunate that slate has been given a bad name from older homes where tree-damaged roofs or roofs undermined by rotting wood supports caused by a lack of proper ventilation result in loose and fallen slate roofing. People have heard horror stories about the high costs of repairing old slate roofs and have unjustly grown overly wary of slate shingles. Like the substitutes available for real cedar shakes and shingles, if you can't afford real slate, a number of synthetic slate roofing lines made from recycled, injection-molded rubber and plastic are acceptable substitutes.

Tile or Cement Shingles

Clay or cement tile shingles are especially popular in the sunbelt areas (Fig. 15.5). They come in all kinds of decorator shapes, colors, and textures. They're simple to install but physically taxing because of their incredible weight—from 800 to 2,600 pounds per square. As with slate shingles, a tile roof needs to be well braced to support its own weight. The tiles are apt to be expensive, especially in areas where they aren't used frequently (outside of warm-climate locations), but they are durable and have a long life expectancy. They're very fire resistant.

Clay or cement tile shingles should be used sparingly for flat-sloped roofs and generally should be applied where the pitch is steep enough for water to run down quickly to avoid water backup and leaking roofs. Clay terra cotta tiles are durable and handsome. Their regularly rough configurations provide natural airflow and ventilation where installed, which is gladly accepted in the warm locations in which they're generally found. Cement tiles made with portland cement and sand/stone mixes are also good at reflecting heat. They're usually less expensive than clay tiles and stand up better to impacts such as from hail or a stray

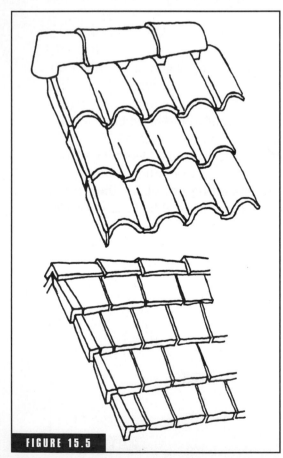

FIGURE 15.5

Tile shingles (clay or cement).

baseball. One drawback to tiles is that they can be difficult to walk on if there's work to be done on a roof. Noncorrugated tiles are best installed over a thin ventilation space. Modern tiles are much less brittle than older versions and frequently contain materials such as rubber, fiber/cement, and various plastics and composites to provide additional strength and long-lasting performance in the face of extreme weather conditions.

Fiber/cement shingles are a mixture of portland cement and cellulose fiber. They come in many shapes and styles and are durable but brittle and may not stand up to hail or being walked on.

Metal Shingles and Roofing

Metal roofs, especially those made of high-quality copper or terne (tin/lead alloy), used to be very popular, but they're rarely used anymore owing to safety and environmental concerns—they leach harmful chemicals and pollutants. Anodized aluminum shingles and sheet roofing with factory finishes are very durable (Fig. 15.6). At the same time, they're relatively expensive and can be noisy to the point of aggravation in a rainstorm. Aluminum shingles are lightweight compared with other roofing materials (about 40 to 60 pounds per square) and come in many modern colors, shades, and styles, mostly in a shake-type texture. They'll last a long time if fastened securely with aluminum nails.

The king of metal roofing, however, is steel. Steel shingles and sheeting come with maintenance-free baked-on, factory-applied paints of all colors and reflectivity levels. They're ideal for the installation of cool roofs—roofs with light, reflective coatings or surfaces that reflect much of the sun's heat—and can save home owners up to 40 percent in cooling costs. Coated-steel roofing products are extremely durable, resistant to fire, can contain a high percentage of recycled content, and look good. Many easily qualify as top-rated Energy Star products owing to the amounts of heat they reflect away from the roof. Like other rigid and semi-rigid roofing, some metal shingles also can benefit from a ventilation airspace between the shingles and the roof deck or sheathing.

ROOFING COLOR

If your roof is a complex one, with many dormers, valleys, and varying planes, medium to dark roofing shingles will tend to pull it all together in a nice way. Whether or not you value appearances more than the roof's ability to reflect heat may depend largely on where the house is built. Be aware that a light-colored roof reflects heat and is more desir-

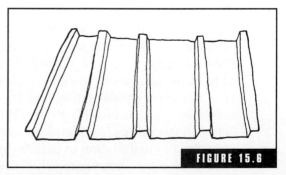

FIGURE 15.6

Metal shingles.

able in areas where air-conditioning is the greatest energy user. Most asphalt shingles used to be black. They absorbed about 95 percent of the sun's heat and were great in locations concerned primarily with heating costs. Black roofs were (and are) a main cause of urban "heat islands" being present in cities from the high levels of heat being absorbed during the day and given off throughout the night. Whites and light grays are the most effective shades when it comes to keeping roofing and attics cool under strong sun rays. They can reduce cooling costs by about 20 to 25 percent. Other colors and darker shades convert more of the sun's rays to heat.

Check other houses that are already completed in the area or on the street on which you're planning to build. If several or many of them are using similar colors, it might be wise for you to select something different so that your home doesn't "blend in" with the rest of them and to break the monotony.

In humid locations and places where tree leaves and debris tends to fall on roofs, algae and mildew growth may be a problem. This can be seen as dark areas or streaks on light-colored roofs. If your site has these conditions, select algae-resistant shingles. They have a slight amount of copper in the surface granules. Copper ions retard the growth of algae.

If you live in a warm climate and still decide to select a dark-colored roof, make sure that you have sufficient ventilation, insulation, and air cooling to negate the additional warmth absorbed by the shingles.

VENTILATION AND SOFFITS

The roof and attic should be assured of adequate ventilation to allow for the escape of heat and humidity (Figs. 15.7 and 15.8). All ventilation units installed on the roof or in gable ends should be designed to shed rain and snow and not permit any moisture penetration. In addition, the free-opening vent areas must be screened to protect against entry by insects, bats, rodents, squirrels, and similar invaders. Soffits, the flat painted surfaces under a roof or overhang, should be constructed of prepainted or vinyl-coated sheets that are maintenance-free (Fig. 15.9).

Soffits are available with either a smooth unbroken surface or with perforated or slotted surfaces that will encourage ventilation of the attic or roof space. You need a steady pattern of perforated soffits to ensure effective airflows for circulation. Eave soffit vents work by allowing circulation of air through an attic to prevent moisture condensation and its consequential damage to roof structure and insulation. When installing the soffit vents, insulation must not plug the spaces between the rafters just above the exterior walls. To prevent this from happening, consider the installation of baffles that will allow air to move past the insulation. Also remember that venting the eaves alone is insufficient. Because warm air circulates upward, roof or gable vents, mentioned earlier, should be used in

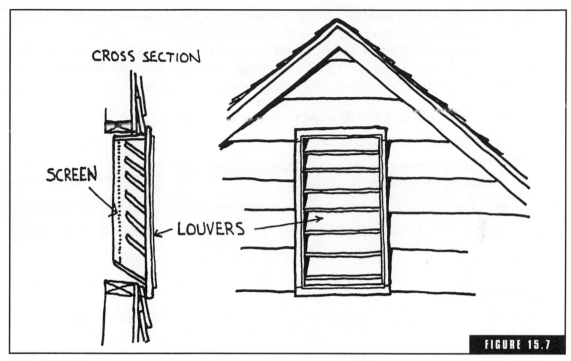

CROSS SECTION

SCREEN

LOUVERS

FIGURE 15.7

Gable ventilation.

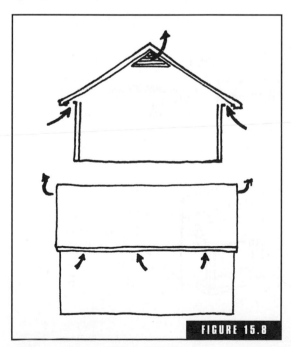

FIGURE 15.8

Soffit and gable ventilation action.

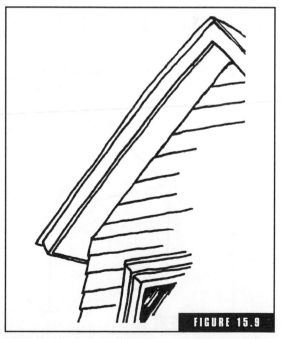

FIGURE 15.9

Soffit under an overhang.

addition. There also must be enough free-opening areas near the top of the attic to match the collective opening space of the eave soffits.

Because ventilation is so important, a ventilation system may include soffit vents with a combination of roof ridge vents, louver vents, metal-dome vents, gable vents, and turbine vents, any combination of which will

- Allow outside air to flow naturally upward and out of the attic
- Promote a cooler, drier attic
- Prevent moisture from becoming trapped within insulation, structural wood, shingles, and roof decking
- Help to prevent rot, mildew, drywall damage, peeling paint, and warped siding
- Provide year-round performance for consistent ventilation, lowering the overall energy consumption

FLASHING

Protecting framing and insulation from rain, snowmelt, and moisture is critical. All can cause great amounts of damage and inconvenience. At the very least, uninvited moisture in its many forms can reduce the insulating value (reducing energy efficiency) and damage your ceilings and walls.

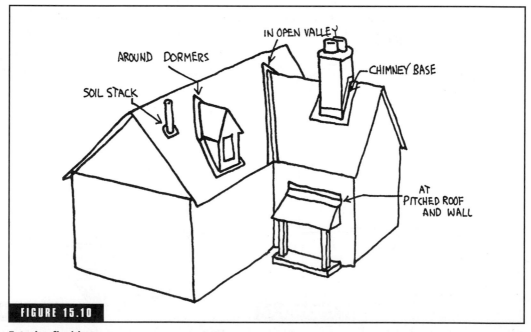

FIGURE 15.10

Exterior flashings.

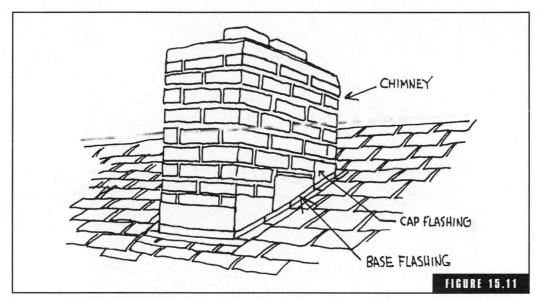

FIGURE 15.11

Flashing around a chimney.

Flashing is sheet metal or other material used to prevent the leakage or driving in of rainwater and general moisture infiltration at joints near openings or where different materials or planes meet, such as around chimneys, vents, roof valleys, and stacks (Figs. 15.10 through 15.13). If a material projects horizontally from the surface of the house, such as at window and door trims or at the insulation around a foundation, flashing is required. It's also needed wherever roofs and walls join, such as with a split-level or a two-story house having an attached garage (Fig. 15.14). Flashing is important at the juncture of a dormer's siding with a main roof to prevent water from leaking through (Fig. 15.15).

Aluminum is the most common flashing material. It's produced in long rolls in several widths and is inexpensive, lightweight, and resistant to corrosion except in industrial areas and near the seacoasts. It has one drawback—a shiny appearance that must be painted—and aluminum does not paint well.

Galvanized steel and terne are also employed as flashing; but they also must be painted. Stainless steel, zinc alloy, and even lead all have been used in similar fashion. Another durable, though expensive choice for flashing is copper. It seems to last forever and requires almost no

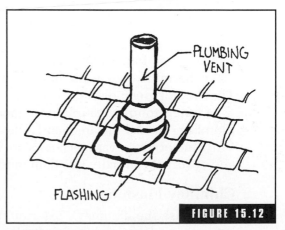

FIGURE 15.12

Flashing around a vent pipe.

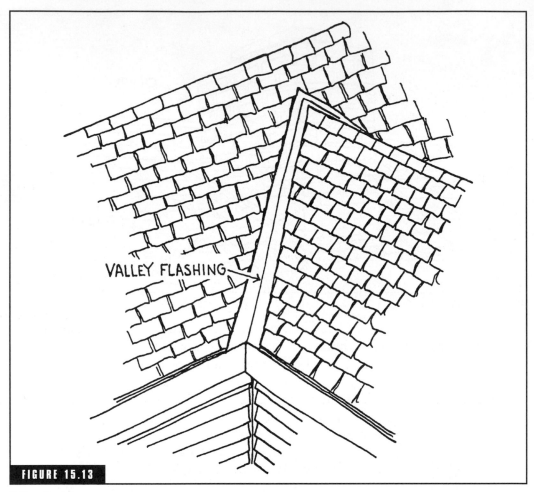

FIGURE 15.13

Valley flashing.

maintenance. One advantage it has is that its corners can be soldered for a water-tight connection. Unfortunately, these nonaluminum bare-metal flashings can leach harmful chemicals and pollutants into rainwater and snowmelt runoff. They're not green options.

Asphalt roofing material is sometimes used for valley flashing on roofs, and plumbing stacks are frequently flashed with special neoprene plastic collars. Vinyl materials in various colors are also on the market. Vinyl is a durable choice and costs substantially less than most other flashing materials.

Chimney Flashing

Because the chimney's exterior can be a frequent source of unwanted water intrusion, a few words on its flashing will perhaps save considerable trouble in

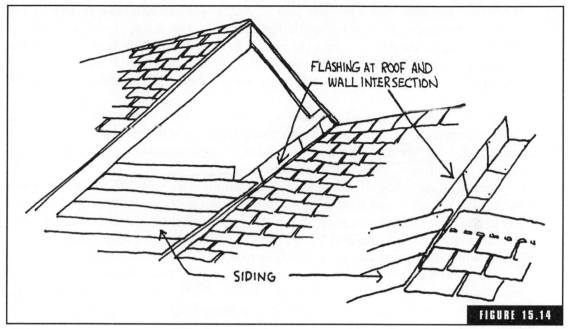

FLASHING AT ROOF AND
WALL INTERSECTION

SIDING

FIGURE 15.14

Flashings at roof and wall intersections.

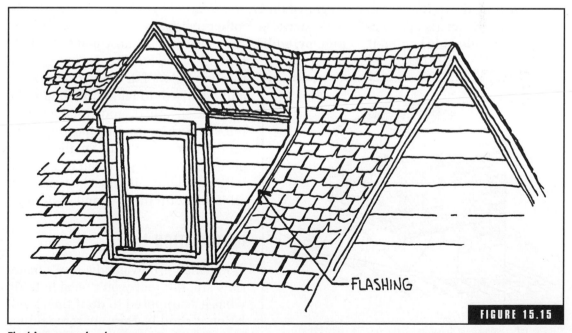

FLASHING

FIGURE 15.15

Flashing around a dormer.

the future. For sure, water seepage around a chimney can enter the attic or spaces beneath the roof and ruin the insulation there, do damage to the roof sheathing and framing, and eventually ruin the ceiling below. When there is such a leak, the problem is usually with the chimney flashing. The sheet-metal flashing around the chimney is supposed to keep the intersection between the chimney and roof watertight.

An effective way to seal a chimney is with two flashing layers: flashing and counterflashing. The first layer is called *step flashing*, where sections of L-shaped sheet metal are "woven" into the surrounding shingle courses and lapped snug up against the chimney sides.

This flashing is installed in a stair-step fashion starting at the bottom or lower side of the chimney and working toward the upper part, fastened to the roof only, not to the chimney. Next, a small lip of the counterflashing metal is embedded in the chimney mortar joints and folded down to cover the tops of the step flashing. Then, when the roof moves with winds or from shrinkage, the two pieces of metal flashing move or slide against each other to prevent bending or damage while maintaining protection from water. The corners of this arrangement are especially vulnerable, and an effective installation will leave only a small spot that must be sealed with high-quality caulk.

A special situation occurs when a chimney is positioned at or near the bottom of a roof slope. In such a case, a *cricket* or *saddle* should be installed at the intersection of the chimney's high side and the roof to divert and prevent water from rushing down the roof into or against the up-roof part of the chimney (Fig. 15.16).

A cricket also prevents leaves, twigs, and other debris, as well as snow and ice, from collecting behind the chimney, which can cause rain or snowmelt to back up beneath the shingles and leak through the roof. If the cricket is large and exposed to view, it should be framed, sheathed, and finished with the same shingles and flashing used on the rest of the roof. Smaller crickets unexposed to view can be covered with metal but still must be flashed at all joints with the roof and chimney.

FIGURE 15.16

A chimney cricket or saddle.

INSTALLATION

No matter how good a roof's materials are, the roof won't be able to do what it's supposed to do if the installation is shoddy. Here are some things to watch out for:

- The ice and water guard or similar underlayment, which is needed to protect your roof deck from ice damming and wind-blown rain, should be flexible, self-adhesive, and waterproof.

- A 3-inch galvanized metal drip edge eave should be installed nailed at least 10 inches on center. Roofing ice and water guard or a similar underlayment should go beneath this drip edge.

- All roofing felt should have at least a 6-inch vertical overlap.

- Ice and water guard, a water-resistant underlayment (see Fig. 15.2), provides superior roof deck protection and helps to prevent damage caused by freeze/thaw cycles, pooled water, wind-driven rain, and normal water flow that occurs around roof valleys, vents, skylights, and chimneys. It also should be installed under shingled roofing eaves to protect against water backup from ice dams and hard rain.

- When anchoring the underlayment and topping materials, power staple guns are the most economical way to go, *but* they don't do as sturdy a job as nails do. If your roofing is self-sealing asphalt shingles (shingles with glue underneath each tab that will stick to the shingle below it when baked in the sun), consider that it takes at least one and preferably two hot summers for them to "melt" together to form a strong bond. Until that time, staples will not provide the holding power of wide-headed nails. High winds are more likely to blow stapled shingles from a roof.

- Roofing nails must meet the shingle manufacturer's specifications to protect the shingle warranty requirements. At the very least, roofing nails will have very sharp points, flat head diameters, and length long enough for full penetration of the roof sheathing.

- All roofing nails should be nailed flush with shingles.

- When wood shakes and shingles are applied, the manufacturer's installation instructions must be followed exactly, especially regarding spacing and fastening.

- Because of the high asphalt content in asphalt and fiberglass shingles, it is recommended that temperatures be over 50°F when they are installed because they are susceptible to cracking in cold weather.

- Make sure that masonry and metal chimneys, skylights, and other obstructions are in place before the roofing begins. Otherwise, the roofers will have to make an extra trip to complete the remaining shingles and flashing at extra expense.

- All materials should conform to or exceed requirements of the local building code.

WATER DRAINAGE

Gutters and downspouts work together to collect runoff water from the roof and divert it away from the house so that foundation seepage can be prevented (Figs. 15.17 through 15.19). They can divert water away from foundations, plantings, decorative details, basements, siding, sidewalks, driveways, and roof edges while increasing the width of roof overhangs and helping to prevent snow and ice slides during winter. They're vital necessities in most cases but can be troublesome to maintain—tree leaves, seeds, and twigs tend to collect in them and clog the downspouts, squirrels and chipmunks use them as freeways and store winter food in them, and they can be damaged by ice that collects and hangs from their not-too-strong edges. Here are some important points to consider when planning gutters and downspouts:

1. The least-expensive gutters to buy are galvanized steel models, but they have to be painted before they can be secured to the fascia or rafter ends of a roof.

2. Another inexpensive option is to use unpainted aluminum. It's durable enough unless exposed to salt air near seacoasts or air laden with chemical contaminants. Even when no pollutants are present, however, this gutter should be painted for the sake of appearance.

3. Your other choices of gutter materials are much better: aluminum with factory baked-on enamel and aluminum covered with a thin layer of vinyl. Vinyl

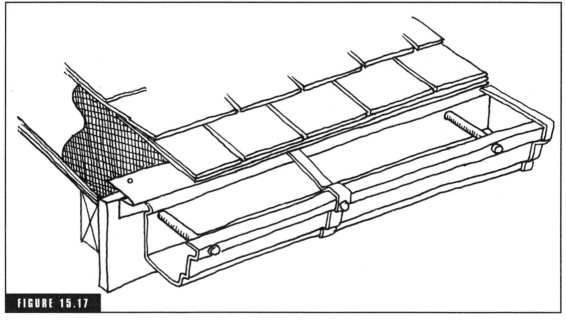

FIGURE 15.17

A roof drainage system.

gutters (solid vinyl) are also available. All three are in the long run durable, economical, and require little maintenance. Vinyl tends to be brittle in very cold weather, but it never requires refinishing because the color is integral to its form. Copper gutters are also available at substantially higher prices than the others.

4. Metals used in gutters and downspouts vary in thicknesses; 26-gauge galvanized steel is quite strong and common, but 24-gauge galvanized steel is stronger.

5. Cleaning gutters and preventing downspouts from getting clogged can be done easily if you specify removable caps or screens. Then you can just pop off the caps or screens when necessary and flush the small accumulation of silt from the gutters with a garden hose.

6. Gutters should be mounted on the fascia boards (especially when the fascia is not made of or coated with vinyl) so that the gutter backs are offset slightly, with an airspace between the fascia, so that the fascia surface will not deteriorate from lack of ventilation.

7. Large houses with great expanses of roof require that both the gutters and the downspouts have sufficient capacity to handle expected volumes of rainwater. While 5-inch gutters are common, 6-inch gutters may be required to handle roofs having very long spans.

8. A roof plane will collect water during any rainfall, especially if there is wind. The higher the roof ridge, the

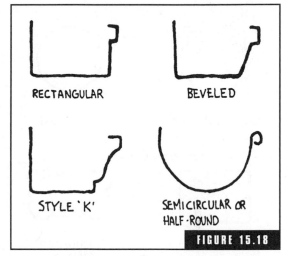

Metal gutter shapes.

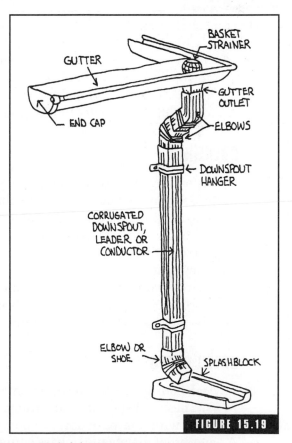

A gutter and downspout arrangement.

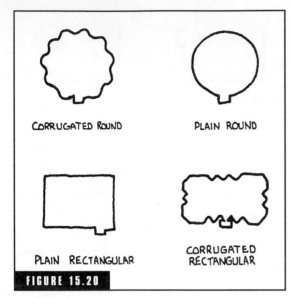

FIGURE 15.20

CORRUGATED ROUND

PLAIN ROUND

PLAIN RECTANGULAR

CORRUGATED RECTANGULAR

Standard downspout shapes.

more true roof area there is, and the faster water will race into the gutters. If you plan a steep roof, try to be generous with gutter sizes regardless of the roof area.

9. Gutter troughs are to be sloped toward downspouts approximately 1 inch for every 12 lineal feet.

10. Your downspouts may be rectangular or round and plain or corrugated (Fig. 15.20). In cold-climate locations when there is a possibility of standing water freezing in the downspouts, the corrugated type is preferable because it can expand without damage.

11. Downspouts are to be fastened to the wall every 5 to 6 vertical feet.

12. The water discharge can flow from the downspouts into drainpipes that run to storm sewers or to a natural runoff area, perhaps to the street or a storage cistern or rain barrel—as long as it meets building code requirements and does not run into the foundation or form a swamp on adjacent ground.

COLUMNS

Depending on the construction of your house, unsupported roof overhangs can protrude from the house a considerable distance. But beyond a certain point, they must be supported around the outer edges by columns (Fig. 15.21).

Although wood columns, except in very small sizes, are hollow, they still have the strength to bear a substantial load. The trouble is, they're so intricately made that they cost a fortune.

Factory-painted aluminum columns are the answer. They cost considerably less, are maintenance-free, and because they're hollow—made only of thin metal—they can be installed around a weight-bearing wood or steel post.

GREEN ROOFS

And here we really mean green roofs. They're living roofs, also called *grass roofs*. These are specially constructed installations of flat or gently sloped roofs surfaced with a layer of soil or other organic substrate in which plants can grow. A waterproof membrane or base supports the growing medium, and native grasses

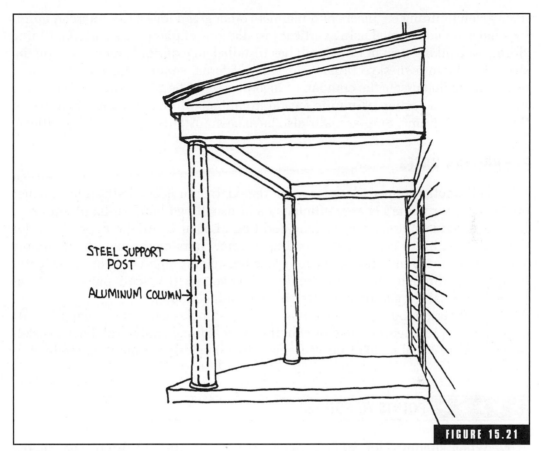

STEEL SUPPORT POST

ALUMINUM COLUMN→

FIGURE 15.21

A column.

or ground cover, wildflowers, and even low-lying shrubs and ground-clinging evergreen trees are planted. This is quintessential green! The plants, selected for their hardiness, require almost zero maintenance and will reduce rainwater runoff, take carbon dioxide out of the atmosphere, and return oxygen to the air. The plants also help to keep the roof cool in summer and provide—with the growing medium—insulating qualities during winter. Of course, not a lot of roofing contractors are installing them, but for professional contractors, they're not all that difficult to learn how to complete. Indications are that green roofs will make slow inroads into the roofing industry as home owners and builders start seeing more of them installed.

Other green roof benefits include reduction of noise levels, reduction of heating and cooling costs, increasing the useful lifespan of the building's entire roofing structure, filtering the storm water not used by the plants, and providing wildlife habitat for birds and beneficial insects. As a related point, the green roofs have given building engineers and planners other green ideas. Commercial buildings have already started using vertical installations of plants as a sort of building siding—a banking firm in Pittsburgh has installed an exterior "green wall" on the side of a downtown skyscraper consisting of ferns, sedum, brass buttons, and other plants that create the company's logo in green. The 2,380-square-foot living wall replaced a section of granite facade from the building and was anchored to the building's frame. Similar walls also have been installed in other large cities.

REMODELING NOTES

This is another opportunity for green remodeling projects that can have major effects on your home's energy efficiency and usually go hand-in-hand with roof framing remodels either through the addition of solar heating components—for the space heating of water or the heating of water coursing through the plumbing system for direct water heating or for space heating through water or other liquid heating—or through the installation of photovoltaic (PV) cell panels or thin-walled materials as part of an electricity-generating system.

For a lesser remodel, just selecting different shingles can have a major impact on energy requirements to heat or cool the home. Shingle color, thickness, installation, and material content all can affect how much solar energy is retained or reflected.

▶▶▶▶▶ POINTS TO PONDER

1. When shopping for roofing, pay particular attention to fire resistance, the severity of weather the roof will face, the roofing's life expectancy, and the roof's appearance.

2. It takes about the same time, effort, and cost to put on a low-quality marginal roof as it does to install one of the highest quality.

3. Roofing material should not be skimped on. The roofing market is competitive, and you'll usually get what you pay for. It's worth doing comprehensive reviews and inspections of a wide variety of materials and models.

4. Selecting premium roofing materials is almost always a wise decision. They not only last longer and provide better protection against the elements, but they'll also make your home look considerably more handsome.

5. If your roof is a complex one, with many dormers, valleys, and various planes, medium or dark roofing shingles will tend to pull the roof together in an attractive way.

6. Be aware that light-colored roofs reflect heat and are more desirable in areas where air-conditioning is the greatest energy user.

7. In colder climates, the reverse is true. Black absorbs heat from the sun, so a darker color is clearly the more practical choice.

8. The roof and attic must be assured of adequate ventilation to enable heat and moisture to escape.

9. Flashing is an important component of roofs. It belongs where different construction materials or planes meet, such as around chimneys, vents, roof valleys, and stacks, and when materials project horizontally almost anywhere from the surface of the house. Simply put, it prevents water, air, dust, and other materials from entering cracks and gaps in the roof and in the rest of the home's outer shell.

10. Be generous with large, quality gutters and downspouts that are appropriately selected to complement the appearance of both roof and outer shell.

FINAL INSPECTION

- Shingle pattern and color should be even and uniform from close up and far away.
- Shingles should fit tightly around all stack vents and skylights. Areas should be well sealed with an asphalt roofing compound.
- Shingles should lie flat with tabs sealed/glued down.
- Shingles should extend over the edge of the roofing deck by at least 3 inches.
- Shingles should match or exceed the required fire rating stated by the local building code.
- Vents and roof flashing should be painted the proper color with exterior rustproof paint.
- Check vents to make sure that they are not blocked with insulation or other obstructions.
- Make sure that adjustable attic and other vents and louvers work correctly.
- Downspouts should be secure so that a strong wind will not affect them.

Exterior Wall Finishing

The exterior wall covering is the single most dominant feature of a home's outer appearance; its color and texture are the first things noticed by anyone approaching the house. Good design calls for simple lines, common sense in the selection of materials, harmonious textures and colors, and good proportions and scale. A hash of materials such as a bit of stone here, some brick over there, with shingles and clapboards and stucco all mixed above will give the impression that the house is desperately trying to trick observers into liking *some* detail and more often than not will ruin the dwelling's appearance. On the other hand, there are so many different building products to select from when deciding on your new home's exterior that green choices are available for most of them.

Beyond its cosmetic nature, the exterior wall covering also acts as the final protective layer between a home's occupants and the great outdoors. More specifically, it is this outer "sandwich" layer that, along with its interior counterpart, envelops whatever insulation is chosen to help protect family members from temperature extremes and minimizes the need to import or purchase additional energy for comfort. Attached to the frame or masonry walls can be wood siding in various forms, brick, stone, stucco, aluminum and vinyl sidings, shingles of metal, asphalt, or plastic, and many other lesser used siding materials.

MATERIAL REQUIREMENTS

When selecting the material for your home's siding, consider how the following characteristics stack up against the materials in the running:

- Cost of the material

- Cost of installation labor, ease of handling by size, weight, and shape
- Resistance to natural weathering, chemical attack, and atmospheric pollution
- Resistance to scratching and impact
- Appearance of color and texture
- Dimensional changes resulting from temperature and moisture
- Resistance to moisture penetration
- Combustibility
- Sound insulation and absorption
- Strength under conditions of compression, bending, shear, and tension to carry applied loads and resist the pressure of wind
- Adaptability to future expansions and other modifications
- Susceptibility to insect damage

ALUMINUM AND VINYL SIDINGS

Aluminum and vinyl sidings are available in many different colors and shades, textures, and forms for both horizontal and vertical installation. When used alone or in combination with each other to cover exterior wood surfaces, they'll practically eliminate the need for future wood refinishing and painting chores. These sidings also can help to provide additional thermal and sound insulation when installed over polystyrene or similar backer boards. When choosing exterior siding, look for maximum-length panels to minimize seams that allow for air infiltration.

Indeed, recent manufacturing innovations enable many sidings to have wood-grain finishes or textures that look and often feel just like painted wood, smooth "clear" cedar, cedar shakes, weathered cedar, teak, or fir, roughsawn barnboard, and other varieties. All feature sturdy locking mechanisms so that individual panels will resist wind and weather. For example, horizontal siding panels generally interlock where they overlap, as do the panels of double 4-inch, double 5-inch, and triple 3-inch clapboard, plus double 4½-inch wood-grain shiplap (Fig. 16.1).

Aluminum Siding

Aluminum siding is a low-maintenance exterior wall covering that won't rust in the ordinary sense. Its baked-on finish lasts for 20 to 40 years depending on the grade purchased. Aluminum siding won't rot, split, warp, or crack. It's manufactured in a wide variety of colors and shades from light pastel tints to whites to deep rich tones and comes in numerous textures and finishes—some resembling wood siding. The difference in price and insulating qualities is small, but if you're planning top-notch construction that calls for aluminum siding, opt for the

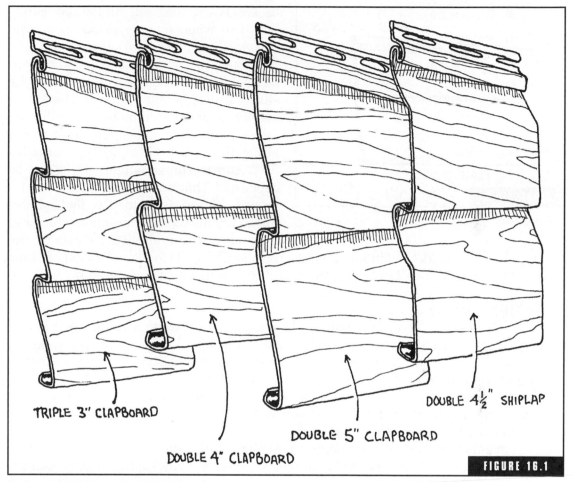

TRIPLE 3" CLAPBOARD

DOUBLE 4" CLAPBOARD

DOUBLE 5" CLAPBOARD

DOUBLE 4½" SHIPLAP

FIGURE 16.1

Horizontal siding types with wood grain.

thicker gauge because it's stiffer and holds up better to abuse. The width of the horizontal type of aluminum siding is a single panel of 8 inches or "double-four" panels that are essentially single panels, each having a horizontal crease across the middle so that it resembles two 4-inch-wide lengths of clapboard (Fig. 16.2). There are also clapboard-like panels with 5- and 9-inch exposures and two beveled edges to give the appearance of two strips of bevel-edge siding.

For vertical applications, aluminum siding is available in many of the same colors and finishes as the horizontal panels, so the two materials can be mixed and matched on the same dwelling. The vertical siding comes in 10-, 12-, and 16-inch-wide board and batten strips, as well as in V-groove and other styles.

There are several drawbacks to aluminum siding that you should know about. First, unless reinforced by being installed directly over a stiff polystyrene or Styrofoam

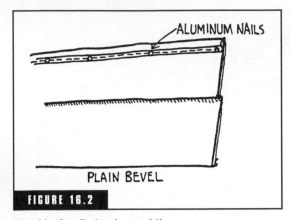

FIGURE 16.2

"Double-four" aluminum siding.

backer board material, aluminum siding will dent when soundly struck by a baseball, rock, or other hard object flung by a neighbor's 10-year-old son. Second, the surface color can be scratched off, exposing the silvery bare aluminum beneath. Third, bare aluminum exposed to industrial pollutants and seacoast environments can react gradually with airborne chemicals in a negative way. And fourth, aluminum siding can be expensive. This is so because the cost of aluminum siding is naturally tied almost directly to the cost of aluminum, which can fluctuate considerably owing to overall supply and demand. Conditions involving wars, tariffs, or the industrialization of China and other nations all can have dramatic effects on the price of aluminum.

Vinyl Siding

Vinyl siding is another popular low-maintenance wall covering that's manufactured essentially in the same forms as aluminum siding. As with aluminum siding, vinyl can be backed with a polystyrene or other board reinforcement to give the siding both a strong base and an insulating R-value (especially when also backed with several layers of house wrap). A major advantage to vinyl siding is that the color is molded throughout the entire thickness of the material, so a scratch will do little damage (Fig. 16.3).

Neither will vinyl siding dent; it's resilient nature allows it to spring back into shape after all but the most violent blows. Look for a vinyl siding that's a double-thick 0.088-inch rolled-over nail hem design that increases wind resistance and stiffens the panel. Such a design may withstand wind load pressures of up to 180 miles per hour when installed with nails and up to 235 miles per hour when installed with staples.

This siding panel should feature a true 0.044-inch thickness for outstanding strength and durability. Most modern vinyl sidings have one-step panel-locking systems for secure installation and perfect horizontal or vertical alignment. In addition, the color goes clear through the vinyl, so scratches won't show, and a special sunshield technology is often used to protect the surface from harmful ultraviolet rays.

Drawbacks to vinyl are that it's inclined to buckle or ripple if not installed exactly correctly, and it's not as readily adaptable as aluminum is to cover unusual or unique exposed wood trim.

No matter which type of aluminum or vinyl siding you select, make sure that the contractor correctly applies caulking around the doors, windows, and corners—

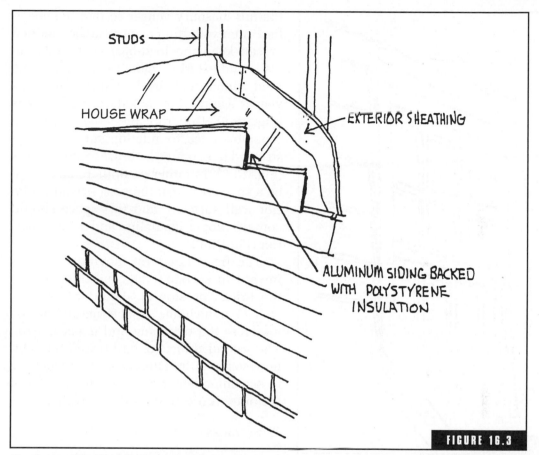

STUDS

HOUSE WRAP

EXTERIOR SHEATHING

ALUMINUM SIDING BACKED WITH POLYSTYRENE INSULATION

FIGURE 16.3

Aluminum siding installed with backer board.

wherever the siding forms a seam across its grain or meets with different building materials (Fig. 16.4). The contractor also should use aluminum nails for fastening the siding materials to exterior walls. Aluminum nails won't rust and form unsightly streaks.

MASONRY EXTERIOR WALL COVERINGS

Masonry exterior walls of brick and stone have always held a certain attraction for individuals who prefer the beauty, feel, and apparent strength of brick and stone construction. Masonry also enjoys an intangible prestige value that houses sheathed with wood, aluminum, or vinyl sidings seem to lack.

It's true that brick and stone sidings are more expensive than most other exterior wall coverings mainly owing to installation costs. To use brick or stone, a contractor must either move exterior walls inward 5 or more inches to allow space for

FIGURE 16.4

Caulking around a window.

the full masonry veneer so that the specified outer wall dimensions can be retained or can keep the load-bearing foundation walls and exterior walls true to their specified dimensions by installing the brick veneer against the outside of those walls (Fig. 16.5). To permit the latter method, a separate outer foundation must be constructed to support the brick or stone walls (Fig. 16.6). In either case, there also must be a space between the masonry and interior wall surfaces, and this space should contain proper insulation and a vapor barrier (Fig. 16.7).

The first choice (of moving the walls inward to accommodate the thickness of the bricks or stones) should require no change in the home's roof structure, particularly to the overhang and exterior trim. The second choice (of building out) might, however, require alterations in these areas to accommodate the wider dimensions of the outer limits to the exterior walls.

ADVANTAGES

1. Brick and stone make beautiful, unique exterior wall coverings.

2. They hold onto their looks indefinitely, with little maintenance.

3. Brick and stone houses historically have held their value well and have enjoyed good resale demand.

4. They're durable and have a reputation of permanence.

5. Because of their strength, they don't "sway" as much in the wind as wood-sided homes and will not develop as many interior plaster or drywall cracks and imperfections as in less rigid nonmasonry dwellings.

6. Their resistance to fire is excellent.

7. They help to reduce exterior noise.

DISADVANTAGES

1. Brick and stone add considerable extra expense to the purchase price of a house.

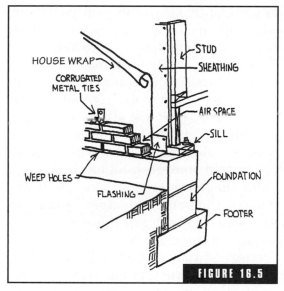

Masonry/brick construction.

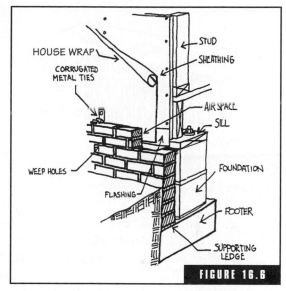

Masonry/brick construction on supporting footer.

2. It's difficult and expensive to make modifications to the exterior walls or additions to a structure. Removal of part of an old wall is expensive, and matching up the brick for the new wall can be difficult.

3. Brick and stone have low insulating values. Despite popular belief, even the thickest masonry offers exceptionally poor insulation properties, which is why masonry houses seem particularly cold and are hard to heat. Consequently, the proper amount of exterior wall insulation must be insisted on regardless of the type of brick or stone used.

Brick

Brick makes a very attractive exterior, with numerous colors and textures available. All of one color can be used, or a mottled effect can be had by using many different shades or colors in the same surface. The best way to arrive at what you'd like is to take a drive through neighborhoods that have plenty of brick homes. A few color snapshots of what most appeals

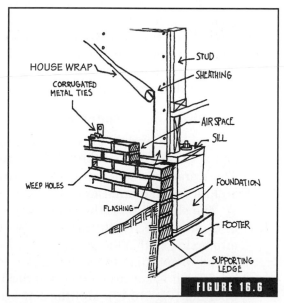

A space between the brick veneer and frame wall.

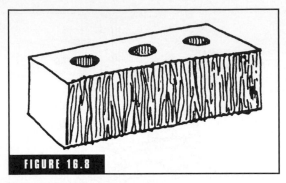

FIGURE 16.8

A textured brick.

to you can be handed to your contractor, who will be able to tell you where those bricks can be purchased or ordered.

It should be noted that most bricks are manufactured with holes in their centers. When mortar is applied to the bricks, some of it fills those holes and provides additional bonding strength when dried. If the top of any bricks need be exposed, enough solid bricks without holes should be ordered along with the others. The same principle applies to textured bricks, where typically only one side—the exposed side—is textured (Fig. 16.8). When bricks need to have a textured surface exposed on two, three, or four surfaces, special bricks that are textured all around will have to be ordered. Remember that a brick wall will cover a structure but won't support it. The stud wall provides the support. Instead, metal anchors tie the brick wall to the frame wall.

Make sure that the contract specifies that the masons must finish the job by cleaning the brick with the brick manufacturer's cleaning solvent. Muriatic acid can stain brick.

Stone

Stone also makes an attractive exterior that's durable and practically maintenance-free. It has most of the advantages and disadvantages of brick.

Stonework is usually more costly than brick. In general, stones cut with rectangular corners are used more commonly for covering exterior walls. Rubble or fieldstones having irregular shapes and no corners can be employed in a feature wall for dramatic effect to create a rustic appearance.

Openings in Masonry Exterior Wall Coverings

Given the weight of brick and stone, door and window openings require special supports to hold the brick or stone securely in place above those openings. There are three common ways to provide such support: steel lintels, curved brick arches, and flat brick arches.

The steel lintel is the simplest to install (Fig. 16.9). It consists of "angle iron" of appropriate length that overlaps the top of the door or window opening on either side so that the weight of the brick or stone above the opening can be transferred to and distributed throughout the adjacent masonry structure. The curved brick arch is constructed of standard size and shape bricks or stones to span the opening (Fig. 16.10), and the flat brick arch is formed with specially cut bricks (Fig. 16.11).

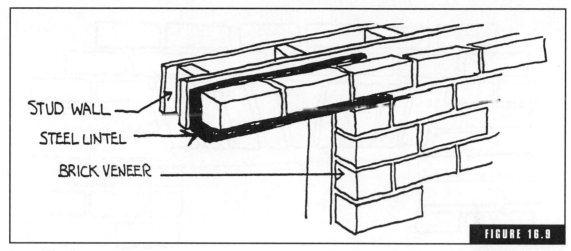

A steel lintel.

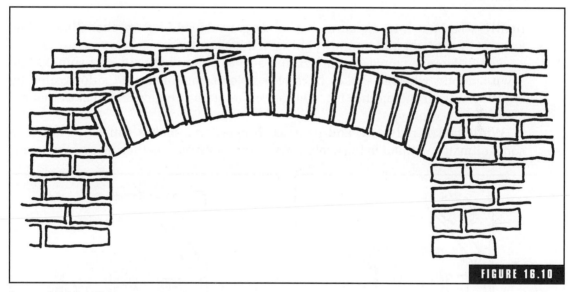

A curved brick arch.

WOOD SHINGLES AND SHAKES

Wood shingles and shakes are usually made of cedar but can be made of red-wood or cypress (Figs. 16.12 and 16.13). Cedar shingles or shakes are used as siding when a home buyer wants an eye-catching rustic appeal to the home and a "warm" siding that's naturally resistant to decay and is an excellent insulation. Cedar has a golden brown color when new that gradually darkens with age and

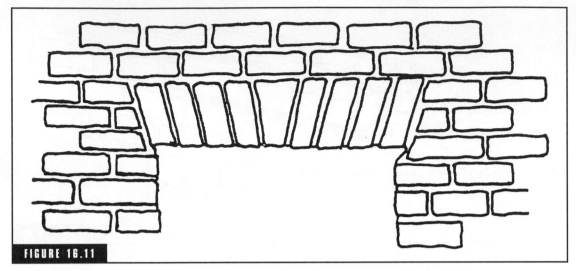

FIGURE 16.11

A flat brick arch.

finally weathers into an attractive silver-gray depending on the climate (the amount of sunlight and humidity) in which it's located.

The difference between shingles and shakes is that both sides of shingles are sawn smooth, whereas shakes have at least one rough-textured side created by splitting it from the mother log. These are the same shingles and shakes that are also used for roofing.

While cedar, redwood, and cypress shingles and shakes can be installed in some climates without being coated with preservatives, weathering everywhere is

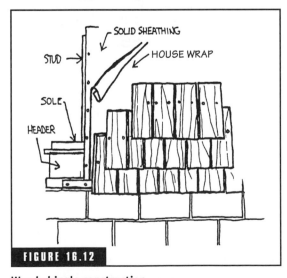

FIGURE 16.12

Wood shingle construction.

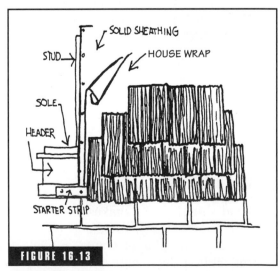

FIGURE 16.13

Wood shake construction.

best controlled by applying recommended weatherproofings every 5 or 6 years. Pressure-treated Southern yellow pine is also an acceptable substitute, when available.

The best wood shingles and shakes are free from knots and pockets of pitch. You can tell the difference between the best and lower grades by the wood grain—it should be regular and clear with few or no defects.

Drawbacks to wood shingles and shakes include their cost: They're expensive and time-consuming to apply. Unless you opt for shingles and shakes prefabricated into 8-foot panels, each shingle or shake must be hand nailed into place, one at a time. They're also susceptible to fire.

Only nonrusting nails that provide sturdy holding power should be used to fasten wood shingles and shakes to the walls. Common nails won't hold well enough and will rust and streak the siding.

Formed or Molded Plastic and Metal "Cedar" Shingles

Some molded shingles that look like wood are available in vinyl, polypropylene, and other plastic materials. Models include both half-round shingle panels and "full perfection" shingle panels. While offering the look of real wood, these panels are practically free from splitting, warping, cupping, twisting, fading, or streaking. They also need no painting or repetitive surface protection. The panels typically are about 0.100-inch thick with ribbed backer components that add structural stability. These molded shingles hold up well in rainy, windy, and coastal climate locations, especially when backed with reflective building foil (Fig. 16-14). Another option is metal prepainted and finished panels made to look like wood shingles. They supply the look without the maintenance hassles and are completely recyclable. Green features of these nonwood sidings are in their durability, low maintenance, and the way they prevent mature trees from being cut up for shingles, shakes, and planks. When the entire life cycles of wood and nonwood sidings are compared, the nonwood versions often seem more eco-friendly.

SOLID WOOD SIDING

Almost any type of wood can be used for solid plank siding, including such species as cedar, redwood, fir, cypress, pine, spruce, and hemlock. Redwood siding in particular is very durable. It resists deterioration from the weather and from insects. Unpainted redwood surfaces will darken season by season to a deep grayish brown.

Solid wood siding comes in many styles for horizontal and vertical application, including beveled, dropped, and beaded planks for horizontal sidings and V-groove, tongue-and-groove, board-and-batten, and channel vertical sidings (Figs. 16.15 through 16.17).

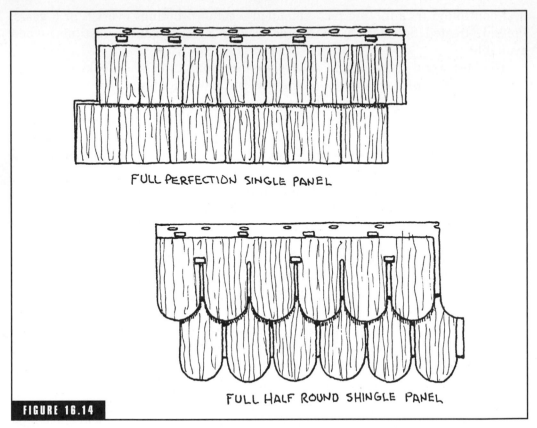

FULL PERFECTION SINGLE PANEL

FULL HALF ROUND SHINGLE PANEL

FIGURE 16.14

Molded "cedar" shingles.

Beveled horizontal wood siding is probably the most popular of all solid wood exterior wall coverings because it so nicely complements most styles of architecture. It consists of long boards, available in varying thicknesses and widths, that have beveled edges and are tapered to exaggerate the deep, long horizontal shadow lines at the lower edges of the planks, which help to provide character to a dwelling's appearance. The individual boards usually are installed over a sheathing and building paper, nailed through them to the exterior wall studs. Corners are covered with either metal corner pieces or wood corner boards (Figs. 16.18 and 16.19). The thickness of the corner boards should be at least 1 inch to provide a substantial caulking base. The old-fashioned clapboard siding that once covered (and still covers) many a home consists of wood planks of uniform thicknesses.

All solid wood sidings should be weatherproofed with water-repellent treatments, oils, varnishes, preservatives, or exterior paints and other coatings that will have to be renewed periodically as needed. A vapor barrier beneath the wood siding is also required to prevent condensation from within the home from causing paint to peel and wood to rot.

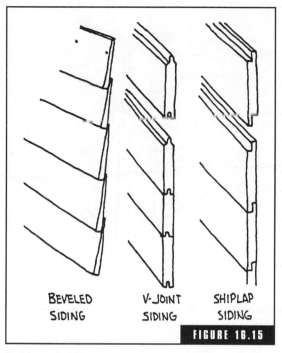

BEVELED SIDING   V-JOINT SIDING   SHIPLAP SIDING

FIGURE 16.15

Solid wood siding.

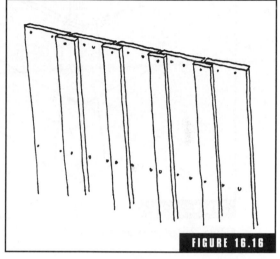

FIGURE 16.16

Board-and-batten wood siding.

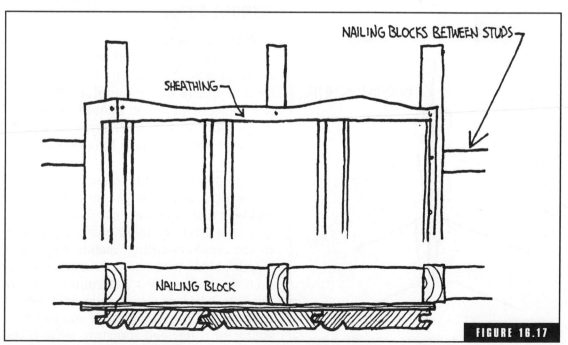

NAILING BLOCKS BETWEEN STUDS

SHEATHING

NAILING BLOCK

FIGURE 16.17

Vertical application of wood paneling.

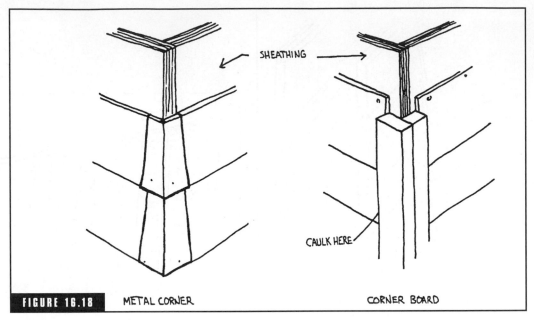

FIGURE 16.18   METAL CORNER   CORNER BOARD

SHEATHING

CAULK HERE

Siding corner construction.

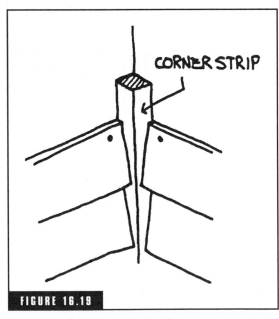

CORNER STRIP

FIGURE 16.19

Siding interior corner construction.

PLYWOOD SIDING

Plywood siding can be supplied in many varieties of wood and patterns at varying costs (Fig. 16.20). Check with your local suppliers to see samples. Only exterior types of plywood should be considered—those having their layers of veneer bonded together with a tough waterproof glue.

Plywood panels are manufactured in 4-foot widths and 8- to 12-foot lengths that, owing to their size and ease of installation, help to hold down labor costs. If you plan to use plywood siding, match the correct length panels to the requirements of your home to have as few horizontal joints as possible because such joints will detract from the overall appearance and can be a source of water and moisture leaks if the panels are not installed correctly. Because

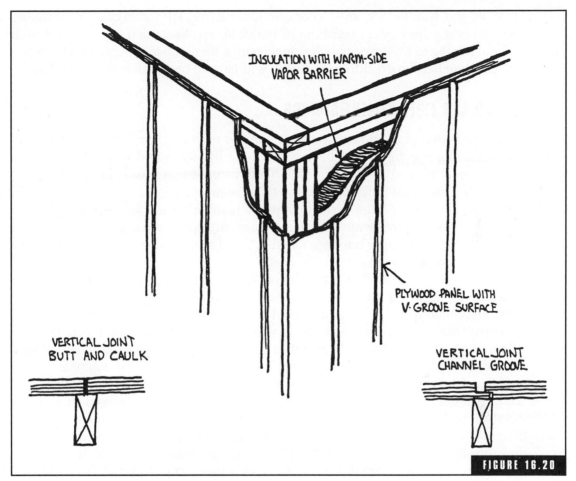

Plywood panel vertical application.

of its strength, plywood siding is sometimes applied directly to the wall studs without the use of an underlayment sheathing.

HARDBOARD SIDING

Some hardboard sidings are manufactured panels consisting mostly of wood products. They come in more finishes and textures than plywoods but are not as strong.

On the positive side, factory-made hardboard sidings are free from natural defects. Their panels are stiffer and less likely to warp or bend. Both the texture and depth of wood are presented in authentic-looking wood grains and grooves. The better hardboard or wood fiber sidings are over 50 percent denser than real wood planking and won't crack, split, check, or delaminate. They also can be purchased primed—ready for custom finishing in multiple lap sheets that are easy to install without having to nail narrow individual boards. Remember, though, that even factory-finished hardboard sidings probably will have to be refinished eventually.

STUCCO AND FIBER-CEMENT SIDINGS

Stucco is that plasterlike material so popular with English Tudor construction. It's an excellent exterior finish, having a long life span and needing very little maintenance. It's really a version of portland cement that's troweled on like plaster to either masonry or frame walls with no seams or joints. It's usually made in white but can be colored with any paint manufactured for application over masonry. There's also a wide selection of pigments available that can be added to the stucco mix. If deeper hues are desired, the stucco can be painted in the same fashion as concrete block.

Stucco can be applied as a finish coat to both existing houses and new construction. It can be finished to give a number of interesting textures to conform with traditional or modern architectural styling.

Three coats with a total thickness of about ¾ inch generally are recommended. When stucco is applied over the sheathing of a wood-framed house, a layer of stucco wrap can be placed over the sheathing. Stucco wrap is a type of engineered construction fabric or membrane (also see Vapor- and Air-Infiltration Barriers). Stucco wrap creates a drainage path for water and moisture to escape. It will take water and moisture that may enter the walls from the interior spaces and around windows, doors, and other joints and channel it outside. It thus helps to prevent water and moisture from harming the sheathing, framing, and insulation—which can cause expansion and contraction, leading to stucco fractures and cracking.

Stucco wrap is also good at managing the hydration process of the stucco material during curing. The scratch, or first, coat will not absorb water from the other stucco coats because, again, the stucco wrap channels the water and moisture toward the outside. Because the scratch coat will not absorb extra water, it won't expand and contract much during curing. The result is a dramatic reduction of cracking in the scratch coat. This helps to create a strong, stable stucco, with each layer drying at a similar rate, front to back. A white stucco wrap is often preferred because it won't absorb much heat from the sun, and the cooler surface further extends the stucco drying time so that cracking is even less likely. Fewer stucco cracks makes a more solid, energy-efficient exterior wall.

Next comes the application of metal lathing nailed to the exterior wall. The lathing should be self-furring or should be applied with self-furring nails. The most important point in the application of stucco is that the scratch coat of material must be pushed through the metal lathing and behind it to form a solid layer between the lathing and studs or sheathing.

Where stucco is applied over large uninterrupted areas, control joints should be installed to permit expansion and contraction of the stucco material. Without these control joints, the stucco will crack. As a general guide, control joints are planned for at least every 3 feet of travel.

The second coat is applied over the scratch coat (the first coat) after allowing sufficient time for the first coat to dry. And finally, after the second coat has dried, the third and finishing layer is applied with whatever pattern you have selected—smooth, stippled, swirled, or other (Fig. 16.21).

When applying stucco over masonry, the finish coat can be troweled directly on the block or concrete. Make sure that exterior outlets and fixtures aren't accidentally covered, and ask about the stucco warranty. Strong stucco will better withstand building movement, wind pressure, and other stresses.

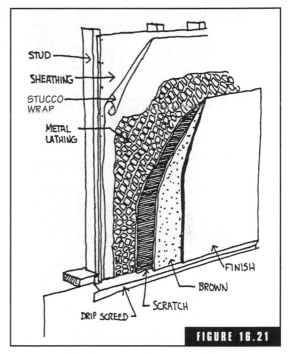

Stucco application.

Fiber-cement siding panels, often in 4- by 8-foot pieces, can mimic the look of stucco. These heavy siding panels are low-maintenance products that wear incredibly well. Fiber-cement siding comes in a variety of sizes and styles, and even though its manufacture is somewhat energy-intensive, it more than makes up for that energy by lasting for years and years with very little maintenance effort along the way.

VAPOR- AND AIR-INFILTRATION BARRIERS

It was apparent decades ago, since the 1950s, that builders needed to protect their houses from the harmful effects of unwanted air drafts and moisture. Back then, they used tar-impregnated paper and similar building papers and sealing materials.

The living areas between the exterior walls should be sealed with appropriate material applied to the inside of the walls to prevent the movement of unwanted air and moisture from the outside in and also from the inside living areas into the exterior wall insulation and outer wall coverings (Fig. 16.22).

To reinforce why vapor- and air-infiltration barriers are needed, it's been estimated that the typical home can have close to a half mile of undesirable cracks

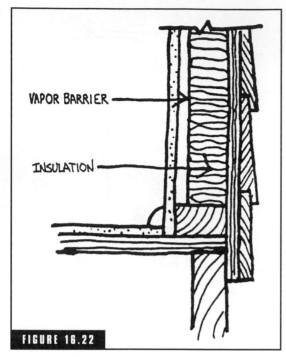

VAPOR BARRIER

INSULATION

FIGURE 16.22

A vapor barrier view.

and crevices in its outer shell that can let out warm air during winter and cooled air during summer. In addition, unwanted moisture that enters walls can lead to mold, mildew, and rot. Wall moisture originating from within a building sometimes can be more damaging than outside moisture penetration.

Daily activities within a household such as showering, cooking, washing clothes and dishes, and even breathing produce moisture vapor that needs to escape. Again, without proper vapor barriers, as the temperature increases within a home, inside water vapor is transmitted into walls, where it condenses. This condensation results in a wetting of structural materials and a loss of the insulating qualities of exterior walls. It also gives rise to such serious problems as chemical, physical, or biological deterioration of the wall materials and promotes corrosion of metal, spalling of brick, and rotting of timbers.

House wrap—an engineered construction fabric or membrane—can be used on the outside of a wall, against some wall sheathings, to protect the sheathing from water and moisture. If installed properly, exterior house wrap placed over certain exterior sheathings can improve comfort and energy efficiency and will protect against moisture and water damage.

Installed over wood or certain insulation sheathings and under siding or other exterior coverings, house wrap provides a protective barrier that helps to seal against leaks and drafts (air infiltration) yet lets moisture that may have been generated inside the living areas escape. It "breathes" similar to a high-tech rainwear fabric that prevents water from entering yet allows perspiration to evaporate to the outside.

On the other hand, as some manufacturers of rigid sheathing panels point out, if their panels are properly installed, there should be no air leaks through cracks or seams (or very few air leaks). If this is true, they say, then additional installation of house wrap over those panels actually may create harmful conditions by trapping eventual residues of wood starches from siding materials and from cleaning detergents that may become trapped within the house-wrap fabric (thus plugging the fabric meshing so that it can no longer breathe).

In many other situations, though, house wrap works hand in hand with insulation. Using a clothing analogy, the home's insulation traps air in tiny pockets (like a thick cable-knit wool sweater does) to slow the transfer of heat, whereas house wrap functions like a Gore-tex windbreaker does, when layered over the wool sweater. Where used properly, house wrap thus should cover or seal

- Gaps between sheathing pieces or panels
- Joints between the sill plate and subfloor along exterior walls
- Gaps in drywall or plaster board and top and bottom wall plates
- Where framing members meet in an outside intersection and form a crack
- Around window and door frames
- Electrical and plumbing penetrations through top and bottom wall plates

An effective house wrap design resists tears in all directions and stands up to windy conditions with good tensile strength. Also, it should enable condensation to evaporate or drain away from the house sheathing. Around windows and doors, house wrap can be used in the sill rough openings before a window or door is installed. A straight flash wrap is available for straight heads and jambs of windows and doors to effectively seal gaps. House wrap tape is manufactured for taping house wrap seams, tears, and openings such as holes and open spaces around electrical boxes, venting ducts, and similar construction components and materials. Before deciding on a vapor/air-infiltration system for your home, at least be aware of the various strategies, and discuss them with your builder. In some cold and cooler locations, the vapor barrier works best when facing the inside of a heated space. Homes in hot and humid climates should have their barriers installed against the outer wall surface, before the siding goes on. Never rely on building wraps to be the only defense against air infiltration. Other building techniques, including paying close attention to all joints and transitions from one construction material to another and all pop-outs or small sections that push out from the main wall planes, must be done correctly to prevent drafts from reducing the home's insulation capabilities.

Make sure that the particular house wrap or rigid panels are compatible with the planned siding. For example, certain cedar and other wood siding may need special add-ons to enable the siding to breathe from both sides. Consider that many new products are in the process of coming to market, so carefully research their pros and cons, and then consider your house style and the weather conditions in your locale. It's far less expensive and a much simpler process to design the barrier system for installation during construction than to try to upgrade or change systems at a later date.

Insulating batts in the exterior walls should have a vapor barrier backing such as treated kraft paper with the vapor barrier on or toward the living-area side. If blown-in insulation or unfaced insulation is chosen, aluminum foil–backed drywall can be used, or friction-fit or other types of insulation can be applied after polyethylene sheet material is stapled or nailed to the interior of the wall studs and ceiling joists. The polyethylene film should not be less than 3 mils thick.

INSULATION

Underneath the sheathing and exterior wall covering, between the studs, one of the following types of insulation generally will be used:

- *Batts or blankets.* These are prepared thicknesses of expanded glass, mineral, or organic fiber that are placed in the walls between the studs. They should be faced (having a vapor barrier on one side) in order to hold their form well.

- *Blown in or poured.* This is composed of loose expanded mineral or organic fibers that are placed or blown into frame spaces. This material is more useful for insulating existing buildings when it would be impractical to completely remove the inner or outer wall sheathings. On the down side, blown-in or poured insulation may settle eventually and lose some of its insulating value.

If you choose to use vinyl or aluminum siding, remember that polystyrene and similar backer boards can be used behind the siding panels to provide extra insulation as well as added strength.

This leads us to another recent product development that's become especially pertinent in this time of rising fuel costs—*exterior rigid foam insulation.* Exterior rigid foam insulation is made of extruded polystyrene or similar material that has an R-value of about R-5 per inch of product thickness. It contains literally hundreds of millions of densely packed air cells. Since air is one of nature's most effective insulators, the sheer volume of this compressed trapped air gives this insulation exceptional thermal performance. It also prevents air infiltration and resists moisture penetration.

In some cases, these panels can be installed over exterior sheathing (as long as the total vapor/air-infiltration barrier system isn't overengineered to prevent at least some healthy "breathing"). For example, a cost-effective way to achieve a R-19 wall system is to install 1-inch extruded polystyrene foam insulation to the exterior sheathing of a 2- by 4-inch wall cavity filled with R-13 fiberglass insulation. Exterior sheathing, siding, and interior drywall typically provide an R-value of R-1. A 2- by 6-inch wall cavity filled with fiberglass insulation will give an even greater R-value. The exterior layer of foam insulation also will help to reduce road noise, will help to prevent air infiltration, and will increase comfort through less radiant heat loss because the entire mass of the wall structure is covered.

Again, when dealing with barrier products, it's important to have a strategy that manufacturers and builders will somewhat agree on so that the combination of several different products will work in your favor—and will not inadvertently cause moisture or air-circulation/breathing problems.

ENERGY-SAVING OUTDOOR PAINT

Many of these paints use microscopic insulating ceramic spheres in their composition to help create a sturdy reflective, radiant barrier to ward off the sun's heat, especially in white and lighter shades of color. They also protect against moisture and provide an excellent choice when sealing joints and narrow cracks and spaces around vents, trim, and fastening devices.

Paints with insulating ceramics resist stains, corrosion, mold, and mildew and can be scrubbed clean, help to deaden sound, and are effective in hot and cold climates. They can be applied with brush or roller and are simple to use for touch-up tasks. Table 16.1 lists insulation values of sidings.

TABLE 16.1. Insulation for Resistance Values of Siding Material

Material	Thicknesses, Inches	Resistance Rating
Airspace	¾ or wider	0.91
Aluminum foil (sheet type with ¾-inch airspace)	—	2.44
Blanket insulation	3	11.10
Common brick	4	0.80
Cinder block	8	1.73
Concrete	10	1.00
Concrete block	8	1.00
Gypsum board	½	0.35
Insulation board	1	3.03
Plywood	⅜	0.47
Roofing roll vapor barrier	⅛ to ¼	0.15
Sheathing and flooring	¾	0.92
Shingles	—	0.17
Stone	16	1.28
Wood siding	¾	0.94
Window glass (single)	—	0.10
Window glass (double)	—	1.44

FIGURE 16.23

Dryer vent.

INTAKE/EXHAUST HOODS

Request that the siding contractor provide waterproof maintenance-free hoods in colors that match your siding for dryer and other intake/exhausts. Dryer vents and exhaust fans should have dampers that open and close freely. These seals between vents and walls must be tight when needed, and should also be able to be disconnected and opened in order to vacuum the piping from the outside (Figs. 16.23 and 16.24).

MOUNTING PLATES

Color-matching mounting plates for mailboxes, hose reels, electrical outlets, coach lamps, and other lights and fixtures usually are available in vinyl and plastic. While these may sound like "small" details, they can all contribute to a handsome exterior—without ungainly distractions caused by mismatching hardware (Fig. 16.25).

ILLUMINATED HOUSE NUMBERS

Many police, paramedic, or fire department personnel will tell you about the amount of time lost trying to locate a house for an emergency call at night when the home's address numbers are not readily identifiable. Consider asking the con-

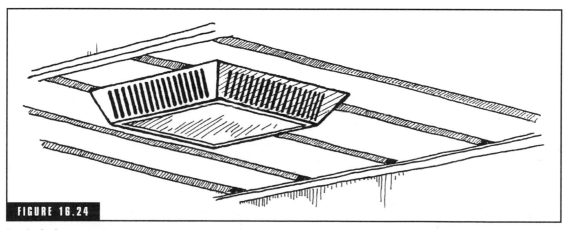

FIGURE 16.24

Intake/exhaust vent.

tractor to quote on a decorative low-voltage address number fixture.

Such fixtures are inexpensive to operate and easy to read, day or night. They're made from maintenance-free vinyl or plastic products that also come in colors to match the siding (Fig. 16.26).

AWNINGS

There's something old-fashioned about a good set of fabric awnings. Maybe it's the additional level of privacy they provide when installed over windows, doors, decks, or patios. Or maybe it's the additional color they add or their ability to be adjustable. They also protect—to a certain extent—against rain, wind, and sunlight. In fact, canvas and other fabric awnings

FIGURE 16.25

Hose faucet mounting plate.

block out or absorb up to 99 percent of the sun's harmful ultraviolet rays and can reduce the amount of sunlight and glare passing through windows by as much as 94 percent. Awnings thus can reduce heat gain through windows—up to 77 percent on eastern and western windows.

Awnings also will protect indoor furnishings such as carpeting, curtains, and furniture from sunlight fading while keeping the inside environment cooler with lower air-conditioning costs. On the down side, awnings eventually wear out. They'll need maintenance and eventual replacement as well as routinely being put up and taken down, depending on seasonal weather patterns; this could raise safety issues, especially with second-story installations. One possible answer to durability concerns is that of rigid awnings, awnings constructed of aluminum, plastic, or composite materials. Especially where snow and ice are not issues, rigid awnings can provide many of the advantages of their fabric cousins and can be left in place year-round.

There are many types and styles of awnings. Consider these features if you decide to investigate their use on your home:

■ Do the units require minimal maintenance?

■ Are they self-storing?

FIGURE 16.26

Illuminated house number.

- Is the awning material resistant to ultraviolet light, mildew, and water?
- Is the awning operated with a manual crank or motorized?
- Is it an under-the-eave mount or flat-wall mounted?
- Does it have stainless steel or other hardware that will not rust or deteriorate?
- Are there oil-impregnated bearings so that there's no need for lubrication?
- Do the units have strong, lightweight, rustproof frames with a baked enamel finish?

VENTILATION GABLES

Ventilation gables can be critical to planning for sufficient air movement into an attic or other "open" space beneath upper reaches of the roof. Air movement will help to remove dampness and hot air, thus helping the insulation and lumber there. Some manufacturers offer copolymer construction gable vents with ultraviolet-stabilized colors molded throughout and fully screened for insect, bat, and bird protection. These units can be installed on all types of exteriors, including wood, vinyl, aluminum, stucco, hardboard, stone, and brick.

SIDING GENERAL CONSIDERATIONS

- It's a good idea to view the work of masons the builder is planning to use on your siding. Ask to see recent completed projects whether they're in brick, stone, or stucco.
- Decide if you want a matching stone or brick mailbox or light posts on either side of the driveway or walk before masonry siding is applied.
- It should be stated in the contract that the builder should see that only Occupational Health and Safety Administration (OSHA)–compliant scaffolding is used for all elevated work.
- The exterior siding contractor also should quote on any wrought iron railings needed.
- The exterior siding contractor should figure in trim around the doors and windows and at the corners of the home. Flashing must be installed at the head and sill of all door and window openings. Trim should be securely fastened and well caulked wherever needed. Request tinted caulk that matches the color of the siding.
- House wrap fastened over plywood will help to keep out wind and water. Flashing at the base of the wrap will help carry off water from the wall, and

weep holes between bricks, stones, or in the vinyl or aluminum siding will allow water to escape.

■ Wood siding should clear the ground surface for less chance of wood-boring insect damage and decay from moisture.

■ The agreement should specify if any brick, stone, shingle, or shake siding must be treated with water repellent after the siding has had sufficient time to "dry out." For example, the contractor should not paint right after installation of wood but should wait until the wood has a chance to dry. If it shrinks after being coated, that will leave unpainted strips of wood where the pieces overlap.

■ No matter which siding you plan to use, ask the contractor to hand pick the best material for the front and back of the home, where appearance is most important.

■ See that only exterior, nonrusting fasteners are used in all siding applications.

■ Nails must be driven flush or countersunk.

■ All laps of siding must be parallel, and all joints should be staggered between courses.

■ All porch lights, fixtures, outside outlets, phone, cable, electric service holes, and faucet hose bibs should be neatly sealed against the siding.

REMODELING NOTES

As part of the home's exterior wall system, the outer siding plays a major defensive role between the elements outdoors and living spaces inside. Consider an insulated siding that includes a rigid foam insulation layer that's fused behind the exterior surface of the siding panel. A number of exterior siding layers, including vinyl, aluminum, and others, come with the insulated backing. Correctly installed, such insulated siding panels are fit in place without air gaps that otherwise can increase heating and cooling demands. These sidings are especially effective when additional insulation is desired for older homes having narrow walls without much between-the-wall space because they can add another R-3 to R-4 of insulating value to what's already there. With newer homes where greener framing techniques have not been used, insulated siding helps to negate the presence of bridging through wooden wall studs that otherwise could make up almost 25 percent of the exterior wall surface's backing. Again, an analysis of heat loss makes sense, and the new exterior wall finishing often must be done in tandem with new insulation and air/moisture layer planning.

> > > > > **POINTS TO PONDER**

1. The exterior wall covering is the single most dominant feature of a home's outer appearance; its color and texture are the first things noticed by anyone approaching the house.

2. Good design calls for simple lines, common sense in the selection of materials, harmonious textures and colors, and good proportions and scale.

3. A hash of contrasting materials, such as a bit of stone here, some brick over there, and shingles, clapboards, and stucco all mixed together can lend an unattractive garish look to the dwelling—even though individually those sidings are quite attractive.

4. Brick and stone are more expensive than most other wall coverings mainly owing to installation costs. But they do make beautiful, unique exteriors, hold their looks indefinitely, need little maintenance, and have reputations for durability and helping home resale values.

5. Although cedar, redwood, cypress, and pressure-treated Southern yellow pine shingles and shakes are sometimes installed in hot, dry climates without being coated with preservatives, weathering everywhere is best controlled by applying the manufacturer's recommended weatherproofing every few years.

6. Only nonrusting fasteners should be used to attach exterior wall siding to prevent unsightly rust leaching and staining.

7. Stucco is a plaster-like material so popular with English Tudor construction. It provides an excellent exterior finish that has a long life span and needs very little maintenance. It's really a version of portland cement that's troweled on like plaster to either masonry or frame walls with no seams or joints.

8. The vinyl, aluminum, and related siding industry is constantly engineering improved materials. Do a thorough review of these sidings before making a final decision. Consider the material's appearance, as well as its ability to resist dents and scratches, to hold its color and resist fading, and to provide insulation value. Again, it costs about the same to install an inferior material as it does to put up quality siding.

9. After you decide on what kind or kinds of siding you want, select only high-quality siding(s) and sealing caulks.

10. If your home is being constructed near others, consider how the appearances of those neighboring dwellings may affect or limit your own siding (and roof) selections. In other words, it's prudent to consider the appearance of your home within its setting.

Stairs

Who can forget the dramatic confrontations in *Gone with the Wind* between Rhett Butler and Scarlett O'Hara on a huge, spectacular staircase—the dominating structural feature of the Deep South estate of Tara? And what about the shrieking panic of Martin Balsam in Alfred Hitchcock's *Psycho* as he tumbles backward away from the murderer—down a stark wooden flight of stairs?

No doubt, staircases are custom-made for grand entrances and exits. At the same time, stairways can be convenient and dangerous, healthy and harmful, attractive and ugly, space-saving and space-stealing. They're less expensive and much more practical than elevators, escalators, or other people movers, and they enable us to make better use of small building sites by permitting several living levels to be positioned one atop another. Staircases can be made of wood, metal, stone, concrete, or any combination of green construction materials having the strength to do the job.

Some people view staircases as unfortunate necessities, whereas others consider them works of art. On the green side, stairways don't have quite the range of possibilities or implications enjoyed by other home design and construction components. They require a certain amount of energy to be climbed or descended, although it's sustainable energy considered to be healthy for most people—a source of exercise. Given their potentially open nature, they can be positioned almost anywhere and not be in the total way of interior sunlight and ventilation. The materials the stairs are constructed with can be one or more types—recycled or new steel, wood, engineered wood, or any product that qualifies as a green material. Of course, their design could employ less material—stringers and open treads, for instance.

Because stairways generally are found as complete units, with each part intact, they make excellent candidates for reclaiming and recycling. Staircases and steps built with old-time craftsmanship have been disassembled and moved from vintage homes, stores, doctor's offices, churches, and schools to be reinstalled as architectural focal points in numerous commercial and residential structures. It will take some research and looking, but used building material entrepreneurs in your area may be able to do the looking for you. They frequently hear about upcoming demolitions and may be able to broker a staircase reclamation to fit your home and construction schedule. Sometimes the railing will be the best and only reusable part of a vintage set of stairs. If so, it's a wonderful way to showcase recycled wood, and it will provide a special feature to be enjoyed for decades. Such rails are available from various demolitions, but they may be hard to come by when needed and typically must be scrounged well in advance.

Again, if possible, place stairways where they do not block or screen intended sunshine or where they do not block the flow of ventilation, air or makeup air, or trap it into stale pockets. Consider the traction levels afforded by the treads, and avoid slippery material. If wood treads are new, use Forest Stewardship Council (FSC)–certified products. Avoid substrates and carpeting with formaldehyde and high–volatile organic compound (VOC) backing, binders, and adhesives.

Light is important for stairs. Design for natural light when available, supplemented with energy-efficient electric fixtures.

A *stairwell* is the term for a shaft or opening through one or more floors of a house in which a staircase is constructed or placed. A completed stairway consists of the following (Figs. 17.1 through 17.3):

- *Stringers*—diagonal or circular supports for the steps
- *Treads*—the horizontal upper surfaces of individual steps, the part your foot steps on
- *Risers*—the vertical pieces between the treads (Some basement stairways don't have risers but are wide open between the wooden treads.)
- *Handrails*
- *Newel posts*—the posts at the top or bottom of a flight of stairs that support a handrail or the central upright pillar around which the steps of a winding staircase turn
- *Balusters*—any of the small posts that support the handrail of a railing (In olden times, these were frequently elaborate woodwork. Latter-day balusters, railings, and posts are more likely to be black wrought-iron or simple wooden handrails attached to the sides of the stairwell walls.)

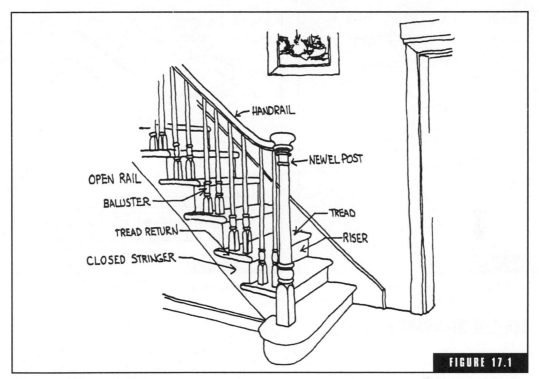

FIGURE 17.1

An open main stairway.

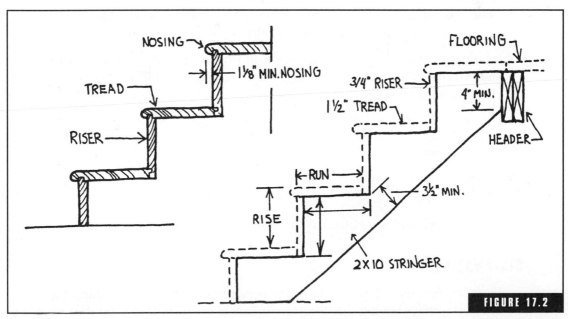

FIGURE 17.2

Staircase parts.

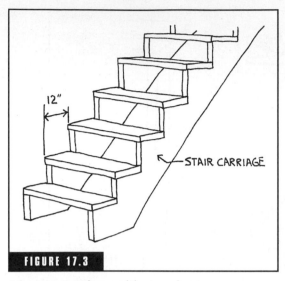

FIGURE 17.3

A basement stairway with open risers.

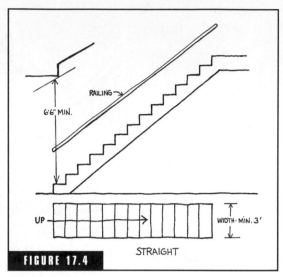

FIGURE 17.4

Stairway dimensions.

GENERAL STANDARDS

1. *Stairway angles.* In staircase design and construction, you'll find a rise and run similar to that of a roof's slope. The angle of a stairway is determined by the arrangement of the tread depths and riser heights.

2. *Stairway treads and risers.* For safety's sake, all treads should be equal and all risers should be equal in any one flight.

3. *Stairway widths.* Main stairways should be at least 3 feet wide, clear of the handrail(s) (Fig. 17.4). A basement stairway can be slightly narrower, with a minimum clearance of 2 feet 10 inches.

4. *Stairway landings.* The minimum dimensions for a regular stairway landing is 3 feet square. For safety, landings must be level and free from intermediate steps between a main up flight and a main down flight.

5. *Stairway framing support.* This is the required vertical structural framing built to support all stairways from underneath.

Table 17.1 provides a checklist for interior stairways.

STAIRWAY TYPES

There are four basic types of staircases used in modern houses: straight stairways, L-shaped stairways having a landing or winders at the turn, U-shaped stairways having a landing or winders at the turn, and spiral staircases (Figs. 17.5 and 17.6).

TABLE 17.1. Checklist for Interior Stairways

	Minimum	Best Quality
Vertical rise	7½ inches	6½ inches
Horizontal run	10 inches	12 to 14 inches
Tread width	36 inches	48 inches
Railing	Firm	Solid
Baluster spacing	10 inches	6 inches
Number of landings	0	2
Natural lighting	Fair	Excellent
Artificial lighting	Fair	Excellent
First-floor foyer	Skimpy	Generous
Second-floor stair hall	Skimpy	Generous
Two-story-high walls	2	0

Straight

Straight stairways are by far the stairways used in most house construction today.

ADVANTAGES

1. They cost the least to build.
2. They're the easiest to carry bulky items and materials on.

DISADVANTAGES

1. They're dangerous. If someone happens to trip at the top, a fall all the way to the bottom could result. Small children especially must be protected from them.
2. They're tiring to climb because there's no space to stop and catch your breath.
3. They're not very attractive.

L-shaped and U-shaped

Both these stairway types were used frequently during past decades when individual carpentry efforts were more predominant than today's prebuilt and space-saving methods.

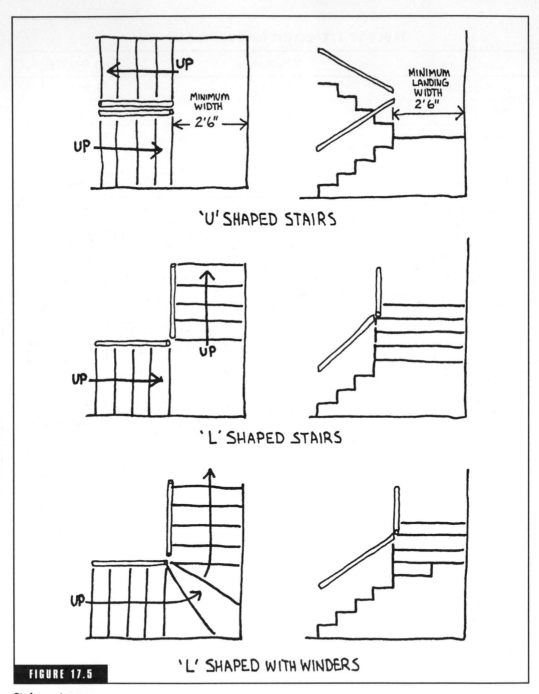

'U' SHAPED STAIRS

'L' SHAPED STAIRS

'L' SHAPED WITH WINDERS

FIGURE 17.5

Stairway types.

ADVANTAGES

1. They have landings to rest on to catch your breath.

2. The landings provide good spaces to hang decorations or art.

3. They can be so attractive as to add character to a house.

DISADVANTAGES

1. They're more difficult to work into a house's floor plan.

2. They're more expensive to build.

3. They make it harder to carry large items such as bedroom furniture up and down. This is especially true of narrow U-shaped stairways.

Spiral and Circular

Only people thoroughly familiar with spiral staircases should plan them into their houses.

ADVANTAGES

1. They save space. Spiral stairways can be installed where you cannot possibly fit conventional stairs.

2. Because they're rarely enclosed, they serve as attractive decorative units that generally become focal points of the rooms they're in.

3. They're good for outdoor use to provide access to second-story balconies, decks, and regular rooms.

DISADVANTAGES

1. The treads are not full depth at both sides. If you fall from the top you can tumble a long way. Most people aren't used to them. Spiral stairways require a different gait to ascend than to descend; visitors unaccustomed to them might find this a nuisance.

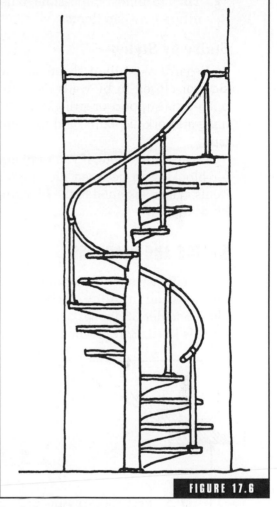

FIGURE 17.6

A spiral staircase.

2. They're almost impossible to use for moving large items such as bedroom furniture between floors.

Stairway Styles

Regardless of their shape, stairways can be open on both sides, open on one side, or closed in by walls on both sides. The most attractive seem to have one open-type support or stringer. In this way, at least one wall provides a surface to hang artwork or plants, and the stairway still looks and feels spacious—even if it isn't.

As an added note, if you're planning to use stairwell walls as a gallery, arrange for blocking in between the studs while the wall is being erected. Then heavy items can be fastened to the blocking if need be and not just into the weaker plaster or drywall.

WIDTHS AND HEADROOM

A staircase should be wide enough so that two people can pass each other on the steps and furniture can be transported up and down with a minimum of trouble. Consider 36 inches as a minimum width to be safe; 42 inches, if space permits, is ideal. Extra inches are especially handy if a staircase is closed or makes a turn and involves winders as in the L- and U-shaped types. If wider, they're a lot easier to maneuver large pieces of furniture on.

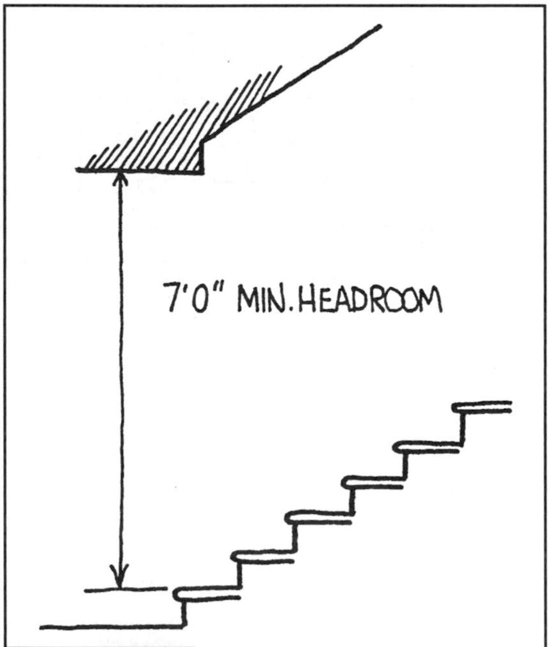

The stairs also should be plenty deep for a good step. Twelve to 14 inches deep for individual treads is both the maximum and ideal range. The headroom between any part of the tread on any individual step and the nearest vertical obstruction should not be less than 7 feet, preferably 7 feet 6 inches (Fig. 17.7).

RAILINGS

Stairway railings can be fun to think about. Should you have a flashy brass rail? Or maybe an intricately carved wooden one? Then again, maybe it would be better to put up a half wall and top it off with a nice modern slab of sanded-smooth oak with a great round finial (ornamental post

7'0" MIN. HEADROOM

FIGURE 17.7

A stairway's minimum headroom.

top) at the bottom to keep youngsters from using the rail as a slide. Above all, a railing must be sturdy. Although local building codes must be followed or exceeded, they often define *sturdy* as being able to support a weight or push of 200 pounds at any point along the rail.

Stairway railings can add a lot to the safety and decor of your home, so keep the following in mind:

- Stairways should be equipped on each side with permanent and substantial handrails 36 inches in height from the center of each tread. Narrow stairs can get along with one rail, but wide stairways should have two.

- The railings should be continuous from floor to floor, even when there are landings.

- All handrails should have rounded corners and a surface smooth and free of splinters.

- Since you're going to need some kind of railing(s) anyway, you might as well use railing that adds to the attractiveness of your home.

FOLDING AND EXTENSION STAIRWAYS

Folding or extension stairways are widely used for necessary and convenient access to attics, finished living quarters, or out-of-the-way closet storage spaces (Fig. 17.8). Some models, especially the wider ones, have handrails on both sides. These are preferable.

Many of the narrower models, with only a single handrail, are best installed to drop down along an adjacent wall, if possible. The use of these stairways also saves the floor space of the room or area below the device, which allows for freer planning. Most folding or sliding extension stairways come completely assembled for installation in a prepared opening and are attached to a ceiling door so that you just have to reach up and pull them down. The two most popular types are rigid extension units that slide up and down parallel with their pull-down door and three-section units held together with hinges. When not in use, the hinged sections fold up into a compact bundle that's stored on top of the closed door.

FIGURE 17.8

A pull-down extension staircase.

Although these setups provide a somewhat less sturdy means of access than access gained by permanently fixed stairs, the folding and extension models are not used as frequently and are the better choice for top-level spaces.

The folding units fit into homes with floor-to-ceiling heights of 7 feet 6 inches to 8 feet 9 inches. Rigid extension stairways are available in many more sizes ranging from 7 feet 6 inches to over 16 feet.

All folding and extension staircases that fold or slide up into unheated areas such as attics must not be overlooked when it comes to insulation and air infiltration. The door of a pull-down stairway should be hinged on one side of the frame and equipped with latches so that, when closed, the door can be snugly pulled against a rubber seal to prevent drafts.

Insulation to match the other parts of the attic floor then should be placed on top of the door and around the sides of the frame. Caulking compound can be applied around the seam at the juncture of the door frame and subfloor.

EXTERIOR STAIRWELLS

Exterior stairwells that lead from basements and lower living levels directly to the outdoors face special problems that are solved by construction specifications that are different from those used for inside stairways (Fig. 17.9).

1. Exterior stairwell sidewalls normally are formed with poured concrete or concrete blocks.

2. The steps are practically always made of poured concrete.

SAFETY POINTERS

BASEMENT STAIRS

Given the "hard" nature of typical basement staircases, coupled with the fact that they usually lead to a plain concrete floor, take extra precautions to safeguard them from babies, toddlers, and other young children. Consider the use of a closure on the basement door, one that slowly shuts the door after someone goes through, similar to the setup on a storm door. To remain effective, the unit should also have a cylinder that can hold the door open if something needs to be transported up or down the stairs. Another feature to arrange for is plush-type padded carpeting at the bottom of the basement stairs securely fastened to the floor or placed with nonslip backing so that it won't pose a tripping hazard. If someone accidentally slips down the stairs, the plush carpeting at the stairs' bottom will help to soften the impact.

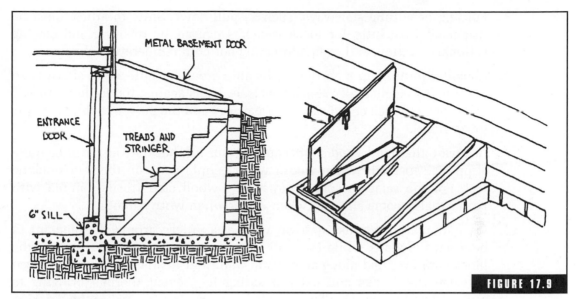

Outdoor basement stairs.

3. The entrance doors, single or double, can be wood but should preferably be steel with a wood center or core. These composition steel/wood doors hold up very well against moisture in all climates.

4. The bottom of an outside stairwell should be lower than the basement to prevent a direct flow of water into the house. A 6-inch sill is standard, with a stairwell drain installed to convey excess water into an appropriate drainage area.

▷▷▷▷▷▷ POINTS TO PONDER

1. Although stairway appearances are important, they're not as important as stairway safety. Safety considerations should come first with stairways.

2. Main stairways should be at least 3 feet wide.

3. Stairs should be plenty deep for a good step. Twelve to 14 inches deep for individual treads is an ideal range.

4. The headroom between any part of the tread on any individual step and the nearest vertical obstruction should be between 7 and 7½ feet.

5. There should be at least one sturdy handrail on each stairway.

6. Stairways must be well lit, with lighting controls at the top and bottom of each stairway.

7. Folding or sliding stairways, such as pull-down units to attics, must be inspected frequently for loose fasteners caused by opening and closing actions, vibration, and even alternating hot/cold temperature changes.

8. Consider putting up a barrier in the attic around a pull-down stairway so that no one accidentally steps, kneels, or leans against the folded stairway from above (which could cause the stairway and the person to tumble to the lower floor).

9. Be aware that hardwood stairs can be beautiful, but they also can be quite slippery, especially when wet or when people walk on them in stocking feet. For the same reason, avoid having wood stair treads painted with paints that become slippery when wet or when worn smooth.

10. If you're planning to use stairway walls as a gallery, arrange for blocking in between the studs while the wall is being erected. Just make sure, if the blocks are installed along an outside wall, that insulation board is placed between the blocks and exterior siding to prevent thermal bridging to reduce heat loss or gain. Then heavy items can be fastened to the blocking if need be and not just into the weaker plaster or drywall.

Windows

Imagine a house without windows, and you're likely to conjure up some prison-like dwelling or subterranean earthen home constructed into the side of a hill. Windows, large and small, perform many important functions in the typical home. First of all, they are one of the most recognizable features of a house. Their design and position in outer walls play a major role in helping to create a dwelling's first impression. Inevitably, we are drawn toward windows—especially windows lit from the inside at night—with the hopes of seeing what's inside. Second, during the day, windows provide natural lighting. Third, they admit fresh air for ventilation and allow oxygen-depleted used air to be expelled. They also provide access for passive-solar-heating sun rays and openings in the house's outer shell for air-conditioning units. From within the house, they enable the occupants to attain a visual continuity with the outdoors and provide exits to the outside in emergencies. After the construction of efficient outer walls and roofs containing healthy types and amounts of insulation, windows (and doors) have the next greatest influence on energy demands for space heating and air-conditioning.

Since windows make up between 12 and 20 percent of a home's outside wall area, they must be as efficient as possible to help contain conditioned warm or cool air. Another general window measurement describes a home's ratio of window area to heated floor area: 12 to 15 percent seems to be tops; otherwise, the home may lose too much heat or gain too much heat through its glass. Although windows are unlikely ever to be as energy efficient as a properly constructed and insulated outer wall, they do supply offsetting benefits such as passive-solar heat gain, natural lighting, and ventilation. The goal toward maximizing window efficiency is to recognize the best types of windows to position in their correct sizes, numbers, and locations.

In a nutshell, four main factors are critical to a window's energy performance: effective installation techniques, frame construction, the glass, and the spaces or material that separates or is placed between individual panes of glass.

GENERAL CONSIDERATIONS

When planning for and selecting windows for your house, keep the following points in mind for each potential window candidate:

- *Insulating and anti-air-infiltration properties.* Some windows types give inherently "looser" fits. You need to weigh various convenience and security factors as well.

- *Rain and snowmelt leak prevention.* Your brand new windows might not leak when they're installed, but as a house settles and ages, slight cracks can open between the window framing members and siding, or even between one pane and another, or an edge seal. One way to prevent eventual leaks is to have the window installers include what's known as pan flashing—really, a mini-gutter that prevents water from entering on the bottom and sides of a window.

- *Ease of operation.* Who will be living in the home? Someone who lacks hand, wrist, and arm strength? Will the windows need to be opened and closed frequently to be cleaned or to function as part of a natural ventilation system?

- *Necessary maintenance.*

- *Ease or difficulty to clean.*

- *Its style and how it will fit in with your overall exterior scheme.*

- *Price.* A cheap window could cause a loss of any initial savings through consequential increases in heating, cooling, and maintenance costs.

DRAWBACKS

As with any other feature in a house, windows also can have their drawbacks:

1. Large expanses of glass increase heat loss during periods of cold temperatures and become a source of unwanted and at times uncontrollable solar heat gain during warmer months.

2. In the summer, windows not only let the hot sun in to make the inside of a house uncomfortably warm, but they also permit sunlight to fade the color from carpeting, paneling, furniture upholstery, and practically anything else.

3. In addition to providing views that might not always be pretty, windows can turn a house into a goldfish bowl by enabling outsiders and strangers to see into the interior living areas.

4. Windows require a fair amount of washing—a chore no one enjoys. Every now and then a child's softball smashes through one or a limb from a nearby tree gets blown too close, and they must be replaced.

5. Windows are the first surfaces in a house to fog up when the interior humidity rises. They can stream with condensation, which might ruin the finish on the sills.

6. Windows can admit annoying neighborhood noises.

7. When not secured properly, windows provide encouragement to burglars and intruders.

8. Windows become ugly black mirrors from inside when you turn on the lights at night.

9. Windows require expensive curtains, draperies, and blinds that also need periodic cleaning.

10. If not carefully and tastefully selected and located, instead of improving the appearance of a house, windows actually can detract from it.

11. Problems include heat loss, overheating through solar gain, and poor sound-proofing.

WINDOW RATINGS

Because windows come in so many types and sizes, ways to rate them were developed to help home designers, architects, and engineers make appropriate selections. Thermal performance was a chief concern of the National Fenestration Rating Council (NFRC), a nonprofit hybrid public-private organization mutually put together by manufacturers of windows, skylights, and doors. The NFRC licenses manufacturers to display certification labels on windows that qualify with energy-efficiency performance features expressed in ratings such as U-factors and solar heat gain coefficients (SHGCs). Other listings reference information about glazing coatings as well as the manufacturer, model, style, and materials used in the window's construction.

Since the quality and energy efficiency of windows continue to improve, the desirable basic window is somewhat of a moving target.

U-Factor or U-Value

You already know that R-value is a measure of a material's or product's resistance to heat or cold (lack of heat) transfer and that it's one of the ways that energy efficiency is measured for insulation products. The higher the R-value, the greater is the material's resistance to temperature change. Windows have a similar measure called *U-values*, which measure, instead of resistance, the opposite process—a window's rate of heat transfer from within the home to the outdoors. U-values are expressed as the inverse of R-values. In other words, to arrive at U-values, simply divide 1 by a material's R-value. This comes into serious play when the temperature inside the house is considerably warmer than the temperature of outdoor air, as it often is during winter in many northern locations. In such cases, the lower the U-value, the better, and the greater the window will block the transfer of heat. A plain, single pane of glass has a U-value of about 0.90. Common U-values range between 0.20 and 1.20 (the value actually can be worse than a single pane of glass if you count an inefficient frame and poor insulation). High-tech, superinsulating three- and four-pane windows can have a U-value of 0.15 and lower. Modern double-pane windows typically run between 0.30 and 0.50. The greater the amount of window square footage you plan for your home, the greater is the need for window efficiency. For minimum levels of performance, insist on U-values below about 0.32. In very harsh climates, for window and door insulation levels, look for U-values approaching 0.18. For skylights, look for U-values between 0.50 and 0.35, depending on the locale's temperature ranges. Remember, the U-value is the inverse of the R-value, or 1 divided by the R-value. For the latest specific information on U-values recommended for your location, check the Energy Star Web site. Given all the attention energy-efficient windows have been receiving lately, the minimum values continue to be adjusted downward as new technological advances are made.

Remember to consider that the window frame material and design also contribute to a window's performance. Aluminum frames without thermal breaks (between outer and inner frame material) are about the least efficient when it comes to U-values. Aluminum frames with thermal breaks are a lot better. Next in efficiency come many windows made of wood and vinyl combinations, and some of the best, most efficient frames are being made from insulated vinyl and fiberglass. But you should be able to compare the offerings by reading their NFRC rating stickers.

Solar Heat Gain Coefficient

The *solar heat gain coefficient* (SHGC) is a simple measurement of how well the window will block the sun's heat as it tries to enter the home. It's expressed as a number ranging from 0 to 1, and the lower the number, the better. This means that windows with lower SHGC ratings are better insulators. A window with an SHGC of 0.35 means that 35 percent of the heat reaching the window is able to pass through the glass. With this knowledge, you can determine which windows are better for your location. When you want high levels of heat to enter through windows, such as in cold northern locations, choose windows with higher SHGC ratings, especially for the southern side of the house, to allow the low-winter sun entry during the coldest months of the year. In the same home, the use of lower-SHGC windows on the west and east sides can help to avoid too much heat gain during the summer months. Conversely, in climates where cooling is more important that heating, windows with lower SHGC ratings are favored. A plain, single pane of glass has an SHGC of about 1. This number is greatly reduced for high-tech window assemblies, which have been shown to be lower than 0.07. Lower SHGC-rated windows can reduce air-conditioning needs considerably when used in homes located in warm climates. In general, look for windows with a minimum SHGC level of about 0.25. Because windows with different SHGC ratings are available, the various windows planned for your home can be "tuned" exactly for each particular geographic location and orientation depending on each window's location and use. This means that one kind of insulating window can be used on one side of the house, and a different insulating window can be planned for other sides, resulting in an overall coordinated window strategy. For example, windows that can easily transmit solar energy should be installed on exterior walls having southern exposures in cold-winter climate locations. Because of the sun's low angle in the sky during winter, more solar heat reaches inside when needed, and when not needed—during hot summer months—it's not as readily admitted in the same windows because the sun travels higher overhead and cannot reach inside with the same low-angled success. If heat gain is more of a problem, say, in hot, arid climates, windows located on west and east walls should be able to block most of the heat from those positions. In any case, one kind of window rarely fits all purposes on a single dwelling.

Air Leakage

Air leakage (AL) is another important window measurement. When designing a home's thermal envelope, unwanted air leakage is a critical factor to heating and cooling calculations. This is typically where older homes lost a lot of heated or cooled air, through gaps and cracks around poorly designed and poorly installed windows. Today's windows, as a class, are leaps and bounds beyond older versions when it comes to efficient sealing. AL values generally range between 0.1 and 0.3, meaning the number of cubic feet of air that passes through a square foot of window area when the window is fully closed. An AL value of 0.2 means that $\frac{2}{10}$ of a cubic foot of air passes through cracks in the window assembly per square foot of window.

Condensation Resistance

Condensation resistance (CR) measures a window's resistance to the formation of condensation on the inside surfaces and is expressed as a number between 1 and 100, with higher numbers equating to greater resistance to condensation.

Visible Transmittance

Visual transmittance (VT) identifies the see-through quality of the glass, measuring how much visible light enters a window when the sun is shining through. Like some of the other measurement values, it is expressed as a number between

0 and 1, indicating the percentage of available light that comes though the window. Lower numbers mean that less light is transmitted. Many windows are rated between 0.25 and 0.85, meaning that between 25 and 85 percent of the available light is allowed to pass through the window. Windows with high visible transmittance are easy to see through and admit plenty of natural daylight. The VT in residential windows ranges from a shady 15 percent for some tinted glass up to 90 percent for clear glass (the higher the number, the clearer is the glass). To most people, glass with VT values of 60 percent or more looks clear. Any value below 50 percent begins to appear dark and/or reflective. Besides giving you a nice view, high-VT windows can save energy in certain conditions because you'll need less artificial illumination. But can you have your high-tech insulated glass and see through it too? Not all the time. Some tints and coatings that block heat also reduce visual transmission, so make sure that you actually *see* and *look through* any special glass you may be considering before specifying it for your home.

WINDOW TYPES

When selecting basic window types for today's modern houses, you can employ two or three or more types as long as they look nice together. At the same time, you can combine one type of movable window with a fixed window or even with another type of movable window in the same opening. The tightest sealing and most energy-efficient window types, including casement, hopper, tilt-turn, and awning windows, use long-lasting compression-type weather-strip seals.

Casement Windows

A casement window is a miniature version of a hinged door, except that it's opened and closed with a crank or lever mounted on the inside of the window sill (Fig. 18.1). Thus you don't have to disturb a screen or additional storm sashes, which might be mounted on the inside—although add-on storm windows and screens also can be installed on the outside of casement windows. A latch locks each sash tightly.

ADVANTAGES

1. Because of their method of operation, casement windows are ideal for installations behind counters and hard-to-reach or difficult-to-move furniture. Wherever you can't stand right next to the window for leverage or can't reach the entire window owing to its high placement, you won't be able to comfortably position a double-hung window and should opt for the casement.

2. They offer excellent sealing against air infiltration when they latch against compression weather stripping.

3. Depending on the particular design, interior and exterior surfaces can be cleaned from inside the house.

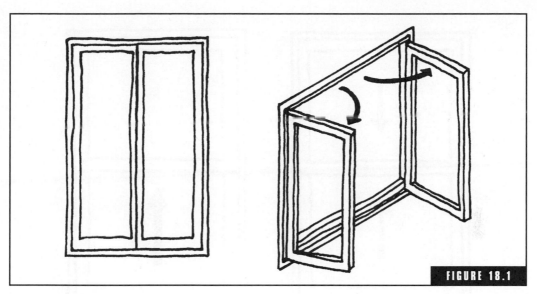

FIGURE 18.1

Casement windows.

4. Since the entire sash opens, a casement window admits 100 percent of an available breeze.

5. Casement windows can be outfitted with automatic openers.

6. Casement windows are effective for scooping up breezes and directing them inside.

DISADVANTAGES

1. You have to carefully consider where you locate casement windows in relation to outdoor activities. They shouldn't open out onto terraces, porches, decks, or sidewalks where people can bump into them.

2. Because the screens or storm windows are fastened to the inside, they hinder fast exits through the window openings if necessary during a fire or other emergency.

Double-Hung Windows

These are the most common windows found in construction today. The double-hung window has two sashes or panes that slide up and down in channels or tracks called *stiles*. As a rule, the sashes are the same size, but in some cases, the bottom sash is taller than the top sash. The two sections are held in place by either springs or friction. If held by friction, this is a sign of a good, tight fit (Fig. 18.2). Look for models with ventilation limit latches that enable the windows to vent in a partly open position, for recessed tilt latches that allow easy window cleaning access, and for a sloped sill for rainwater runoff.

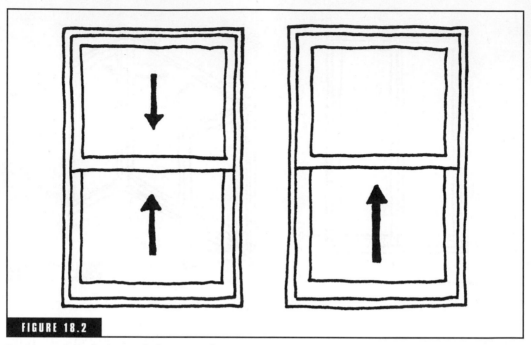

FIGURE 18.2

Double- and single-hung window operation.

ADVANTAGES

1. Because they're held firmly in place, double-hung windows rarely warp or sag.

2. Unless they're painted shut, double-hung windows are simple to open and close as long as you can stand directly adjacent to them for good leverage.

3. Relatively little air leakage occurs around the edges.

4. They can be cleaned from the inside if the sash is removable. The older models had pulleys and weights suspended within the walls to help the windows open and close—they had to be cleaned from the outside. Some modern double-hung window sashes can be popped out of their stiles to the inside for convenient cleaning and replacement.

DISADVANTAGES

1. If you will have to reach over a counter or piece of furniture to open and close them, double-hung windows will be difficult to operate and shouldn't be used.

2. These windows can never open to more than half their total area.

3. Even when they're open only an inch or two, double-hung windows are likely to admit hard-driven rain.

4. If the sashes aren't removable, the only way to clean them is from the out-side—with a ladder when they're located on second-story levels.

Single-Hung Windows

Not as popular as its double-hung cousin, the single-hung window looks exactly like the double-hung unit but differs in that the single-hung window's top sash is fixed. It can't be moved. Only the bottom half of the window can be screened.

ADVANTAGES

1. Because half this window is sealed shut, there's somewhat less maintenance and less chance of air leakage.

2. The cost of a single-hung window is less than that of a similar double-hung model.

DISADVANTAGES

1. Ventilation is limited to the bottom part of the window opening.

2. Washing a single-hung window can be a problem unless the lower sash is removable.

Awning Windows

Awning windows are hinged similarly to casement windows, but along their top edge so that they swing out and up when you turn a crank or lever or simply give them a push (Fig. 18.3). Some units are made with special hardware that provides pivot action—the top of the sash moves down as you push the bottom outward. The screens and storm windows are installed from the inside.

FIGURE 18.3

An awning window.

ADVANTAGES

1. Awning windows can be opened wide enough that you can get almost 100 percent of possible ventilation—even during a rainstorm—without letting in water.

2. They can be used as clerestory windows, placed high in walls to provide

natural light and ventilation while ensuring privacy and leaving a maximum amount of wall space for furniture placement.

3. They offer an excellent seal against air infiltration when they latch closed against compression weather stripping.

DISADVANTAGES

1. Awning windows shouldn't be installed overlooking porches, decks, terraces, or sidewalks because someone might run into their open projecting sashes.

2. Because they slant, open sashes are so exposed that they become dirty in short order and require more frequent washing than any other type of window.

3. As with casement windows, having storm windows and screens mounted on the inside can hinder a quick escape.

Hopper Windows and Tilt-Turn Windows

Hopper windows are the reverse of awning windows. Hinged or pivoted at their bottom, they open inward and downward from their top so that the entering air flows upward (Fig. 18.4). Operated by a lock handle at the top of the sash, they're used most commonly in basements and clerestories. Screens and storm windows are installed on the outside.

A tilt-turn window is a variation of a hopper window in which, by turning one handle 90 degrees, the window switches from a hopper design (tilts in at the top just a little) to a swing-in casement window (Fig. 18.5). In the hopper position, the window can be left open in a rainstorm without water leakage. In the casement position, the window is easy to clean from indoors. Tilt-turn windows are also very airtight and efficient because the weather-stripping seal gets compressed when the window is closed.

ADVANTAGES

1. Hopper windows provide almost 100 percent of possible ventilation.

2. Both their inner and outer surfaces can be washed easily from the inside.

FIGURE 18.4

A hopper window.

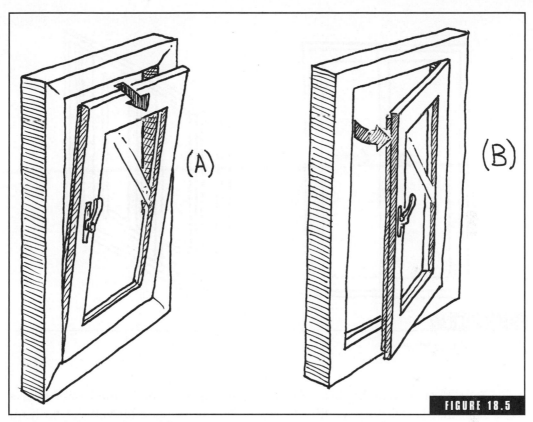

Tilt-turn window opening positions.

3. They offer an excellent seal against air infiltration when they latch closed against compression weather stripping.

DISADVANTAGES

1. Hopper windows interfere with draperies and curtains and are impossible to darken with shades when opened.

2. Because they stick out inside a room or hallway, they can cause traffic problems in living areas of a home.

3. Because of their unusual open position, they can be difficult to exit from in case of an emergency.

Horizontal Sliding Windows

In effect, a horizontal sliding window is a double-hung or single-hung window laid on its side (Fig. 18.6). With some units, both sashes slide from side to side in a channel; in others, only one sash (usually the right sash) slides. In still others

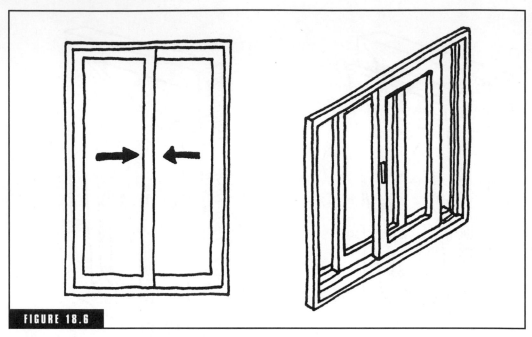

Horizontal sliding windows.

made with three panels of glass, the two outer sashes slide to the center over a fixed sash that is twice the width of each sliding sash. Look for ventilation limit latches that enable the windows to vent in a partly open position, for recessed tilt latches that allow easy access for window cleaning, and for a sloped sill for rain-water runoff.

ADVANTAGES

1. As with double-hung windows, because they're held firmly in place, horizontal sliding windows won't warp or sag.

2. They're easy to open and close as long as you're standing next to them.

3. Relatively little air leakage occurs around the edges.

4. Washing is usually easy because many sashes can be removed from inside the house.

5. Horizontal sliding windows are a good choice in locations where you want an operating sash with a large expanse of glass and a minimum number of framing members to obstruct the view. No other operating unit fills this requirement as well.

DISADVANTAGES

1. Horizontal sliding windows cannot be opened to access more than 50 percent of their possible ventilation space.

2. They will admit driving rain into the house.

3. If you must reach over a counter or piece of furniture to open and close them, horizontal sliders are difficult to operate and should not be used.

Fixed Windows

Fixed windows are panes of glass mounted in frames that are installed directly into a wall (Fig. 18.7). They can't be opened and closed and can be ordered in a variety of sizes, shapes, and glass types.

ADVANTAGES

1. Fixed windows are the most weather-tight windows available.

2. Because they can't be opened, they don't require screens or hardware.

3. They're less expensive than other windows.

DISADVANTAGES

1. They can provide no ventilation.

2. They're impossible to exit from in case of an emergency.

3. They must be cleaned from the outside.

FIGURE 18.7

Fixed windows.

Glass Block Windows

Glass block windows are installed like concrete blocks, course by course. Glass blocks allow light to enter a room and, at the same time, provide privacy. Standard (plain) as well as fancy "designer" glass blocks are available. These blocks are not solid glass. Instead, each unit consists of two hollow ¼- to ¾-inch-thick glass half-blocks fused together under high temperatures. As the air inside the fused block cools, an insulating partial vacuum is formed within the block (see Fig. 18.7).

ADVANTAGES

1. When set in mortar, glass blocks are airtight, reducing the likelihood of drafts, dirt, allergy-causing particles, noise, and even burglar entry. They're efficient year round and minimize interior glare and the fading of carpet, furniture, and furnishings.

2. Some "designer" glass blocks have patterns etched in their glass such as wavy finishes, raised diamonds, stippled textures, or fluted surfaces. Any of these can add character to a room.

3. Glass blocks can be purchased with color tints to blend or contrast with interior designs. Patterns made with various color, shades, translucence, and textures can help to improve solar control and energy efficiency.

DISADVANTAGES

1. They can't be opened or seen through.

2. They can't be escaped through.

Bay Windows

A bay window consists of three adjacent windows or sections of windows in a series. Two side sections are angled back from each side of a straight center window or section of windows (Fig. 18.8). An entire bay window unit can be made from combinations of windows such as casement or double-hung windows on the sides and a fixed center section.

Bay windows are ideal when you want to increase both the real and apparent size of a room. They'll also add a graceful note to an otherwise rather severe facade.

ADVANTAGES

1. Bay windows open up a 180-degree view and add space to a room.

2. They not only increase ventilation but also enable you to scoop in breezes traveling parallel to the house walls.

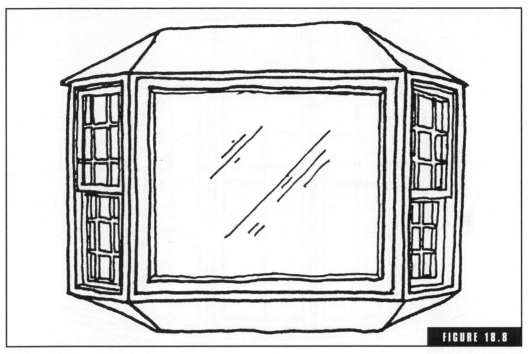

A bay window.

FIGURE 18.8

3. They form a delightful niche for sitting or dining. They're often featured in designer rooms and houses, and they provide considerably more light than conventional window arrangements do.

4. They provide an excellent place for growing houseplants.

5. Bay window roofs may be shingled to match the house roof, or they can be roofed with copper for a distinctive traditional look.

DISADVANTAGES

1. At least the center part of a bay window must be cleaned from the outside.

2. Because this arrangement protrudes out from a wall, it's not as energy efficient as other window installations.

Bow Windows

The bow window is a close relative of the bay window, and they're often confused with each other (Fig. 18.9). The bow window is gently curved rather than angled and is considered a more graceful feature when used in a house's living area. The bow window receives its name from the arrangement of a series of windows that arc out from the house's exterior walls.

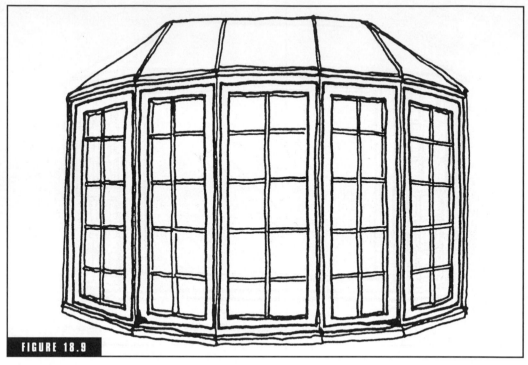

FIGURE 18.9

A bow window.

Because of their curved shape, bow windows are necessarily made up of relatively narrow sashes or of many small fixed panes. When sashes are used, they're generally the casement and occasionally the double-hung type. With casement windows, either all the sashes can open, or only the two end panels or only the end panels and every other intermediate panel can open. When double-hung windows make up a bow, only the end panels open. Bow windows are also available in models in which none of the sashes open, with fixed large- or small-pane styles.

ADVANTAGES

1. Bow windows open up a 180-degree view.

2. Not only do bow windows increase ventilation, but they also enable you to scoop in breezes that run parallel to the house walls.

3. They form the same kind of delightful niche found with bay windows for dining, growing plants, and sitting.

DISADVANTAGES

1. Because they protrude, they are not as energy efficient as windows closer to the walls.

2. These windows are usually narrow or small, so there's little opportunity to escape through them in case of an emergency.

3. Some of their sections are normally fixed, and cleaning will have to be done from the outside.

Garden Windows

Garden windows, also referred to as *greenhouse windows*, project from a home's exterior by about 12 inches and have glass roofs as well as vertical glass panes (Fig. 18.10). Inside glass shelves or expanded metal shelving across a garden window allows the placement of plants and admits sunlights from top to bottom. The insulated glass and tight seals minimize winter heat loss. Some models have insulated center window sections that eliminate the need for center frames. Others use side-opening casement windows that hinge on the side near the house. Many come with double-lock latches on each side for security and an airtight seal when closed and latched.

Numerous units employ vinyl frames (some foam-filled for extra insulation value) that come in white, tan, and brown. For severe cold climate locations, certain models afford extra protection for the plants during winter with rigid foam insulation sandwiched between the seat and sides.

FIGURE 18.10

A garden window.

ADVANTAGES

1. Garden windows offer practically the same excellent spaciousness and ventilating possibilities as bay windows.

2. They are great for growing cooking herbs in or near the kitchen.

DISADVANTAGES

1. They cannot be easily escaped through.

2. They may be difficult to clean.

Jalousie Windows

A jalousie window is made up of a series of narrow horizontal panes or glass slats that open outward with a crank (Fig. 18.11).

ADVANTAGES

1. Jalousie windows can be opened far enough to gain virtually 100 percent of available ventilation.

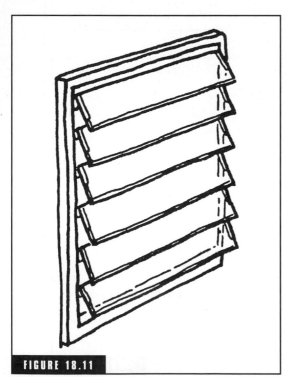

FIGURE 18.11

A jalousie window.

2. They can be opened during rainy weather without admitting water into the room.

3. The airflow from jalousie windows can be adjusted in any amount or vertical direction.

4. They're easy to open over a counter or furniture.

DISADVANTAGES

1. They possess many small glass sections that need to be cleaned.

2. They're difficult to wash from the inside.

3. They're very poor for preventing air infiltration.

4. Jalousie windows are impossible to exit from in case of an emergency.

Skylight Windows

Skylight windows do two things better than other windows can: They admit more natural light, and they distribute the light more evenly. When operable (can be opened or closed), they also can help to ventilate a home by releasing unwanted warm air at night and drawing cooler makeup air through other vents and openings into the house.

They can make rooms look larger and help to equalize the light in a room that might have windows on only one side. Frequently, owing to cost restrictions, the skylight chosen is a fixed window unable to be opened. Fixed skylights come in many shapes—dome, smooth, low-profile curb, pyramid, and ridge (Fig. 18.12). The same windows also are available in models that can be opened and closed and, again, can provide ventilation when needed. Low-e coatings are especially important for skylights and other roof-located windows because they admit the direct, high-angled sunlight that provides high heat gain and very bright ultraviolet (UV)-bearing natural light that can be tough on both furnishings and occupants. Gas fills are also a good idea for overhead window assemblies to prevent heat loss during nights and times of cold temperatures.

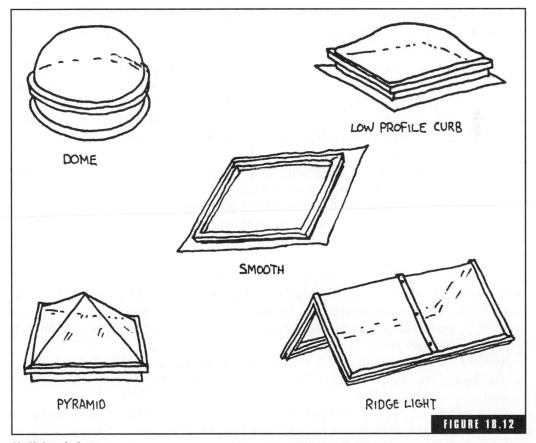

DOME

LOW PROFILE CURB

SMOOTH

PYRAMID

RIDGE LIGHT

FIGURE 18.12

Skylight windows.

Another kind of roof skylight window is a single sash that pivots at the sides about a third of the way down from the top. When opened, the bottom swings out, and the top swings in. It can be held open at any angle—and it even can be completely reversed for easy washing from the inside.

In a third type of roof window, the sash is hinged at the top and raises like an awning window to give an unobstructed view while keeping rain out. The outside of the more progressive models is washed with a special tool provided by the manufacturer.

Skylights and roof windows generally should be installed on the south side of homes located in cold-climate areas or on the north side of dwellings located in warm-climate places. In colder areas, consider a clear skylight or roof window combined with an insulating shade or storm window. In warmer areas, use frosted or tinted skylights that open to vent excess heat and have shades for blocking out the sun when needed. The tinted glass will help to reduce illumination while cutting down on glare and heat gain.

Sun-screening capabilities with skylight or roof windows include venetian blinds, pleated shades, and roller shades. Venetian blinds come in thermal units operated manually or electrically. Pleated shades offer lighting gradations from soft filtered light to darkness.

For the reasons of increased natural lighting and ventilation features, skylights are great, but consider that they also reduce what is usually the most energy-efficient part of a home's thermal envelope—the roof—and replace perhaps an R-40+ layer of insulation with a window that's far less energy efficient. This is why the most energy-efficient models should be used, all with low-e glass. (Low-e coatings—special coatings affixed to glass that reduce heat transfer through windows—are especially important for skylights and other roof-located windows because windows without low-e glazings freely admit the direct, high-angled sunlight that provides high heat gain, and very bright UV-bearing natural light that can be tough on both furnishings and occupants. See the Additional Glass Options section later in this chapter for a more detailed discussion on low-e glazings.)

In warmer climates, skylights are easier to justify but often can be replaced with clerestory windows located high in wall insets, where they can be protected from midday sun by roof overhangs. Small windows called *roof monitors* also can be used in small, raised areas of the roof ridge, usually sheltered from high sun with glass window sides.

Various colors and shades are available, with different insulation values. Roller shades are often a choice of home owners looking to work within a limited budget.

Roof windows can be installed in convenient-reach locations such as attics and extra or nook rooms. Some of these windows open to a full 45-degree angle to satisfy egress requirements for emergency escape.

Ventilating skylights are available in low-e insulated glass with optional insect screens. Units positioned out of a person's normal reach can be operated with a number of control systems (with manual or motorized control rods), including the following:

- Electric programmable units with timers that can be set to open or close the windows automatically at desired times
- Electric control systems with switch keypads
- Units with infrared remote controls similar to a handheld television remote control for convenient operating of vent skylights and sunscreening accessories

ADVANTAGES

1. Skylight windows permit installation of smaller and fewer windows and simplify interior decoration and furniture placement by allowing more uninterrupted wall space in a room.
2. They can be used to illuminate rooms and areas that share no outside walls for regular windows, such as inside bathrooms and halls.
3. They supply privacy without sacrificing any natural lighting. Also, some models open for fresh air.
4. Skylight windows can provide more flexibility in the planning of a house because you needn't include sidewall windows in every room and because skylights can effectively add useful space (such as in attics) to spaces otherwise dark and dreary.
5. During winter, the pros and cons of a high-quality skylight are about a wash because the skylight loses more heat than does an insulated attic floor or ceiling, but it does reduce the need for electric lighting during the day and provides some passive-solar heat gain during sunny weather. However, during summer, a vent skylight is an energy saver because the hottest indoor air rises to the ceiling, where the skylight vent exhausts it. This creates a natural airflow, drawing the fresh cooler outside air indoors.

DISADVANTAGES

1. Because heat rises, skylight windows tend to be less efficient than a plain windowless roof or ceiling in cold weather, especially during times when the sun is not shining. Because of this, consider only skylights that have a minimum of double-glazed glass (not all of them do).
2. They can be difficult to clean. The fixed types must be cleaned from above. Leaves, dust, and even ice buildup during winter can pose real problems.

3. Provisions need to be made for draining off water—either condensated moisture or water that collects from rain and melting snow.

SOLAR LIGHT TUBES OR TUNNELS

Solar light tubes or tunnels are discussed in more depth in Chapter 23, but in some ways, they function similar to windows by conveying natural light into a home's interior through a domed collector on the roof via a reflective tube that's attached to a fixture in the ceiling of the room being lit, where the light is dispersed. They're ideal for bathrooms, hallways, closets, and other areas within the core of a home, where windows are not an option because there are no outside walls or roof access to the target spaces. Because of their ease of installation and their relatively inexpensive construction, light tubes are often less expensive than skylights, and if they are insulated when they are run through unheated areas such as attics, they provide more energy efficiency than skylights.

TYPES OF GLASS

Three types of glass panels typically are used to construct modern windows: plate glass, tempered glass, and insulating glass.

Plate Glass

Plate glass is the standard glass normally used in house windows. It can be plain or tinted to reduce glare and can be doubled up to sandwich in a thin airspace for insulating qualities. When struck or put under stress, it shatters into pieces that are usually very sharp. It's an excellent material for windows, though, because it can be manufactured free of flaws and distortions.

Tempered Glass

Tempered glass panes are three to five times stronger than those made of ordinary plate glass. Tempered glass should be used in doors and in glass panels adjacent to doors and other areas where it is likely that people, especially children, might run into or fall against them. In fact, many building codes require the use of tempered glass in wall areas that are within 4 feet of any door. When struck or put under stress, tempered glass develops hairline cracks or breaks into many small, rounded pieces instead of the sharp, ragged pieces that come from standard plate glass. Auto windshields are a common example of tempered glass.

Insulating Glass

In this day and age, it no longer makes sense to install windows having only a single thickness of glass. Instead, all exterior windows located in living areas or heated areas of a house should be double- or triple-paned or, as in some "superinsulated" models, even quadruple-paned. Who knows where this multi-

plication of panes will stop? Some of these "superwindows" have been rated with R-values that approach those of energy-efficient outer walls to the lower teens. They include insulated, gas-filled, high-tech multicoated glazing, heat mirror film, foam-filled fiberglass frames, warm-edge construction—you name it. The additional expense, though, is well worth it. The resulting savings in fuel and energy costs should more than make up for the initial investment within a few years.

Using double- or triple-pane windows as opposed to a combination of single-pane sashes and storm windows has several other advantages. Multipanel windows offer a better appearance, are easier to clean, and provide increased sound-proofing, a permanent installation, and even a better overall price. This glass usually exists in two forms. One is a special double or triple (or more) sheet of glass separated by an airspace(s) with the glass edges welded or formed together to make airtight center spaces much like the liner of a thermos bottle. To a certain point, the wider the separating airspace, the greater is the insulating value. Cheap, poorly designed insulating windows have very narrow separating airspaces. The other type consists of two or three (or more) sheets of glass held in the frame with insulating airspaces in between. Double-pane insulating glass used in many stock windows is made of two panes of sheet glass having an airspace between each pane. Triple-pane glass windows consist of three panes of glass with airspaces between each pair of panes (Fig. 18.13). Again, such insulated glass contains at least double panes surrounding a sealed airspace, offer-

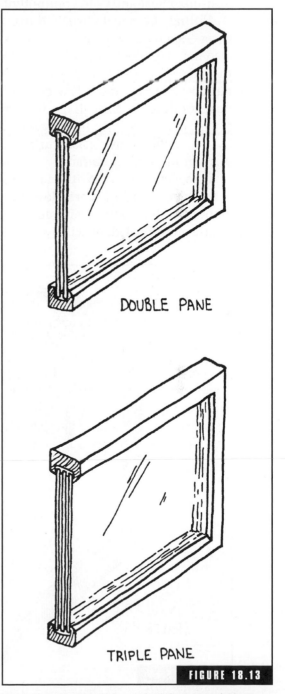

DOUBLE PANE

TRIPLE PANE

FIGURE 18.13

Insulating glass double- and triple-pane windows.

ing an insulated layer between you and the elements, plus warm-edge spacers that minimize heat and cold conductivity between outdoors and indoors.

Filling the gap between the panes with a low-conductivity harmless inert gases—such as argon or krypton—adds more insulation value to the window and also helps to block out noise (Fig. 18.14). In the manufacturing process, air inside the space between two glazing layers is removed and replaced by one or a combination of several inert, low-conductivity gases. Argon and krypton gases reduce heat conduction through the window and also eliminate convective currents otherwise created within the space by the constant movement of air as it gets cooled by the colder inner glass surface of the window and draws warmth from the warmer inner glass surface.

One disadvantage with stacking multiple layers of glass in double, triple, or more layers within a window frame is that collectively they will reduce the amount of heat gain available through the window. A single pane of glass will admit more heat than will two or three layers of the same glass. This heat gain

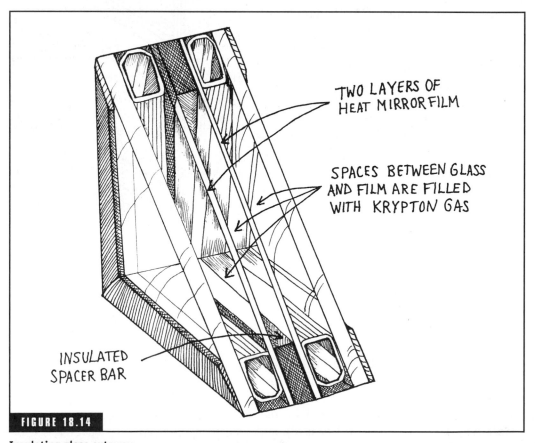

TWO LAYERS OF HEAT MIRROR FILM

SPACES BETWEEN GLASS AND FILM ARE FILLED WITH KRYPTON GAS

INSULATED SPACER BAR

FIGURE 18.14

Insulating glass cutaway.

reduction needs to be taken into account when windows are being planned for locations desiring high levels of heat gain—such as passive heat design, where as much solar heat as possible is expected to warm up a solid stone wall or concrete floor—for slow heat release later. This is why it's so important to pay attention to the heat-related window ratings—so that windows designed for heat gain can be installed in the right places and so that windows engineered for blocking heat can be used appropriately.

Self-Cleaning Glass

Several manufacturers produce windows made of glass that's designed to self-clean. Owing to chemical compounds embedded within the surface of the molten glass during manufacturing, when the window is exposed to sunlight, a chemical reaction helps to disintegrate many foreign materials that collect on the glass, such as tree sap, pollen, and dead insects. Also, water doesn't bead up on self-cleaning glass; instead, it spreads out in sheets that wash away loose debris like a squeegee.

While windows with self-cleaning glass cost more, they enable more of the sun's rays to enter through the cleaner glass—warming interior spaces during winter and helping to reduce energy costs.

Additional Glass Options

- As mentioned earlier, *low-e glazings* are special coatings that reduce heat transfer through windows. They can be used to either block heat from entry or restrict heat from getting out, depending on the climate and which conditioning task is most important: heating or cooling. The *e* stands for *emissivity*, a measure of the ability of glass to reflect or block out long-wave radiant energy or heat and UV rays. The coatings are thin, almost invisible metal oxide or semiconductor films placed directly on one or more surfaces of glass or on plastic films between two or more panes. They enable visible light to enter the home while preventing the unwanted infrared heat energy from getting through. Instead, the e-coating often reflects that energy back into the space between glazings, where it warms that space. When extra heat is desired inside the home, the window is constructed with the e-coating film facing the inside of the home. The lower the emissivity, the better are the insulating qualities of the glass. Low-e glazing and coatings reduce the fading of furniture, curtains, carpeting, artwork, and paint. The coatings prevent heat loss during winter and slow heat from entering the house in the summer. A low-e window will reflect your own body heat back toward you, so you won't feel cold while standing right next to the window.

 Two main types of low-e coatings are used, depending on whether heat gain needs to be either blocked or admitted. The sputtered, or soft, coating is used on windows designed to admit low to moderate levels of solar heat, and they are popular in warmer climates. The pyrolitic, or hard, low-e coating is used for windows designed to admit high levels of solar heat. An incredible amount of research is being done with low-e coatings and has resulted in a wide variety of coatings, some combining two, three, or more layers that result in the ability of more visible light to enter while at the same time blocking more UV radiation.

■ *Spectrally selective coatings* are considered to be the next generation of low-e technology. These coatings filter out from 40 to 70 percent of the heat normally transmitted through clear glass while allowing the full amount of light transmission. Spectrally selective coatings offer optical properties that are transparent to some wavelengths of energy (visible light) and reflective to others (infrared radiation). The most common spectrally selective coatings are tints and certain varieties of low-e films. Light-tinted glazings are yet another way to reduce solar heat gain by reducing heat without much darkening of the glass.

■ *Heat-absorbing glazings* are panes of glass that have tinted coatings to absorb some solar heat (but they can't absorb it all). Some heat continues to pass through the glass by conduction and reradiation.

■ *Warm-edge technology* uses low-conductance spacers, often butyl rubber, silicone foam, epoxies, or composites, to reduce heat transfer near the edges of insulated glazing and in some cases to stretch glazing films over. The edge spacers are what hold the panes of glass apart and provide an airtight seal in an insulated glass window. If the spacers break or otherwise come apart, the gas or air will escape, and replacement air and moisture can enter the space and cause condensation and reduced insulating values. Less efficient spacers are made of metal, which increases undesirable thermal bridging and heat loss while lowering U-values. The better window models carry a long warranty against spacer and seal failure. New glazing technologies with warm edges and insulated frames not only reduce energy costs but also make homes more comfortable as well, even helping to reduce incidents of frost and condensation.

■ *Reflective coatings* greatly reduce the transmission of daylight through clear glass. Although they typically block more light than heat, reflective coatings, when applied to tinted or clear glass, also slow some heat transmission. These coatings are commonly applied in hot-climate locations, where protection from the glaring sun is critical to comfort. Care must be taken, though, because the reduced cooling energy that results may be somewhat offset by a resulting need for additional artificial lighting.

CONTROLLING HEAT

Windows, for all their wonderful qualities, also can be considered as thermal holes or passageways. An average home may lose up to 30 percent of its heat or air-conditioning energy through low-quality windows. Energy-efficient windows save money every month. Their higher initial cost can be offset in many ways. One way is that a smaller, less expensive heating and cooling system would be acceptable. Energy-efficient, durable windows will certainly cost less in the long haul because of the lower energy use, lower maintenance costs, and avoidance of replacement expenses that otherwise inevitably will come into play if inferior windows are selected.

In addition, the occupants will be a lot more comfortable in a dwelling that's built with good windows—owing to the ways the windows help to control heat. In short, when sunlight strikes a window, visible light, UV rays, and heat are either reflected, absorbed, or transmitted into the building.

During winter, a window with a lower glass temperature feels colder partly because more heat is radiated from a person's body toward the window than from the window to the person. Cold glass also can create uncomfortable drafts as air next to the window is cooled and travels downward to the floor. This sets up an air movement pattern that feels drafty and promotes heat loss. High-performance windows installed with efficient weather stripping result in higher interior temperatures in winter and thus greater comfort. During summer, windows with low solar heat coefficients reduce the solar radiation coming through the glass with its overly warm discomfort.

Windows lose and gain heat by conduction, convection, radiation, and air leakage (Fig. 18.15).

■ *Conduction* is the movement of heat through a solid material. With less conductive material, head flow is

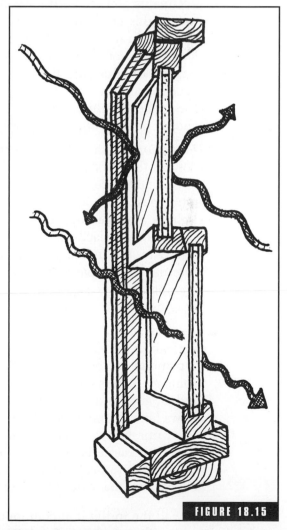

FIGURE 18.15

Windows lose and gain heat.

impeded. To control conduction, look for multiple-glazed windows with an approved low-conductance, inert, harmless gas trapped between panes of glass. Thermally resistant edge spacers and window frames will reduce conduction further.

■ *Convection* is another way heat moves through windows. In cold weather, heated indoor air presses against the interior surface of window glass. The air cools off, becomes dense, and sinks toward the floor. As this cooled air drops, warm air rushes in to take its place along the surface of the glass. The cycle then repeats itself over and over or at least until the glass becomes too warm to continue to cool the indoor air. What actually happens is that the occupants feel too cold for comfort and turn up their thermostat. Unfortunately, this is where excessive energy costs come into play. Each 1 percent increase in thermostat setting requires an increased home energy usage of about 2 percent. This heat loss or transfer is expressed with U-values, or U-factors. U-values are the mathematical inverse of the R-values commonly used to measure the effectiveness of thermal insulation. This means that the lower the U-value, the higher its insulating value. Your window U-value should be below 0.35 to be efficient.

■ *Radiation* is a third way heat can enter or leave a dwelling. You can help to control this process to your advantage with low-e glass coatings, transparent metal oxides that reflect up to 90 percent of long-wave heat energy while passing shorter waves of visible light. The shorter-wavelength visible light is absorbed by the floors, walls, and furniture. It reradiates indoors from those surfaces, all while the long-wave heat energy is reflected back outdoors. For heating, low-e coatings thus work best when applied to the internal or interpane surface of the interior window pane. Conversely, for cooling, low-e coatings work best applied to the interpane surface of the window's exterior pane.

■ *Air leakage* is a fourth way that heat is lost (or gained) from a home. In short, air leakage siphons a large percentage of an average home's heating and cooling energy to the outdoors. Some of this is unavoidable, of course. When someone enters or exits a dwelling, there's bound to be some exchange of indoor and outdoor air. It's the avoidable air escape and exchange that windows (and doors) must address. To control air infiltration, quality windows need durable weather stripping and secure closing devices. Hinged windows such as casement and awning types tend to clamp more tightly against weather stripping than do double-hung windows. But the difference can be slight; well-made double-hung windows are certainly acceptable.

How well the individual components of the window are joined also can affect air leakage. Glass-to-frame, frame-to-frame, and sash-to-frame connections must be well fit and tight. The technical measurement specification for window air leakage is measured in cubic feet of air per minute per square of window. Look for windows with certified air-leakage rates of 0.01 to 0.06 cubic feet per minute per foot or less. Lowest values are best.

TYPES OF WINDOW FRAMES

There are three primary types of materials used in window frame construction: wood, metal, and plastic.

Wood Frames

Wood frames are the most handsome window frames available and are often preferred for this reason alone. They can be purchased with their exterior and side surfaces (the parts that abut the tracks or stiles and face the outdoors) covered with a layer of tough vinyl or a layer of aluminum with a coat of factory-applied baked-on paint. The only part of such a window frame that retains its wood surface is the interior section—the part that faces the inside of a room. This inside surface is the most important part of a window frame from an appearance point of view. It can be stained, varnished, or painted to match or complement the rest of the room's decor. The choice of colors for either the vinyl- or aluminum-clad surfaces is usually limited to white, brown, or bronze.

Because no staining, varnishing, or refinishing is ever required to the nonwood surfaces, maintenance there is extremely infrequent. And the wood part of the frame, the part you can see from inside the room, rarely will need attention either, because it isn't exposed to the elements. Vinyl- or aluminum-clad factory-finished wood frames are excellent choices (Fig. 18.16).

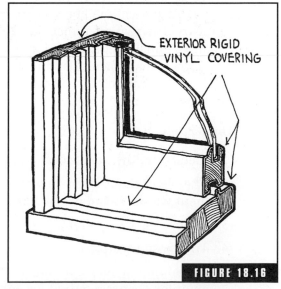

EXTERIOR RIGID VINYL COVERING

FIGURE 18.16

Vinyl-covered window construction cutaway.

ADVANTAGES

1. A primary advantage of wood-framed windows is their appearance. They look less clinical than aluminum or steel sashes. As such, wood is favored in many residential applications because of its appearance and traditional place in house design.

2. Condensation is not much of a problem with wood frames, as it is with steel and aluminum frames.

3. Wood frames can be used successfully with all architectural styles.

4. Wood frames are poor heat conductors, so they provide effective insulating qualities.

5. Provided that you select the wood frames having vinyl- or aluminum-clad exteriors, the outer and inner track surfaces will be practically maintenance-free.

6. The interior surfaces of wood sashes can be painted to match any color scheme or can be stained and finished in natural tones to match inside wood baseboard and other trim. Exterior surfaces of wood sashes also can be painted to easily change color schemes if desired.

DISADVANTAGE

1. If the exterior surfaces are not vinyl or aluminum clad, they'll need refinishing, especially if no awnings or substantial overhangs are in place to shield the windows from rain, sun, and snow. If uncovered wood frames are not treated to resist decay and moisture absorption, they'll rot in short order.

Metal Frames

Metal window frames are available in aluminum and steel models, in natural finishes or various selections of anodized coloring. Aluminum windows became popular because people thought they suffered from none of the problems associated with wood—that they wouldn't rot, swell, contract, warp, or need refinishing. This, however, proved not altogether true. Near seacoasts and corrosive industrial locales, aluminum frames can corrode so badly that they need to be painted for protection. For these reasons, it's advisable to purchase aluminum or steel windows that are protected by factory-applied finishes.

A traditional heat-conduction problem for aluminum frames can be addressed during their manufacture by including a thermal break, splitting the frame components into interior and exterior pieces, by using a less-conductive material to join them.

ADVANTAGES

1. Metal window frames cost less than wood frames.

2. They lend themselves nicely to places that receive rugged use, such as basement windows and garage windows.

3. They're easy to operate.

4. They won't warp.

5. Aluminum window frames are light, strong, and easily extruded into the complex shapes required for window parts.

6. Aluminum frames are available in anodized and factory-baked enamel fin-ishes that are extremely durable and low maintenance.

DISADVANTAGES

1. Because aluminum and steel are excellent conductors, they permit high heat loss from within a house through the window frames.

2. Also, owing to their conductivity, they cause excessive moisture condensa-tion on the interior portion of the frames when significant temperature dif-ferences exist between inside and outside the windows. If you insist on aluminum- or steel-framed windows, make sure that you select a brand that has a thermal break—where an insulating material separates the interior and exterior sections of the frame. The most efficient and practical insulating materials include plastic, urethane, epoxy, and vinyl.

3. Aluminum and steel frames often provide a looser fit than wood frames, allowing for more air infiltration.

Vinyl Frames

Vinyl is an option for your consideration. Vinyl allows very little heat and cold transference and is practically maintenance-free. Vinyl-clad wood makes for top-quality frames that combine wood's extra insulating properties with vinyl's easy care. Most vinyl-framed windows use multichambered hollow extruded frame and sash sections. These chambers create multiple "dead" airspaces that provide insulation U-value and strength. Several manufacturers offer foam insulation inside the frame chambers. The major difference between insulated vinyl and standard vinyl frames is improved thermal insulating capabilities.

ADVANTAGES

1. Vinyl window frames are energy efficient and help to reduce noise transmission.

2. They have good air and weather seals for reducing dust and pollen.

3. Vinyl comes in wood-grain finishes, and one model actually has a real wood composite on the side that faces the inside of the home.

4. Vinyl window frames do not require painting. Because the color goes all the way through, the finish can't be damaged and will not deteriorate; therefore, the surface is maintenance-free.

DISADVANTAGES

1. Extruded vinyl frames may shrink and expand with changes in temperatures enough to allow more air infiltration than expected, unless high-quality weather stripping is included with the units.

2. Low-quality vinyl frames that look remarkably similar to high-quality vinyl frames can confuse buyers who do not insist on thoroughly researching the brands.

Plastic Frames

An available option on some window types is plastic frames. Plastic frames are lightweight and corrosion-free.

ADVANTAGES

1. Painting is never needed unless you decide to change their color.

2. Plastic frames are easy to operate.

3. They're not as expensive as wood frames.

4. Plastic is not a good conductor; it doesn't have the condensation or heat-transfer problems of aluminum or steel.

DISADVANTAGE

1. The main drawback is their lack of strength. Wood, aluminum, and steel frames are much stronger. Plastic frames are more likely to break, especially during cold weather, when plastic turns brittle.

Fiberglass Frames

Fiberglass-framed windows can cost a bit more, but they may be worth it to you. They seldom need to be caulked or painted and possess high insulation values. Some fiberglass windows are available with real wood interior sides. The strong fiberglass exterior sides provide the stability and can resist gale winds and driving rains, whereas the wood interior sides give the home a warm, comfortable look and feel. Fiberglass window frames are a relatively recent window option. Some manufacturers have been filling hollow fiberglass frames with urethane foam insulation, making those windows excellent choices for cold climates.

ADVANTAGES

1. Fiberglass-framed windows remain airtight because fiberglass frame material expands with temperature changes at almost the identical rate as window glass, so the fit stays true during temperature swings.

2. The fiberglass exterior provides excellent strength and rigidity, which makes these windows favorable choices in rough-weather locations subject to gale-force winds and driving rain. Models are available in many colors, and since fiberglass resists high temperatures, the paint can be baked on. These frames

also can be hand painted with good success should you decide to change the decor of a single room or of the entire house.

2. Many fiberglass-framed windows offer optional foam insulation filling for additional energy efficiency.

3. Because fiberglass is stronger than most vinyl/plastic, it can have smaller cross-sectional pieces and thus provide a proportionally larger clear window area, allowing more free passive-solar heating during winter.

WINDOW SIZE AND ALIGNMENT

Make certain that the size of some windows, particularly in bedrooms, is large enough to escape from in case of a fire. As mentioned previously, all sleeping areas should have at least one easy-to-open window having an opening of not less than 7 square feet. Check local building code requirements for window opening width and height, as well as the sill height above the floor.

Also be aware that the size and placement of windows will limit where you can comfortably arrange furniture. Major items such as desks, sofas, bureaus, dressers, china cabinets, and buffets all normally require wall space. However, if window sills are high enough, some furniture can be placed beneath them. Many pieces of furniture are only 30 to 32 inches high.

Windows should be aligned in a pleasant manner, especially when viewed from the outside. This typically means that windows across each living level conform to one long horizontal line. Small windows should line up with the top or bottom halves of large windows. Then, for maximum effect, have the tops of exterior doors line up with the window tops on the first level (Fig. 18.17). When possible, arrange vertical window placements directly above one another.

WINDOW LOCATION

No matter where you locate your windows, all exposures will be able to provide a sufficient amount of natural light (Fig. 18.18). Southern exposures, with their high sun angle, offer the most light and the best

FIGURE 18.17

Comparison of poorly and correctly aligned windows.

FIGURE 18.18

Good window location.

opportunity to control and use sunshine to good advantage. East and west exposures are the most difficult to control, having low-angled rays, with the west being particularly troublesome. Northern exposures, lacking direct sunlight, are the easiest of the four to control. For the typical home, windows on the north side of the house are discouraged. However, when windows are required owing to an unavoidable or advantageous orientation or positioning of the dwelling—such as a master bedroom overlooking a scenic view—a northern exposure can be well suited to the dwelling.

Other points to remember:

- Horizontal window openings are especially useful for controlling light from southern exposures.

- Vertical window openings are most useful for controlling light from eastern and western exposures.

- Windows located high in a room offer the most illumination and the deepest penetration by natural light.

- Clerestories and skylights offer good possibilities for lighting interior spaces in a home.

- In southern hotter climates, a variety of shade screens can be planned for windows facing south, east, and west—if not already shaded by roof overhangs, a porch, vegetation, or trees. In these cases, solar heat gain can be minimized by reducing south-wall window coverage and maximizing the square area of windows facing north.

- As mentioned elsewhere, simple roof overhangs work well on south-facing windows to block high summer sun while allowing lower winter sun rays free entry.

- When in concert with an overall thermal envelope plan, windows should be located to illuminate parts of a house or room where specific tasks need to be accomplished.

WINDOW VENTILATION

In addition to providing natural light, the second major function of windows is to provide ventilation to get rid of stale air in the home (Fig. 18.19), a function provided by the deliberate placement of operable windows—meaning windows that you can open and close.

The amount of airflow through a window opening depends on the size of the open area that the window's design provides. Naturally, the larger the open area, the greater ventilation "breezes" can be. Since large openings allow for the best natural ventilation when arranged to encourage cross-currents of air, consider the opening-area capacities provided by individual window types. Experts concur that for enough outside air to enter a room or combination open living space for healthy air exchanges to take place, combined total window-opening capabilities should be between 12 and 15 percent of the room's or area's floor area.

In general, estimated percentages of effective open areas of the following window types are

- Single-hung 45 percent
- Double-hung 45 percent
- Hopper 45 percent
- Sliding 50 percent
- Awning 75 percent
- Jalousie 75 percent
- Casement 90 percent

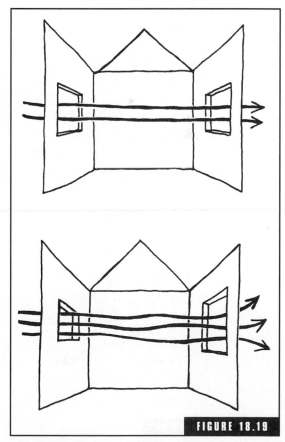

FIGURE 18.19

Window ventilation.

Openings should be oriented to pick up prevailing summer breezes. As those breezes blow against windows and exterior walls from outdoors, the pressure on the side they first meet your home (the upwind side) is naturally greater than on the opposite side of the home (the downwind side). Thus air usually will enter open windows on the upwind side—but only if there's a way to push out the same amount of "used" or "stale" air that's already inside the house—through open or partially open windows positioned on the downwind side of the dwelling or through windows on other walls. Windows positioned on those two or more other sides of the home, the sides that are parallel to the prevailing wind direction, can be outfitted with casement windows that can open in a direction that will effectively "scoop" air as it blows by and redirect it inside for extra ventilation when desired (Fig. 18.20). Hinges for those casement windows must be positioned on the downwind sides of the frames. Conversely, if you want to ventilate air out from a room, simply use casement windows with their hinges positioned on the

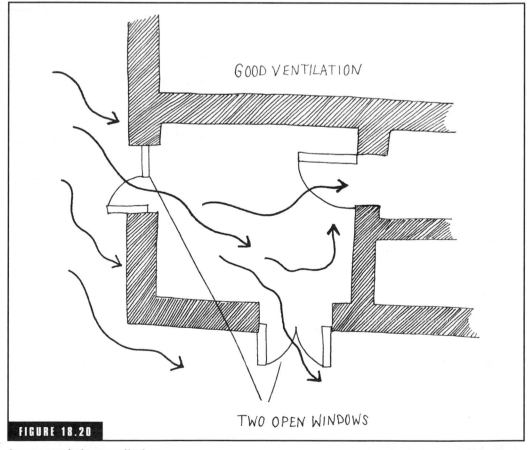

FIGURE 18.20

Casement window ventilation.

upwind side of prevailing breezes. Double-hung windows can be considered "great equalizers" because when both halves are slid toward the middle of the frame, cooler air can enter through the bottom opening, and warmer air is released through the top open space.

Good airflow occurs when the inlets and outlets are approximately the same size. Better airflow can be attained by having a larger ratio of outlet-to-inlet area. A combination of openings can direct airflow as desired; openings placed lower in wall surfaces result in better cooling than those placed higher in a room. Exterior features such as overhangs, porches, fences, garages, shrubs, and trees can be used to block or encourage airflow.

If you plan to install central air-conditioning in the house and that central air-conditioning will be run most of the time, you won't need side windows for cross-ventilation. By not putting them in, you'll save their installation costs, plus money on energy costs.

STORM WINDOWS

At one time, storm windows were early forerunners of modern insulating glass windows. By adding another layer of glass and a healthy airspace, they turned ordinary single-paned windows into much more energy-efficient units. They could be put up when needed and taken down when cold weather passed. They're still an option that can be installed on the inside or outside of "regular" insulating glass windows for additional R-values, and over the years, have morphed into less expensive, cheaper versions—customizable glass or clear flexible plastic sheets that can be affixed to existing windows, usually to the inside framework. They also employ a sealed insulating air gap that must be present for the storm or "secondary" windows to achieve appreciable energy savings.

Storm windows cut down on conductive heat losses and gains, depending on the season, by impeding air infiltration and by providing an airspace between inner and outer panes of glass. On most types of windows (double-hung, single-hung, awning, sliding, and jalousie), conventional storm windows are put up in the fall and taken down in the spring. But they also can be used to keep cool, conditioned air in a home during summers in warm-climate locations. On casement windows, storm windows are frequently fastened to the outside of the sash.

Combination aluminum-framed storm windows and screens are used on double-hung, single-hung, and sliding windows. In cold-climate areas, in general they have replaced conventional storm windows because combination storm window/screens can be left in place year round. In winter, they keep out the cold, and during summer, they keep out insects.

Two kinds of combination storm windows are commonly available: double-track and triple-track. Both include an upper panel of glass, a lower panel of glass,

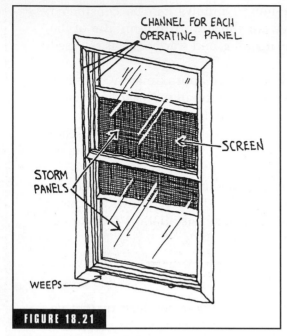

CHANNEL FOR EACH OPERATING PANEL

SCREEN

STORM PANELS

WEEPS

FIGURE 18.21

A triple-track storm window arrangement.

and a single panel of screen. In the double-track arrangement, both glass panels are fitted into separate channels or tracks so that they can move up and down independently of each other. In summer, when ventilation is required, the lower panel of glass slides to the top of its track, and the screen panel is inserted into the lower half of the track. During winter, the screen is removed entirely and stored.

The triple-track storm window arrangement eliminates the necessity of putting in and taking out the screen because each of its two glass panels and the screen all fit into their own tracks (Fig. 18.21). You can convert from a storm window to a screen simply by sliding the lower glass panel up and pushing its replacement screen down. In winter, the screen conveniently can be stored in the top part of the frame, within its own track. Although definitely more expensive, this setup is highly desirable if it fits into your budget. You gain the flexibility of having screens at a moment's notice or storm windows, and it sure beats having to lug and store screens someplace where they could get damaged during the off-season.

When planning for storm windows, consider that caulking is needed around permanently installed units at the outer edges of their frames. Two weep holes must be kept open at the bottom edges of each storm window to provide drainage and some ventilation, or wooden sills might rot. To prevent corrosion and maintain a good appearance, select only storm windows that have frames finished in baked enamel or that are coated with a layer of maintenance-free vinyl or similar material.

Key points to look for in a storm window include

- Installation with quality stainless steel screws
- Low air-infiltration rating
- No-gap weather stripping (The entire perimeter of the closed sash should be sealed.)
- Baked enamel finish on the frames
- Tie-bar horizontal stiffeners for a more rigid assembly

- Double-strength glass

- Thick-gauge aluminum

- Low-e coating

- Adjustable sill extender for a tight fit, even on uneven sills

- Energy Star labels

SCREENS

Most screens installed in today's homes are made of aluminum mesh (Figs. 18.22 and 18.23). Screens are wonderful conveniences. They let air in (or out) and keep out insects and vermin. One recent innovation is a window with built-in screens that pull down and roll up out of sight within the window frame.

Aluminum Screening

Aluminum screening is rustproof and resilient. It comes in bright or natural (silvery) finish, charcoal, and black. Charcoal and black tend to be the most popular because they provide excellent outward visibility. Black aluminum is a top-of-the-line screening product. It actually seems to disappear into the background while you look through it to the outdoors.

Fiberglass Screening

Fiberglass screening typically is vinyl coated for strength and durability. It's especially well suited for coastal areas. It will not corrode, rust, or dent and is very easy to handle.

Solar Screening

Solar screening products are made of vinyl-coated fiberglass, heavy-duty vinyl-coated polyester, and louvered aluminum.

FIGURE 18.22

A screen in place.

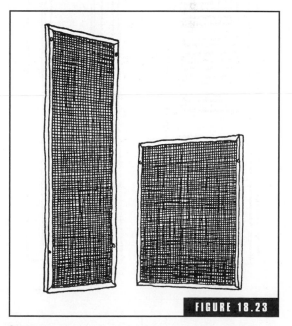

FIGURE 18.23

Screens.

They provide protection against insects while blocking out two-thirds of the sun's heat and glare—and still allow good outward visibility. Less heat and less glare mean less summer energy consumption. One screen design reflects the sun's rays and heat before entry, before the sun's rays even penetrate the window's glass.

Pet Screening

Pet screens are heavy-duty pet-resistant screens made from strong materials such as vinyl-coated polyester. This screening fabric resists tears, punctures, and other damage caused by pets, toddlers, or heavy wear in high-traffic areas. They're available in black and gray and are ideal for windows, doors, and porches likely to take abuse.

SHUTTERS

The main purpose of outside shutters is to beautify the exterior of a house by harmoniously balancing out the appearance of the windows. Maybe years ago they would prevent an arrow, a marauder's bullet, or grizzly bear's paw from entering a window, but they don't anymore. In fact, most of them no longer even close.

LOUVERED   RAISED PANEL

FIGURE 18.24

Shutters.

You can save money by using ornamental shutters made of vinyl, plastic, or aluminum. Vinyl and plastic shutters typically are available in maintenance-free colors and shades that will match or contrast with whatever siding you choose. Their rigid one-piece construction comes with the color molded throughout that doesn't chip or flake like the finishes of traditional painted shutters. Deep wood-grain-textured models are also on the market in both open-louver and raised-panel designs. They're less expensive than wood and don't require costly operating hardware. Vinyl, plastic, and aluminum shutters are made in louvered and raised-panel designs—usually in black, brown, green, or white (Fig. 18.24). Aluminum units are the strongest of the three, but because the finish is only baked on, and they're exposed to the rain, sun, and snow throughout the year, they'll eventually need repainting. Vinyl-covered shutters, on the other hand, are integrally colored, so they don't have to be touched up even if damaged.

Shutters typically are installed by fastening them to window casings or adjacent wall surfaces with screws. But this also means that there's no easy way to clean out wasps' nests, bats, or debris that can accumulate behind them. Wood shutters present an additional problem: If they're not treated adequately with wood preservative, they'll rot. They require frequent stripping, sanding, and painting or staining, which can be quite a time-consuming process, especially if the shutters are louvered. As with other site-painted items, painted wood shutters won't clean as easily as those having factory finishes. On the positive side, wood shutters can be custom finished and refinished to match any decorating scheme.

DIAMOND AND RECTANGULAR PANES

If you'd like to have windows with either small diamond- or rectangular-shaped panes, you could invest a small fortune in obtaining them. Alternatively, you could buy single-pane windows and turn them into multipane ones with devices called *snap-in muntins*. The muntins are made of plastic or wood that is painted or coated to match the window frames. They snap onto the back of the window, on the inside, depending on the style of window. You can remove them quickly when you wash the windows, and then snap them back into the sash when the glass is clean (Fig. 18.25).

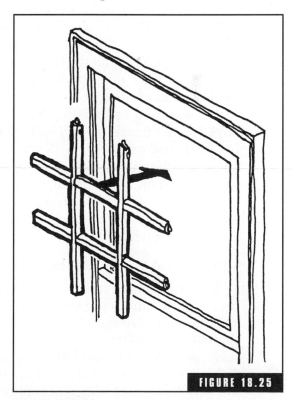

FIGURE 18.25

Snap-in muntins.

Seen from the inside of a house, muntin inserts are difficult to distinguish from permanent muntins. From the outside, although you might be able to tell that they don't project through the glass, the insets impart an appearance and effect of the real thing at a much lower cost.

EXTERIOR CONTROL OF SUNLIGHT

Regular double- or triple-pane windows, even though they're great for controlling the loss or gain of heat through conductivity, cannot prevent the sun's rays from entering and heating a room. This is good in winter and bad in summer. There are tinted window coatings that act like

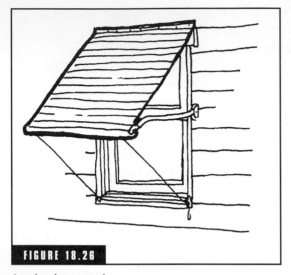

FIGURE 18.26

An aluminum awning.

tinted glass when applied (as in a car windshield) or, to a certain extent, like sunglasses. From a green perspective, whenever possible, it's far better to plan windows that admit solar gain during times of cooler and cold temperatures and resort to external shading during summer hot weather when heat gain is not needed than it is to install windows designed to prevent solar gain year round.

Wide roof overhangs, like wide-brimmed hats, will shade south-facing windows effectively. The same overhangs also will admit winter sun that strikes at a much lower angle. Overhangs, though, are not very effective at shielding east- and west-facing windows because the morning and afternoon sun rises and sets at low angles all year round.

Canvas, plastic, or aluminum awnings can provide the overhang needed to shade most windows successfully during warm weather (Fig. 18.26). Retractable awnings can be used in cold and warm months. They can reduce solar heat gain by up to 75 percent and lower inside temperatures by between 10 and 15 degrees.

Also consider motorized awnings, which can enhance the appearance and comfort of an existing porch, deck, or patio while stopping direct sunlight from hitting windows and raising the house's temperature. In addition, they protect carpeting and furniture from fading and stop the associated degrading effects that gradually weaken the fibers of indoor furnishings. Beyond installing canvas, plastic, or aluminum awnings, deciduous trees can be the answer. Deciduous shade trees planted on the southern, western, and eastern sides of a home will provide much appreciated shade during summer, and because they lose their leaves toward the end of each autumn, sunshine will be let through when you need it the most—during winter.

Sun-Control Window Film

Window film is a relatively inexpensive feature to consider from day one with your windows. It should be installed and approved by the window manufacturer to protect the window warranty. It's a clear high-tech protective layer that's applied over window glass to increase the window's visual clarity, shatter resistance, and UV- and other light-blocking ability. The film is treated with a variety of thin metal coatings that result in a wide range of colors or shades, appearances, and performance. Quality sun-control window film has the following features:

- The film can block up to 99 percent of the sun's harmful UV rays. UV light causes most of the deterioration and discoloration in furnishings.

- It also helps to block out intense visible light that contributes to fading of more sensitive colors and materials such as natural dyes and fibers or works of art on paper.

- Window film can reduce the amount of solar heat that passes into the home. Solar heat levels build up on and damage furniture and fabrics, which get almost hot to the touch. This causes temperature changes that lead to dryness, warping, and general deterioration—particularly with wood, paper, and natural fabrics.

- Window film can provide a clear, practically colorless appearance that's critical for a good view—while reducing glare and eye discomfort (similar to what a good pair of sunglasses does for the eyes).

- It is wipable and scratch resistant.

- It helps to hold the glass together if struck, for additional security against violent weather, intruders, and accidental breakage and personal injury.

- It saves energy by reducing cooling needs during summer and by reflecting heat back inside the home during winter. It effectively increases the insulation value of windows.

INTERNAL CONTROL OF SUNLIGHT

Sunshine, for lighting purposes, is typically regarded as a good thing because it reduces a home's dependence on electric lighting. Direct sun rays provide the most powerful source of light, but daylight—light still available even on a cloudy day—is still capable of supplying illumination through windows. Even moonlight, on clear nights featuring full moons, can provide considerable amounts of light through clerestories or roof skylights.

To take full advantage of such free light sources, consider how the sun "works" in your locale. Especially critical is the angle at which the sun shines on your home as the seasons of the year play out. The higher the sun is in the sky, the brighter and hotter will be its rays. People realize that the sun tends to be the hottest around the world's equator and "cools off" as geographic locations approach extreme northern and southern positions on the globe. In northern states and countries, sunlight approach angles are considerably lower and more acute most of the time, so they are a source of sunshine that is less bright and less hot. However, because of their low angles, they penetrate far deeper into a room through wall-mounted windows. Such low-angled rays don't require clerestory or skylight windows to enter the home from above. Therefore, in places that have a lot of direct, higher sun angles, the concern is how to block out and reduce the sun's overpowering heat and light in order to maintain a comfortable indoor environment. On the other hand, in places that mainly have access to indirect light and weaker and less hot sunshine, the concern is how to maximize the use of what's available. This handling of sunlight and indirect light can be approached in a number of ways.

Planning the locations of rooms to take advantage of how sunshine and daylight occur throughout the day is one method of ensuring maximum use of natural lighting. For example, eastern morning sun exposures can brighten bedrooms and kitchens during wakeup time without much heat gain and glare. Kitchens benefit from clerestory windows and north- or east-facing skylights that brighten work areas even on the most cloudy days. Small windows near the sink can supply ventilation, whereas the positioning of large south- and west-facing windows should be considered carefully owing to the inordinate amount of heat gain they could admit. Although north-facing windows are usually minimized, their selected inclusion can supply daylight without heat gain from strong midday sunshine. The type of home and floor plan will influence how creative you need to be when planning natural lighting features. Homes with interior "lightlocked" areas (where natural light is not directly available through windows placed in outer walls) may require components such as light tubes or tunnels.

Another way of using natural light is to use it in its reflected form, a kind of double dipping with available illumination. Light-colored interior surfaces (versus dark-colored surfaces) of walls, ceilings, floorings, and even furniture and other furnishings all reflect daylight, which makes a room brighter. A window located at a room's corner also will increase lighting levels by illuminating the adjacent wall and enabling light to be reflected from that wall into the room. Two windows, again located on both sides of a room's corner, will admit and reflect twice as much natural light, which can be far more effective than having two equal-sized windows located on the same wall. Further, light-colored surfaces outside windows also can reflect natural light indoors. This is why various outdoors landscaping accents and features, such as a light-colored patio, wall, walkway, or garage, or light-colored silver or gold vegetation with flowers, or the shimmering and sparkling surface of a filled swimming pool all can reflect additional sunlight and daylight inside a home.

With all that natural light entering a room, glare can become a problem. Glare occurs when most of a room's lighting source comes from one direction. Glare can be reduced or balanced out through the use of small skylights or clerestory windows positioned near an opposite wall.

A third way of working with available natural light indoors is through the use of clear, semitransparent, or translucent visual views. If you can see through one or more walls within a living space, light also will be able to pass from one place to another. Fixed window panes; stained-glass windows; glass blocks; and metal, composite, and wood screening within interior walls all can enable natural light to reach deep within rooms that otherwise may be illuminated only by electric lighting.

Be aware that curtains and drapes can be purchased with linings that provide considerable insulating values. Look at the options before making a choice. In addition to conventional curtains and draperies, you also can help to control energy loss with roll-up shades, honeycomb shades, cellular shades, venetian blinds, and vertical blinds. Roll-up shades come in many colors, patterns, and textures. The least-expensive ones are made of a thin layer of vinyl. Vinyl-coated cotton shades are better. Fiberglass laminated to vinyl results in the most durable and nicest looking shades available. While most of these materials are translucent or semitranslucent, some are designed to give complete darkness. Also on the market are shades that are coated on the back to prevent and reflect the incoming sun's rays. The alternatives to fabric shades are those constructed of slender strips of wood, metal, or semirigid vinyl.

When choosing blinds, honeycomb shades made of spun polyester are extremely flexible, making them good choices to fit windows with unusual shapes. The combs give this product a distinct look. They do a fine job of trapping air for good sound and thermal insulating qualities. Double- and triple-honeycomb design shades are highly energy efficient. They trap insulating air within their cells, are lightweight, and are relatively easy to clean. Their R-values even can approach 5, which is a big help when added to a plain, low-e double-glazed window with an R-value of only about 3.5. Other insulating shade designs include fabrics with black linings and woven shades "fabricated" with green materials such as bamboo and other grasses. Cellular shades are also good sound and thermal insulators, whereas the use of venetian blinds is another common way of regulating available sunlight (Fig. 18.27). Venetian blinds of horizontal wood, metal, or plastic strips or louvers are made in two basic styles. The standard blind features 2-inch-wide slats held in place by wide cloth tapes. The miniblind has 1-inch-wide slats held

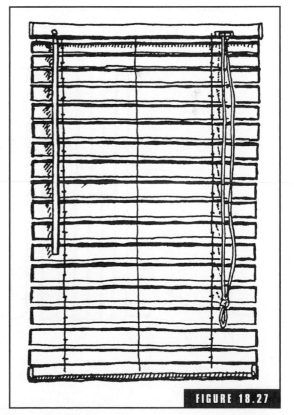

FIGURE 18.27

A venetian blind.

by slender cords. Simply because it's made of heavier material, the standard blind is more rugged, flaps less in a breeze, and can be used to darken rooms more effectively. But the miniblind is more attractive in every way, and when it's opened wide, the slats are almost invisible. These and other sized units come in a great range of colors and dimensions up to a maximum of about 100 square feet.

Vertical blinds are, in effect, venetian blinds turned on their side (Fig. 18.28). They take the place of draperies and conventional blinds or shades on windows of above-average size and are particularly suited to unusually tall or wide windows. They're ideal for glass sliding doors because they can be set to shut out glare without barring the view, and they won't catch in the doors as draperies will.

When choosing blinds, consider the single-cord control, which eliminates the looped-cord design. Better yet, some advanced models operate on a remote-control system—no cords, no wiring, just batteries. A few even feature a memory stop system to adjust the shades to the same desired position each time.

FIGURE 18.28

Vertical blinds.

AVOIDING HEAT LOSS THROUGH WINDOWS

Heat can be lost through windows in a variety of ways. It can be lost through radiation directly through the glass surfaces. Heat can be conducted through the spacers that separate two adjacent glass panes at the edges and through the window's frame. Heat also can be convected away by air movement within the spaces between adjacent panes when air picks up heat from the warmest pane surface and carries it past the colder side of the space. And finally, heat can be lost through the gaps and abutting movable parts of the windows. Again, some windows allow more air infiltration by their design. Double-hung windows, for example, typically have slightly "looser" fits than do casement windows that are closed tightly by cam-action locking mechanisms.

The loss of heat through window openings can be reduced by

- *Adding additional layers of glass (storm sashes or panels) and low-e coatings.* Since much of the thermal loss by a window is through thermal radiation from the warm pane to the adjacent colder pane, a low-e coating on the colder pane, facing the warmer pane, will prevent much of the potential heat transfer. The air gap between sheets of glass adds insulating value.

- *Including inert gas between glazings.* Inert gases such as argon and krypton have far more insulating value than air's R-5 value per inch. Argon is R-7, and krypton is R-12.

- *Sealing cracks around glass, sashes, and window frames* prevents air infiltration.

- *Making sure that weather stripping and thresholds seal the window edges tightly.*

- *Installing heavy drapes* on the inside to trap an additional layer of air next to the glass.

- *Providing shelters for window openings* in the form of overhangs, baffles, recesses, or plantings.

WINDOW INSTALLATION

- Proper installation will protect the indoors from wind and moisture and will help to lengthen a window's useful lifespan.

- The rough opening for the window should be wrapped with house wrap or prepared using an equally efficient insulation material.

- As the frame is set into the opening, it should be adjusted to be perfectly square, plumb, and level. The distance between the frame sides should be measured precisely to make sure that there is no bowing that would result in overly tight or loose sashes.

■ After the frame is fastened in place, the top must be flashed with a copper or aluminum cap. To be effective, the cap must extend up under the siding.

■ The gap between the window frame and wall frame should be filled with a nonexpanding approved insulation.

WINDOW QUICK-SELECTION CLIMATE STRATEGIES

In climates having

■ Cold winters and cool summers, choose insulated-glass models with argon gas and low-e coatings for high solar gain during winter and with low U-factors (0.35 or below) to help keep the home's heated air from escaping and an SHGC of 0.60 or higher to permit more heat to enter the home. The coldest winters can benefit from triple-glazed or even quadruple-paned windows with multiple low-e coatings and gas fills. Place fewer window's on the dwelling's colder north side.

■ Cold winters and warm to hot summers, select insulating windows with argon or krypton gas and low-e coatings to insulate in winter and partially block solar heat gain during summer.

■ Mild to cold winters and hot summers, go with low-e coating windows to moderate the heating effects of the sun.

■ Practically no winters and very hot summers, windows with multiple low-e coatings and gas fills to reflect solar heat gain and strong sunlight exposure.

In hot, dry climates such as the southwestern United States, west-facing windows gain too much heat and radiation for comfort. Windows with low-e coatings, specifically designed for such hot weather conditions, should have an SHGC of 0.40 or less. Windows should be arranged to admit general or indirect daylight rather than direct sun rays.

WINDOW ENERGY-SAVING CONSIDERATIONS

■ Grilles mounted between double-glazed windows eliminate the task of removing and replacing standard grilles whenever the windows need cleaning. With the use of interior grilles, all you do is wipe the glass clean.

■ The same goes for blinds that are enclosed between glass layers—their individual slats won't need meticulous cleaning over the years, and they're protected from being accidentally caught and damaged by children, cats, or clumsy bystanders. Cordless models are available in which a sliding handle can raise, lower, and tilt the slats. Some are adjustable by remote control.

■ Keeping the glass clean will help to take advantage of solar heat in the cold months and will admit higher illumination levels all year around, reducing the need for indoor artificial lighting.

■ Gaps between window frames and rough framing will sabotage the best windows and wall systems. Such installation voids must be filled with insulation and/or with an expandable polyurethane foam if the leaks are discovered after construction has finished.

■ Double weather-stripped window sashes and compression seals all the way around save energy.

■ In warm climates, look for windows with double glazing and spectrally selective coatings that reduce heat gain.

■ In climates with both heating and cooling seasons, select windows with both low U-values and low SHGCs.

■ Another quality to look for in windows is an air-leakage rating of 0.01 to 0.06 cubic feet of air per minute or less.

■ Quality-built windows help your house to stay cleaner owing to less air infiltration. Humidity is easier to control, and less electricity will be used running vacuums for cleaning.

■ Awning windows can stay open through more types of weather without allowing the weather into your home.

■ Windows should be located for cross-ventilation to help reduce cooling system use. Also, try to locate them away from high-noise areas so that you will be able to leave them open more often and for longer durations. In general, try to avoid placing windows on the west side in hot-climate locations and on the north side in cold-climate locales.

■ General window features to look for include tilt-in sashes for easy cleaning, removable screens, double- or single-hung or sliding windows with interlocks at the panel's meeting rails to seal out air and water, tempered or "safety" glass for shatter resistance, and fusion-welded frames for superior strength and weather resistance.

■ Energy Star labels on the windows mean energy savings at home.

■ Multipane windows having ⅜- to ½-inch spaces between panes that are filled with low-conductivity inert gas.

■ Windows traditionally have been a weak link in a home's exterior when it comes to insulation capabilities. Insist on windows with high R-values (or low U-values). This means storm window arrangements and at least double-pane (and sometimes triple-pane) windows made of glazed low-e glass. What's next? Researchers have discovered that thin transparent films made from metallic compounds such as nickel hydroxide and titanium dioxide, when sandwiched around window glass, can yield effects similar to those available from "reactive" sunglasses that automatically darken as light levels increase. Simply, these "smart" windows can remain transparent or clear when the sun is low in the sky (or not out at all) and will slowly darken as the sun rises and shines more forcefully later in the day. By blocking out midday heat from the sun, these photochromatic windows will reduce the amount of energy needed to run air-conditioning and cooling units. As the sun sets and outdoor light levels decrease, these windows gradually turn clear again.

REMODELING NOTES

■ If ever there was a remodeling "low-hanging fruit" to pick, it's windows. Simply, if windows are drafty, old, loose, dry-rotted, warped, displaying condensation, or are single-paned with gaps around the sills or frames, they need to be replaced. But those aren't the only reasons to remodel with windows; it's not such an open-and-shut case. Even fairly good windows, in the wrong places, can benefit from a well-thought-out remodeling plan.

■ There are three main ways to remodel with windows, and they all can be done at the same time. First, old, inefficient windows—those mentioned in the preceding paragraph—can be replaced with new windows of about the same size, unit per unit. Second, some of the old windows could be replaced with different-sized newer, more efficient windows at about the same places as long as the wall structure can accommodate such a plan. The third option is a wholesale swap and upgrade of window models and placements, with larger or smaller window sizes and types, some at different places in the outside walls, and possibly with different total numbers of windows—again, as long as the exterior wall structure supports the changes.

■ To accomplish the latter remodel option, analyze the windows already present. How old are they? What type? Of what construction and condition? Where are they located, and what percentage of adjacent room floor area does their square footage "cover" on each side of the dwelling? From the previous sections of this chapter, determine the ideal window placements for the home in question based on floor plans for each level and on directional (south, west, east, and north) orientations. Are there too many windows on the south side, without the benefit of a roof overhang, awnings, or trees that shade summer midday sun? Are the windows on the east and west sides too large to make energy-efficient sense? Perhaps there are too few small windows, poorly positioned. Instead of just assuming that old windows simply should be upgraded in place, take the replacement as an opportunity to maximize the benefits windows can afford. Remember, they'll also aid in ventilation, natural light allowance, and potential views of the outdoors.

■ Contact representatives of a full-service window supplier that handles brand-name or comparably constructed models and installs replacement windows as well. The installation is critical to how well the windows will perform. Be extremely wary of companies advertising unrealistic 50 percent off deals. Such businesses are notorious for supplying mass-produced mediocre windows and hiring out-of-town inexperienced crews that are given a few hours of training and turned loose on unsuspecting customers. These companies make their money by selling lots of these low-priced windows and by not paying their installers much. They're also not overly concerned about establishing satisfied repeat customers. Instead of mediocre units, get the best-quality windows you can afford. They'll pay for themselves in a short time and will provide far greater levels of comfort.

■ After the windows are installed, perform (or hire someone to do) an energy survey of the rest of your outside walls, doors included. Make sure that gaps and leaks are sealed. This will help the windows achieve the level of energy efficiency for which they were designed.

▷▷▷▷▷▷ POINTS TO PONDER

1. Windows provide natural lighting, ventilation, passive-solar heat, openings for air-conditioning units and fans, visual contact with the outside, and exits during emergencies.

2. Consider the following characteristics when selecting windows: insulating properties, ease of operation, necessary maintenance, simplicity or difficulty to clean, how the style fits in with the overall exterior scheme, and price.

3. Avoid making decisions on window selections mainly on price. Inexpensive windows could really cost literally thousands of dollars worth of unnecessary heat loss over the years.

4. When choosing windows, ask yourself where and how the windows will be used, and then match your needs with the most logical window types that will satisfy them.

5. When comparing windows, carefully review their insulating values.

6. All sleeping areas should have at least one easy-to-open window having an opening of not less than 6 to 7 square feet. Check the local building code for the required opening height, width, and sill height from the floor.

7. Be aware that the size and placement of windows will limit where you can comfortably arrange furniture.

8. Horizontal window openings are great for controlling light from southern exposures; vertical window openings work well with light from eastern and western exposures.

9. Windows located high in a room offer the most illumination and the deepest penetration by natural light.

10. Clerestories and skylights offer good possibilities for lighting interior spaces in a home.

11. Avoid skimping on basement windows. Windows installed in a basement well should be of the same quality as in the rest of the house. Traditional single-glazed windows with metal frames are a huge waste of energy and are among the least secure units available.

12. Kitchens are good candidates for installing vent skylights to exhaust moist, heated air and cooking odors.

13. Homes with second or higher floors should have safety escape chain ladders that will reach ground level available in every upper-floor bedroom.

14. Certain windows are designed to accept "between the glass" shades or other decorating, insulating, or privacy treatments. Such treatments are shielded from dust and dirt and don't interfere with window washing and cleaning.

15. Some casement window screens are retractable—they roll up and out of sight when not in use. They're a lot easier to deploy than separate screens are, and they actually increase the number of times screens are likely to be used instead of air-conditioning.

16. Cam-style locks on windows hold sashes in a weatherproof seal while securing the opening. Such locks also must be easy to open in case of an emergency. Although fixed windows tend to have fewer air leaks, operable windows having closures that pull the operable window panel and sash tightly against the frame are the next best models.

17. High-quality windows usually have heavy-duty, durable hardware and solid construction, enabling them to operate more smoothly.

Doors

There's absolutely no doubt about it: You can't have a usable house without doors. Even primitive people had them—hides draped from poles or vines. The Egyptians used woven reed mats that rolled up and down, and early Britons employed huge stones that pivoted in a circular fashion. Doors as we know them came into vogue during the Middle Ages—sturdy wooden models held together by strips of wrought iron or tightly fitted dowels.

A door provides a lot more than a simple entrance or exitway in a house. A main outside door is more often than not the architectural feature that first draws our eyes. It's the point of entry behind which is a mysterious inside. A door is a moving part. It lets in fresh air when open and seals out weather, dirt, and noise when closed. It takes up space, gets in the way, batters walls and furniture, and gets battered in turn.

Doors protect our privacy and belongings. They keep out the heat and cold and allow ventilation of a closed-in space through screens, even when shut. They provide an access for natural light and bring the outdoors inside. They'll hold warmth-giving heat indoors during winter and cool air in the summer. They'll even pull teeth in a pinch.

Greenwise, doors are not an open or shut case. Since many contain either no glass or small panes, panels, or sidelights of glass, and these glass pieces are firmly set and sealed within the doors, doors aren't as likely to cause as much heat loss as windows do. Indeed, individual doors are usually not the culprits; it's rather their installation—how the door frames are attached as transitions from house to door and door to house. Since a door typically swings open and closed, it requires space between the door and frame so that this can happen—plus an extra measure for shrinkage and expansion in response to temperature changes.

The usual green products can be rallied to manufacture doors that may be purchased in styles featuring appropriate wood and recycled materials. In fact, entire doors are often refurbished and recycled. Some doors, owing to the volume of glass in their makeup, are little more than expanded window cases. As such, sliding glass doors that access an outdoor deck, patio, or porch require sealing mechanisms that restrict the amount of air infiltration when the door panels are closed. Doors with large glass proportions are tested by manufacturers and testing organizations in the same fashion as windows are. Thus many of the same product rating systems can be applied—which are especially helpful when comparing various installations of front doors, glass side panes or panels, and sliding glass doors having fixed and convertible glass/screen inserts.

Remember the seals around pet doors, basement doors, and inside doors separating heated or cooled living areas from those areas that might not be heated or cooled, such as attics, garages, and in some cases basements and crawl spaces. Seals are also important behind bedroom built-in drawer units that may protrude into unconditioned areas or spaces such as attics. Be careful of built-in bookcases and interior soffits harboring recessed lighting, both of which may protrude into an unheated section of attic. Temper all this with the realization that failing to supply proper fresh air exchange can result in oxygen-depleted rooms that could be uncomfortable or even dangerous to live in behind closed air-sealed doors when employing space heaters, cooking, water heating, or otherwise using combustion that could quickly deplete available oxygen or emit carbon monoxide.

When considering the entrances/exits that your house will have, here are some questions to ask yourself about each door:

- Will it operate easily and reliably?
- Will it close securely?
- Will it permit easy passage of people and objects?
- Will it interfere with the use of space on either side of the door?
- Will it effectively close off whatever is supposed to be closed off?
- Will it retard the spread of fire?
- Will it minimize the transmission of sound?
- Will it permit you to see through to the other side?
- Can you hang things on its back side?
- Can it cause injury if someone walks into it?

DOOR TYPES

There are five main types of doors that a house can contain: exterior, interior, storm, patio/garden, and basement.

Exterior Doors

In addition to providing privacy and security, exterior doors can serve as effective weather barriers and sound reducers (Fig. 19.1). They're about 1¾ inch thick, 3 feet or more wide, and at least 6 feet 8 inches high. There always should be a secure layer of weather stripping around an exterior door's edges to ensure a tight weather seal. Exterior doors require the ability to resist moisture that otherwise could cause mischievous warping and misfitting, especially with wood and doors having wooden structural components—even if shielded with metal, fiberglass, or other materials.

A house's front door deserves extra attention because it's the part of a home visitors see first. The main entrance can make an impression that adds considerably to a dwelling's appearance and even to the home's value and salability. Because of the special importance of front doors, they're constructed differently

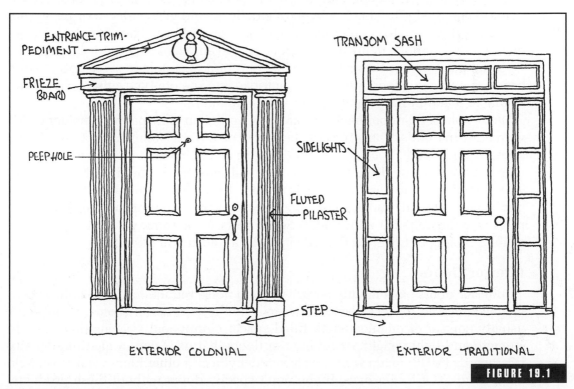

ENTRANCE TRIM·
PEDIMENT

FRIEZE
BOARD

PEEPHOLE

EXTERIOR COLONIAL

TRANSOM SASH

SIDELIGHTS

FLUTED
PILASTER

STEP

EXTERIOR TRADITIONAL

FIGURE 19.1

Exterior doors.

in some respects from just "plain" exterior doors. Details such as door caps, exterior moldings and panels, windows or lights in or to the side of the door, and reeded or fluted pilaster trim at the jambs all help to make the front door something to be approached by its own sidewalk, lit up from the outside at night, flanked by landscaped shrubbery beds, and protected by a roof overhang.

Home security should not be forgotten in connection with any exterior doors. Security means a combination of the proper door locks and hardware plus the ability to see who is calling before the door is opened. One way that front entrance visibility can be accomplished is by the installation of sidelights. Sidelights are narrow glass panes or panels that run the height of an entrance door and are placed either at one or both sides of the door for added beauty and natural light. Two drawbacks are their relatively poor insulation value and their susceptibility to intruders who, if the sidelights are not positioned correctly in relation to the door's locks, can break the glass and then reach inside to unlock the door. Sidelights vary in size but normally are less than 1 foot wide. They're available in many finishes and textures, some with low-e insulated glass for increased energy efficiency. The larger door and side glass panels let plenty of light in but can leave the entrance vulnerable to break-ins, even if double glazing of tempered glass is used. What good is a strong entry door if an intruder simply can break a glass and then reach in and open the lock? This is why most sidelights and glass entry door panels are either small enough to prevent such reaching in or are located far enough above the door handle and lock to prevent illegal access, even when the glass is broken.

If there are no see-through sidelights, opt for a peephole to see who's outside before opening the door. Electronic touch-pad and remote-type entrance locks are available that eliminate fumbling for keys at night.

For a side or rear door having clear energy-efficient glass panes, consider a unit with built-in blinds. The blinds can be closed on a warm summer day to minimize excessive heat gain. Because the blinds are sealed between tempered safety glass, there's no dusting or cleaning of the individual slats; they should operate for years with practically no maintenance involved. Such inside-the-door or -window blinds will tilt a full 180 degrees, which allows you to control sunlight levels and privacy with fingertip adjustment. Some units even come with an option that enables raising or lowering the slats just like a traditional blind.

Interior Doors

Interior doors exist mainly for privacy and noise reduction. Many hollow-core models are used for bedrooms, bathrooms, and other interior rooms. Their cores usually consist of engineered air-filled spacer component systems that provide strength and light weight. Avoid interior doors that use Luan or medium-density fiberboards (MDF) made with urea formaldehyde and other high–volatile organic compound (VOC) adhesives. If you don't specify doors without these products, you may well find them being used in your home.

To be effective for each room, the doors must be well fitted. However, if the house heating system depends on a free flow of air from room to room, interior doors should be undercut at least ½ inch above the finished floors to permit air passage. Although this doesn't apply to areas having their own air supply and return outlets, remember that door fit is still important. You don't want doors to work too tightly, especially over carpeting, because large amounts of friction will be created when the doors are opened and closed, and excessive effort will be needed to operate them.

Interior doors are available, in addition to flush and paneled models, in full louvered, top and bottom louvered, or partially louvered models with either a top or bottom of paneling (Fig. 19.2). Louvered doors, while more expensive than flush or

FIGURE 19.2

A louvered door.

paneled doors, are particularly useful in locations requiring a free flow of air—namely, closets or rooms containing mechanical or electronic equipment that must "breathe" or emit heat to operate safely and efficiently, such as some water heaters and certain heating units and furnaces. On the other hand, avoid using louvered doors when the opposite is true—when you want to prevent air from traveling from one space to another—say, from an attached garage to a kitchen.

Storm Doors

If you elect to include an enclosed patio that leads to your back or side door, it will provide an efficient air lock when you enter the house from there during cold weather. Otherwise, storm doors provide protection from harsh weather and direct sunlight for your primary doors. They supply additional security, offer natural ventilation in the summer, and help to control heat loss and drafts during winter and cool air loss during summer (Fig. 19.3), when, in both seasons, the storm door creates an insulating dead air space around the main door it protects. Most storm doors are designed for easy changeovers from screens in summer, with fiberglass or other screening that will not rust or corrode, to energy-efficient glass inserts during winter. A storm door is nothing to skimp on: Good styling on the front-entrance storm door can add a lot to the appearance of a house and also can cover up a nondescript front door.

One potential trouble spot for a storm door—especially one having a full face of glass—is that the space between the glass and the entry door—especially if the

FIGURE 19.3

A storm door.

door faces strong sunlight for hours at a time—can create extremely high temperatures. Think of how hot it gets inside a vehicle with closed windows parked in the sun all day. Those high temperatures may fade or warp the best entry doors over years of such abuse. To prevent that from happening, simply select storm doors with half-glass panels instead of full-length glass. In the summer, the screen provides increased cross-ventilation, thus reducing the amount you may need to operate air-conditioning.

When selecting your storm doors, look for the following:

■ The main frames and frames for the glass and screen inserts should be strong. If you can easily bend or flex the frames, they're too weak to make an adequate door.

■ A wrought-iron door with deadbolts and heavy hinges makes a secure and decorative storm door. But well-constructed storm doors are available in many other materials as well, including wood, aluminum, steel, and fiberglass.

■ Doors having a foam insulation core between their outer panels or skins are very efficient. This sandwich-style construction forms a rigid door with airtight seals, some with refrigerator-type magnetic closure strips.

■ A functional design typically will enable you to remove the glass and screen inserts from the inside of the house in a simple manner. Separate screen doors with particleboard or wood cores beneath their outer skins are rigid and durable.

■ A front storm door with a lot of screen/glass having attractive bevels or stained glass provides efficient ventilation and an attractive entrance.

Home's Appearance

The most decorative glass panes are beveled, etched, frosted, colored, or accented with brass and other accompaniments. Smaller windows, such as ornate ovals, are energy efficient. Low-e glass with insulating inert argon gas in the gap is one of the most energy-efficient panes available.

- For the front storm door, select glass that helps to enhance the appearance. In some models, the decorative glass panes are further sandwiched between two outer panes, creating additional insulating air gaps.

- For a functional rear screen door, consider a unit having less glass and an extrastrong frame. In hot climates, tinted glass panes will help your air conditioner.

- Look for weather tightness to prevent the entrance of water, cold air, dust, and insects. A triple-track system is one of the best designs, especially for the back storm door. If you lower the top glass and raise the bottom glass panels a little, it creates a natural air current ventilation path. With such a system, you never need to remove the screen or glass panels.

- For ease of maintenance, a storm door with a self-storing glass or screen has less glass area, so the glass or screen panel can be slipped down and hidden inside the door.

- Make sure that storm doors have easy-to-work locking mechanisms. Some of the most secure units feature decorative wrought-iron or aluminum channels, reinforced latches, antitheft stops, deadbolt pins resembling the pins from bank vaults, and nonremovable pin hinges. In addition, there is an increasing demand for storm doors having keyed deadbolts that you can lock from the outside for additional security.

Screening

RETRACTABLE SCREEN SYSTEMS

In our ever-present quest to save energy whenever possible, consider that improving natural ventilation instead of using air-conditioning can help to lower utility bills and improve indoor air quality. Enter retractable screen systems.

Retractable screen systems feature a narrow tubular housing mounted vertically on a door frame (Fig. 19.4). One small aluminum track is attached to the floor and another to the top of the door opening.

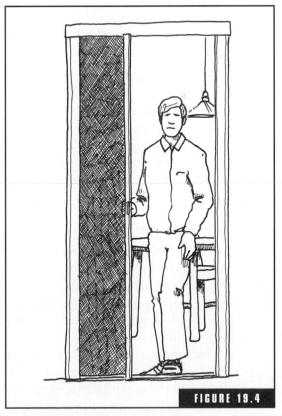

FIGURE 19.4

A retractable screen.

A magnetic latch is fixed on the other side of the door opening, as seen in the figure. When you open the door to go in or out or just for ventilation, you pull the handle on the screen that's coiled up within the cassette housing. The screen unrolls from the cassette housing and adheres to the magnetic latch; there is a slight spring tension on the screening to keep it taut and attractive. Premium screening kits use ball bearings in the cassette for smoother operation. Nylon or other reinforcement strips along the upper and lower edges of the screen increase the unit's durability.

Sun- and Pet-Control Screening

This screen material can be used to block intense summer sunlight when a window is open and also when the same window is closed because the screening is located on the outside of the window. A durable woven vinyl-coated fiberglass product, its ribbed weave is designed to block up to 70 percent of the sun's heat and glare. In addition to reducing the amount of solar heat gain (and keeping insects out) during summer, it also can reduce heat loss during winter. Another handy option for pet lovers is special dog- and cat-resistant screening made of vinyl-coated polyester. It's about seven times more tear-resistant than ordinary screening.

Awnings

An alternative to a storm door is a retractable awning installed above the exterior door. Many retractable awnings open or close in just a few seconds. An awning can protect the door from rain and sun. Blocking the sun will reduce heat buildup within the house. It can keep the outer surface of the exterior door from getting wet—which also prevents water from dripping off the door onto the interior floor each time the door is opened when wet. An awning will give you the chance to open an umbrella as you first go outdoors and an opportunity to be out of the rain as you unlock the door to go inside.

Patio/Garden Doors

Sliding glass doors and French doors will bring the outdoors inside and will provide convenient access to a patio, deck, or garden. They can make a room seem and feel, by extending the inside to the outdoors, larger than it really is, and they'll supply a flood of natural air and light when their screens are in play. Practically any house built today will use one of these doors somewhere within its outer walls (Fig. 19.5).

Factors to consider when selecting patio/garden doors are thermal insulation quality, weather tightness, a secure locking system, and a nice appearance. Since sliding doors essentially look and operate like large windows, they need effective weather stripping and insulating glass. Sliders with "super" insulating glass are available now for use in northern climates.

FIGURE 19.5

A sliding-glass patio door.

Sliding-glass doors generally are the bypass type. Most units include at least one fixed and one sliding panel. Some three-panel models are available that have a center panel that slides open in one direction. For larger wall spans, four-panel models can be installed that have two center panels opening in opposite directions to make a convenient access to large decks or patios. Sliding glass doors cover a large span, so the strength of the frame is critical. Typical frame material options include fiberglass, vinyl, wood, vinyl- or aluminum-clad wood, or aluminum. Wood frames allow for a great range of styles and contours; they should come treated with a water-repellent coating.

Fiberglass frames are very energy efficient, easy to maintain, and durable, and they can be painted easily. Fiberglass expands and contracts with temperature changes at a rate similar to the glass panes. This reduces stress within the door and results in a long-term airtight seal that helps to prevent fogging. Fiberglass or vinyl frames should contain foam or similar insulation inside the cavities for improved comfort and lower utility bills. For a wood door appearance, select a model having real oak or other veneer fastened to the fiberglass. A patio door has

FIGURE 19.6

French doors.

a large amount of glass area compared with the frame area, so the type of glass you select has a greater impact on energy efficiency than does the frame material. For hot climate locations, consider doors with tinted glass. For cold climate locations, opt for triple pane systems with low-e glass.

French doors generally have a single panel that swings while the other panel remains stationary (Fig. 19.6). Their wide frames are attractive and strong and can be energy efficient because there is less glass area through which to lose or gain heat. Grids inside the panels have thick rails, stiles, and transoms with stained, beveled, or etched thermal glass. For exterior wood French doors, look for units that have a waterproof material inserted in the bottom of each door stile to prevent moisture damage. The block is covered by veneer so that you can't see it, and the bottom rail and stile are secured with glue and dowel pins. The bottom rail needs to be sealed with waterproof material.

Basement Doors

Outside basement doors allow you to transport such items as screens, storm windows, and garden tools inside and out without lugging them through the living areas. As mentioned earlier, basement doors are ideal for lower-level laundry rooms and will provide children with a means of getting to the back and side yards without having to pass through the rest of the house. A basement door should be at least 36 inches wide to accommodate large appliances.

Although basement doors should be able to withstand the weather and provide security against theft by themselves, attractive basement stairwell covers can be purchased in ready-to-install packages for use in all types of houses. They're typically steel double door covers that enclose and protect the outer stairwell leading to the basement door.

DOOR STYLES

There are six basic styles of doors used throughout today's modern house: hinged, bifold, sliding, pocket, folding, and café.

Hinged Doors

A hinged door is essentially a simple rigid panel that swings open and closed on hinges. It's the most common type of door. Hinged doors come in several architectural styles: flush, contemporary, colonial (six-panel), and glass (Fig. 19.7).

FLUSH   CONTEMPORARY   COLONIAL WITH GLASS

FIGURE 19.7

Hinged doors.

ADVANTAGES

1. When closed, hinged doors seal very well, curbing energy loss and limiting the amount of sound transmission.

2. They're initially one of the least costly types of doors to purchase and hang.

3. They require a minimum amount of maintenance and cleaning.

4. They're great for providing (on their back sides) space for door-hung shoe racks, necktie racks, and belt racks and for fastening all-purpose hooks.

DISADVANTAGE

1. Hinged doors take up precious room to swing in. Consequently, they can't be used where there's an obstacle in the way of their swing.

Bifold Doors

Bifold doors are similar to those used in telephone booths, except house bifolds open outward (Fig. 19.8). They're used indoors only because there is no way to seal the cracks around their edges. The most common bifold door consists of two fairly narrow vertical panels that are hinged together. One panel pivots next to the door jamb; the other glides in an overhead track. To open a bifold door, you either shove the track-mounted panel toward the opposite door jamb or pull the knobs fastened to the panels near the hinged edges. Both methods of opening force the panels to fold together back to back at right angles to the doorway opening.

For small openings, a single bifold door with two narrow panels is adequate. For larger openings, the door is made with wider panels or a double bifold door is employed that has four panels hinged together. These doors are designed to be operated from one side only and are best suited for closets. They're useful in providing wide door opening coverage to shallow closets, making the most of the available square footage.

ADVANTAGES

1. When both sections of a bifold door are completely opened, you have an almost clear view through the doorway. Or you

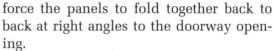

FIGURE 19.8

Bifold doors.

can have access to one-half of the same closet without disturbing the door covering the other half.

2. Bifold doors are ideal in places where there is little room to swing a regular door outward.

3. They allow the maximum opening to a closet with minimal extension into the room. Extending the height of the doors a full 8 feet to the ceiling eliminates headers and permits full-width shelves and access to the upper area that otherwise would be lost.

4. In walk-in closets, the space used for the "walking in" cannot be used for storage. In shallow closets with bifold doors, however, the users do not enter the closets—so almost all the space within is available for storage.

5. Bifold doors come in styles that include solid or louvered panels. The louvered doors have a beautiful appearance that alone makes them popular with many home owners.

DISADVANTAGES

1. Bifold doors can come untracked or malfunction easier than simple hinged doors can. They won't take the abuse that other types of doors can take.

2. Bifold doors are somewhat more expensive than their counterparts.

3. Bifold doors cannot be used where a tight weather seal is required, nor where the door must be operated from two sides.

4. Bifold louvered doors are time-consuming to clean and difficult to repaint or resurface because of the many individual slats.

Sliding Doors

Sliding doors consist of usually two and sometimes three door panels that slide by each other (Fig. 19.9). These units hang from and move along double or triple tracks installed against the underside of conventional head jambs. To prevent operating problems, sliding doors made of glass should be of top-quality construction with sturdy tracks, double or insulated shatterproof glass, and mohair or other stripping laid along the door's tubing edges for maximum insulation.

FIGURE 19.9

Sliding doors.

ADVANTAGES

1. Sliding doors can be used wherever doors are needed but door swing space or projections are not permitted.

2. Sliding doors are easily maintained and cleaned.

3. Glass sliding doors are wonderful for expanding a view and for making rooms seem a lot larger than they really are.

DISADVANTAGES

1. Sliding doors give access to only half (or, when three doors are involved, to one-third) of an opening at once.

2. These doors are sensitive to any settling that might occur in a house. The sliding doors can stick against the bottom floor guide, which causes the doors to ride up and either jump or damage the hanging tracks and trolleys.

3. Sometimes the screen inserts to glass sliding doors can be a nuisance if they're not fitted exactly because they tend to pop out of their tracks. The rollers may eventually wear out and may have to be replaced. It's an inexpensive precaution to purchase a few spare sets when the door is ordered, so you won't have to search around at a later date.

4. A cheaply made closet sliding door, when handled gently, will do the job, but a cheaply made glass slider that isn't weather tight and fitted correctly will let in a lot of cold or hot air and can be difficult to operate.

Pocket Doors

A pocket door slides in and out of a pocket built into the wall framing of partition walls. Their use with load-bearing walls is usually impractical. One excellent use is with a small bathroom or mudroom to prevent the room's occupant from having to squeeze around the door (Fig. 19.10).

These space-savers can have silent-action rollers and rubber stopping bumpers inside the pockets so that the doors will work without clatter. A pocket door recedes or slides in and out of a pocket built into the wall framing instead of swinging out in an arc like a hinged door does. Standard hinged doors waste a lot of space; they take away from possible furniture placements, picture hanging, shelving installations, and the like.

A well-placed pocket door will save roughly 8 to 10 square feet of floor space. Also, while pocket doors themselves may not lower your utility costs directly, they will allow you to build a smaller square footage house that provides the same usable amount of floor space. A smaller house has less wall and roof footage and thus less area to heat and cool.

Another energy benefit of pocket doors is that they allow heating and cooling systems to operate more efficiently because when you open a pocket door, there is

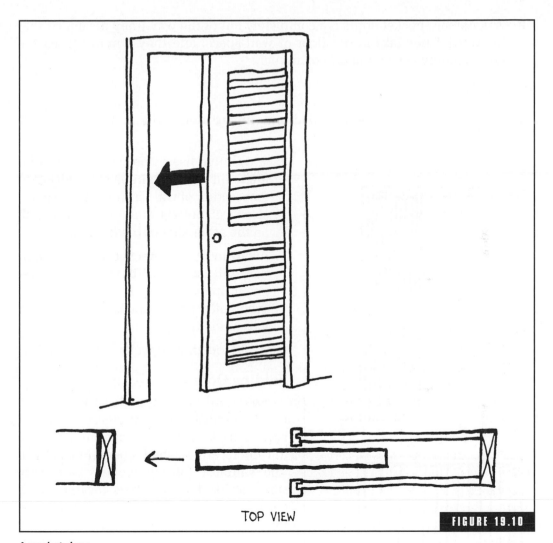

TOP VIEW

FIGURE 19.10

A pocket door.

no restriction to air movement, allowing better circulation. Standard hinged doors can hinder air movement and cause (however slightly) heating and cooling systems to work harder. Manufacturers offer beautiful wood pocket doors made from oak, cherry, walnut, and others, supported by sturdy steel-reinforced split studs.

ADVANTAGES

1. Pocket doors are useful in locations where there is little room to swing a standard hinged door out of the way owing to interference with traffic or the operation of other doors.

2. When open, pocket doors are completely out of the way (they disappear into the wall). They take up no floor or wall space, and they don't obstruct the door opening even a fraction of an inch.

DISADVANTAGES

1. Pocket doors should be installed only in partition walls, not walls that are load bearing.

2. A wall that has a door pocket built into it should not contain electric wiring in that section of wall. You'll have to place electrical outlets and the light switch on the other side of the doorway.

3. Avoid locating a pocket door in a wall that will be tiled. Vibrations from frequent opening and closing of the door eventually could crack the grout and loosen the tiles.

4. Avoid locating on walls with plumbing.

Folding Doors

Folding doors are made of many thin, narrow vertical strips or creases that fold back to back into a compact bundle when the doors are pushed open (Fig. 19.11). The simplest folding models have very small strips that are tied together with cords. Most, however, have wooden or metal slats about 4 inches wide that are hinged together with vinyl fabric. In all cases, these doors hang from and run in a track. They open and close between the door opening's side jambs.

The main applications for folding doors are in closets, laundry niches, and some storage pantry–like areas in the garage, basement, or hallways. They also can be used to divide large open spaces into two smaller rooms.

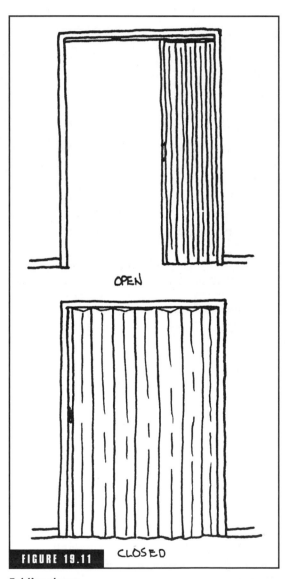

OPEN

CLOSED

FIGURE 19.11

Folding doors.

1. Folding doors don't swing out or protrude from doorway openings. Their accordion sections fold up into a small bundle when open.

DISADVANTAGES

1. Folding doors give scant protection against fire and noise.

2. They don't operate very smoothly. They're not made as sturdily as other doors and cannot stand heavy use well.

3. A main objection of home owners is that folding doors *don't* look like doors. Rather, they resemble stiff draperies. Folding doors generally are neither strong nor secure, and they have a tendency to wave in a strong draft.

Café Doors

These are the doors you've probably seen a thousand gunslingers walk through into television and theater saloons. They're the double swinging doors on the short side—about 30 to 60 inches long—installed on opposite sides of an opening roughly midway between the top and bottom of a passageway (Fig. 19.12). They're attached to the opening's walls or jambs with gravity pivot hinges that enable the doors to be pushed open in either direction, only to be closed automatically once a person passes through. Café doors are available in both louvered and paneled designs.

Because you can push your way through them without using your hands, these doors come in handy in places where you're likely to have your hands full, such as between a kitchen and dining room, where the cook is likely to shoulder his or her way from the kitchen carrying a holiday turkey. Café doors don't provide much privacy from noise or odors (then again, who wants to hide the delicious smells that waft from a kitchen stove?), but they will block the sight of stacks of dirty dishes in the kitchen sink from guests in the dining room.

FIGURE 19.12

Café doors.

ADVANTAGES

1. Café doors are inexpensive and easy to install.

2. They're simple to use.

3. They add a unique and attractive character to the interior of a home.

DISADVANTAGES

1. Café doors provide little protection from fire and noise.

2. Because people are constantly pushing against them, they're difficult to keep clean. If louvered, they're time consuming to wash or resurface.

3. Children can be injured running in and out of them.

DOOR OPENINGS

Door openings are permanent features of a house that should be well thought out in advance. Here are some pointers to consider:

1. Door opening heights should be a minimum of 6 feet 8 inches or 7 feet. For greater flexibility, though, consider a front door opening that's 8 feet tall and 42 inches wide for moving large pieces of furniture through. An alternative is to select a door having a decorative sidelight panel that opens. The extra 14 inches or so will greatly save time that otherwise would be spent by movers who must carefully lift and manipulate large furniture pieces sideways, backward, or upside down.

2. A front door should be a minimum of 36 inches wide—this is still a tight fit for numerous oversize pieces of furniture available on the market today. If the front door width is any less, then the house should have another outside door that is at least 36 inches wide so that you'll have the ability to move large items in and out. The recommended thickness of a 36-inch+ exterior door is at least 1¾ inches.

3. Secondary outside door openings to a basement, kitchen, laundry, or garage can be 32 inches wide with thicknesses of 1¾ inches.

4. If you happen to position a bedroom door at a right angle to the end of a hallway, make sure that the hallway is extra wide and the door opening is 36 inches, or you'll never be able to maneuver large pieces of furniture such as dressers and headboards into the room.

5. Consider each individual passageway if you want interior doors to open inward or outward as safety and convenience dictate. Basement stairway doors always should open away from the stairs.

6. When planning patio/garden openings, figure that they consist of sliding and stationary glass panels with widths of at least 36 inches per panel.

HINGED DOORS

Because hinged doors are used in every house in some fashion, exterior or interior, they deserve additional comment:

1. They are easier to open and close than all other doors except swinging cafe doors.

2. They permit you to use their backsides for storage space, a major advantage in closets.

3. Their operation is noiseless except when slammed.

4. When hung properly, exterior models close tightly and stop drafts, dirt, and insects from penetrating around the edges.

5. Exterior and interior doors should be hung with three hinges. Ball-bearing hinges typically provide the smoothest operation. The middle hinge helps to support the door while maintaining correct alignment. At the same time, on hollow-core doors, typically a horizontal reinforcement board is placed through the door center to provide a sturdy base or support for the doorknob hardware. If you plan to install a doorstop with a hollow-core door, position the stop where that center reinforcement board runs. If the doorstop is placed elsewhere, it may punch a hole in the unsupported facing.

6. Interior doors should swing into the rooms they close off from hallways. Otherwise, they interfere with hallway traffic.

7. Doors on hall closets obviously must swing into the hall, and it's often advisable to swing a kitchen door into a hall so that it doesn't create traffic problems within the kitchen work areas.

8. Whenever possible, bathroom doors should swing in, but if the bathroom is too cramped, the door can be hung to swing outward.

9. Doors between adjoining rooms other than bathrooms can be swung whichever way will cause the least inconvenience.

10. Doors at the head of stairways must swing away from the stairs.

11. Whether a door should be hinged on the right or left depends on which position will interfere less with furniture placements and passage through the doorway.

12. Ideally, storm doors should be placed so that they can swing back into a corner out of the way.

13. Every exterior hinged door (and other types for that matter)—front, back, or side—should have a step down to the outside, a sill forming the bottom part of the frame and entrance. This 8-inch step down is to prevent water from entering the house during heavy rains or snows.

PET DOORS

In warm-climate regions, if you own a dog or cat, you might consider installing a pet door next to one of your side or rear entrances (Fig. 19.13). Several companies manufacture ready-to-install units that are two-way, self-closing, silent, chewproof, energy efficient (fitted with a weather seal), and lockable.

The main reason that pet doors are energy efficient is because a pet exiting and entering through a small pet door prevents the full-size exterior door from opening for those same tasks. A full-size exterior door opening allows a substantial amount of heated or cooled air to escape outdoors. Then, whatever conditioned air is lost must be replaced, thus increasing energy usage and cost. Units are also available with foam insulation inside the metal rise and height-adjustment components for further energy savings and noise reduction.

Consider that pet doors are available for practically any situation, even panels constructed to fit in a glass or screen door track, as are units available having ½-inch dual-pane insulated glass with foam weather stripping on both edges. Some models have a locking steel close-off cover that keeps animals in or out. A pin lock is available for security.

ADVANTAGES

1. You needn't be present to let your pet in and out during the day or night.

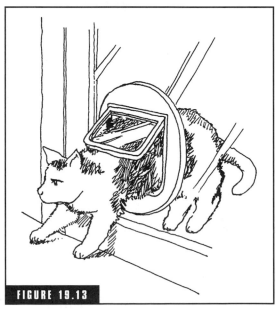

FIGURE 19.13

Pet door.

2. You needn't worry about heating or cooling the great outdoors by leaving a front or rear door propped open while you peer into the darkness and whistle for your pet to come home.

DISADVANTAGE

What might happen if your neighbors install the same type of door for their pets?

PET DOOR CONSIDERATIONS

■ Units can be purchased that mount between 2 × 4 or 2 × 6 framing studs. Other designs include units that are complete panels that mount in a sliding-glass patio door track with a pet door built in at the bottom. Units are also on the market to custom-frame in an irregularly sized door.

- The pet door or panel should have a fully weather-stripped, soft, two-way flexible flap with magnetic closures to keep the flap secure or an electromagnetic release equipped with two collar keys that have a beeper to indicate when a unit's battery is running low. A collar key is a tiny device that attaches to the pet's collar—typically operating on two AA batteries. Without a signal from the key, the pet door will not open. This system effectively keeps out neighbor's pets, as well as squirrels, rodents, and other wild animals.

- Some models have settings such as "in only," "out only," "locked," or "full open" in case special circumstances arise, such as your cousin visiting with his or her pet that also needs to go in and out throughout the day.

- Several units come with an "in/out" indicator that lets you know which way the pet went last: in or out.

- A "break-in" alarm is available on some models, which goes off or "chirps" if the pet door is forced open or smashed in.

- Some manufacturers claim that their doors will to help wipe off mosquitoes and other bugs as the pets come and go.

DOOR CONSTRUCTION

The construction of interior doors versus exterior doors is substantially different (Fig. 19.14).

Interior Doors

Interior doors can be built out of wood, plastic, metal, or any combination thereof. A solid-wood door is the best and most expensive interior door available. Solid-wood doors do a good job controlling sound between rooms. They are made by sandwiching a wooden core between two sheets of high-quality hardwood veneer such as birch, oak, mahogany, or pine. Lighter-duty hollow-core doors can have the same expensive veneer faces, but sheets of sturdy wood-grain plastic also make a practical, easy-to-clean surface. The lowest-priced hollow-core models frequently are covered with less durable wood composition board.

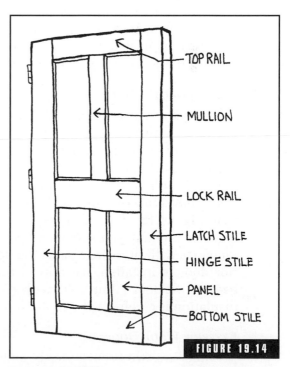

FIGURE 19.14

TOP RAIL

MULLION

LOCK RAIL

LATCH STILE

HINGE STILE

PANEL

BOTTOM STILE

Door construction.

When selecting door veneers, keep in mind that birch and oak doors hold up better than mahogany or pine. Oak and birch are harder woods that can resist greater impacts.

Exterior Doors

Exterior doors can be categorized as wood, steel, and composition patio doors. There are some great-looking entry doors in the marketplace, many of which are now being constructed with green components. But consider that even the best doors will not be as energy efficient as well-designed, well-insulated walls. Recommendations for door insulation: R-5 minimum; better yet, greater than R-5.

In addition, every time an exterior door is opened in hot, cold, or moist weather, conditioned air from within the home will escape, and unconditioned air will enter. One way to minimize these effects is to plan and include small entry rooms, mudrooms, confined foyers, or, when positioned at the side or back, sheds that act like airlocks and confine the air exchange to a small location, keeping cold and moisture out and heat inside. These don't have to be ugly little spaces, like old farmhouse sheds used to be. They can be tastefully integrated into the front, side, or rear entries, and when fitted with inside storm doors, they will help to prevent air infiltration and dirt from being tracked into the house. One design feature that might fly in the face of green, however, is the big, multistory entry foyer. The big entry foyer has been popular for many years but has been losing favor recently owing to the large amount of unusable space it requires—space that unavoidably also must be heated and cooled for no good use. See where those exterior entry doors can lead to? To the threshold of discussing door parts.

THRESHOLDS AND SILLS

No matter what kind of door it is, a sturdy threshold is needed. Door models having an adjustable threshold are excellent choices. An adjustable threshold can be adjusted easily up or down with a screwdriver—which can help to make and keep the door airtight, quiet, and energy efficient while sealing out dust, dirt, moisture, and drafts (Fig. 19.15). At the same time, located on the bottom of exterior doors, a multifin threshold seal provides further defense against air penetration (Fig. 19.16). For ultimate protection in high-exposure severe-weather areas, look for a composite substrate bumper swing-out sill. The accompanying seal increases with pressure against the door to keep out air and water. When an exterior door is installed, it's critical that a generous amount of caulk be applied beneath the door's threshold, with a few beads run on top of the sill plate, and that insulation is carefully placed around the rest of the door frame to keep out drafts.

EXTERIOR WOOD DOORS

There are two basic styles of exterior wood doors: flush and paneled. Flush doors are simple flat-surfaced doors that can be constructed with particleboard

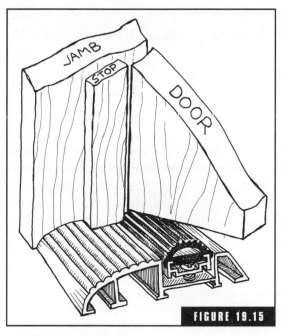

FIGURE 19.15

An adjustable threshold.

FIGURE 19.16

A multifin threshold.

cores between two outer surfaces of a durable wood such as a high-grade fir or a solid-lumber core between the two outer faces. The latter are much stronger—a better choice, and the most expensive. Paneled doors have decorative designs cut into them. Both flush and paneled models can be made with various amounts and shapes of glass inserts. If you desire the highest insulating efficiency along with the beauty of real wood, several manufacturers produce real wood exterior doors having insulated cores and, for a weather-tight fit, triple-weather-strip seals. There are even models featuring engineered wood for additional strength.

ADVANTAGES

1. They're beautiful, particularly when stained to show off their grain.
2. They lend themselves to an infinite variety of designs and even can be customized to your specifications by the manufacturer.
3. They can be sawed and planed to fit existing door openings or new openings that are not carefully made or openings that later warp because of settling.
4. Solid-core and insulation-core wooden doors have good insulating qualities and are relatively soundproof.

DISADVANTAGES

1. If not taken care of, exterior wood doors may expand, warp, crack, shrink, and cause sealing problems.

2. They must be refinished periodically.

3. Wood doors are combustible.

EXTERIOR STEEL DOORS

Most steel doors are really part steel and part wood—steel sheets fabricated around a wooden frame in which urethane foam or another insulation material is sandwiched to provide outstanding protection against cold and heat. Steel doors are more practical than doors made of wood. They're designed to prevent the principal cause of wood door failures—warpage that results in improper closure and air infiltration. They also resist cracking, splitting, splintering, shrinking, and bowing. Newer door frames provide a thermal break between interior parts and exterior surfaces, eliminating winter condensation inside. Overall, insulated steel doors generally are several times more efficient than solid-wood doors.

Other features that apply to many steel door models are adjustable thermal-break thresholds, magnetic weather stripping for uniform sealing, and fire-resistant qualities that result in excellent safety ratings. The steel-skin design makes these doors efficient and maintenance-free, with the thickness of the steel skin and door width being fairly good indicators of overall door quality. Thicker steel provides better stability and dent resistance and offers considerable protection against intruders.

Remember, when comparing steel doors, a lower gauge number represents a thicker steel skin. Partly for security and partly to maintain a tight fit, units are available with a multipoint deadbolt lock—the deadbolt engages the door's frame in three locations from top to bottom and is operated by a sturdy rack and pinion system hidden inside the door. Another safety feature of quality steel doors is a rugged heavy wood lock block. The insulated foam placed in the hollow can provide insulating values of R-14 and greater.

Exterior steel doors come in many styles and finishes and are commonly fitted with glass inserts and peepholes for viewing. They're also available with real natural oak and other veneers permanently bonded to the steel skin all sandwiched around a core of insulation. The steel doors with magnetic gaskets along their edges grip like seals on a refrigerator door and give the tightest seal against the weather. For ease of installation, they're available with integrated framing systems that coordinate framing components, sills, door bottoms, corner pads, and weather stripping as a single packaged unit, completely prehung with hinges. The cost of steel doors is quite competitive with the costs of wood doors.

Make sure that any steel door you buy is predrilled by the supplier to accept the door hardware (handles, knobs, and locks) you desire. If you don't, it could cost you extra to have it done on the job site because some carpenters don't have the right tools to drill this type of door.

ADVANTAGES

1. Steel doors provide an excellent seal against air infiltration; some have magnetic seals.
2. They're well insulated.
3. They're difficult to force open, cut open, or break through.
4. They're not affected by moisture and won't crack, rot, or warp.
5. They're fire resistant.
6. Plastic decorator panels are available for some steel door models to provide elaborate and varied finishes.
7. They come in 20-gauge, dent-resistant wood-grain finishes that are stainable to achieve the warm look of wood.
8. Steel doors can be purchased with stained wood, steel, or vinyl-coated aluminum surfaces.
9. Steel doors are available with fully adjustable oak or vinyl caps to provide energy-efficient fits.
10. Multiple-blade sweeps (on door bottoms) eliminate drafts.

DISADVANTAGE

Steel doors come in standard sizes and are not easily adjusted to slightly uneven or odd-sized openings.

EXTERIOR FIBERGLASS AND CARBON DOORS

Factory-finished or stainable fiberglass and carbon doors have a sturdy construction and a foam core that gives them high insulating values. These doors will hardly shrink or expand with changing seasons, maintaining a tight air and moisture seal that is often further ensured by the use of magnetic weather stripping with brass-plated steel trim strips inlaid in the door's edge. Of the two, carbon expands or contracts less with temperature changes, making a tighter seal. As with steel insulated doors, fiberglass and carbon insulated doors are also several times more energy efficient than solid-wood doors.

Carbon door skins also require less forming pressure during the manufacturing process, so the surface remains more porous and able to take stain very well. When compared with steel-clad doors—especially those with thinner steel cladding—fiberglass is considerably more dent resistant. Triple-locking mechanisms with heavy-duty blocks such as those found on better wood and steel doors are also available on fiberglass and carbon door models.

COMPOSITE PATIO DOORS

Patio doors typically are sliding-glass doors framed with steel, aluminum, or wood or French doors that provide access to a patio, porch, deck, or garden. The wood frames are frequently clad in vinyl to eliminate the need to repaint or refinish the wood.

Double- or triple-pane glass that has a good insulating value should be used in these doors, and weather stripping must be included along the door edges. Design improvements have separated the inner and outer faces so that the frames will not easily transmit heat or cold.

ADVANTAGES

1. Glass allows a view of the outside surroundings.
2. They require very little maintenance.
3. They're great if lots of light and sunshine are desired.

DISADVANTAGES

1. They're easy to force open if proper precautions are not taken.
2. Poorly constructed ones will sweat.
3. When constructed without thermal-type double or better glass, they have poor insulating value.
4. Even with the better patio doors, the wear and tear caused by regular door movement across the sealing material is prone to allow leaks in the sealing that will permit air and moisture infiltration.

GENERAL DOOR CONSIDERATIONS

Make sure that you check the operation of each door after the doors are installed. Because doors are used so often, minor imperfections or operating deficiencies can become very annoying.

See that

■ All knobs, locks, and deadbolts work properly, without sticking, and that doorknobs and latches line up with latch inserts. You shouldn't have to yank a door closed to latch it or push downward or upward on the handle to engage the latch. This is especially important for a basement door. If it won't close securely, a small child could open it and fall down the stairway.

■ Doors hang level, with hinges that don't squeak or bind. All doors should swing freely, without noise or obvious friction. The door installation must be square, with an even gap between the door frame from top to bottom.

- Opened doors should hold their position and not swing closed or farther open by themselves.

- Door frame and casing nails should be set below the wood surface and puttied.

- There should be no leaks around the weather stripping or thresholds.

- When choosing interior doors, you can increase the appearance of interior lighting while making the room look larger by selecting mirrored doors. Interior doors are available having mirrors built into one side. Mirrors reflect lighting, so the lighting travels around the room farther, illuminating things on its way. At least one manufacturer offers doors with framed and frameless mirrors on them that swing, slide, and bifold open and closed.

- At times, we all receive unwanted visitors at our front door. During summer or winter, heated or cooled air is lost when the front door is opened so that unrequested solicitors can be spoken to or asked to leave. For safety's sake, and to limit the need for opening the door unnecessarily, consider the installation of a wide-angle peephole. Models are available that offer excellent views of the outside. One unit even projects the view onto a screen that's several inches wide.

- To protect a door's integrity, install a door stop that will protect both the door and its adjacent wall. Look for a model that does not put pressure on the door itself.

- For exterior doors, consider a built-in battery-operated burglar alarm that, when the door is locked, any shaking of the door sets off an audible alarm for a short time. The alarm sensitivity level can be adjusted.

REMODELING NOTES

Exterior doors mean a lot to the appearance and first impressions of a home and to street appeal for resale and home value. The appearance usually does not have a major effect on the performance, and since the door will not be as energy efficient as a well-planned exterior wall, it's a necessary appendage to the home that should be considered as well for its security purposes.

You may be able to find an old door that could be used, but old doors typically are not as energy efficient as more modern doors designed with energy in mind. The installation is very important and should be water- and airtight with sealing edges and frames that have insulation applied all around with no gaps or cold spots in the abutting walls around the door frame.

Interior doors are another matter. You have a lot more leeway in selecting them because they don't need to be as energy efficient. There's typically no advantage to segregating heat within interior rooms unless your home has sophisticated or dedicated zones that are heated with exact controls as you are in various locations. Interior doors—unless there's a need to block sound transmission—require no insulation. Older doors made of wood, of solid construction, often can be found from deconstructed homes, schools, and office buildings. When trimmed to size and installed with original hinges, they can be nice accents to inside decor and are good ways to reclaim existing doors that otherwise might be landfilled. Some of these doors include panels of oblique or translucent glass that allow the passage of light and can reduce reliance on electric lighting in certain cases. Some have frosted panes with words or logos or colorful panes of stained glass that can add to the unique decor in the home. The knobs also can be interesting, of cut glass or solid billiard-ball-quality plastic or other unusual accents. You can replace cheap hollow plastic doors with ones with more character if you can find them in junk yards or where deconstruction building materials are sold. If you're planning to use doors made of forest-initiative wood, try to get the ones made of veneers rather than solid wood.

Other door remodeling projects could include the following:

1. Replace noninsulated exterior doors with insulated models. Sandwich-type door construction having a foam insulation core between outer panels or skins forms a rigid door with tight seals, some with refrigerator-door style magnetic strips. Storm doors with this construction are also available.

2. Consider side or rear exterior doors with energy-efficient glass panes having built-in blinds. The blinds can be closed on a hot summer day to minimize excessive heat gain.

3. Wide-angle peepholes are fairly simple to install and can help to screen unwanted visitors and prevent outside doors from being opened without good cause. This not only increases security but also saves conditioned air from being lost whenever the door is opened.

4. No matter what kind of exterior door is installed, an adjustable threshold— that can be moved up or down with a screwdriver—will allow you to fine-tune the door's seal so that it is airtight, quiet, and energy efficient.

5. Installing storm doors will supply additional security, afford natural ventila-tion, and help to control the loss of heated and cooled air. For storm doors, look for weather tightness to prevent entrance of water, cold air, dust, and insects. A triple-track system is one of the best designs, especially for back storm doors. If you lower the top glass and raise the bottom glass panels a lit-tle, this creates a natural air ventilation path. You rarely need to remove the glass or screen panels. During summer, the screen will enable improved cross-ventilation, reducing the number of times air conditioning may be run.

6. Trade a regular swinging interior door for a pocket door if the affected wall construction permits. Pocket doors allow greater use per square foot of living

area in the rooms in which they are located. They also permit more efficient air circulation and use of conditioned air because they don't restrict air movement.

>>>>>> **POINTS TO PONDER**

1. When selecting a door, ask yourself if it will operate easily and reliably, close securely, interfere with the use of space on either side of itself, retard the spread of fire, deaden sound, and allow you to see to the other side.

2. A home's front door is often the first thing a visitor (or potential buyer) sees. It helps to form an impression of the rest of the home, for good or for worse. In short, the main entrance can make an impression that adds considerably to a dwelling's appearance and even to the home's value and salability.

3. A little extra invested for a unique entrance door that's more attractive than those typically found with comparable homes will be worth it in the short and long run.

4. Storm doors for all outside entrances/exits are a must in cold-climate locations and also are desirable in warmer locations because they can help to conserve cool air, screen out insects, and provide ventilation.

5. If you've ever seen or had a child accidentally run through the regular glass panel of a storm door, you know why only safety glass should be used with storm doors.

6. Pocket doors, once popular years ago, are useful in locations where there is little room to swing a standard hinged door out of the way owing to interference with traffic or the operation of other doors.

7. For security's sake, exterior hinged doors must have standard hinges positioned on the interior side of the door so that the pins can't be removed by a potential intruder to gain access.

8. Make sure that all latch mechanisms line up correctly with their matching plates so that the doors can be positively closed and won't accidentally swing open in response to window or fan drafts or pets or toddlers pushing on them. This is especially important with bathroom and basement doors.

9. For ease of operation, European-type latch handles provide greater leverage and a more comfortable grip than do round doorknobs.

10. Bifold doors are ideal for closets. They allow a maximum opening with minimal extension into the room. Extending the height of the doors a full 8 feet to the ceiling eliminates the need for headers and permits full-width shelves and access to the upper area that otherwise would be lost.

Garages

Garages supply some of the least expensive spaces in today's home. Depending on the climate in which your home is constructed, a garage can help to make the house more energy efficient by being built between prevailing cold winds and the main dwelling.

DETACHED OR ATTACHED/INTEGRAL?

The garage is one area of the home where green construction goals may be in conflict with themselves. The main green contention is about where the garage is located. Should it be an actual part of the house, also called *attached* or *integral*? Or is it best built detached, apart from the rest of the home? Green arguments can be made for either case. Although some building sites may not be large enough or configured properly to include a detached garage, if one could be constructed, here's a synopsis of both views.

Attached or Integral Garage

If the garage is attached to the house with just one wall, then fewer materials and resources are needed to build it because it shares an entire wall with the house. Garages should share only a single wall with the main dwelling. Avoid building garages beneath or surrounded by more than one wall because that greatly increases the likelihood of noxious fumes entering living areas. The attached garage can act as a buffer from cold winter winds or strong sunlight patterns during summer, and a sloped or flat garage roof can be a convenient on-dwelling surface for locating solar panels or water-heating systems.

Conventional thinking over the past few decades has resulted in mostly attached garages being planned and built. At first glance, the conveniences of initial construction, maintenance, and home-owner traffic patterns of an attached garage seem to far outweigh the disadvantages—until home air quality is considered. On the negative side, attached or integral garages may enable vehicle exhaust, gasoline, and other noxious fumes to loft into the house. Consequently, an attached garage requires safety features not necessary in detached models. Carbon monoxide fumes can gather within integral garages and seep into the house's living quarters. Carbon monoxide fumes are heavier than air and can travel into a basement or lower living level if the garage is on that same level or higher. To prevent this from happening, your building code should state the required stepdown measurement from the house to the garage. A curb can also be a partial remedy. In any case, if you plan a house with an attached garage, realize that there will always be a potential danger with exhaust fumes if a car is allowed to idle in the garage with the garage door closed. Safety at times will depend on the behavior of the occupants. Is a car being started and warmed up in the garage during winter with the garage door closed? Certainly, to prevent fire, the ceiling and wall connecting the garage and house should be painted plaster, masonry, or some other fire-retardant material, and the door from the garage to house also should be rated to stop or hinder the spread of fire.

Ask yourself exactly what you want your garage to provide. Do you plan to refinish antique cars in one of the bays? Do you need a lot of storage? A floor with a strip drain? Sinks for washing and cleaning fresh vegetables and fruit? A place for hanging kayaks or bicycles? What is most important to you: energy efficiency or lifestyle requirements?

Green construction emphasizes the air-quality side of things. The Leadership in Energy and Environmental Design (LEED) for Homes guidelines stress pollution protection as the primary garage concern. As a prerequisite to LEED for Homes qualification, no unsustainable mechanical heating or cooling of garage space can occur. In other words, garage square footage is not to be considered as part of the home's conditioned-space envelope. Therefore, points are awarded when penetrations and connecting or adjacent framework and surfaces between the garage and the home's conditioned spaces are tightly sealed. In addition, another point can be secured by installing a continuously operating exhaust fan in the garage or a fan otherwise triggered by the garage vehicle door opener or by a carbon monoxide detector. Another way to arrive at LEED for Homes points for garage construction is simply to build a detached garage or no garage at all (Fig. 20.1)

The Detached Garage

One argument commonly used against having a detached garage, especially in a harsh climate area, is that you'll constantly be fighting snow or rain from house to garage and back. This can be averted by installing a simple covered walkway

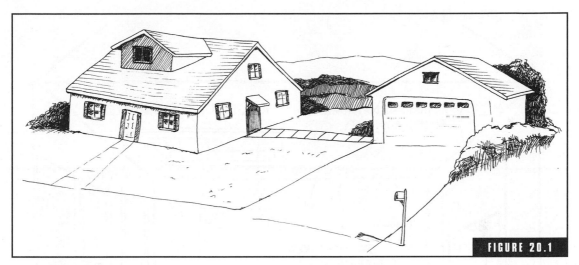

FIGURE 20.1

Home with detached garage.

constructed in minimal fashion in a style that blends in with the home's layout and landscaping. The sides needn't be fully enclosed.

Yet another way to satisfy LEED for Homes requirements is to include an Energy Star indoor air package with the home—a comprehensive system having a variety of components that will ensure a healthy air exchange rate.

Although green construction stresses minimal-sized spaces, consider that garage square footage costs run far less than those of living areas: Unconditioned garage space doesn't have as much electrical, plumbing, lighting, or floor or interior wall finishing costs. Sometimes, a larger garage can allow the home builder to go with a smaller floor plan or fewer rooms in the home plan and less ongoing energy costs (Fig. 20.2). Again, review your garage-use intentions, and build accordingly.

General Considerations

When you do plan your garage, here are some ideas to keep in mind:

1. Request a minimum of two electrical wall outlets in the garage, as well as an outlet or outlets centered above the overhead garage door(s) so that you can put up an automatic door opener at a later date if desired.

2. Besides having at least two overhead lights installed in the main level of the garage, if there's a garage attic in your plan, specify a light fixture there also.

3. Provide adequate ventilation in any garage attic.

4. If you want to heat the garage, have the outer walls as well as those of adjoining living spaces insulated.

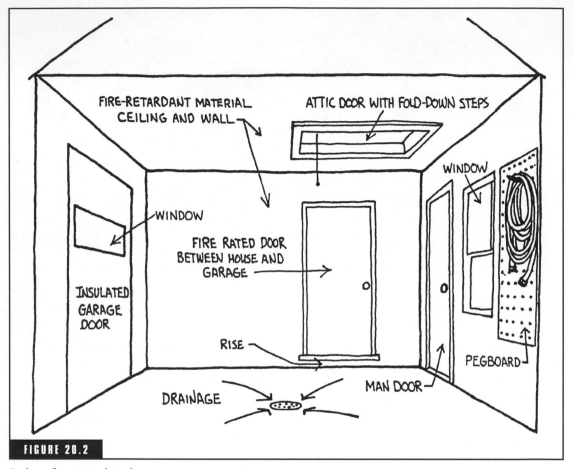

FIRE-RETARDANT MATERIAL CEILING AND WALL

ATTIC DOOR WITH FOLD-DOWN STEPS

WINDOW

WINDOW

FIRE RATED DOOR BETWEEN HOUSE AND GARAGE

INSULATED GARAGE DOOR

RISE

DRAINAGE

MAN DOOR

PEGBOARD

FIGURE 20.2

A view of a garage interior.

5. Proper flashing should be installed between the garage roof and the wall of the house, or vice versa, to prevent water seepage there.

6. If the back of a fireplace chimney will protrude into the garage, make sure that you take this into consideration when planning the garage's length.

7. To keep out the elements, soil, and energy-wasting summer and winter temperatures, make certain that the garage car doors will seal tightly against the floor and sides of their tracks when closed.

8. For appearance's sake, specify whether you desire the trim around the car doors to have "cut corners" at the top. This can add an interesting flair to a garage for a minimum cost.

9. If you're building a two-car garage, decide if you'd prefer two separate car doors or a single larger model. Two doors might look more attractive, but they require two separate door openers and need a support post in the center, which reduces the opening clearance that might be wanted for maneuvering a boat trailer in. Such a center post between two doors also can become an expensive obstacle for inexperienced drivers to crunch into.

10. A single-car garage should be no smaller than 12 by 14 feet to provide enough space for an automobile plus general equipment such as lawn mowers, snowblowers, ladders, garbage cans, bicycles, and other sports items. A two-car garage should be at least 24 by 24 feet to comfortably handle two cars and equipment storage. The ceiling height in either case should be at least 12 feet, with plenty of room to install an electric garage door opener.

11. Have a water faucet installed somewhere inside the garage. The best place is usually on a common wall with the living quarters of the home to avoid winter pipeline freeze. An ideal arrangement is a utility sink center. A utility sink center will allow you to complete cleanup chores before going into the living areas of the house. This includes messy tasks such as bathing a pet and washing off fruit, tools, greasy hands, or clothes. A number of units are available. An inexpensive one that does a good job is a plastic sink 24 inches wide, 24 inches long, and 12 inches deep.

12. A telephone in the garage offers numerous conveniences. When you're working in the garage or yard, it will save you from tracking through the house in dirty clothes, and you can at times grab a call you'd probably otherwise miss.

13. Having a window or windows (other than in the garage door) helps to increase illumination and air circulation. From a safety standpoint, this means that you can see more of what you're doing, and you can get rid of fumes from a car's exhaust. An awning window is a good choice because it can be cracked open for ventilation even in times of inclement weather.

14. Depending on your garage's design, you may want to consider one or more skylights for additional natural light and ventilation. Skylights also can help to dissipate heat during summer, when having a cool garage will help to prevent the rest of the house from becoming uncomfortable or needing air-conditioning. Electric venting skylights are available to be operated from either a remote control or a convenient fixed location near the entrance door to the garage from the house. Some models even feature rain sensors that automatically cause the window to close at the first sign of rain or other moisture. A model that fits perfectly between the trusses or other roof supports should be selected.

In some climates, not enough heat from the home radiates into the garage, especially during winter. A heat vent or wall heater installed in the garage is frequently the answer. Either one offers the following benefits:

- Snow and ice will melt/dry off cars and the garage floor.

- Fluids and foods stored in the garage will not freeze.

- Working on a car, snowblower, and any other project can be done in relative comfort.

- You won't have to scrape ice and frost off your car windows in the morning.

GARAGE DOORS

Since a home's garage car door often makes up a major part of the dwelling's structure and curb appeal, it's important to select a door that will contribute as much beauty, security, and insulation as possible. This means avoiding marginal-quality units that eventually may shake, rattle, warp, stick, and deteriorate and selecting only quality garage door and opener systems.

Modern car doors on garages either swing or roll up out of the way. Old-fashioned sliding bypass types and hinged garage doors are much less practical. The typical single garage car door is 7 feet high and 9 feet wide, whereas a double garage car door is the same height and at least twice as wide (Fig. 20.3). Some doors have reinforced, high-impact nylon rollers with solid-steel shafts. These rollers enable the door to glide easily, smoothly, and quietly.

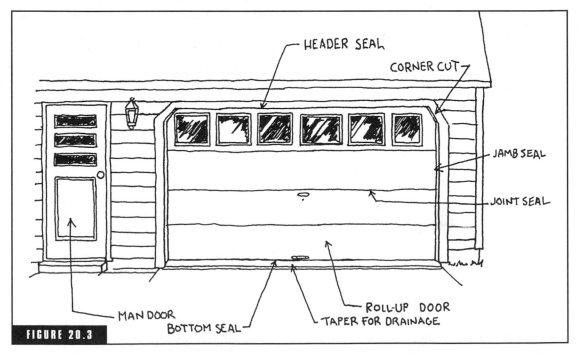

FIGURE 20.3

Garage doors.

Insulation values can range from about R-6 and up. Windows in the door typically will lower the overall insulating value. Naturally, favor doors with higher R-values. Also, review the various decorative window design options available with doors you are considering. There are frosted and beveled panes and assorted decorative glass inserts. All, however, should be the shatter-resistant type. In general, the better units feature strong warranties on the doors and their openers.

Garage doors are constructed in a variety of materials. Below are the pros and cons of each type of construction.

WOOD DOOR CONSTRUCTION
Advantages

1. The wood can be painted or stained to a desired color or finish.
2. Intricately carved or rough-sawn panels are available to suit a home's exterior decor.
3. Wood doors can be precision cut from solid ¾-inch redwood or hemlock, offering a beautiful natural finish when stained and covered with a clear-coat protectant.

Disadvantages

1. Wood doors will need to be repainted or refinished periodically.
2. Wood doesn't clean well.
3. Wood is capable of warping and rotting.

FIBERGLASS DOOR CONSTRUCTION
Advantages

1. Fiberglass is light in weight and easy to lift without an automatic opener.
2. Fiberglass doesn't need to be painted or stained.
3. Fiberglass can be cleaned easily.
4. Fiberglass is resistant to salt and air corrosion and to rusting and warping from exposure to moisture.
5. Fiberglass is relatively inexpensive and requires little maintenance.

Disadvantages

1. Fiberglass is low in strength.
2. Some fiberglass doors come with minimal insulation.
3. Fiberglass doors are not as strong or secure as steel doors.

STEEL DOOR CONSTRUCTION

Steel door "sandwich" construction is by far the most popular with builders and home owners. It consists of two outer steel "skins" sandwiched or pressure bonded around a rigid polyurethane foam, polystyrene core, or similar panelized material. Panelized insulation materials offer added strength plus predictable heat and consistent noise insulation qualities, whereas injected foam insulation may decompose and develop cavities. In short, this method of construction results in high-strength, dent-resistant, well-insulated, attractive doors. Additional desirable steel door features include the following:

- Heavy-gauge high-tensile-strength steel skins (26 or 24 gauge) with deep embossing that helps to resist denting.

- The steel skin "layering" can include zinc/steel plating, hot-dipped galvanizing, primer coatings, and exterior/interior finish coatings to resist rust formation. Paint colors are often white, tan, brown, almond, or others. Some doors feature wood-grain outside finishes and textured inside coatings that simply wipe clean, like those of a kitchen range or refrigerator.

- Durable heavy-duty hinges that are galvanized and coated.

- Heavy-duty steel backup plates laminated under the inside steel skin to support each hinge.

- Painted galvanized steel end stiles to give hinges and rollers extra support and a clean interior appearance.

- Heavy-duty steel step plates, inside and out, which help to make the door easy and safe to close without the automatic opener.

- Steel door panels that are mechanically interlocked along their entire length for additional strength.

- Steel door panel joints should have seals to prevent wind, rain, and snow from entering between sections. There are two popular types of panel seals—compression and tongue and groove (Fig. 20.4). The compression-type seals have an excellent seal but tend to wear over time. The tongue-and-groove-type seals are effective and almost maintenance-free.

Advantages

1. Exterior skins of at least 26-gauge steel have good strength and durability.

2. The insulation value, given a thickness of 2 inches of material, is about four times that offered by a conventional wood door.

3. Painting maintenance will be minimal as long as the exterior and interior door skins are precoated with an epoxy primer plus a top coat of polyester white, brown, or other color of baked enamel.

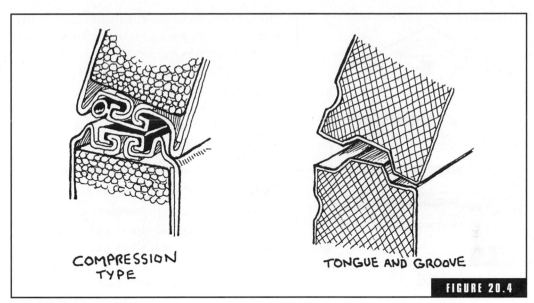

COMPRESSION
TYPE

TONGUE AND GROOVE

FIGURE 20.4

Steel door panel joint seals.

Disadvantages

1. Steel doors are heavy.

2. If scratched, touch-ups are difficult to complete.

3. Cleaning is often difficult.

ALUMINUM DOOR CONSTRUCTION

Advantages

1. Aluminum doors are light in weight.

2. Painting and maintenance needs are minimal, given the primer and enamel precoatings similar to those available on steel doors.

Disadvantages

1. Some models are lacking in strength.

2. Scratch touch-ups are difficult to make.

3. Cleaning can be difficult.

Swing-Up Doors

These are less expensive than roll-up doors. They can be made on the building site from the same materials used for the house's siding. Often, though, swing-up

FIGURE 20.5

Swing-up type of garage door.

doors consist of thin sheets of exterior plywood that are easy to work with and light enough for the owner to open with little bother. The drawbacks to this type of door are that it's so lightly constructed, it often has problems operating on its tracks, it can warp easily, it's not very energy efficient, and it's not as attractive as roll-up doors (Fig. 20.5).

Roll-Up Doors

Roll-up doors are the most popular and practical garage car doors available. They come in wood, steel, aluminum, fiberglass, plastic, masonite, and composite models. Insulated garage doors made of plastic, aluminum, or steel having fiberglass insulation inside are terrific for saving energy. The plastic doors are also maintenance-free, with the door's color an integral part of its makeup so that it never needs resurfacing. Any roll-up door should be trimmed on the bottom with an astragal (rubber) strip to ensure a tight seal with the floor.

Specify the type of roll-up door propelled by torsion springs for operating safety and ease. All roll-up doors can be efficiently connected to automatic door openers.

Garage Door Features

Perimeter weather sealing with jamb and header seals along the exterior sides and top of the door is critical. To prevent air infiltration, the door should be equipped with the following factory-installed seals (Fig. 20.6):

- Between each section joint
- Self-adjusting jamb seals on the end stiles
- Top section header seal
- Adjustable U-shaped bottom rubber or astragal seal with the ability to conform with irregular floors to effectively seal out the elements

Look for a garage door bottom weather seal that can be easily replaced once it's worn. The bottom weather seal retainer should be made of aluminum or other rustproof sturdy design; its thickness likely will affect the door's durability. At least 2 inches of insulation, pressure bonded between the sheets of steel or other material, reduce energy loss and improve noise reduction.

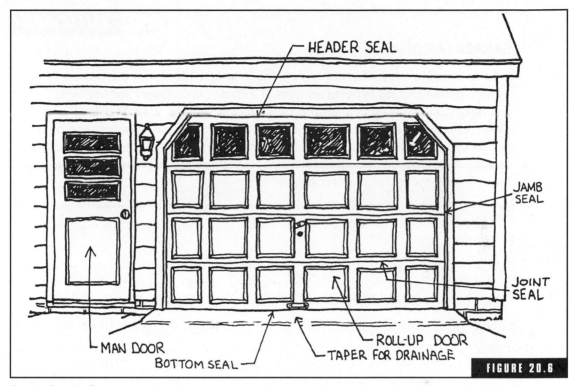

HEADER SEAL

JAMB SEAL

JOINT SEAL

MAN DOOR

BOTTOM SEAL

ROLL-UP DOOR

TAPER FOR DRAINAGE

FIGURE 20.6

Garage door seals.

Tongue-and-groove section joints provide excellent weather sealing. Look for a door model with a pinch-resistant joint design that helps to prevent fingers from getting caught in the door panel joints. A full plastic thermal break will reduce metal-to-metal contact between the interior and exterior of the door's surface while adding to insulating efficiency. Garage door windows should be watertight and at least double-glazed.

Torsion springs should be computer-calibrated to match your door load. The springs should be made from oil-tempered wire and must be mounted on a continuous cross-header tube or shaft that's appropriate to the door's torque load. Torsion springs mounted without a tube or shaft are dangerous because if they snap unexpectedly, they'll whip through the air with a powerful force.

Automatic Door Openers

It's nice to come home late at night in a thundering rainstorm or blizzard and push a tiny button from within your car so that your garage door raises open for you like magic. For the sake of convenience and safety, automatic garage door openers are relatively inexpensive and reliable contraptions.

GARAGE CAR DOORS

Some garage car doors feature "safe" hinges designed to reduce the chances of fingers getting pinched between sections of a closing door. Finger shields "hide" and restrict access to section joints on the door's outer side. Other brands offer pinch-resistant designs where the closing sections actually push fingers away from the section panel joints as the door closes. The parts of some of these pinch preventers are made from the same prepainted steel as the door panels themselves, so they blend in with the rest of the door face.

ADVANTAGES

1. *Convenience*. You never have to get in/out of your car to open/close the garage door, especially in bad weather. An inside wall button lets you open and close the door while standing at the garage human door from the house.

2. *Safety*. A built-in lamp brightens the way as you head into or out of the garage.

3. *Security*. The opener itself acts as a garage lock, making it difficult for anyone to jimmy open the garage door. In addition, the door is automatically locked when closed.

4. *Weather protection*. The opener's shock-absorbing spring(s) allow the door to close tightly against the floor, ensuring a good weather seal.

Check for the following features:

1. There should be an easy-to-disconnect pull cord for manual operation in case of a power failure or other emergency. It should reconnect automatically when the radio control or wall pushbutton is pressed after the power is restored.

2. A ⅓-horsepower motor will handle a single-car door, but a ½-horse-power unit is recommended for double doors.

3. There should be separate up and down door travel limit nuts that are easy to adjust for fine-tuning of the desired open and closed positions.

4. A heavy-gauge metal cover should protect the inner workings. It should have a maintenance-free decorative surface.

5. There should be safety switches that are obstruction sensitive. They'll make the door automatically reverse itself if it contacts any object.

6. An electric eye. Even if you aren't planning to have children or pets, include an electric eye to supplement the obstruction switches. It will stop a descending door and send it back up when a child or animal passes through the beam.

7. A keyless entry mounted on the garage overhead door jamb that allows access from the outside via a private (and changeable) security keypad code, thus eliminating the need to leave the garage door open for long periods just because someone will be arriving later and needs access (such as children or other relatives). This also comes in handy when there aren't enough door remote units to cover all the family vehicles.

8. Plastic strap track drives, belt drives, and worm screw drives are quieter than chain drive openers.

9. Remote-control coding so that the code can be changed by flipping small switches in the remote to any up/down configuration you desire.

10. A high-impact plastic light cover for the lamp that turns on automatically for 5 minutes when the door is either being opened or closed.

11. Consider an opener with two-socket lighting. This allows for two light bulbs to do the illumination. When one bulb burns out, the other will continue to provide some light, providing time for the bad bulb to be changed. This is particularly important for someone with limited mobility who needs help changing out an overhead bulb.

12. A vacation switch. This switch renders the opener deaf to all radio signals, including those from its own remote, while you're gone.

13. Some units come with a lighted keyless four-code entry pad that installs unobtrusively on the outer door frame. It has its own flip-up weather protection cover and allows the home owner to press in the correct code from the outside to open the door.

14. Fixed door opener codes can lead to thieves stealing or cracking the code with sophisticated code-cracking devices; then, while you are away, the thieves may open the garage door to survey what they could take. Even if nothing appeals to them, they may leave the door up during the middle of winter as they disappear, allowing cold air in and leaving your garage open for further vandalism. To defeat these thieves, some keyless entry pad systems feature antiburglary coding mechanisms that automatically change the access code to one of billions of new codes selected each time the remote control unit is activated.

15. Consider a unit with a soft start/stop that prevents jerking when starting or stopping. Again, make sure that the opener you select will reverse itself automatically if it encounters any obstacles (such as a small child) while closing

toward the garage floor. Also arrange for the control buttons to be positioned high enough so that children can't reach them. This is especially important for the buttons near the inside garage human door to the house. Children sometimes will push a control button to close the door and then attempt to dash through the opening before the door is fully lowered.

16. Units are available that operate off a direct current (DC) motor instead of a standard alternating current (AC) motor. The DC motor can operate on less energy, will provide a soft start and stop feature for smooth operation, less noise, reduced door wear, and greater reliability.

17. A polymer-lined rail reduces metal-to-metal contact between movable parts for less resistance and noise during operation.

18. Units are available with a light control having an energy-saver shutoff. There's also a motion-detecting control panel that will turn the garage door opener lights on when someone enters a dark garage from inside the home. A timer should automatically shut off the same lights after a few minutes. Another option is a multifunction remote control that will turn on the opener's lights independently of the garage door operation and even activate or deactivate house lights. This is helpful when a person must enter through the small door and wants the lights on in advance.

19. Consider the feature of having a red light inside the kitchen or other room that goes on whenever the garage car door is in a raised position. This may save the door from being accidentally left open all night. It also prevents the need to open the inside human door, allowing cooled or heated air to escape just in order to see if the garage door is open.

Garage Door Screens

If included, this handy feature offers the pleasure of using your garage during warm-weather days and evenings for sitting, socializing, and partying without being annoyed by insects or dampened by rain.

Man (Woman or Human) Doors

A man (woman or human) door entrance to the garage should be included to permit access into the garage from outdoors without having to raise the garage overhead door. An outside man (woman or human) door in the garage provides many benefits. First, from a safety standpoint, it allows a quick and easy exit. Second, it eliminates the need to constantly open the big door every time a person enters or exits. Opening the big garage door enables heat to enter in the summer and to escape during winter, increasing both your space conditioning and electrical consumptions. The best man (woman or human) doors are steel covered. They're strong, burglar-resistant, and fare well against the weather. As with all other outer man

---

SAFETY*NOTE*

GARAGE DOOR OPENERS

Remember, a photo-eye positioned near the floor across the garage door's plane of travel must not be the automatic door opener's only or main method of preventing injury. Although the photo-eye beam mechanism—when working correctly—will prevent someone from being struck and will reverse the door's travel, it does not react on the door's edge striking something on its way down. Indeed, sunlight, rain, or snow can make the photo eye malfunction, as can collections of dirt or other debris on the lens, and even a simple bump of the eye by a child's foot or basketball can disable the beam from proper operation. Instead, the unit's main safeguard must be a sensor in the opener's drive mechanism that is set so that the door will automatically and immediately stop and reverse its travel on encountering a change in pressure or resistance (such as the presence of a child's head or arm) when the bottom edge of the door strikes the same on its way down.

SAFETY*NOTE*

GARAGE DOOR OPENERS

Some manufacturers offer a wall control inside the garage with an illuminated open/close button in case the door must be opened in the dark.

(woman or human) doors, garage entrances should be insulated with weather stripping. Depending on your lot, if the back of the garage faces the backyard, you might consider having a second man (woman or human) door installed there.

GARAGE FLOORS

The following points should be considered to ensure a trouble-free garage floor:

1. It should have a 4-inch gravel base covered by a sheet of polyethylene or similar moisture barrier. Drainpipes should be laid under the gravel, and the gravel should be tamped before the concrete floor is poured.

2. If no garage floor drains will be installed, the garage floor should be poured so that it begins about ½ inch above the driveway's surface and then slopes up to about 2 inches toward the back of the garage.

3. If possible, include floor drains, one for each car space. Naturally, the floor should be sloped toward the drains to prevent any standing water.

GARAGE DOOR OPENERS

Monthly

- Examine cables for fraying. Carefully run a rag along the cables. If the rag catches or tears, have the cables inspected by a professional.
- Inspect the garage door springs, rollers, pulleys, and other hardware for signs of wear. Make sure that nuts and bolts are tight. If any component is broken, contact a professional for repairs, and avoid using the door until the repairs are completed.
- Per the manufacturer's instructions, periodically lubricate the door rollers, bearings, hinges, and drive mechanism.
- Test the emergency release used for power outages, and then test the balance of the door to see if the springs are adjusted properly. Follow the manufacturer's guidelines, or close the door and disconnect the automatic operator. You then should be able to lift the door waist high with relative ease. The door should stay open in that position by itself. If it doesn't, the door spring tension should be adjusted by the door company repair person until it does.
- Test the reversing features on the opener monthly by seeing if the photo eye works and by placing a 2- by 4-inch block of wood on the floor to obstruct the door to see if it will reverse direction, as it should. If either of these safety features fails, disconnect the door opener until it's repaired.

4. To support the edges of the garage floor where the fill around the footer might settle, specify 6- by 6-inch reinforcement wire to be used throughout the entire floor.

5. The concrete should be poured at least 4 inches thick.

6. The garage (and basement) floor should be steel-troweled to achieve a smooth finish. This is a time-consuming task that requires going over the surface with a trowel many times during an 8-hour period or until the surface hardens.

7. The part of the garage floor that sticks out past the garage door—normally about 6 inches—should taper away from the door down toward the driveway, ending ½ to 1 inch higher than the driveway surface. By tapering it down toward the driveway, rainwater and melting snow will not drain into the

garage. Keeping the floor slightly elevated prevents water from backing up into the garage from the driveway.

8. Before parking cars on a new garage floor, the floor should be cleaned with a solution of muriatic acid and then coated with two or three applications of a clear sealer. The sealer improves the floor's appearance by preventing oils, grease, and dirt from staining the concrete and by making the floor a lot easier to clean. It also will prevent cement/concrete dust from rising and will help water flow more quickly toward the drains.

GARAGE ATTIC STORAGE

The garage attic, even when trusses are running through it, can be used to store off-season equipment of all types, including holiday decorations, lawn furniture, spare tires, kids' swimming pools, bicycles, and gardening supplies. To make this space accessible, cover or "finish" the attic floor, and specify a set of pulldown steps. Folding or rolldown stairways (Fig. 20.7) are in most cases the best option. At the same time, with attic space in the garage quite high off the garage concrete floor, these types of stairways are far safer than using conventional stepladders.

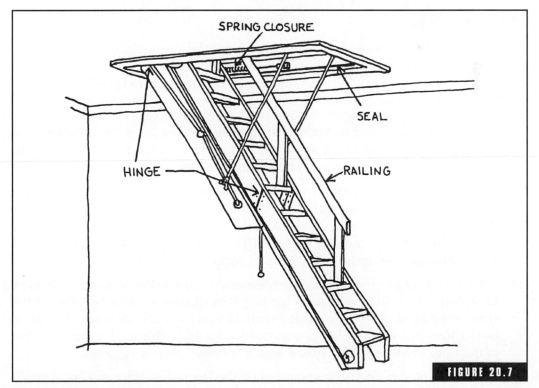

FIGURE 20.7

Folding pulldown stairway.

Make sure that whichever model you choose has handrail(s). Also, when closed, the unit should latch securely against a rubber seal to prevent drafts and insects from entering the attic.

There should be adequate lighting installed in the garage attic so that you can see and move freely about in a safe manner. The switch for the light ideally should be located on a wall in the garage so that you can turn it on before climbing the stairs. A less desirable alternative is a pull string that you can grab as you reach the top of the attic stairs.

If it applies to your location, use fluorescent bulbs designed for outdoor use, which will activate relatively quickly in cold temperatures. Also make sure that exposed bulbs are not situated where they'll be bumped into easily and broken.

An important consideration for a garage attic is ventilation. A thermostatically controlled ventilation fan is an excellent choice to help remove excess summer heat and car exhaust fumes. Such a system also will prevent dampness and mold problems. Ridge, roof, gable, and soffitt ventilation a can lso be employed with satisfactory results.

Electrical outlets should be installed throughout the attic so that you can plug in tools or a vacuum cleaner.

GARAGE STORAGE

In years past, there was a time when garages fit the automobiles for which they were built like a glove. Now garages are erected not only to hold cars but also to shelter a wide variety of other work, maintenance, and leisure-time items.

Consider the following ideas when planning your garage storage space:

1. Provide enough space to store lawn mowers, snow blowers, bicycles, and other bulky objects along a side wall and a place to keep even larger items such as garden tractors or small boats along the back wall.

2. No matter what size garage you plan, many cubic feet of relatively inactive storage space can be salvaged by building one or more shelves 24 to 30 inches deep around the two sides and back of the garage about 6 feet above the floor attached by brackets fixed to the walls. This will accommodate the storage of spray cans, garden tools, auto parts and supplies, and so on.

3. A huge rack for storing screens, oars, water skis, and other long articles can be hung from the ceiling over each car bay. If built over a "walking area" at the sides or in front of where a car is stored, the rack should clear the floor by at least 7 feet. But where it hangs over the car, it can be dropped to within 6 feet of the floor because it isn't over a highly traveled pedestrian zone.

4. The more you can keep items elevated off the floor, the easier and faster you'll be able to clean out the garage.

5. You'll find it handy to leave one wall with the framing studs and planks exposed—not covered with plaster or drywall board. This permits you to attach large sheets of Peg-Board directly to the studs and will provide an air-space to arrange hanging pegs into the Peg-Board itself. Peg-Board is ideal for hanging all sorts of hand tools, garden tools, hoses, and many other items. If Peg-Board will be secured to finished walls, you must leave an airspace behind it using 2- by 2-inch studs to establish a gap.

6. Heavy garden tools and items such as hand mowers, empty lawn rollers, and long wooden extension ladders can be hung from 4-inch boards nailed across open studs when steel brackets are fastened to the top edges of the 4-inch boards.

7. A lockable tool/equipment cabinet keeps small items and tools organized and extra secure.

8. On the bottom of the exposed stud walls and below areas having Peg-Board, you can build 12-inch shelf inserts between the studs on top of the block at an elevation approximately 12 inches above the floor (Fig. 20.8). This will work well for storing wash pails, step stools, jack stands, bags of seed, fertilizer, and so on.

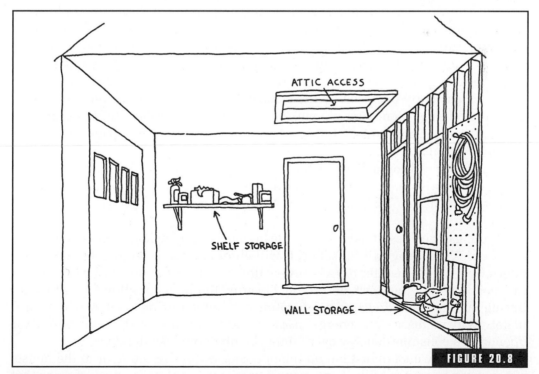

FIGURE 20.8

Garage storage.

GARAGE POSITIONING

This subject is also touched on in Chapter 33 on house orientation and positioning. In simplest terms, the garage must fit on the lot without encroaching on an adjacent site. It also should conform to the slope of your lot. For instance, when a garage must be planned for a downward side-sloping lot, instead of completely lowering the garage to meet the natural lot line or placing load after load of fill dirt to raise the lot level, it might be best to split the difference—reaching a conservative compromise between both solutions. From a green (and air-quality) perspective, a detached garage incurring no ongoing expenses to heat and cool is preferred.

When possible, position the garage to help reduce energy loads. In cold-climate areas, garages should be located toward the northern part of the house, if possible. In hot-climate areas, a garage is best suited on the east or west side of the home to help reduce unwanted heat gain.

REMODELING NOTES

Remodeling an integral garage may be undertaken in a number of ways. To achieve an improved indoor air quality, if at all possible, another garage—a detached, separate garage—could be planned and constructed. It would be a tradeoff of sorts, depending on what is most important to you. You could work with the attached garage, and make sure that its construction will keep vehicle emissions and soil from entering and being tracked into the living areas, or you could—as long as there's enough room and building and zoning codes permit—build another garage apart from the home. The next question is what to do with the space currently enclosed by the garage? Again, that depends on your needs, your home's floor plan, your climate, and whether it is heated and has plumbing access. It may be able to take the place of a room addition or expansion you had already been planning.

Consider installing a light in the house somewhere that indicates when the garage car door is up. This prevents the need to open the inside human door, allowing cooled or heated air to escape, just to check whether the garage door is up or down.

If your garage doesn't have an outside human door, consider adding one. It will allow quick and easy exit for safety. It will eliminate the need to open the garage door every time you enter or exit—every time you take the dog for a walk, go get the mail, take out the trash, and so on. Opening the big door allows heat to enter during summer and freezing temperatures to enter during winter, which ultimately will increase your energy usage. In addition, use of the automatic door opener also consumes energy every time you open or close the door.

By installing an exhaust fan on the opposite wall from the door to the house, exhaust can be sent outside. Some people wire it to the electric garage door so that it runs whenever the door goes up and down to exhaust any fumes. Make sure that leaks between the garage and the living area are all sealed, such as the bottom plate of the wall between spaces and any penetrations through the wall. Use a steel insulated garage door with a good jamb, header, and bottom seals. Look for a garage door bottom weather seal that can be replaced easily once it's worn. If the garage attic does not have a roof ventilation fan, consider having one installed to help reduce heat in the summer, which will help the rest of the house because garages often are not insulated and may be positioned to act as a buffer between extreme weather and temperatures.

Sunlight tubes in the garage will supply an inexpensive source of natural illumination.

> > > > > > **POINTS TO PONDER**

1. A garage costs considerably less per square foot than the rest of the house. Instead of planning a garage that's just large enough for your needs, go a few steps further. It won't cost much more.

2. A garage can be positioned as a buffer between cold prevailing winds and home living spaces or on the east or west side of the dwelling to help shade interior living areas depending on your location and climate.

3. If you plan to heat the garage, have the outer walls, as well as those of adjoining living spaces, insulated. If you insulate, consider that when a warmed car is pulled into the garage after a drive, heat radiating from the parked vehicle will be retained longer within the garage and will even help to insulate the adjoining part of the house.

4. Have a water faucet or utility sink center installed somewhere on a common wall with the living quarters of the home.

5. Install a garage floor drain or, better yet, a strip drain (a rectangular lengthwise concrete drain covered with pieces of removable grating for cleaning mud or debris) so that the floor can be hosed down when needed throughout the winter.

6. A telephone located in the garage provides numerous conveniences. Otherwise, the opening and closing of the house door will waste energy as the home's heated or cooled air is lost. Also consider installing a cable television outlet there, for watching favorite programs while waxing a car or pursuing various hobbies and housework activities.

7. Automatic garage door openers must have automatic reverse safety features and also should have an electric-eye beam that stops the door's downward travel when someone or something crosses the floor in the door's path.

8. It usually makes sense to have a garage attic that can be accessed by a set of pull-down stairs.

9. Garage attics should have lighting, a sturdy floor, and adequate ventilation.

10. Plan garage shelves, Peg-Boards, racks, and hangers with the goal of keeping items in the garage stored off the floor so that the floor remains uncluttered and easy to keep clean.

11. Fluorescent lighting will allow you to spend long periods of time performing various activities in the garage without receiving a high electricity bill.

12. Sunlight tubes installed in the garage can help to provide an inexpensive source of natural illumination.

13. To maximize lighting efficiency, have the walls painted white or another bright, light color or shade.

Plumbing

The plumbing and electrical systems in any dwelling can be considered the actual lifelines of the house. Without them, practically all modern conveniences would be impossible. Given their importance, both systems are strictly regulated by local and national codes, and both are included in ambitious inspection programs required to ensure the safety of occupants. This chapter focuses on plumbing. Since plumbing processes, heats, and distributes water needed for daily living, it presents one of the greatest opportunities green components and design have to reduce natural resource and energy use throughout the life of the home. In a nutshell, overall water conservation, efficient water heating, and ways to reduce the proportion of potable or drinkable water you use are the keys to green handling of this precious resource.

Water conservation typically saves in a number of ways. It obviously saves the water you do not use, but less apparent is excess water sent down a sanitary sewer or storm sewer to be processed. Or the warm/hot water you don't use saves on the energy required to heat and store it while hot. Water conservation can be accomplished through water-efficient and low-flow fixtures such as aerated faucets, low-flow toilets, front-loading clothes washers, top-rated dishwashers, and ultra-low-flow showerheads. It can be accomplished by more efficient water piping configurations. And it can be accomplished by occupant behavior changes. Is the water turned off intermittently during teeth brushing, showering, rinsing vegetables, or dishwashing? Is drinkable water being used to wash a car or water a lawn or garden? Consider that only about 1 percent of the entire water supply in the entire world is clean enough to be used for drinking. Through a combination of these efforts, thousands of gallons of water can be saved in a typical household each year.

Efficient water heating can be accomplished in many ways. Through solar heating, tankless heaters, combination water- and space-heating boilers, drain-water heat-recovery systems, and quick hot-water delivery piping.

Ways to reduce the proportion of drinkable to nondrinkable water used include recognizing opportunities where drinkable water can be reserved for activities requiring clean water and finding ways to satisfy nonpotable water needs by other means. This might mean catching and storing enough rainwater to be able to wash your car or water your garden. It could mean diverting and using bathwater or kitchen sink water to flush your toilets as part of a graywater system. Or it could mean figuring out how to have less-thirsty or less-water-dependent landscaping plants by using more native vegetation or drought-hardy grasses.

Most people got haven't a very good idea of how much water they are currently using—or how their water bills specifically relate to the amounts of water that various appliances, fixtures, and activities use. An excellent exercise to prepare for designing your plumbing system is to determine how much water your residence is using now. By understanding your current use, you can get an idea of what reductions can be made for your new home and how best to plan them.

The entire plumbing system of a house can be broken into five basic categories: water supply, pipe types, fixtures, water heaters, and drainage.

WATER SUPPLY

Your water source can be either public, private, or a combination of both. Public water systems are the most worry-free from a home owner's point of view. Large water pipes called *mains* deliver the water directly to your house in practically all urban locations, ensuring adequate water pressure and supply. Large private water systems often do the same thing for subdivisions beyond the reaches of public water mains. These full-blown water systems, both public and private, have strict rules and codes to follow that guarantee proper hookups to residential and other dwellings (Fig. 21.1).

Homes with basements should have as much plumbing as possible run parallel along the floor joists and then up through the floor. Try to minimize the number of holes drilled so that piping can run perpendicularly through the joists. Similarly, don't allow notching of the bottoms of the joists to make room for piping. In both cases, the holes and notches reduce the carrying strength of the joists. If piping absolutely must go through joists, the holes should be cleanly drilled through the center of a joist, just large enough for the pipe (or wire) with some clearance to prevent a hot pipe from contacting a wood joist (Fig. 21.2). Check the local building code for guidelines. All told, it's best to discourage hole drilling.

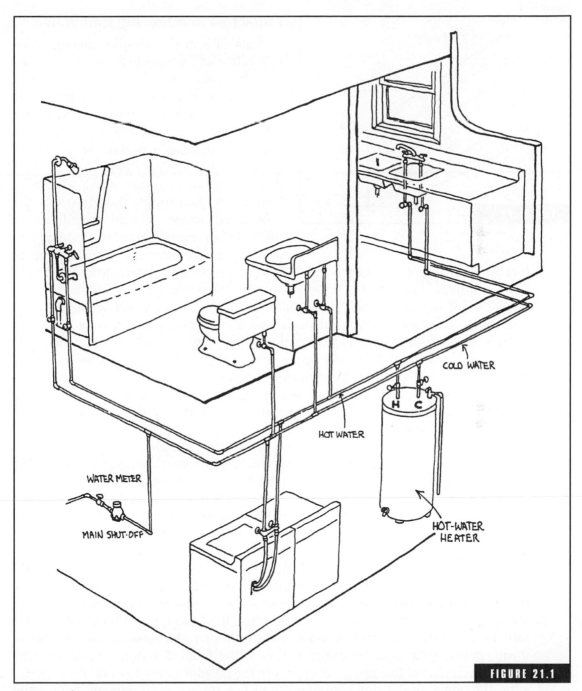

Water supply system.

FIGURE 21.1

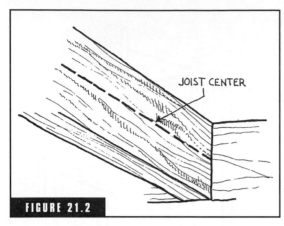

Joint center.

Collecting and Storing Rainwater

This is really a simple concept. The rain is free and available for harvesting. It's usually clean, and if it is collected in a clean manner, it can be used safely for activities such as car washing, lawn and garden watering, and any other use not requiring drinkable water. Very simple systems can be installed directly onto downspouts from gutters using a barrel, a filter pump, and supply lines to where the recaptured water is made available or used. Other more complex systems are available to collect, store, filter, and make that water available to your main plumbing to help with toilet flushing and washing machines. Such systems typically require large storage tanks, tanks that are often buried below ground out of sight. This also depends on what the local plumbing codes will allow. Rainwater and other water-reuse systems typically will require a local permit, so be sure that you review your plans before your system is set up. With all the publicity green building has been getting, more leeway is gradually entering our building ordinances and codes as large cities experience serious droughts and are realizing the importance of water conservation and how the use of rainwater-capturing systems and graywater systems can help to conserve drinkable water supplies.

If you design a more sophisticated rainwater-collection system and add a number of testing and/or treatment and sterilization steps, you even may be able to get a permit to drink the collected water and use it for potable water activities. For centuries, native civilizations all over the have world relied on rainwater harvesting to meet all their daily needs. Since most collection occurs from roofs, it stands to reason that the roof must be clean and must not leach harmful chemicals or lots of particulates into the water. This points to factory-coated metal roofs as the most logical choice. Then, even though the roofing may be cleanly manufactured, when most of the rainwater is collected—during rainstorms—there may be an initial water burst or runoff in the first few minutes that carries away collected dust, leaf particles, seeds, and bird droppings that would contaminate the collected rain that immediately follows the opening deluge. Some means is usually planned to separate that initial flush of water—perhaps it goes into a precontainer that must fill up before the cleaner rainwater that follows can enter the larger, designated container for usable storage. And depending on what the first flush of water may be used for—say, watering the garden or lawn, for example—it will work fine.

The storage container should be large enough to help out during times of drought. It should be covered to prevent sunlight from entering, which could produce algae, and also to prevent insects such as mosquito larva and any other creatures (including children) from access. Screens can act as simple filters to keep larger organic debris such as leaves, pinecones, seeds, and bits of bark from entering. All sorts of containers have been set up for rainwater storage, including old wood tanks and wine barrels, plastic farm tanks, galvanized steel tanks from various industrial processes, concrete tanks, fiberglass, polyethylene, and others. Naturally, the containers need to be cleaned out before being installed.

Again, if the collected water is planned to be used as drinkable water, it should be tested and probably will need to be treated to eliminate the possibility of bacteria or other biological or harmful organic contaminants. Various filtration and treatment systems are available, and water treatment experts in your area will know which will likely work for your situation. It could be extremely fine filtration, ultraviolet (UV)-light treatment systems, or the use of ozone treatments.

Graywater Systems

Another potential type of water-reuse system is a graywater system that takes drain water from bathroom sinks, from showers and bathtubs, and from clothes washers and laundry sinks and, with possible minor treatment, uses it for toilet flushing, car washing, watering landscaping, and other nonpotable water uses. The graywater otherwise would head down the sanitary sewer line or flow into a septic tank for treatment. Water from toilets, kitchen sinks and sink disposals, and dishwashers traditionally is considered "black" water, which could have high organic content, and typically is sent to the sanitary sewer or septic tank and normally cannot be reused. On the other hand, some individuals are starting to think that kitchen sink waste water also can be included in graywater systems, as long as means are included to segregate materials such as animal waste (meats, fats, and grease) from vegetable matter. Again, these kinds of systems take careful planning to make sure that contaminants do not either get into drinkable water systems or are used in ways that could be dangerous to the occupants. A usable option is adding a kitchen sink for saving the water that otherwise runs down the drain while you wait for the temperature to heat up or while processing vegetables and fruits. That water could be piped into your graywater system and used for almost any nonpotable purpose, unlike graywater that would have soap or cleaning chemicals and would need minor treatment before being reused. This is another case of think safety—*then* think green. Why bother with graywater? If this sounds like a lot of trouble to you, consider that if you live in an area where rain falls infrequently, graywater could reduce your dependence on rainfall and eliminate the need for extralarge storage tanks. You'll have a continuous source of graywater available as long as people are living in the home.

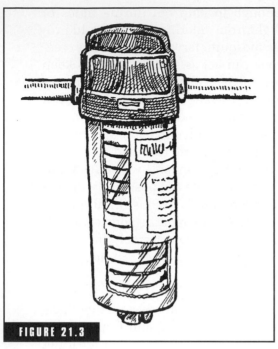

FIGURE 21.3

Water filter.

Water Filters

If you simply have a main supply of water and plan to filter all your water, you might as well have a filter unit installed on the main water supply pipe as soon as it enters the house (Fig. 21.3).

- A filter can remove sediment, lead, rust, sand, silt, sulfur, dirt, excess chlorine, and many other undesirable elements—depending on what's in your water supply.

- By removing impurities, a filter can reduce odors and improve the water's taste.

- Installing filters from the start protects pipelines and water equipment (water heaters, cooling equipment, washers, dishwashers, and ice makers) from any harmful scale elements.

- Installing filters possibly can protect household members from potentially harmful elements.

Water Wells

Beyond the big water supply systems, things get personal. Since the first settling of America, private wells or springs have provided rural farms and homesteads with their water. Wells are not as regulated as large water systems, and if you need one, it's best to consult local professionals familiar with the conditions and special situations that exist in your area. There are certain constants, however, you should be aware of when putting in a well as your main source of water supply:

1. Locate the well as close to the house as possible yet as far away from any septic disposal system as practical—preferably uphill from it. You certainly don't want to contaminate your water with sewage leachate. Also consider the possibility of sewage systems that future neighbors might install to the sides or back of your property, and keep in mind that presently uncontaminated rivers, streams, lakes, ponds, and swamps might not always remain so. Try to position the well at least 50 feet away from any of them.

2. When the well is completed, have it tested for water flow, purity, taste, and even color. If any irritating characteristics persist, such as "hard" water (having

higher than usual concentrations of dissolved solids), a metallic taste, or a cloudy or off-color appearance, determine if those qualities can be handled effectively with a water softener/treatment unit that attaches to the well.

3. Protect the pipe that transports water from the well to the house from freezing temperatures. This can be achieved by burying the pipe below the frost line, lagging or wrapping it with insulation, or attaching electrically heated wire to the pipe (heat tape). It won't matter how good the rest of your plumbing is if the supply line freezes in midwinter. Frozen pipes are expensive to thaw and can cause a lot of damage if they burst.

PIPE TYPES

Cast-Iron Pipe

Cast-iron pipe might be heavy and awkward to handle, but it's so strong and durable that it's been in general use for drain, sewer, and vent lines for many years. Compared with plastic pipe, cast iron has two major advantages. First, it delivers its contents with much less noise. If you can't avoid running a waste pipe through a wall adjacent to a living or dining room, cast-iron pipe will prevent many uncomfortable moments you would otherwise be spending listening to water and waste gurgle through the line. Second, cast-iron pipe is more durable and able to withstand the rigors of the Roto-Rooter and other mechanical and chemical pipe-cleaning equipment.

Galvanized Steel Pipe

Galvanized steel pipe is what was most commonly used for transporting water before copper lines gained widespread acceptance. It's available in various lengths and diameters and has a rust-resistant coating on its inner and outer surfaces. Connections are usually made by cutting threads into the pipe, and because this is done after the protective coating is applied, any exposed threads will rust.

Because of its strength and wall thickness, steel pipe has a long life expectancy even when buried and is frequently used to supply natural gas as well as water. It's still a popular choice whenever a "rough" plumbing line is called for. The principal drawback is the pipe's roughness, which contributes to water-flow friction and the collection of mineral deposits and sediments that over the years tend to reduce the inside diameter of the pipe in the same way that cholesterol can accumulate and restrict a person's arteries.

Copper Pipe

Copper makes an excellent pipe. It comes in soft, flexible, and hard varieties; has a very long life; and—if not spliced into galvanized steel pipe—is generally not affected by corrosion. It's the number one choice to supply hot and cold water throughout today's modern houses. Copper lines are somewhat more expensive than other piping, and so is the labor needed to install them. Individual pieces are connected by soldering them to copper unions, tees, elbows, and other fittings. A major advantage of copper pipe is that it can be bent or curved rather easily, a characteristic not available with cast iron, galvanized steel, or most plastics. However, given their nature, copper pipes require special pressure chambers to prevent *water hammer*—a shuddering, rapping noise created by a sudden turning off (or on) of the water. As with most other pipes, copper can be ruptured by water freezing inside.

Plastic Pipe

Plastic pipe is substantially less expensive than copper, galvanized steel, or cast iron. Plastic pipe is also simple to install and keeps labor costs low. There's no need to solder with torches and no measuring and threading the ends of galvanized steel stock. There's only convenient plastic fittings, easy-to-cut plastic pipe, a can of plastic cement, and a brush. Almost anyone can do it.

There are other advantages to plastic pipe. It's extremely lightweight and easy to support. Plastic is chemically inert and unaffected by corrosive materials. The smooth inside surface of plastic pipe aids the movement of materials through the lines.

A few major disadvantages, though, eliminate the use of plastic lines from several parts of a house. It's not as strong as cast iron, galvanized steel, or even copper, and it doesn't have the bending capability of copper. Because of its tendency to crack under heavy loads or stress, it shouldn't be used beneath or within a concrete slab, where long, strong lengths of pipe having no splices are needed. As mentioned earlier, to the unwary, the noise that water makes when running through plastic lines can be a serious source of irritation if used above or near first-floor living areas, especially in multilevel houses. Plastic pipe also will burst when water freezes inside it.

A good-natured battle wages between the proponents of cast iron, galvanized steel, copper, and plastic for dominance over the entire house plumbing material question. The most sensible approach, and one favored by many residential plumbing experts, is to employ each kind of material where its strong characteristics can be used to best advantage. This means cast iron and steel for drainage pipes and for piping that's embedded in ground or concrete, copper for water supply, and plastic for venting.

PEX (cross-linked polyethylene) is narrow, flexible reinforced tubing that—owing to its narrow diameter—can reduce hot water wait time at various fixtures when used as a fixture supply line. It can be used to make continuous runs, eliminating many elbows and joints in a line, and doesn't sweat under high-humidity conditions. It's resistant to bursting but potentially can melt if run next to exhaust vents on water heaters.

PIPE INSULATION

While traditional construction methods prescribe that pipes—especially water pipes—exposed to cold temperatures should be insulated to conserve warmth or prevent freezing, we take pipe insulation recommendations to another level. Indeed, consider having every pipe—hot or cold—insulated with heavy-duty fiberglass or polyethylene foam tubes, their seams sealed with insulated tape. This should be done in the home's initial construction stages. Early on, it's simple and inexpensive to do. Later, once walls, ceilings, and floors are enclosed or covered, simple access will be lost.

A couple of points to consider regarding insulating pipes follow:

- Piping in attics, garages, crawlspaces, and outside walls is especially vulnerable to freezing if it is located near cracks and other openings that let in cold air. If any areas of piping will be exposed to extremely cold temperatures, consider using a combination of insulation sleeves or tubes with electrical heat tape or a thermostatically controlled heat cable. Insist that the contractor use only products approved by an independent testing laboratory such as Underwriters Laboratories, Inc., and make sure that products intended for outdoors use are labeled that way. Manufacturer instructions must be followed precisely.

- Insulated pipes, hot or cold, will maintain more consistent water temperatures. They will prevent hot water from losing heat and cooling off within the line and, conversely, will prevent cold water from absorbing heat and warming up while it sits in the line. With insulated piping, water won't have to run as long to reach the desired hot or cold temperatures at the faucet. In other words, more hot water will stay hot longer within an insulated line so that it comes out of the faucet at the desired temperature sooner than would hot water standing in an uninsulated line that loses its heat in a cool basement and has to run out (being wasted) at the faucet until hot water fresh from the water heater can be drawn into its place. Thus insulated pipes deliver water at desired temperatures with less waiting, less wasting of water, and less energy needed for heating. This is a savings of water, time, and money.

PLUMBING FIXTURES

Plumbing fixtures include the water heater, sinks, tubs, showers, toilets, and even outside faucets. The time and effort you spend planning their locations will be the most important part of their installation. Naturally, with green guidelines come low-flow fixtures. These are discussed in greater detail in Chapter 27 on bathrooms, but they typically involve ways that improved fixtures can accomplish the same work with less water, often by mixing air with the water flow to achieve a flow that feels and looks like a regularly sized stream but isn't, or by providing the ability for a user to easily and temporarily stop the water flow between various steps of an activity, or by having engineered more efficient mechanical operating improvements for a new design to an old fixture, such as a low-flush toilet.

A major consideration is where to position the water heater and how to keep as much of the plumbing as possible concentrated in one area of the house. Hot water will cool off if it must stand in sizable lengths of pipe or travel long distances between supply and outlets.

For ease of installation and savings on materials, bathroom fixtures should line up along one wall, and depending on the floor plan, the other side of such a "wet wall" full of plumbing could perhaps accommodate the plumbing support systems of a kitchen, a laundry, or another bathroom. Compact fixture placement will keep the plumbing clean and simple.

Another benefit of compact plumbing is that certain fixtures can share vents. Whenever possible, locate the toilet between the tub and sink so that the vent from the toilet can perform extra duty. Rookie bathroom planners sometimes ask builders to put the toilet on one wall, and the bathtub on the opposite wall. This causes unnecessary piping to be installed at an extra cost.

To save yourself from headaches later on, make certain that every fixture can be turned off, preferably via a local or easy-to-get-at water shutoff valve, in case

⟨**F**⟩**OCUS**

SHUTOFF VALVES

A shutoff, or isolation, valve stops water or other liquids or gases at some point within a pipeline or tank system, typically so that maintenance, repair, or installation work can be performed downstream from the valve. Localized shutoff valves should be installed for all individual fixtures, such as faucets, bathtubs and showers, hot-water heaters, boilers, dishwashers, and others. Don't allow the plumbing and fixtures to be installed without these shutoffs, or future maintenance will be difficult to accomplish without shutting off and draining main portions of the home's plumbing. Shutoff valves should include the following:

- Valves should be located beneath each faucet in the house.
- Shutoff valves should be present at the washing machine, dishwasher, and refrigerator ice maker.
- Toilets will have one cold-water valve usually installed under the water tank.
- Hot-water heating systems have a cold-water shutoff valve near their boilers.
- Bathtub and shower valves should be located behind the faucet controls.
- In addition to providing shutoff valves, the contractor should cut an access door or a simple rectangular hole in the back of the plumbing wall that can be kept covered with a thin, discrete removable cover—they're often located out of sight within an abutting hallway or bedroom clothes closet. The door will allow access for any needed maintenance once the plumbing is isolated.
- The plumbing system should have an indoor shutoff valve to each sill cock (outdoor) faucet that enables those faucets to be shut off and drained from the pipe to the faucet—reducing the risk of water freezing in the outside part of the faucet and piping during winter (see Fig. 21.18).
- Each plumbing system also must have a main shutoff valve, typically located where the waterline enters the house and just before the water meter on municipal water systems (see Fig. 21.1). The idea is to be able to quickly shut off the entire water supply in response to serious leaks or emergencies. Again, if the water must be shut off at the main valve, remember to follow the boiler or water-heating tank instructions for proper shutdowns. Remember that any fire-protection sprinkler system will lose its water pressure as well.
- Test all shutoff valves, from the main valve to the individual fixture shutoffs, with the entire plumbing system activated to see if they individually work or hold.
- Insist that the contractor tag basement shutoff valves with labels that tell what each valve shuts off to prevent errors from being made if you ever have to activate them during an emergency.

it's necessary to isolate the fixture so that it can be serviced or repaired. Don't ignore the economy that can be realized through careful planning of the house's entire plumbing system.

DRAINAGE

Sufficient capacity and pitch, tight sealing, proper venting, and provisions for cleanouts are all important to a good, effective drainage system. Used water and the waste it carries must be disposed of both for convenience and for the sake of your health. Waste creates unpleasant and potentially harmful gases that must be expelled. A drainage system therefore has two functions: to transport water and solid wastes to a sanitary sewer or septic tank and to dispel noxious gases into air you won't be breathing.

If everything has been well planned, the waste water and materials will flow by gravity alone. Consequently, all drainage parts must be pitched or sloped downhill. These parts must be connected with special fittings and be large enough in diameter and smooth enough inside to prevent accumulation of solids at any point. This also means the fewer drainage parts, the better. This might not sound very exciting, but it's true: The entire plumbing installation generally is planned around the drainage system—to drain as many fixtures as possible with the same main pipe, and the fewer main pipes, the better. This setup makes venting easier, too.

There are four topics important enough to discuss by themselves when it comes to drainage: the plumbing lines that drain the house's internal plumbing fixtures, the private individual sewage system or septic tank, cleanout plugs, and venting.

Fixture Drainage Lines

All drainage lines must be pitched toward the sewer pipe. Tests have proven that a ¼-inch pitch per foot of run will allow practically all waste to move freely, even though it doesn't seem like much of a slope. At the other extreme, a pitch of 45 degrees or more (1 foot of pitch per 1 foot of run) provides a much stronger flow. If a straight run can't be accomplished with a sizable pitch of ½ inch per foot maximum, the largest part of the run should be made using the latter pitch and the remainder sloped at 45 degrees.

Drainage line piping should use 45-degree elbows to minimize flow resistance instead of 90-degree elbows. Using 90-degree elbows will slow down the drainage flow and increase the chance of a drainage plug up.

The slope and size of the trenches required to be excavated for the disposal lines are also important and depend on the type of soil and the contour of the land. Ideally, excavators will dig all the drainage trenches at the same time they are completing the foundation preparations.

Septic Systems

Because drainage systems that malfunction can affect the health of the entire community, there are usually stringent regulations governing private or individual sewage systems. The best all-around individual sewage system is a septic tank (Fig. 21.4). The septic tank system consists of a house drain, a septic tank, an outlet sewer, a distribution box, and a disposal or leachate field.

The location of a septic tank and leachate field on a building site will be partly determined by the lay of the land because the drainage must be downhill and

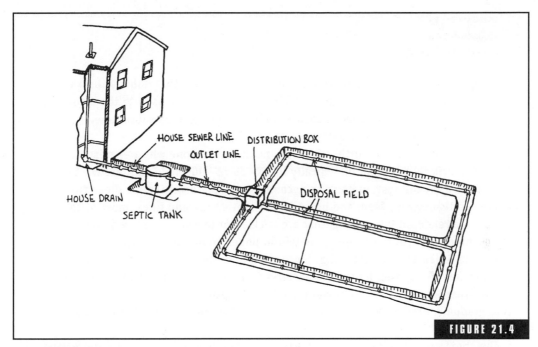

FIGURE 21.4

A septic tank system.

away from the water supply. Also remember that you need access to the tank when it must be serviced or repaired.

The *soil pipe* is the main drain from the house to the septic tank. It's usually made from a sturdy 5-inch cast-iron pipe that's pitched at an ideal slope.

The septic tank most frequently will be tar-coated steel or concrete (Fig. 21.5). Concrete costs more but lasts longer. When raw sewage enters the septic tank, bacterial action breaks down the solids into liquids and gases that drain off through an outlet sewer into a box that distributes them into the disposal field. This field is an area beneath the surface of the ground that "absorbs" and "cleans" the waste through natural processes of decay. The size of a septic tank is important because a tank that's too small will accumulate sludge that can back up into the house.

If you will need a septic system, be careful when you select your building site. Building sites seem to be getting smaller all the time. Once wide-open land is being

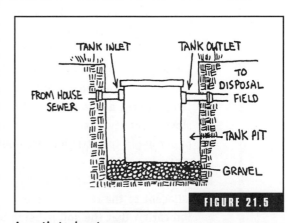

FIGURE 21.5

A septic tank cutaway.

FOCUS

SEPTIC SYSTEMS

A septic system is one of those hidden support systems that nobody thinks about until something goes wrong with it. To city dwellers who are used to the effortless convenience of sanitary sewers, septic systems are mysterious subterranean pipes and tanks that surely must take care of themselves.

Well, nothing could be further from the truth. Ask anyone who was raised on a farm. A septic tank system biologically breaks down household sanitary wastes. Bacteria within the system helps to decompose the solid wastes. As these tiny microorganisms grow, feed, and breed in the septic tank and lines, most of the wastes are rendered into liquids that are trickled or leached into the ground through a "leaching field" of perforated pipe laid in underground beds of gravel. Some of the waste-laden sewage water that leaches through the disposal lines is additionally decomposed or purified by natural bacteria found in the ground from 2 to 6 feet deep. Other wastes, however, remain inside the septic tank in the form of a sludge that gradually accumulates. A wide variety of factors can influence a septic system's operation.

The contractor who installs your septic tank should supply you with information so that you can inspect and arrange for maintenance services on the entire system. The following points are likely to be similar to the advice you should get.

SEPTIC SYSTEM INSPECTIONS: WHAT TO LOOK FOR

■ Septic tanks that are filling with sludge. Remove the access cover or cap, and measure the depth of sludge by inserting a long stick into the tank. When the total depth of solids exceeds one-third of the tank's capacity (certainly no more than one-half), it's time to have the tank pumped out and the solids removed. On many septic systems, if the sludge is allowed to accumulate, it eventually will fill the tank so that there is no room for waste to enter from the house. If this happens, the tank may overflow and saturate the surrounding grounds with horrible-smelling raw sewage.

■ Sluggish or plugged waste in sewer lines. When septic tanks are not functioning properly, a side effect is that lines running from the home's toilets are slow to convey wastes from the toilets to the septic tank. Solids and waste paper begin to settle and accumulate in the lines. Eventually, the whole system could back up.

■ Unusual foliage displays above leaching fields. Look at the grounds above and adjacent to the leaching field. Abnormal or luxuriant lawn conditions are an indication that the soil is being overloaded with waste-laden nutrients. Wet, soggy soil is another characteristic of failing absorption fields or clogged septic tanks. A good time to inspect leaching fields is during very wet weather. The size and composition of the leaching field should be sufficient to absorb household wastes and rainwater at the same time. If a heavy rain overloads the system and turns the leaching field into a swampy mess, improvements should be considered—perhaps adding more lengths of drainage pipe. Most problems are caused by the quality of soil around the leaching field. If there's a lot of clay present in the soil, good drainage will be almost impossible to achieve.

■ Trees and large shrubs growing on leaching fields. Roots can reach into the absorption beds and clog perforated piping. Make sure that trees and large shrubs are not encroaching over or immediately adjacent to septic system leaching fields.

SEPTIC SYSTEM REPAIRS AND MAINTENANCE

As far as repairs go, few individuals look forward to working on septic systems. Special tools and equipment such as heavy-duty pumps and vacuum units are often required.

1. Septic tanks should be cleaned periodically, or when they need it. Most should be checked at least once or twice a year to see that they're in working order. Typical septic tanks need cleaning about every 2 or 3 years. Ideally, the cleaning can be done in the spring. Because the waste material can give off obnoxious odors and may contain disease bacteria and warm weather accelerates bacteria action, it's best to pump and get rid of the waste before hot weather sets in. Cleaning a septic tank is not recommended as a do-it-yourself project. There are qualified companies that specialize in working on septic, well, and similar plumbing systems. They'll have the knowledge and equipment, and they'll also know where to get rid of the waste. It can't and shouldn't just be dumped anywhere.

2. Leaching fields should be kept free of trees and shrubs.

3. Avoid connecting nonessential home waste-water streams to a septic system. Runoff from gutters should be channeled elsewhere, as should discharge water from swimming pools and sump pumps.

4. Review with other family members what household wastes should not be put into septic systems.

   ■ If you have a kitchen garbage disposal, try not to grind and dispose of large amounts of vegetable and fruit matter. It's much better to dispose of them in an aboveground composting bin or pen, along with grass clippings, leaves, and similar vegetable and plant matter. Kitchen sink waste that's introduced to a septic system takes more time to be broken down by bacteria than do human wastes. If kitchen sink wastes are sent to the septic system, it probably will mean more frequent septic tank pumping and cleaning.

■ Avoid using drain cleaners and high-foaming detergents if the plumbing they go into is connected to the septic lines. Those substances will kill bacteria that's needed by the septic system to break down regular wastes. Low- and nonfoaming detergents are okay to wash with. So are nonphosphate and biodegradable laundry soaps.

■ Never let petroleum products, paint thinners, solvents, cleaning fluids, dyes, cigarettes, plastics, or similar materials enter a septic system. Most are harmful (or neutral) to the bacteria that grows, feeds, and breeds in the septic tank.

■ Grease from cooking juices and related activities should be reduced as much as possible. Grease, animal fats, and related food particles tend to float and accumulate in the top layer of lighter-than-water scum and slime that's present in all septic tanks. It's usually pumped out during regular maintenance of the tank. Naturally, never pour grease down a kitchen sink. Instruct family members to scrape and wipe as much grease as possible from cooking pans before immersing the pans in soapy water.

■ Also avoid placing modern "flushable" sanitary napkins into a septic system. Naturally, this goes double for regular types of sanitary napkins as well.

NEW SEPTIC INSTALLATIONS

When planning a new septic system, the most critical factor is the type of soil the ground is made of. Soil having good drainage will make things easier. As a general rule, a three-bedroom house should have, at minimum, a 900-gallon septic tank. A four-bedroom dwelling should have a tank with at least 1,150-gallon capacity. Since the septic tank and system are so critical to the daily operation of a household, leave nothing to chance. Get some professional help. Check with companies that have installed systems near your location. They'll know what to look for and what to look out for as well. Also consider the following options, all designed to take the pressure off the septic system:

■ In many areas, building codes insist that all toilets must be connected to a sanitary sewer or septic tank. These codes have not caught up with all the advances made by toilet manufacturers. There are toilets available that perform their own decomposing operations, channeling the waste (along with a very small amount of water) to relatively small tanks that usually are installed in a basement. These tanks need to be emptied as few times as once per year. And by then, the waste has been broken down into a practically odorless material. Composting toilets thus greatly reduce the amounts of solid wastes going to a septic tank and the overall amount of water used in a bathroom.

■ A less radical option is one of a number of new toilets designed to use less water per flush. Since even now, at this very moment, new designs are on the drawing board, check with local plumbing supply houses for news on the most water-efficient models.

■ Another workable idea is to use two separate septic tanks: one for solid waste and the other for what's known as graywater. Graywater is waste water that's not heavily laden with solids. It includes rinse and other water from clothes washing machines, dishwashers, showers, bathtubs, and even sump pumps. The graywater can be routed through its own tank to the leaching field so that it won't overload the main septic tank.

NOTE

■ Large vehicles should not be allowed to drive over septic tanks or leaching fields. Be especially wary of large, heavy rigs such as concrete trucks, front-end loaders, bulldozers, drilling outfits, and the like.

SEPTIC TANK QUICK CHECKLIST

1. A septic tank should be cleaned out when the total depth of solids within it exceeds between one-third and one-half the tank's capacity.
2. Have septic tanks inspected at least once a year, typically during spring.
3. Keep trees and large shrubs from growing over the system's leaching field.
4. Avoid routing graywater or nonsanitary waste water to the septic system.
5. Keep kitchen wastes out of the septic tank. The same goes for petroleum products, paints, solvents, and similar materials.
6. Don't use drain cleaners or high-foaming detergents if the plumbing they drain into is connected to a septic tank.

built up. The space required for safe waste disposal is dwindling and, in some close-quartered neighborhoods, nonexistent.

Cleanout Plugs

The importance of cleanouts in a plumbing system becomes apparent as soon as there's a blockage somewhere. Plumbing stoppages occur for a number of reasons, including the following:

- Foreign objects lodged in a drainage line
- An accumulation of hair or other matter
- Deposits of grease, fat, or other congealed substances

These materials can completely block the discharge through drainage lines or at least greatly reduce effective flows. Complete blockages cause considerable damage to the lower floors when wastewater backs up. Even partial stoppages can create conditions in drainage lines that interfere with proper venting. In turn, poor venting results in the escape of foul gases and odors into the living areas of the home.

Pipe drainage cleanouts should be accessible for servicing. The contractor should provide an out-of-sight access door for any that are located within a wall.

Venting

A *plumbing* or *building trap* is a device installed in plumbing that prevents the intake of sewer gas into the interior piping system. A cleanout at the trap offers access to the house's sewer line between the dwelling and the outside street sewer facilities. Other gases and odors in a home's plumbing are kept in check and vented from the house through piping that runs up through the roof. At the same time, this prevents gurgling or sucking sounds after a fixture is drained and protects trap seals from siphonage and backpressure.

It's best to specify that the vent pipe or pipes be installed near the rear of the house so that they're not readily visible from the street (Figs. 21.6 and 21.7).

WATER HEATERS

Until fairly recently, most home owners had only one basic water heater type available for their home hot-water use: a tank water heater. Today, tank water heaters still make up the majority of water heaters sold and installed for home use. But other types of systems are likely to continue to gain wider acceptance in the near future: tankless water heaters and solar water heaters. Currently, most water heaters are heated by either natural gas, propane, oil, or electricity.

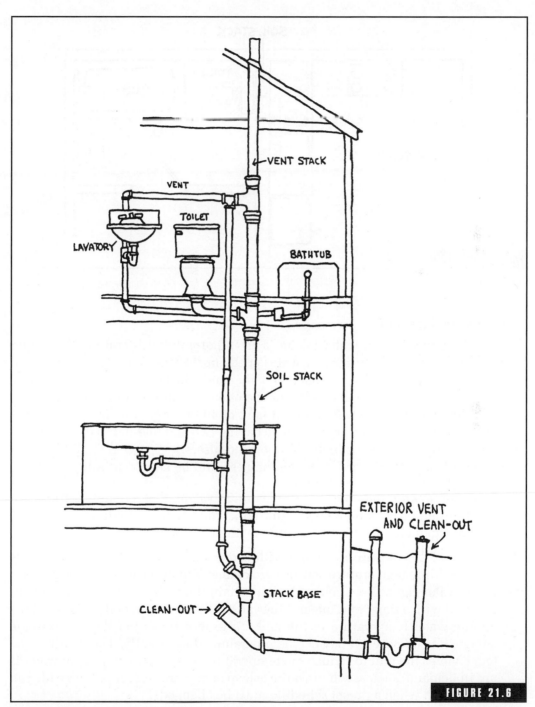

A drain/waste/vent plumbing system.

VENT STACK

VENT

TOILET

LAVATORY

BATHTUB

SOIL STACK

EXTERIOR VENT
AND CLEAN-OUT

CLEAN-OUT →

STACK BASE

FIGURE 21.6

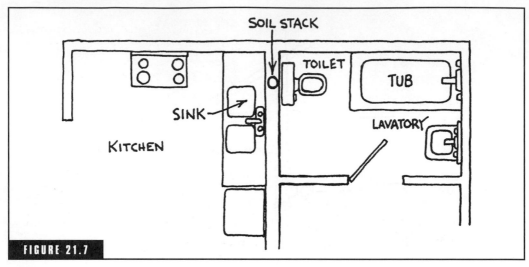

FIGURE 21.7

Toilet venting.

Tank Water Heaters

The capacity of a tank water heater is an important consideration. The water heater should provide enough hot water at the busiest time of the day or night. The ability of a water heater to meet peak demands for hot water is indicated by its *first-hour rating*, which accounts for the effects of tank size and the speed at which cold water is heated. A standard tank of 40 or 50 gallons is usually sufficient for a family of four living in a house having two and one-half bathrooms, but larger tanks are available for high-volume water users.

A number of points regarding water tanks should be kept in mind:

1. Look for a unit that has a self-cleaning system that creates a turbulent swirling action as water enters the tank, thus fighting sediment buildup, improving operating efficiency, and lengthening tank life.

2. Some tank heaters are available with setback-adjustable thermostats. Units with multiple temperature settings are convenient and can save energy costs when water can be kept cooler during certain times. Some models are manufactured with a timer and integral thermostat that automatically raises or lowers the water temperature in the tank up to four times per day to conserve energy. If need be, each day can be programmed differently. This control system enables the unit to reduce the temperature temporarily when hot water is not in demand, such as when you're asleep or at work. A manual override can be accessed when a preset schedule must be changed.

3. Install water heaters near the highest hot-water demand areas in order to reduce wasted energy from running the water long distances. If your house

will have two equal demand areas, try to center the water heater between them. If your furnace and hot-water tank vent through the chimney, logically they will need to be near each other. However, many of the high-efficiency furnaces and hot-water tanks have their own direct-vent system, allowing them to be vented straight to the outdoors. Because a hot-water heater or tank will wear out in time, you should be able to access it easily for removal, and the inspection panels and drain valve must also be simple to get at for maintenance and repairs.

4. Look for models with longer warranties (10 to 12 years) with maximized isolation and heat transfer and larger heating elements.

5. The water heater should be easy to shut down and start up. Favor an ignition device that automatically lights the pilot as it's needed.

6. Check to see if adding insulation to your water heater will affect the warranty. If additional insulation is desired, follow the instructions from the water heater manufacturer.

7. A water heater tank must have a drain near the bottom so that you can easily drain the tank when needed and can flush out sediments that collect at the tank's bottom periodically. Unless you have soft water, it's important to drain water from the bottom of a water heater tank periodically to help remove hard-water deposits that may accumulate on the tank's bottom. These deposits effectively act like insulation. They eventually surround the heating element and force it to work harder and harder at heating the tank's water. Removing these sediments by periodic draining of small amounts of water from the tank's bottom will help to keep the system healthier and less expensive to operate.

8. When locating a gas water heater in a garage, keep it raised off the floor so that when the pilot ignites the gas burners, it doesn't cause any floor-hugging gasoline fumes from a lawnmower or auto to explode.

SAFETY»NOTE

HOT-WATER-HEATING SYSTEM SHUTOFFS

When shutting the water off to the boiler or other parts of a hot-water heating system or to a hot-water heater (tank), carefully follow the manufacturer's instructions. If a boiler or hot-water heater runs out of or is low on water, serious damage (including explosion and fire) and injuries can result.

(F)OCUS

WATER SOFTENERS

Also referred to as *water conditioners*, when the quality of available water is less than ideal, the installation of water softeners or conditioners can provide a number of major benefits, including:

- Filtering potentially harmful contaminants out of the water
- Removing miscellaneous unpleasant tastes and odors from the household's drinking water
- Softening hard water reduces buildup of hard-water soap curd, which can gum up the insides of appliances. Less soap-curd deposits can mean that dishwashers, clothes washers, and water heaters will operate more efficiently and for a longer lifetime.

Hard water typically contains unusually high amounts of minerals and metals, including iron, calcium, and magnesium. This water can wreak havoc within a home, causing soap scum and lime deposits to form on numerous appliances, fixtures, and plumbing components. Hard water will leave streaking windows, bathtub and toilet rings, tainted appliances, plugged showerheads, restricted flows in pipes, and other nagging problems. Water softening is by far the most common treatment required for hard water supplied by wells and some private or municipal water authorities. Advantages of softening hard water are many. They include the following:

- Hard water causes lime scale buildup. Lime scale coats moving parts in appliances, causing them to operate less efficiently. Lime scale collects within water heaters, reducing heat-exchange efficiencies and increasing the cost of heating water. Lime scale clogs pipes and fixture internals and slows the delivery of water throughout the home.
- Hard water will discolor bathroom and kitchen fixtures.
- Soft water works far more efficiently with soaps and detergent cleaners. For clothes, shorter wash cycles and cooler water will suffice when soft water is employed. In some cases, for the same results, twice as much cleanser is needed when used with hard water. Hard water also can reduce the life span of clothes when lime curd deposits cause difficult-to-remove yellowish or gray stains. For people and pets, bar soap and shampoo usage will be reduced with soft water. Hard water can dry skin and hair because the minerals within the water combine with the soap to form a sticky residue that's hard to rinse away. People who use hard water tend to use more skin-softening lotions and hair conditioners.

SELECTING WATER SOFTENERS/CONDITIONERS

Consider the following points when reviewing your water softener or conditioner needs:

- First, test your water so that you know exactly what problems, if any, you need to solve. A local water treatment company expert can perform a preliminary analysis, usually at no charge.
- Conventional softening equipment works via an ion exchange. The softening tank is full of tiny porous plastic spheres that attract hard calcium and magnesium ions. When the spheres are full of these hard ions, a regeneration cycle starts to clean off the spheres so that they can be used again to soften more water. For maximum savings, look for a sphere-cleaning system that uses a salt solution and water. Further, a demand-initiated regeneration system actually meters water usage and only regenerates on demand—unlike units that use timers to regenerate at preset intervals, which can require twice as much salt and water. Give serious consideration to a twin-tank system that allows switching from one softening tank to the other as they exhaust their softening capability to provide an uninterrupted flow of soft water 24 hours per day.
- Lean toward reliable systems that are not subject to electric timer malfunctions or power outages. Cost should not be the main issue when it comes to water softening and conditioning. You'll want equipment that operates without interruption, is easy to care for, and produces consistent desired results.

High-Efficiency Gas Storage Water Heaters

High-efficiency gas storage water heaters take the standard gas water heaters a few more green steps forward (Fig. 21.8). Like standard water heaters, they consist of a glass-lined steel tank in which the water is stored and heated by a burner located at the bottom of the tank. The improved units are more efficient because they have better insulation, heat traps, and more efficient burners. These improvements bump the price of a high-efficiency water heater up a little over that of the standard models, but it's worth it when the cost of heating water is figured over the life cycle of the tank. The high-efficient gas models provide an average of over 7 percent greater efficiency. For even greater savings, some manufacturers increase the venting capability of combustion gases with a power vent.

Gas-Condensing Water Heaters

These water heaters also work much like regular gas water heaters, but instead of venting combustion gases outside, those gases are captured and used to heat the

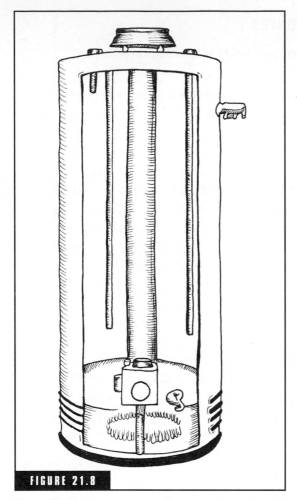

FIGURE 21.8

High-efficiency gas water heater.

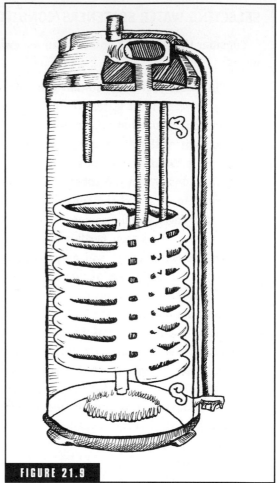

FIGURE 21.9

Gas-condensing water heater.

water even more. A standard gas storage water heater can be thought of like a simple water tank sitting on top of a gas fireplace with the chimney running straight up through the middle, exiting at the top. A gas-condensing water heater has its "chimney" or flue designed with greater surface area (Fig. 21.9). As shown in the figure, the heat and combustion gases have much farther to travel before they exit the water tank, so more heat can be transferred to the water in the tank before the gases depart, creating greater efficiency.

Heat-Pump Water Heaters

Heat pumps are efficient ways to heat water as another part of an overall home space-heating and -cooling system (Fig. 21.10). They're like a refrigerator that can work in either a regular fashion or in reverse. A refrigerator removes heat from an insulated, enclosed "box" and expels the heat to the surrounding air. Instead, a heat-pump water heater takes heat from surrounding air (or in-the-ground water) and transfers it to the water in an enclosed storage tank. A low-pressure liquid refrigerant is vaporized in the heat pump's evaporator and sent into the compressor. As the pressure of the refrigerant increases, so does its temperature. The heated refrigerant runs through a condenser coil within the storage tank and transfers the heat to water stored there. As the refrigerant delivers its heat to the water, it cools and condenses and then passes through an expansion valve where the pressure is reduced so that the cycle can start all over again.

Solar Water Heaters

Solar water heating systems are fairly simple to install, maintain, and operate, but even so, it's best, and sometimes mandatory, to have licensed installers who are experienced with solar heating do the work. Florida and California have had solar water heating for decades, since the early 1900s. There were times when solar heating made inroads, but the low cost of other fuels years ago discouraged solar

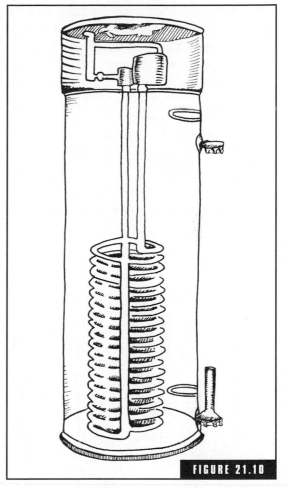

FIGURE 21.10

Heat-pump water heater.

systems from being produced and installed. In response to the fuel embargo in the 1970s, solar installations were making a comeback in part owing to federal tax credits that went with them, and a large number of companies started to make, install, and service solar heaters. Then the federal tax credits were discontinued, and energy prices dropped again. Most of the newly started solar companies dropped out of sight. Some persisted, though, and helped to develop the technology further. Now solar is back. When the sun is shining, they work very efficiently. When cloudy days persist, they still provide some heat, but probably not enough, so another water-heating source must be available. Solar systems consist of—in addition to interconnecting piping—a number of control devices, collectors that absorb heat from the sun, and a storage tank and/or distribution setup to hold the heated water until it's needed. Solar systems can stand alone or can be integrated into regular tank water-heating units and piping. Some solar heaters serve as preheaters for conventional gas or electric tank heaters or for water that enters a tankless on-demand heater. They do an excellent job—think of the temperature water can reach from sitting in a rubber hose that's stretched along the lawn on a cloudless summer day. All told, solar water heating is a feature that should be considered by anyone planning a new home. At this time, it's much easier and considerably less expensive than planning and installing a solar system for electricity generation.

There are different styles of collectors and many variations of each style (Fig. 21.11). Most are usually mounted on a roof or the ground facing south, southwest,

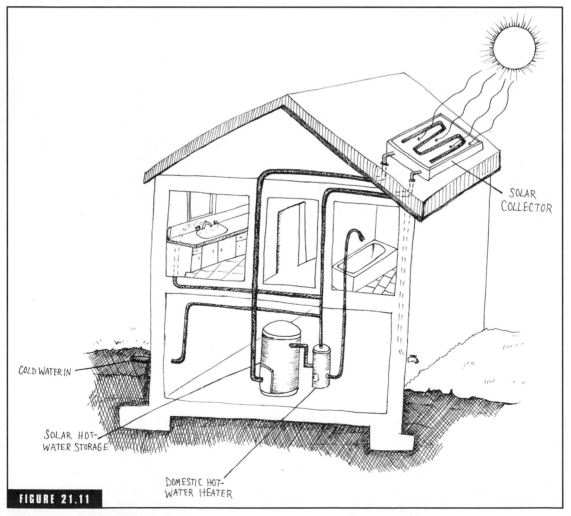

SOLAR COLLECTOR

COLD WATER IN

SOLAR HOT-WATER STORAGE

DOMESTIC HOT-WATER HEATER

FIGURE 21.11

Solar water-heating system.

or southeast. Some use several roof panels that resemble skylights and fit into traditional window decor so well that a casual observer may not even be able to tell that they're solar panels.

Both active- and passive-solar water-heating systems are available. The active systems heat water indirectly by means of a heat exchanger inside a hot-water tank. A pump is used to circulate water to and from the solar collectors. Passive systems heat the actual water that goes through the home's fixtures and appliances by circulating the water through the solar collectors often as part of a continuous loop before it arrives at the use points. The water moves throughout the system via simple thermosyphoning—as the water in the collector tubes heats up, it becomes lighter, rising into the storage tank, leaving more room for cold water to take its place. The household hot water then gets used out of the hot-water tank, which opens up more space for the replacement water heating inside the collector tubes, and so on.

Solar Collectors

FLAT-PLATE COLLECTORS

The most popular systems use flat-plate collectors—copper tubes that are mounted to a flat absorber plate surrounded by an insulated black box that's covered with plastic or tempered glass. The absorber plate heats up from sunlight and then heats water or another heating fluid such as antifreeze as it is pumped through or flows through the copper pipes. This hot water or fluid then is either stored in a tank or pumped through the copper piping to a heat exchanger or through a heating coil in a storage tank, where it heats the water outside the coil in the tank. Flat-plate collectors are considered to be effective no matter what climate they're used in.

INTEGRAL COLLECTOR STORAGE

Nicknamed *ICS* or *batch systems*, these solar collectors are constructed with black tanks or tubes, again positioned in an insulated black box that's covered with a glass or plastic top. Like all solar collectors, they're mounted facing as south as possible. The sun's rays heat cold water as it flows through the collector, no matter what the outside temperature is (think of how hot it can get inside a car parked in a sunny location, even when the outdoors temperature is cold). These collectors are best used in mild-weather locations, where exposed pipe between the collector and inside hot-water tanks will not freeze during winter.

EVACUATED-TUBE SOLAR COLLECTORS

These collectors consist of parallel clear glass tubes, each consisting of a vacuum-sealed outer tube with an inside glass or metal absorber tube containing water or heat-transfer fluid fixed to an absorber fin. The fin collects solar energy,

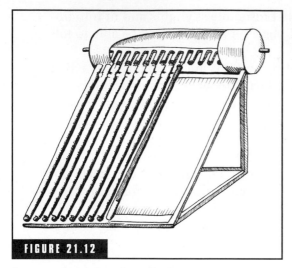

FIGURE 21.12

An evacuated-tube solar collector.

which is used to heat water (Fig. 21.12). The space between the inner and outer tubes is a vacuum, so very little heat is lost from the fluid. Although these collectors can cost considerably more than flat-plate collectors, they're very efficient and work well even in overcast conditions and in below-zero temperatures.

Tankless Water Heaters

Also called *demand water heaters*, these tankless units provide an alternative to the standard hot-water tank. Why consider tankless units? There's less risk of a water rupture—with all the water damage such an unexpected event can cause. Also, tankless water-heating equipment likely will last longer than components of a tank heating system. Tankless components are less subject to corrosion. The highest-quality models use stainless steel, copper, and brass for parts that contact water. If a component malfunctions, it can be repaired. There's no tank to rust out, so the entire unit never has to be replaced.

In addition, tankless systems provide hot water where and when you need it, without relying on a preheated inventory of heated water. Considerable energy is lost from heated water that simply stands in the tank all day and all night. Tankless units also virtually eliminate standby water heat losses—energy wasted when hot water cools down in long pipes or while sitting in a storage tank. By providing heated water immediately where it's used, tankless water heaters waste less water. People don't need to let the water run as they wait for warm or hot water to reach a remote faucet. A tankless water heater, correctly sized, provides almost unlimited instant heated water as long as the system is used within its capabilities.

For example, when someone opens a hot-water faucet within a home's plumbing system, the tankless water heater "senses" this—starting the gas burner or the electric elements that heats the water as it flows toward the faucet. By using standard energy sources such as electricity, gas, or propane, these remarkably efficient tankless water heaters can reduce a household's water-heating bill by 10 to 20 percent or more. The top models have modulating gas valve or electric heat output, and solid-state controls maintain a steady hot-water temperature. These designs ensure a constant water temperature from a faucet's trickle to a shower's full-force spray.

As a rule, tankless water heaters are a lot smaller than tank water heater; some are only 36 inches high and hang on a wall (Fig. 21.13); others are about the size of a bread box. When compared with bulky water tanks, these units use far less valuable square footage of living space. Direct-vent models are available, as are

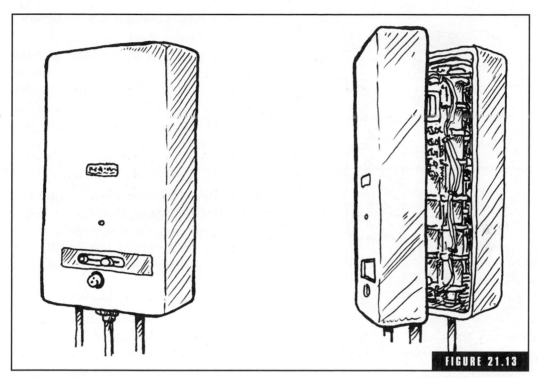

Tankless water heater.

units with electronic ignition to save energy otherwise consumed by a continuously burning pilot light. When the demand for water ceases, the tankless unit shuts down and uses no energy. The compact design affords you almost limitless options so that you can locate the unit strategically for maximum performance and energy efficiency. The tankless unit saves on square footage in a home.

Whole-home gas tankless water heaters are larger units (Fig. 21.14) that can heat adequate amounts of water, enough to supply average demands in most households. Again, when a hot-water tap is turned on in the home, cold water is drawn into the water heater, where a flow sensor activates the gas burner, which warms the heat exchanger. The incoming cold water circles through or around the heat exchanger and leaves the heater at a preset temperature. The combustion gases exit safely through a dedicated, sealed vent system.

Are there any downsides to installing tankless water heaters? One could be that in the event of an electrical failure, a tank full of already heated water is *not* available, on standby, as would be with a tank hot-water system. Another could depend on the affected electrical power utility—tankless electric units draw more instantaneous power than tank water heaters because water must be heated quickly to the desired temperature. If electric rates include a demand charge, operation could be relatively expensive.

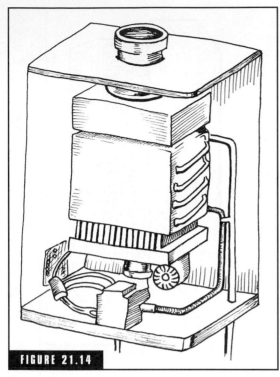

FIGURE 21.14

A whole-house gas tankless water heater.

A hot-water dispenser is a small electric water heater that can be located beneath your sink with a spout near the faucet. Typically, it contains an insulated ½-gallon water tank. Combining the hot water in the tank with the output of the heating element, enough hot water is produced for about 50 cups per hour. In an otherwise traditional water distribution system, the water-heater dispenser can lower utility bills because every time you turn on the hot-water faucet, the entire hot-water pipe from the water heater in the utility room or basement has to fill with hot water before it even gets to the sink.

Creative Ways to Heat Water

For years, experienced plumbers have been devising ways to squeeze the last few degrees of warmth from drain water. Whether it comes from sinks, showers, or clothes washing machines, wherever hot water drains through a home's lines, someone has figured out how to use that warmth to power a heat exchanger such as the one shown in Figure 21.15. As long as the code permits, such a heat-recapturing arrangement could be an energy saver.

PLUMBING INSPECTION

It's likely that the plumbing in a new house will be put together satisfactorily from a technical viewpoint because local codes usually specify that licensed plumbers must perform the work and that all of that work must then be inspected and certified. But no matter what the situation is with your house, it's still up to you to determine if the plumbing is installed in a fashion that you feel is adequate. Here are some guidelines to help you to evaluate your plumbing system:

1. All piping must be well supported. Nothing should just hang there, wobbly or vibrating when liquids and waste materials pass through.

2. Pipes should run parallel to inside wall studs. If any pipe runs parallel to an exterior wall stud, make sure that insulation is arranged between the pipe and both the interior and exterior parts of the wall.

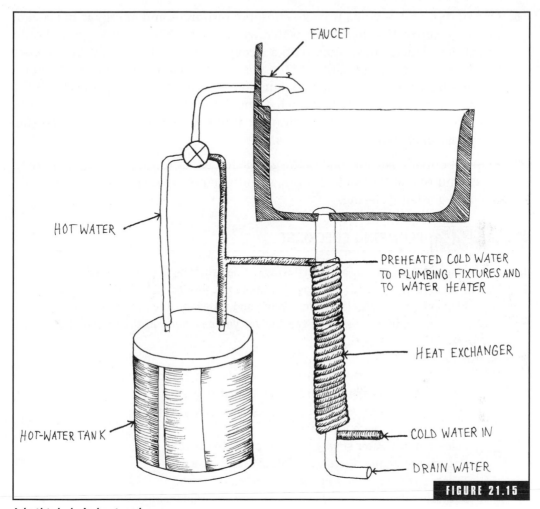

FAUCET

HOT WATER

PREHEATED COLD WATER
TO PLUMBING FIXTURES AND
TO WATER HEATER

HEAT EXCHANGER

HOT-WATER TANK

COLD WATER IN

DRAIN WATER

FIGURE 21.15

A bathtub drain heat exchanger.

3. Check to see if the plumber installs the correct number of shutoff valves and cleanouts as called for in the plans.

4. Before the walls and floors are closed up by the contractor, the rough plumbing must be inspected by the municipal inspector. You also should make a mental note (or drawing) of what's getting covered up. Check that all water piping has been insulated.

5. The regular plumbing lines should be water tested and inspected for leaks, and if there's a gas line, it must be subjected to a pressure leak test as provided by the building code.

6. One of the most obvious ways to conserve resources and energy is to prevent leaks. A faucet that leaks hot water wastes both. This is why you should select only faucets that come with a strong warranty. The extent of coverage specified is a good indication of the manufacturer's quality standards. For a top-notch faucet, look for an all-inclusive warranty, one that applies to all the parts as well as to the outside finish. Consider washerless, drip-free faucets as desirable alternatives to old-fashioned units with washers and seals—the main reasons for troublesome leaks.

7. Request outside faucets: one in the garage (on a warm wall), one at the home's front, and two at the back to allow simultaneous lawn sprinkling, car washing, and garden watering.

 **PLUMBING CHECKLIST**

Few things in a house can be as irritating, as destructive, and as expensive to repair as plumbing. When it's working, it's taken for granted. When it's not, look out. Keep yours out of trouble by identifying and following the applicable items in this checklist. And also be aware of the choices you can make in the selection of various fixtures.

1. Plumbing item specs:

_____ Sewer pipe from street to house: Preferably cast iron or steel.

_____ Sewer pipe under the house: Preferably cast iron.

_____ Exposed sewer and vent pipes: Plastic, cast iron, or copper.

_____ Cleanouts in enough locations.

_____ Cold- and hot-water supply pipes: Preferably copper.

_____ Natural gas piping: Preferably "black" steel pipe.

_____ Toilet: Specify type, manufacturer, model, and color.

_____ Bathtub: Specify fiberglass, steel, or cast iron and manufacturer, model, and color.

_____ Molded shower/tub unit: Specify type, manufacturer, model, and color.

_____ Bathroom vanity top/sink: Specify porcelain or cultured marble or other and type, manufacturer, model, and color.

_____ Kitchen sink: Specify stainless steel or enamel and type (single-, double-, or triple-basin), manufacturer, model, and color.

_____ Faucets: Specify single- or double-handle type, chrome, brass, or other, and manufacturer, model, and color.

_____ Refrigerator: Include a water connection for an ice maker.

_____ Shower heads: Specify type, manufacturer, and model.

_____ Garbage disposal: Specify manufacturer and model.

_____ Dishwasher: Specify manufacturer, model, and color.

PLUMBING CHECKLIST *(Continued)*

_____ Clothes washer and dryer: Specify type, manufacturer, model, and color.

_____ Laundry tub: Specify manufacturer, model, and color.

_____ Water heater: Specify electric, natural gas, or oil heat source, gallon capacity, and manufacturer.

_____ Water softener: Specify manufacturer and gallon capacity.

_____ Water wells and pumps: Specify size and type.

_____ Septic tank: Specify size and type.

2. Plumbing minimum drain specs:

_____ Toilet: 3 inches.

_____ Shower stall: 2 inches.

_____ Clothes washer: 2 inches.

_____ Laundry tray: 1½ inches.

_____ Tub and shower: 1½ inches.

_____ Bathroom sink: 1½ inches

_____ Kitchen sink: 1½ inches.

_____ Dishwasher: 1½ inches.

3. Pipe insulation:

_____ Bare pipes do not conserve energy, so they should be insulated. Insulating cold-water pipes prevents cooling the warm air around them during winter, which can cause a heating system to run harder than necessary.

_____ Insulating hot-water pipes is useful year round. During late spring, summer, and early fall, pipe insulation will prevent the heat from the hot water inside the pipes from radiating and warming the surrounding air, which forces the air-conditioning system to run more often. Insulating hot-water pipes also helps to prevent hot water in the lines from cooling off before it reaches its destination faucet or appliance.

_____ For pipe insulation, consider ¾-inch-thick preformed pipe insulation tubes, some constructed of flexible rubber or polyethylene foam. These tubes can be purchased in bulk or by the piece, often 3- or 6-feet long, preslit and self-sealing.

_____ Make sure that whatever type you choose is rated to safely handle the highest temperature your system can produce. If the insulation is not suited for the application, the insulation could deteriorate or even catch fire. Insulate bare steel-jacketed burstproof hoses with flexible pipe-wrap insulation with ¾-inch-thick walls.

4. Miscellaneous plumbing points:

_____ You should be able to conveniently turn off the water or gas supply pipes to each plumbing fixture in the house with shutoff valves (Fig. 21.16).

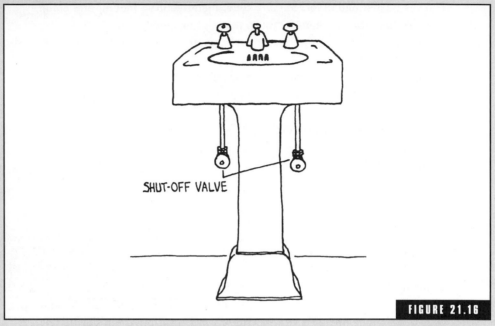

FIGURE 21.16

Sink shutoff valves.

_____ A neat way to arrange the plumbing needed by the clothes washing machine and laundry tub is to have the plumber install an in-the-wall-plumbing box (Fig. 21.17). This box will dress up the installation and provide protection to any plaster or drywall that might be placed behind your laundry area. It's a good method to achieve the plumbing compactness mentioned earlier. All the faucet, supply, and drain piping is conveniently tied together. A laundry room clothes washing machine will be safer and more energy efficient if insulated steel-jacketed burstproof water supply hoses are used.

_____ Make sure that piping run through the basement does not "break up" otherwise usable living space.

_____ Include enough sill cocks. A *sill cock* is nothing but an outside cold water tap for lawn watering, car washing, and other outdoors use (Fig. 21.18). A typical dwelling should have at least two of them, and very large houses may need as many as four—so you needn't rely on excessively long and unwieldy garden hoses. Have the sill cocks staggered around the house, with one near the driveway. In cold-weather locations where freezing occurs, sill cocks should be of the freeze-proof variety to protect your exterior faucets from freezing and rupturing. A freeze-proof outside faucet having a long stem

PLUMBING CHECKLIST (*Continued*)

An in-the-wall plumbing box.

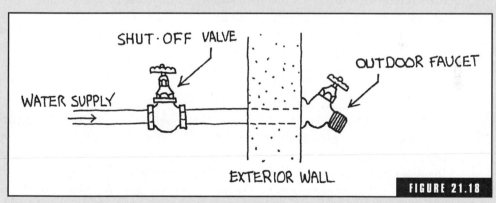

A sill cock.

shuts water off a foot or two back within the house, where things stay warm and above freezing.

____ Locate a sill cock or water faucet in the garage, preferably on an inside wall bordering the heated part of the house.

____ Insist that single-unit bathtubs or shower stalls be installed while the house is being framed for a more custom built-in look.

____ Even if you're not including a basement bathroom with the initial construction, it's a good idea to include a *service stub,* or connection arrangement,

✔✔✔✔✔ **PLUMBING CHECKLIST** (*Continued*)

for one sink, one toilet, and one tub/shower unit so that they can be installed easily later.

_____ Vinyl, ceramic tile, and wood flooring should be installed in rooms that will receive plumbing fixtures. You'll have a much neater looking floor if these materials are laid down first. If carpet is the selected floor covering, the carpeting underlayment should be installed before the plumbing comes through, and then the carpet itself can be laid after the fixtures have been set.

_____ To prevent cluttering up the appearance of the front of the house, have waste vents exit through the roof at the rear of the house.

_____ All roof stacks should be made of galvanized or other nonrusting metal or material.

_____ Avoid plastic ice lines for icemaker feeds. Consider a stainless steel braided hose line for leak and breakage prevention.

_____ A floor pan should be installed under a clothes washer if the washer is located upstairs.

_____ Use smooth steel round ducting with smooth walls to vent the dryer. The smooth walls will resist collecting lint and are easy to clean.

_____ Keep the dryer vent pipe run as short and straight as possible. Avoid elbows that impede airflow and lessen efficiency.

_____ Avoid dryer vent pipe joints whenever possible—lint can build up and also hurt pipe efficiency.

_____ No screws or fasteners should penetrate the dryer vent pipe.

_____ An efficient dryer vent pipe arrangement is through an exterior wall behind the dryer, with the pipe going from the back of the dryer straight through the wall to outdoors.

_____ The dryer should be positioned to allow easy access to clean the lint off the screen as well as inside the dryer housing and underneath the unit behind the toe kick plate.

_____ The dryer vent cap should be positioned to permit easy disconnecting and cleaning.

_____ Always insist on gas-line connection leak tests when a new appliance, fixture, or line is installed.

_____ For toilets, consider using stainless steel braided hose to prevent possible line breaks.

_____ If your plumbing code allows PEX supply lines for water supply, consider them.

PLUMBING

1. Bathtub/shower hot and cold faucets operate correctly, with no dripping when shut off. The drains work quickly.

2. All sink faucets and drains work as they're supposed to.

3. Toilets flush properly, fill to correct lines, with no seepage or running sounds.

4. Turn on all sink faucets and flush all toilets at the same time to see if they'll all work without a major reduction in water flow.

5. Allow faucets, tubs, and drains on upper floors to run for a while. See if any stains form on downstairs ceilings beneath those fixtures. Best to catch problems early, before the home is painted or wallpapered.

6. Garbage disposal operates smoothly.

7. Dishwasher operates evenly, with no leaks. Run through an entire cycle.

8. Run the clothes washing machine; make sure the drain discharge doesn't leak.

9. No scratches, dents, or chipped surfaces on appliances.

10. Test the water-heater drain valve. See if it opens easily and seals shut when closed.

11. Operate the sump pump, the humidifier, the baseboard heat, and all other plumbing components that may apply. Check for leaks.

12. Try all outdoor spigots. Make sure they close easily and completely.

13. Check that isolation valves are tagged as to what they shut off. Test the isolation valves, with the system activated, to see that they hold. Make sure with hot-water heaters and boilers that the manufacturers' instructions are followed.

14. If the home has natural gas, ask the utility company to test or "sniff" the gas lines, gas appliances, and areas in which those components are present for leaks, loose fittings, and other problems. Many utility companies will do such a check as a complimentary safety service.

REMODELING NOTES

For sure, have your water tested and plumbing lines inspected. Your lines may have been put together with solder containing lead, depending on what material the plumbers used. If so, replace the lines to ensure safe drinking water.

One of the easier remodels that can pay back big time is a water heater replacement. There are so many options to select from because it's such a large user of electricity, gas, or other fuel, and there are so many ways to save. See if tankless water heaters would fit your lifestyle and make sense. How much hot water do you use, and when do you use it? Look at your water and electricity bills. How do they compare with the bills of other family members or friends? You can consider renewable-energy participation with passive-solar heat tubes positioned on the roof or elsewhere outdoors. You can tie in a geothermal heat exchanger or combine your potable water heating with a boiler used for space heating, or you can simply wrap insulation around your existing water heater if it's relatively new and somewhat energy efficient. Since water heating is such a huge issue, look at your remodel options, and this is one remodel that can start paying off immediately and still will be a major sales feature when it's time to move out.

>>>>> POINTS TO PONDER

1. The time and effort you spend planning the location of plumbing fixtures are the most important parts of their installation.

2. A major consideration is where to position the water heater and how to keep as much of the plumbing as possible concentrated in one three-dimensional area (from basement or lowest level to top level) of the home.

3. The plumbing should be planned, if possible, so that waste water and materials flow by gravity alone.

4. Drain a few gallons of water from the water-heater tank at least once a month. At the same time, check the tank's pressure valve.

5. Know where plumbing shutoff valves are. The contractor should label each valve as to what it shuts off. Operate each valve several times a year to keep all valves in working order.

6. All piping must be well supported to prevent wobbly or hammering lines.

7. For maximum energy savings, insulate water-heater tanks (following the manufacturer's instructions) and water lines. Install water heaters near the highest hot-water demand areas to reduce wasted energy from running the heated water long distances.

8. When planning your landscaping, keep large trees and large shrubs from being planted over septic tank leaching fields and also avoid, if possible, connecting nonessential home waste-water streams to a septic system. Runoff from gutters should be channeled elsewhere, as should discharge water from swimming pools and sump pumps.

9. If a gas water heater is located in a garage, make sure that it's raised off the floor so that when the pilot ignites the gas burner, it doesn't cause any floor-hugging gasoline fumes from a lawnmower or auto to explode.

10. Whenever you have the option, elect water-saving appliances such as low-demand toilets, smaller bathtubs, and low-flow faucets and showerheads.

Electric

If there is one system in a house that shouldn't be skimped on, it's the electrical system. Like the plumbing in a house, the electrical system is taken for granted until something goes wrong with it or there's not enough to go around. To properly understand your prints and drawings, familiarize yourself with the symbols in Table 22.1.

TABLE 22.1 Basic Electrical Symbols

1.	⊖=	This is a duplex wall outlet. This supplies your power to lamps, vacuum cleaners, and other household devices and appliances.
2.	S	This means a single-pole switch. This provides on and off control to outlets from one position
3.	S_2	This signifies a double-pole switch. This provides on and off control from two locations. For example, it lets you turn off lights from either of two entrances to a room.
4.	S_3	This is a three-way switch.
5.	S_4	This is a four-way switch.
6.	Ⓢ	This is a pull-switch in the ceiling.
7.	S_{CB}	This is a circuit breaker.
8.	=⊖wp	This means a weatherproof outlet.
9.	⌀	This denotes a ceiling light fixture.
10.	TV	This is a television antenna outlet.

POWER SUPPLY

The minimum power supply recommended for most houses today is a three-wire 240-volt, 200-ampere service, especially if the house is larger than 3,000 square feet, if heavy-draw electric appliances such as electric cooking ranges or clothes dryers are planned, or if such features as central air-conditioning and swimming pool pumps will be installed. A good indication of the power supply available at any site is whether two or three main wires enter the weatherhead fitting on the roof or side of the house. If only two wires are present, the dwelling has 110–120-volt power throughout. If three, then 220–240-volt power is available at the meter.

The circuit box is where the main electrical service is split into separate circuits. There should be at least 24 to 36 circuits to handle the electrical needs of most homes. The cover on the panel should be able to be tightly closed, and the main wires entering the box should be neatly and securely affixed to the wall. Home wiring must be grounded properly. Proper grounding provides a path for electricity to safely travel from a defective appliance, tool, outlet, fixture, or other component to the earth, or ground. Your local building code will state what is required for proper grounding in your area.

Renewable-Energy Power Supplies: Solar, Wind, and Hydroelectricity Generation

Until recently, practically all electricity came from organizations running large-scale generating facilities. And yes, even though you may have been hearing a lot about sustainable energy, it still does come from mostly the same places. About half our electric supply is produced by huge coal-fired boilers. Most of the rest is distributed from nuclear power plants and natural gas– and oil-fired boilers. A small percentage continues to be produced by hydroelectric plants, and the last few percent hails from other sources—including solar and wind generation. There are big plans to make sustainable energy a larger part of the picture, but a number of things have to happen before this occurs. The main thing we need is an effective distribution system. Even if the amount of sustainable energy generation increases geometrically, large streams of solar- and wind-generated electricity just couldn't be "plugged into" the existing electrical grid. Major improvements are required for control, storage, distribution, and coordination efforts.

On a smaller scale, for residential electricity generation, household by household, the technology is available now and is getting more efficient and less expensive by the week. But it's still not being installed as a matter of fact. There are numerous variables involved and some costs over and above what's typically expended for more traditional electrical supply. Solar and wind power for homes is still not a financial slam dunk. So you need to line up all the costs of the system you'd like, and then study them. In most of the United States, you can drive around from subdivision to subdivision and try to count the solar arrays on rooftops or wind turbines in backyards, and you will find few. In fact, try to find any. It depends, of course, on where you'll be driving. There are places in the Sunbelt states where solar photovoltaic (PV) systems are up and generating, as there are small-scale wind turbines here and there—mostly on larger properties with acreage, but the typical newer home is more than likely using electrical energy from the local grid alone. This is so because "regular" local grid energy is still often the cheapest electricity. A loosey-goosey guideline per kilowatt for residential systems has been about $10,000. This would equate to about $30,000 for a no-frills 3-kilowatt solar or wind system powerful enough to operate and contribute to a household that keeps its energy usage at a very conservative level. And it could easily be two or three times this, depending on the situation. Naturally, someone may be able to purchase some of the components cheaper or may have a brother-in-law who could do the installation, so it could be considerably less expensive. If the numbers for your area are different, just use your initial setup cost and divide it by the number of kilowatt-hours the system will generate over its useful lifetime, and then compare the kilowatt price with your current and projected utility rates. There also could be grants, tax credits, low-interest energy mortgage loans, rebates, or other incentives you could take advantage of before you do the math. All these variables need to be taken into account.

Yes, the systems work. They're getting better and more efficient as time goes on. The point is that it still may take quite a few years to break even by waiting for all the avoided electricity costs you would have been purchasing from your local utility to exceed the cost, installation, and maintenance of your own private solar or wind system. Then again, you may not be installing sustainable-energy-generating systems only for a financial reason. Many good reasons exist for going to solar electricity generation. This leads us back to your motives and strategy.

Some of this may be getting ready to change. Backlashes against high energy prices have started to nudge the government scales toward sustainability. Politicians are beginning to get seriously involved, finally, with more than just talk. Monies for grants and tax incentives are starting to appear in budgets and plans that reach states, municipalities, agencies, private organizations, and even individuals. As mentioned in Chapter 1, we appear to be entering a pivotal point in green construction and sustainable-energy generation, a "wild west of green energy," where there will be all kinds of activities, developments, and various green skirmishes before organized patterns of products, systems, and installations begin leading the way. But you still need to do your homework and understand the various costs associated with generating your own electricity. Reputable solar and wind turbine companies often will do a lot of the financial figuring for you—they've done their homework already and can quickly share what they've learned. But you still need to check what they supply to see if it's backed up with data and if it sounds reasonable based on your own independent research.

For residential new construction, there are two types of sustainable-energy systems challenging each other for acceptance (and sometimes working together at the same time): solar and wind.

Solar Electricity-Generating Systems for the Home

Solar electricity-generating systems create energy by converting sunlight to electricity by a process called *photovoltaics*, in which light particles from sunlight are "captured" by photovoltaic cells or modules constructed from silicon semi-conducting material—the same stuff that computer chips are made of. These captured particles are turned into a direct electric current (DC)—a current that must, in turn, be further converted into alternating current (AC), the form of energy most of our appliances and electronic devices need to operate. Although the earliest PV cells or modules were developed over 50 years ago during the space program, their efficiency levels were too low and costs too great to be practical. It hasn't been until recently that PV cells have been reaching efficiency levels that could be used to drive residential generating systems at a more reasonable cost.

Some solar PV systems stand alone and are not attached to the commonly shared electrical grid operated by utility companies and related organizations. In order to supply electricity to a home when the sun is not shining—at night or on cloudy days—the electricity generated during the day must be stored for later use. A series or bank of deep-cycle batteries typically must be included in the system for such storage. Other home solar generating systems are tied into the public grid and use purchased electricity when the solar generation can't keep up with the home's electrical needs. When the solar system produces more electricity than the home is using and the batteries are also full, the home system then provides the excess to the grid, and the utility company compensates the home owner in some way for the power accepted. In order to provide a partial incentive to home owners who install these "net metering" systems in which they can supply electricity to the grid, some states have written net-metering laws that allow the same meter through which their purchased electricity is measured to be used to send home-generated electricity back into the utility's grid. The meter simply runs backward when power is being sent to the grid from the house. Compensation for that surplus energy, however, is not always the same as the price charged by the utility. In other words, no one who generates solar (or wind) electricity is going to make a fortune selling it to the utility companies.

A convenient characteristic of solar components is that they are typically modular and can be expanded easily if the need or financial resources change at a future date. Solar components, as demand increases, are bound to become more efficient and reasonably priced, in the same way that most electronic devices such as DVDs, flat-screen televisions, cell phones, and personal computers have. But will they drop enough to make home solar systems competitive with grid-supplied electricity? You'll have to research your own situation. The question, "Is solar electricity generation feasible for your new home?" can be answered after reviewing your overall strategy and compiling information on the following:

- *Location.* Where you live will directly affect how much your system will cost in a number of ways.

  - Places receiving lots of sunshine will be more efficient, meaning that smaller systems in such a sunny location will produce more energy per day per square foot of solar collector modules than the same-sized system located in a place where the sun doesn't shine as much. How much sunlight will reach the modules? You need a realistic idea of how the sun "travels" throughout the year and where it is in the sky on its shortest and longest days. Are there trees or other natural or human-made objects that will prevent the sun's light from reaching your house? What if your neighbor plants a row of fast-growing evergreens on his or her property line between you and the sun's path? Is your climate typically cloudy and wet? What is the average number of days receiving sunshine in a typical year?

  - Find out what your city or town solar permitting regulations are. Are expensive construction and installation stipulations required? Are there large inspection fees and local utility hookup fees? Do you need to submit elaborate feasibility or engineering studies or extra insurance policy riders? Obtaining the proper building and electrical permits can be challenging.

  - Consider how much your local utility charges for electricity. Naturally, the more it charges, the more attractive self-generation becomes. Then you'll need to estimate what your total usage will be in your new home. Next comes the math—What will your total generating system cost to permit, install, and maintain over its expected useful life versus the projected cost of grid-supplied electricity for the same time period? Typical American homes use an average of between 10,000 and 12,000 kilowatt-hours annually. Of course, many homes use considerably less and many use considerably more kilowatt-hours.

- *Space availability.* The total area or square footage of the solar collection modules depends on the type of system and its efficiency in converting sunlight to electrical power. An average-sized 2-kilowatt system for a family of three or four would require about 170 to 200 square feet of module space, but smaller and larger systems could range from 50 to over 1,000 square feet depending on where you live, available roof or ground space, the amount of energy your household needs, and how much you have available to spend. Naturally, the more efficient (and smaller) a comparable system is, the more it costs to purchase and install. If you don't have enough room to install all the modules you want, you'll need more efficient PV modules to produce the extra energy required. What are the slopes of your roof, and which directions will your roofing planes face? Your solar distributor can assess your options and suggest the most feasible type of system. The type of solar modules used also can affect how much room is needed and how the modules are installed. Some units are starting to resemble roofing surfaces and practically blend into the roofline—almost camouflaged (Fig. 22.1).

■ Are there any energy grants, tax rebates, credits, or low-interest loans available for solar systems where you plan to build? State, local, or utility-sponsored programs are quickly starting, stopping, and restarting—depending on money availability and the political mood. The easiest way to find out what's available up to the minute is to contact solar businesses that make a

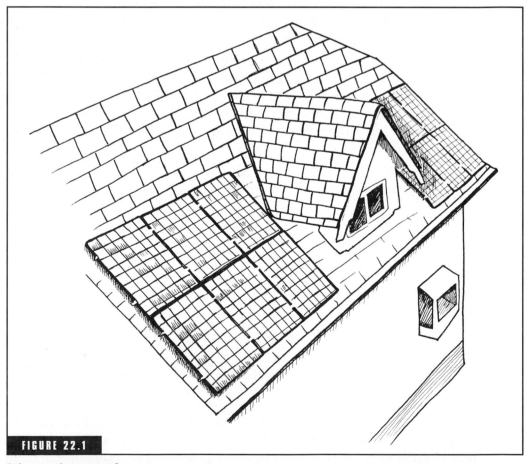

FIGURE 22.1

Solar panels on a roof.

point of showing prospective system buyers where money or reasonable financing terms can be found.

- Can you arrange—through energy conservation and by installing energy-efficient systems and appliances—to use minimal amounts of electricity? If you use small amounts of electric power, you simply may opt to skip your own generating system and just purchase electricity from the grid. In some cases, electricity that's generated through sustainable means can be requested through the same grid as an option your utility company provides so that its customers can support green energy production.

Wind Turbine Electricity-Generating Systems for the Home

Wind power is really a form of solar energy because the sun, by its heating of the atmosphere, causes wind currents to form when warmed air interacts with cooler air, and one displaces the other. Wind flow patterns then are influenced by the earth's surface—by mountains, hills, valleys, plains, and various bodies of water. The wind's energy motion or flow then can be used for sailing a boat, flying a kite, or generating electricity with a wind turbine.

A wind turbine produces electricity by mechanical means—the wind turns the blades that spin a shaft that connects to a generator that creates electrical energy—as long as the wind continues to blow and the shaft continues to spin. There are two basic types of modern wind turbines based on the positioning of the axis around which they spin: horizontal-axis units and vertical-axis varieties. Most horizontal-axis models have two or three large blades that function similar to a child's toy windmill. In its simplest description, the wind blows into the blades, and the blades spin around. The three-bladed units are operated "upwind," with their blades facing directly into the wind. The vertical-axis models stand perpendicular to the ground and are ready to catch wind that blows from any direction (Fig. 22.2).

Because wind generation so depends on a steady supply of wind, these turbines are often designed as part of a hybrid system that combines the wind generation with another source of power such as the local electrical grid or a backup diesel or other-fuel generator, a bank of batteries, or even a separate solar PV electricity-generating system. The main idea, though, is to let the wind provide as much free or low-cost electricity as possible—so that other electricity will not have to be generated by fossil fuels and be purchased from the local utility company. These systems, though probably more expensive to install than regular electrical company hookups, can come in handy, especially when a home will be located far off the beaten path, far away from the nearest electrical grid supply line.

Wind turbine systems typically are not designed for small building sites or urban lots owing to the size of their components. An exception can be made for very small units that can be installed relatively close to the ground, having rotors between 3 and 4 feet or less long. For larger units, the consensus seems to be that

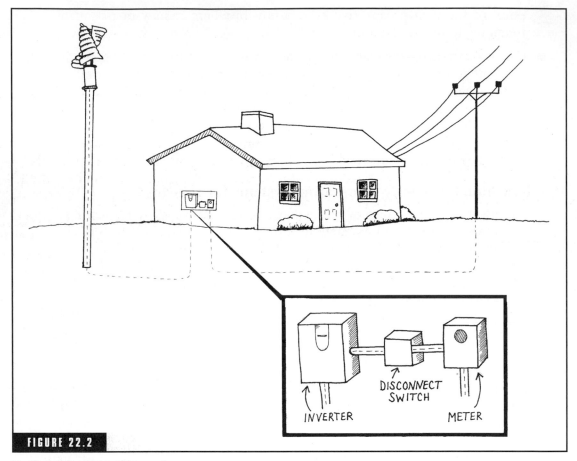

FIGURE 22.2

Vertical-axis wind turbine system.

you need at least an acre of space, and the larger the site, the better. The blades on average residential units easily can be 20 feet or more in diameter, with a tower between 80 and 120 feet high.

As with a solar-powered PV generating system, a wind turbine generating system may be installed for a variety of reasons, not all of them financial. Wind-powered electricity certainly is a sustainable energy that does not become depleted through use. It does not produce harmful emissions such as greenhouse gases. You potentially can avoid connection fees and ever-increasing electricity rate increases from your local utility. It can be considered one of the most meaningful green steps you could take to express your pro-environment values. And then again, it may allow you to take advantage of a "screaming deal" government grant, tax credit or rebate, low-interest loan, or other financial incentive.

Most residential systems, however, work hand in hand with the local utility. When there's enough wind blowing to generate a sufficient supply of energy (when winds are between about 7 and 10 mi/h), your wind turbine supplies the power. If the winds die down to below those cut-in speeds and your system cannot make the electricity your home needs, the local utility's electricity takes over, and you pay for what you use from the utility. If wind speeds increase beyond the cut-in speed and your turbine starts making more electricity than you can use. If your state and local utility allow a net-metering mode, your electrical meter may spin backward as you supply excess electricity back to your utility company, for which it may pay you a certain "home supplier" rate or give you a credit toward your total bill.

Will a wind turbine save you money over the long haul? This depends on how large your system is, how much it costs to purchase and set up, and how strong and frequent the winds are. Most manufacturers suggest that average wind speeds need to be at least 10 mi/h for the financials to make sense. There are wind maps available for average wind speeds for whatever location you are considering, but always keep in mind that wind speeds could be influenced by local factors—by what's constructed upwind of your location and by the positions of trees or waterways or other natural or human-made features. The financials also depend on how much the local utility plant charges for electricity and how often your system needs repairs and maintenance. As an order-of-magnitude estimate, most families use about 800 kilowatt-hours of electricity a month, or about 9,600 kilowatt-hours per year. The turbine systems are often sold by individual components but also may be marketed as part of a complete package to satisfy a specific situation. For example, a relatively powerful 10 kilowatt-hour per-month system for utility bill reductions, complete with the wind turbine, 100-foot tower, wiring, shipping, sales tax, permit costs, foundation and tower erection, electrical hookups, and inspection fees, easily could run about $75,000 when provided and installed by a certified dealer. Okay, now deduct whatever amount is available through government grants or rebates and any other financial incentives that you can find at the time. Depending on the size, quality, and efficiency of the turbine and system equipment—and also depending on how much work you could contract or perform yourself—that amount could be whittled down considerably. But remember that municipal permits may insist that a qualified contractor must do the installation. There's a safety issue present whenever you're working with electrical supplies and systems.

Hybrid systems providing similar amounts of electricity generation easily could go over the $100,000 mark and much more if banks of batteries, diesel generators, and various other options are selected. Again, from a purely financial viewpoint, where does the initial investment become too large to a home owner who originally intends to reduce or eliminate an electricity bill that may only (and here *only* is in reference to tens of thousand of dollars worth of wind turbine purchase and installation costs) amount to a few hundred dollars a month.

A way to reduce the initial investment is to consider smaller systems, but they still require permitting, towers or platforms, electrical connections, inverters, and controls. Smaller systems, again, depending on their quality, efficiency, and your situation, could run between $6,000 and $25,000 installed. Many smaller systems have been installed on farms to power pumps to supply water for irrigation or drinking water for livestock. In truth, though, wind turbine prices can be all over the place. With increased demand and manufacturing efficiencies, costs are bound to drop in the near future. If you are interested, you need to look at your own situation, price out systems, speak with others who are already making electricity with wind power, and decide for yourself.

Hydroelectric Generation

This, of course, isn't the large-scale hydroelectric power generated by the great Niagara or other rivers. We're talking small-scale hydroelectric, sometimes referred to as *micro-hydroelectric power*, where running or falling water is used to produce electricity. With small-scale residential hydroelectric systems, some water from a stream or river is continuously routed through an electricity-generating system and then returned to its source. While this may be a possible way to provide a sustainable supply of energy, satisfying watershed environmental and wildlife regulations may be way too difficult and expensive to be worth the trouble.

✔✔✔✔✔ APPLIANCE WIRING CHECKLIST

When you think of it, there aren't many modern home conveniences that would work without electricity. Here's a checklist you can use to help plan your electrical service. Consider electrical service for the following:

___ Telephones (kitchen, living areas, bedrooms, basement, garage)

___ Doorbells (front and side or back doors with different tones) with illuminated buttons

___ Refrigerators (kitchen plus spare for basement, garage, or wet bar)

___ Freezers (kitchen plus spare for basement or garage)

___ Furnace blowers

___ Thermostat controls

___ Cooking ranges/stoves

___ Microwave ovens

___ Water heaters

___ Televisions (electrical, cable, antenna service)

___ Smoke alarms

APPLIANCE WIRING CHECKLIST *(Continued)*

___ Carbon monoxide alarms

___ Video players and games

___ Personal computers and Internet access

___ Attic fans

___ Bathroom fans

___ Garage door openers

___ Dishwashers

___ Clothes washers

___ Clothes dryers

___ Hi-fi speaker systems

___ Intercoms/cassette or stereo systems built into walls

___ FM antenna hookups

___ Burglar alarms

___ Garbage disposals or compactors

___ Electric grills

___ Sun lamps in bathrooms

___ Water pumps

___ Sump pumps

___ Vent hoods for cooking ranges

___ Central air-conditioning

___ Dehumidifier

___ Humidifier

___ Jacuzzi motor with timer switch

___ Overhead circulating fans and whole-house attic fan with timer switch

___ Electric heat-circulating fan built into a fireplace

___ Bathroom heater, vent fan, lights

___ Attic power ventilator

___ Electric baseboard heaters, if main or supplementary heat source

___ Central vacuum system

Electric clothes dryers and cooking ranges require special 240-volt receptacles. These receptacles differ slightly but significantly, so make sure that the dryer and range receptacles will fit your appliances. Electric water heaters are wired directly to the house's electric cable. Electric ranges can also be wired directly.

Because most major appliances run on electricity, you'll want to

- Make sure that the brand is reputable.

- Consider whether the features of each appliance will do what you need them to do.

- Evaluate the warranties on each one.

- Check for energy efficiency.

- Know if service contracts are available.

ELECTRICAL OUTLETS AND SWITCHES

The rule for electrical outlets is one duplex outlet for every 12 linear feet of wall because lamps and household appliances usually have 6-foot-long cords. When a doorway comes between, the outlets around it should be located closer than 12 feet apart, or you might have to use extension cords in that part of the room. Kitchen outlets are best located above the countertop to handle appliances safely. A duplex wall outlet for every 4 linear feet of kitchen counter space will do nicely.

Here are some other guidelines:

1. There should be light switches at every entrance to every room and, for safety's sake, at the top and bottom of stairs and at garage and basement doors. These switches should be about 1 foot away from the steps so that the user will not trip on or down the steps while trying to access the light.

2. Insist on intermediate- or specification-grade outlets and wiring. There are also competitive grades of cheaper quality for only a minor difference in cost. Specification grade, the best of all, is usually recommended for heavy-duty commercial installions, but they are worth the extra cost if you want top quality, particularly in the kitchen and in all switches.

3. Wall switches should control overhead lighting. If a room has more than one entrance, install double- or triple-pole switches so that these lights can be turned off and on from each doorway.

4. If a room has no overhead lighting, such as a living room or family room, wire at least one duplex outlet to a wall switch so that a lamp that's plugged into the outlet can be turned on and off at the switch on a wall near the room's entrance.

5. Include at least three outside electrical outlets (two in front, one in back) and, for a large, sprawling ranch home, four. They should be equipped with ground-fault circuit interrupters for protection from the electrical hazards posed by wet lawns and driveways, as well as a weatherproof cap that covers each receptacle.

6. Install ceiling outlets in the garage for an automatic garage door opener even if you're not planning to use an opener at first. If you decide to add such a convenience later, you can do it without having to spend a hefty price for a service call.

7. Be certain to plan several receptacles in the garage for power tools, an extra freezer, a vacuum cleaner, and other items.

8. All ceiling fixtures such as lights and fans must be securely fastened to the house framing structure and not dependent on the outlet for anchoring.

9. There should be at least one ground-fault circuit interrupter (GFCI) duplex safety outlet above each bathroom vanity top for hair dryers, electric shavers, and other personal care appliances. Such outlets will help to prevent shock.

10. All receptacles should be the three-hole grounded type. These are much safer than the old two-hole ones. If an appliance becomes faulty, the current will pass through the third wire (the ground wire) in the receptacle rather than through you.

11. Make sure that you allow for a sufficient number of outlets throughout the home, especially for plugging in and unplugging electronic equipment. Many of today's home electronic items use electricity even when turned off—they go into standby mode so that they'll be instantly ready when needed. This standby energy loss is sometimes referred to as *leaking electricity*. Consider that to keep this type of energy from enlarging energy bills, try to remember to unplug home electronics and appliances when they're not in use.

12. It's easy to overlook the basement when planning for outlets. Consider that refrigerators, freezers, hand tools, vacuums, dehumidifiers, sump pumps, and extension cords all require electricity.

13. The locations of certain light switches and outlets you want in special places can be marked in advance with chalk.

LIGHTS AND LAMP WIRING

1. Wire for overhead lights in the dining area, kitchen, kitchen sink and counter, laundry room, bedrooms, bathrooms, hallways, garage, and basement.

FIGURE 22.3

Closet recessed lighting.

2. Avoid putting recessed lights in ceilings with unheated space above. They can't be insulated properly and will leak air badly. Recessed lights should be the insulated ceiling (IC) type. Confirm from the manufacturer that the units will not become hot enough to be fire hazards.

3. Include recessed lights in all closets, with wall switches mounted outside the closet near the closet door (Fig. 22.3). Even shallow closets having bifold doors will need lighting on occasion.

4. Consider some outside spot or floodlights to provide illumination for general use of the yard and for security reasons. Ideally, some yard lighting should be controlled from the master bedroom as an additional security measure.

5. Make sure that there's wiring for lighting at the front and back doors and wherever someone can enter the house, with convenient switching at those locations. Lighting should be wired near the main electric service panel so that you can see the circuit breakers and their labels without using a flashlight.

SURGE PROTECTORS

A power surge may not sound dangerous, but if it strikes your personal computer, TV, or other piece of electronic equipment, it can cause expensive problems. The average home gets almost a dozen surges from lightning every year—power surges that can damage electronic microchips. And lightning is not the only source of high-voltage surges. Local businesses and utility companies with electrical equipment going off and on also can help to create potentially damaging power surges.

These surges may not damage an electronic device right away, but the cumulative effects can definitely ruin equipment over time. Each surge results in an electrical "hammering" that wears and tears at the weakest parts of the electronics, eventually causing failure. Power surges come from both outside and inside a home, for numerous reasons, and even can travel through phone and cable television lines.

The remedy? In addition to individual outlet plug-in surge protectors, whole-house voltage surge protectors are available for installation with a home's main electrical system. Such a combined two-stage method protects electronic equipment from almost anything short of a direct lightning strike.

Whole-house surge protectors help to protect every television, phone, computer, modem, microwave oven, programmable thermostat, stereo, fax machine, security system—the list goes on and on. Some whole-house surge protectors are installed at the circuit breaker box, whereas others are engaged at the electric meter—generally installed by the supplying utility company. These surge protectors use very little energy and can literally save hundreds of dollars in appliance repair and replacement costs because modern appliances are often operated through delicate electronic controls that can be instantly damaged by high-voltage surges.

With fewer power spikes and surges traveling through the home, appliance energy-efficiency capabilities and life expectancies are increased; even simple light bulbs will last longer and burn brighter. The surge protectors should have monitor lights that indicate if the units are working. Before specifying whole-house surge protection, discuss the options with your builder or electrical contractor.

ELECTRICAL INSPECTION

Here are some wiring features to watch for as the house nears the plaster/drywall stage and how the electrical inspection proceeds:

1. See that in exterior walls cables installed horizontally run along the top of the bottom plate. This provides the least interference with wall insulation. Most electric cable is sufficiently flexible to comply.

2. Be careful how electric wiring is installed in bathrooms. It should not be run through the area around the bathtub. Wiring also should stay clear of places where long screws may be used to fasten shelving, soap dishes, or towel racks to the wall.

3. Wires should not be placed too close to any plumbing to avoid damage from the plumber's propane torch.

4. After all the rough wiring is completed—known as the *roughing out*—and checked over, the electrician will contact both the Underwriters Laboratories inspector and the local building code inspector, who will inspect everything and, if satisfied, will issue a certificate and notify the utility company. The utility company then will send a representative to connect power to the house.

HOME CONTROL SYSTEMS

Individuals with busy schedules can employ relatively sophisticated home control centers simply by touching bedside controls or clicking the mouse of a personal computer. These units can operate various home equipment functions even from remote locations through code numbers sent via touch-tone phone lines. Home owners can better manage their heating, cooling, and ventilation systems to save money and increase comfort. These electronic units can control such functions as the following:

- Setting/checking security systems before leaving the home or retiring at night
- Setting lawn sprinklers for the next morning or evening
- Automatically turning off/on house or Christmas lights
- Setting what time a VCR/television should wake you up or record a program
- Automatically starting kitchen or other appliances

5. The electrician now can wire all the outlet box receptacles as soon as the walls are insulated and covered. To finish this work, the electrician must know how you plan to complete the walls so that the boxes can be set to project the right amount through the finished walls.

SPECIAL ELECTRICAL FEATURES

Remember to give some consideration to the following features:

1. *Noiseless, no-click light switches.* There are also silent touch-button switches that require only slight finger pressure. There are flat-plate models that are set flush against the wall. Slight pressure on the top turns a light on, and pressure on the bottom turns it off.

2. *Ivory, colored, metallic, and other decorator switchplates.* These are available instead of the standard plastic brown, off-white, or tan models that might clash with your decor. Electrical and lighting suppliers carry them in a wide variety of models and materials. These unique switchplates can give your house an interesting finishing touch overlooked in most dwellings today.

3. *Dimmer controls.* These enable you to adjust lighting intensity up or down according to your needs. Illumination in a room can be dimmed to a candle-light glow for a dinner party, kept subdued for television watching, or turned up brightly for reading. Dimmers are used chiefly for living and dining rooms but can also be used in a bathroom night-light arrangement.

4. *Automatic switches.* You can have built-in automatic switches that turn on the closet lights when the doors are opened and then turn them off again when the doors are closed, similar to the refrigerator interior lighting setup.

5. *Remote-control lighting.* This is surprisingly simple to install. It can permit you to turn indoor and outdoor lights on or off from a central location such as the kitchen or master bedroom. A remote kitchen switch can control front door or garage lights, for example. A control panel next to your bed can eliminate that final tour of your house and grounds every night to turn out all the lights.

6. *Electrical snow-melting panels.* These are available for sidewalks and driveways, and electrical snow-melting wire strung along your roof gutters will prevent the accumulation of dangerous snowdrifts and icicles on roof slopes and gutters (Fig. 22.4).

FIGURE 22.4

Snow-melting wire.

7. *No-shock outlets.* These can be installed to prevent children (who frequently insist on jabbing hairpins or anything metallic into receptacles) from receiving shocks.

8. *Safety-type grounded outlets.* As mentioned earlier, these can be added protection against shocks and help to prevent the possibility of electrocution in a bathroom. A ground fault is a partial short circuit in an electrical device. A person can be the electrical ground (electricity will travel from an outside source through the person and into the ground) when using an appliance or tool in a damp or wet area such as a bathroom, laundry room, basement, garage, or backyard. The partial short circuit allows a small amount of electric current to flow through the individual's body—a condition that could be harmful or even fatal. Regular household appliances work by drawing power from one side of a wall receptacle through one prong on the plug and returning it through the other prong to the other side of the receptacle. If the ground-fault circuit interrupter (GFCI) detects extra current within the circuit, it will trip a little breaker within itself and interrupt the current. GFCIs belong wherever household members are likely to encounter wet or moist

FIGURE 22.5

Ground-fault circuit interrupter.

conditions (Fig. 22.5). The socket simply can be reset with the push of a button. As with any bathroom receptacles, these outlets should not be within reach of a bathtub or shower.

9. *Alarm system.* Even if you don't initially plan to have a security alarm system, the wiring for one can be easily installed within the walls at the time of construction. The system then can be completed inexpensively at a later date, if desired.

10. Electrical equipment that can be shut off when not in actual use should be on electrical outlets or "smart" power strips that can be turned off between appliance uses to reduce needless phantom electrical draws that keep the equipment in an energy-drawing standby. You could have certain electrical wall switches wired to perform outlet shutoff functions.

REMODELING NOTES

If your current home's electrical service is seriously undersized, you probably know it from the number of times you've had to replace fuses or reset breakers. If the old knob-and-tube wiring setups are still visible in the attic and basement, you should have an electrical inspection and get a number of quotes for electrical upgrades. Don't wait another day because way more than energy efficiency is at stake here. We're talking about safety. Nothing can cause a fire quicker than electrical systems that aren't meeting code minimums.

If there's one remodel you do first, it should be to bring your electrical system into the modern age. Electricity is invisible, and the deficiencies may not be readily apparent unless something smells funny or the power quits—and really, long before those signals appear, get an electrician in there to look things over. Do not delay.

Then explain to the electrician that you are looking to remodel with an eye toward energy efficiency and that you might be adding a variety of renewable-energy com-

CHILD-SAFE ELECTRICAL OUTLETS

SAFETY POINTERS

For electrical protection of children, consider installing outlets with a night-light on the top outlet and with the bottom outlet blocked with a cover that flips down when electrical access is needed.

FINAL INSPECTION

ELECTRICAL

1. Furnace/heating unit starts and stops okay.
2. Cooling system runs.
3. Washer, dryer, sump pump, and outlets are operational.
4. Central vacuum system works.
5. Bathroom vents and heaters work.
6. Jacuzzi pump motor is operational. Timer switch is not reachable from the tub.
7. Electric range/stove operates properly. Electric pilot light on gas range is connected and working correctly. Range hood, downdraft, and light work.
8. Garbage disposal, dishwasher, and trash compactor all work. Refrigerator outlet is functional.
9. All lights work.
10. Door chimes work.
11. Garage door opener works.
12. Thermostat/power ventilators on roof are connected and working.
13. Electronic security system is operational; each individual sensor has been tested.
14. No scratches, dents, or other damage is seen on electrical appliances.

ponents such as PV panels, a tankless water heater, a whole-house fan, and the like, and you need access to enough safe power in the home.

At the same time, have the electrician include wiring and suggested ballast fixtures for energy-efficient fluorescent lighting to replace expensive-to-operate and often air-leaking halogen recessed floodlights in the kitchen and other areas where contractors used to install them. They looked good but were incredibly inefficient. The lights burned hotly and didn't last very long. Ask the electrician about the possibility and for his or her suggestions on trouble-free inexpensive-to-run fixtures and where they could be installed easily.

▷▷▷▷▷ POINTS TO PONDER

1. Insist that no competitive or cheaper grades of electrical wiring and related components are used.

2. Make sure that the main electrical supply wire is grounded properly and attached sturdily to the house and free from encroaching tree limbs or other wires and cables.

3. Remember to specify electrical outlets in the basement, garage, and attic, plus near outdoor front and rear entrances and patio and deck areas.

4. All circuit breakers in the home's main circuit box must be clearly marked by the electrical contractor so that electricity to certain parts of the home can be turned off if necessary and so that areas where electrical overloads occur can be identified.

5. Major appliances that are heavy users of electricity should have individual circuits to themselves.

6. For a modern look and ease of operation, consider using large push-on, push-off light switches instead of standard wall switch controls.

7. Any electrical outlets positioned in areas where water is expected to be present, such as outdoors and in kitchens, bathrooms, laundry rooms, and garages, or near swimming pools, need to be ground-fault circuit interrupters (GFCIs).

8. To protect against appliance- and computer-damaging power surges, have a whole-house voltage surge protector installed with the main electrical system.

9. Research available electronic home communication and control systems for possible installation and use in your new home.

10. Consider wiring the home for motion-detector lighting, outdoors and indoors. Motion-sensing wall switches exist that activate when a person enters a room or area.

Lighting

A long, long time ago, before humans discovered how to use fire, when it got dark, it got dark. There were no switches to flip on and no battery-powered flashlights to illuminate pathways. Once we mastered fire, we not only increased our comfort, safety, and gastronomic enjoyment, but the light we gained supplied us with more time to work constructively. We were able, for the first time, to light the night.

The first lamp easily could have been a lit pool of fat drippings that shimmered in a shallow depression near the glowing embers of a cave campfire. Then clay and stone lamps came onto the scene—little more than saucer- or cup-shaped receptacles for oil, grease, or tallow. They were either open or covered, with a carrying handle on one side and on the other a small trough or gutter in which a wick rested. This simple lamp persisted for about 10,000 years, resisting change even into the eighteenth and nineteenth centuries, when people were still using dangerous iron lamps that burned disagreeable-smelling whale oil.

Throughout the ages, light has always been something sacred to humans. It has been a symbol of religion, of ideas, of knowledge, and of understanding. It has enabled us to take advantage of our most important sense: sight.

Lighting these days, however, often takes a back seat. We have access to free natural light for nearly half of each day. For the remaining time, there are lighting fixtures and bulbs powered by electricity that luminate on demand. People frequently will buy lights because they fancy the fixtures, not the effects those fixtures will provide. When you think of it, this is kind of silly. It's like buying food only for its looks or for how it might conveniently fit into a refrigerator or freezer, with no regard to taste or nutritional value.

There's often little advance planning for lighting. While home owners pride themselves on knowing the last little detail about stereo systems, kitchen ranges, or video players, the lights that illuminate their private worlds are completely taken for granted. This is too bad because precise lighting can create a variety of moods within a room and can help to exaggerate strong points while downplaying shortcomings. Lighting can increase efficiency in work areas. Consider how important lighting is to theater and dance. What show, what film, what live performance have you ever seen that didn't include strategic lighting as a major part of its overall effect? Consider museums and art galleries and how they can make their showcase works stand out merely by lighting them properly.

The same principles hold true for lighting in home use in the average household. Unfortunately, most people are afraid to make advance plans that they feel might be too radical or too difficult to change. Nothing radical is needed, however, to lend a home a pleasant lighting scheme. It doesn't take many built-in lights to add a distinctive touch.

TYPES OF LIGHT SOURCES

Sunlight

In the world of green construction, the use of natural light to illuminate spaces within a home is called *natural daylighting* and is accomplished through passive-solar arrangements of various windows, doors, traditional skylights and glass panels, transparent roof panels, mirrors, reflective coatings, and tubular skylights.

People and plants function better in a natural light–filled environment. Sunlight or "natural" daylight has numerous positive effects on the human psyche. It tends to make people feel better about whatever they're doing or thinking about. It has a naturally uplifting effect. It provides strong, comprehensive illumination required for performing close-up, intricate tasks. Sunlight also allows colors to be seen in their most natural state. Of course, sunlight intensity can be somewhat reduced by clouds, weather, and foliage, as well as the seasonal position and tilt of the earth's axis. Days get longer and shorter and longer again, and some sunlight is considerably stronger in certain locations and places. Unfiltered sunlight or rays strengthened and concentrated by certain types of glass and windows can send ultraviolet (UV) and other light waves into the home to discolor and fade furnishings and to dry out and burn skin on people, pets, and plants.

Naturally, the chief source of natural light is glass in windows, skylights, and doors. One way to increase the entry of natural lighting during the day, especially in homes with thick outer walls, is to install splayed or angled window sills that angle light rays to larger perimeter dimensions as they enter the room's living space (Fig. 23.1).

In earlier editions of this book, discussions about skylights were presented only in the chapter about windows, where they were mentioned regarding their roles providing ventilation and natural light. Numerous advances in skylight technology, however, made it far more logical to include some information in this, the lighting chapter, as well.

For a home to take full advantage of natural daylighting, the configuration and floor plans must be chosen carefully in relation to seasonal available sunlight. Window and door positioning and the inclusion of other components that can provide natural light are also important. Analyze your living habits and those of your family members, and try to plan room locations so that they take advantage of

FIGURE 23.1

Splayed or angled window sill.

available light. For example, if you plan your day around getting up at the crack of dawn and having a leisurely breakfast, reading the paper, and planning your day in the kitchen, then try to plan exposure to morning sunlight on that side of the house while keeping the bedrooms on the opposite side out of the morning sun's access. Perhaps the children's bedrooms should have access to late-day sunlight, when they are active in their rooms doing homework or playing, or perhaps you want the family room, where those same activities can take place, to receive late-day sunlight.

Electric Lighting

Until recently, there were only two major kinds of electric lamps or bulbs, as most people call them: incandescent-filament lights and fluorescent lights. Now a third type has gained a foothold—light-emitting diodes (LEDs)—and others are being developed to take advantage of new technology aimed at further reducing our reliance on electricity.

INCANDESCENT-FILAMENT LIGHTING

The first practical incandescent-filament lamp was perfected by Thomas Edison in the late 1800s. Not much has changed with them since. They're based on that same very old design. An incandescent lamp produces light when its filament (usually made of tungsten) in a glass bowl or bulb filled with argon gas is heated by an electric current to a regulated temperature, at which point it glows

FIGURE 23.2

Incandescent-filament light.

and emits the amount of light for which it is engineered (Fig. 23.2). Incandescent lamps are only about 10 to 15 percent efficient in converting electricity to light—most of the wasted electricity is given off as heat. This is why they'll burn your fingers if you try to unscrew one that's been on for a while. They operate under the same electric resistance category that other high-cost-use electrical appliances employ. Because of the high heat they generate, they usually last only about 1,000 hours—the time it takes for their metal filament to decompose or burn up. The quality of light from incandescent-filament bulbs is warm in color and gives a friendly, homelike feeling to interiors. Beneath incandescent lights, colors such as oranges, reds, and browns are enhanced, whereas the cool colors such as blues and greens are subdued.

Tungsten-halogen lamps use halogen gas instead of argon, and they are about twice as efficient as the older style incandescents. Their wattages can be lower because they concentrate the light generation into a smaller area, which increases the brightness effect cast in directional beams instead of a general spread. Their life expectancies range from 2,000 to 4,000 hours. They require a transformer that can be located in the fitting base or in the wiring within the wall or ceiling. Some can be used with dimmers, but the not-so-green feature of halogen bulbs is that they contain mercury vapor and halogen gases, which are definite pollutants. They generate enough heat to create a safety hazard, and fluorescent bulbs are at least twice as efficient.

Incandescent bulbs provide a source of light that can be focused or directed over a restricted area, if desired, and because most incandescent household bulbs have the same size base, the lighting from fixtures or lamps can be increased or decreased within limits by changing to bulbs of different wattages. Most types of incandescent lights are less expensive than fluorescent lights. And the incandescent lighting fixtures themselves are generally less expensive to purchase because they require no ballast or starter—a part of a light bulb that provides a high voltage for starting the bulb and a low voltage for running it.

FLUORESCENT LIGHTING

Fluorescent bulbs operate by an entirely different principle. They've typically been long and tubular in design, either straight, circular, or angular in the case of neon signs used for advertisements. They're coated on the inside of the glass with phosphors, substances that give off light when subjected to ultraviolet radiation generated by a low-pressure electric charge. The low-pressure electric charge is regulated by the starter or ballast that forces the charge through mercury vapor inside the bulb (Fig. 23.3).

Fluorescent bulbs offer greater lighting efficiencies, up to three or four times as much light per watt of electricity as incandescent bulbs have. They'll also last from 7 to 10 times longer, largely owing to their cooler operating temperature range. Hot-burning incandescent lights, by their very nature, burn themselves out more quickly.

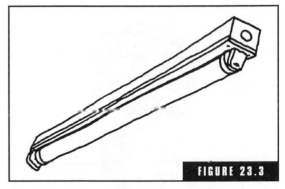

FIGURE 23.3

Fluorescent light.

Fluorescent bulbs provide lines of light and are excellent choices in work areas where light coming from several angles is needed to effectively eliminate bothersome shadows, such as work rooms, utility areas, garages, attics, and basements. These lines of light are also frequently used over mirrors and kitchen work surfaces; in window valences, corners, and covers; and with other architectural features. Given their long life spans, fluorescent bulbs are favorites in places that can't be reached conveniently for bulb changing. Circular fluorescent tubes traditionally have been used in high kitchen ceilings, for example.

When considering their use, remember that some older-style fluorescent bulbs (also called *lamps* by the lighting industry—because some lights are no longer bulb-shaped) weren't as quiet as incandescent lights. This is so because earlier magnetic ballasts tended to hum while starting, while trying to operate in cold conditions, and when starting to fail. A newer wrinkle to the lighting scene has been the emergence of smaller, more compact straight-tube fluorescent bulbs or lamps. These newer, more advanced lamps with electronic ballasts are quieter and take less time to turn on. They're also manufactured with fewer toxic materials and are smaller in design for equal wattages of light generation. The smaller, thinner T-8 straight lamps that replace their thicker brothers, the T-12s, are equipped with these newer electronic ballasts and produce over 25 percent more light per watt. This is improved performance for less energy—a very green feature. And by the time you're ready to select lighting, there might be even newer, more energy-efficient models replacing the T-8s. Things are moving that quickly.

Compact Fluorescent Lights

As a general guideline, although they can cost many, many times what a comparable incandescent bulb costs, compact fluorescent light bulbs are about four times more energy efficient, provide equivalent illumination for considerably less wattage, produce less heat, and last up to 6 to 10 times longer. Many take the form of coil-type spiral bulbs that will fit in traditional incandescent fixtures (Fig. 23.4). Others are manufactured in straight, longer styles that may not fit tradi-

FIGURE 23.4

A compact fluorescent spiral bulb.

tional fixture shades or globes designed for incandescent bulbs.

For sure, compact fluorescents are great for hard-to-reach places where changing bulbs may be both an inconvenience and a safety issue. When planning your lighting, remember that not all compact fluorescents are equal. Some are constructed with electronic/iron ballast in each bulb; cheaper models with this kind of accompanying ballast tend to flicker at startup and may buzz. When planning for compact fluorescent fixtures, consider fixtures with built-in ballasts that take pin-based replacement bulbs (Fig. 23.5), which will save money because you won't have to replace the ballast within the bulbs every time you change a bulb. Screw-in fixture types, however, are more commonly available, so you might have to make an extra effort to get the stab-in fixtures.

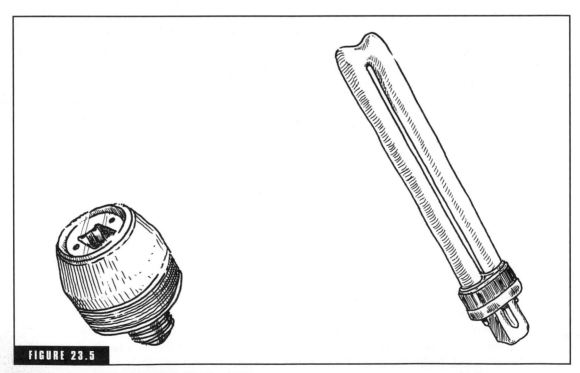

FIGURE 23.5

Compact fluorescent ballast and pin-type bulb.

Just be sure that you know how much the replacement bulbs will cost, where to buy them, and that pin-type fixtures will not accommodate standard screw-threaded incandescent bulbs. Also be aware that many compact bulbs cannot be dimmed with dimmer switches. If you want to dim one, you'll need to purchase a bulb designed for dimming. If applicable and desired, make sure that the same bulb can be used with photosensors, electronic timers, and motion detectors. Fluorescent bulbs come in numerous makes, models, and sizes, including three-way and floodlight styles.

Some, however, have certain restrictions on what they should be used for, such as indoor use only, outdoor use, low-temperature use, cannot be installed within a glass globe, or cannot be installed in an inverted position. Compact fluorescent lights are components that are constantly being improved, and you can expect numerous advancements in the near future

Light-Emitting Diodes (LEDs)

You're probably already somewhat familiar with LEDs from seeing them as red and green on/off indicators in electronic equipment. LEDs are incredibly efficient and durable tiny lights that use electricity to create light when fast moving electrons emit photons. The subsequent beams of light are very concentrated, which enables them to be tightly focused. While incandescent lights may last around 2,000 hours and fluorescent up to 10,000 hours, the useful life of LEDs can be 50,000 hours and longer. White LEDs became popular in small flashlights, night lights, and solar landscape lights, as well as later in a variety of architectural accent and task lighting fixtures that use many of the LEDs in a concentrated array (Fig. 23.6). As the technology improves, many more applications will become available. Municipalities have begun using LEDs in traffic lights owing to their longevity and durable nature, where they are saving considerable amounts in energy and maintenance. The lights do not use mercury and are not considered to be hazardous waste when disposed of, as are fluorescent and compact fluorescent bulbs. When planning fixtures for your new home, anywhere you can use LEDs will prove to be a long-lasting source of energy savings and light bulb replacement avoidance.

Skylighting

Again, you'll find a separate discussion of skylights in Chapter 18 on windows. Although it's hard to review the same subject here without some overlap, there are several important points worth reviewing.

A skylight is basically a casement window mounted in a ceiling or section of roof framing to provide natural daylight (and sometimes ventilation) so that the need for additional active daytime electric light (and possibly powered ventilation) is reduced. Since hot air naturally rises, opening a vented skylight will exhaust such heated air and create a comfortable breeze inside the dwelling

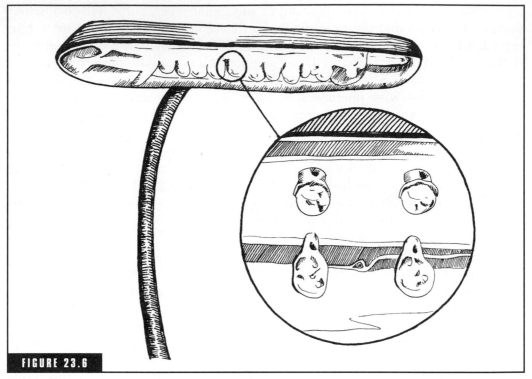

FIGURE 23.6

LED lamp.

without relying on air-conditioning. Some models are fixed in place and do not open or vent at all.

On skylights that do open or vent, control options range from a manual crank to an electric motor operated by sophisticated electronic and/or hand remotes. Many skylights come with laminated or tempered glass having low-emissivity (low-e) and tinted coatings that effectively control heat transmission and UV radiation. Compare U-value and heat- and light-transmission rates of all skylights you may consider for your home. Although most skylights are serviceable and provide excellent sources of natural light, they can let too much heat in during the summer and allow for too much heat loss during winter. Their glass should be of the superinsulated variety.

Sunlight Tubes or Tunnels

Sunlight tubes or tunnels are essentially highly reflective cylindrical skylights that run from the roof down into an interior room or space (Fig. 23.7). These natural sunlight skylights are complete roof-to-ceiling systems for efficiently bringing natural sunlight into the home. Look for models with gaskets and flashing that effectively prevent air loss through the tube. When installed correctly, they'll provide high levels of free natural light to windowless places in the home without the unwanted heat loss or gain of skylights.

In frequently used rooms requiring ongoing lighting, a sunlight tube or tunnel offers natural lighting that saves turning on electric lights every time you enter, say, a bathroom, kitchen, or other room where such a natural lighting system is installed. There are lots of makes and models available, but they all operate under the same principle. Sunlight enters through a clear acrylic plastic or similarly made dome on the roof and is directed to exactly where you want it—typically a space having no windows, such as a hallway, bathroom, storage area, and even basement. The light is "transported" within the tube through a series of mirrors positioned within the reflective interior surface of the tube. Because most of the bendable tubes are narrower than 16 inches in diameter, they'll easily fit between roof trusses or rafters in traditional and advanced fram-

A sunlight tube.

ing sections. The installers won't have to cut out or build framing around the tubes; they'll easily fit at any stage of early or late wall construction. From the hallway or room, the tube diffuser looks simply like any ceiling fixture. In fact, some come with light diffusers that can double as a sunlight distribution lens and a lens for an electric light and fixture that's used at night.

Acrylic does not yellow from sun exposure, and it naturally filters out some of the damaging UV rays from the sun. The top of the tube is dome shaped, and it is very resistant to breakage, even from hail. Rain usually will be enough to keep it clean. Some domes incorporate a prismatic lens, like a "fly eye," that helps to bend and collect low-angle or early-morning light and late-afternoon light down into the tube or tunnel. Some units provide interior seals and a double-insulated diffuser lens component that creates insulating dead-air pockets similar to those of a thermal pane window.

The insulation rating on some models is as high as R-22. Collected sunlight travels from the roof dome through a rigid or flexible tube or tunnel. The rigid tube or tunnel is lined with one of several types of silvery, highly reflective linings of aluminum or equally good-quality reflective material. A rigid tube is fine for passing through an open attic; the fewer bends (elbow joints), the better, because even though the tube is highly reflective, some light intensity is lost each time the light bounces back and forth inside the tube. Flexible tubes or tunnels employ sturdy construction that can be easily bent around obstacles such as chimneys, furnace ducting, beams, and other construction components without using elbow joints. The captured sunlight, after being transported down the tube or tunnel, is then diffused into a room or space through another prismatic diffuser lens.

On sunny days, this natural skylight easily can provide the equivalent of between 600 and 700 watts of incandescent light. Even on cloudy days, there is still enough natural light to approach the illumination level of a 100- or 150-watt bulb, and what's more, on nights with a clear sky and full moon, an out-of-this-world moon glow within the room is not out of the question.

Transparent Roof Panels

In places where hot summers rarely exist and heating needs far exceed cooling use, transparent roof panels make sense for allowing even more natural daylight to enter the interior of a home. These panels have been used for years in commercial and industrial buildings to save electricity and lamp replacement costs when the roofing needs are partly combined with daylight illumination.

HOME LIGHTING USES

Few homes will rely on one or another type of bulb exclusively. Most dwellings now employ a combination of incandescent, fluorescent, and compact fluorescent fixtures, and as newer LED models are becoming available, those are also being included. What follows are three different ways in which these types of lights can be used in modern dwellings.

General or Background Lighting

General or background lighting is a low level of illumination required for general living activities. It's the level of lighting provided by ceiling fixtures such as overhead lights in a bedroom or from lighted valances (shields affixed to the wall that direct light from a source behind them upward, downward, or both ways), coves, cornices (shields affixed to the ceiling that direct light from a source behind them downward), and wall lighting or portable lights in groups of three or more that cast relatively low but adequate levels of light throughout a room.

Local or Task Lighting

Local or task lighting is the light you want focused on relatively small areas or limited areas used for specific activities such as reading, playing cards, typing at a computer keyboard, playing billiards, sewing, painting, shaving, cooking, and eating. These are the lamps and fixtures people are most familiar with, including floor, desk, and table lamps and other lighting arrangements such as recessed ceiling downlights in a bathroom to illuminate a bathtub or hand basin.

Accent or Decorative Lighting

Accent or decorative lighting comes from fixtures planned to create certain moods and atmospheres, plus fixtures designed and positioned to emphasize artwork, plants, and any other items important to a person's lifestyle or interior decor. Many different kinds of fixtures and bulbs can be used in creative ways here, limited only by the owner's imagination. Spotlights, floodlights, all sorts of decorative lights, and even candles will create a host of effects.

While planning your home, you have to decide how much of each of the lighting types you need. Then look through designer books, magazines, and lighting sales literature for ideas, and if possible, visit actual houses that pay attention to lighting schemes. It doesn't take many well-placed lighting built-ins for a house to be considered unique, and such a home will gain a special quality not found in the vast majority of dwellings that treat lighting merely as a necessary afterthought, not a part of the house to be carefully planned for maximum effect.

With general lighting, the light rays are usually diffused over a wide span. This diffusion is best accomplished by translucent glass or plastic. In a room in which the light is completely diffused, it will be coming from all sides, either directly or indirectly (bouncing off other surfaces), including the floor and ceiling, so that no shadows are cast.

Dimmer Lights

Dimmers can be useful to increase control over a variety of lights by taking charge of the voltage or current applied to the bulb or tube, thus giving a full range of light intensities. Dimmer light switches that come with intensity slide on-and-off controls (Fig. 23.8) allow you simply to turn a light on or off without setting or resetting the dimmer intensity level each time. By operating lights at less than their maximum output, energy savings can be

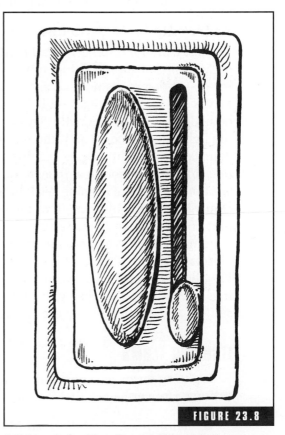

FIGURE 23.8

A light switch with a dimmer slide control.

realized. Dimming also can add an interesting mood to a room while quietly extending the life of affected light bulbs. Light bulbs dimmed just 10 percent on a regular basis are estimated to last about twice as long as a bulb burned at full brightness. For flexibility, dimmer switches are available that allow dimming the same light fixture from multiple locations.

Under-Cabinet Lights

The kitchen is one room to consider for the installation of low-voltage under-cabinet lighting that will make counters brighter and safer at a savings compared with operating overhead fixtures that illuminate the entire room. Because basic kitchen lighting can place the fixture at the center of the ceiling, cooks working at counters frequently find themselves working behind their own shadows. This will make food preparation difficult and sometimes even dangerous. Under-cabinet lighting gives an effective lighting output that can be focused directly on tasks at hand. Fixtures are available with swiveling heads that allow home cooks to pinpoint illumination exactly where it's desired.

Automatic Light Switches

Also called *motion-activated light switches*, these automatic controls (see Focus on Motion-Detector Lighting) typically are activated by a sensor that detects a moving object that emits heat, such as a person or animal. When the activating creature leaves the room, the light will turn itself off automatically, preventing lights from being left on unintentionally. These switches also should have electric eyes so that the lights do not come on if there is already enough daylight present. Units having adjustable daylight sensors for this purpose will allow the level of darkness to be preset for when motion will begin to turn the lights on. For rooms where you spend a lot of time in the evening, watching television or reading, you can install a light control that gradually brightens the lights as night falls. The control senses the current conditions and maintains a preset desired brightness level within the room. Automatic light switches can be great indoors for bedrooms, kitchens, stairwells, closets, garages, attics, and laundry and utility rooms. It's nice not having to reach for a light switch if your hands are full of groceries or laundry. The electricity savings from not leaving the lights on by accident will quickly pay back the cost of the switch, and when children are involved, the savings can be even greater.

LIGHTING TERMS

Lighting terms are constantly being tossed about by various experts and publications. Here are a few that you should be familiar with:

- *Semidirect.* Light directed 60 to 85 percent downward.
- *Semi-indirect.* Light directed 60 to 85 percent upward.

FOCUS

MOTION DETECTOR LIGHTING

Motion-detector lighting can provide both convenience and cost efficiency. No more fumbling for light switches when entering a closet, garage, basement, attic, or laundry room—especially when your arms are full of groceries, tools, or laundry. Feel more secure when you come home to an illuminated entryway, deck, or patio (Fig. 23.9). Some units can be adjusted to sense motion up to 50 feet away and within a 120-degree radius. It's also convenient for visitors to park their vehicles outside in a well-lit driveway and to approach the home's entrance on illuminated walkways. Motion-detecting units can come with solar-powered security lights. The solar panels normally are tethered with long cords so that the panels can be located in remote places. Solar units

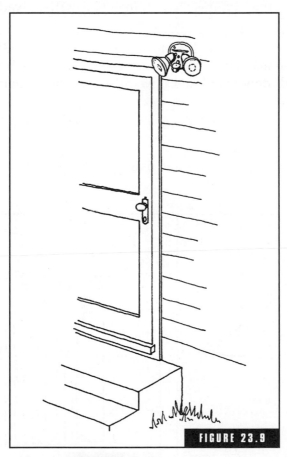

FIGURE 23.9

Motion-detector lighting.

are also available with amorphous collectors that make use of energy present in low-light levels during morning or dusk and even on overcast and rainy days. Heavy-duty batteries allow the units to work in below-freezing temperatures.

Indoors, why allow lights to be on for long periods of time, especially if you have children who are constantly forgetting to turn them off? Motion-sensing wall switches exist that activate when a person enters a room or area. Lights can be easily "tuned" to stay on for 1 to 10 minutes after no motion is detected. Sometimes, a wide field of view for a sensor works best for a particular situation, and other times a narrow field is desired. Motion-detecting units are available for both. Installation of these convenient components can be specified along with the main electrical system.

- *Recessed*. Lighting fixtures affixed flush to a ceiling, wall, or other surface (Fig. 23.10).

- *Valance*. Light source shielded by a panel attached parallel to a wall, usually employed across the top of a window. Valance lighting provides illumination both downward and upward unless the valance possesses a top (Fig. 23.11).

- *Indirect*. A system in which over 85 percent of all the light is cast upward toward the ceiling.

- *Direct*. Over 85 percent of all the light is cast downward toward the floor.

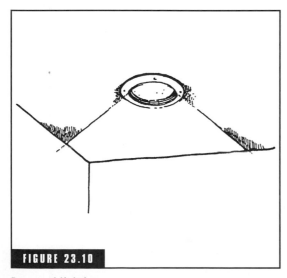

FIGURE 23.10

Recessed lighting.

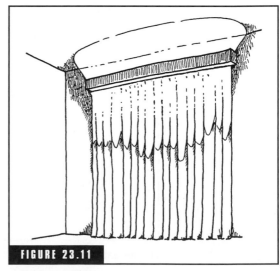

FIGURE 23.11

Valance lighting.

FIGURE 23.12

Accent light.

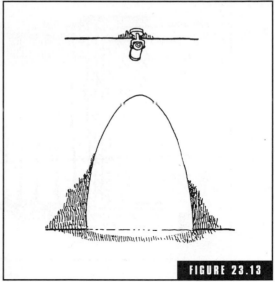

FIGURE 23.13

Accent light.

■ *Accent.* Directional lighting to emphasize a particular area or object (Figs. 23.12 and 23.13).

■ *Cornice.* Light sources shielded from direct view by a panel of wood, metal, plaster, or diffusing plastic or glass parallel to the wall and attached to the ceiling and casting light over the wall through direct or downward lighting (Fig. 23.14).

■ *Cove.* Light source shielded by a ledge and casting light over the ceiling and upper wall, usually through indirect or upward lighting (Fig. 23.15).

■ *General diffuse.* Almost an equal amount of light produced in all directions, such as the light emitted from a suspended globe (Fig. 23.16).

■ *Luminous.* A lighting system consisting of a false ceiling of diffusing material with light sources mounted above it (Fig. 23.17).

■ *Track.* One electrical outlet supplying a number of separate fittings that can be positioned anywhere along a

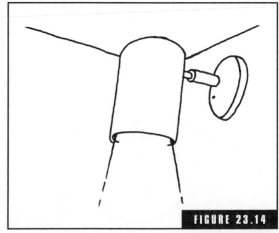

FIGURE 23.14

Cornice lighting.

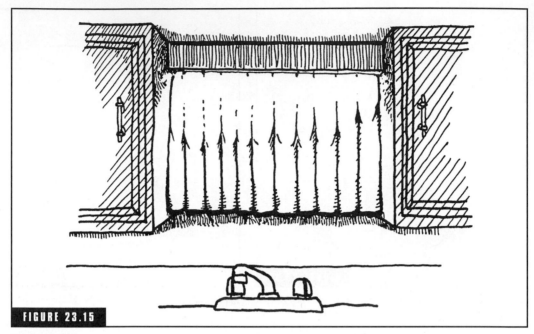

FIGURE 23.15

Cove lighting.

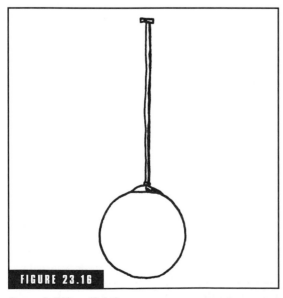

FIGURE 23.16

General diffuse lighting.

FIGURE 23.17

Luminous lighting.

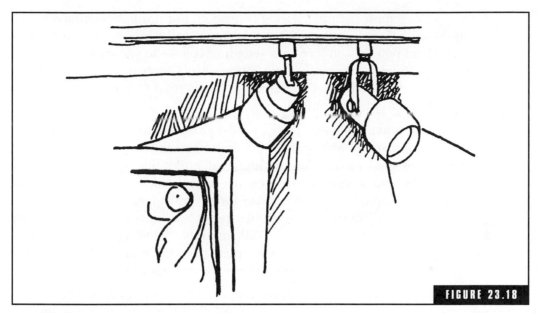

FIGURE 23.18

Track lighting.

length of electrified track. It's very versatile for ceilings or walls with vertical or horizontal tracks (Fig. 23.18).

■ *Wallwashers.* When installed about 3 feet away from a wall, wallwashers will light up the wall evenly from top to bottom or bottom to top without spilling or wasting light away from the wall into the room. Angled closer to a wall of paintings or art groupings, wallwashers will splash light onto varying surfaces, leaving interesting shadows contrasted in between.

■ *Downlights.* Round or square metal canisters that can be recessed into a ceiling, semirecessed, or ceiling-mounted to cast pools of light on the floor or on any surface below them. They can be a spotlight, a floodlight, or an ordinary bulb. A spotlight will throw a concentrated circle of light. A floodlight will cast a wider, cone-shaped light. An ordinary bulb will provide soft, diffuse, all-over lighting.

■ *Uplights.* Fixtures put on the floor behind sofas, plants, or other appointments, under glass shelves, and in corners where they will lend a beautiful dramatic accent, bouncing reflected light off ceilings and into the room and creating moods that could hardly be imagined possible by day.

Exterior Lighting Considerations

■ Consider solar-powered security lights (Fig. 23.19), where solar panels collect free natural light during the day and store it as energy in rechargeable batteries. No exterior supply wiring is needed. For motion-sensing models, at night, a halogen bulb turns on automatically when any motion is detected and remains on a certain length of time—30 seconds or so—after the motion stops. Other models are triggered by timers or automatic photo-cell electric eyes set to specific darkness levels (that turn on automatically at night and off in the morning).

■ There are units available that work by solar panels so that the light itself can be located in a shady area if need be. Some can function in temperatures reaching 40°F below zero. You can aim, test, and adjust the solar lights via test switches, and weatherproof housings seal them for protection against the elements. Some units will operate for several nights without an intermediate charge. Different styles of solar-powered lights can solve a variety of specific lighting challenges. Wall mounts, hanging units, column-mounted coach lights similar to a lamppost, pagodas, and tier lights that are wall mounted or ground supported cover most situations.

■ For entryways, decorative lantern units are common choices. Many have adjustable motion sensitivity and manual override so that you can activate the light from a standard wall switch. Motion-sensing flood lights directed at rear and side entranceways or walkways are recommended by many security experts. Even on cloudy days, built-in batteries will keep them working. At dusk, an electric eye automatically switches on an accent amber LED. When motion is detected within about 20 feet of the light, a bright halogen bulb comes on for about 3 minutes to scare away unwanted visitors. Remember that the key factors to consider when selecting a motion-sensing light are the sensitivity range and field of view. Those two factors determine the area of security coverage for an individual light fixture.

FIGURE 23.19

A solar-powered security light.

■ To assist evening delivery persons, visitors, emergency service providers, and others, solar-powered house number lights are available. Numbers 4 inches high illuminate at night and can be seen clearly from the street. They need only a couple of hours of sun during the day and are completely weatherproof. Mailboxes with solar-powered lights also use rechargeable batteries that can be activated at night by a remote-control feature that allows you to turn on the lights from inside your home.

- Hanging garden lights are another outdoor option. They come with an adjustable-height hanging hook. They're ideal for illuminating steps, walkways, entryways, porches, decks and patios.

General Lighting Considerations

- Use lower-watt bulbs for nonworking spaces.

- Choose light fixtures that are easy to access and clean. Remember that dirt absorbs light.

- To get the most from your lamps, walls and ceilings painted white will maximize the amount of reflection into the room.

- Lighter colors and shades of furnishings such as carpeting, draperies, and upholstery will minimize the amount of artificial light required by a room.

- Mirrors spread light within a room. By strategically placing mirrors where they will not be blocked by furniture, illumination can be spread and extended to where needed.

- Selecting LED-, compact fluorescent- and other fluorescent-bulb fixtures over incandescent-bulb fixtures results both in energy savings and longer individual bulb life.

- Bulbs having the Energy Star label, though they typically cost more to buy, run with less pollution and less energy and will last longer.

- Use lamps and other fixtures having three-way controls (for bulbs having three separate wattage levels, such as a bulb for a table lamp set up as a reading light, with the brightest intensity setting to read by). Three-way bulbs enable you to use the lower settings when the brightest is not necessary.

- When choosing night-lights, consider 4-watt minifluorescent or electroluminescent models. Some require as little as a few cents per year to operate. Some have auto-off features that will turn the light off after 10 to 30 minutes; after 9 or 29 minutes, the bulb will blink twice—signaling that it is only 1 minute away from turning itself off.

- Have you ever been frustrated by children who leave closet lights on forever? Then consider door-frame buttons that turn on the light as the door opens—similar to that of a refrigerator. As the door is closed, it pushes the button in, and the light turns off. Of course, you've got to train those same children to keep the closet doors closed or install an automatic door closure.

- To provide cost-effective security lighting while you're gone, consider electronic timer/light switches. The best ones enable you to set different light schedules (six on/off times) for each day of the week. Some even have random lighting schedules. Even for just an evening out, it's an effective strategy to have indoor lights go on at dusk or at other times while no one is home.

■ Remote-control entry door locking and lighting controls allow you to illuminate and unlock an entry door from as far as 30 feet away, providing both security and convenience. This helps to save energy by eliminating the need to leave your outdoor lights on all evening until you return and allows you to use both hands to carry items to the door instead of using one hand for keys. With the remote, you may need one less trip back to the car, as well as one less opening and closing of the entry door. Each time the door is opened, heated or cooled air can escape.

REMODELING NOTES

Because remodeling the lights fits so naturally with electrical remodeling issues, it's best to handle them at the same time. Before that, though, think where the possible addition of natural lighting could partially eliminate the need for electric lights, especially in bathrooms, hallways, foyers, laundry rooms, and other areas that may not have windows.

Light bulbs or lamps are available in so many types, sizes, shapes, and levels of power. There's rampant innovation involved because they're so closely tied into the cost of illuminating homes and commercial and industrial properties—really all types of indoor and outdoor spaces. Overall, lighting is a huge energy user that just will not go away. People want more light for less money, and lighting equipment manufacturers are giving them that. LED lamps and fixtures are becoming more commonplace, and so are solar lighting fixtures. It's another way to help wean yourself from the higher electricity prices of the future. Through the use of lighting aids such as solar tubes, the bouncing of light from room to room with mirrors, and light-colored paints and surfaces, you can make do with less light inside.

Architects, interior designers, and home planners have been aware of the importance of light for many years, and there are tricks of the trade to squeeze more lumens out of less wattages. Look through lighting catalogs, and speak with salespersons from lighting fixture specialty stores who have seen the changes that are happening and have been around for years. Their opinions can help lead you to trouble-free fixtures and lamps that can save big time.

If you have children who are forever forgetting to turn off lights, consider timers or switches that act like a timer in a sauna that automatically turn off after the original number of minutes set. Again, pinpoint control—whenever you can include increased control over an energy expenditure—that's part of the battle. And once a system is set up, it might be more expensive to begin with, but it can pay off very quickly with cumulative savings on energy. Consider motion-sensor switches for some lights. This is why sometimes in major grocery chains, within long banks of freezers or refrigerators, the inside freezer or cooler lights go off automatically when no one is in the aisle. Why have lights on when no one is using them? The same goes for certain rooms in your home. As long as safety is not compromised, consider how any automatic lighting (such as motion-sensor rear porch or garage walkway lighting) will save energy, similar to the lights that come on and off automatically with automatic garage door openers. How many times do they save six or eight lamps from burning all night long by automatically shutting off?

A sun tunnel or tube lighting can be an excellent remodeling project to bring natural light into an otherwise dark area inside the home such as a hallway. The installation of dimmers can help to save considerable amounts of energy and dollars and may extend the useful lives of light bulbs that will not burn as hotly as they do at full strength. Outdoor solar lights can easily replace their wired electrical versions. Also consider that some can be brought in at night in case of a power outage or emergency.

> > > > > > **POINTS TO PONDER**

1. Built-in lighting, as opposed to lighting fixtures simply added on after the rooms are planned, will add a distinctive touch to any home.

2. Fluorescent lamps offer greater lighting efficiencies than do incandescent-filament lamps. Initially, setting up for fluorescent lighting is more expensive, but those expenses eventually will be recaptured with lower energy costs.

3. Fluorescent lamps—owing to their cooler operating temperature range—typically will last up to 10 times as long as many incandescent bulbs. This is why fluorescent lamps and compact fluorescent bulbs should be considered in places that can't be reached conveniently for bulb changing.

4. If absolute quiet is a major factor, such as in a small office or library, remember that fluorescent bulbs aren't as quiet as incandescent light. Most fluorescent models produce faint humming sounds. On the other hand, so do personal computers—and few individuals notice or complain about computer background noise.

5. Most homes are constructed with plenty of general or background lighting, such as overhead lights in bedrooms. Identify places where local or task lighting will be needed, and try to plan recessed or track lighting units to focus on those areas.

6. Dimmer switches make sense wherever accent or decorative lighting is installed. Dimmers increase control over lamps by taking charge of the voltage or current applied to the bulb or tube, thus allowing a full range of light intensities.

7. Make sure that fixtures are rated for the bulb wattages you plan to use in them. For example, avoid burning 100-watt bulbs in fixtures rated for only 60 watts.

8. If your children are notorious for leaving certain lights on all the time, such as bright lights over a makeup table, consider putting the lights on a 15-minute (or so) timer switch that will automatically turn off the lights unless the timer is reset manually.

9. Make sure that all stairways have adequate lighting that's controlled by switches at both ends of the stairway.

10. Consider twice before installing fixtures in places that are extremely difficult to access, such as in vaulted ceilings and two-story-high entrance foyers. At the very least, plan how the bulbs will be replaced without the use of extra-long ladders. Also, avoid putting recessed lights in ceilings with unheated space above. They can't be insulated properly and will leak air badly.

11. Tips for effective and efficient lighting:

   ■ Provide brighter, more focused lighting for tasks instead of raising the levels of overhead or background lights.

   ■ When planning lighting for rooms that need a lot of light, such as the kitchen, start with a bright central overhead fixture rather than loading up on background or accent lighting.

   ■ Install dimmer switches for better control on appropriate fixtures. Dimmers allow you to set the right mood with different light levels and also help to save energy during times when you don't need full lighting.

   ■ If you leave some lights on for security when you're away from home, use timers to save energy and create a more realistic impression that you're there.

   ■ Replace standard outdoor flood lamps with outdoor-rated compact fluorescent lamps. Wattages of 9 to 18 watts are recommended for reducing glare and improving nighttime visibility.

   ■ Use solar-powered fixtures for landscape and other outdoor lighting. These are free to operate and can be installed anywhere because they don't have to be wired to a house circuit. Virtually every type of popular outdoor fixture is available in a solar version, including path and driveway lights, patio lights, floods and spotlights, and utility lights for outbuildings.

■ Control outdoor lights with timers, photocells, or motion sensors so that lights go on only when they're needed.

■ When using incandescent bulbs, remember that a single high-wattage bulb is more efficient than multiple low-wattage bulbs. For example, a 100-watt bulb produces the same light as two 60-watt bulbs or three 40-watt bulbs. But never exceed a fixture's maximum wattage rating.

■ Turn off the lights when you leave a room. This familiar parental reminder seems to have been lost on many of today's home owners. It's time to get back into the habit of basic conservation.

12. Additional tips:

■ Install as many energy-efficient lamps as possible.

■ Design lighting for maximum task efficiency.

■ Turn lights off when not needed.

■ Use time switches or sensors on external lights so that they are not left burning all night.

■ Why leave lights on when there is no one in a room? Consider installing occupancy sensors that detect motion or infrared heat. These switches can trigger a switch that turns the lights on instantly when someone enters the room.

Heating and Cooling

Space—although it may have been the final frontier for Captain Kirk and his crew—should be one of the first concerns for the planners of a new home. Indeed, how a home heats, cools, and freshens its interior atmosphere and spaces is of prime importance for the completion of any successful green dwelling. Handling of interior air is usually accomplished by the most expensive to install and costly to run and maintain system in the home. These same installation, running, and maintenance tasks also present great opportunities to conserve energy and resources while helping to create a comfortable, healthy inside environment. This chapter—the longest in the book—discusses many heating and cooling options available for both green and not-so-green construction. And where there is heating and cooling, ventilation can't be far behind.

Topics such as makeup air, air changes, drafts, air tightness, building envclopes, cross-ventilation, thermosiphoning, and other related concepts all become involved with any heating and cooling discussion worth its efficiency. Heating and cooling cannot be reviewed within a vacuum; many other chapters interact simultaneously, such as those on insulation, windows, landscaping, and orientation.

Certainly, you could plan the most attractive and utilitarian home design imaginable, locate it on a site with a breathtaking view, and furnish it with the finest appointments, yet unless the temperature and humidity within such a dwelling are maintained properly, the house would be unpleasant to live in. Heating and cooling systems are probably the hardest working components of any home, especially homes located in climates having temperature extremes.

There's a good reason for the existence of the oft-referred-to acronym *HVAC*, which stands for *h*eating, *v*entilation, and *a*ir-*c*onditioning. The letters tie interrelated concepts together, all needing to be addressed when planning space heating and cooling. Simply put, the green home should be serviced by a correctly sized and balanced heating, ventilation, and if absolutely needed, air-conditioning system. In such a system's most efficient state, indoor air is exchanged with outside replacement air that is partly preheated or precooled by stale air as it passes from inside the home to the outdoors.

For discussion purposes, space conditioning equipment typically involves four main components:

1. A *fuel* or *power source*, such as electricity, solar, or fuels that are burned, including natural gas, oil, propane, wood, and biomass products.

2. *Conversion equipment* that converts the fuel or power source into heating or cooling operations. This equipment includes furnaces, boilers, water heaters, heat pumps, condensing units, wood or biomass stoves, and solar collecting systems.

3. A *distribution system* that transports the heat or cooling to where it will be used. This can include air ducts, pipes of air or liquid, or wiring for electricity.

4. A *delivery method* using air registers, radiant wall or floor heaters or panels, fan coils and blowers for cold or warm air dispersal, and electric resistance heaters.

TYPES OF FUEL OR POWER SOURCES FOR HOME HEATING

Types of noncombustion fuel or power sources available for home heating use include electricity (generated by utility, commercial, and private means), solar, wind, hydroelectric, ground-source heat, and air-source heat. Combustion fuel or power sources include natural gas, propane, fuel oil, biodiesel, wood, switch grass, corn, wood pellets, and other biomass burnable materials.

Electricity

Electricity is readily available almost anywhere. Although technically not a fuel, electricity is a source of power that's generated by a variety of methods, most often the combustion of coal, oil, natural gas, and other biomass products, all of which produce harmful greenhouse gases when burned. Unfortunately, the combustion-generation process is so inefficient that most of the fuel's energy potential gets wasted as heat. Smaller amounts of electric current are also being generated by nuclear and chemical reactions and by harnessing potential energy using moving water, wind, and solar installations. After the generating is done, however, electricity is a very clean and efficient source of power. However, as a ready-made "fuel" for heating or cooling, it can be quite expensive. From a green perspective, the purchase of electricity from renewable suppliers is an option becoming more cost competitive as additional renewable capacity comes online. Of course, another strategy involves generating your own electricity from small solar photovoltaic (PV) or wind turbine systems.

Home electricity-generation systems using sustainable means—also called *microgeneration systems*, are becoming more popular as their technologies improve and their costs come down, but they're still not affordable enough to entice many home owners, even with the inclusion of tax rebates, credits, and grants. Difficulties that still pose stumbling blocks include

- *The intermittent nature of wind and sunshine.* They're not always present or available.

- *Restrictive zoning or building codes.* These may stop or discourage home owners from installing a wind turbine or solar system

- *The expense of tying into the local electric grid system.* Together with the initial capital outlay for generating and storage equipment, this can be quite restrictive.

If a household uses large amounts of electricity, generating systems and even purchased electricity that would satisfy such demands may be cost-prohibitive. However, when high levels of insulation, passive-solar design, reasonably sized spaces, zoned heating with programmable thermostats, natural ventilation and cooling, and other green energy-saving features are present, electric-resistance heat may be a reasonable option. Because only small amounts of heat may be needed to satisfy an extremely efficient home, a small, inexpensive electric heating system may be able to replace more sophisticated, costly other-fuel furnaces or boilers often planned for green dwellings. If electricity is the desired heating power source for homes requiring larger electric loads, then a heat pump system may be a reasonable choice.

ADVANTAGES

1. Electricity is a clean power source that leaves no residue to contaminate the house or the atmosphere.

2. It requires no chimney to vent exhaust fumes and smoke.

3. It's a power source that can be depended on in the future because it can be produced from almost any type of fuel—gas, oil, coal, nuclear, solar, wind, and hydroelectric or water power.

DISADVANTAGES

1. Its rate charge depends on the local utility company.

2. Breaks in the main supply line could leave you and your neighbors temporarily without supply.

Fuel Oil

Like electricity, fuel oil enjoys a comprehensive, efficient distribution that makes it readily available practically everywhere.

ADVANTAGES

1. If the oil fuel burner is routinely serviced and adjusted for maximum efficiency, fuel oil is a relatively clean source of combustion—but still dirtier than most other fuels.

2. The supply is stored on the property. Once it's in place, there's no worry about it being cut off.

DISADVANTAGES

1. Fuel oil must be stored in a tank that's usually located underground. The tank requires certain safety and fireproofing precautions, all of which combine to make the initial setup cost fairly high.

2. Money is tied up in the inventory stored.

3. The use of fuel oil may require a chimney.

4. If burned in an out-of-tune unit, fuel oil will give off dirty emissions that will soil the interior of a home.

5. Fuel oil is not a renewable resource.

Natural Gas

Natural gas is combustible mixture of hydrocarbon gases (mostly methane) commonly delivered by a network of utility company pipelines and used as an energy source for commercial, industrial, and residential heating. Natural gas is not available everywhere, though. It's most often found underground, near deposits of oil. Unlike oil, coal, wood, and some other fossil fuels, natural gas is clean burning and emits few pollutants. It is a popular first choice to fuel household furnaces, boilers, water heaters, ovens, and cooktops.

ADVANTAGES

1. Natural gas is a clean fuel.

2. Natural gas requires no on-site storage.

3. Many space- and water-heating appliances have been designed for this fuel.

DISADVANTAGES

1. The natural gas supply and rate depend on the local utility company.

2. Poorly maintained equipment and pipelines can result in dangerous natural gas leaks.

3. Natural gas is not a renewable resource.

PROPANE OR LP GAS

Propane is another combustible hydrocarbon used as fuel. It's also called *liquefied petroleum gas* (LP gas or LPG). It's made from equal amounts of crude oil refining and natural gas processing. It's stored in pressurized tanks as a liquid and is used in heating equipment as a vapor.

ADVANTAGES

1. Propane is a clean fuel.

2. Propane can be used where there are no natural gas or electric lines that service the site.

3. Propane vaporizes and dissipates into the air if spilled.

4. Propane gas is usually not as volatile as natural gas (but still can be dangerous).

DISADVANTAGES

1. The propane supply and rate depend on the local utility company.

2. Storage tanks and fittings can leak.

3. It ties up money in inventory.

4. Propane is not a renewable resource.

Coal

Coal is an old-fashioned fuel that, while remaining a popular fuel supply for the generation of electricity, is rarely used any more to heat individual homes. It's not readily available in all areas.

ADVANTAGE

1. The supply of coal can be maintained on the property.

DISADVANTAGES

1. If you've ever read Victor Hugo's *Germinal*, then you know what a dirty, filthy substance coal is—even *before* it's burned.

2. Coal is dirty when burned, too.

3. Coal leaves large amounts of ash after combustion occurs.

4. Naturally, the use of coal requires a chimney.

5. Coal is a hot-burning fuel that possesses an above-average risk of starting house fires.

6. The supply of coal requires substantial storage capacity, as well as money tied up in inventory.

7. Coal is not a renewable resource.

Wood

The availability of wood depends on the local supply of hardwoods such as oak, ash, maple, cherry, and elm. It can be a reliable fuel source, especially in rural areas, but not without some environmental consequences. Still, because it's a renewable resource, burning wood in newer, energy-efficient fireplaces and stoves can prevent the burning of nonrenewable fuel sources such as natural gas, propane, and oil.

ADVANTAGES

1. The wood supply can be maintained and even grown on the property.

2. If you have the equipment and time, you can procure the supply yourself.

3. Wood is a renewable resource if grown and harvested responsibly—so the forest from which the wood is taken will be maintained in good health for future generations.

DISADVANTAGES

1. Substantial labor is required to place or have the hardwood put in storage, to move it to a stove or fireplace, and to remove the ashes after combustion.

2. Reliable sources of firewood may not be available nearby.

3. If handling and preparing the wood yourself, there's danger involved with using chainsaws, hand axes, and mauls and power splitters.

4. The inventory takes up a lot of room and ties up money.

5. The use of wood requires a chimney.

6. There's some risk of house fires.

7. Wood can bring dirt, insects, and fungi into the house.

8. The combustion of unseasoned wood can cause smoke to taint interior furnishings.

The possibility of additional environmental regulations and building code restrictions is likely. Given the pollutants and safety concerns associated with burning wood, this source of fuel may fall out of favor. Certainly, burning wood in a conventional fireplace or stove gives off large amounts of particulates, unburned hydrocarbons, and gases such as sulfur dioxide, carbon dioxide, and carbon monoxide. More environmentally friendly, tightly sealed fireplaces and stoves do a lot better job, but even so, wood is not one of the cleanest, greenest options.

Pellets of Wood, Corn, Switchgrass, and Other Biomass Products

Pellets are made from clean wood waste products from sawmill, furniture, and other basic wood-product and wood-fiber manufacturing operations. Pellets are a convenient source of fuel that, once stored on site, can be delivered to the combustion chamber of a stove, a fireplace insert, or even a boiler or furnace automatically by means of an electrically run auger. Because pellets burn so completely, there is less smoke and pollution than from burning equal amounts of firewood. Wood is not the only material from which pellets are made. Switchgrass is a crop grown in South America for use as fuel and other products and is a crop that is starting to catch on in other places. It's a rapidly growing grass that does not need to be planted from scratch each year and thrives on inhospitable weather and soil conditions and needs almost no help from fertilizers or pesticides. Corn is another renewable resource from which pellets can be made.

ADVANTAGES

1. Pellets are clean to store, handle, and burn.
2. Pellets can be made from a variety of renewable materials, such as wood, corn, and switchgrass.
3. Pellets do not involve splitting, dirt, insects, seasoning, or heavy lifting.

DISADVANTAGES

1. Pellets can be more expensive per British thermal unit of heat than other biomass fuels.
2. Sometimes pellets become hard to find, particularly toward the end of a burning season.

Solar

Solar energy depends on the amount of sunshine available. Sometimes it's available. Sometimes it's not. It's certainly not available at night, nor when blocked by thick clouds or by shadows from trees, hills, or adjacent buildings. The conversion of sunshine into enough electricity to satisfy typical individual housing demands is still a fairly expensive proposition for most home owners, even when partial grants, tax credits, and other financial stimuli are available. Solar thermal collection processes, however (instead of solar electricity production), a more direct use of the sun's power, are more affordable systems. The collection of solar energy to heat water or other materials that can, in turn, help to heat a home's living spaces is an age-old process that's currently using modern technology and products. This happens in a wide variety of closely related ways, one of which involves directly heating coolant or water that courses through piping or tube collectors located on roofs or elsewhere and then circulating the heated liquid through a coil within an insulated water storage tank, where water used for heat distribution is warmed. And certainly, some level of passive-solar heating and cooling design is a realistic possibility and very affordable to all dwellings, from older homes to high-tech new construction.

ADVANTAGES

1. It's clean.
2. There's no charge for sunshine.
3. It should be readily available for the next few billion years.
4. It lessens the reliance on endangered and imported fuels.

DISADVANTAGES

1. Unless substantial expense is incurred, not much long-range solar energy can be stored up. Even at best, it's minimal when compared with the storage capacity of other fuels.
2. How often have you known your local weather forecaster to be 100 percent accurate? There's an inability to predict with assurance the amount of sunlight that will occur during any one season.
3. Backup systems are needed.
4. It's relatively expensive to plan and install a solar system.

TYPES OF HEAT PRODUCTION AND DELIVERY SYSTEMS

When it comes to selecting a space-heating system, numerous types can be considered, including forced-air and hot-water systems, heat pumps, and solar and electrical systems. Although major improvements have been made with heating and air-conditioning systems in the past few years, taking advantage of them requires attention to supporting green construction details and features. Certainly, home-heating energy consumption depends on the climate, the home's insulating and thermal envelope package, daily activities of the occupants, and the efficiency of the dwelling's heating system. How can you tell what a heating system's efficiency rating is? Efficiency is expressed as a ratio of heat energy output to fuel energy input. The U.S. Department of Energy (DOE) has a specific test for heating appliances that results in what's known as the *annual fuel utilization efficiency* (AFUE) rating, measured as a percentage. It's an all-around indicator of how the tested unit performs under average conditions it would face in a yearly operation, and it can be found on those yellow Energy Guide stickers or tags attached to all new heating equipment, along with estimates for annual operating costs. The higher the AFUE percentage, the greater is the fuel usage efficiency. The Energy Star program uses AFUE numbers to help qualify heating units for its efficiency program. For example, furnaces need to reach 90 percent or above to qualify for Energy Star, whereas boilers make the cut at or above 85 percent. The term *high efficiency* traditionally has meant 90 percent or higher efficiency and is often applied not only to the best gas furnace models but also to condensing-type units that capture some of the heat energy that is usually lost to vaporization of exhaust and flue gases.

Another efficiency rating is the *steady-state efficiency* (SSE), a measurement of how much energy carries over from combusted fuel to the unit's distribution system after its burning. Again, the higher the percentage number, the greater is the efficiency rating. To find this number, the amount of energy lost to the combustion process owing to incomplete fuel burning, combined with the heat energy lost up a chimney after combustion takes place, is subtracted from the fuel's energy content. Because SSE numbers do not take into account starting or stopping times, SSE levels may be slightly higher than AFUE percentages.

The efficiency of equipment that burns fuel depends on a number of basic factors, including how completely the fuel burns, how much of the combustion heat reaches the air or water being heated, how much of the heat is lost through the equipment during standby and operating times, and how much heat is lost in exhaust or up a chimney during standby and operating cycles.

Additional factors that support operating efficiencies include correctly sizing the units and matching them with precise control instrumentation. All heating and cooling units need to be sized for projected and actual heating or cooling demands to prevent frequent startups and stops of furnaces, boilers, and other units. Oversized equipment will cycle on and off way too frequently, increasing equipment wear, and rarely will oversized units reach the efficient operating "sweet spots" for which they were engineered. They also cost more to purchase, install, run, and maintain. Today, it's more important than ever to get the sizing right because old rule-of-thumb square footage guidelines likely don't take into account increased equipment efficiencies, greater levels of insulation, passive-solar design features, and airtight thermal envelope construction. If these green features aren't considered, larger heating and cooling systems than needed could be installed. On the other hand, grossly undersized equipment may run continuously and may not satisfy heating or cooling requirements. One way to correctly determine equipment size is for a competent HVAC engineer or contractor to do a load calculation based on the specific construction plan and HVAC variables involved, using recognized guidelines and software such as that available from the appropriate resources of the Air Conditioning Contractors of America (ACCA).

In a second-to-last last note about sizing heating and cooling units, it may be best to err slightly on the small side. As long as a heating or air-conditioning unit can keep up with space-conditioning demands most of the time, jumping up in size just to take care of a few yearly extreme-temperature days may not be worth the infrequent annoyance of temporarily having to put on a sweater or set up a few portable fans.

And the last note—a note of of caution: Efficiency percentages (like all percentages) can be misleading if the situation they're related to is not considered in its entirety. Some electric space and water heaters have very high efficiency ratings, approaching 100 percent, but this doesn't mean that they're the cheapest units to run. The cost of electricity may be far greater than the cost of other fuels or power sources, proportionately, for the amount of heat energy received per dollar. Understand where the efficiency rating of equipment you're considering fits within the total process of purchasing, installing, maintaining, and running the heating or cooling unit over its useful life.

Furnaces: Forced-Air Heating Units

These popular systems burn fuel to create a supply of warm air that's blown (or forced) by a fan through a duct system to various parts of the house. During its operation, this type of furnace heats air that's drawn from the rooms and then sends it back through ducts and registers out again into the rooms (Figs. 24.1 and 24.2). The enclosures that route the air back to the furnace are known as the *return ducts*, and those supplying the air are *supply ducts*. Before the air comes back into the furnace from the return ducts, it goes through an air filter where most of the fugitive airborne dirt and dust is filtered out to protect the furnace from fouling its working parts.

Most furnaces are run on natural gas or propane. Some, however, use other fuels or power sources, including electricity, fuel oil, and biomass products. Electric furnaces heat air or water by direct current through heavy-duty heating coils. They work fine, but they can be expensive to operate owing to the cost of purchased electricity. Oil-fired furnaces employ high-pressure oil burners that shoot high-pressure mists of oil and air into a combustion chamber, where ignition occurs by electric sparks. Oil is not as cleanly or efficiently burned as natural gas or propane and must be trucked to storage tanks kept on site. Biomass furnaces use wood, pellets, or other combustible fuel sources. Again, their operation is considerably less efficient and more polluting than furnaces powered by natural or liquid gas.

In short, forced-air gas furnaces can work very well, especially if natural gas is available nearby and you design a well-insulated, efficient thermal envelope that will keep the conditioned air from leaking out.

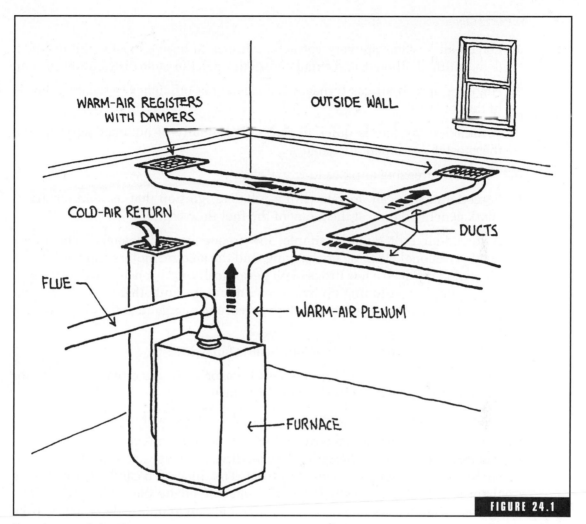

WARM-AIR REGISTERS
WITH DAMPERS

OUTSIDE WALL

COLD-AIR RETURN

DUCTS

FLUE

WARM-AIR PLENUM

FURNACE

FIGURE 24.1

Forced-warm-air heating system.

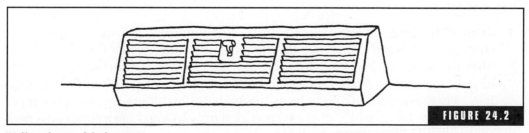

FIGURE 24.2

Wall register with damper.

ADVANTAGES

1. Forced-air systems are very versatile. Air can be heated, cooled, humidified, dehumidified, filtered, and circulated all through the same distribution system.

2. High-end forced-air gas furnaces can operate at efficiency percentage levels in the mid-90s.

3. A forced-air system is quick to respond manually or automatically via the thermostat to temperature changes.

4. There's no freezing of pipes to worry about.

5. Forced-air units can operate with a pilotless ignition that uses an electrical spark generated only at the moment the fuel flow begins.

6. A forced-air unit requires simple, low-frequency maintenance. The filters need occasional cleaning or changing, and the electric motors and a few moving parts may need a few drops of oil periodically. Only once a year will a typical furnace need tuning up by a professional. In units that are heavily run, though, such tuneups usually will save more in energy than they cost to have done.

7. The installation price of forced-air heat is fairly low.

8. The distribution system requires less floor or wall space than radiators for water or steam heat or electric baseboard heat.

9. The forced-air system is adaptable to most burnable fuel supplies.

10. Forced-air systems can be designed with more than one blower or with special devices so that the heated air can be directed to particular locations, with each location having its own thermostat. The ducts also can have fins inside them or movable baffles that can be used to regulate the airflow to various rooms. Thermostats can be used to automatically control flaps that can be closed or opened (fully or partially) as needed. A less expensive way to accomplish zoning would be to locate manually operated dampers that can be accessed easily by hand when needed.

DISADVANTAGES

1. Some of the by-products of combustion—the unburned gas, oil, soot, or other contaminants—can come out through the registers. A poorly maintained, dirty forced-air furnace, for instance, inevitably will transport small amounts of airborne soot through the supply ducts and onto walls, floors, and furnishings. This process is likely to be so gradual and insidious that the graying of white walls, for instance, might be revealed only by washing a small area near one of the registers or by removing a picture from a wall.

2. Another disadvantage of forced-air heating is heat cycling. Because the blower operates on an off-and-on basis, the room temperature varies near the thermostat setting from an overwarm to an underwarm condition and then back again. There's a constant overcompensating going on.

3. If a blower motor is too large or a duct system has not been designed properly, the movement of air in a room can be uncomfortable.

4. The sounds of the blower unit can be conveyed all over the house through the ductwork.

FORCED-AIR HEATING CONSIDERATIONS

1. Consider opting for a forced-air furnace with a high-efficiency (>90 percent efficiency) condensing unit that exhausts directly outdoors via a pipe. Condensing furnaces can use true sealed combustion air drawn through a small pipe, minimizing the chances of backdrafting, carbon monoxide poisoning, and chilly indoor drafts. A lower-cost alternative is an energy-efficient (>80 percent efficiency) conventional forced-air furnace that exhausts through a chimney flue.

2. The furnace's casing and blower compartment should be insulated.

3. Furnace operation should be quiet, with a direct-drive blower.

4. Look for an easy-to-change filter arrangement. Some units have filter doors/covers that attach magnetically, enabling the cover to be pulled off and put back on without the use of tools. If it's difficult to access the filter, you'll be less likely to change it as often as you should. The filter should be replaced or cleaned regularly to remove accumulations of dust and other particles.

5. See that there's a drain installed for condensation discharge.

6. The air-intake pipes and furnace exhaust port should be located above the snow line in cold-climate locations. In all areas, they must be kept unobstructed and clean.

Some forced-air furnaces are two-stage models with low and high heat-output levels. They use two-stage burners, operating in low-output mode during moderately cold weather and high-output mode during cold temperatures. The furnace adjusts its own mode of operation to best suit the circumstances. Since the furnace runs longer in a low-heat stage (than it would in a high-output stage), there is more continuous air circulation for household comfort and more effective air cleaning.

Two-stage heating models offer the following advantages:

- Increased heating comfort

- Quieter operation
- High heating capacity to ensure comfort on coldest days
- Longer and fewer heating cycles
- Increased air circulation
- More consistent house temperatures
- Improved indoor air quality
- Reduced drafts
- Less wear and tear on the furnace

Sealed combustion furnace installations use direct venting to the outdoors for both air intake and combustion exhaust, so there's little chance of backdrafting in negative-pressure scenarios. This also eliminates the need to draw heated indoor air for combustion, saving the additional energy it would take to heat the replacement air again.

Condensing furnaces (and boilers) with acid-resisting liner pipes can reclaim some of the waste heat that otherwise would be lost up a chimney. The temperature of exhaust gases from noncondensing furnaces easily can reach 400°F compared with about 100°F in a condensing unit. The difference in reclaimed heat can be distributed inside the home instead of the outdoors.

Variable-speed blowers that automatically adjust to heating needs are superior to single-speed blowers and are able to deliver better air quality and comfort. This is so because different airflow capacities are needed for different heat output levels. Once a furnace starts its cycle, the blower motor on a variable-speed unit operates slowly and then softly ramps up to full speed—preventing chilly drafts while conserving electricity. When shutting down, the variable-speed unit ramps down into slow speed and brings itself to a stop. These highly efficient motors can take full advantage of electronically controlled brushless operation by automatically adjusting their speed based on a variety of operating factors, including duct pressure and preset requirements. They're most efficient when used on systems with high run times.

Variable speed motors offer the following advantages:

- Quieter heating and cooling operation
- Improved electrical efficiency all year long
- Increased comfort in both heating and cooling
- Economical use of a continuous fan
- Increased cooling efficiency

■ Better humidity control in cooling

Important features can be had with variable-speed blowers:

■ Furnaces with soft start and soft stop are considerably quieter and use less energy than units without those features. They maintain a more constant temperature without the push and pull of cold and then warm and then cold and then warm corrections that commonly occur with single-speed blowers.

■ They also achieve better humidity control while cooling the household air because they run longer in the low speed.

■ They reduce furnace-caused drafts and minimize the shock of blowers that abruptly come on at full speed and abruptly stop.

Forced-air *zoning* features a system that operates via individual area thermostats and motorized duct dampers. This arrangement allows a home to be segmented into zones that are individually controlled with their own thermostats. The units typically come with a clean-air filter reminder and indoor relative-humidity display, with fully modulating dampers and adjustable temperature set points. Energy is saved by cutting back heat to zones where and when it's not needed.

Boilers: Hot-Water (Hydronic) Heating Units

With this type of system, water is heated in a boiler by a gas, oil, or other burner and then pumped throughout the house via a piping network equipped with radiators that ultimately distribute heat into the rooms (Fig. 24.3). Radiators work more by convection than by radiation because they heat air with the radiator fins, and the air rises into the room, cools off, and then heats up and rises again in a continual cycle as hot water circulates through copper pipes inside the radiator. A boiler is efficient in its use of electricity as well. Furnaces use considerably more electricity to distribute their heat. Water can hold over 3,300 to 3,400 times more heat than can an equivalent volume of air at equal temperatures. Two basic types of radiators are used. One is the familiar under-the-window style modernized with an attractive grilled cover (Fig. 24.4), and the other is the low-profile baseboard radiator (Fig. 24.5). The disadvantages of the former are that they jut into a room and interfere with furniture placements and drapes. The baseboard system gives more outside wall coverage and efficiency. For these reasons, it's generally the favored of the two. The best baseboard models are the long, low kind about 6 to 10 inches high and up to 10 feet long and longer. They're often made with copper or aluminum heating fins. The most elite, quiet, and expensive baseboard units are the cast-iron ones.

When selecting a boiler, consider a high-efficiency low-mass model that will hold between 3 and 6 gallons (versus at least 10 or more gallons for high-mass units). The

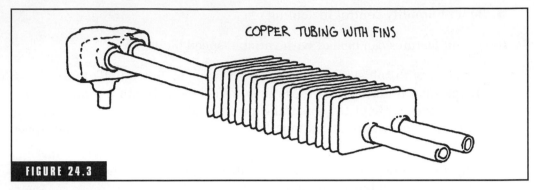

FIGURE 24.3

Hot-water radiator.

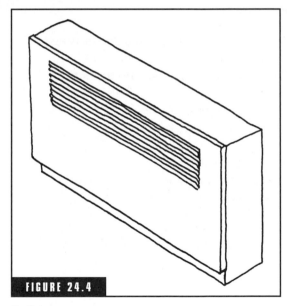

FIGURE 24.4

Radiator.

smaller unit will heat up quicker and supply hot water through the pipes sooner than will larger units, and less heat will be tied up in the water during times when the boiler is resting. In all cases, when considering and sizing any main heating or cooling power plant, make sure that your decision is made with the approval of a professional HVAC contractor.

Biomass boilers can burn wood, wood chips, corn, or switchgrass pellets or any burnable fuel that can be placed or fed into the boiler's combustion chamber—as long as it's approved by the boiler's manufacturer. Residential biomass boilers operate similar to those powered by natural gas or oil. If biomass fuels are readily available at reasonable cost, a biomass central boiler

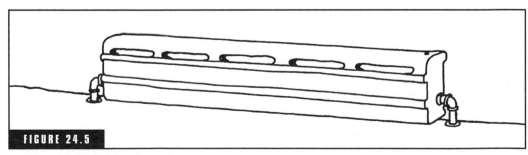

FIGURE 24.5

Cast-iron baseboard heating unit.

can be a less expensive heating option, especially if the home is rather small and well insulated.

Biodiesel fuel—heating oil blended with certain percentages of recycled vegetable oil or refined animal fats—also can be used to fuel boilers and furnaces. Biodiesel, although greener than many fossil fuels, can be more expensive and is not universally available just yet.

ADVANTAGES

1. Hot-water heat is a clean, effective, and fairly quiet way to heat a home (except for a little gurgling here and there). It requires very little energy to move water from a boiler.

2. Hot-water heating systems are adaptable to many of the more popular solar heating arrangements.

3. Hot-water heating can be zoned to allow you to maintain different temperatures throughout the various parts of your house.

4. Hot-water heat is a more even heat than the heat supplied by forced-air systems.

5. Hot-water gives a moist, warm heat that won't dry people or furnishings out.

6. Hot-water does not create or stir up dust, relieving allergies and easing home cleaning requirements.

DISADVANTAGES

1. Humidifiers, dehumidifiers, air cleaners, and air conditioners must be added as separate systems, thus incurring extra expense. There's also no duct work already in place to provide for the movement of air needed by such add-ons.

2. Hot-water units can be difficult to keep clean. The insides of the pipes can develop mineral deposits that reduce heating efficiency.

3. Some hot-water systems tend to rattle and clink when the heat goes on and off.

4. If a pipe breaks, a whole floor could get soaked.

5. The actual production of heat is not spontaneous; it takes time for the process to start up and become operational. The complete cycling of the water takes time initially compared with the immediacy of forced-air heat.

6. This type of heating system generally is more expensive than forced-air units to purchase and have installed.

7. Having to keep furniture away from the radiators can be annoying.

8. If a home with hot-water heat will be idle during periods of freezing temperatures, there's the possibility of frozen and broken pipes, or else the entire system might have to be winterized.

Hot-Water Heating Considerations

1. Look for a gas or oil high-tech hot-water boiler heating unit with direct venting for greatest efficiency.

2. If your home is in an area with frequent temperature swings, a two-stage low/high-output noncondensing gas boiler will allow for increased efficiency. When temperatures are extremely cold, the burner operates in the high-output mode. The rest of the time the boiler will run in low-output modes. This translates to less energy use and increased comfort.

3. A water-heater coil can be added to hot-water home heating systems to increase water-heating efficiency.

4. Try not to locate radiators on outer-wall sides of rooms; some of the heat invariably will be drawn outside, unless preventive layers of extra insulation and reflective membrane are installed.

5. If flat-against-the-wall radiators are used, wooden spacer blocks used to hang them can help to increase their effective heated air flow.

6. Dust on radiators or baseboard units acts as insulation and wastes heat. These components must be accessible to be kept clean in order to operate efficiently.

7. All pipes leading to and from a boiler should be insulated.

8. Within a room or area, a series of small radiators or heaters can supply more comfortable heating patterns than can one large radiator.

9. Programmable thermostats should be installed on and used to control each heating zone.

Radiant Floor Heating Systems

Radiant floor heating can provide a cost-effective, quiet, gentle heat, with delivery by warm-water piping or electric wiring floor panels or mats. If you're serious about investigating radiant floor heating possibilities, consider meeting with contractors experienced in their installation. There are numerous flooring situations for which this type of heating will work, but the components must be customized and installed to suit the type of floor planned. For instance, hydronic (liquid) hot-water piping systems use small-diameter piping laid within the floor in "wet" installations, where the tubing is embedded in a concrete foundation slab, over a previously poured slab, or even within a relatively thin thickness of concrete that's been poured over the top of a subfloor. Special narrow-diameter cross-linked polyethylene (PEX) piping is easily embedded in poured concrete floors and lined beneath other floors. Ceramic tile typically has been the floor covering of choice for radiant heating, but this has been changing lately as radiant floor heating options expand. "Dry" installations still involve tubing, but the tubing is either suspended beneath the subfloor, is laid between two subfloor layers, or is actually built into a sandwich-style subfloor.

This form of home heating has seen considerable innovation recently, so do a last-minute check on what's available before making a decision. Some new installations are being paired up with solar water heating and geothermal systems that supply efficient sources of hot water. In any case, the piping or tubing holds hot or warm water heated by a gas, oil, or similarly fired boiler and/or a circulation pump (or geothermal or solar heat pump) that circulates the water to heat the flooring. Solar water-heating systems also may supply enough preheated or heated water to run radiant floor applications. A manifold of valves controls the water distribution, and a thermostat controls the temperature—some control the temperature of water in a boiler, whereas others may control the room temperature. Another alternative for smaller homes or homes in locales with low heating demands is simply to use a standard water heater/tank to supply the radiant floor heating. Water piping systems may cost a bit more to install, but they're very efficient.

Carpet, tile, vinyl, and engineered-wood flooring types all can be positioned over the hot-water piping that's typically installed in a masonry floor by a plumber or HVAC contractor. Electric panel elements provide another option for radiant floor heating. They're relatively inexpensive to install but may cost more to operate, especially if reduced off-peak energy rates are not available from the local electric utility company.

As comfortable as radiant floor heating is, it may not be your best option. Unless sustainable solar or geothermal systems can supply preheated or heated water, radiant floor heating systems are only about as energy efficient as other hydronic radiant heating systems using boilers or heat pumps. If lots of heat is constantly needed to warm a home, then radiant floor heating may be a good choice. But if a well-constructed green home is designed and constructed to require only small amounts of space heating, then radiant floor heating might be too much of a good thing. Why install a rather expensive heating system to supply only small amounts of heat? Also, the slow response or time lag of radiant floor heat can result in far too much heat given off for what's needed. Quick adjustments to heat delivery rates are not able to be made at the thermostat—as they are with forced-air systems. The time frames between when the floor begins to heat up, heats up, starts and continues to deliver heat, then stops and cools down are all fairly long and must be planned for considerably in advance of when needed. In other words, you can't quickly turn on, adjust, and turn off the heat. There's a learning curve required to control the system to prevent under- or overheating scenarios.

ADVANTAGES

1. Radiant heat is quiet, even, and comfortable.

2. It's clean, and there's no dust generation.

3. Radiant heat does not dry out the air, there are no drafts, and there is less outside-air infiltration.

4. It's invisible, blending nicely into the home's structure, with no bulky ductwork or registers.

5. It's a safe heat, with no or very few moving parts.

6. It's energy efficient in that a radiant floor system is fairly easy to split into separate individually controlled heating zones and because it lends itself nicely to solar and geothermal water systems.

7. It warms from the floor up and feels great on the feet.

DISADVANTAGES

1. Maintenance on the piping or electrical panels can be costly.

2. Water damage from leaking pipes or tubing is always a possibility.

3. A separate system is usually needed for cooled-air delivery.

4. It's not as responsive as other forms of heat; it takes a long time for a floor to heat up.

5. Electric heating can be relatively costly unless the electric company offers off-peak rates when radiant floors can be heated up or "recharged" at night.

RADIANT FLOOR HEATING CONSIDERATIONS

1. Recent innovations in concrete and other masonry flooring make suitable matches with radiant floor heating. Consider that contractors specializing in custom-concrete countertops, tabletops, and other furniture and furnishing innovations are rapidly becoming more available to general contractors, architects, and the housing industry in general.

2. Laminated wood flooring is often preferred over solid wood, which reduces the possibility of wood shrinking and cracking.

3. Early versions of radiant floor heating systems often failed owing to leaky tubes caused by corrosion from chemical reactions that took place between the metal piping and the concrete. Now plastic, ceramic-coated, rubber, copper, and other noncorrosive tubing is in use by most manufacturers.

Electric-Resistance Systems: Electrical Heating Units

Another popular but less used heating system than forced air and hot water is electrical. Straight electrical heating systems use electricity directly as a heat source. In essence, electricity is converted to heat when it moves through conductors that resist the flow of current. The conductors or heating elements become hot and give off heat. The heat is then typically distributed via baseboard heaters that come in a wide range of sizes (Fig. 24.6) with different output ratings so that they can be used for general heating or for supplementary purposes.

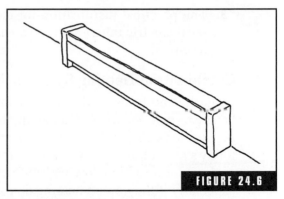

FIGURE 24.6

Electric baseboard heating unit.

ADVANTAGES

1. An electric heating system is one of the simplest and least-expensive heating systems to install. There's no ductwork, plumbing, or expensive furnace or boiler needed.

2. It's an unobtrusive and practically silent heat.

3. Depending on the circumstances—where and how it's used—electric heat can be very cost-efficient. Each room can have its own control, permitting variations in the amount of heat provided. If these controls are used judiciously, the cost of operation can be quite low.

4. Maintenance is practically nonexistent. There's no furnace or boiler to service, repair, or replace.

5. Electric heating units offer the cleanest heat available.

6. Because no fuel is burned, there's no need for a chimney.

7. Electric heat is adaptable to wind and other locally powered electrical sources.

DISADVANTAGES

1. Electric heat is a very dry heat. Humidification is usually necessary during times of low humidity.

2. Sometimes electrical heating element surfaces get hot enough to pose a danger to young children.

3. The practical justification for electric heat can depend heavily on what the local electric rates are in the area and how they compare with other fuels economically.

Combination Heating Systems: Heat Pumps

Earlier editions of this book contained brief discussions about heat pumps because years ago the verdict on them was still out. Now the verdict is in, and heat pumps certainly are heating and cooling systems that are making a difference in today's green homes. Just ask your local electric company. They provide effective options for any home owner who chooses electricity to power a heating system, especially if the home's heating demands are too great to be met by less expensive electric-resistance systems.

In essence, there are two basic types of heat pumps: air-to-air (or air-source) and geothermal (ground-source) heat pumps. They collect heat from the air, ground, or water outside the home and concentrate it for use inside. They both also function as central air conditioners, cooling by collecting heat inside the house and then effectively pumping it outdoors.

AIR-SOURCE HEAT PUMPS

These units (Figs. 24.7 and 24.8) employ air to store and deliver both heat and coolness, depending on which is needed at the time. The most common is the

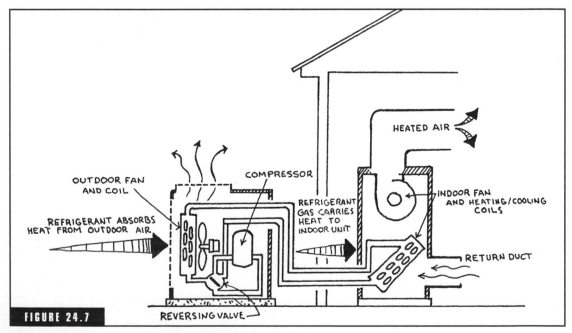

FIGURE 24.7

Air-source heat pump system, winter mode.

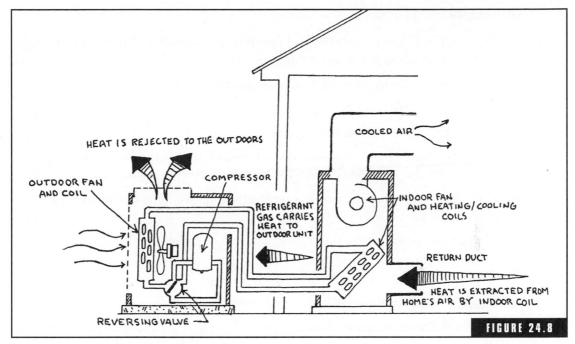

HEAT IS REJECTED TO THE OUTDOORS

COOLED AIR

OUTDOOR FAN
AND COIL

COMPRESSOR

REFRIGERANT
GAS CARRIES
HEAT TO
OUTDOOR UNIT

INDOOR FAN
AND HEATING/COOLING
COILS

RETURN DUCT

HEAT IS EXTRACTED FROM
HOME'S AIR BY INDOOR COIL

REVERSING VALVE

FIGURE 24.8

Air-source heat pump system, summer mode.

split-system heat pump. The main compressor, fan, and heat-exchanger coil are located outdoors in a unit that looks like a central air-conditioning compressor. Another fan and heat-exchanger coil are located inside the house within a unit that resembles a furnace.

In simple terms, an air-source heat pump heats the home during times of cool or cold outdoor temperatures by pumping refrigerant through a tubing or piping system that absorbs heat from the outside air (believe it or not, there is heat available to be drawn from cold air) and carries the heat into a coil within the indoor unit, where a blower forces the heated air through ducts to various rooms. Because heat can be drawn from outside air only when that air is warmer than between about 30 to 40°F, when temperatures fall much below freezing, a backup electric strip-heating system kicks in to help deliver heat throughout the home. Consequently, air-source heat pumps are better suited to milder climates where electric-resistance heat won't be needed often. During times of warm or hot outdoor temperatures, the heat pump refrigerant absorbs heat from the air inside the house and then pumps it through the outside tubing or piping, where the heat is released outside the home.

Advantages

1. One unit can provide year-round comfort, with heating during cold weather and cooling when hot temperatures persist.

2. Air-source units are less expensive to install than ground-source units.

3. The units are fairly quiet.

4. There are no fuel delivery problems.

5. The units operate cleanly—no ash, smoke, or soot is created. The walls, furniture, and draperies stay clean longer.

6. Units are safe—no flames, no combustible gases, no storage of flammable fuels, no flue.

7. There is no worry about the future availability of heating fuels.

Disadvantages

1. Supplemental heating will be needed in areas with extreme cold temperatures.

2. Air-source heat pumps are less energy efficient that ground-source heat pumps.

Air-Source Heat Pump Considerations

1. Look for two-level output capability: either two separate compressors (a large and small one) or a single two-speed compressor, both with variable-speed blowers. With two-level output, each setting can be tuned to run at the most efficient speed. The low-output level will be run most of the time and will switch to the higher level during very cold or hot weather.

2. Also look for external fittings installed in a totally sealed manner to prevent system leaks.

3. To reduce compressor operating sounds, a well-insulated compressor compartment is necessary.

4. Air filters should be located within the return air duct or at the indoor section of the system.

GEOTHERMAL OR GROUND-SOURCE HEAT PUMPS

Geothermal units take advantage of the earth's relatively constant ground temperature to provide very efficient heating and cooling in any season. These are also referred to as *ground-source* or *water-source pumps*. After all, the earth is like a huge solar sponge, soaking up energy from the sun and holding it about 6 feet below the surface, where the soil's temperature is between 50 and 55°F. Instead of burning natural gas or oil to provide space heating, geothermal ground-source heat pumps require relatively small amounts of electricity to run their compressors. Thanks to the ability of the ground to absorb or give off heat at a steady, dependable rate, that heat can be moved or transferred in either direction—into or from the ground—by means of liquid-filled coils depending on the relative temperature inside the home, where a temperature modification is desired. Thus geothermal heat pumps, via heat-transfer solutions (antifreeze-type liquids or refrigerants in climates where freezing temperatures persist) traveling through horizontal loops of piping buried 6 to 8 feet underground use the natural thermal mass of the earth to withdraw heat during cold weather and to transfer heat into during hot weather. If a site does not have enough room for large horizontal loops to be installed, the piping loop(s) can be installed vertically—after a rather expensive drilling process is completed—for similar results. Ground-source heat pumps can be between 30 and 40 percent more efficient than the more commonly found air-source heat pumps mainly because rapidly changing air temperatures outdoors rarely provide a dependable source of accessible heat. When compared with electric air-conditioning systems, geothermal heat pumps can save as much as 70 percent for equal amounts of conditioning. A comparison with gas furnaces finds the geothermal heat pump up to 50 percent more efficient.

Geothermal heat pump systems are essentially made of two main components:

1. The indoor unit has a compressor to circulate refrigerant, an evaporator coil to provide heat exchange between the heat-transfer solution and refrigerant, a reversing valve to "switch gears" from heating to cooling or cooling to heating, and a blower fan to send warm or cool air through the household.

2. The underground heat-exchanger piping that's run underground allows the heat-transfer solution to collect heat from the ground during winter and disburse home-captured heat to the ground during summer. The term *geothermal* also can include water in its process. Heat can be absorbed from the air in the home during summer and then "dumped" into the cooler water or a pond, river, lake, or well instead of the ground.

A geothermal heat pump does not create heat; rather, it just moves heat from inside out or outside in with continuous cycles that include evaporation, compression, condensation, and expansion. For both situations, the heat pump uses the difference in temperatures to its advantage as it pumps and pressurizes the refrigerant liquid in a sealed system, further increasing or decreasing desired temperatures. In moderate climates, a backup electric-resistance heating system or a warm-air furnace may not be needed. However, in extreme climates, such a backup system should be in place.

■ With auxiliary electric-resistance heat, consider getting a "smart" controller that monitors the home's temperature level and brings up just enough resistance heat, in small stages, to raise the outlet air temperature as needed.

■ When a warm-air furnace is the backup, electronic controls choose between the operation of the heat pump or the furnace depending on the weather. As the outside temperature drops, the heat pump becomes less efficient (it's harder to draw heat out of colder air). When the outside temperature drops to the point where it's no longer economical to run the heat pump, the controls automatically switch the heat pump off and turn the furnace on. In this way, the heat pump and furnace operate at maximum efficiency. Installation of this system costs more than a typical heating system, but it's very efficient and results in very low energy usage.

There are two basic types of piping delivery/collection systems: closed end and open end. A closed-end system uses a solution of water and antifreeze that circulates (is pumped) through a closed ground loop of pressurized piping that's connected to the indoor heat pump. The earth has the ability to store heat energy. To use this stored energy, heat is extracted from the earth through the liquid antifreeze solution and is pumped to the heat pump or heat exchanger. There, the heat is used to heat the home. In the summer, the process is reversed. Indoor heat is extracted from within the home and then transferred back to the soil, where it dissipates. The ground pipes typically are buried in narrow trenches 6 to 8 feet deep. In a small yard, the pipes can be placed in vertical holes drilled deep into the ground. To save the possibility of expensive repairs later on, make sure that the installing contractor pressure tests the piping loop before covering up the trenches (Fig. 24.9).

The other option exists for home owners with access to a pond or well—an open-end system for drawing water from a well, lake, or pond and using it as a heat-transfer solution. Since groundwater is at a relatively constant temperature year round, it provides a good heat source. First, however, because of strict water usage regulations, check local and state laws, ordinances, codes, covenants, and/or licensing requirements to see whether a geothermal heat pump is even an option. Also understand the quality of the water that will be used. It should be tested for hardness, acidity, and iron content before the heat pump is installed. Unacceptable water quality can cause mineral deposits to build up inside the piping and related components, which could clog the system and make it inoperable within a relatively short time (Fig. 24.10).

The installation of geothermal units should be completed only by experienced contractors who know how local building codes apply, who know exactly what to do, and who supply the home owner with accurate, detailed records of the heat-exchanger piping arrangement and location. Such information will be necessary for any future construction or maintenance required by the system.

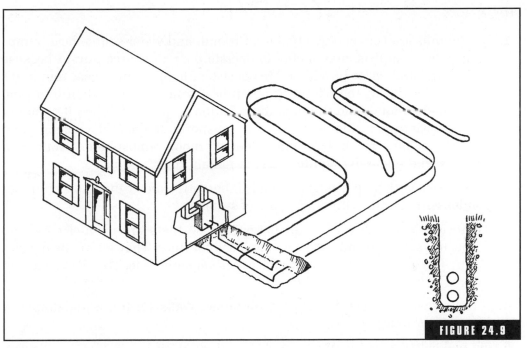

Closed-end geothermal heat pump system.

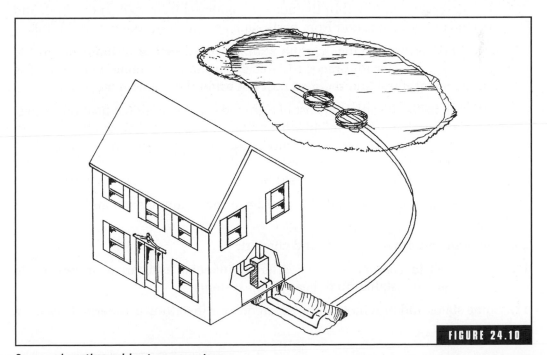

Open-end geothermal heat pump system.

ADVANTAGES

1. These units are very energy efficient. Ground- and water-source heat pumps require less supplemental energy to operate than air-source pumps because the ground and water provide more consistent temperatures year round. It's much easier during the winter to pump heat from 55°F soil than it is from frigid outdoor air. In the summer, the situation is reversed, when it's simpler to draw heat from inside the house and transport it to the 55°F cooler ground than to, for instance, a 92°F, moist, midafternoon atmosphere. Geothermal systems lend themselves quite nicely to radiant floor heating.

2. The closed earth loop piping system is inherently quieter than noisy outdoor condenser fan units with other types of systems.

3. There is added safety with geothermal units—there are no fuel tanks, no flame, no fumes, no emissions, and no need for flues. They eliminate dangerous by-products of combustion, such as carbon monoxide. This also results in improved household air quality.

4. A clean energy source—no ash, soot, or fumes. Walls, furniture, and draperies stay cleaner longer.

5. No fuel delivery problems.

6. The geothermal unit within the home is sheltered from rain, snow, hail, and extreme temperatures and from pests such as squirrels, rodents, and birds.

7. Additional energy savings can be realized by diverting indoor heat to the home's water heater for practically free hot water all summer and for adding supplementary heat and reduced-cost hot water during winter.

8. Although initial installation cost of a ground- or water-source heat pump system is higher than that of many other systems, when comparing all fuel types, these heat pumps are among the most economical heating and cooling alternatives available today. Such a system, with its low energy consumption, will be an attractive feature for buyers if the home is ever put on the market.

9. Geothermal systems are reliable and have low maintenance and a long life span.

10. One unit can provide year-round comfort.

11. Some electric companies have offered financial assistance or rebates to encourage the installation of heat-pump systems.

12. Some states and provinces have tax credits for installing geothermal systems.

DISADVANTAGES

1. Supplemental heating may be required in areas of extreme cold temperatures.

2. Initial installation costs probably will be higher than those of other heating/cooling systems.

GEOTHERMAL HEAT PUMP CONSIDERATIONS

1. Cabinet and compressor compartments should be insulated for noise control.

2. Look for two-level heat-pump output capability and a variable-speed blower.

3. Consider purchasing an optional water heater that can be used for heating the house water with the heat pump. Some manufacturers offer a hot-water desuperheater that produces hot water for household use whenever the unit runs in the cooling mode.

4. Another option is the space-heating-priority water-heating system. If both the house and water-heating tank need heat, the heat pump first kicks in to take care of the home heating system and then to take care of the water heater.

5. Check out the warranty on the system's underground piping. Naturally, the longer the warranty, the better. Fifty years is not unheard of.

Combination Heating Systems: Electric Thermal Storage Units

An electric thermal heating system can be an excellent solution for new homes, can meet the requirements of hard-to-heat rooms, and can be easily added at a later date for additions to home living spaces or basements. These units employ electricity to create heat and store it in ceramic bricks, crushed rock, or water for later use (Fig. 24.11). If the home owner's electric utility company offers lower rates for consuming electricity during off-peak hours, this type of heating system can have considerable cost advantages.

Electric thermal heating systems come in central heating systems and individual room systems. These heating units create enough heat to warm the home immediately at night and heat their storage medium (e.g., ceramic bricks, crushed rock, or water) during off-peak hours when electrical demand is least (and less costly), typically late at night. Then, during peak electrical usage times, typically during the day and early evening, the heating elements are automatically turned off or down while the stored heat is released to warm the household. It's a great way to use electricity late at night when it's less expensive and convert the energy into heat and store the heat for later use.

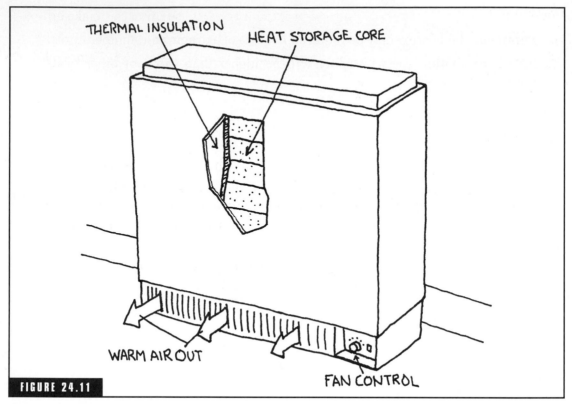

THERMAL INSULATION   HEAT STORAGE CORE

WARM AIR OUT

FAN CONTROL

FIGURE 24.11

Electric thermal heating system.

Various types of electric thermal storage heat delivery systems are available:

- Forced-air systems
- Radiant baseboard hot water
- Radiant/convection room heaters

ADVANTAGES

1. Units operate fairly quietly.
2. Units are dependable, the heating elements have no moving parts, which means long life.
3. Units are located indoors out of the weather.
4. No fuel delivery problems.
5. The units operate cleanly; no ash, smoke, or soot is created. The walls, furniture, and draperies stay clean longer.

6. If the electric utility offers low off-peak hour rates, these units can make efficient use of electricity.

7. Units are safe—no flames, no combustible gases, no storage of flammable fuels, and no flue.

8. No worry about the future availability of heating fuels.

DISADVANTAGES

1. If individual room units are used, and their placement in rooms will take up wall space.

2. These units are designed for heating only; cooling would involve separate equipment.

ELECTRIC THERMAL STORAGE UNIT CONSIDERATIONS

An option in some units, when stored radiant heat isn't enough to keep the room temperature at the desired thermostat setting, is a quiet fan that circulates air through the core of heated medium and warms the spaces by convection.

Solar Heating Systems

PASSIVE-SOLAR DESIGN

Passive-solar design—taking advantage of existing sunlight and, as much as possible, prevailing winds—begins with careful and deliberate planning. In fact, planning for a passive-solar home often requires more design expertise and cost than does planning for a conventional dwelling. Experienced professional solar home designers use computer modeling programs and proven guidelines to ensure a high-performance dwelling. The designer reviews and enters data into interactive software about the home's geographic location, possible orientations, square footage, proposed heating and cooling systems, window placements and sizes, window glazing types, overhang dimensions, floor plan configurations, and other related information. What's critical to the success of a passive-solar home is how the various green features work together. Optimal sizing is important; no component should be too small or too large. The insulation package, the home's orientation, the floor plan traffic and zoning setup, the windows, the HVAC systems, and related options all need to function as a single unit, complementing one another with their individual operations. Such efforts are usually rewarded with comfortable homes that not only save money on energy but also are less expensive to build because they can be heated, cooled, and ventilated with smaller and simpler HVAC systems.

Total passive-solar heating means that once the home is built, it is thereafter heated and sometimes cooled without using mechanical devices such as furnaces or boilers or nonrenewable fossil fuels. Instead, the sun supplies most of the power. That solar power is captured as heat energy within the home and later gets released slowly into the living areas. The DOE points out that passive-solar homes share five fundamental components for effective heating designs, and all five must be closely interrelated with each other to result in an effective heating system.

1. There needs to be apertures or collectors, typically large glazing surfaces through which sunlight enters the home. Thanks to low-emissivity (low-e) coatings on high-efficiency windows, greater window areas now can be planned without having large amounts of heat loss at night. For greatest efficiency, the aperture should face within 30 degrees of true south and should have full access to the sun from 9 a.m. to 3 p.m. during all days in the home heating season. For all-around positioning of glazing surfaces, see Chapter 18 on windows. In general, though, east- and west-side windows usually should be designed to block or screen solar heat gain, with lower solar heat-gain coefficients. For the south side, typically windows with higher solar heat-gain coefficients work best.

2. An absorber must be in place to accept available solar heat—an exposed heat-collecting structure such as a masonry wall, tile floor, tank of water, or similar component located in the direct sunlight.

3. There must be a component with thermal mass. This component or material is not necessarily exposed to direct sunlight but is used as a heat sink for the heat that is accepted by the absorber. The thermal mass component is what stores the heat after the heat is gained through the absorber and actually can be attached to or a large part of the absorber. This works great during spring, fall, and winter, but throughout summer cooling seasons, this same thermal mass is best screened or shaded from the sun to prevent uncomfortable amounts of heat gain from entering the home. Climates where passive thermal mass heating excels are either cold and sunny, or the days are hot and sunny and the nights are cool to cold.

4. There must be a means of distribution, or a way to move the heat from storage to living spaces. Passive-solar heat systems rely only on natural heat-transfer methods: conduction, convection, and radiation. Steps beyond these methods also can include the use of fans, ducts, and blowers.

5. Controls must be present that prevent the gain of unwanted heat, including landscaping, roof overhangs, low-e windows, vents, blinds, shades, and awnings.

In addition to individual windows positioned for heat gain, common passive-solar heating designs include systems for direct heat gain, for thermal storage walls or floors, and for rooms called *sunspaces*. Direct-gain systems offer the simplest and least expensive methods of passive-solar heating. They operate by enabling sunlight to warm a home's interior atmosphere, surfaces, and furnishings whenever the sun is shining. By design, available sunlight will reach indoors where and when it's needed, most often at low angles through carefully placed windows, clerestories, and skylights.

The lightest-duty direct-gain passive-solar system design is seen when one of the home's longer walls faces south for maximum positioning of sun-gathering windows, but no other arrangements are made for thermal mass storage or warmed-air circulation. This type of home orientation can be referred to as sun tempering. At the same time, strong overhead sunshine is blocked or screened out to avoid summer overheating.

Fully planned passive-solar direct-gain systems are much more effective. When planned correctly, such systems allow healthy quantities of heat to be absorbed by a home's inside walls, floors, and furnishings and then slowly released at night to reduce supplemental space heating demand. Selection of high-mass wall and floor coverings such as tile, brick, concrete, plaster, and dry wall, as well as dark-colored furnishings, helps to increase this free collection and distribution of solar heat owing to their excellent heat-absorbing qualities. Care must be taken not to oversize the solar components: Too many south-facing windows and too much high-mass floor and wall thermal mass easily can overwhelm a home with heat, as occurred in many of the early passive-solar homes built decades ago, before more reasonable window-to-floor-space ratios were established. Sometimes temporary shading with overhangs, screens, portable insulation panels, foliage, trellises and louvers must be used during summer weather.

Although direct-gain passive-solar systems are simple to maintain and require no special air-handling equipment or fans, upfront consideration must be given to how the sun "travels" around the home at different times of the day and the seasons to arrive at an effective, comfortable overall design.

The construction of thermal storage walls within the home is another way to provide passive-solar heating capability. A stone, brick, concrete, narrow-water-tank, or other high-mass wall (sometimes referred to as a *Trombe wall*, named after a French engineer) is built closely parallel to a south-facing similarly sized exterior window or glass panel that allows easy heat gain from outside. Sunlight passes through the glass and heats the wall. As enough heat is absorbed to slowly pass through the wall, the heat slowly begins to be given off into living spaces. The heated wall will continue to deliver its warmth throughout the night, making heat available when direct-gain solar heat is no longer accessible. Vents generally are included in the wall with one-way flaps that prevent convection at night and also remain closed during summer when additional heat is not desired. Although during normal operation some heat is lost back through the glass to the outdoors, the amounts are minimized thanks to heat-blocking low-e coatings on the glass that enable heat gain to enter while preventing absorbed heat from passing back from indoors to outside. Some Trombe walls also incorporate windows for additional natural lighting. The indoor sides of these walls can be finished with any high-mass masonry material such as stucco, tile, or even drywall or plaster.

Another type of passive-solar design results in the sunspace—an individual room built on the south side of a home, constructed with a high percentage of windows or fixed glass panes. The sunspace is somewhat insulated from the rest of the home; the wall it shares with the rest of the home has its own door or doors to the sunspace, as well as operating windows and vents. The end result is a sunroom that can be shut off from the rest of the home and can be used to heat air, walls, floor, and furnishings by sunshine. When the heat is needed during the day or later at night, the door(s) and windows to the adjacent living areas are opened, and the warm air circulates into the home or is moved by fans through vents or ductwork. The same sunspace room also can be used in reverse, to access cooler evening air, which then can help to cool down living spaces when needed. Sunspaces are sometimes called *isolated-gain systems* owing to their ability to be shut off from the rest of the home.

ACTIVE-SOLAR SPACE HEATING

A solar heating system that uses the sun for a primary energy source typically includes four major components:

1. Collectors to harvest sunlight and convert radiant energy to thermal energy.

2. A storage medium that can hold enough heat to last through a night or through periods of cloudy weather.

3. A distribution system to convey the heat to points of use.

4. A backup system that will take over when stored solar heat is exhausted because the sun has not been cooperating.

5. Typical active-solar space-heating systems are expected to supply only a portion, often about half, of a home's living area heat during the coldest months of the year. The collector is often a heat-absorbing metal plate with an array of tubing that can be an integral part of the plate or merely bonded to it. Usually this assembly is in a black frame with a layer of insulation at the back and a glass- or plastic-covered airspace on the surface that should face the sun. As long as the heat collectors have an unobstructed southern exposure, collection will occur year round, regardless of outside temperatures.

The heat transfer is made through liquid or air that passes through the collector, picks up heat, transports it to storage, and later distributes it throughout the house. Of course, an alternate way of heating water or air is required at night or during the day when not enough sunshine is available.

Solar-heated water can supply radiant floor heat by circulating through tubes under tile, concrete, bamboo, composite, or other flooring. Other than the pump that circulates the water or coolant, solar water-heating systems don't need much maintenance, although protection from subfreezing temperatures must be provided during winter weather if water is the collection agent within the outside piping.

Solar-heated air thermosiphoning panels constructed of materials such as glass, corrugated metal sheets, airspaces, and other components within a wood or other case can be integrated into an outside wall and use either natural convection processes to move warm air into the home or are fitted with small electric fans that circulate the heated air in an even manner. Simply, the sun's rays strike the collector's outside surface, which is often covered by a heat-absorbing dark glass; then heated air enters the home through top vents in the wall panel, and cooler air is siphoned out of the home through bottom, floor-level vents in the wall panel. Larger collectors, of course, will provide greater quantities of heat, and the panels using fans or small blower systems provide the most effective distribution of heat. This system works fine when heat is needed, during times of cool and cold weather, but during summer—when additional heat gain is not desired, wall units must be taken offline, and in cases where they stand alone without fans or blower systems, they must be protected or shaded temporarily so that they won't overheat and send unwanted hot air indoors.

Radiant floor heating systems that use copper or plastic piping to circulate heat from the collectors are excellent setups to provide welcome warmth to kitchens, bathrooms, and other spaces.

SPACE HEATERS

Fireplaces

The first fireplaces were logical extensions of an open campfire—functional features that were designed to provide heat, illumination, and a way to cook foods in early dwellings. They were originally a necessity in all but the warmest climates and supplied home owners with basic needs for centuries.

Then, rather quickly, other mechanisms were invented that more efficiently heated our houses, illuminated our rooms, and cooked our foods. Consequently, fireplaces lost some of their functional value and became more decorative options than necessities. They still, however, remained a part of our houses for the atmosphere they created and the warmth that home owners appreciated on cold winter evenings. Once the energy crunch hit, however, fireplaces were accused of being the energy-wasters they really were and fell further out of favor.

Not to be upstaged, hundreds of large and small companies set out to modify the standard fireplace into units that, through various add-on tubes, gadgets, and heat exchangers, would burn fuel much more efficiently. Therefore, today's fireplaces can be divided into two main types: those used primarily to heat a room, area, or an entire house and those used primarily as decoration or novelty. Even with continuing concerns for energy usage, the latter models—the fireplaces installed for decoration and atmosphere—are still the most popular. They're included in modern homes because of what they add to a room in ways that excite our senses of sight, sound, and smell. They're a bit of the past to which we still cling.

Any fireplace should at least do five things:

1. Permit combustion of fuel.
2. Exhaust the by-products of combustion from the house.
2. Deliver as much heat as possible into the house.
3. Function safely.
4. Be located so that people sitting in all areas of a room can enjoy it. In a long, narrow room, for example, it's better to plan a fireplace on one of the long side walls than on a short end wall. Because people tend to cluster around a fireplace, if it's located at one of the short walls at the end of a long room, the opposite end of the room (without a fireplace) likely would go completely unused.

ADVANTAGES

1. Fireplaces can provide additional heat.
2. They can provide *all* the necessary heat in mild-climate locations.
3. They enhance the appearance and comfort of any room in any house in any climate.
4. They provide a traditionally romantic and reassuring atmosphere.
5. They can burn as fuel certain combustible materials that otherwise would be wasted, such as coke, briquettes, and scrap lumber.

DISADVANTAGES

1. A major concern with a typical fireplace is that it uses substantially more air than needed for combustion. The room air used for fireplace combustion has already been heated by the primary heating system, and much of it is ultimately lost up the chimney. Rather than assisting the primary system in its heating function, the fireplace can interfere with its operation and usually increases the workload of the primary system. As much as 80 percent of the heat produced by a wood fireplace can dissipate up and out the chimney. To address this concept further, you can review the Fireplace Energy Efficiency points toward the end of this chapter.

2. A fireplace heats by radiation only. Much of the air that comes into contact with the hottest surface of the fireplace ends up outdoors.

3. Some warm air from the house will go up the chimney even when a fire is not lit and the damper is closed.

4. Because brick and stone are poor insulators, a fireplace and chimney can create a thermal opening in the wall of a dwelling if it is located somewhere in the building's outer shell.

5. A fireplace adds to the cost of a new house.

6. When positioned within a building, a fireplace occupies valuable floor and wall space.

7. When positioned in an exterior wall, a fireplace can occupy scarce land.

8. A fireplace requires periodic maintenance and occasionally the services of professional chimney cleaners.

9. Fireplaces can be messy. Storage space for wood and other fuel is needed, and so are places to keep dirty fireplace tools such as pokers, tongs, and shovels.

10. Fireplaces can be dangerous when incorrectly built, installed, or used. They can be hazardous when small children have free rein throughout the house.

Types of Fireplaces

With the development of modern manufacturing processes, materials other than traditional stone and brick have been made available for fireplace construction. Today, there are numerous fireplace designs that come ready-made or can be custom-built to suit any application.

MASONRY FIREPLACES

These are the original models that are still popular today. They consist of a stone or brick exterior having a lining of fire-brick—a brick that can stand the high temperatures encountered when wood or other fuels are burned. Of course, built into the masonry are various operating accessories such as grates to hold the wood while it's being burned and dampers to regulate the amount of airflow through the chimney passages (Fig. 24.12).

There are several basic masonry fireplace designs, including fireplaces with a single opening constructed against a single

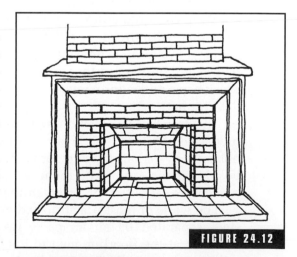

FIGURE 24.12

An all-masonry fireplace.

wall (the most popular); fireplaces constructed into a wall that divides two rooms so that the fireplace has two openings, one per each of the back-to-back rooms; fireplaces built into an outside corner, open to two sides; and even circular fireplaces of brick and stone having sheet metal chimneys suspended from the ceiling that flare out over the round firebox like an inverted funnel.

Because these masonry units must be built from scratch on the building site, the labor construction costs of masonry fireplaces are high. Once a masonry fireplace is up, however, its maintenance expenses and efforts are minimal. The beauty, durability, and reputation of its brick or stonework can enhance the overall appearance of a house's interior and exterior and will increase the home's salability and value.

Stone generally costs more than brick and requires a higher degree of skill on the mason's part. If you opt for an all masonry fireplace, make sure that whoever will be putting it up has had experience completing others as well. There are many tricky steps to masonry fireplace construction, and unless they're all done exactly correctly, they can cause serious structural and safety defects that may appear years later. All-masonry fireplaces, because of their weight, require at least an 8-inch-thick concrete footer for adequate support.

MASONRY AND STEEL-BOX FIREPLACES

This type is similar to the all-masonry fireplace except that the firebox, or where the fuel is burned, is prefabricated of steel instead of being constructed from firebrick. The rest of the fireplace is all masonry. Masonry and steel-box fireplaces are less costly than all-masonry units, and they still retain a handsome appearance and low-maintenance characteristics (Fig. 24.13).

CIRCULATING FIREPLACES

A typical circulating fireplace consists of a specially designed prefabricated steel shell with firebox and damper. It greatly simplifies construction because all a mason has to do is build the foundation and hearth, set the prefabricated fireplace shell on the hearth, and lay finishing bricks or stones up around the shell. The shape and approximate exterior dimensions of the fireplace are already determined.

The prefabricated shell more than makes up for its restricted authenticity with increased efficiency. The real advantage of a circulating fireplace is that it heats not only by radiation (as a conventional fireplace does) but also by circulating heated air directly into a room or adjacent area. As a result, it provides almost twice the heat output of a conventional fireplace.

The walls of most prefabricated circulating fireplaces consist of two layers of steel separated by an airspace. Cool air enters the airspace through grilles installed at the floorline next to the fireplace. As air passes through the bottom grilles and moves between the hot layers of steel, it gets heated and then expelled

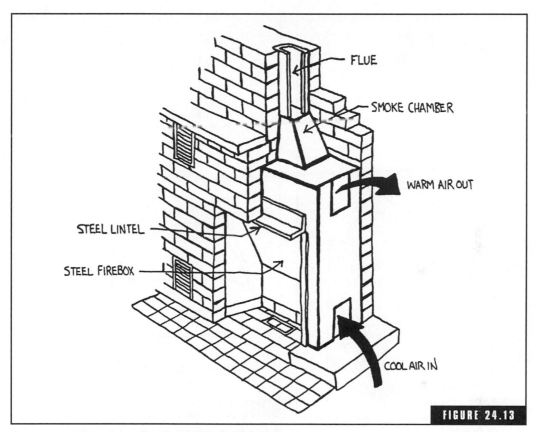

A masonry and steel-box fireplace with circulator vents.

through other grilles installed near the top of the firebox or high in the wall. To encourage constant air movement and an even amount of heat, manufacturers offer air inlets containing electric fans. Fans also can be used with the warm-air outlets placed in adjacent rooms. The chimney may be of conventional masonry construction or made of prefabricated steel.

PREFABRICATED BUILT-IN FIREPLACES

This type of fireplace not only reduces construction costs but makes it possible to install a traditional design almost anywhere in an existing house. The prefabricated built-in fireplace consists of a steel firebox complete with hearth, damper, and a prefabricated chimney as well. Prefabricated built-in fireplaces are made with either one opening in the front or with one front and one side opening. Most are constructed with close clearances. The manufacturer should detail the necessary clearances and proper floor construction required. Choose a unit that bears the Underwriters Laboratories label, and check what clearances your building code specifies (Fig. 24.14).

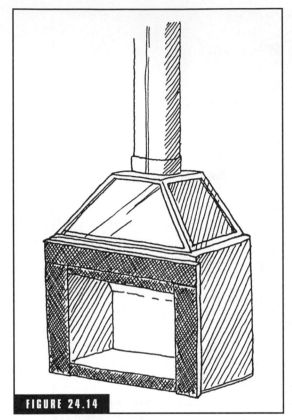

FIGURE 24.14

A prefabricated fireplace.

FIGURE 24.15

A freestanding fireplace.

Another advantage to the prefabs is that they don't weigh much, so there's no need to place them on an elaborate and expensive masonry foundation. Instead, they can be set directly on a noncombustible floor, and a fire-resistant forehearth can be integrated into the finished flooring directly in front of the fireplace's main opening.

FREESTANDING FIREPLACES

Freestanding fireplaces are the least-expensive fireplaces and the easiest to install. All it takes to erect one is to set it in position and run a flue through the roof or the nearest exterior wall. Freestanding units are usually made of steel or cast iron and come in a variety of designs and shapes—round, square, hexagonal, egg-shaped, and even triangular. They're typically finished in bright porcelains or enamels of red, green, yellow, black, white, and other tones. They're modern looking but give off plenty of old-fashioned heat because the sheet metal chimney, in addition to the firebox, also gives off radiant heat directly into the room (Fig. 24.15).

These fireplaces can be placed right against unpainted masonry walls, but if a wall is constructed or surfaced with combustible materials, a clearance of several inches is needed behind them, and an even greater safety margin is required on the sides.

Biomass (Wood and Other Burnable Fuel) Stoves

To someone looking for more heat than glamour, a wood- or other biomass-burning stove is a good choice (for residential use, coal is no longer a fuel of choice). Made of either steel or cast iron, freestanding stoves can provide over 90 percent of the available heat from wood or coal combustion. And because they're not constructed at the building site, they'll definitely keep installation costs low. Another plus is that many models have doors that can be swung open so that all the pleasures of an open fire can be enjoyed (Figs. 24.16 and 24.17).

In rural areas where firewood is inexpensive and plentiful, a wood-burner can make a lot of sense. The trouble is—unless they're the most high-tech models, complete with almost airtight fireboxes, catalytic converters, recirculating air chambers, and attached to professionally built chimneys—they can spew dangerous fumes, gases, and smoke, they can cause fires, they can pollute inside and outside atmospheres, and they can need frequent tending and maintenance. Still, for many, a wood-burning stove or a fireplace is a novelty that adds an old-fashioned characteristic to the home. Its sounds, its odors, and its way of radiating heat can be attractive, romantic, and comforting to some. In many ways, a space-heating stove shares many similarities with fireplaces. If logs are used for fuel, someone has to cut the trees down—a dangerous task. Then someone has to haul, cut, split, pile, and season the cut wood—also not for the weak or timid. The pieces have to be carried into the house and fed into the stove. Ashes need to be removed

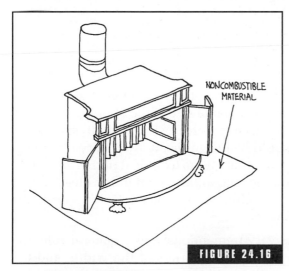

FIGURE 24.16

A Franklin wood stove.

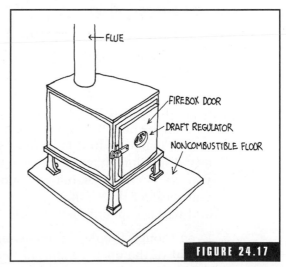

FIGURE 24.17

A wood stove.

periodically. Chimney flues need to be cleaned, inspected, and maintained. If you decide to buy ready-cut, seasoned, delivered wood, that can be expensive.

When strapped for funds, a home buyer can elect to install a freestanding wood-burning stove after the house is constructed without much trouble. Like freestanding fireplaces, stoves must be set out from combustible walls, and although most of them stand on legs, they should be centered on a noncombustible pad of some kind.

FIREPLACE DESIGN

Fireplace efficiency depends largely on proper design (Fig. 24.18). Here are some important considerations to review if you're thinking about including one or more fireplaces in your house:

1. A common but inefficient way to include a fireplace in a home is to have it built so that it employs a chimney at a side or end of the house where three sides (the back and two sides) of the chimney are exposed to the weather (Fig. 24.19). As discussed in Chapter 25 on insulation, brick and stone are of limited insulating value. They'll lose much more heat to the outdoors than they'll save for the indoors.

2. Don't settle for a fireplace with a large throat and a flue without an adjustable damper. An adjustable damper will limit the amount of warm air lost up the chimney to only that necessary to remove the smoke.

3. The best place for a fireplace to be located is away from outside walls so that most of the heat stored in its brick, stone, or metal parts is eventually delivered into the house.

4. A low chimney is a dangerous design feature.

5. The most efficient fireplaces follow established guidelines and mathematical relationships between the firebox, opening, throat diameter, and flue diameter dimensions. If the front opening is proportionally too large, the draft will be poor. A cheap way to decrease the acceptable size of the opening would be to raise the hearth, but because a fireplace requires a sizable draft, savings on energy expenses in this manner would be insignificant—and very often negative. You don't have to actually *know* what all the technical points are before you plan a fireplace, but you should be able to throw out a few ideas so that your builder thinks that he or she is dealing with someone who understands and will accept only letter-perfect work.

6. Even though fireplace dimensions vary tremendously, as a general rule, the height of the opening should be about three-quarters of the width, and the depth of the firebox should be two-thirds to three-quarters of the opening

height. For openings up to 6 feet wide, the height usually should not exceed 3½ feet; 4 feet is a good maximum for fireplaces over 6 feet wide. The average fireplace has an opening 30 to 40 inches wide and 30 inches high. The depth is between 18 and 24 inches. A typical fireplace facing will be 6 feet wide all the way from floor to ceiling.

7. A fireplace should be more or less in scale with the room in which it will be located. As a rule of thumb, there should be 5 square inches of fireplace opening for every square foot of floor area.

8. Each fireplace should have its own flue, and it's not a sound idea to vent any other heating unit, such as a furnace, into a fireplace flue.

9. Glass doors will eliminate lazy drafts and reduce smoking, plus they're good safety features to have.

10. If natural gas is available in your area, it's smart to include a gas starter in a fireplace for convenience. Make sure that an isolation valve is included on the gas line to the starter in case eventual repairs or maintenance tasks are needed.

11. To operate safely and efficiently, a fireplace should be positioned level with the floor.

Where to Locate a Fireplace

Keep in mind that once you decide where a typical fireplace will be positioned, and once it's installed, you won't want to move it to somewhere else in the house. Whenever possible, outside wall locations should be avoided. Why heat the

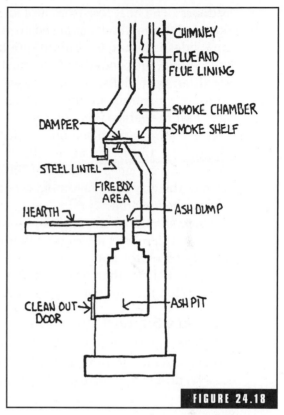

FIGURE 24.18

Cross section of conventional fireplace design.

FIGURE 24.19

A three-sided fireplace chimney exposure.

outdoors? The heat loss from a placement along an outside wall is nearly 25 percent. A chimney that's exposed to the weather along its entire length on one or more sides is bound to cool off quickly when the fire is low. Then, when the fire is rekindled, the products of combustion must try to force their way out of a chimney filled with dense, cooled gases. In contrast, heat that escapes through the chimney walls from an inside-wall fireplace will help to warm the house or at the very least the garage (Fig. 24.20).

By locating a fireplace on any inside wall, especially the wall separating the garage from the living areas, the part of the fireplace and chimney facing the garage does not need a facing of finished brick or stone. Thus, by locating a fireplace in the way most favorable for energy savings, material and installation costs also can be lowered.

There should be ample room around a fireplace for furniture. But the furniture placement shouldn't interfere with traffic in and through the room, and it shouldn't be situated closer than 6 feet from the fireplace front opening. Chairs and sofas positioned closer than 6 feet likely will make occupants uncomfortably warm no matter what the outdoor temperature is.

Fireplace Support

A masonry chimney is usually the heaviest part of a house. It must rest on a solid foundation to prevent settlement. Concrete footers are recommended. They must be designed to distribute the load over an area wide enough to avoid exceed-

FIGURE 24.20

A fireplace chimney through a garage.

ing the safe load-bearing capacity of the soil. They should extend at least 12 inches beyond the chimney on all sides and be at least 8 inches thick for single-story houses and 12 inches thick for two-story houses with basements. If there is no basement, the footers for an exterior-wall chimney should be poured on solid ground below the frost line.

Chimneys

Stone and brick fireplace chimneys can be dominating features no matter whether they're located at the exterior of a home or in the interior. The more massive the chimney, the more heat it can retain. Such retained heat can help the central mechanical heating system by reducing the time it needs to operate.

Chimney Walls

Walls of chimneys with lined flues, not more than 30 feet high, should be at least 8 inches thick if made with brick or reinforced concrete and at least 12 inches thick if made of stone. Chimneys can contain more than one flue. Building codes generally require a separate flue for each fireplace, furnace, or boiler. If a chimney contains three or more lined flues, each group of two flues must be separated from the other flue or groups of two flues by *buck divisions* or *wythes* at least 3¾ inches thick.

Neither the chimney nor the fireplace should touch any wood or flammable materials in the house structure. Check the local building code for the proper clearance the chimney must have from any combustibles as it passes through floors, walls, and roofs.

Chimney Height

Proper chimney height on any house depends on the shape of the house's roof as well as the positions and sizes of surrounding trees, buildings, and even hills. The chimney should extend or rise at least 3 feet above flat roofs and at least 2 feet above a roof ridge or raised part of a roof within 10 feet of the chimney. A chimney hood should be provided if a chimney cannot be built high enough above a ridge to prevent trouble from wind eddies caused by breezes being deflected from the roof or nearby trees. The open ends of a chimney hood should be parallel to the ridge (Fig. 24.21).

Chimney Lining

Although a chimney can be lined with brick, there's less chance of soot accumulating inside the flue if a clay tile lining at least ⅝ inch thick is used instead. The joints between such tiles must be completely filled with mortar and finished smooth on the inside. The lining is surrounded with a brick, stone, or concrete block wall at least 8 to 12 inches thick. The inside of the fireplace will be finished with firebrick on the sides and back.

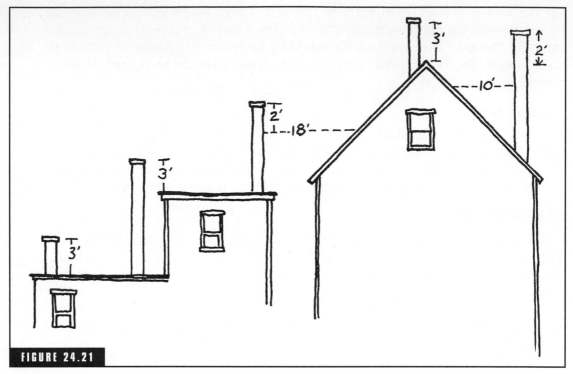

FIGURE 24.21

Chimney heights.

Chimney Mortar

Brickwork around chimney flues and fireplaces should be laid with cement mortar. It's more resistant to the action of heat and flue gases than is lime mortar. Firebrick should be laid with fire clay. Mortar will not stand up to intense heat as well as fire clay will. This is an example of why it pays to have only experienced masons work on fireplaces. It's a shame, but they're a disappearing breed, the fireplace specialists—going the same way as plasterers and stone masons. Even some of the masons who claim to know what they're doing do not. They leave behind a trail of fireplaces that smoke, draw poorly, and have flues that are constantly accumulating thick deposits of creosote. This is why, when putting up a masonry fireplace, it's best to select someone (or make sure that the contractor chooses someone) who is a proven professional.

Chimney Damper

The fireplace and chimney are large heat gobblers, particularly when they're not in use. Because of this, a fireplace chimney should be equipped with a metal damper that can be closed when the fireplace is not in service to prevent a continual draft. The damper should be the kind that opens and closes by increments so that airflow can be regulated when the fireplace is needed. A fireplace damper typically is about 36 inches wide.

Chimney Cap

The chimney cap, by definition, is placed at the very top of the chimney (Fig. 24.22). The top surface of the chimney cap should be given a slight downward slope for water to run off. This watertight cap prevents moisture from entering the brick, stone, and flue lining. Typically, the cap is made of concrete.

Spark Arrestors

Each year many fires are caused by sparks or flying embers escaping from chimneys. Those same sparks and embers

FIGURE 24.22

Chimney cap.

also can damage roofs. A chimney spark arrestor is a metal device with metal caging on the sides and a solid metal top. It is fastened over the chimney top opening not only to stop sparks, embers, and pieces of burning material from getting out of the chimney but also to prevent rain, leaves, and animals from entering. Spark arrestors also can reduce *downdrafting*, which is smoke that either starts to travel up the chimney but then backs down the chimney or smoke that has escaped from the top of the chimney that "pushes back" into the chimney owing to wind or air-movement patterns created by nearby structures or trees. Select only spark arrestors that are Underwriters Laboratories labeled.

Chimney Flashing

The intersection of the chimney and roof should be flashed with metal shingles that extend at least 4 inches under the roof shingles and 4 inches up the outer face of the chimney. They also should overlap each other by 3 inches to provide a watertight seal along the chimney. Counterflashing should be installed over the top of the metal shingles, again overlapping by at least 3 inches. Counterflashing should be embedded at least 1 inch into the masonry (accomplished, of course, as the chimney is being constructed so that the 1-inch counterflashing lip can be mortared in between a course of bricks or stone) to prevent water from running behind the flashing and into the house. The flashing seams where it meets the shingles should be caulked and then coated with a rustproof paint (Fig. 24.23).

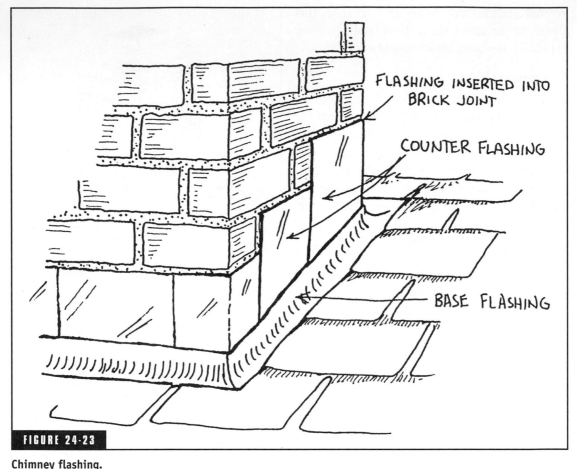

Chimney flashing.

Chimney Sealing

Once the chimney is complete and cured, the contractor should seal the out-side masonry with a transparent penetrating water-repellent sealant developed for stone, brick, concrete, and general masonry. It should be a sealant that's specifi-cally made for the application—that establishes a moisture barrier yet allows the surface to breathe.

The exterior walls and cap naturally will encounter rain, snow, ice, wind, and other conditions as time goes on. Those exterior chimney components, if not treated, eventually may absorb water. If water gets into the chimney wall, it could cause cracks and chipping, especially in cold climates, with their alternating freeze/thaw cycles. Eventually, the moisture could work its way into the house and cause damage to your insulation and ceiling. The masonry sealer will help to keep your chimney in good condition from the very start, and it also will help to prevent spalling and efflorescence. It should be reapplied as recommended by the manufacturer as a planned preventive maintenance measure.

Chimney Cleaning

All wood fires produce some creosote, and flues should be inspected periodically to check the amount of creosote present inside them. Creosote can build to thick deposits that become extremely flammable and can result in dangerous house fires.

When the flue's insides are coated with uneven surfaces of black gummy-looking material and you can't discern the tile and mortar joints, it's time for a cleaning. The term *chimney sweep* isn't really accurate. Creosote is so hard and gummy that it can't be swept loose. Rather, it has to be chipped away from the masonry with a blade. In the meantime, care must be taken not to knock out mortar joints or damage the flue lining. Because it's such an infrequent and important task, and specialized tools are needed, it's best to hand the job over to a commercial chimney sweep or cleaning outfit.

Hearths

The fireplace hearth is really an extension of the fireplace floor that protects the surrounding room floor area from catching fire. Typically, it's the brick, stone, or concrete pad beneath and in front of the firebox. Practically any noncombustible material can be used, including brick, concrete, adobe, terrazzo, quarry tile, marble, mosaic tile, slate, field stone, and even bronze or copper if laid over a noncombustible base.

Because the hearth cannot safely rest on the floor or wood framing, it should either be cantilevered out from the foundation or the foundation should be extended under it. It must be supported from the ground up, beginning with a concrete pad 12 inches thick or more typically part of the entire fireplace footer and then brought up to the subfloor level with concrete block.

A hearth should extend at least 20 to 24 inches into the room and at least 6 to 8 inches on both sides of the fireplace opening. It can be flush with the floor so that sweepings can be brushed into the fireplace, or it can be raised. Raising the hearth to various heights and extending its length are a common practice, especially in contemporary designs. This can create a natural seat for people to rest on and warm up for brief periods after a cold winter evening of skiing or tobogganing. When done on a smaller scale, though, raised hearths also can present a hazard for tripping over.

Covers and Screens

Suitable screens should be placed in front of all fireplace openings to minimize the dangers from sparks and exploding embers and to keep young children from playing with and in the flames. Some wire-mesh screens tend to be messy looking, especially when they're not permanently attached to the sides of the fireplace opening. It's better to go with ones that are suspended across the opening and can be removed when the fire needs tending. Glass screens or doors are even better because they're ideal for safety, are attractive, and can be closed at night to reduce heat loss that otherwise would go up the chimney during cold weather. They also can be used to prevent any smoke from being blown back down the chimney into a room by a strong fluke downdraft.

MANTELS

There's no strict rule dictating that every built-in fireplace must have a mantel. Many do not; quite a few contemporary designs carry the wallcovering material—usually brick or stone—right up to the edges of the fireplace opening. Most traditional fireplaces, however, still have mantels. Mantels can be made of practically any sturdy material, from a slab of rough-hewn oak to granite, marble, slate, and even concrete. Some consist of elaborately carved wood.

All wood mantels must be set back from the fireplace opening edges to keep the wood from catching fire. The minimum clearance from the front of a fireplace is at least 14 inches away from the opening.

Ash Pits

A fireplace ash pit or soot pocket is formed in the hollow space within the foundation walls and is connected with the fireplace by a small metal door called an *ash dump*. Some fireplaces have them, and others don't; it depends on the fireplace design and how often the owners will be burning wood. With an ash pit, to get rid of ashes and soot, you simply open the ash dump door and scrape or shovel the ashes into the pit. Then they're removed through a tight-fitting metal cleanout door (about 10 by 12 inches square) located in the foundation wall of the basement. In houses without basements, the pit takes the form of a metal bucket that is lifted out through the hearth when full.

In recent years, the ash pit is often placed on the outside of the chimney. This arrangement is workable in houses with or without basements, providing access to the ash pit from the outside, where the ashes are ultimately disposed of anyway.

DIRECT-VENT GAS FIREPLACES

Are you reluctant to fuss with all the activities associated with wood-burning fireplaces, such as the procurement, cutting, storage, and handling of firewood; disposing of ashes; and performance of chimney and flue cleaning and maintenance? Then consider direct-vent gas fireplaces.

Direct-vent gas fireplaces come in a variety of attractive designs. Contemporary models include corner, three-sided peninsulas, see-through, arched, bay-front,

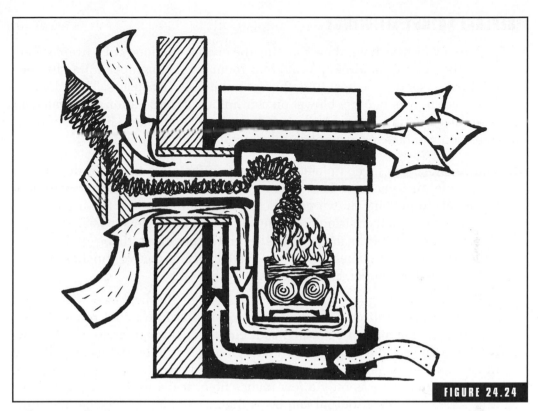

A direct-vent fireplace.

and other styles. The burning process is totally sealed from indoor air. Combustion air is drawn from outdoors, and the flue gases go back outside through one special dual-channel pipe. No air is lost during the process, and there are no drafts or dust involved. They burn clean, efficient gas and need only an access through an outside wall right behind or above the fireplace for the exhaust hardware (Fig. 24.24). No expensive chimney is required.

Direct-vent gas fireplaces are efficient, too, up to 80 percent. Using one of these units can cut utility bills because it allows the home thermostat to be set lower. For convenience, you can select a model with a handheld remote control, which allows you to simply push a button to start a fire in the hearth. Other remote buttons control flame size, heat output, room temperature, and optional blower speeds.

Many of the better models have optional battery-powered ignition systems or generate their own electricity from a pilot light. They will operate during an electrical power outage even when your furnace won't.

FIREPLACE ENERGY EFFICIENCY

The two major keys toward maximizing the energy efficiency of a fireplace are to reduce the amount of already heated-up room air that escapes up a chimney and to direct or send more heat from the fire out into living spaces. Then, by running a furnace blower or other blower on continuous air circulation, the heated air in the fireplace room can be distributed throughout the home. There are numerous steps you can take to accomplish this, including the following:

1. The fireplace can be completed with tight-fitting glass fireplace doors with adjustable air openings. These glass doors block large amounts of indoor heated air from being drawn up the chimney not only while the fire is burning but also when there is no fire. Some models use magnets to keep the doors closed; others use cam mechanisms. High-temperature silicon gaskets provide excellent seals. These doors are available in attractive finishes such as polished nickel, copper, and pewter.

2. A heat-circulating grate and blower installed in the fireplace will greatly assist heat distribution. The quiet built-in blower draws cool room air into the grate so that air can be heated as it circulates through grate tubes before being blown back out into the room. The grate is typically constructed of steel pipes, that, again, enable cooled air to enter and heated air to be blown out. Since the grate base is only a few inches high, it fits under the glass doors (Fig. 24.25). The heat output can be as high as 40,000 British thermal units per hour.

3. Models with a built-in thermostat and a variable-speed blower provide the most control over heat output and noise levels. The thermostat turns the blower on automatically when it senses about 110°F and off again at about 90°F.

4. Consider the installation of a fireback, made of heavy cast-iron plate. Such a fireback positioned at the back of the fireplace will get very hot. It helps to absorb—and then radiate—additional fireplace heat into the room, heat that's otherwise lost up the chimney. Many commercial firebacks have decorative patterns cast into their face (Fig. 24.26).

FIREPLACE CONSIDERATIONS

1. Before you rule out a fireplace, check with local real estate brokers. Buyers in your area, when looking at homes similar in type and size to the one you're building, may expect at least one fireplace to be included. If you don't put one in your home, it eventually may hinder the resale value or your ability to sell.

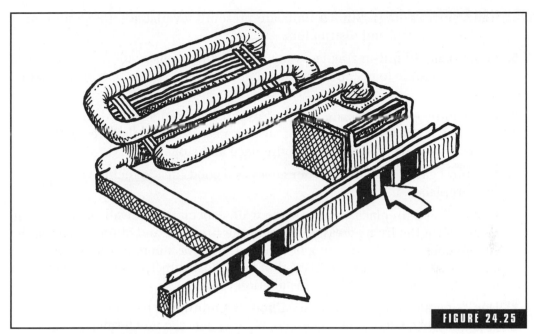

FIGURE 24.25

A heat-circulating fireplace grate.

2. Many people install fireplaces but are reluctant to use them because they have installed a light-color plush carpeting in the room, they have no place to stack the wood, or they simply don't want the ashes and debris from burning and handling wood in the house. If you definitely plan to use your fireplace(s), plan the room's furnishings and wood supply storage accordingly so that a bit of ash or dirt here and there won't create a federal case.

3. Why not select fireplaces that deliver as much heat as possible into the house? Even though they may be more expensive up front, they'll have a continuing positive effect on energy consumption during cool to cold weather conditions.

4. For hundreds of years, Europeans, Russians, and numerous other groups have been using modular masonry fireplace units in which hot fires are stoked with wood or coal, and the surrounding firebrick and attractive glazed tile absorb the heat, store it, then gently release/radiate it throughout the day or evening, warming the

FIGURE 24.26

A cast-iron fireback.

unit's surroundings. Similar units are presently available through a number of manufacturers and distributors.

5. Prefabricated built-in fireplaces not only reduce construction costs but also make it possible to install a traditional design almost anywhere in an existing house.

6. Freestanding fireplaces are the least-expensive fireplaces and the easiest to install. They're typically made of steel or cast iron but also are available in soapstone—a handsome, durable fireplace and stove material.

7. If natural gas is available in your area, it's a good idea to include a gas starter in a fireplace.

8. By locating a fireplace on any inside wall, especially the wall separating the garage from the living areas, the part of the fireplace and chimney facing the garage does not need a facing of finished brick or stone, plus absorbed heat can radiate into the garage instead of being lost directly outdoors. This will save energy and material and installation costs.

9. Don't operate an open fireplace without the minimum protection afforded by spark screens. Glass screens and doors, however, are much safer.

10. For safety's sake (and to ensure operating efficiencies), fireplaces, flues, and chimneys need to be put on a routine cleaning, inspection, and maintenance schedule.

EARTH SHELTERING

A few decades ago, settlers in the Midwest and Great Plains used to build low, earth-sheltered dwellings to insulate and protect their families from subfreezing and blistering hot temperatures, as well as from tornadoes and powerful wind storms. Today, some homes, typically sprawling ranch types constructed in wide-open spaces, still lend themselves nicely to earth sheltering, where a full or partial buildup of earth against moisture-protected outer walls help to protect the home from extreme temperatures and winds. Usually walls that face the hottest sunshine (west side) and the coldest winds (north side), when landscaped with rising aprons of soil, will help to moderate those warmest and coldest months of the year by the steady temperature of the earth (it's always about 50 to 55°F between 36 and 48 inches deep and is proportionately influenced by ground-level air temperatures as the depth gets closer to the surface).

COOLING SYSTEMS

Space-heating and -cooling systems are usually the largest energy-consuming systems in a home, especially in homes located in climates where extreme cold and hot temperatures occur. The Leadership in Energy and Environmental Design (LEED) for Homes guidelines require that both heating and cooling systems meet the minimum legal requirements to qualify for Energy Star ratings as a jumping-off condition to be awarded LEED for Homes points. What's needed is professional HVAC design and installation, high- or very high-efficiency heating and cooling units, qualified programmable thermostats (except for heat pumps and hydronic systems), and tight, no-leak distribution systems. Different climate areas have different requirements.

The greenest homes do not rely on ozone-destroying refrigerant-type air-conditioning to keep things cool. In some climates, though, especially where hot temperatures and high humidity are both prevalent, powered air-conditioning systems or systems that rely on ozone-safe refrigerants are planned to satisfy occupant comfort and health needs.

In addition to window- or wall-mounted air-conditioning units that cool one room or area at a time, whole-house air conditioners, or *central air*, usually are integrated with a forced-air furnace that shares a delivery system of ducts, vents, and registers. Because all the same ductwork will be shared, most forced-air heating units readily adapt at a modest surcharge to include mechanical air-conditioning. The heat pump automatically includes it because the same equipment is used for both heating and cooling operations. If your primary heating system is not one requiring ducts, and you still want central air-conditioning, it will have to be a separate system.

For the highest comfort, a multilevel cooling output model is best. It matches the cooling output to the changing cooling requirements of the home. A two-speed unit is like having two systems in one: a low-speed system for mild days and a high-speed system for hot and humid days. Such a dual system usually operates about 80 percent of the time at low speed. Longer low-speed cycles mean better dehumidification, air cleaning, and air circulation for increased household comfort. Some available cooling systems have two separate, different-sized compressors in the outdoor unit. When the outside air temperature is below about 85 to 88°F, the small compressor runs the system. When the outside air temperature reaches the high 80s and beyond, the system switches to the larger compressor. On very hot days, when neither compressor alone can handle the desired cooling requirements, both compressors kick in at once for maximum effort. A second style of multilevel output unit employs two-speed compressors. These multilevel output units are most effective when they use variable-speed indoor blowers that automatically adjust to match the cooling output required. The blower motors should have a quiet soft-start feature so that they'll slowly ramp up to full speed and then slowly ramp down when proper cooling levels are reached.

There are a number of important points that shouldn't be overlooked when you're considering the installation of air-conditioning:

1. When comparing bids from air-conditioning contractors, look at the seasonal energy efficiency ratings (SEERs). This is how the various units are compared. A rating of 17 or 18 is excellent, a rating of 15 or 16 is good, and a rating of 13 or 14 is acceptable.

2. Don't oversize a system in the hope of getting quick cooling. If oversizing is much greater than 15 percent, a fast cool-down of the air will occur, but without efficient moisture removal. The result will be cold, clammy, very uncomfortable air.

3. If possible, locate outdoor compressors away from decks, patios, bedroom windows, and dryer vents. Also avoid interior corners that tend to accentuate the compressor noise. Try instead for a shaded area out of the limelight. In this way, the noise won't bother anyone, and no direct sunlight will unnecessarily increase the compressor coil's workload.

4. A well-designed unit's top will keep dirt, leaves, and debris from clogging the insides so that hot air can be discharged upward away from adjacent plants, patio, or grounds.

5. If you're not starting out with air-conditioning and you plan to add it later, arrange for a large enough heating equipment room so that the air-conditioning coil, air cleaner, and humidifier can be comfortably installed.

6. Provide a means of draining condensation water from the coil to a nearby fixture.

7. If you plan on expanding your home at a later date, make certain that the size of your air conditioner will accommodate it.

8. If you're not going to have a forced-air system with ductwork, consider having the proper ductwork for air-conditioning installed when the house is being constructed even if you're going to wait to have the air-conditioning put in.

9. Make sure that refrigerant used by any proposed cooling system will be readily available in the future and is not being phased out to comply with existing or expected environmental regulations. The refrigerant must be safe for both the ozone and the environment.

DUCTS

Ducts can be considered the main delivery vehicles for heated and cooled air within a home having heating and cooling systems serviced by some type of air-moving blower unit. Two kinds of materials are used in combination to manufacture ductwork for forced-air heating and independent air-conditioning or cooling systems: galvanized sheet metal and fiberglass.

Galvanized sheet metal ducts are manufactured in a shop and brought to the job site for installation. These ducts offer good support and are put together using strong fasteners, including rivets. By themselves, however, sheet metal ducts can be annoyingly noisy. Insulating the outside of the duct with 2-inch-thick fire-resistant fiberglass duct wrap insulation with a vapor-retarding face or liner will cut down on noise vibration, will help to control moisture condensation, and will give thermal support by preserving the heated or cooled air temperature as the air travels to its destination. When the sheet metal ducts are manufactured or installed, the seams, joints, and corners should be of a good design and craftsmanship, tightly fitted to form a good seal. Sheet metal construction offers numerous advantages: It's durable, its smooth surfaces offer little resistance to air flow, it can be custom fitted to odd shapes and sizes, it isolates the outer insulation jacket from the airstream—preventing penetration of the insulation by dirt and dust—and cleaning can be easily accomplished on the smooth surfaces with yearly dust vacuuming or in response to special situations such as smoke or ash contamination from a fire. Another type of ductwork is called *flex duct*, and it is inexpensive, flexible ducting that's simple to install because it will bend around obstructions. Although it eliminates the need for piecing together elbows and other fittings to form efficient ductwork runs, the internal wire reinforcement structure of flexible ducting tends to increase air turbulence and reduce airflow capabilities within the ducting, especially when installed with sags or droops in horizontal runs.

Duct System Considerations

1. Sheet metal ducts are an excellent green duct choice because they are made from recyclable material. They're less likely to sag than flexible ducts. Their smooth walls won't interfere with airflow. They won't contribute any fibers or contaminants to indoor air.

2. Since sheet metal is very conductive to heat, to prevent heat loss along the delivery system, insulate the outside of sheet metal ducts using 2-inch-thick fire-resistant fiberglass insulation with a vapor barrier. At the same time, avoid any ducts that are lined with fiberglass. You don't want fibers to escape and be carried into living areas where they could be breathed in by family members.

3. Maximize the use of straight ducts for greater airflow efficiency. The fewer elbows, turns, and sharp angles, the better.

4. Because duct tape eventually will dry out and fall off, mastic or metal tape should be used instead to seal joints, small holes, and gaps.

5. To make cleaning easier, access port doors or covers can be installed. Although few builders or home buyers think of this, duct access ports provide the means

for vacuuming collected dust from ductwork once a year. It will keep the system, the air it supplies, and the entire household cleaner and healthier.

6. With forced-air units, total duct travel distances, as well as the number of bends and turns in the ductwork, should be minimized. The more 90-degree bends or tees used, the shorter the allowable or functional run can be owing to increased resistance to the airflow experienced by air swirling and losing momentum in curves and bends. Wherever possible, 45-degree bends should be used instead of 90-degree bends to improve airflow efficiency. Ducts with curved sides move air more efficiently than ducts with sharp corners.

7. In cold climates, have ducts run within heated areas of the house. This will help to maximize the amount of heat retained within the ducts and will place more heat where it's wanted at a lower cost. Avoid running ducts up exterior walls, where they'll take up valuable space that could be given to insulation instead and will enable conditioned air to be affected by outside temperatures.

8. If there's a basement, make sure that a few heat outlets are placed there to help supply warmth when needed and to cut down on dampness. They simply can be adjustable louvers installed in one of the main heat supply ducts.

9. Warmed or cooled air that's blown down a main or *trunk* duct line will bounce off an end cap and disperse down the various branch lines. If there's a duct opening or open line at the end of the trunk, much of the conditioned air will take the path of least resistance and continue down that path—starving the rest of the ducts.

10. There should be dampers on each branch where the branch comes off the main trunk so that the amount of air entering any particular duct branch can be somewhat controlled. An unused bedroom thus may be "sealed off" during winter and left unheated if desired. To set dampers once the system is running, use a thermometer to check individual room temperatures, and then adjust the airflow dampers as needed.

11. Ducts with humidifier connections will need a nearby water source and drain.

12. Finally, do not locate air return ducts in bathrooms or kitchens; they will pull undesired humidity back into the system from showers, baths, and cooking.

In short, carefully plan the location of furnace ducts and their outlets. Once your house is finished and occupied, you must keep furniture, rugs, and other obstructions away from the return registers, heating and cooling vents, and related components.

REGISTERS

The purpose of heating and cooling outlets or registers is to supply the heat or cooled air where it's most needed, usually near the exterior walls and windows (Fig. 24.27). Two or more registers often are needed in large rooms or along extended walls beneath long picture windows. What's needed is a "curtain" of warm or cold air thrown up (or down) from the registers around the perimeter of the house between the occupants and the outside temperatures. The heat sources work best when they're located along the bottom of a wall beneath the windows. This position counteracts the most likely places where cold might seep into the room. In warm-climate areas, the registers instead can be located in the ceiling, directly over windows on exterior walls, because cool air falls.

Here are some other considerations:

1. Make sure that no registers contribute to unwanted noise transmission between rooms. Two-sided or double-opening registers that serve two rooms at once are fine in certain instances, but be on guard against any doubling up

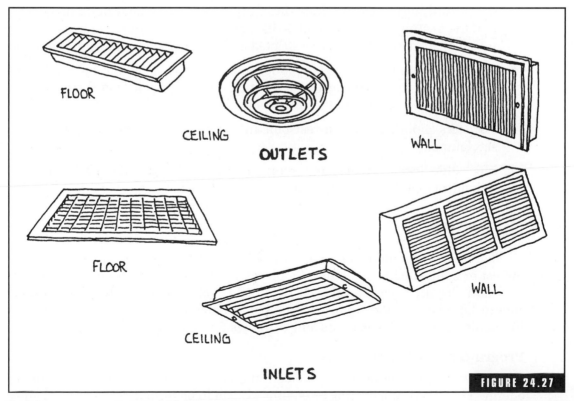

FLOOR

CEILING

OUTLETS

WALL

FLOOR

CEILING

WALL

INLETS

Registers.

that violates someone's privacy. These double registers can be a big source of interroom noise transmission.

2. Floor-mounted supply registers are more efficient than the baseboard type. It remains a good practice, however, to use the baseboard registers in rooms such as kitchens, bathrooms, and laundries to prevent water, wax, or other materials from entering the duct system.

3. Return registers are best mounted on the walls in the interior of a home. They should be positioned near the floor in cold-climate areas and along the ceiling in warm-climate locations.

4. After completion of the heating/cooling rough-in, the heating contractor should install temporary covers over all outlets and registers, both supply and return, to prevent debris, dust, and other materials from getting into the ductwork during the remaining construction. If temporary covers are not installed, fine dust particles will enter the duct work and eventually coat every room in the house when the blower is turned on. Even so, it's a good idea to request that air ducts be cleaned at the end of construction because even with attempts to temporarily cover the registers, some dust, dirt, and debris still may enter the ducts inadvertently. On a related note, make sure that the heating/cooling system is disconnected and cannot operate when the registers are covered because restricted airflow can damage the entire system.

5. The more areas that can be tapped for return air, the faster and more efficient the system will be. The best systems include many more than the minimum number of inches required for return air.

6. Registers should be scratch-resistant and rustproof, with easy to operate and set dampers.

7. If possible, locate registers and return vents so that they will not be in the way or behind main furniture and drapery placements.

THERMOSTATS

Thermostats shouldn't be placed where they'll be affected by drafts, in the hottest or coldest parts of a home, in places where they'll interfere with furnishings and decor. Place thermostats on inside, not outside, walls. Thermostats should be located away from heat sources such as fireplaces and registers and from cold sources such as doors and windows for dependable readings.

Programmable Thermostats

Programmable thermostats are electronic conveniences that can save lots of energy. They'll allow a heating or cooling system to be turned down or back automatically at preset times so that heating or cooling units won't be running full blast while occupants are sleeping or away. Although some of these controls aren't recommended with heat pumps or radiant flooring heating systems—units meant to be run under steady operation or systems that are difficult to shut on and off—they work wonders with many other systems. More sophisticated programmable thermostats and controls are being developed all the time. Some will adjust heat or coolness output in response to a whole series of variables, including outside temperature and humidity or family member activity levels indoors.

PROGRAMMABLE THERMOSTAT CONSIDERATIONS

1. Look for a programmable controls that can store and repeat multiple daily settings for wake-up, daytime, evening, and sleep times. Some "smart" units will even learn how long it takes to heat or cool the house so that it "knows" when to start heating or cooling in the future. Many of these units are also able to remind the occupants when to clean or replace the system's air filter.

2. Thermostats for heating and air-conditioning should be positioned on an inside wall where they will not be subject to draft or heat from televisions, lamps, and other appliances.

3. Units exist that retain programmed settings during a power outage. Better units need no batteries and operate off memory chips.

4. Some models offer a temporary program override feature for away-from-home vacations or holidays. You can override the program and set the temperature down for the time you will be out of town.

5. If you go with zoned hot-water heat or have adjustable fans on your forced-air system (dual-control fans), consider having more than one thermostat strategically located in the house.

6. One of the newest designs is a thermidistat. It controls the furnace, air conditioner, blower, and humidifier independently for total comfort.

NOISE

A noisy heating or cooling system can be annoying. There's no justification for such noise, except that it costs the manufacturer a trifle less and saves the builder a trifle more. Ask to be taken to a home that already employs the heating/cooling system that you're considering. Listen to it start, operate, and stop. Be sure that you do all three because sometimes a burner fires with a bang or pops when the flame goes out. Sometimes the motor that runs a circulating pump or blower is noisy. Fan noises can be transmitted through the ductwork (like through an old-fashioned speaking tube), and quite often the noises created in boilers are carried throughout the house in the metal piping. How much attention you pay to these noises depends on your sensitivity to disturbing sounds.

SIZE AND LOCATION

You shouldn't go with an oversized furnace or air conditioner unless it's in anticipation of a room or space you plan on adding at a later date. An oversized unit will run inefficiently in a smaller space than it was engineered for.

Try to locate the furnace/air conditioner in as central a location as possible to get an even distribution of heat and coolness. The air conditioner's outside compressor, as mentioned earlier, should be installed in an out-of-the-way place in the shade where it won't annoy anyone.

AIR CLEANERS

Forced-air heating and air-conditioning systems are ideal for the application of electrostatic air cleaners. They not only clean the air, but they also tend to make it smell fresher too, which is a feature that's becoming more important with today's comprehensive sealing of houses. The accompanying reduction of air infiltration actually has reduced the amount of fresh air that used to move into homes through various uninsulated surfaces and cracks in the outer shell.

Air cleaners remove up to 95 percent of airborne dust, bacteria, and even viruses. Indeed, air cleaners have many benefits:

- They can filter out unseen microscopic particles that float in the air, including dust, pollen, mold, plant spores, bacteria, viruses, dust mites, pet hair, dander, cooking smoke, and other miscellaneous particles—making the air cleaner and more comfortable for everyone, pets included.

- Air cleaners also keep heating and cooling equipment coils cleaner, protecting operating efficiencies and lowering costs.

- Cleaner air minimizes the time required for cleaning dust and soil throughout the home.

The other types of heating systems aren't so accommodating to the air cleaners, and separate units must be installed in individual rooms.

HUMIDIFIERS

Heat tends to dry out the air inside a house and make it uncomfortable. This is particularly true of forced-air systems. If mechanical means for supplying moisture are not available, the humidity inside the home can drop to the level of dryness found in a desert. This condition causes shrinking of wood and other materials, which might open gaps in the house structure and shell and permit air infiltration.

Low humidity causes a variety of problems:

- Dry, itchy skin, dry-throat coughs, and cracked nasal membranes on people and pets

- Sharp static electrical shocks

- Ceiling and wall cracks that may allow hot or cold air to enter, hurting energy efficiency

- Dehydration of some house plants

- Excessive wear of fabrics, carpets, and other furnishings (Wood shrinks, floors creak, banisters wobble, drawers loosen, and gaps appear in moldings.)

- Household members often feel colder in homes having dry air.

As with air cleaners, humidifiers can be installed directly onto a duct system (Fig. 24.28). They can be hooked up to a constant water supply so that they'll continually and automatically put needed moisture into the air. For houses heated with systems other than forced air, humidifiers must be placed in appropriate areas throughout the home to accomplish the same thing.

Dehumidifiers also can be needed in certain locations and at certain times of the year, usually in basements during hot and wet-weather conditions. Individual units run by electricity usually do the job.

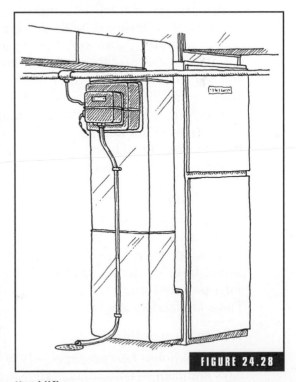

FIGURE 24.28

Humidifier.

FANS

Fans are remarkable mechanical inventions. Next to methods of natural ventilation, where air movement alone—through open windows and vents—cools and ventilates a home, fans are probably the next least expensive and most efficient way of accomplishing the same thing. They use small amounts of electricity to push and pull quantities of air from one place to another, and when coordinated with passive-solar design, natural ventilation methods, and assorted powered heating, cooling, and ventilation units, they provide flexibility and comfort by helping to regulate the indoor atmosphere of a home. Fans placed throughout a home can make occupants feel cooler than they really are—by the evaporative effect that moving air has on bare skin. If the occupants feel cooler than they really are, there's less need to turn down the air-conditioning, if air conditioning is present. By drawing cooler outside air indoors and exhausting warmer "stuffy" inside air to the outdoors, "local" bathroom, kitchen, and laundry fans also help to adjust and maintain desired indoor temperatures. Window fans are best used with rooms having opposite-wall windows so that straight-line exhaust/makeup air paths can be established. They also work—though not as efficiently—with only a single window present. Intake fans should be placed on the room's cooler side, on the shadier part of the home, and exhaust fans on the other side.

Ceiling Fans

Running a ceiling fan allows you to raise an area's air-conditioner thermostat by as much as 5 degrees for the same effective result. In winter, reversing the fan's rotation direction will send warm air near the ceiling to gently flow outward and down along the walls. These fans are incredibly efficient, with some running on as little energy as it takes to operate a 100-watt light bulb. Some ceiling fans also function as air cleaners, with air filters hidden inside each blade. As the fan circulates room air, the air constantly passes through and is cleaned by the blade filters. The blades usually can be turned on by either a pull chain or a wall switch and are able to turn at two or three speeds. Ceiling fans are available in several sizes and an enormous range of styles, with or without integrated light fixtures. For correctly sizing a fan for a room or space, consult the manufacturer's guidelines. Areas wider or longer than 16 to 18 feet may need two fans for adequate airflow. Most manufacturers recommend installing the fan so that its blades are 10 to 12 inches below the ceiling and 7 to 9 feet above the floor.

Attic Fans

Attic fans exhaust hot air from an attic and draw cooler fresh replacement air from outside. An attic fan must be sized properly so that it won't pull conditioned or moist air from lower inside living areas and should be well insulated and air sealed from the living spaces below. Because attic fans are so close to the roof, solar-powered units are available and a very green option for cooling an attic. There are models available for both roof and gable installations.

Whole-House Fans

Whole-house fans are especially popular in locations with climates having hot days and cool to cold nights. They're large, powerful fans mounted in an upper-floor hallway ceiling or open-foyer ceiling or other upper-floor accessible room ceiling They work in a remarkably simple but effective way, drawing cool night air from all partly opened lower-floor and other-floor windows throughout the home—creating a kind of "power" night air flush. Simply, a whole-house fan uses this newer, cooler air to replace hot air collected during the day throughout the home. The heated air gets exhausted along with additional hot air accumulated within the attic through attic gable and roof vents. The vents are equipped with air-sealed louvers or manual covers used during the heating seasons so that warmth is not lost inadvertently during those times. It's also important to have no air leaks between the attic and living areas, and the fan should be able to be covered with insulation and be sealed off from the outside during winter and other times the fan will not be in use.

Because the sizing and control of a whole-house fan are so important to its effective operation, it's best left to an HVAC professional who will also take the rest of the heating and cooling system into account so that all components and functions work efficiently together.

Heat Recovery/Energy Recovery Ventilation

These units are complete whole house ventilation systems that incorporate a supply motor and an exhaust motor in one unit. The supply motor draws fresh air in from the outdoors and the exhaust motor pushes stale contaminated air outside. The two air systems are separated by a heat/energy recovery core which tempers the air and results in a comfortable, healthy indoor environment.

Some benefits are:

- Brings a continuous supply of fresh, filtered outside air into the home
- Exhausts environmental contaminants for improved indoor air quality
- Saves energy by recovering heat from exhaust air during winter
- Cools incoming air during summer
- Helps control excess humidity

COOLING WITH VEGETATION

Trees, in addition to blocking some hot summer sun rays, can cool the atmosphere surrounding a home in another way—through a process called *transpiration*. Humans perspire. When our bodies are under stress or are heating owing to the temperature around us or the amount of activity we're performing, the body cools itself by allowing water (sweat) to evaporate off our skin. Trees, shrubs, grass, and other vegetation transpire in a similar manner, and when they do, they have a cooling affect on air around them. Naturally, the same vegetation also can have a cooling effect on walls, roofs, and other house components by directly blocking the sun. Awnings and other human-made products can perform the same kind of cooling sun-blocking functions.

GENERAL HEATING AND COOLING EQUIPMENT CONSIDERATIONS

1. No matter what type of heating/cooling unit is selected, the indoor mechanical equipment location must not break up the interior floor plan. If the main unit is placed in the basement, consider how it will affect the living spaces there, but remember that it will need plenty of air circulation and must be easily accessible for maintenance and repairs.

2. For the sake of noise reduction, the main unit should be placed away from quiet living spaces such as bedrooms, family rooms, and offices or libraries.

3. A whole-house humidifier adds needed moisture to the air in a home during seasonal dry spells and other times of low humidity. Properly humidified air feels warmer than drier air of the same temperature, so you can effectively lower your indoor settings and still enjoy comfortable conditions.

4. Wherever it's placed, the mechanical equipment needs to be accessible for maintenance. Filters should especially be easy to get at, with an overhead light nearby.

5. For any heating unit that's exhausted through a chimney, make sure that the chimney has the proper liner to safely handle the exhausting. Water vapor is a by-product of fuel combustion and can condense on inside masonry chimney surfaces, especially those on exterior walls. Resulting water then can be absorbed by the chimney and transferred through walls. This can result in damp patches on interior and exterior walls, blistering paint, peeling wallpaper, stains on the ceiling around the chimney, and white stains on the outside surfaces of the chimney itself. During winter, chimneys may be subject to numerous freezes, where the condensation freezes and expands. This "works" on mortared joints, bricks, or blocks and may cause cracks and crumbling masonry, which could, in turn, lead to openings in the flue and possible incursions of dangerous carbon monoxide into the home.

6. Rubber isolator (vibration) pads placed beneath the corners of a forced-air furnace or heat pump blower unit will help to absorb vibrations and lessen operating sound levels.

7. If you choose hot-water baseboard heat but also want separate forced-air central air-conditioning, the air-conditioning sheet metal ductwork with outside insulation should be installed overhead with outlets in the ceiling. The most efficient air-conditioning is where outlets are overhead (cool air falls). The most efficient heating runs along the floor (heat rises).

8. If you're putting in hot-water baseboard heat and know that you'll want central air-conditioning at a later time, prepare for that eventuality by having the sheet metal ductwork with outside insulation installed overhead, complete with ceiling outlets.

9. If possible, avoid running ducts and air handlers in attics and other unheated or unconditioned spaces. Some heated or cooled air will be lost unnecessarily, and if the ducts or air handlers leak, all the worse. Instead, run them through a conditioned space such as an attic having an insulated roof or an insulated crawlspace or basement.

10. It might sound convenient, but approving framing crews to build HVAC air returns in outside wall stud cavities simply by fastening sheet metal across existing wall studs usually will result in leaky returns that easily can cause backdrafting and the unwanted entry of moisture, dust, pollutants, and even conditioned air from inside the house.

11. Consider that the greater the energy efficiency of a heating system, the more completely the fuel is used, and the less incomplete combustion losses go up a chimney.

12. To reduce or minimize off-cycle heating losses when a heating or cooling unit is starting or stopping, make sure that the systems are correctly sized. If too large for the area they have to condition, they'll cycle on and off too frequently and will rarely reach their operating "sweet spots." If too small, they won't be able to keep up the demand on the coldest or warmest days.

13. Standby loss is heat emitted or lost through the actual heating plant and distribution system components themselves. Minimize such losses by properly sizing, insulating, and sealing piping and ducts where possible and, when using a boiler, by selecting a low-mass type.

14. A disadvantage of designing long flue runs with several or more elbows is the need for power vents. Even though power vents can handle the removal of flue gases, the air needed for combustion and drafting still must come from within the dwelling. In some cases, the power vent's fan could create negative pressure in a utility area or basement, where a water heater or other combustion-type appliance could be included in a backdraft.

15. The selection of sealed-combustion heating appliances, with their concentric-pipe flue-within-a-flue (incoming air and outgoing exhaust) construction and installation, is encouraged both for safety and for operating efficiencies.

16. Of course, always consider how you can deliberately reduce heat gain while you're trying to cool things down inside. Remember how to use windows properly, how using fluorescent instead of incandescent lighting can reduce

inside temperatures, and how light-colored paints, carpeting, tile, roofing, and other surfaces can reflect heat.

REMODELING NOTES

Like-system furnaces and air-conditioning units that can use existing delivery systems can be relatively simple remodeling projects. Start trying to hook together dissimilar components, and things can get complicated and expensive. Your best course of action is to get the opinions of at least three experts—experienced representatives from well-known local heating and cooling companies. They'll be able to quickly look at your system and recommend the most compatible remodels based on the brands they handle. It's usually a good idea to include the company that does your yearly tune-ups and safety checks as one of the three. If you've been doing research on ideal systems, bring your thoughts up, and see how the reps react. At the very least, have them comment on improving your control of the equipment you already have. Can you separate portions of the home into zones by reapportioning the delivery system and installing localized thermostats? There's typically no advantage to segregating heat within interior rooms unless your home features sophisticated or dedicated zones that are heated with exact controls as you are in those various locations. It's another case of the more precise your controls are, the less energy you'll have to expend. Let's say that you're the only one living in the home. Ideally, if the home is zoned, you can heat various portions of it as the day and night unfolds. When discussing heating and cooling remodeling projects, ask the contractors how expensive it would be to create such a system.

Ask them what they would do to become more energy efficient if they had your systems in their homes? If you're planning to sell your home in the near future, consider how much the improvements would save energy in the meantime and how much the investment would be reflected in your home's market value.

▶▶▶▶▶ POINTS TO PONDER

1. Forced-air heating and cooling systems are very versatile. Air can be heated, cooled, humidified, dehumidified, filtered, and circulated all through the same distribution system.

2. A hot-water system is a clean, effective, and fairly quiet way to heat a home. It can supply heat to specific areas or zones in a house and withhold heat from seasonally unused parts of that same house. It also can be adapted to some household water heaters and some solar heating arrangements.

3. An electric heating system is one of the simplest and least expensive heating systems to install. There's no ductwork, plumbing, or expensive furnace or boiler needed. Unfortunately, if purchased electricity is needed to run the system, it can be quite expensive.

4. Although initial installation costs of a ground- or water-source heat-pump system are higher than that of many other systems, when comparing all fuel types, these heat pumps are among the most economical heating and cooling alternatives today—when their low energy consumption is considered.

5. Don't oversize an air-conditioning system in the hope of getting improved performance or quicker cooling. If oversizing is much greater than 15 percent, a fast cool-down of the air will occur, but without efficient moisture removal.

6. If possible, locate outdoor air-conditioning compressors away from decks, patios, bedroom windows, and dryer vents.

7. In warm climates, it's better to place heating and cooling registers in ceilings. In cold-climate locations, they should be positioned at floor levels. If you have separate heating and air-conditioning systems (i.e., hot-water baseboard heat and forced central air), the heating should be at floor level and the air-conditioning in the ceiling.

8. If you're not going to have a forced-air heating system with ductwork, consider having the proper ductwork for air-conditioning installed when the house is being constructed, even if you're going to wait to have the air-conditioning put in.

9. Heating and air-conditioning ducts should be insulated on their outside, not inside.

10. To prevent "false" readings, thermostats should be located away from heat sources such as fireplaces and registers and from cold sources such as doors and windows.

11. Discomfort from heat within the home is related to temperature, humidity, and air movement or convection. Reduce or eliminate the need for air-conditioning by temporarily increasing shading when needed to prevent solar radiation from entering living spaces, by increasing the building's reflectivity, by increasing ventilation—especially by "night flushing" when cool evening air replaces or "flushes out" warmer daylight air—and by identifying and minimizing activities that generate humidity and heat within the home.

12. Be aware that for every degree you raise your thermostat control during warm weather, you'll lower your air-conditioning cooling bill by about 2

percent. Lowering your thermostat setting by a single degree during cold weather can save between 2 and 3 percent on heating costs. This is why programmable thermostats can easily have a major cumulative influence on energy usage, especially when combined with regular heating and air-conditioning system maintenance tune-ups.

Insulation

There aren't many people who live in a climate where they don't have to worry about protecting themselves from temperatures that are periodically too hot or too cold. Since the oil embargoes and the realization that many of the energy sources on which we depend are not unlimited, insulation in houses has taken a position of high priority, no matter what the location. It's a matter of keeping inside and outside air or atmospheres separated from each other. When it's cold outside, insulation keeps the conditioned, warmer air inside and prevents the home from losing its heat through the outer walls, roof, and basement. The insulation works by holding air stationary or captive in numerous pockets or voids in the insulating material. This is why all insulation is relatively light and squeezable—it's full of tiny air pockets. And to be most effective, insulation should be installed in airtight cavities or places where air cannot leak or travel through the space, stealing precious heat as it goes.

Different materials conduct heat at different rates based on their density and composition. Insulation is designed to transfer heat as slowly as possible. It provides a thermal break—stopping heat transfer—in whatever it is insulating. Both wood and metal products transfer heat much faster than insulation does. This means that framing members made of wood or steel, as well as metal window and door frames, can provide thermal bridges within the exterior walls—enabling unwanted heat to partially bypass the insulation and enter or exit depending on which side of the wall is exposed to warmer temperatures. Thermal bridging, or places in an outer wall having 2- by 6-inch studs every 24 inches or more, reduces the overall R-value of the wall section by whatever lesser R-values the wood studs provide. This situation can be corrected by adding a layer of rigid foam insulating panels to the outside of the wall, effectively cutting off the energy-wasting thermal bridges caused by the 2 × 6 wooden wall studs.

In its most universal application, insulation belongs inside or against any barrier located between a heated space and an unheated space or between a cooled space and an uncooled space. Applied to the structure of a house, this means that insulation should be within all exterior walls, in attics or under roofs, beneath floors exposed to the outside, as well as floors covering unheated crawl spaces or slabs, and in extremely cold locations on walls in a heated basement.

Insulation is a needed component, but again, it must be installed as only part of a well-designed outer wall or roof. If moisture or air is allowed to infiltrate the wall or roof or an outside wall is full of framing members, plumbing, and heating, ventilation, and air-conditioning (HVAC) ductwork, the insulation may not work correctly, or simply, there may not be enough of it present. In some cases, heated or cooled air could easily escape through gaps around doors and windows. Both insulation sheathing and cavity insulation should be installed as stick-built outer walls are being constructed (Fig. 25.1). Of course, if structural insulated panels (SIPs) are being used for walls, they already come equipped with insulation.

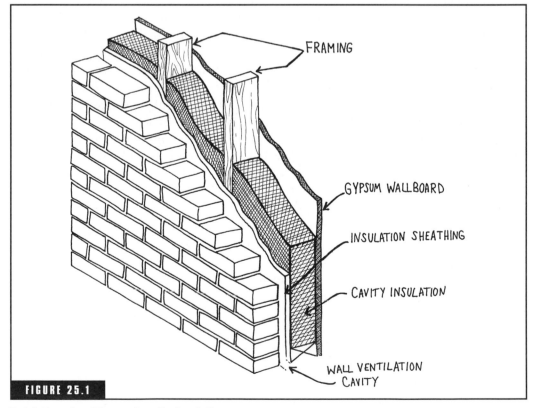

FRAMING

GYPSUM WALLBOARD

INSULATION SHEATHING

CAVITY INSULATION

WALL VENTILATION CAVITY

FIGURE 25.1

Insulation sheathing and cavity insulation.

In short, insulation should envelop all living areas of your home, leaving no openings except doors, windows, and necessary vents. As discussed in Chapters 21 and 24 on plumbing and heating, the heating or cooling ducts and hot-water heater and pipes must be insulated to provide energy efficiency, especially when such ducts and pipes pass through unheated or uncooled spaces—usually a poor location for ducts and pipes anyway.

Fortunately, sealing a home against heat conduction and air infiltration is a relatively simple process if done during construction of the house, and it's fairly inexpensive, considering the energy saved in the long run. If insulation and air-tightness are not properly planned and must be added at a later date after the house has been completed—now that can run into big problems and big expenses. Stationary air is a relatively poor conductor of heat, but once it's allowed to move freely from the outside in or inside out, it will create quick avenues for heat to be gained or lost through convection.

Most insulation is installed after the framing is complete and the electrical, plumbing, and heating systems have been roughed in and inspected. In other words, after everything else goes into the wall, the remaining space is used for insulation. This is why recent advanced framing techniques try to minimize the overall space taken up by the framing members. The greater the open space in stud or joist bays, the more insulation can be installed in the same-size wall. Larger inside wall spaces can be achieved by using fewer or smaller (thinner) framing boards or members, as long as enough strength is maintained. Remember that heat always travels from hot to cold. To put it simply, insulation is a nonconductive material designed to slow the movement of heat from passing through the building envelope from inside out or outside in. During cold winter seasons, it means keeping warm, conditioned air within the home. When uncomfortable, hot summer days persist, it means keeping those high temperatures from entering the home's living spaces and keeping cooler, conditioned air indoors.

Insulation is one of the most important components of green construction. Compared with other building materials, it's a huge bargain with tremendous payback. Attics and upper-story ceilings generally have been the easiest places to install thick layers of insulation, which ends up working well because that's where the warm, conditioned air rises to, where the greatest heat transfer could take place if there was no attic or ceiling insulation.

Green homes have been gradually including more and more insulation, and the insulation used is being manufactured to provide increased energy efficiency. Of course, higher levels of insulation make sense in warmer and colder climates. Exactly how much is most cost effective? Various agencies and organizations have issued numerous guidelines, but it's often a matter of personal preference.

Regarding insulation products, they include a handful of popular types: batts, loose or blown-in insulation, rigid foam boards, and spray foams. The type of insulation to use in a particular case will depend on how large the spaces are, how they can be accessed, and what else will the material be sharing the space with. Could the insulation be subject to moisture or the effects of gravity? Cost might be an issue, and so may the amount of recycled materials that go into the material's manufacture.

The question "How much insulation is enough?" is asked frequently. The most recent answer is, "More than has been traditionally thought." Can there be too much insulation? There is a point at which adding more insulation will not really make sense. Who wants to live in a bunker with window ledges 3 or 4 feet thick. Even if you splay or angle the windows, it's probably not financially worth it, plus the windows will not be as energy efficient. There have been attempts at designing superinsulated dwellings with insulation levels all over R-70 for roofs, R-60 for floors, and R-55 for walls, with triple-glazed, inert-gas-filled windows, and those units then were able to be heated with little more than their own lighting, appliance use, and the heat generated by the occupants' own bodies. Naturally, superrated insulation levels would make little sense in milder climates but could result in the need for smaller, less expensive heating systems, plus great ongoing energy savings and increased comfort in hot or cold climate areas.

R-VALUES

Insulation quality is often expressed in R-values. An *R-value* is a numerical expression of the ability of any material to resist the conductance or potential passage of heat. All building materials have R-values. The higher a material's R-value, the slower heat will move through the material by conduction, and the better is its insulation value. For example, a fiberglass batt 6 inches thick has an R-value of approximately 19. The same material in batts 12 inches thick will possess an R-value of about 38. R-values can be added together, and multiple layers of insulation or even different material layers will yield higher overall totals of insulating R-values. R-values actually are based on scientific measurements of heat loss called *U-values* (see the next section). Essentially, an R-value is the thermal inverse of a material's ability to conduct heat. The simple equation is R-value = 1/thermal conductance, expressed in R-value per inch. Of course, such measurements are made for ideal conditions—when materials and components are installed properly without construction mistakes such as building material gaps, compressed sections of insulation, damp materials, or air leaks. Squeeze 6 inches of fiberglass batts into a space 3 inches deep, and the material's resistance to heat conductance will be greatly reduced. It's important for you to know what the insulation plan is for your home.

Unfortunately, just because walls are fitted with R-19 insulation doesn't mean that the entire wall ends up with an R-19 real performance rating. Remember that insulation usually needs to be placed between and behind framing members such as 2 × 4s or 2 × 6s, and other lumber for window and door openings, bays, trusses, and similar components. These components typically have smaller R-values and less heat-passage resistance, so thermal bridging occurs where wood, steel, or similarly dense materials take the place of insulation. In addition, the insulation contractor may not install everything correctly. Insulation gaps or too much insulation squeezed into a space both could result in reduced insulating efficiency. From a practical point of view, this means that these possible inefficiencies should be planned for in advance by specifying wall systems rated at greater R-values than perhaps originally called for.

The performance of all insulation products can be compared by each individual product's R-value number or range. Table 25.1 provides a comparison of insulation materials. Table 25.2 lists some of the same kinds of insulations and shows approximations of what their most common thicknesses equal in insulating values.

Because heat rises, the potential heat loss in a house is greatest through the roof and least through the floors. Therefore, different recommendations exist for insulating those areas as well as the walls—each with a different appropriate R-factor. Here are some conservative recommended R-values for your house: walls—R-20; floors—R-27 (above grade), which includes overhangs, cantilevers, and below projecting windows; and ceilings—R-40.

Table 25.1 Comparison of Insulation Materials

Form	Type	Approximate R-Value per Inch of Thickness	Relative Cost 1 = least, 5 = most
Blankets and batts	Fiberglass	3.1	1
	Rock wool	3.7	1
Boards	Fiberglass	4.5	5
	Polystyrene	3.5 to 5.4	5
	Polyisocyanurate	6.0 to 8.0	5
	Polyurethane	6.0 to 8.0	5
Loose	Rock wool (blown)	3.0 to 3.3	1
Spray foam	Fiberglass (blown)	2.2 to 2.7	1
	Cellulose (blown)	3.2 to 3.3	1
	Polyurethane (closed cell)	6.0 to 6.5	5
	Polyurethane (open cell)	3.0 to 4.0	5

Table 25.2 Thicknesses of Various Insulations and Approximate Insulating Values

Form	R-11	R-19	R-22	R-30	R-38
Fiberglass blankets/batts	3½–4 in	6–6½ in	7–7½ in	9½–10 in	12–13 in
Rock wool blankets/batts	3–3½ in	5–6 in	6–7 in	8–9½ in	10½–12 in
Fiberglass loose/blown	5 in	8½ in	10 in	13½ in	17 in
Rock wool loose/blown	4 in	6½ in	7½ in	10 in	13 in

U-VALUES

On occasion, you might find the thermal qualities of an insulation material expressed in terms of U-values. What *U-values* refer to is the thermal conductance of a certain material. More specifically, the U-value represents the amount of heat that passes through a square foot of the material in an hour when the temperature difference between one side and the other of the material being measured is exactly 1°F. The U-value is the reciprocal of the R-value and can be determined by dividing the R-value into the numeral value. For example, a fiberglass batt having an R-value of 19 has a U-value of 1/19, or about 0.053. Because U-values are expressed in ratios, U-values of different materials, even though installed against one another, cannot simply be added together for an accurate total. Basically, the lower the U-value, the greater is the thermal resistance of the material, and the better is its insulation quality. Again, remember that test ratings such as these are made in ideal situations, where the material (insulation, wall section, siding, or other product) is installed as designed and not compromised in any way. And also consider that what's measured here is conductive heat loss—not heat loss resulting from radiation or convection. If insulation gets wet or sloppy construction allows air to blow or move through the insulation, U-values will test much higher because the material will not be as effective, and other factors will impede resistance against heat conduction.

TYPES OF INSULATION

While it's true that each material used to make up your house possesses some insulating value, the effectiveness of individual types of materials varies greatly. For example, a 1-inch-thick blanket of fiberglass insulation has the same insulation value as approximately a 3½-inch-thick layer of pine wood planking, a 22-

inch-thick wall of common brick, a 40-inch-thick layer of solid concrete, or a 54-inch-thick (4½ feet!) layer of stone.

The most popular types of insulation used in modern homes are blankets and batts of fiberglass and rock wool, rigid boards of polystyrene, fiberglass boards, rigid foam boards, and various loose forms of fiberglass and rock wool.

Fiberglass and Rock Wool Blankets and Batts

These two products make up about 90 percent of all home-owner insulation (Figs. 25.2 and 25.3). Fiberglass has been used as cost-effective insulation for over 75 years. It's made from sand and mostly recycled glass that's melted and spun into a material that's in effect "glass wool." These compressed fibers come in continuous-roll form (blanket) or in rolls having perforations along every few feet or yards so that you can pull off regular rectangular pieces (batts). Both blankets and batts are available in various densities, thicknesses, widths, and lengths, some with or without facing material or vapor barrier material (foil or kraft-faced vapor "retarder" barrier layer) on one side—which needs to be installed toward the warm or conditioned side of the wall's cavity. Look for batts or blankets that are formaldehyde-free. Fiberglass blankets and batts are mostly pink or yellow in color and are great in accessible locations such as open attic floors and wall or interior roof framing bays and other spaces. Some are sandwiched within sheets of plastic to help reduce the irritating itchiness that loose fiberglass or rock wool can cause when handled. They greatly lose their effectiveness when damp, compressed, or installed too loosely to cover an entire section or surface or when air is permitted to blow through the fibers, causing convective heat loss. One drawback of fiberglass blanket or batt material is that small pockets or voids around electrical boxes, heating and cooling ducts, plumbing, and wiring must be done with great care and are tempting places for insulating contractors to short change. Cramming or squeezing fiberglass insulation into tight spaces greatly reduces insulating values because very little air can remain trapped within the fibers.

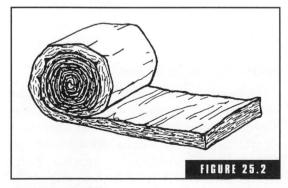

FIGURE 25.2

Blanket insulation.

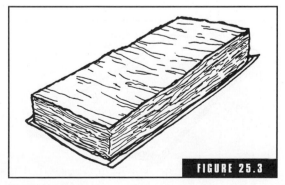

FIGURE 25.3

Batt insulation.

Different density versions of fiberglass blankets and batts are available and may be selected to closely match the desired R-values.

Fiberglass and rock wool also come in shredded forms for hand-pouring or machine-blowing applications. Be aware that both these materials can be irritating if they come into direct contact with your skin. Rock wool is the less bothersome of the two. Although loose insulation is more economical to purchase and install, it eventually will settle and lose some of its insulating value, and it's difficult to move out of the way if need be.

Fiberglass and rock wool insulation can be used throughout the entire house for ceilings, walls, floors, basements, around windows and doors, or anywhere else energy otherwise might be lost to conductivity and air infiltration. They both have good insulation values and are among the most economical types to purchase.

Rock wool insulation batts are available in semirigid models with unique flexible edges designed to compress as the batt is placed into walls, attics, ceiling, and floor frames. The flexible edge springs back, expanding against whatever it is filling, to give a tight fit.

Rigid Boards

Rigid insulation panels or boards are used for basement walls, concrete slabs, cathedral ceilings, exterior walls, and roofs before finishing (Fig. 25.4). A 1- or 2-inch layer of rigid foam panels on the outside of walls and roofs creates a sturdy structural layer that provides an effective thermal break between wood or steel framing members and the outer finishing materials. It is especially important when using steel studs in outside walls because steel efficiently transfers heat back and forth between inside and outside spaces at rates 8 to 12 times that of wood framing members. Rigid boards are manufactured in a variety of materials, some with foil facings for extra efficiency (they can add another R-2 to the boards), in different thicknesses, such as ½ inch with approximate R-2.5 value, 1 inch at about R-5 value, 1½ inches at approximately R-7.5 value, and 2 inches at about R-10 value. They also come in individual sheets with different edge styles, such as tongue and groove or interlocking and fanfold panels.

POLYSTYRENE RIGID BOARDS

Polystyrene is a plastic that, in rigid board form, dents easily and is highly combustible, but it is also very resistant to weather and moisture. Also known as *Styrofoam* or *molded expanded polystyrene* (MEPS), it's good for below-grade or exterior wall applications. Used indoors,

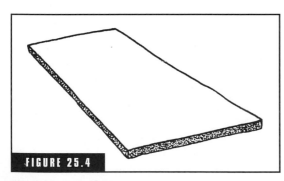

FIGURE 25.4

Rigid-board insulation.

these boards are a fire hazard unless covered by ⅝-inch-thick sheets of fire-resistant gypsum board. They typically have no facing.

FIBERGLASS BOARDS

Fiberglass boards are made of compressed fiberglass wool sandwiched between tough facing materials that together form a semirigid board. Its insulation value is average among the rest of the rigid-board insulation family. It's often covered by ⅝-inch-thick fire-resistant gypsum board on interior walls and ceilings.

RIGID FOAM BOARDS

These boards have the highest insulating qualities of all rigid-board materials. They form their own vapor barriers, too. Some of these plastic foam boards dent easily and must be handled gently. Most rigid-board insulations, though not easy to catch fire or flammable, will burn if started and will give off toxic fumes and gases, so foam boards should be covered by ⅝-inch-thick fire-resistant gypsum board on interior walls and ceilings, as usually prescribed in local building codes.

Spray Foam Insulation

Spray foam is a wonderful insulation invention; it's great to stop air infiltration from small cracks and holes. You may already be familiar with those cans of expandable foam marketed to fill small voids, cracks, and spaces around windows, doors, and various small openings in exterior walls and other places. Similar expanding foams are also available to insulate larger voids and entire sections of walls, roofs, and floors using special equipment that distributes the material in steady, even streams. Applying spray foam is an art that must be learned, though, and if done incorrectly, the results can be uneven and will not deliver desired R-values. The foams are usually sprayed with water as a spraying agent into a cavity—expanding on contact to fill any voids. Spray foam is perhaps best known for retroinsulating older homes by filling hard-to-access wall and other voids, where installing boards, batts, or blankets would involve taking apart walls and other main components. One potential drawback to using spray foam with new construction is that once it expands into walls or other cavities, after it solidifies or sets, it's literally attached to and envelops everything it comes in contact with. To modify electrical wiring, plumbing, or other wall components at a later date becomes difficult to impossible. Other nonadhesive materials such as fiberglass blankets, batts, and rigid foam can be removed and replaced a lot easier.

There are two main types of spray foam: open cell and closed cell. With open-cell foam, tiny cells of the foam remain partly open so that air fills all the cells and can migrate through portions of it. It's fairly soft and easy to squeeze. Closed-cell foam has similar cells that, as you might guess, are closed. The air or gas stays where it already is and results in a denser, heavier insulation that provides more strength per inch of thickness and higher R-values.

Be aware of how permeable the foam you plan to use is. If it is impermeable, plans must account for preventing the trapping of moisture in wall or roof assemblies.

Loose Insulation

Loose insulation can be hand poured or blown into walls and other voids (Fig. 25.5). Generally blown against an air-permeable backing and into framing member joist or stud bays, it fits tightly around wiring components, electric boxes, pipes, and other in-the-wall components. Loose insulation can consist of fiberglass, recycled newspaper, or other cellulose products and mineral wool. For installation on horizontal surfaces, such as in floors or attics and some roofs, the material just piles loosely. When blown into walls, it's usually mixed with a "sticky" binder that helps to hold it vertically in place and prevents settling. There's a considerable amount of skill involved in effective installation, and the contractors must be both experienced and responsible—because once it's done and the walls or ceilings or floors are sealed, it's very difficult to determine the work's coverage quality.

FIBERGLASS AND ROCK WOOLS

Fiberglass and rock wools are efficient and inexpensive. They can be applied using very little binder because they have a tendency to stick and pile up within gaps and voids around pipes, wiring, electrical boxes, and other wall obstructions and irregularities in wall and floor spaces. Although often more expensive than cellulose, fiberglass and rock wools will not shrink or absorb moisture (although they can become wet if no ventilation is provided) and are resistant to mold.

CELLULOSE

Cellulose, an organic insulation made from pulverized or ground-up newspapers and other wood or paper fibers, can be either dumped or blown into horizontal or vertical surfaces (often blown with a damp or "sticky" binder into vertical spaces). Cellulose insulation should be treated with fire-retardant and insect-preventive borate chemicals. Avoid cellulose that contains ammonium sulfate. It's an inexpensive material usually applied by experienced installers with air pumping equipment and wide hoses (Fig. 25.6). Its insulating value is only about R-3.5 per inch, but it's easily installed in deep thicknesses for greater total R-values, typically depending on how deep the open framing cavities are. It's a good material for filling

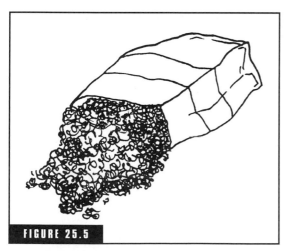

FIGURE 25.5

Loose-fill insulation.

Cellulose insulation.

irregular voids, where access is somewhat restricted or hard to reach. When compared with spray foam insulations, loose cellulose is a little easier to partially remove if additional wiring or plumbing lines need to be run later on. One negative feature of cellulose is that it can absorb moisture, especially if proper ventilation is not arranged with the installation.

INSULATION INSTALLATION

It's more difficult to say than to do, yet some installers just can't get the hang of it. Unless insulation is deliberately and correctly applied—without taking shortcuts—it quickly loses its advertised R-ratings and value. Voids that may occur owing to incomplete coverage or unwanted airflow can slash insulating values in half. So can unwanted moisture. Batt and blanket fibers must be equally lofted, with no gaps, voids, or compressed sections. When things are correct, the air between the fibers or cells is stationary and in equal proportions throughout. Seams along rigid foam panels must be taped. Places where foam board meets other materials must fit tightly so that no air can flow around the edges. Spray foams also must provide uninterrupted coverage, and the material should be as uniformly applied as possible.

PLACES TO INSULATE

Even if you live in an area having a mild climate, your home will be more comfortable if it's well insulated. It's not possible to have too much insulation in the walls and top-floor ceiling or in floors over carports, garages, porches, and other areas exposed to the weather, provided the insulation is installed correctly.

To prevent fire hazards, always keep insulation away from chimneys, exhaust flues, attic ventilators, and in general, all other heat-generating components and fixtures. Local building codes and product manufacturers provide clearance guidelines and requirements. It's usually best to insulate to the highest valued recommendations, and lately people have been going beyond those.

Recommended Insulation Values:
U.S. Department of Energy Recommendations

- *Warm climate:* Southern states with air-conditioning but little heating:
  - Gas or oil heat: Ceiling—R-22 to R-38; wall—R-11 to R-23; floor—R-11 to R-13; basement crawl space—R-11 to R-19
  - Electric-resistance heat: Ceiling—R-38 to R-49; wall—R-13 to R-25; floor—R-13 to R-19; basement crawl space—R-11 to R-19
- *Mixed climate:* Middle-tier states with moderate heating and cooling requirements:
  - Gas or oil heat: Ceiling—R-38; wall—R-11 to R-22; floor—R-13 to R-25; basement crawl space—R-11 to R-19
  - Electric-resistance heating: Ceiling—R-49; wall—R-11 to R-26; floor—R-25; basement crawl space—R-11 to R-19
- *Cold climate:* Northern states and mountainous regions with heavy heating loads:
  - Gas or oil heat: Ceiling—R-38 to R-49; wall—R-11 to R-22; floor—R-25; basement crawl space—R-11 to R-19
  - Electric-resistance heat: Ceiling—R-49; wall—R-11 to R-28; floor—R-25; basement crawl space—R-13 to R-19

There are six primary areas that should not be overlooked: basements, floors, walls, attics, ducts and plumbing, and cracks and joints that require caulking.

Basements

Insulation should not be installed against a wet or damp wall. Before insulation can be applied, a dry wall is necessary; after, basement or masonry interior walls may be insulated by several methods:

■ One method is to put up furring strips followed by applying insulating blankets or batts in the usual way, with a vapor barrier facing the living area of the basement

■ Another method is to attach rigid-board insulation to wood nailing strips that are bolted to the walls. Sheets of extruded polystyrene foam are very efficient per unit of thickness. The foil-faced vapor barrier should be placed toward the living spaces.

For either insulating method, consider using a separate vapor barrier on the backside of the insulation to prevent moisture from wall dampness from entering or collecting against the insulation.

After basement insulation is put up, it should be covered with an approved fire-safety-rated finishing material such as ⅝-inch-thick fire-resistant gypsum board. Find minimum guidelines for this in your local building code.

In general, rigid sheets of extruded polystyrene foam are the most efficient per unit of thickness. They're good to add to any masonry or concrete surface.

The exterior of basement foundation walls may be insulated with extruded polystyrene rigid foam insulation. Rigid foam insulation, with its tongue and groove design, also makes an excellent barrier against moisture and air infiltration. It can be used below grade because of its exceptional moisture resistance for applications such as concrete and masonry walls.

When foam panel board installation is complete, all joints should be sealed with construction insulation tape.

Floors

Prudent insulation of floors can save 5 to 15 percent of your heating costs. It's easy to insulate under floors during construction and not very expensive. Here's what to consider:

1. Insulate between the top of the foundation wall and the sill plate under the first-floor decking. This will stop air infiltration more than it "insulates," which is important when it comes to overall energy efficiency and savings. Resilient polyethylene foam insulation strips are used to make an airtight seal between the masonry foundation and the sill plate (Fig. 25.7).

2. The subfloor junction with the sole plate should be sealed. The framing crew can place a double bead of caulk on the subfloor before the sole plate is put in place (Fig. 25.7).

3. Under-floor insulation is important unless the first floor sits over a heated basement. In a house with a basement, typically the furnace is located in the basement with ducts (if a forced-air system) running to the upper floors. Some heat will be released from the furnace and ducts in the basement, heat that rises and helps to warm the floor above. If your house is instead built over a crawl space, consider that a floor over an unheated crawl space can be insulated by laying blanket insulation with a vapor barrier that faces up (Fig. 25.8). The insulation bottom must be covered with approved material per your local building code so that it's not exposed. To insulate over a concrete slab, lay a hard rigid board such as plywood over the top of the slab.

4. Seal where pipes, electric wires, or telephone and television cables penetrate the sole and top plates.

5. Seal around plumbing drains and beneath bathtubs by blocking large openings with pieces of construction sheathing and sealing the remaining cracks with expanding foam.

6. For soundproofing, insulate the floors between a first and second story. You can use blanket or batt fiberglass or rock wool insulation.

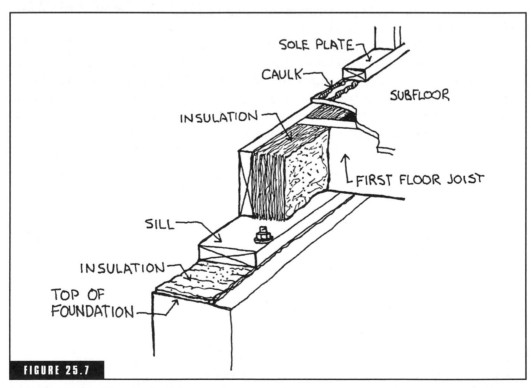

FIGURE 25.7

Insulating under sill and sole plates.

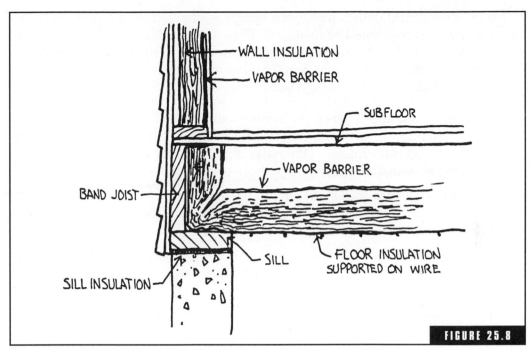

Insulation cutaway.

7. Fiberglass batts are excellent for insulating along or between the perimeter joists. There should be a vapor barrier that faces the living side, and the insulation should be covered with a fire-safety-rated material that's specified or approved by your local building code. One example may be ⅝-inch thick fire-resistant gypsum board.

8. All floors above cold spaces, such as vented crawl spaces, must be insulated, and so must floors in a room that is cantilevered beyond exterior walls below.

9. Floors of slabs built directly on the ground need insulation.

10. With crawl spaces, the insulation should be positioned with the vapor retarder toward the warm side of the structure (in cold-weather climates). The insulation can be supported with nylon banding or metal insulation supports. The bottom of the insulation should be protected or covered by a material specified or approved by your local building code.

Walls

Sides, tops, and bottoms of windows and doors should be insulated, with all cracks around window and door sashes and frames filled with insulation loosely pressed into place and then sealed with strips of vapor barrier tape, which serves as a vapor barrier. Tape should be stapled into the wood so that it holds firmly.

Conduit, electrical outlets (notorious energy wasters), switch boxes, and other fixtures and built-ins should be insulated. Fiberglass can fill larger holes and gaps around the conduit, electrical outlets, and switch boxes. Heat-generating electrical items must have a clearance from insulation. Reference your local building code and the fixture manufacturer's recommendations.

1. The openings formed near corner studs, cavities, and T-junctions created during the framing construction all should be filled with insulation before the entire framing is completed. Otherwise, it will be very difficult, if not impossible, to get insulation into some of those places.

2. The spaces between wall studs should be lined or filled with blankets or batts during framing. The insulation should be placed in the stud cavities with a vapor barrier facing the living area of the house.

3. For additional R-value, use insulated sheathing or apply rigid-board insulation to the outside of regular sheathing that might have a low insulation value.

4. Interior walls should be insulated if you want soundproofing. Fiberglass works well for sound control.

5. If the exterior walls of a house are covered with house wrap prior to application of the siding, air infiltration will be greatly reduced.

6. Drafts can be prevented around electric light switches and wall outlets with inexpensive fire-retardant plastic foam gaskets that fit behind the cover plates. The contractor should use only Underwriters Laboratories–approved products.

7. Insulation should be placed behind plumbing access panels and warm-air registers.

8. Insulating the garage walls and enclosing them with drywall or plasterboard will help to retain the heat from your vehicles during winter.

9. Knee walls are partial walls that extend from the floor to the rafters, commonly found in one-and-one-half story homes and used most frequently for bedrooms or bonus spaces. They should be insulated.

10. Stipulate in the contract that the contractor is responsible for the initial cleaning, both interior and exterior, of windows. Dirty glass can block as much as 40 percent of available solar energy coming through during the day, which could contribute to as much as 3 or 4 percent of your heating bill.

11. If your walls have metal frames, consider having continuous insulation sheathing placed over the outside of the wall framing, between the metal framing pieces and your exterior siding.

12. Consider having window coverings quoted as part of the house contract. Window insulation is available in a variety of shutters, shades, draperies, and panels. Most curtains, blinds, shades, and drapes provide some insulating value when closed over a window. During sunny winter days, windows receiving direct sunlight should be uncovered because they will let in more heat than they'll lose. Qualities to look for in window coverings include the following:

- Flame-retardant materials that won't produce dangerous fumes if ignited
- Moisture resistance
- Durability
- Quality of opening/closing mechanisms
- Ease of operation

13. Unless exterior doors come with bottom seals, request that door sweeps be installed and positioned so that the door bottoms seal when closed.

14. Openings that have been made in walls for plumbing or heating components should be plugged to keep air and sound from traveling through. Larger openings and gaps where the walls and floors were drilled for pipes and wiring can be packed with unfaced fiberglass insulation. Smaller cracks and openings can be sealed with silicone caulking.

15. Insulate behind bathtubs with moisture-resistant insulation before the tubs are installed.

16. Foam panels installed over the outside of exterior wall sheathing can increase insulating values. Some tear-resistant foam panels unfold over sheathing to form a nearly airtight seal all around the house. This rigid foam panel board siding is made of fan-folded panels that minimize the number of seams and greatly reduce the potential for air infiltration. Once the few existing joints are covered with construction insulation tape, an efficient seal is complete. Again, rigid foam insulation applied to the outside reduces thermal bridging and air infiltration, increasing the R-value of your walls. It also reduces the risk of condensation inside wall cavities.

17. Exterior walls can receive added protection from the application of house wrap after taping the joints or sheathing and caulking, which helps to block the chill from wind, rain, and snow.

ATTICS

Particularly in a single-story house, most heat loss occurs through the attic. By installing sufficient attic insulation, and by sealing connections between the heated space and the attic such as plumbing and vent stack openings, you can cut up to 30 percent of your fuel bill. Depending on where you live, the U.S. Department of Energy recommends that R-values for insulation should range between R-38 and R-50. Realistically, and to a point, the more the better.

1. The most common method of insulating an attic is to staple blanket insulation between the ceiling joists with the vapor barrier on the side closest to the home's living areas (Fig. 25.9). Attic insulation should be at least 15½ to 18 inches of standard fiberglass batts. In cold-climate areas, consider insulation with even greater R-values.

2. Another way is to use loose-blown insulation (see Fig. 25.6). This can be a very effective way as long as you're not planning to use the insulated area for storage.

3. If you have cathedral ceilings, one way to insulate is to install batt material between the roof rafters against the underside of the roof sheathing or deck before the installation of dry wall or plasterboard (Figs. 25.10 and 25.11). There should be an airspace of at least 3 inches between the top of the insulation and the underside of the roof sheathing or deck. This space is needed to ensure proper ventilation and to provide enough space for attic rafter and other vents to function properly.

4. An easier way to accomplish the insulation of cathedral ceilings is simply to use structural insulated panels (SIPs) in their construction—then the rigid foam insulation is already sandwiched between the outside and inside panel layers.

5. Any attic overhead pulldown doors should be hinged on one side of the door frame and equipped with springs so that when closed, the door can be

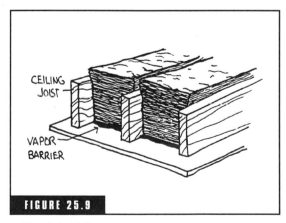

FIGURE 25.9

Ceiling insulation.

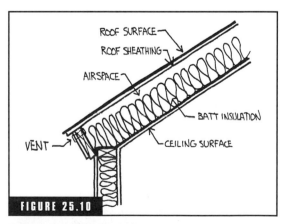

FIGURE 25.10

Cathedral ceiling insulation.

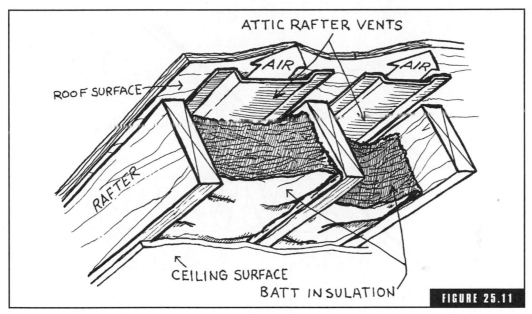

ATTIC RAFTER VENTS

ROOF SURFACE

AIR

AIR

RAFTER

CEILING SURFACE

BATT INSULATION

FIGURE 25.11

Cathedral ceiling insulation with attic rafter vents.

secured snugly. The insulation that fits over the attic side of such a door should be able to be pulled over the opening before the door is closed unless it's permanently attached to the top of the attic door itself. There also should be a rubber seal around the door frame to stop any possible air infiltration.

6. In homes where ductwork must be installed directly through the attic, the roof and the attic ceiling both need to be insulated to minimize the influence attic temperatures have on conditioned air in the ductwork. This complicates attic and roofing ventilation needs, though, and separate ventilation needs to be arranged where the sheathing is installed and where considerable temperature differences may occur.

7. Soffit vents must not be blocked by insulation. In the attic ceiling, baffles can be placed where the attic ceiling insulation approaches soffit vents to help maintain the airspace required between insulation and roof sheathing. The baffles help to prevent insulation from blocking soffet vent airflow into the attic and help to prevent insulation from blowing into unwanted areas (Fig. 25.12).

Attic baffles typically are extruded polystyrene used to help maintain constant airflow from soffit vents through the attic to the ridge vent, preventing heat buildup. They increase attic cross-ventilation; reduce cooling-energy loss; minimize moisture buildup, heat gain, and roof ice dams; and help to extend the useful life of the roof. They also keep insulation out of unwanted

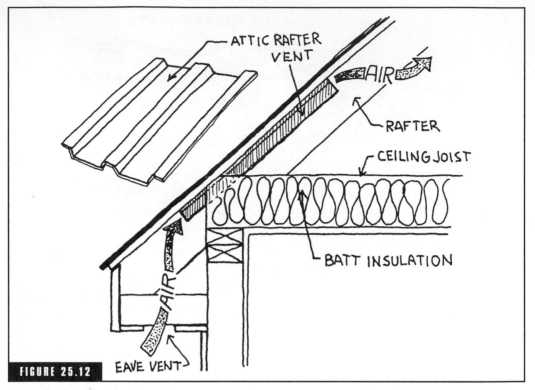

FIGURE 25.12

Attic rafter vent baffles.

areas, prevent insulation from blocking airflow from soffit vents into the attic, and keep loose-fill insulation away from recessed light fixtures or other heat-producing devices and from spilling over attic hatch door openings.

8. Attic accesses should be insulated—the back of the hatch or door with a piece of fiberglass blanket or rigid board. The bottom of the hatch or door should be weather-stripped to prevent heat from transferring into the attic from below.

   One access cover design available is molded from lightweight polystyrene to form a hollow shell. The shell is then filled with fiberglass insulation. The insulated cover is large enough to cover attic stairs. Double foam weather-stripping seals are attached to the bottom edge, providing an airtight seal around the opening. It's hinged on its side to attic joists for easy opening.

9. Recessed lighting fixtures can be a major source of heat loss, but you need to be careful how close insulation is placed next to a heat-producing fixture unless the fixture is marked "I.C."—which means "insulated ceiling," which further means "designed for insulation contact." Resist the temptation to stuff insulation around and directly next to the fixture. Properly made can lights should come with or specify a protective cap made of rigid foam insulation to

prevent the passage of conditioned warm or cool air up into the attic or above the living area. For all recessed lighting fixtures, verify local building code and light fixture manufacturer recommendations for proper insulation clearances.

10. Radiant barriers such as those made with aluminum foil are not exactly insulation, but they do keep heat from being absorbed by an outside surface, especially in hot climates. Foil-covered flexible plastic sheets, kraft paper, rigid foam board, oriented strandboard, plywood, and other sheathings installed in roofs can help to keep attics cooler when installed over ventilated backings.

11. Insulating housewraps are available that provide another R-2 of protection where installed. They can provide two-way heat protection while still allowing the walls to breathe.

Ducts and Plumbing

By insulating heating and cooling ducts, pipes, and water heaters, you can reduce your annual heating costs by as much as 10 percent.

1. Wherever heating ducts run through unheated parts of a house, such as through attics, basements, or garages, they can waste as much heat or more than they deliver. This means that the occupants pay for a lot more heat than they receive. Two-inch-thick foil-faced fiberglass blanket insulation is manufactured in sizes designed for wrapping around ductwork and pipes (Fig. 25.13). The foil barrier prevents condensation and mold from forming on the duct or pipe. It also helps to prevent banging noises caused by flexing and vibration.

2. Seal all duct seams and metal duct seams with metallic tape rated for the temperature.

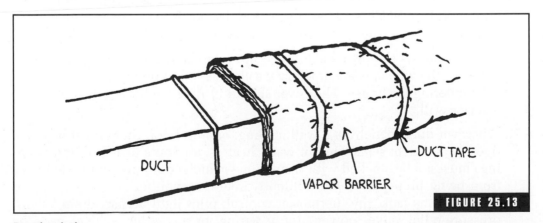

DUCT

VAPOR BARRIER

DUCT TAPE

FIGURE 25.13

Duct insulation.

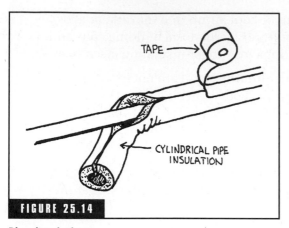

TAPE →

CYLINDRICAL PIPE INSULATION

FIGURE 25.14

Pipe insulation.

3. Well-sealed vapor barriers should exist on the outside of the insulation on cooling ducts to prevent moisture buildup.

4. Water pipes need insulation, too, especially cold-water pipes exposed to freezing temperatures in winter and hot-water pipes installed between a water heater and fixtures. Preformed polystyrene insulation tubes easily snap into place around pipes, or pipes can be wrapped in strips cut from fiberglass batts (an old-fashioned, messy way). The pipe insulation also will muffle gurgling noises and will prevent the irritating problem of condensation during warm temperatures when cold-water pipes tend to "sweat" and drip condensate onto basement floors, carpeting, and furnishings (Fig. 25.14). For pipes running through an unheated crawl space that's exposed to freezing temperatures (generally not a good idea), insulate both hot- and cold-water lines or protect with heat tape.

5. For hot-water tanks, carefully read the manufacturer's instructions to see if additional blanket insulation is allowed. Some companies may void the warranty if insulation is applied over the tank. If additional insulation is permitted, instructions must be followed to the letter because many critical parts cannot be covered safely or effectively. The top or bottom of the tank, the thermostat control, pilot access, drain valves, pressure-relief valves, power-supply wiring, air vents, hood drafts, and other components could become hazards if covered with additional insulation. In all cases, make sure that the tank air vents and hood draft are clear at all times for safe ventilation to the outdoors. If a tankless water heater is selected, follow the manufacturer's instructions as to where pipe insulation can be installed.

6. Outside faucets should be able to accept a premade foam faucet insulation cover for the winter as a temporary weatherization to prevent freezing winds from entering the house. The cover should fit flush and securely against the exterior wall.

7. Wherever ducts penetrate a wall, ceiling, or attic floor, there must be effective fits and tight seals. On hot-water heaters, air vents or hood draft openings must not be blocked with insulation—which could prevent toxic fumes from being properly vented outdoors. Likewise, neither should the top or bottom of the tank, the thermostat control, pilot light access, drain valves, pressure-relief valve, power-supply wiring, or any other critical parts be

blocked. Follow the instructions from the water heater manufacturer for installing insulation.

CAULKING

A house is made of many different materials. With age, temperature changes, vibration, and general wear, cracks will develop where the different construction materials meet. Even when doors and windows are weather-stripped, air can infiltrate through these other cracks and joints in the floors, walls, and roof. Individually, these small cracks might seem insignificant, but together they can cause chilly drafts and raise heating or cooling costs.

They also invite insects, leaks, and rot-causing moisture. Although you can't expect to seal up your house completely, by caulking it thoroughly, you can curb most of the drafts and heat loss. It's a simple and inexpensive process, yet it can cut up to 10 percent off your heating bills. Advances in caulk manufacturing have been outstanding. If you remember that sticky, runny, or too-thick-to-adhere caulking of years ago, today's caulk literally can run seams around them. There are acrylic and tripolymer caulks that make experts out of novices. Insist that your contractor and all subcontractors use a high grade of caulk for all their sealing tasks. Between caulk, spray foam, and weather stripping, accidental seams and inadvertent air leaks can be sealed to prevent heat-robbing drafts.

The caulking itself is an ideal solution for sealing narrow gaps and cracks. It's a soft, rubber-like material that will conform to any opening, will stay supple, and won't crack or deteriorate for at least several years or—depending on the type of caulk used and the application—for many years. The following checklist presents key areas that should be caulked in the typical house.

CAULKING CHECKLIST ✔✔✔✔✔

___ Around window and door frames

___ Anyplace a crack occurs between brick or pieces of siding

___ Between the foundation and the house framing walls

___ Around the outside of an air-conditioning unit that protrudes from a window

___ Where the wood sill meets the foundation

___ Where exhaust hoods and fan covers pass through a wall

___ Where plumbing pipes enter the house (Severe cold wind chill at a tiny opening can cause a pipe to freeze.)

___ Where telephone, cable, and electric wires enter the house

(Continued)

✔✔✔✔✔ **CAULKING CHECKLIST** (*Continued*)

___ Where trim meets wood siding, brick, mortar, and other materials

___ Where door or window frames meet walls

___ Under window sills

___ Where floors meet walls

___ At corners formed by siding

___ Between porches and the main body of the house

___ Where chimney or masonry meets siding (Chimney caulk is needed here.)

___ Around fireplace glass door jambs (Special heat-resistant caulk is needed here.)

___ Around heating and cooling ducts and pipes running from a separate outside central air-conditioning unit

___ Around pipes going to sinks and behind toilets

___ Around roof flashing, vents, and pipes

___ In gutter and downspout joints

___ Around vents and fans

___ At mortar joints

___ Where two building/siding materials meet (i.e., brick meets stucco or wood)

___ Around exterior basement doors

___ At window stops

___ Make sure that weep holes at the bottoms of storm windows are not caulked or otherwise plugged. They allow moisture from condensation to drain out or evaporate.

___ At exterior penetrations in the sheathing (porch light fixtures, outdoor outlets, phone, cable, electric service holes, etc.)

___ At tub drain penetrations

___ Backsides of window flanges to the sheathing during installation

___ Between door thresholds and subflooring

___ At baseboards and quarter-round moldings

___ At gaps beneath escutcheons on plumbing pipes

___ At seams between door jambs and door stops

___ Underneath metal or wooden door thresholds

CAULKING CHECKLIST *(Continued)* ✔✔✔✔✔

___ Between window and door drip caps and siding

___ On split or broken siding

___ Where framing meets flooring

___ On gaps in the attic around pipe penetrations under the insulation and anywhere else cracks or gaps exist between the living area and attic

Note: Silicone caulk stays flexible and is ideal for gaps where movement or seasonal expansion/contraction occurs. However, most makes of silicone caulk cannot be painted. They need to be purchased in appropriate colors. When caulking, for gaps of ⅜-inch or more, the crack should be packed with foam backer rod before the caulk is applied, so the seam won't crack later.

In addition to insulation, a home's living areas also should be sealed with appropriate material (called a vapor barrier) applied along the inside of the studs, the ceiling joists, and the floor joists—mainly to prevent the movement of moisture from the living areas into the insulation. Insulation loses some of its efficiency when it becomes damp or wet, and if moisture is not retained inside the living spaces of a home, the occupants won't be as comfortable and will need more heat to achieve a satisfying inside temperature. In humid locations, however, where air-conditioning is often running to remove moisture from the inside air, the vapor barrier will prevent outside moisture from entering the living areas.

Vapor Barriers for Walls and Ceilings

There are three methods for applying a vapor barrier to exterior walls or ceilings:

1. Install insulating blankets or batts having faces of vapor barrier backing such as treated kraft paper or aluminum foil placed on the living area side of the wall or ceiling.

2. When unfaced blanket or batt insulation is used, a separate vapor barrier must be provided. Aluminum-backed plaster and drywall are not effective choices because their seams don't overlap.

3. Staple or nail polyethylene sheet material to the interior of the studs and ceiling joists. This is probably the most effective vapor barrier. Installation details are extremely important. Polyethylene tape is also available for sealing seams and wrapping loose sheet material ends. The fewer seams, the better, and the material should be attached before the interior partitions are installed for an effective, continuous seal.

Vapor Barriers for Floors

If blanket or batt insulation is applied between the floor joists, a vapor barrier (per local building code specifications) should be installed against the subfloor. The covering of the insulation on the bottom likewise should be per code specifications.

A Safety Note

Peel back insulation and flammable vapor barriers away from the heat-producing components or features in a house. Chimneys, flues, stoves, electric fans, and heating sources all can be potential fire starters. The heat-producing equipment manufacturer and your local building code should provide guidelines for proper clearance.

✔✔✔✔✔ SOUND CONTROL INSULATION CHECKLIST

___ Consider using fiberglass insulation in walls, ceilings, and floors to control sound.

___ Install thick padding and carpeting to reduce impact sound. Heavily padded carpets absorb sound far better than bare or tiled floors.

___ Choose solid-wood (not hollow core) interior doors with threshold and jamb seals where privacy is desired.

___ Have all windows, wiring, and piping holes caulked.

___ Use at least double-pane storm windows to help reduce sound transmission.

___ Telephone hookups, doorbells, intercoms, or audio built-ins should be installed on interior walls only, never on common or corridor walls.

___ Wiring, where it penetrates connecting structures, should be insulated with non-hardening caulk or dry packing.

___ Ceiling fixture openings need to be sealed using before-mentioned precautions around heat-producing components.

___ Electric outlet holes should be neatly cut out to reduce sound leaks.

___ Fire-retardant plastic foam gaskets may be included behind all electric outlets and switch covers on both sides of common walls they're placed in, blocking a direct route between rooms for airborne noise.

___ A well-planned layout will minimize flowing water noise.

___ Plumbing fixtures and wall plates need caulking.

___ A nonhardening silicone or butyl-based caulk is also needed for the perimeter of drywall panels. Caulking around the floor, corner, and ceiling of drywall or plas-

SOUND CONTROL INSULATION (*Continued*)

terboard must be done before the panels go up against the wood studding. This makes sure that acoustical gaps from warped or uneven studs are filled. The flexible caulk will help to reduce vibration.

___ Window treatments can help to minimize sound transmission from the outside. Heavy draperies and quilted or pleated shades will help to absorb noise better than thin metal or vinyl blinds or curtains will.

___ An additional sound control relies on resilient channels, U-shaped metal strips, applied to wall studs and ceiling joists with a ½- by 3-inch gypsum nailing strip at the bottom. The channels help to break up sound waves and isolate noise. Fiberglass or mineral wool batts should be stapled in the stud spaces. Since the channels are resilient, they deaden sound transmission (Fig. 25.15).

___ Another sound-controlling wall features studs that are staggered within the wall so that no individual stud actually touches both inner surfaces of the wall. Insulation is snaked through the studs along the entire length, leaving no gaps for sound to get through.

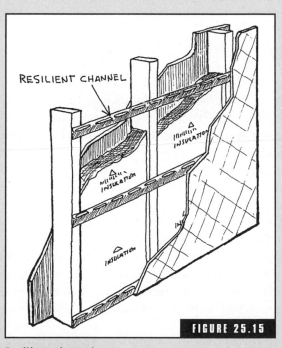

Resilient channels.

INSULATION

- All insulation is tightly installed, with no air gaps.
- Vapor barriers face the interior of the home sides that are heated.
- No punctures have been made in vapor barriers. Any rips or tears have been repaired.
- Ductwork is insulated.
- Plumbing is insulated throughout the house.
- All openings to the outside for plumbing, wiring, and gas lines are sealed.

SUMMER AND WINTER PROTECTION

Where possible, provide shade for sunny east, south, and west walls and windows. Use roof overhangs, shade trees, sun screens, shades, or interior draperies. Try to be flexible; shade makes for easier cooling in summer, yet sunshine streaming in through a window in winter can be a welcome sight. Consider placing evergreen trees on the north side of the house to help block the cold northern winter winds.

REMODELING NOTES

Insulation ranks toward the top of green remodeling strategies involving energy investments and quick paybacks. Some homes have generous cavities whose inside levels of insulation have compressed, otherwise degraded, or absorbed moisture over the years, rendering the original insulation ineffective. A thermal survey quickly should be able to point out the efficiency even with sealed walls. The help of several professional insulation companies should be called on. If the survey is done during winter, a plan can be arrived at involving the best way to upgrade the insulation—Can the cavities simply be refilled or topped off with new insulation, or must the existing insulation be removed and replaced?—a far more extensive job. Or can additional insulation be added to the outer wall surfaces and new siding added? This can be done in stages during nicer weather as the budget permits. The installation of air-impermeable membranes also must be included as part of the entire wall strategy. Once you open things up, the exterior walls must work in tandem with the windows as well. It's not as simple as just replacing what's inside the walls.

Some older walls simply are to narrow and too full of plaster, lathing, wood, and other materials to do anything other that sandwich with insulation. And then, care must be taken to handle moisture and air infiltration. Moisture needs to be blocked from entering but allowed to escape from within the walls. Ventilation becomes an issue when sandwiching insulation around old existing walls. Can the existing siding be removed intact, with the ability to be put on over the new insulation? Or must you plan new siding?

Other options include building a wall around or outside a wall with SIPs or even insulated concrete forms. This is a bit more elaborate but would, in effect, be like having an entirely new thermal envelope. Care is required to reconcile the places where the walls meet, such as at windows and door frames, and accommodation is needed for the exceptionally deep depths of window and door sills. However, if you have an acceptable floor plan and a good location and serviceable plumbing and electrical supplies, it's an option. You need to evaluate your situation.

▶▶▶▶▶ POINTS TO PONDER

1. Insulation should envelop all living areas of your home, leaving no openings except doors, windows, and necessary vents (which may, in turn, be individually insulated, too).

2. Heating and cooling ducts and water piping should be insulated to provide energy efficiency.

3. Much of the insulation should be installed after the framing is complete and the electrical, plumbing, and heating systems have been roughed in and inspected.

4. Because heat rises, the potential heat loss in a house is greatest through the roof.

5. Although interior walls and floors are not exposed to outside temperatures, they also should be insulated to provide sound barriers between rooms.

6. Insulation belongs between the top of the foundation wall and the sill plate under the first-floor decking. Insulation also should be stuffed into the cracks and small spaces between rough framing and the jambs, heads, and sills of windows and doors and used to fill spaces behind conduit, electric outlets, switch boxes, and other built-ins. Enough airspace should be included between insulation and any devices that produce heat or get hot.

7. Seal where pipes, electric wires, or telephone and television cables penetrate the sole and top plates. Insulating foam is a viable alternative to caulk when large gaps must be sealed because foam fills cracks, holes, and other voids, assuming the shape of the cavities. It does not shrink and sticks to most surfaces, including wood, metal, masonry, glass, and most plastics.

8. Make sure that contractors don't skimp on the quality of caulking they use. There isn't much additional cost that separates medium-quality caulking from top-quality caulking. If special color caulking is used (as with stucco), see that you receive a few tubes for future touch-ups and so that you can purchase more of the same caulk later.

9. Insulation loses effectiveness when damp or wet. Vapor barriers must be applied between the living areas and insulation to prevent movement of moisture from the living areas into the insulation.

10. Where possible, provide shade for walls and windows with roof overhangs, trees, blinds, shades, or interior draperies, and plant evergreen trees and shrubs for wind blocks.

11. Consider adding insulation backings to interior wall coverings and furnishings such as wood paneling, wall hangings, and even large built-on or -in sections of book shelves or other shelves. For years, Europeans have been hanging weighted curtains that can be temporarily pulled over doors to reduce drafts. Blinds and shutters are available with insulated panels and inside layers of reflective foil to help prevent solar heat gain during summer days and to prevent cold winter radiation from the windows at night.

12. Remember that drywall can be used as an insulating air barrier if caulk, glue, or gaskets are used with the installation to prevent moist, warm air from entering the walls from interior living spaces.

CHAPTER 26

Wall Covering and Trim

The materials you select to cover your inside walls, plus the trim that's installed along corners and joints, are features that should or will ultimately weigh heavily in your decorating scheme. They're part of a home's inside cosmetics—what you and your visitors will see—the home's inner facings that can influence the home's air quality if unhealthy materials are used.

Interior wall and ceiling surfaces function a lot like skin. They're what we see, feel, and even smell inside the home. Although their volume altogether isn't much when compared with other building materials, area-wise, they're the largest surface type in almost any space, and they influence rooms and home areas by attracting or reflecting heat, absorbing or reflecting light, absorbing or reflecting sound, emitting or gasing off chemicals and odors and affecting the home's air quality, allowing or stopping moisture to pass through, and even creating desired moods through colors or textures.

They might be the first thing a visitor will notice when entering your home and often will set the tone for how you've planned your green construction. Instead of a considerable financial payback from lower energy bills, green wall coverings and trim offer a home's occupants a healthy environment from safe materials that will not negatively affect their surroundings. Basic selection guidelines must consider

- *Health and safety.* For decades, common building products sacrificed healthy characteristics for manufacturing ease and toxic materials. Building materials and furnishings gased-off inside the house and spoiled air quality. Now, select low– or no–volatile organic compound (VOC), formaldehyde-free, water-based sealants, paints, stains, and other coatings. Use similar types of healthy adhesives and binders in cabinets, doors, and trim. Reduce the amount of carpeting throughout each floor plan.

■ *Durability.* Although they're usually a bit more expensive to begin with, in almost every case, the lifetime costs of such materials offer much better values. They're more comfortable. They don't break down as frequently, require less maintenance and replacement, and are even easier to keep clean.

■ *Resource conservation.* Why waste raw materials that aren't readily replenishable when sustainable substitutes are available? The list of green products gets more extensive every year. Companies are practically falling over each other trying to engineer green characteristics into their offerings. Wall coverings and trim are no exception—there are unique, excellent-performing renewable products to choose from right now. Can you use reclaimed and recycled products or materials made with recycled content? Do you really need a "finished" surface? Or would you be better off simplifying the construction by letting the structural components stand with their own finished surfaces, such as a tinted natural clay plaster wall or ceiling or a tinted sealed concrete floor instead of a concrete floor topped with tile. Another way to further reduce the amount of finished wall space required is to do away with some nonbearing walls and similar room dividers. Open interiors are often healthier spaces that live larger than they really are.

■ *Green products or green results?* A product manufactured in a nongreen way or using nongreen materials sometimes can provide durability and cost-effectiveness, resulting in a green use. Think of some of the functional components resulting from vinyl or aluminum. The greenness of many green products easily could become the subject of high school debate teams, with logical-sounding arguments coming from both sides. How the materials are manufactured and how they need to be maintained also can be debatable green issues.

There are a number of possibilities to select from when it comes to covering or finishing off the inside walls. The most popular materials are drywall, plaster, and paneling. If drywall or plaster is selected, then specify whether you want the finished surfaces painted or wallpapered. Old-fashioned clay plasters have been becoming more popular, made from clay with natural binders and pigments. But make sure that you know where your products are coming from. There have been instances where cheap structural wall covering such as drywall, imported from places having few quality standards, were made from contaminated materials that soon caused widespread mold growth after installation, to the point where every wall they were in had to be ripped out and rebuilt.

DRYWALL

Drywall is by far the most often used structural wall covering in new homes today. It's available in 4- by 8-foot and other size sheets and typically is made of a sturdy layer of gypsum sandwiched between two layers of paper that help give it such a smooth, unblemished look and feel. Greener drywall is available containing between 10 and 15 percent recycled gypsum and 100 percent recycled paper. It's also available in a paperless version, which makes it less likely to be affected by moisture and molds, which tend to degrade the paper facings. Paperless drywall is faced with fiberglass instead, which has greater strength and water and mold resistance than paper. The gypsum inside is also reinforced with fiberglass strands that result in a very sturdy wall board similar to the underlayment boards for tile floors and walls. Like paper drywalls, paperless versions also can be smooth-faced and then painted or wallpapered. Another type of drywall is available when soundproofing features are desired. *Sound transmission class* drywall products are designed to deaden sounds that occur on either side of the wall. This can come in handy if you build on a small lot and have close neighbors or are near a highway, business, school, or other operation that frequently gets noisy. Or maybe you want to stop noise from exiting your home—from a teenage son's rock band practice or a loud stereo.

One more type of drywall is beginning to be installed, called *phase-change drywall*, which has been developed to assist passive-solar design. It's unique makeup enables this "high mass" drywall to absorb heat from the sun and then release it later into the house. It does so by changing a waxlike substance it's built around back and forth from a solid to a liquid then back again to a solid. When it first changes from a solid to liquid, it absorbs considerable amounts of heat from the sun. Later, when the sun is no longer directly heating the drywall, the liquid core starts solidifying back to its original state—changing its phase—and giving off heat that helps to warm the home's interior when extra heat is needed.

Drywall Installation

Panels are measured to fit, cut to fit, and screwed (or screwed and glued for extra strength) to the rough walls (Fig. 26.1).

- The screws must be slightly countersunk or driven so that the heads pass slightly through the surface of the drywall.

- A smooth, continuous surface is achieved between adjacent panels by filling in and troweling over the joints, cracks, and spaces with a plasterlike joint compound after a thin water-saturated paper tape has been applied to each crack or space.

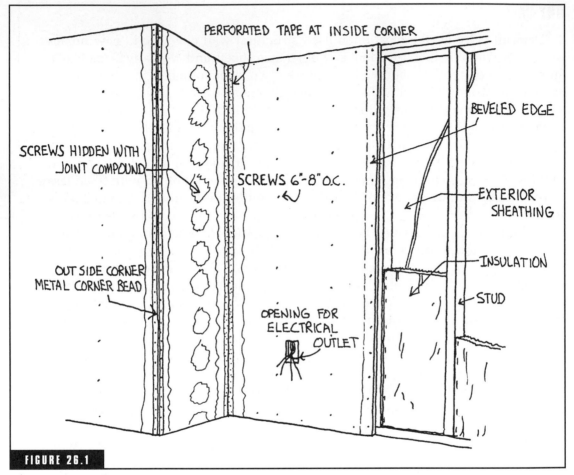

PERFORATED TAPE AT INSIDE CORNER

BEVELED EDGE

SCREWS HIDDEN WITH JOINT COMPOUND

SCREWS 6"-8" O.C.

EXTERIOR SHEATHING

OUT SIDE CORNER METAL CORNER BEAD

INSULATION

STUD

OPENING FOR ELECTRICAL OUTLET

FIGURE 26.1

Drywall—vertical application.

An optional installation can include gaskets attached to framing and walls behind the drywall's edges and around any rough openings such as those for doors to make for an airtight seal. This can be especially important when planned for a wall that's shared by the living area and an attached garage to prevent carbon monoxide and gasoline fumes from entering the house. The gaskets also can be used in all outer walls and places where plumbing and electrical building envelope penetrations occur to help form an effective air barrier. This use of drywall as an air seal is sometimes referred to as an *airtight drywall approach* (ADA). Another way to achieve a similar type of air seal with drywall is to use silicon caulk or closed-cell foam instead of gaskets.

■ Screw depressions from the countersunk screws are filled in with the same joint compound and then troweled smooth.

- Lightweight but sturdy metal angles are installed wherever two pieces of drywall form right angles to strengthen the corners. Edges then are troweled smooth with a thin layer of joint compound.

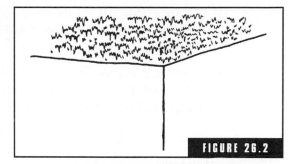

FIGURE 26.2

A textured ceiling—dappled finish.

- Once the joint compound dries, it's smoothed out with fine-grit sandpaper. A second coat of joint compound then should be applied and also sanded smooth when dry. The second coat then should be followed by a third and final coat.

Final finishing is accomplished with more sanding and by last-minute "point up" work—taking care of any minor irregularities and making edges sharper. When everything is dry and sanded smooth, the entire surface is painted, usually white. Once painted, there should be no evidence of panel joints or nail indentations.

At an additional cost, special finishes may be applied to drywall (and ceilings) in skim coatings of topping compounds similar to plaster. A skim coat can be left smooth, swished, dappled, ridged, or otherwise finished to obtain a variety of unique textures (Fig. 26.2). Some contractors will apply a coating of material, and while it's still wet, take a large sponge and press it against the surface, drawing out the plaster-like material in many tiny points that look like miniature stalactites. It's a way to have your own walls and ceilings finished in a manner that you'll find nowhere else.

DRYWALL CONSIDERATIONS

- Drywall should not be applied in extreme heat or cold to avoid the possibility of warping or shrinkage.

- Drywall should be carefully fit to minimize the number and sizes of gaps.

- Specify that contractors must use approved scaffolding for reaching ceilings and high walls. Some contractors actually use stilts to reach indoor heights—a dangerous practice.

- When specifying drywall, look for ⅝-inch-thick fire-resistant gypsum board. Check to make sure that it meets your local building code.

- When extra strength is desired, wall adhesive can be applied to all studs before installing drywall.

- Screws provide better holding power than nails, with less chance of "pop outs," where fastener heads loosen and work their way back through the surface of the drywall.

- Request that all joints be taped, with three separate coats of joint compound, each sanded smooth. Each successive coat should leave a wider swatch or track and a smooth finish.
- Special moisture-resistant gypsum drywall must be used along all wall areas around shower stalls and bathtubs—and wherever else there's the likelihood of water or moisture present.

ADVANTAGES

1. Drywall is relatively inexpensive to purchase and install.
2. It's less inclined to crack than plaster.
3. It's easier to repair than plaster.
4. Drywall can be installed quickly and doesn't take as long to set up as plaster does. The rest of the finishing work can proceed without much delay.

DISADVANTAGES

1. Drywall must be painted because its finished appearance is not uniform. All joints, screw indentations, and repairs are whiter—owing to the joint compound—than the rest of the drywall surfacing, which is a gray or buff color (whatever the shade of the drywall's outer paper layer).
2. The modular construction and taping of drywall sections sometimes can be discerned, especially if it's a less-than-perfect installation. This can be worse than an occasional crack in a plaster wall.

PLASTER

Before drywall was invented, plaster was the number one way to finish off a home's interior walls. Plasters made of natural clay, lime, and gypsum are some of the earliest wall finishes still in use. Clay is a wonderfully green material, available

✔✔✔✔ DRYWALL INSPECTION CHECKLIST

The following is a checklist of items that shouldn't be overlooked with drywall:

__ Cuts should be clean around register openings, wall switches, and outlets so that covers and fixtures do not allow gaps or exposed spaces in the drywall.

__ When viewed lengthwise, there should be no warped or bumpy surfaces. Nor should there be uneven surfaces to the touch.

__ Inquire as to how long the contractor will guarantee the drywall against defects.

practically anywhere. It's inexpensive to process, is harmless and biodegradable, and can be purchased in all sorts of unique colors and breathable finishes, including lime paints and various color washes. If you'd rather not apply any finishes, that's fine, too. These natural wall and ceiling surfaces need no paints or wallpaper to fit well with most decors. Recently, a raft of designer earth- and bright-colored tinted plasters has been gaining traction with interior designers.

Plaster Installation

Plaster is a mudlike building material that needs to be applied to some type of structural base. It can be applied over masonry in thin coats. It also can be applied over plaster-board lathing, which provides a secure base or adhesive priming coat to which the plaster adheres. Lathing is a wallboard that usually has a gypsum core sandwiched between layers of paper and a cardboard or foil backing that serves as a vapor barrier. The outer layers of paper absorb water quickly so that plaster sticks to the lath before it begins to slide. The inner layers are treated to resist moisture.

- Specify ⅝-inch-thick fire-resistant gypsum board if it meets your local code.

- Gypsum lath should be applied to the studs with screws. If extra strength is desired, it also can be glued to the studs.

- The lath may be solid or perforated. Perforated material improves bonding capabilities between the plaster.

- Gaps between applied sheets should be minimized.

- Plaster typically is applied in either a single ½-inch-thick layer or two ⅜-inch-thick coats, one on top of the other.

PLASTER CONSIDERATIONS

- Plastering should not be done in extreme heat or cold.

- Contractors should use approved scaffolding to reach high areas (not stilts).

- Screws, not nails, should be used to fasten lath to studs; for extra strength, also apply glue to the studs.

- Plaster can be finished in smooth or textured surfaces to complement any decor. Ask the plaster contractor to show you samples of the various options. If possible, view homes featuring different plaster options to compare looks.

- Specify how you want the plaster finished in each room. In bathrooms and kitchens, consider smooth surfaces for easier cleaning.

ADVANTAGES

1. Together with its lathing, a plaster wall is thicker and provides better insulation values than drywall.

2. A plaster wall is more fire resistant than a surface finished with drywall.

3. Plaster, with its lathing screwed to the studs, is more rigid than drywall and less likely to bend or buckle.

4. It provides better soundproofing than drywall.

5. With plaster, a wider variety of creative artistic effects is possible. The topping layers on drywall cannot create such startling designs and surface modifications.

DISADVANTAGES

1. Plaster costs more to install.

2. Plaster cracks easier than drywall and is more difficult to repair.

3. Plaster takes longer to install. It takes time for it to dry or set up that otherwise could be used for completing more of the wall finishing work.

CERAMIC TILE

You're probably already familiar with ceramic wall tiles that line shower enclosure walls or provide a colorful kitchen accent above countertops and below cabinets. Wall tiles are usually thinner and lighter weight than floor tiles. Of course, wall tiles just have to look good and fend off splashed water, cooking grease, and other errant ingredients. They aren't walked on, furniture isn't placed on them, and cooking pots or heavy drinking glasses aren't dropped to their

---

✔✔✔✔✔ PLASTER INSPECTION CHECKLIST

The following is a checklist of items that shouldn't be overlooked with plaster:

___ Cuts should be clean around register openings, switches, outlets, and fixtures so that no voids in the plaster show.

___ When viewed lengthwise, there should be no undulations or bumps in the plaster's surface. Nor should there be any uneven surfaces to the touch.

___ Inspect closely for cracks.

___ Ask how long the contractor will guarantee the plaster work against cracks and other defects.

surfaces. They come in a huge variety of sizes, colors, patterns, and finishes and are easy to clean and maintain—especially on the walls. Some interesting tiles made with recycled glass, stone, coarse sand, and other granules are available for lending that unique decorating touch. Just be careful that healthy, low-VOC adhesives are used to fasten them.

WALLPAPER AND OTHER NONSTRUCTURAL THIN-SHEET COVERINGS

Wall coverings are being made from a huge assortment of green materials nowadays. In no particular order, they include drawn and woven glass fibers, sisal, jute, straw, sustainable wood pulp, bamboo, embossed paper, honeysuckle vine, silk, linen, recycled cotton, hemp, flax, various grasses, cork, and of course, paper. Some wall coverings are available in sheets, whereas others can be purchased in sheets or tiles. Thinner versions of materials commonly thought of as flooring choices can make excellent wall coverings. Ceramic and recycled glass tiles can create interesting, colorful walls. Other recycled materials are being used creatively.

Vinyl wall coverings still enjoy a wide following, but given their environmental characteristics and impermeable nature, they may not be acceptable choices. If vinyl wallpaper is used, make sure that the adhesives are no- or low-VOC materials. Be aware that there's an ongoing debate among vinyl wallpaper manufacturers and anti-vinyl activists. The vinyl manufacturers claim that vinyl is so inexpensive, durable, easy to clean, and maintenance-free that its often nongreen manufacturing techniques and disposal results should be overlooked. Unless ventilation precautions are taken in the wall's construction. impermeable wall coverings can trap moisture within the wall and create a safe haven for mold.

Natural cork wall tiles and sheets are great materials for children's rooms because they dampen sounds and act as wall-to-wall bulletin boards a child can pin artwork and photos to. Polyester, nylon, and similar synthetic materials are also made into wall coverings. Many unusual lines are coming out to satisfy demands for green products. Creative recycling uses include old phone book paper, three-dimensional tiles made of recycled paper and pulp, or a type of papier-mâché. Natural-looking textiles are being offered. Flexible sheets of linoleum make excellent green selections for bathrooms, kitchens, and other areas where water and moisture frequently may be present. Solar-powered wallpaper is available that, after absorbing energy from the sun, will provide a certain amount of lighting for the room at a later time of day or night—depending on preset lumen levels from built-in light sensors. Some models allow for manual control of the lighting levels provided by the wallpaper. Some of these unique wall coverings may be a bit overpowering when used for an entire room, but on a single wall or wall section, they can accent the room just right.

Wallpaper manufacturers have made efforts to design environmentally safe products and have all but eliminated previously relied on toxic materials such as vinyl chlorides, formaldehyde, cadmium, and plasticizers.

PAINT AND OTHER LIQUID COATINGS

When paint is the wall covering chosen, select solvent-free, no- or low-VOC paints with natural tints. Oil-based paints and varnishes traditionally have caused a lot of environmental pollution during their manufacture, throughout their useful life in homes and other buildings, and by their disposal. These high-solvent paints are giving way to newer latex versions that are becoming more durable than ever. Water-based wood finishes are also providing greener coatings that take the place of petroleum-based high-VOC varnishes and shellacs. Natural paints are available, made with tree resins, natural latex, citrus fruits, vegetable extracts, seed oils, soils, ground minerals, and numerous crushed plants. Old-fashioned and sometimes homemade milk paints, with their beautiful soft blues and other pastels, can add lots of character to a room with zero health issues. In essence, such paints are simple concoctions of milk, lime, and clay or other soil pigments. Limewashes, distempers, and casein paints are also made from natural ingredients such as chalk, limestone and burnt limestone, milk extracts, eggs, and vegetable and other seed and plant oils.

The two-part polyurethane varnishes relied on for so many years were exceptionally dangerous coatings. They contained harmful chemicals that off-gased during application and long after from the wearing surface. High percentages of solvents helped the stain or clear wear coat to be effectively absorbed into the wood's grain. Nasty chemicals present often included potent anines and iso-cyanates. Instead of using paint, natural oils and waxes can be rubbed into wooden surfaces. Reliable air-friendly coatings include boiled linseed oil and tung oil. Beeswax and carnauba wax coatings are also both harmless and effective. They have to be reapplied every so often but frequently are preferred to paints. When looking for interior coatings, avoid paints and other coatings marketed for outside use—they may contain fungicides you won't want off-gasing inside.

PANELING, TRIM, AND OTHER DETAILS

Panels consisting of bamboo, hardwood veneers, and formaldehyde-free medium-density fiberboard (MDF) are all available for wall coverings. Versions using milled wheatboard or hempboard also have become available. Of course, so are solid-wood panels. Cherry, oaks, maples, ash, and pines and various exotic woods have been lining home interiors for ages. It's generally better to use paneling sparingly so as not to overwhelm a home with its intense presence. If possible, wood used in any type of paneling should come from Forest Stewardship Council

(FSC)–certified forests. Some beautiful sections of paneling can be reclaimed from old homes, churches, and commercial buildings. Reclaimed and recycled solid-wood flooring also can be used as paneling but may need to be resized and usually will need to be refinished. Older versions of wood paneling made from particleboard containing formaldehyde and other harmful chemicals should be avoided.

Prefabricated panels of wood and other materials are used to cover walls because of the panels' beauty, variety, low-maintenance qualities, and simple installation methods (Fig. 26.3). In fact, the finishing job on drywall or plaster walls that will be covered by paneling can be less than perfect, thus saving time.

You can find panels constructed to look and feel like a wide selection of building materials, including marble, stone, brick, and stucco. There are even panels that simulate a wallpapered surface. These handy prefabricated sheets are becoming increasingly popular in kitchens, bathrooms, foyers, and even main living areas planned in today's modern dwellings. They are still not, however, as widely accepted as wood and wood-simulated paneling designs.

Plywood makes a sturdy paneling for walls. It's durable and can add an old-fashioned informal look to a family room, recreation room, study, den, or dining area. Wood species such as elm, pecan, birch, and certain kinds of walnut lend themselves nicely to use as plywood veneers.

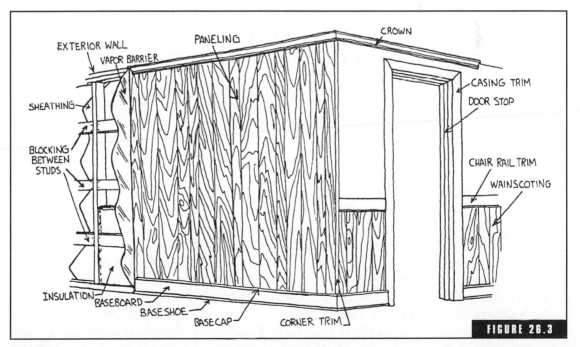

FIGURE 26.3

Paneling.

Paneling should be installed against walls that have already been roughly finished in drywall or plaster so that the paneling will have sufficient backing to prevent waviness or buckling. Another method is to fasten wall paneling to wooden battens on the wall, but care must be taken to ensure that all sections of paneling are plumb and fitted tightly together with adequate nailing along their edges.

ADVANTAGES

1. Paneling will not show cracks in the walls.
2. It is easy to install.
3. It adds to the insulation and soundproof values of the walls.
4. It can create many different moods for a room or area.

DISADVANTAGES

1. Making repairs to damaged paneling can be very difficult.
2. Paneling adds to the overall expenses of wall finishing beyond the cost of drywall or plaster.
3. It's another step in the construction of a house that takes additional time.

TRIM

Look in any home and you'll see wood or other trim installed wherever different construction finishing materials intersect: along joints, for instance, and in corners, at door frames, and around windows and other built-in house features. Trim makes an otherwise unattractive meeting place of two planes or surfaces (such as plastered walls and wood flooring, drywall and carpeting, wood paneling and vinyl flooring) into an attractive border accent.

Trim also can have functional applications: It can tightly hold down edges of paneling, carpeting, and linoleum, and when placed in dining areas at chair-back height from the floor, it will prevent the chairs from scratching the walls.

Most wood trim used to be milled from clear, knot-free quality wood stock that typically had to be cut from older trees. It was used for almost all applications, even for wood that eventually was painted. This was an extremely wasteful practice, but it was done that way because knots, even if they were sanded, tended to show through the paint. Fortunately, a number of improvements resulted in trim engineered from many shorter pieces bonded together smoothly in finger joints. It's not only more resource efficient, but it also results in straighter pieces at reduced cost. Trimwork milled from medium-density fiberboard (MDF), made from compressed wood fibers with no formaldehyde binders, is another excellent product. If you plan to stain the trim, products are available covered with thin layers of veneer that will accept staining. If solid-wood trim is decided on, make sure that it is FSC-certified, or use reclaimed or recycled material.

The cost of a house's interior trimwork will vary depending on what you specify. Here are some general points to consider before planning the trim for your house:

1. Even though hardwood trim is more expensive, it's the best and most common choice because it's more durable than softwood trim.

2. Decide whether you want the trim to be stained, sealed, varnished, or painted. Some contractors will charge extra depending on how the trim will be finished.

3. Specify where you want trim to be used. Some places in a house are not necessarily trimmed unless you make specific arrangements for them, such as around open doorways or around closet exteriors.

4. Be careful not to mix or have too many different molding shapes. Match up the kind of trim material you select with the basic style of your home.

TRIM CONSIDERATIONS

- If you plan to have bookshelves, get quotes along with the trim.

- Trim needs to be protected before installation. It should be kept out of main traffic areas to avoid dents, scratches, and waste.

- Whenever possible, all the trim should be purchased from the same supplier so that pieces match. Otherwise, different shades, grades, finishes, and dimensions may not match well together. Top-grade no. 1 trim material is well worth the relatively minor extra cost.

- Specify the finish in which you want the trim stained.

Types of Trim and Moldings

The following types of trim are a good representation of what's available on the market and what each is most commonly used for (Figs. 26.4 through 26.11).

CASING TRIM

Casing trim is the molding applied around doors and windows to cover the junctions of the door or window frames and finished wall. It's available in several styles and sizes. Doorway casing runs all the way to the floor, past and adjacent to baseboard trim that stops snugly against it.

BASE OR BASEBOARD TRIM

Base trim or molding covers the gaps between the floor and the finished walls. Its style is usually the same as the door and window casing but larger in size.

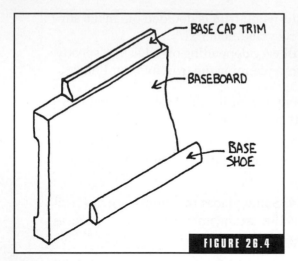

Trim/molding.

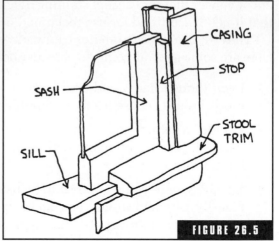

Trim/molding.

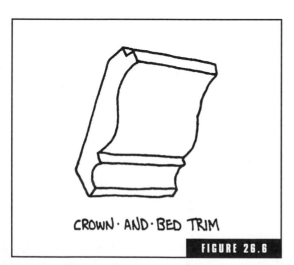

CROWN · AND · BED TRIM

Trim/molding.

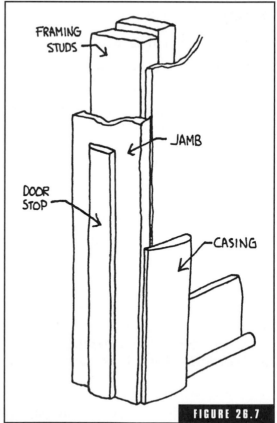

Trim/molding.

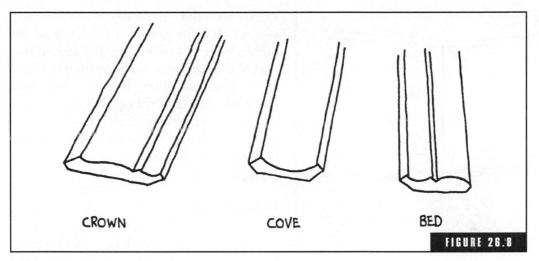

CROWN   COVE   BED

FIGURE 26.8

Trim/molding.

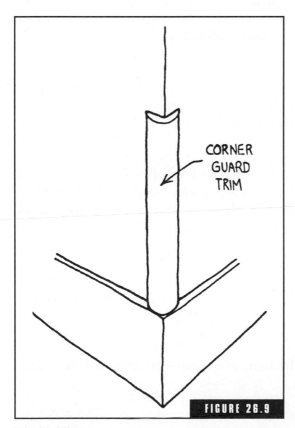

CORNER
GUARD
TRIM

FIGURE 26.9

Trim/molding.

SIDING

FLASHED METAL DRIP

DRIP CAP

WINDOW
CASING

SASH

FIGURE 26.10

Trim/molding.

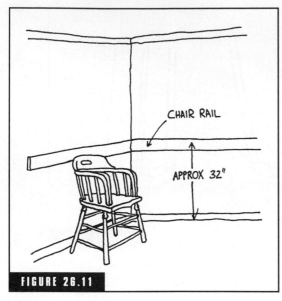

CHAIR RAIL

APPROX 32"

FIGURE 26.11

Trim.

Plasterers and drywall finishers will assume that the baseboard is at least 2½ inches high and will leave unfinished that part of the wall which is less than that distance from the floor. If you select base that's less than 2½ inches, check with your contractor to ensure that the drywall or plaster walls will be finished near enough to the floor so that no unfinished wall will show above the baseboard.

BASE SHOE TRIM

Base shoe trim is molding applied between the finished floor and the baseboard. It's very flexible and can fit tightly along both the floor and baseboard trim despite any irregularities of the structure that can be present even in the best of wood construction.

BASE CAP TRIM

These narrow sections of trim may be used to handsomely "cap" the tops of plain flat baseboard moldings. If you choose to use them, they'll also close any gaps that might exist between the wall and the baseboard.

CROWN-AND-BED TRIM

Crown-and-bed trim is a decorative molding used to soften sharp lines where two planes meet. Usual applications are at corners where walls and ceilings intersect. Such moldings are ideal for decorative trimwork around a fireplace mantel, for instance, or to make picture frames. The backs on most crown trim sections are hollow.

STOP TRIM

Stop trim is molding nailed to a door jamb to stop a closing door. It's also used on windows with sliding sashes.

STOOL TRIM

Stool trim is molding used at the bottoms of windows to provide a snug joint with the lowered sash.

PICTURE TRIM

Picture trim molding was so named because it was designed originally as a perimeter trim from which pictures could be hung. It still can be used that way, but a more modern application is to use it as a substitute for crown trim.

SHELF EDGE OR SCREEN TRIM

This molding is designed to cover the raw edges of screening on doors or windows, to decorate the edges of wood members such as shelves, or to conceal exposed plywood edges.

CORNER GUARD TRIM

Corner guard trim is used to protect and finish outside corners.

DRIP CAP TRIM

Drip cap trim can be installed for use at top edges on the exterior sides of doors and windows to prevent moisture from getting inside the walls.

CHAIR RAIL TRIM

Chair rail trim is a decorative and functional molding installed about 32 inches above the finished floor or at whatever height is best for a particular application that would protect the walls in a room from dining room chair or other furniture damage.

WAINSCOTING

Wainscoting can be wood planks with tongue-and-groove arrangements, paneling, or other similar materials installed on the lower portions of interior walls, often between the baseboard and a chair rail. The wainscoting is applied first, and then the chair and baseboard trims are fastened over the wainscoting's bottom and top edges.

PLY CAPS

Ply caps are moldings used at the top of wainscoting to provide a smooth finish. They're also effective for edging plywood and for framing any panel, especially if the panel will be used as a slab for, say, a table top.

ROUNDS

Rounds can be purchased as quarter-rounds, half-rounds, and full rounds (Fig. 26.12). Typical applications for full rounds are as closet poles, curtain rods, and banisters; for half-rounds, as decorative surface trim or seam covers; and for quarter-rounds, as decorative trim for inside corners and as shelf cleats.

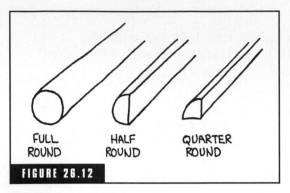

FIGURE 26.12

Rounds.

HANDRAILS

Handrails are installed along one or both sides of a staircase (Fig. 26.13).

REMODELING NOTES

This is another ready-made surface full of green remodeling opportunities. And it's another feature where the impact can be felt throughout the home with minimal effort and cost and major impacts on indoor air quality. As long as the wall

FIGURE 26.13

Stairway with a handrail.

structure is sound and square, the installation of various green wall coverings can be accomplished. Wall surfaces are far less likely to receive hard wear—except in the case of young children who may have their hands all over them, draw on them, and otherwise abuse the surfaces or in rooms where moisture or cooking juices and oils could spatter or condense, such as bathrooms and kitchens. Be sure to remove the old wall covering in a manner that does not damage the supporting wall—unless there is the ability to cover what's already there with the new material. Remember that qualities can be added other than the simply visual. Cork tiles or wall sheathing not only look nice, but they also stop sounds from reverberating through and within rooms, and so can various fabrics. In some cases, the use of patterns or images integrated within the wall covering can do double duty as artwork and will result in interesting points of focus in a room, which will even reduce the amount of decorating and hanging of artwork from the walls. You can opt for a minimal decor look, which has a cumulative effect of the items you keep and must clean and move. Carpet tiles can be used partially up a wall or to create interesting patterns of focus on a single wall in a room.

Painted walls can be employed if you like to change, dramatically, the wall decor base colors every so often, with the only effort required being occasional fresh coats of paint.

▶▶▶▶▶ POINTS TO PONDER

1. When planning major installation wall coverings such as wood paneling, stone, and tile, give them plenty of thought because they're expensive and difficult to replace.

2. Even heavy-duty paneling should be installed against walls that already have been finished in drywall or plaster so that the paneling will have sufficient backing to prevent waviness or buckling.

3. Consider that paint and wallpaper are the simplest wall surfaces with which to make subtle and dramatic decorating changes.

4. Between drywall and plaster, remember that drywall is less expensive, easier to repair and work with, and less inclined to crack than plaster. Plaster, however, lends itself to a wide variety of finished textures when applied professionally. A plaster wall also is more rigid, more soundproof, and more fire resistant than drywall.

5. Whenever you have a choice, go with stain-resistant, washable wall surfaces. Avoid the use of flat paints for kitchens, bathrooms, and children's rooms. Instead, opt for semigloss or gloss coatings.

6. Even though hardwood trim is more expensive, it's a good choice because it's more durable than softwood trim. If the trim will be painted, though, softwood can be an acceptable choice (dents and scratches can be filled with wood filler and coated with touch-up paint).

7. Any home can benefit from the use of unique molding. Moldings can provide architectural details—at relatively small cost—that can make the interior decor of a home far more attractive than it otherwise would be.

8. Be careful not to mix or have too many different molding shapes. Match up the kind of trim material you select with the basic style of your home.

9. Consider asking the contractor for extra pieces of trim and molding, finished exactly like those used throughout your home, in case you eventually need to replace or add pieces for repair/addition/maintenance reasons. Naturally, make this request before the main trim is installed, and realize that you may have to pay a minimal charge for the extra pieces.

10. Inexpensive vinyl trim is often an acceptable material for use in utility rooms, sunrooms, and basement bathrooms. Extensions of a room's carpeting also can be used as wall trim if it suits the decorating plan.

Bathrooms

In green terms, bathrooms are mostly about water and moisture. How much water is used and where does it go, and how much moisture and condensation are created, and where do they go? The toilet and the bath/shower together make up about half the total home water consumption. This translates to efficient fixtures, water-resistant surfaces, and effective ventilation.

Since bathrooms rank right up there next to kitchens when it comes to the most important rooms in a home, the quality and number of bathrooms in a house can greatly affect both living convenience and the dwelling's eventual resale value. Bathroom components also will contribute considerably to the amount of energy the family uses. Unless these components are chosen with water and energy conservation in mind, too many energy dollars will be going down the drain. Naturally, your family's needs also will help determine how many bathrooms you'll want and how they'll be appointed.

In a nutshell, bathrooms usually consist of a hand sink or lavatory, a toilet, and a tub/shower unit (Fig. 27.1). Bathroom lavatories or sinks are available in numerous types, styles, sizes, and colors. The drywall or other wall and ceiling construction must be able to resist temporary bouts of moisture. Use mold-resistant drywall or cementboard covered with wall tile, especially around tub/shower units and exposed vanity tops and sinks. The flooring also should be water resistant, very durable, and nonslip. For areas of drywall that won't get splashed, a semigloss or eggshell low–volatile organic compound (VOC) paint will take occasional moisture and has the ability to withstand hand washing when needed. Although vinyl wallpaper is used often in bathrooms because it stands up well to water and moisture, unless a version manufactured without traditional methods and VOCs is used, with no harmful adhesives, painted drywall or tile surfaces are greener choices.

FIGURE 27.1

A full bath.

TYPES OF BATHROOM SINKS

The main types of bathroom sinks or lavs include vitreous china, porcelain/enamel over cast iron or steel, marbleized bowls or counter units, solid composites, and concrete.

Vitreous China Sinks

These sinks are inherently acid resistant, and although they can be stained by rust, copper corrosion, and certain other persistent staining substances, vitreous china is considered an excellent material, with good resistance to chipping (Fig. 27.2). Vitreous china also can be formed into very fancy bowls and even into original works of art that are substantially more expensive than most bathroom sink units.

Porcelain/Enamel over Cast Iron or Steel

These are practically the least-expensive sinks you can purchase. They're less durable and more susceptible to chipping and normal wear than the others mentioned here.

Marbleized Bowl/Counter Units

There are two kinds of marbleized bowl and counter units: acrylic plastic and cast methacrylate, both of which can contain veining that simulates, in a highly polished surface, that of marble (Fig. 27.3). They're even referred to as *synthetic marble*. Both come in various colors and finishes, including high-gloss onyx models.

These sinks are frequently integrated into a vanity countertop with one-piece construction. They have a popular appearance, are easy to clean, and can be molded into beautiful patterned bowls (in the form of a seashell, for example).

The main drawback to marbleized surfaces is that the finished layers are very thin. A heavy scratch can penetrate the coating and expose the white material underneath, which is difficult to cover up or repair.

Solid Composites

Sinks and counters made of solid composite materials are made with the color, often a bone white, all the way through the

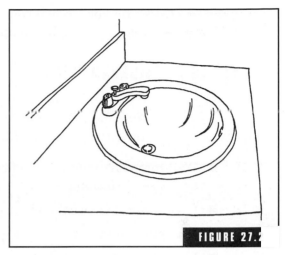

FIGURE 27.2

A vitreous china sink.

FIGURE 27.3

A marbleized sinktop.

material. If scratched, there's no color change, and the mark can be removed easily with steel wool or fine sandpaper. Solid composites also can be sawn, drilled, and filed with standard carpentry tools for custom applications. This is one of the better materials for bathroom (and kitchen) counters and sinks, but it's also one of the most expensive.

Concrete

Sinks and countertops made of concrete that's custom-formed, stained, and sealed can be created right on site by individuals who specialize in finished concrete work (see the section on kitchen countertops in Chapter 28). It's an option that you may want to consider if you like components that are stylish and one-of-a-kind.

STYLES OF BATHROOM SINKS

More and more people are turning to designer and continental-style lavs and lav sets. The following styles of sinks can be purchased in a wide range of materials and prices in round, oval, or sculptured bowls.

- Wall-hung lavs requiring no floor supports or pedestal—for more openness and ease of cleaning
- Lavs supported by cabinets or pedestals
- Lavs supported by metal legs
- Lavs built into ceramic-tile-surfaced counters
- Lavs recessed into countertops of plastic laminate (China sinks are popular with plastic laminate countertops.)
- Single-piece sink and counter units, either molded or sculptured

BATHROOM SINK INSTALLATION

A bathroom sink should be large enough for comfortable use, especially if it must suffice to wash your hair or bathe an infant. Try not to select anything smaller than 20 by 24 inches. In master bathooms, consider a double-bowl arrangement.

Every sink should have at least a narrow backsplash along the back of the wall it's mounted against to protect the wall from spilled or splashing water. A drip edge should be included at the front and side ends of the countertop or around the tops of basin lavatories to prevent water from overrunning the top surfaces onto the floor. Sinks also should have an overflow-prevention catch-hole that drains water after it reaches a certain level in the bowl.

Although many plumbing fixtures such as toilets and some faucets are best not reclaimed owing to their water-wasteful designs or dangerous (lead) components, vanity cabinets and sinks may be found and constructed in numerous unique ways. Salvaged furniture heads the list. People have made bathroom vanities out of old dressers, tables, desks, bureaus, sewing machines, and even television cabinets. Entire books have been written on how to create recycled vanities that are often outfitted with tile or concrete tops.

TOILETS

Toilets, or *water closets*, are made in various grades, from low-cost models to luxurious units with gold-leaf seats. The best buys are usually in the middle of any manufacturer's range. Standard 2- to 2.5-gallon-per-flush toilets typically use up to 40 percent of a household's indoor water. Greener models can be purchased in water-saving designs that operate with far less water than standard models—an especially helpful feature if you simply want green fixtures, if you're in an area that has metered water, if you draw water from a well, or if you experience periodic water shortages. Some low-flush models use as little as 1.5 gallons per flush—which is a huge step down from most toilets manufactured a few decades ago that used between 5 and 7 gallons per each flush. There are also power-assisted or pressure-assisted toilets—electric models that use electronic flushing systems to complete immediate and powerful flushes without the use of a toilet tank. They do, however, require electricity to operate and may frighten someone unfamiliar with the model on first-time use.

Today, overall, less water per effective flush or ultralow flush is what manufacturers are touting. Some models are available with a choice of two different flushes. The first is a regular 1.6-gallon-per-flush type, and the second is a urinal-type flush of as little as a half gallon. Urinals are becoming popular in some new green homes. They're installed next to regular toilets and—especially in a family of mostly males—can make a huge difference in water usage. There are even waterless urinals that are never flushed. Instead, they're plumbed directly into the sanitary sewer line and trapped with valve and drain fixtures that allow the liquid waste to find its way via gravity to the sewer drain without the chance of odors or fumes backing out of the fixture through a series of liquid seals. For the most dedicated, die-hard green home owners, there are also composting toilets that take care of most everything that should go into a toilet. Before you completely dismiss the idea of a composting toilet, consider your building location. If you're on a public or private sanitary sewer line, where the line's construction and operation, as well as the waste-treatment process, are all shared within your neighborhood or community, then tying into that system probably makes sense. But, if you're building out in the boondocks, miles away from the closest sewer line, you may want to consider composting toilets and graywater systems if they could potentially eliminate your need for an elaborate septic tank system.

Because toilets are such personal, frequently used items, it's important that you understand exactly how any unusual models work before piping them into your new home. If you don't like to use them, then no matter how much water they save or how green they are, you won't be satisfied.

Most toilets are made of vitreous china, although some manufacturers carry injection-molded ABS (acrylonitrile butadiene styrene plastic—a common thermoplastic used to make light, rigid, durable products including pipes, tanks, and automotive body parts) plastic tanks as well. The important features to look for in a water closet include

- Sanitary self-cleaning action
- Size of the free-flow water passage
- Quietness of the flushing action
- Water resource savings

Types of Water Closets

There are a number of basic types of toilets that you should be aware of: siphon-jet, reverse-trap, and washdown. The first two are the only ones you should consider for inclusion in your home.

SIPHON-JET BOWLS

The free-water surface in a siphon-jet toilet bowl covers practically the entire visible bowl area (Fig. 27.4). Water and wastes exit the siphon-jet toilet from the rear of the bowl.

1. A siphon-jet bowl is usually manufactured in an elongated oval form that's attractive and comfortable.
2. It's the most sanitary of the three types mentioned.
3. The free-flow water passage is the largest of the three, with less chance of becoming obstructed.
4. It's the quietest type of the three.

5. It's available in a one-piece wall-mounted unit that makes cleaning the bowl itself and the bathroom surfaces around it simple.

6. When made in a single piece, however, the cost is quite high because any chip or flaw destroys the entire unit at the factory and in your home. When the bowl and tank are separate units, the cost for the combination drops.

REVERSE-TRAP BOWLS

A reverse-trap bowl is a shorter type of toilet than the siphon-jet (Fig. 27.5). Like

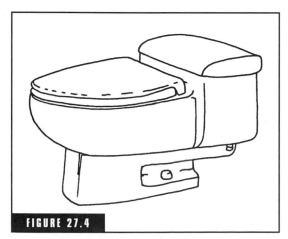

FIGURE 27.4

A siphon-jet toilet.

the siphon-jet, water and wastes exit the reverse-trap toilet from the rear of the bowl. The reverse-trap toilet has a free-water surface covering roughly two-thirds of the bowl area and has a smaller water outflow passage.

1. The reverse-trap toilet is a little less sanitary than the siphon-jet.

2. It's moderately quiet in flushing action, and it is the most popular type with builders of middle-priced houses because it costs quite a bit less than siphon-jet models in similar combinations of tank and bowls.

WASHDOWN BOWLS

Washdown bowls are old-fashioned-type toilets that can be distinguished by their vertical front profiles. They have very small free-water areas, half that of the siphon-jet and the smallest of the three types mentioned. Water and wastes exit the washdown models from the front of their bowls.

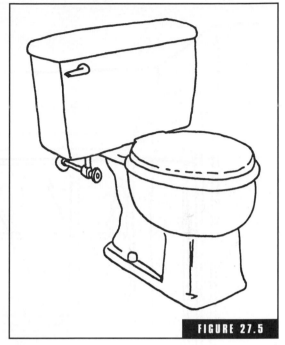

FIGURE 27.5

A reverse-trap toilet.

1. Washdown bowls have a noisy flushing action.

2. They're not effective in self-cleaning.

3. They're the least sanitary of the three types mentioned.

BATHTUB AND SHOWER UNITS

A typical home features one bathroom having a combination bathtub and shower and another bathroom with only a shower (Fig. 27.6).

Bathtub and Shower Sizes

Choose bathtub and shower units that you'll feel comfortable in, and plan them in advance so that the bathroom framing can be erected to size.

Many sizes of bathtubs are available. The usual widths are 2½ to 4 feet, with lengths of 4 to 6 feet. Typical tub depth is 12 to 15 inches above the floor surface. Numerous special models such as sunken units and old-fashioned tubs with legs are on the market. Remember that the deeper bathtubs will result in less water splashing.

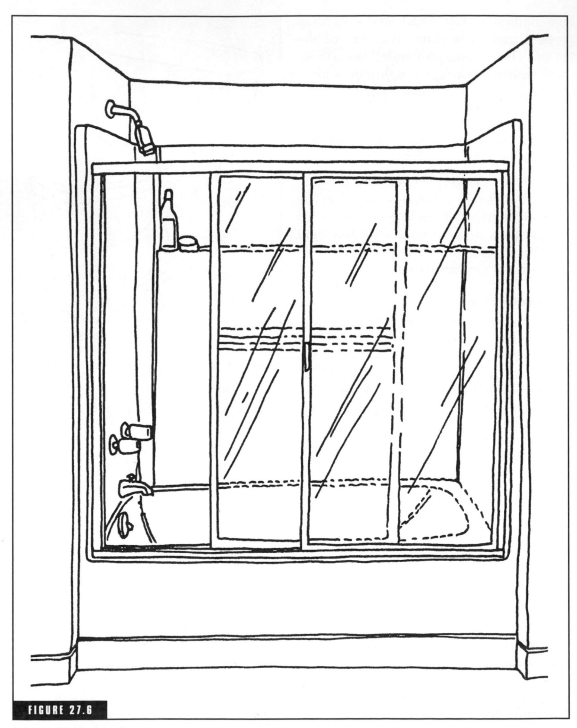

A bathtub/shower unit.

A small shower stall is only about 30 inches square. It's preferable to go with one that's between 36 and 48 inches in both width and depth.

Types of Bathtubs and Showers

FIBERGLASS TUBS AND SHOWERS

Fiberglass tubs and showers are extremely popular units that come either as a single molded piece complete with walls or with separate walls that are assembled around the tub (Fig. 27.7). Most new construction uses the single-unit tubs/showers having molded walls.

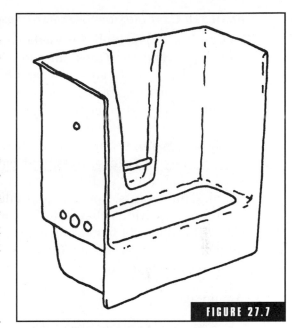

FIGURE 27.7

A fiberglass tub and shower.

Advantages

1. They're easier to clean than other types.
2. They tend to resist mildew better than ceramic tile surfaces.
3. They solve the age-old problem of getting a watertight joint between the tub's edges and the adjoining wall surfaces.
4. These units can be purchased with their own ceilings attached.
5. Fiberglass units are warmer to the touch than the harder models, especially during cold weather.
6. They don't soil as quickly as conventional porcelain.
7. They can be purchased with molded-in soap holders and seats.
8. They're very attractive and come in numerous colors.
9. They're soft and forgiving.

Disadvantages

1. They flex under the weight of even a medium body. Sufficient support must be placed beneath the units during installation to prevent the fiberglass floor from "giving."
2. When the shower water strikes the bottom of a fiberglass unit, it tends to be somewhat noisy unless insulation is installed between the bottom of the shower and the top of the floor to absorb sound.

ENAMELED CAST IRON OR STEEL BATHTUBS

Cast iron or steel tubs finished in regular enamel rarely come in any other color than white. The same tubs finished with acid-resisting enamel, however, come in white and colors. Because you can't tell by observation which grade of enamel is used on white tubs, the manufacturer's warranty must be requested. Elect the models with acid-resistant enamel if a cast iron or steel bathtub best suits your decor.

The walls above a cast iron or steel bathtub can be finished with a number of coverings, including ceramic tile and glazelike hardboards. Tiles come in a huge variety of colors, sizes, and patterns. The glazed hardboards work well when installed with adhesive over a suitable backing material such as gypsum board. Their joints, corners, and edges are trimmed in color-matching metal moldings in various shapes to fit the junctures. A few manufacturers' lines of glazed hardboards have unusual patterns and themes, such as of ferns, lace, multiple lines, metallics, antiqued and textured woodgrains, and other modern surface representations.

Advantages

1. They're exceptionally sturdy.
2. They're a lot quieter than fiberglass.
3. The adjoining walls can be finished off in practically any way that would best suit your decor.

Disadvantages

1. The enameled or porcelain surfaces chip very easily.
2. These tubs tend to show water stains after a period.

CERAMIC TILE BATHTUBS AND SHOWERS

Ceramic tile bathtubs and showers are just that—tubs and showers built in place with walls and floors of ceramic tile. Often people going with this type of bathing facility elect to have the tub sunken beneath the floor level. Ceramic tile applied with cement is the most permanent installation. Tile applied with mastic glues is second best because its performance is highly dependent on well-maintained caulking. If water works its way through the joints, the mastic base could deteriorate.

Advantages

1. They're unique and colorful.
2. They offer unlimited patterns, designs, sizes, and shapes. They can provide the ultimate customizing possibilities.

Disadvantages

1. They're expensive.

2. The tile installation must be of superior workmanship or the tiles eventually will loosen and the tub will leak.

3. Tiles are more difficult to clean than the other types of tub and shower surfaces (especially small mosaic tiles).

WHIRLPOOLS

Whirlpool bathtubs—once found only in expensive, exclusive homes—are now available for most budgets and have become standard fare with many contractors. Whirlpools, in addition to lending beauty to a bathroom, are also functional. Available in a huge variety of attractive materials and colors with many equipment options, whirlpools provide relaxing comfort for their owners and often will improve a home's market value and sale potential (Fig. 27.8).

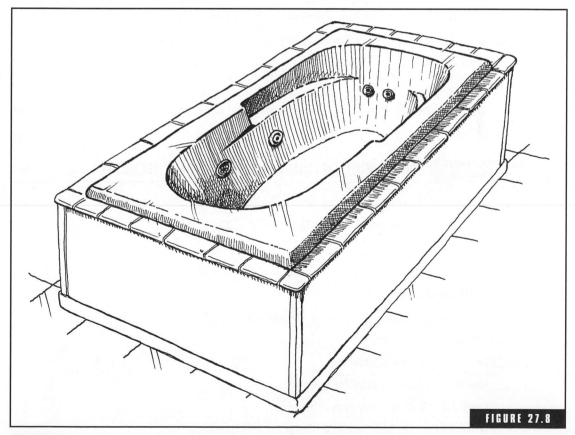

FIGURE 27.8

Whirlpool.

Present-day whirlpools are more energy efficient than ever—some models giving up as little as 1 degree in temperature every 15 minutes, with electricity to run the whirlpool circulation pump costing only a few cents per use. During winter, the warmth that's slowly lost from the hot water can help to heat the surrounding room space. The main cost of operation is heating the water that's used from the hot-water tank.

Some important features to select from are the tub material (cushioned models are available); the number, power, and control of water jets; and the shape and size (gallon capacity) of the tub. Massage jets in the whirlpools inject an adjustable mixture of water and air to control the jet force. The size or horsepower of the pump and number of speeds are often good indicators of the relaxing and massaging capabilities of the unit.

BATHTUB AND SHOWER GENERAL CONSIDERATIONS

- The plumbers should set any tub or shower unit in place before the framing is completed (Fig. 27.9). Some of the larger molded fiberglass units won't fit into the house once the framing work is finished.

- If a tub/shower unit comes from the manufacturer covered with protective plastic or paper, fine. The covers will protect the unit's finish while construction work goes on around it. If not, it's advisable to tape plastic around the inside of the tub, with some thick paper on the bottom for padding, so that somebody can step inside and work around the tub without damaging the finish.

✔✔✔✔✔ WHIRLPOOL OPTION CONSIDERATION CHECKLIST

___ Digital water temperature and timing controls.

___ Waterfalls are available on certain models.

___ Rotating deep massage jets.

___ Review the number, power, and control of water jets.

___ Multispeed pumps.

___ Check the pump size and number of speeds.

___ Colored mood lighting.

___ Check the energy efficiency.

___ Sample the tub material for comfort.

___ Consider the shape and size of the tub.

___ Whirlpool motor accessibility for future maintenance.

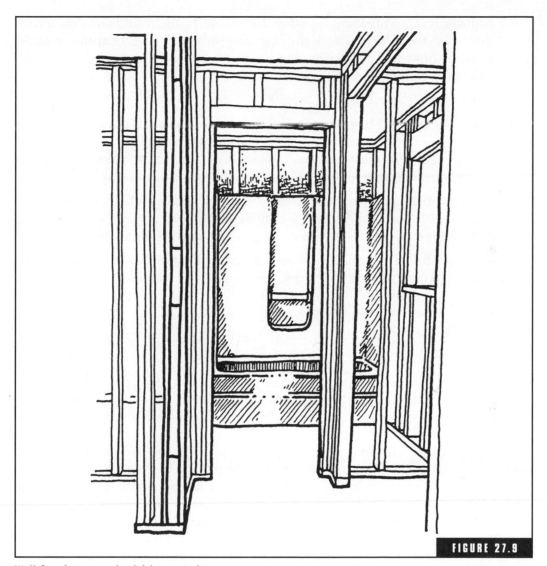

FIGURE 27.9

Wall framing around tub/shower unit.

- A tub/shower unit should be securely fastened to the walls. This is especially important with tubs that use ceramic tile for wall protection. Any movement later on will cause the tub to crack away from the tile.

- The floor of the tub/shower should have a nonslip surface.

- The tub/shower unit should have handles that you can live with.

- Remember not to place the bathtub beneath a window. This design fault will mean providing some form of shower curtain to cover the window, especially if the tub is equipped with a showerhead. In cold weather, a window over the tub can create unpleasant drafts, and whenever the window must be opened, you'll either have to reach across the tub or step into the tub to get enough opening leverage.

- Specify tub/shower color.

- Insulation should be placed in the shower walls, as well as under the tub and in the cavities surrounding it. The insulation will help to retain the heat in the shower stall or tub. Consequently, the tub will require less hot water to stay warm.

- All plumbing holes or penetrations through walls and floors should be sealed with urethane foam or a similar insulation. Remember the hole in the subfloor around the tub drain; it can be a major source of heat loss.

- One additional possibility, when planning tub and shower enclosures, is the use of custom-formed concrete that's stained and sealed. It can be of the same type, style, and finish as concrete that's used for the room's sink and sink countertop.

FAUCETS

The selection of faucets is a matter of personal taste. Many, many styles are available, from high-tech to old-fashioned, constructed with many different materials. One thing is for sure, the quality faucets will last longer and retain their appearance over the long haul.

They also likely will come with aerators or flow reducers. An aerator is another device that can help to save energy within your water supply. Shower and faucet aerators typically are located in place of the standard faucet or shower head screen. They add air to the spray to lower the flow. High-efficiency aerators can reduce water flow from between 2 to 4 gallons per minute to less that 1 gallon per minute, which is sufficient for most bathroom sink activities. Regular aerators reduce the flow to about 1.5 gallons per minute, which also is usually a strong enough flow for all bathroom sink activities. The lower or higher ends of the aerator range are a matter of personal preference. The aerator, usually a disk-shaped perforated fitting that screws into the faucet's end spout, simply reduces the amount of water in the flow by mixing in air, which saves water and also can save the energy that otherwise would have been needed to heat the amount of water saved. There is a slight reduction in flow pressure, but it will barely be noticeable. Flow reducers are similar fittings that don't mix air in with the water flow; they just reduce the amount of water in the stream.

There are three basic grades of faucets: good, marginal, and cheap. Good faucets are constructed with solid-brass innards that have tough coatings of chrome, nickel, brushed or polished brass, or other durable material. Marginal

SHOWER/BATHTUB SAFETY-VALVE CHECKLIST

__ Select a unit that will maintain constant water temperature.

__ Look for a model where you can set the sensitivity comfort zone range between two temperatures so that it's simple to fine-tune water temperatures.

__ Some units feature a preset temperature memory, which lets you set the water temperature where you like it, and the faucet "remembers" to return to that temperature the next time it's turned on. Certain units allow as many as three preset bathwater temperatures to be programmed—to accommodate different people's preferences.

__ The fixtures should restrict water flow entirely until the set temperature is reached to prevent hot- or cold-water shocking.

__ Some units have safeguard rotation-limiting mechanisms or stops that prevent a control handle from accidentally being bumped into a fully "hot" position.

__ Last-temperature memory is a feature that many home owners find convenient.

__ Temperature-limit stops allow you to limit how far the hot water can be turned on. This is a feature that's important when children or elderly users are involved.

__ The best units resist corrosion, clogging, scalding, and erosion.

__ Volume controls allow the water delivery rate to be adjusted as desired.

__ Some are self-cleaning.

faucets usually are made of lightweight zinc or aluminum castings that will tarnish quickly, drip, and look dreadful within a short time. Cheap faucets often can be identified by their crosslike handles with four horizontal spokes coming out from their center.

Faucets really get a good workout from the average family. Cheap faucets just won't do the trick. One drippy faucet may waste as much as 50 gallons of hot water per day! Literally, money down the drain. This is a powerful reason for selecting a quality-made, reputable brand.

In general, faucets having luxury features cost more than the straight models. Push-pull or dual-control handles or single-lever-control faucets are certainly convenient, though, and are made in models of high quality. You might realize a better price if you select all your plumbing fixtures, sink, tub, and shower from the line of a single manufacturer.

Once the faucets are installed, check to see if the cold water is on the right-hand side of each fixture. Believe it or not, people have been scalded while discovering that their faucet handles had been reversed by mistake.

SHOWER NOZZLES

It usually takes substantially more water for a bath than for a shower, as long as a person spends a reasonable amount of time in the shower and doesn't overdo it. Even so, an efficient shower head is a component that can help to save energy and water costs. Regulating the water going through the shower head to match the needs of the task can greatly reduce waste and save on heated-water usage. Flow restrictors with a shutoff valve and temperature controls will help with the shower head's efficiency. Since the early nineties, no showerheads should have been manufactured with capacities for providing more than 2.5 gallons of water per minute. But many models are engineered to give much lower flow rates, as low as 1 gallon per minute. There are numerous options available, including

- *Flow restrictors.* A showerhead flow restrictor can effectively reduce the water flow from around 7 gallons per minute in the heaviest-volume showers to as little as a gallon and a half per minute without cutting back on pressure and without appreciably decreasing the quality and effectiveness of the shower spray. On average, they'll cut a family's total energy expenditure for hot water by over 40 percent.
- *Temperature control.* This is a shower handle control with scald-guard protection that maintains the temperature even if there's a change in water pressure. It prevents wasting water while you try to get the desired temperature setting back.
- *Built-in on/off switches.* A control that is manually operated and easily reached so that you can completely turn off the flow while soaping up and washing, shampooing, or shaving, and then you can turn it back on for rinsing—without having to adjust the temperature.

The shower nozzle you choose should have a flexible ball joint for directional control, plus a control to adjust the spray. Self-cleaning showerheads make the most sense to buy. Consider a unit that's handheld, with a pullout hose and adjustable spray and pulsating massage sprays. Cheap nozzles offer little or no control of spray direction or quality.

An automatic diverter control should come with a combination tub/shower. It automatically diverts the water back to the tub faucet after someone has taken a shower. Such a setup prevents the next person who might want to take a bath from being pelted with hot or cold water. Omission of the diverter, an inexpensive item, also can cause accidental scalding of children.

Shower and Bathtub Shock Safety Valves

Shower and bathtub "shock" occurs when water pressure fluctuates because of changing water supply demands. For example, turn on one faucet, and the water flow may be very strong. Turn on a second faucet at the same time, and the pressure of the first may drop somewhat. If, while someone showers, a toilet is flushed or a dishwasher or clothes washer turns on, the person showering may be jolted by a shocking change in water temperature (for instance, less cold water makes it to the shower, and the shower water comes out hot). With traditional faucets, a sudden change in water temperature is what we notice most. The actual thermal shock event is a change in water pressure. In the case of traditional bathroom faucets, if there is a demand for cold water elsewhere in the house, the cold-water pressure at the faucet is reduced, leaving mostly hot water in the mix. An additional demand for hot water causes pressure on the hot side of the faucet to lessen, leaving mostly cold water in the mix. Flow further weakens with each new water outlet put into operation, causing rapid temperature swings that could either scald or chill.

Water shock can be prevented by specifying bathroom plumbing equipped with either pressure-balance or thermostatic valves. Such valves provide a measure of safety by eliminating surges of hot or cold water from the shower.

Pressure-balancing valves detect changes in pressure and instantly adjust water flow to keep temperatures constant. Pressure-balance valves are designed to keep hot- and cold-water pressure equal at all times. Valves use diaphragms or pistons to accomplish these feats by adjusting the inlet ports of the faucet's control valves. Thermostatic valves cost more but allow you to dial in a desired temperature, which will be maintained even as water pressure varies.

Thousands of people are injured every year from thermal shock. The most severe scalds are caused by high-temperature water flowing into a tub or shower. Young children and the elderly are particularly at risk.

A second common scald injury is when someone slips in the shower or tub and bumps the valve handle or grabs it as he or she falls, and it gets turned fully to hot. If a person who so falls does not move immediately, serious burns can result. The elderly often have reduced temperature sensitivity and can unknowingly scald themselves. Thermal shock also can cause broken bones and other impact injuries that occur as victims try to escape burning or freezing water.

Shower and tub thermal shock can be avoided through the installation of pressure-balancing or thermostatic bathtub or shower fixtures. These fixtures will hold the bath or shower water temperature steady to within a few degrees, even though toilets are flushed or dishwashers are started elsewhere along the home's plumbing lines. The installation of these valves also can save on heating costs and water bills. With fluctuating shower temperatures, time and water can be wasted just trying to arrive at an optimal shower water temperature. Some building codes in areas of the country now require water shock safety-control valves for new construction.

BATHROOM CABINETS

There are two types of cabinets that you should consider for installation in your bathrooms: medicine cabinets and lavatory cabinets.

Medicine Cabinets

Medicine cabinets are used for storing medicines, razors, toothpaste, and other items of personal hygiene. These cabinets come in a variety of styles. Four of the most popular are as follows:

- A rectangular door and mirror with diffusion lighting fixtures above the mirror (Fig. 27.10)

- A sliding-door operation, again with a light fixture positioned above the mirrored doors (Fig. 27.11)

- Hinged mirror-door cabinets with lighting fixtures positioned on both sides (Fig. 27.12)

- More economical cabinets consisting of single-mirror doors on recessed cabinets without lights (Fig. 27.13)

It's not difficult to find cabinets or medicine cabinets made of eco-friendly materials. Follow the usual guidelines of avoiding cabinet frame and side substrates with formaldehyde and high-VOC adhesives, and lean toward durable moisture-resistant surfaces that match or complement the sink and vanity.

FIGURE 27.10

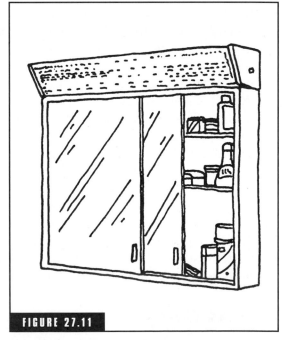

FIGURE 27.11

A medicine cabinet with diffusion lighting fixtures above.

A medicine cabinet with sliding door.

FIGURE 27.12

A medicine cabinet with lighting fixtures at sides.

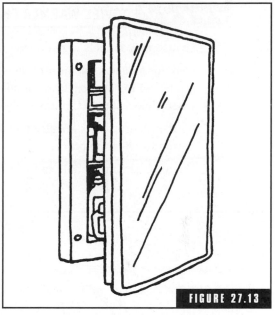

FIGURE 27.13

A medicine cabinet with no lights—the most economical.

Lavatory Cabinets

Lavatory cabinets, also referred to as *vanity bases*, frequently support the sink and sink counter in addition to providing storage space below (Fig. 27.14). They also should be manufactured with durable green components.

Lav cabinets, when compared with the smaller medicine cabinets, offer considerably more storage space. They also eliminate unsightly plumbing connections below the sink, help to develop the bathroom decor, and even can be used to accommodate a built-in clothes hamper.

TOWEL WARMERS

Towel warmers (Fig. 27.15) are clever devices that come in a number of different types and models. All of them supply the luxury of warm towels after a shower,

FIGURE 27.14

A lavatory cabinet.

✔✔✔✔✔ TOWEL WARMER CHECKLIST

___ Choose only models with Underwriters Laboratories approval.

___ Look for models with on/off timers that can be set in advance. Programmable timers can be set to come on 15 to 30 minutes before the warm towels will be needed. These timers should turn themselves off automatically in case you forget to.

___ Built-in thermostats are also nice features that will tell how warm the towels get during the heating process.

___ The units should be able to be installed out of young children's reach.

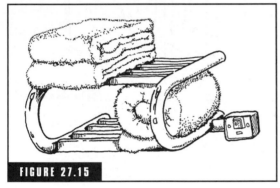

FIGURE 27.15

Towel warmer.

bath, or morning face wash. Some units use electric low-wattage heating elements. Many towel warmer bars or tubes are oil-filled and permanently sealed to provide safe, even heating. Some towel warmers are simply extension units of hot-water radiator/registers and heat the towels while heating the room. Warm towels also can save energy by reducing the need to crank up the heat in the morning for a shower.

SPACE HEAT

Raising the heat throughout the house in order to warm the bathroom is a common practice, but it isn't very energy efficient. When you want a warmer bathroom, it's far more effective to simply raise the temperature there instead. The three most common ways to do this are

1. Electric radiant heating panels installed on walls, ceilings, or floors provide heat on demand. For walls or ceilings, even a small panel can supply the warmth needed. Because of their radiant nature, these panels heat people and objects with a gentle warmth without overheating and drying out the room's air. Radiant units are ideal for just one room. In a bathroom, people can stay warm while in the tub or drying off, even though the temperature of the air in the bathroom is the same as the air in the rest of the house.

2. In addition to the electric radiant panels, radiant floor water-heating systems are particularly popular with people who have allergies. This is so because radiant systems cause very little air movement compared with more traditional

ducted forced-air heating systems. There are fewer fugitive particles in the air, such as airborne dust, mold spores, and animal dander.

3. A third common method of direct bathroom heating is the ceiling forced-air fan heater. Some models also provide a built-in ventilation fan and light.

VENTILATING FANS

Energy Star–rated ventilating (or exhaust) fans, vented to the outdoors, should be installed in bathrooms to control moisture levels. The shorter and straighter the ductwork is from the fan to the outside, the more efficient the fan will be. If the duct must pass through an attic or other unheated space, all ventilation ductwork should be insulated. Remember to include a fan even if the bathroom will have an operating window. A window or windows alone cannot be relied on to provide yearlong ventilation that keeps moisture in check.

Excessive moisture can quickly deteriorate building materials and furnishings, will promote the growth of mold, and can cause allergy problems for many individuals.

Operating a vent fan is typically more efficient than simply opening a window. The fan should be designed to run quietly for the proper amount of time to remove moisture and odors. If it runs too long, it draws excessive heated or cooled air from the house. If it runs too little, then mold, fungus, and wall material damage could occur. One of the best and most energy-efficient features to have is a quiet automatic timer switch (Fig. 27.16). The fan goes on when you start the timer and then shuts off when the desired time period ends.

Depending on how much moisture and humidity are present and what the bathroom temperature is, you simply touch the 5-, 10-, 15-, or 30-minute key to set the timer or bypass the preset keys if a different time is needed. Another reason that having a timer is convenient is that it gives you the ability to remove humidity for up to 30 minutes after you leave the room without the worry of forgetting to turn the fan off later. For maximum efficiency, match the bathroom ventilation or exhaust fan to the size of the room based on the number of cubic feet of air the fan moves per minute. This is typically how the fans are rated.

FIGURE 27.16

A ventilation fan timer switch.

✔✔✔✔✔ VENTILATION FAN CONSIDERATION CHECKLIST

___ Which type of electricity powers the fan motor? Bath vent fans that run on a DC (direct current) motor can adjust for changes in pressure to operate at a constant cubic-feet-per-minute (CFM) output, making them up to 400 percent more efficient than comparable models using AC (alternating current) motors.

___ How is the fan operation vented? Ceiling fans should be vented through the roof or wall. Venting through soffits is not recommended because unwanted humid air expelled can be sucked back into the attic through nearby soffit vents, causing moisture damage.

___ Are exterior wall caps or roof caps—outlets that fan ducts connect to—used for fan ventilation?

___ Wall caps can accept ducts pitched to the outdoors, allowing condensation to drain away from the vent fan, and are less likely to be blocked by snow or ice (a potential issue with roof caps).

___ Roof caps are simpler to flash for watertight installation.

___ The duct path from the vent fan to the wall or roof cap should be as smooth, short, and straight as possible for efficient air flow and noise reduction. Obstruction such as ridges and turns in the ductwork create static pressure and amplify noise. Rigid galvanized duct results in the best performance.

___ When installing rigid duct, 45-degree elbows are best used to create gradual changes in direction to provide effective air flow.

___ Roof and wall caps should be readily accessible to allow inspection.

___ Is the unit approved by Underwriters Laboratories?

___ Is the unit grounded with a ground-fault circuit interrupter (GFCI)?

___ Does the unit have a built-in damper that eliminates metallic clatter while preventing backdrafts?

___ Is there a balanced high-efficiency blower?

___ And a permanently lubricated motor?

___ Resilient motor mounts for isolating vibration?

___ Quiet performance? Listen to a demo unit before agreeing to a particular model.

___ Is there a built-in night-light control switch?

___ Size the vent fan properly for quiet operation. Don't buy more fan than you need. No matter how well the unit is designed, all other things equal, the larger the airflow capacity, the louder is the fan noise.

If your calculation falls between two sizes, look at the different brands and models to find the best match. If there's not a model with a perfect fit, go up to the next-higher fan based on cubic feet per minute. The best exhaust fans will combine a heater, fan, room light, and night-light in a single unit. More advanced units also have heaters that circulate warm air while removing moist air at the same time.

Automatic Ventilation Fans

Automatic ventilation fans, mounted in bathroom ceilings, will automatically activate lamps and ventilation fans (Fig. 27.17) based on the need to help prevent cosmetic and structural problems that can be caused by excessive moisture buildup. Most automatic fans are operated by one of the following:

1. Motion sensing, where sensors automatically turn on the fan, light, or both when a person enters the room. If the user forgets to activate or deactivate the light or fan as he or she enters or leaves the room, the unit will do it anyway. There's typically an adjustable automatic shutoff time, from about 5 to 60 minutes after motion stops. There also should be an adjustable sensor whose sensing field can be modified to match specific conditions.

2. Humidity sensing, where monitors detect rapid increases in humidity brought about by the bath or shower, and the fan turns on automatically.

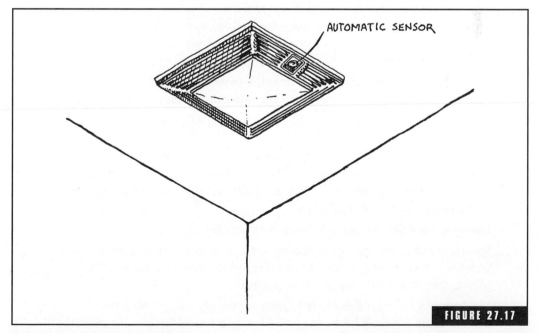

FIGURE 27.17

Automatic ventilation fan and light.

✔✔✔✔✔ BATHROOM CHECKLIST

The following is a checklist of items that shouldn't be overlooked when you're planning bathrooms:

___ A waterproof shower light.

___ A low-permeability vapor barrier on the inside surface of the bathroom framing to help prevent moisture from condensing in the wall cavities.

___ Electrical outlets well out of reach of the shower, tub, and lavatory water.

___ Soap holders at the lavatory, tub, and shower.

___ Toothbrush holders.

___ Shutoff valves at each fixture so that water can be turned off for repairs without turning off the main water supply to the house.

___ Consider having a built-in linen closet.

___ Consider that the plumbing plan include the installation of a polyvinyl chloride (PVC) pan underneath the shower as a protection against leaks.

___ A toilet paper holder located so that it's not subject to splashing from sinks, tubs, or showers or to dripping from washcloths hanging on a towel bar above.

___ A grab bar or safety bar should be installed to serve two purposes: to help a person using the tub to get up easily and to help the bather step out of the tub safely.

___ One 36-inch towel bar (the longest standard bar available) for each person using the bathroom. This gives ample space for a folded bath towel, hand towel, and washcloth. Use towel rings only for supplemental towel or washcloth storage or for drying off wet towels.

___ Install the shower soap dish as far from the shower head and as high up on the back wall as practical. Centering the dish between the ends of the tub or shower stall results in the rapid melting of the soap under prolonged exposure to the water spray.

___ A combination ceiling unit that includes an exhaust fan, an electric fan-forced heater, and a light. A good ventilation fan or exhaust fan is important for removing odors and excess humidity in the air. Such humidity can be harmful to the walls, paint, paper, and insulation.

___ Consider installing several tasteful garment hooks.

___ Specify whether you want glass sliding doors or a shower curtain for your shower. Doors cost considerably more, but to some people, doors are marks of luxury. To others, they represent more surfaces to clean.

___ The best way to select fixtures is to compare brands and see what line of fixtures most appeals to you. Stick to one brand for each line of fixtures. In selecting

BATHROOM CHECKLIST (*Continued*)

colored fixtures such as nonwhite tubs and toilets, remember that there is a good color match between fixtures of the same brand but noticeable variations in the same color when fixtures of different manufacturers are compared.

___ Anywhere sinks meet walls or where tub or showers meet flooring needs to be caulked.

___ Moisture-resistant insulation should be installed along tub/shower bottoms and sides to help maintain constant water temperatures.

___ When selecting faucets, make sure that they're compatible with the models of lavatories you've selected.

___ Have ground-fault circuit interrupters (GFCIs) specified on all receptacles.

___ Allow no electrical switches within 60 inches of any water, if possible.

___ Have a clear walkway space of at least 21 inches in front of the lavatory and toilet.

___ Have the toilet paper holder installed within easy reach of the toilet.

___ Install one or more grab bars for safe bathtub or shower entry/exit.

___ Be sure that all shower and bathtub faucets are protected by pressure-balance temperature regulators or temperature-limiting devices.

___ Be sure that bathroom, bathtub, and shower flooring is slip resistant.

___ Install a removable handheld showerhead for flexibility when showering.

___ Be sure that there is generous storage space, including the following:

    ___ Counter/shelf space around lavatory

    ___ Grooming equipment storage

    ___ Shampoo/soap storage in shower/tub area

    ___ Hanging space for linens

    ___ Towel storage/towel warmers

___ Be sure that bathtub faucets are accessible from outside the tub.

___ Make child toilet seats available. They have smaller openings and wider seat areas to make small children feel secure. They can include molded hand grips on the sides for children to hold onto.

___ Install a toilet tank with an insulated liner to help provide quieter operation and prevent tank sweating that eventually could damage the floor.

___ Be sure that bathroom fasteners are rustproof. Even toilet seat and toilet lid fasteners will rust eventually.

___ Specify the desired colors of bathroom items (tubs, showers, sinks, toilets, and so on) so that it's figured in the quote.

Inline Ventilation Fans

A remote inline vent fan is a quiet and effective bathroom exhaust option. Sometimes called *tube fans*, these units are mounted in attics, attached with a flexible dryer duct to a grille in the bathroom ceiling. Since the fan motor is located away from the bathroom, the operation is practically without sound (but will not have other built-in options such as lights or heaters). Also, the units must be turned on and off as needed with wall switches. By using a tee duct fitting, one inline fan can vent two or more areas simultaneously (such as two separate bathrooms).

ELECTRIC MIRRORS

This interesting product is often overlooked as a possibility, but it's a great bathroom feature. If you dislike waiting for a fogged-up bathroom mirror to clear after a hot shower or bath with the ventilation fan working overtime, an electric mirror could solve the problem. An electric mirror gently warms enough to prevent condensation, thus allowing you to finish in the bathroom more quickly and to waste less energy there.

LIGHTING FOR THE BATHROOM

All bathroom lighting, especially lighting in bathrooms without windows, has to be well thought out. You need general plus very good task lighting for shaving and applying makeup. And don't forget lighting to read by in the bathtub. Of course, natural light from windows is very desirable.

Some of the most successful lighting for bathrooms is created by indirect rather than direct light sources. Light can be bounced off a white ceiling, concealed behind battens, and doubled off mirrors. Where ceilings are low, choose flush recessed fittings so that you won't hit them while toweling off. Energy-efficient fixtures and lamps are a must.

Lighting also can create interesting focal points that are particularly important for internal bathrooms without windows. In fact, lighting even can be employed to create a fake window effect.

REMODELING NOTES

Low-flow showerheads are great. Swapping out a showerhead is simple—just replace the head with an adapter and another more-efficient model. Tub faucets should not be low-flow because they're used mostly for filling—the quicker this is done, the less warmth is lost from hot water and the quicker the warm water can be used. Reasonable-length showers use far less water than baths in tubs (unless someone is taking mammoth long showers). Consider not having a tub. Instead, there are nice shower units with seating and all sorts of amenities.

Low-flow toilets constructed in the early or middle nineties probably used about 3.5 gallons per flush. Today's standard is 1.6 gallon per flush, and because the toilets have been reengineered, they work just as well. Very early low-flush models were not engineered well and simply restricted the water without properly redesigning the trap and plumbing. Dual-flush toilets and urinals also should be considered. Urinal flush mechanisms with electronic sensors eliminate the need to touch a handle before the user has the opportunity to wash his hands—good for a family with young boys who may forget to flush. It senses when a user approaches the fixture and then commands the fixture to flush when the user steps away. This is both sanitary and water-saving. There are lots of high-tech toilets coming out with sleek lines and colors in gravity and pressure-assisted models and power-assisted units. Some are very expensive and use electricity in their operation. Dual-flush buttons allow selecting a low-water-volume flush for liquid waste or a full-strength flush when needed. Composting toilets use little or no water and collect the waste in a bin underneath or in a basement or crawl space, where aerobic microorganisms quickly convert the waste into a dry, almost odorless, and nutrient-rich material that can be spread around ornamental (nonedible) vegetation and trees. See your local codes, though. Make sure that the toilets will either line up with existing plumbing or can be converted easily.

Pull-and-knob hardware fixtures are readily available made of recycled and reclaimed materials. Recycled glass can be especially attractive and durable. Creative toilet paper holders and towel bars can help to make green decorating statements. Some of the reclaimed forged and wrought iron bars or other industrial or commercial use bars and tubes can be bent to fit.

Tile flooring works well for bathrooms, and so does professionally installed radiant floor heat. Vanity tops and cabinetry are additional ways to go green. You need materials that will hold up against moisture to prevent mold. Given those high moisture levels in the air, bathroom vent fans should be used even if windows are present. An electric vent fan is the most convenient way to get rid of excess moisture and odors in a bathroom. A vent fan can be controlled by its own standard wall switch or can be wired to come on with the bathroom overhead light and can be tied to a timer as well. Most vent fans are installed in the center of the bathroom ceiling or over the toilet area. A fan installed over a tub or shower must be GFCI-protected and rated for use in wet areas.

The walls should be made of backer board or other material that's suitable for wet locations. Floors, walls, and ceiling should be covered with water-resistant materials that are easy to clean and highly durable. Tile and hard-wearing paints are common, and because the area is relatively small, you can splurge on quality. Do not use carpeting, unfinished wood, or fabrics with soft porous materials that can trap moisture and airborne contaminants that can quickly lead to mold. Avoid very slippery tiles.

Tile backer can be used in place of drywall. Tile backer won't break down if water seeps behind the tile or paint. Also available are cement board, fiber-cement board, or glass mat, which is a water-resistant gypsum board with a waterproof fiberglass facing.

▷▷▷▷▷▷ POINTS TO PONDER

1. The quality and quantity of bathrooms in a house may greatly affect the home's resale value.

2. Elect water-saving fixtures whenever possible. Toilets, faucets, shower-heads, and even bathtubs all can be purchased in models that take less water per use than standard units do.

3. Remember that many one-piece bathtub/shower units may not be able to be used in bathroom additions or expansions because they're too large to fit through typical stairways. They need to be installed along with the original home wall framing.

4. Make sure that bathtub and shower units have nonslip surfaces.

5. Tub and shower glass doors should be made of safety glass, and so should all mirrors used adjacent to the tub or shower.

6. Bathroom electrical outlets should all be GFCI types.

7. Consider installing safety railings or support handles near tubs, showers, and toilets.

8. Whirlpool off and on switches should be located far enough away from the tub that no one in the tub can turn the unit on.

9. Don't skimp on the bathroom ventilation fans; a quality fan system is required to address moisture control and healthy air movement.

10. You should be able to unlock a bathroom from the outside in case a child or other person locks himself or herself in.

Kitchens

If there's one overall most important room in a typical house, it's the kitchen. Just look through the shelves of any library, bookstore, or magazine rack. Dozens and dozens of books have been written entirely about kitchens, and countless magazines devote their pages to the same subject. Kitchens have spawned enormous manufacturing invention, variety, and capacity with seemingly limitless amounts of materials, appliances, and other items designed and marketed specifically for home kitchen use.

It used to be that the kitchen—with its fireplace in constant use—was the most regularly heated room of the house. It was the family gathering place, where household members cooked, ate, talked, studied, and played cards and other games. Today, even without a wood-burning fireplace, the kitchen is still the most frequented room in the typical home.

Ask any real estate agent which room in a home will best up the dwelling's market value, and he or she invariably will answer "The kitchen." As discussed in Chapter 5, a kitchen functions as the hub in any household. In kitchens, we prepare our meals, eat our meals, socialize, relax, and work.

Today's green kitchens can be very practical rooms, featuring simple food preparation surfaces and cooking and dining spaces and outfitted with energy- and water-efficient fixtures, appliances, lighting, and ventilating systems. One way to look at kitchens is to think of their four major components: dining facilities, countertops, appliances, and cabinets.

DINING FACILITIES

Even if you plan to have a formal dining room—a feature often excluded from green homes to save on square footage—you'll still find dining accommodations in the kitchen a convenient necessity. Consider one or both of the following two options:

1. *A table placed in the kitchen, out of the traffic flow* (Fig. 28.1). Such an arrangement, also referred to as a *breakfast nook*, can be openly situated between the kitchen and another room (a family room, for example). In some homes, the kitchen table is simply put in a corner out of the way. Wherever it's located, the kitchen table and chairs always should be as close as possible to food preparation and cleanup areas.

2. *A snack bar or counter is frequently used instead of a table with chairs* (Fig. 28.2). The counter itself can be employed to separate the kitchen from an adjacent family room or eating area, whether it be a nook or a formal dining room. A counter is especially nice because it encourages excellent communications and socializing; it allows whoever is working in the kitchen to carry on conversations with family members or friends while those guests comfortably enjoy food and drink at the counter.

FIGURE 28.1

A kitchen with dining space.

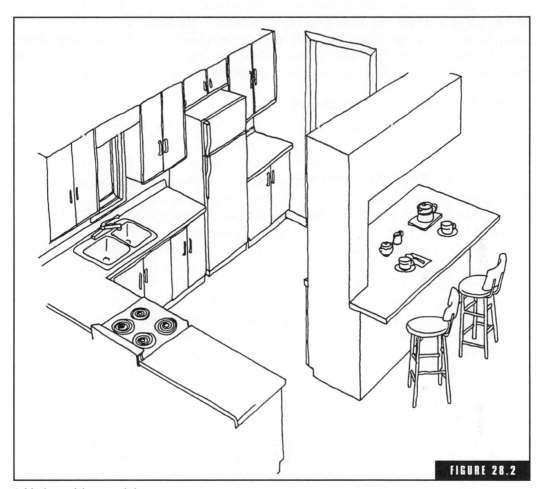

A kitchen with a snack bar.

COUNTERTOPS

Of all parts in a kitchen, countertops get the most use. And they're not only used regularly but also are subjected to the greatest abuse and the most frequent cleaning. To be truly serviceable, a countertop surface must be able to resist moisture, heat, color fading, sharp knives and blows, scratching, and staining from all sorts of nasty foods and substances such as grape juice, beets, and Easter-egg dyes.

Countertop materials include plastic laminates, wood, ceramic tile, solid composites, stainless steel, and concrete. And these are not your old-fashioned versions. A lot of innovative engineering and manufacturing has gone into modern countertops. As a result, they've got great appearances and even greater durability. Most are simple to care for and will last practically a lifetime. Some characteristics of kitchen counters that go against the "green grain" have to do with the substrates and adhesives frequently relied on in countertop construction. Sometimes, even when no substrates or adhesives with formaldehyde or high volatile organic compounds (VOCs) are used, attention is called to the distances that stone or butcher block counters must be transported from where they were manufactured.

Plastic Laminates and Linoleum

Plastic laminate countertops are by far the most popular—owing to a combination of price, availability, and utility. Greenwise, as mentioned earlier, for their price and their durability, they can be a hard value to beat. If the wood structure beneath the wearing surface is made from recycled wood fibers and no- or low-VOC binders or a top-grade medium-density fiberboard (MDF), then the countertop is likely green enough. The plastic laminate surface wear layers are usually between 1/20 and 1/16 inch thick, available in many different styles, designs, and colors in sheets 30 and 48 inches wide in 8- and 12-foot lengths. Some of the most durable versions are factory-made in a single laminated piece consisting of a rigid base, layers of kraft paper soaked in low-VOC binders, covered by the hard, heat-resistant plastic topping. This topping is formed or molded under heat and high pressure with a rolled front edge and a vertical backsplash that abuts whatever wall the countertop is mounted against. These countertop surface layers can be formed to resemble other materials, such as stone, brick, tile, concrete, or butcher block.

Plastic laminate countertops come in two types of construction: custom and postformed. The custom-made top has an advantage of greater flexibility in shape—it's made to fit. But it also has a joint between the top and backsplash section that is difficult to keep clean, plus a seam in front that's exposed to wear and, like all laminate seams, might come apart if the cement fails. A well-made top, though, even with seams, will last indefinitely with proper care.

The postformed top is molded under high pressure by machinery designed specifically for producing countertops. The result is a smooth countertop with a seamless rounded back joint that's easy to clean and a seamless smooth lip or drip edge on the front that prevents spilled liquids from running off the countertop onto the floor.

Although it's not as nice a setup as factory-integrated laminated models, the same kind of hard, heat-resistant types of plastic can be adhered to flat plywood countertops, with square edges finished off in the same plastic through the use of narrow strips that are cemented onto the edge surfaces. The exposed edge corners are dark, showing the thickness of the plastic laminate itself. The edges also can be covered with stainless steel or aluminum trim. In the best countertop installations, there are no joints in the worktop surface.

Less expensive polyester and vinyl plastics can be used instead of the durable plastic just mentioned. But both polyester and vinyl are more susceptible to heat damage from cigarettes, hot skillets, or other hazards and are more likely to have adverse effects on indoor air quality.

Linoleum also can be used to surface countertops. It's essentially the same green material that for years has been popular for kitchen, bathroom, and utility space floorings. Made of linseed oil, pine resin, and wood dust or grinds, it's not as durable as plastic composite, but it won't show every little nick and scratch either. Today there are many more colors and styles of linoleum than those available decades ago. The linoleum should be installed over a green substrate in all cases.

Wood

Wood countertops are constructed of hardwood blocks or boards of maple, beech, birch, or oak glued together in a thickness of about 1⅛ inches or more. These edge-grain or end-grain maple and other hardwood butcher block tops make excellent, attractive surfaces for cutting on and for handling hot dishes, but they require more care in cleaning and maintenance. As hard and as close-grained as maple and other hardwoods are, if they aren't cared for, their surfaces may wear irregularly, may dry out and crack, may suffer water damage, and may harbor harmful bacteria that could infect food and ingredients that come into contact with them. Butcher block tops made from recycled wood from flooring, furniture, and other product manufacturing companies are available. Plywood doesn't make an acceptable countertop by itself but is used commonly as a base for other finishing materials. Again, choose the substrate and framing components carefully, and avoid nongreen lumber, plywood, and adhesives. Wood in the form of compressed hardboards treated with a protective coating of tung or other oil is a low-cost alternative suitable for inexpensive kitchen designs. A high-quality bamboo countertop is another excellent choice.

Ceramic Tile

Ceramic tile makes a beautiful, easy-care countertop if it is well laid. It's colorful, distinctive, and heat- and fade-proof. It's also hard and noisy and can cause dish and glass breakage. Neither does it provide a good cutting surface (a wood or plastic chopping/cutting board can take care of that problem easily enough). Tiles can be large or small, glazed or unglazed with nonporous vitreous bodies, and laid plain or in patterns. Tiles are available with recycled content. The grout and adhesives used in setting tile can pose problems. Specify nontoxic varieties, and then seal the grout regularly at least twice a year to keep bacteria from entering small cracks and voids between the tiles.

Solid Composites

Solid composites are tough, inert, nonporous materials, often plastic-based. They're exceptionally durable and easy to work with. Because of their solid substance and homogeneous color, accidental burns, shallow dings, or scratches can be rubbed out of the countertop with common household abrasive cleaners. These countertops also come with integrated sinks. This material is more expensive than laminated plastic, and the choice of colors is somewhat limited but improving as new lines are being introduced. Some solid composites contain wood pulp from sustainably managed forests or postconsumer recycled pulp.

Concrete

Since the last edition of this book, custom and production concrete countertops have made further inroads. It's not that they haven't been used before. They've been fairly common in many other parts of the world. It's just that these new and improved versions continue to be promoted by high-end users, architects, kitchen designers, writers, and builders. Now more of these countertops are finding their way into typical new construction, although they're still at upper price ranges because of the skilled labor needed to create them—not because of the cost of their raw materials (after all, like other concrete, countertop concrete is made simply of water, cement, sand, stone, and color pigments). When mixed, formed, cured, and finished correctly, concrete countertops can be artistic statements, their design limited by only the imagination. Natural pigments, decorative stone chips, recycled tile and glass inlays, and other surface highlights can result in uniquely green countertops that easily become focal points in a room.

The colorful tile and stone embeddings can offer numerous colors and texture effects, and depending on the skill of the fabricator, features such as integral sinks, drain boards, and decorative splash plates and edges all can be included as part of the countertop, without seams or joints. The counters can be either precast to fit a mold that's designed exactly to your specifications or cast on site. At the same time, some owners opt for matching kitchen tables, decorative tiles, or other products that can be made with the same color and type of concrete. Some manufacturers offer ready-made finished concrete sections that can be arranged and installed as a countertop.

Concrete, though sturdy, does have its drawbacks. It must be carefully sealed in order to resist stains, and the seal needs to be protected with occasional waxings. Even then, the surface may need resealing within a year or so. Cutting on a concrete countertop likely will leave marks. Another possibility is the appearance of cracks. Even the strongest concrete can develop hairline cracks—for no apparent reason. Concrete with fly-ash components is less likely to crack, but it's still a possibility. Again, because the surface of concrete is fairly porous, it must be kept well sealed. A green drawback of concrete countertops is that they all require *some* percentage of portland cement, which is rather energy-intensive to manufacture. On the other hand, when fly ash is added to the mix, the total amount of portland cement that goes into a concrete countertop does not amount to much.

Stone

Stone is inherently a natural green product. Its composition determines if it will make a good countertop. If it contains a porous surface—full of small voids and cracks—it must be sealed regularly to perform well. If it's not sealed, bacteria can grow inside those cracks and voids and can contaminate utensils, hand towels, and food. Kinds of stone most often used are marble, granite, slate, soapstone, and other more exotic types. When sealed properly, such countertops can be considered as green products except, perhaps, for one feature. If you've ever tried to lift a piece of granite countertop—even a rather small piece—you noticed that it was heavy—extremely heavy. Depending on where it was quarried, cut, and polished, it could take considerable transportation efforts to get it to the building site. Stone can come from literally anywhere in the world. Again, this is a question only you can answer. Does the practical performance of stone countertops in the kitchen outweigh your concern with the energy expense it has taken to acquire them? One alternative is to try to find a local product.

Another option is to look at the solid-stone composite countertops currently being sold along with the plastic composite varieties. They consist of mostly quartz granules held together with strong binders. They're even better than stone from a maintenance standpoint because they are more nonporous and don't require the extent of sealing that natural stone products do.

Stainless Steel

Stainless steel is another option. It's the first choice of commercial food service institutions such as restaurants and hotels. Stainless steel is hard, durable, nonporous, sanitary, easy to clean, heatproof, attractive, and expensive. It's usually satin-finished to avoid any evidence of scratches, but constant cleaning eventually will polish the work area anyway. On the negative side, stainless steel is noisy and tough on dishes and glassware. And when dirty with gritty substances, it gives some cooks the shivers when they touch it. Green versions should be bonded to a healthy substrates manufactured without formaldehyde.

Countertop Placement

1. Give careful thought to where you locate your counter space.
2. You'll want some counters near the entrance you use from the garage to set groceries on.
3. Some should be placed adjacent to the refrigerator, where you must put away groceries and take out food for meals.
4. If possible, try to arrange for continuous counter space from cooking range to sink to refrigerator. The refrigerator, however, never should be placed between the sink and the range because it would divide the counter and impede the kitchen work flow.
5. A countertop next to the range is convenient to temporarily put hot foods on before serving them.

6. There should be counter space on one side of the sink and dishwasher for rough cleaning and stacking of dishes and glassware and for placing food brought back from the dining area. Another clear countertop should be planned on the other side of the sink and dishwasher (usually to the left) for placing the washed and drying dishes and utensils.

APPLIANCES

Kitchens typically use a lot of energy through appliances. Refrigerators are the main culprits—they're running constantly, keeping things cold and frozen, making ice, and grinding ice to the tune of about 15 percent. Then there are all kinds of other electric and electronic appliances and gadgets, including dishwashers, disposals, compactors, cooktops, ovens, microwave ovens, toaster ovens, toasters, Crock-Pots, electric fry pans, coffee makers, coffee grinders, blenders, food processors, mixers, broilers, waffle irons, electric grills, ceiling fans, and exhaust fans and, if you've been staying up late at night watching infomercials, probably hundreds of other kitchen slicers, dicers, juicers, can openers, and whatnots. Then what about that flat-panel television, the computer, the clock radio, the phone/answering machine, and numerous overhead lights. For the major appliances and any other applicable appliances and gadgets, think Energy Star and energy efficiency. Energy Star models save, on average, between 10 and 50 percent on water and energy use than non–Energy Star models. Also be aware of the sizes of the appliances you're considering. Is bigger really better? Sure, refrigerators and dishwashers are becoming increasingly energy efficient, but do you really need large family-size models? This is another case where if you're looking at pricing value, you indeed may get more cubic feet of refrigerator or freezer space for your money in a larger unit versus a smaller model. But the larger ones will require more energy than a similarly built smaller model will. If you're always waiting a few days to collect enough soiled dishes to fill an extralarge dishwasher, you probably should consider a smaller model. Use a narrower dishwasher, and you'll save energy and water per load. In general, it's advised to err on the small side when purchasing appliances. Why purchase a huge cooktop with a grill and extra burners you'll rarely use? If additional cooking surfaces are needed for a special occasion, family cooks have found that inexpensive electric frying pans are just as effective as extra burners.

The most basic kitchen planning concepts revolve around a very simple arrangement of three common-to-all-kitchen areas: the food preservation and storage area (refrigerator), the food preparation and cooking areas (range, oven, and microwave), and the food mixing and cleanup areas (sink, disposal, and dishwasher) (Fig. 28.3).

If you're going to have a well-planned modern kitchen, it's wise to outfit it with top-rated appliances. Here are four considerations that you can use to help select individual units:

Kitchen appliances.

FIGURE 28.3

1. Try to favor major appliances designed such that their main components can be serviced and repaired from the front.

2. Self-diagnostic electronic controls make appliances more reliable and make it easier for service technicians or knowledgeable appliance owners to troubleshoot problems.

3. Always compare warranty coverage.

4. Investigate the availability, reputation, and rates of the local manufacturer's service dealer—if there is one.

APPLIANCE EVALUATION AND OPTIONAL SERVICE CONTRACTS

Product Evaluation

This is your first and strongest line of offense and defense against inferior appliances. Product evaluations are 95 percent of finding and purchasing the best values for your dollars. Many builders may be able to purchase whatever appliances you select. If you happen to pick out units that exceed the builder's allowance, you'll likely have to pay the difference, but you'll still be ahead because the builder's cost is typically at a hefty discount.

Here are some guidelines that have worked well for consumers:

1. Select appliances and other items with established brand names known for quality and dependability. Unfamiliar makes can be difficult and expensive to have repaired. Choose a model that best suits your requirements. It needn't be the least or most expensive model.

2. If possible, ask for a demonstration so that you see the item in action and can learn how to operate it.

3. Find out what the availability is of competent service technicians and spare parts. How quickly can a service call be arranged?

4. Read the warranty or guarantee made by the manufacturer. Resolve any questions before making your selection.

Service Contracts or Extended Warranties

It's becoming standard fare. Walk into any appliance store, electronics shop, automobile dealership, or real estate firm. Purchase what's offered, and some salesperson will invariably will inquire if you also want to include, at extra cost, a service contract.

A service contract is really a form of insurance. Consider that no company in its right mind would offer an insurance policy—or a service contract—without fully understanding the possible outcomes based on known mathematical probabilities and without making sure that those probable outcomes favor the company—not the consumer. For example, a 2-year-long service contract on a new clothes dryer might cost $120. You can be sure that the manufacturer arrived at that price based on the knowledge that average repairs on the unit in question during the first 2 years of a typical owner's use will cost considerably less than $120. Well, if that's the case, then why would you ever consider or want a service contract?

There are reasons. Perhaps you're planning to use the appliance more frequently than the typical user does. What if you're the designated uniform washer for a grade school soccer team? You know that for the next few years—during your stint as uniform washer—you're really going to put 10 years' worth of usage into your new dryer. In this case, the service contract likely could come into play on your behalf.

Simply put, purchasing a service contract or extended warranty is a gamble. It's in your best interest to see that the odds are tipped at least as far as possible toward an outcome that will be favorable to you. If you simply feel more comfortable with and can afford service contracts and extended warranties whenever they're offered, so be it. You're well covered, and you'll be unlikely to experience any major repairs. However, unless you plan to use those items harder than most other individuals do, you'll probably be paying a premium for the coverage. For purchases that will be used for routine service, this is why it's important to do your homework before you buy. Find out which makes and models have the least number of problems, are the least expensive to run and own, and are superior performers. If you buy the best-value items to begin with, and if no special or extenuating circumstances exist, you aren't likely to need a service contract. Thus, in a nutshell, before you go for any repair-type service contracts, you must have a clear understanding of what's being promised in all the fine print, and you must do a thorough evaluation of your own needs and how you will be using the item in question.

Here are some additional considerations:

■ Is the contract already covered, in full or in part, by a manufacturer's warranty? This happens. A manufacturer will warrant its product and another company—a different company offering extended or other warranties—will accept payments for the same protection.

■ What does the contract include? Labor? Labor and parts? Must you pay for the repairperson's travel time? Some contracts cover only certain components, such as the motor in a washing machine or the heating elements in an electric range, or the picture tube in a television.

■ What if the repair is needed at night or on a weekend? A hot water heater that fails on a freezing Friday night in February needs to be fixed before Monday morning. If the service contract doesn't specify 7-days-a-week repairs, a costly overtime charge could result.

■ Does the cost of the service contract rise as the item ages? It likely will. Naturally, expected repair costs are minimal during the early life of most appliances and major components. Ask about maintaining the contract in the third, fourth, fifth, or later years.

■ Never take a salesperson's word for what a contract covers. He or she may forget important details or may misunderstand the terms. Find out what a contract includes and excludes by reading it yourself. Pay attention to items such as the following: Where will the product be serviced? In your home? In a repair shop? In a manufacturer's service center? Is the contract transferable if you sell the item? How much time do you have to decide if you want the service contract?

■ Find out who is offering the service contract: the retailer or dealer you're buying the item from, the manufacturer, or an independent third party?

■ Find out who will be performing or who you can have do the repairs. Regarding appliances or individually manufactured units, will repairs be made by technicians trained to service your product?

■ To check on the reputation of a company offering service contracts, ask the Better Business Bureau or your local consumer protection office.

✔✔✔✔✔ APPLIANCE CHECKLIST

__ Prepare before you buy. Compare and evaluate products and services.

__ If reasonable, favor established, reputable local retailers.

__ Buy quality. Generally, select appliances and other items with established brand names.

__ Always ask for a demonstration.

__ Ask about parts and service availability.

__ Favor service contracts (or repair insurance) if you plan to give unusually rough use to whatever you're buying.

__ When purchasing items for normal use, buy models offering superior performance and maintenance records, and you won't need a service contract.

Refrigerators

Today's refrigerators are remarkably energy efficient. Cubic foot per cubic foot, they now use only about a third of the energy they would have used a few decades ago. That's progress. As mentioned earlier, carefully consider what size models you can live with, and err on the small side for additional energy conservation. But don't go too small. You might have to get a larger unit (and you may end up keeping the first one, too—as an unneeded extra). If you get a larger unit than you need, you'll be paying to cool and freeze empty space for years. Unless you're planning to cook for reasons other than normal household cuisine, avoid those huge commercial units. Generally, refrigerators with freezers on top are the most practical and efficient, whereas the side-by-sides cost more per cubic foot to run. Manual-defrost refrigerators, if defrosted regularly so that ice buildups don't occur around their freezers, require less energy to operate than same-size units with automatic defrost.

Consider which modern options, if any, you'd like, such as an automatic ice maker, fast freezer, or ice-water spout. Make sure that the model you want will fit into the spot allocated on the plans. And whenever possible, the refrigerator door should be reversible so that with a simple changeover it can open from the right or the left in case you want to remodel some day or relocate.

Here are some available options for refrigerators:

- Adjustable rollers at the base so that the unit can be moved without being lifted.

- Reversible doors.

- Recessed handles.

- A textured door that won't show dirt and smudges.

- A door heater to prevent excess condensation during hot, humid weather.

- Door lights that signal problem conditions such as power outages, an open door, warm inside temperatures, and dirty condenser coils.

- An automatic ice maker with dispensers for crushed or cubed ice and chilled water, conveniently illuminated by a night-light.

- A front-door compartment that enables a built-in counter to drop out from the door to provide easy access to often-used items such as milk or juice.

- If lack of space is a problem, some units come only 24 inches deep.

- A self-defrosting freezer.

- Ice trays and buckets.

- Removable door dikes that allow you to completely remove the ice bucket.

- Removable covered storage containers/dishes that are designed for freezer, microwave, and dishwasher use.
- A vacation economy setting.
- Adjustable internal and door shelves.
- Humidity-controlled crispers.
- Extracold meat compartments.
- Egg storage bins.
- Extradeep, movable door storage bins for gallon containers, 3-liter bottles, or six-packs.
- Movable retainers on door shelves to keep small, tall, or oddly shaped items in place.
- See-through compartments allowing viewing of food without opening them.
- Sealed snack-pack compartment for keeping items such as cold cuts and cheeses fresh.

Ovens

The oven can be a part of the cooking range, situated under the burners, or it can be a separate unit built into the kitchen cabinets. Consider a double oven if you do a lot of baking or entertaining. Make sure that the ovens aren't placed next to the refrigerator, where cooking heat could affect the operation of the refrigerator. (Commercial appliances are by far overdone or overkill. The British thermal unit outputs are big, and the amounts cooked are generally small. They're loaded with extra capacities and extra features that aren't really needed. A lot of material goes into their construction as well.)

Here are some available options for ovens:

- Self-cleaning.
- Electronic ignition (This takes the place of standard pilot lights in gas ovens to save on fuel.)
- Broiler pan/rack.
- A window plus a hand towel bar on the oven door.
- A clock with an automatic timer.
- A removable oven door.
- An electronic meat thermometer.
- An automatic rotisserie.

- Chrome finish for easy cleaning
- A porcelain enamel-on-steel finish is also excellent.

Cooktops

- *Cooktop/stove.* Inductive cooktops are the most energy efficient (about 90 percent energy efficiency) followed by electric (00 percent) and gas (50 percent).
- *Ovens.* Gas ovens are cheaper to operate that electric ovens (at current average rates). Convection ovens can be the most efficient because they require less cooking time than conventional types.
- *Microwaves, Crock-Pots, and toaster ovens.* These can be far more efficient than full-sized electric ovens because they are smaller and faster.

The range or top burners can be a separate unit built into a countertop, with at least four individual burners. In some makes, the burner tops can be removed temporarily so that other cooking devices such as grills and rotisseries can be substituted.

Popular new types of electric cooktops can be purchased with sealed elements that replace hard-to-clean drip bowls. Food spills end up on the cooktop around the heat element, where cooler temperatures will not "bake" the spilled material onto the finish.

Inductive cooktops are made with electric coils located beneath a glass ceramic surface. Magnetic energy generated between the cooktop coils and the pots and pans placed on the cooktop surface creates heat that cooks the food. Because the glass ceramic cooktop surface is nonmagnetic, the current flows through it, reaches the metallic pots and pans, heats them but leaves the rest of the cooktop surface cool to the touch.

Cooking on inductive stovetops has certain advantages:

- Since the ferrous (magnetic metal) cooking pans absorb heat from electromagnetic energy, once the pans are lifted off the cooktop surface, the spot they're lifted from does not stay hot. Cooking starts or stops immediately, with no preheating or cooldown time required. This means that you can bring milk that is about to boil over back to the preboil temperature within a second of the heat being turned down. It responds quickly to higher and lower temperature setting changes. There's very little cooktop energy that does not go directly into cooking.
- Inductive stovetops can be set to very low cooking temperatures.
- Cleanup is simple because spills don't bake on.

- Only the part of the cooktop that comes in contact with the pan heats, which helps to save energy.

- When cooking, less "fugitive" or excess heat is given off into the kitchen.

- Inductive units are up to 40 percent more efficient than regular electric or gas ranges.

- Inductive stovetops are safer than heating with other cooktop types.

Drawbacks to inductive cooktops are that they only work with ferrous (steel) cookware and don't work with aluminum and many stainless steel pans. Inductive cooktops are also rather expensive.

Glass ceramic cooktops use halogen lamps that provide instantaneous heat on demand. A resistance coil around the element's outer edge ensures even heat distribution.

- Cleanup is easy because the surface of the cooktop around the elements remains cool.

- Heating is uniform across the element, and heat control is very precise. The reheating ability of the elements is extremely rapid.

- For safety, temperature limits are employed to prevent heat surges and to protect the elements from overheating.

- Other considerations for cooktops include the following:

  - Grime-resistant control knobs are the best. The most popular are plastic injection-molded knobs with markings that won't rub off and are flush with the knob so that they don't collect grease, dirt, and grime.

  - Removable cooktop sections that can be replaced with a grill, rotisserie, or griddle having easy-to-clean nonstick finishes.

  - If the cooktop is mounted as part of a range, a cooking light should be furnished.

  - "On" indicator lights will remind the cook when a cooktop surface unit is turned on.

  - Some solid-disk units contain temperature limits that will automatically reduce heat if a pot boils dry or if a unit is accidentally left on without a pot or pan on its surface.

When planning your cooking appliance list, remember to include a place for small cooking appliances. Why crank up the entire oven to cook a frozen pot pie? Think energy efficiency. Think toaster ovens, small electric grills, and Crock-Pots whenever possible.

Cooktop Ventilation

Your first concern should be to establish natural ventilation in the kitchen through window placements. But windows by themselves probably will not get rid of cooking smoke, fumes, and odors. You're going to need mechanical ventilation as well. Whether gas or electric, most grill cooktops have built-in ventilation systems. Their downdraft designs pull smoke, odors, moisture, and grease from the cooktop through a vent to the outside. One perceived advantage to downdraft systems is that they use a quieter and less powerful fan than is required of an overhead ventilation hood. Although this provides a design option for a kitchen that can't accommodate updraft or overhead ventilation systems, it's fighting an uphill battle because the inclination of cooking smoke and moisture-bearing fumes is to rise, nor is there a hood in which to capture the smoke and fumes. Another issue with downdraft systems is that they may effect the efficiency of gas burners by actually pulling down a burner's flame. If the flame wavers beneath a pan, it won't supply the consistent heat needed for cooking.

If your selected cooktop doesn't require a built-in downdraft ventilation system, opt for an overhead vent hood. Overhead vent hoods don't have to work nearly as hard to capture the naturally rising fumes and smoke from the cooktop. But they do have to kick in to push the smoke and fumes outdoors. Consider the following:

- A kitchen vent fan should come with several speed settings.
- It should use removable grease filters.
- There should be a night-light.
- The vent fan, hood, and ducts must be sized correctly to do the job. Just like the size of all heating and cooling equipment, trouble brews with a system too large or too small. It's got to be just about right to function smoothly. Too small a system won't get rid of smoke, fumes, moisture, and odors and may not be able to supply adequate ventilation. Too large a system could cause dangerous backdrafts containing carbon monoxide, caused by negative pressure created if too much kitchen air is expelled at once. If makeup air is not available from places in the house, contaminated air otherwise rising through a furnace or boiler chimney and heading outdoors may be sucked back down into the house to fill the void. This kind of sizing is best left to professional heating, ventilation, and air-conditioning (HVAC) contractors or engineers. It's too dangerous to guess at.

Microwave Ovens

Don't overlook the inclusion of a microwave oven. Inexpensive models are available for placing on a countertop or mounting in a wall cabinet or beneath a hanging cabinet. They're particularly useful in conjunction with freezers because they eliminate the chore of defrosting food beforehand. Combination microwave/convection ovens also are available that offer the best in both cooking methods.

Available features include the following:

- Countertop, built-in, or beneath-cabinet mounts
- A built-in clock/timer
- Window and interior light
- Multiple power levels
- Auto start
- Adjustable shelves
- Meat probes
- Humidity or weight sensors to calculate cooking time
- A defrost setting
- A ventilation system
- Combination cook: microwave and microbake
- Microwave/convection oven capable of cooking, roasting, broiling, baking, toasting, and warming
- A temperature cook/hold setting that allows food to be kept at a desired temperature for up to 1 hour or until the clear/off pad is touched
- Wood-grain cabinets

Dishwashers

Believe it or not, studies have shown that a correctly loaded dishwasher, run on an energy- and water-saving cycle, uses considerably less water and effort than does hand washing the same load. Some people would never have a kitchen without a dishwasher. Others hardly ever use the one they have. It's up to your own personal preference. Here are some features to consider if you're planning to have a dishwasher in your kitchen:

- A warning alarm that signals a blocked drain.
- An energy-saving option that will shut off the heater in the drying cycle to save energy when dishes can air dry overnight or throughout the day.
- A soft-food disposal.
- A choice of wash cycles: normal, short, light, energy saver, china/crystal, rinse only, and air-drying settings.

- Internal water temperature boosters that raise the temperature of wash water inside the unit an additional 20 degrees or so.

- Energy Star models can mean 20 to 25 percent greater efficiency over units that are not rated.

- Changeable front panels that allow damaged panels to be replaced easily or existing panels to be replaced with different color panels to match changing decorating schemes.

Disposals

The disposal is another appliance that draws mixed reviews. Overall, it's not a green appliance—it uses too much clean water and wastes considerable vegetable matter that otherwise could be biodegraded into mulch on site. A disposal also sends additional organic matter through the sewer system for expensive treatment. It's not a good use of water, energy, or resources. Yet some people love disposals—the way they can just whirr through almost anything short of bones. Other people are afraid of them, of the noise and the blades—can they trust them with children?

If you plan to suspend your pursuit of green on this decision and still plan to include a disposal in your kitchen sink, look for the following:

- Stainless steel construction
- A model insulated for sound depression
- Continuous feed
- A noncorroding nylon hopper and polyester drain housing
- Child safety features

Food Processors

These appliances make it quicker and easier for both new and experienced cooks to tackle much of the work involved in food preparation. Small quantities of foods can be minced in seconds—onions, garlic, parsley, raw meat, cooked eggs, practically anything. Look for the following options:

- Continuous feed for processing large amounts
- An S-blade for chopping
- A reversible slicer/shredder disk
- Up-front controls for easy access
- On/off pulse action
- Bowl capacity of 4 dry cups and 2 liquid cups

- Cord storage
- A convenient opening for adding liquids while processing
- A lid to the processing bowl for food storage

Vacuum Meal Sealers

These neat devices seal food into plastic bags. Good points include the following:

- They expel the air from the package/food, locking in flavor and freshness.
- They extend storage life and reduce required cooking and heating times.
- They allow food to be boiled in the plastic bag or heated in a microwave.
- They come with instant on/off controls, a plastic bag cutter, and cord storage.

Automatic Coffee Makers

Consider the following features:

- A capacity for making 4 to 12 cups of coffee automatically
- A removable glass carafe server with cord-free convenience
- Stainless steel pump
- Automatic "keep warm" cycle
- Thermostatically controlled
- An automatic shutoff if left unattended for 2 hours
- A heat-resistant handle and base that stays cool to the touch
- A light-emitting diode (LED) clock/timer
- A 24-hour automatic-perc time cycle on a digital clock auto timer with on/off/auto switch
- A flavor-neutral glass carafe
- Dishwasher-safe glass carafe server
- A removable water container that can be filled right at the sink
- A beverage indicator on an insulated carafe (coffee, decaf, tea, or other)

Cool-Touch Wide-Mouth Toasters

This type of toaster offers many features and advantages:

- Its "cool touch," sleek exterior remains comfortable to the touch, even when toasting.

- It is self-adjusting, capable of toasting thin to extra thick bread, bagels, English muffins, croissants, and more.

- An extrawide, long toasting rack accommodates French bread or oversize rolls.

- An electronic temperature control offers defrosting, warming, and various degrees of toasting.

- A convenient crumb tray makes cleanup a breeze.

Automatic Chrome Can Opener/Scissors Sharpener

This appliance should provide the following features and advantages:

- It will open cans, bags, jars, and bottles.

- It will automatically power-pierce the lid, open the can, and then shut itself off. A magnetic finger securely holds the lid.

- The sharpener hones household knives, shears, and other cutting instruments.

Cordless Wet and Dry Vac

This appliance is designed for wet, soggy, and dry cleanup tasks.

- It's great to have close by for spilled flour, beans, liquids, potting soil—almost anything.

- One option to look for is a motorized brush attachment that cleans carpets, upholstery, and bare floors.

- Other popular attachments include a crevice tool, a ceiling wand, a furniture brush, and a squeegee.

SINKS

Many of the best kitchen sinks are made of either stainless steel or enameled cast iron. Both are easy to keep clean and will retain their good looks over the years. There are also porcelain-on-steel sinks that look like cast iron but are hard to keep clean, chip easily, and lose their gloss quickly. The more expensive line of stainless steel sinks contains higher percentages of chrome alloys, which provide better appearances and a reduced tendency toward "water spotting."

The style of sink you choose should have at least two wash bays or bowls and a rinse spray gun. A triple-bowl kitchen sink (Fig. 28.4) allows hand dish washing in one bowl, rinsing in a reduced-size center bowl, and placing items in a drying rack staged in the third bowl. This quick-wash and dry system enables dish washing to be completed while the washing water is still hot.

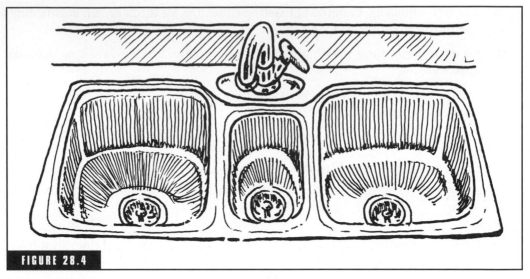

FIGURE 28.4

A triple-bowl sink.

Some stainless steel sink manufacturers offer a single- or double-sided drip-pan sink extension that extends out into the counter area so items can be staged before cleaning or after being washed.

If desired, an optional garbage disposal makes cleaning dirty dishes and cookware faster and easier but can be a headache if not used and maintained properly. Another drawback is that a disposal may result in needless use of drinking water that is typically run whenever the disposal is grinding through vegetable and fruit matter. Better that the nonanimal food wastes from fruits and vegetables are used to make mulch rather than be ground and sent to a sanitary sewer for treatment or to clog up a septic system.

It's not absolutely necessary, but it sure is handy to include an automatic dishwasher. If you decide on one, place it next to the sink, and be sure to allow at least 18 inches between any sidewall or counter running at right angles to the machine's front. If you cram a dishwasher all the way into a corner, then two people won't be able to load or unload it at the same time.

Sink/Pullout Spray Faucets

Consider purchasing a comfortable, palm-fitting pullout main kitchen sink faucet. It will allow easier washing and rinsing of larger items in the sink and the filling of containers that otherwise would be too large for a fixed sink faucet spout to handle. With fingertip control, this faucet's flow can change from an aerated stream for rinsing vegetables or cleaning around the sink to a functional steady stream for basic sink use. A very green feature on these pullout spray or stream faucets (as well as for some stationary faucets) is fingertip, knee, or foot controls that can easily start and stop the water flow, saving water between various steps of a task such as cleaning vegetables or hand rinsing glasses or dishes.

Faucet Filters

When choosing a kitchen sink faucet, consider one with a functional "carbon block" filter. Unless you have included a whole-house water filter with your plumbing, take a look at faucets that come with replaceable filters right inside the faucet's neck, out of sight, and available in pullout models. These faucets and their filters accomplish the following:

- They reduce common impurities such as chlorine and lead.
- They should not remove beneficial fluoride.
- They improve water taste and reduce odor.
- Typically, they can be switched from filtered to unfiltered flow.
- Filter cartridges offer quick and easy replacement, right at the sink.
- Inconspicuous filters are positioned out of sight, inside the faucet.
- The units are stylish.
- They are available with built-in filter life indicators to provide visual and audible feedback signals for remaining filter life, for showing water is being filtered, and for monitoring battery strength.

CABINETS

Kitchen cabinets always have been the focal point of any kitchen (Fig. 28.5). More than anything, they set the flavor of the room and make or break its appearance. It's no coincidence that they're usually the first to be changed when kitchens are remodeled, and countless home-improvement contractors earn their living by replacing or giving face-lifts to kitchen cabinets. Nowhere else in the typical house are so many different items kept. If it weren't for kitchen cabinets and drawers, chaos would prevent numerous cooks from staying organized and efficient in the kitchen.

Most kitchen and other cabinets (bathroom cabinets, for instance) are manufactured in one of three ways: custom-made, factory-made, and custom factory-made. Custom-made cabinets are constructed in a local cabinet shop according to your exact plans. Such a method offers practically unlimited selection as to material, design, and finish, but it's also the most expensive. If your needs are unusual, though, custom-made cabinets could be your best option. Your builder should get bids from several cabinetmakers before you make a final decision.

FIGURE 28.5

Kitchen cabinets.

Factory-made cabinets are built to the specifications of the different lines the factory carries. Your choices thus are limited in the selection of material, design, and finishes. These cabinets range in price from inexpensive to very expensive depending on the individual manufacturers and lines.

Custom factory-made cabinets are assembled at a centralized plant in response to orders taken by local kitchen cabinet outlets. You can expect a much greater choice in material, design, and finish than with factory-made cabinets. Prices usually are less than those of custom-made cabinets and more than those of the medium and economy grades of factory-made models.

For your kitchen cabinets, give careful thought not only to cost but also to what cabinet style, type, sizes, quantities, and accessories will best suit your needs.

CABINET CONSIDERATIONS

- Base cabinet depth should be around 24 inches.

- The floor-to-countertop height should be about 36 inches.

- Cabinets installed over countertops should be at least 12 inches deep and about 30 inches high.

- There should be about 18 inches of clearance between the countertop and the bottom of wall cabinets.

- Solid-wood cabinets can be a beautiful addition to a kitchen, but cabinets built out of veneer can yield practically the same result, with a lot less top-grade dimensional wood used up by their manufacture. Insist upon Forest Stewardship Council (FSC)–certified solid woods if the materials are new.

- Consider recycled or reclaimed cabinets removed from an older home and refinished. Excellent-quality cabinets may be available from local demolition projects if you look far enough in advance.

- Avoid particleboard and plywood substrates held together with formaldehyde glues and binders.

CABINET STORAGE CHECKLIST

Kitchen storage space is obviously most efficient when it's conveniently located. This is particularly true in the cooking area, where most kitchen work is done. It follows that when planning a kitchen layout, you must arrange for enough storage space of the right kinds to be made available near each of the major appliances for utensils, foods, seasonings, cleaning supplies, and other items that are used at the various workstations.

Here are some sample checklists of items for which you should plan storage space for near the kitchen cooking range, refrigerator, and sink.

Near the range:

_ Seasonings, instant coffee, tea, cocoa, flour, cornstarch, cooking oils, and shortening

_ Saucepans, skillets, griddles, roasters, frying pans

(Continued)

✔✔✔✔✔ CABINET STORAGE CHECKLIST (*Continued*)

___ Knives, large forks and spoons, ladles, tongs, shears, carving tools, and measuring cups and spoons

___ Platters, serving dishes, and trays

___ Hand mixers and blenders

___ Cooling racks

Near the refrigerator (this area usually serves as the food preparation area):

___ Baking sheets, pie and muffin pans, rolling pins, sifters

___ Casserole dishes, measuring cups and spoons, mixing bowls

___ Paper towels, sandwich bags, aluminum foil, waxed paper, plastic wrap

___ Seasonings

___ Bottle and can openers

___ Spatulas, ice cream scoops, refrigerator dishes

___ Ice bucket

___ Sandwich grill, waffle iron

___ Bowl covers

___ Bread and cake boxes, cookie jars

Near the sink (and dishwasher if you have one):

___ Soaps, cleansers, detergents

___ Paper and garbage bags

___ Paper towels and napkins

___ Scouring pads

___ Silver-polishing supplies

___ Window-cleaning supplies

___ Appliance waxes

___ Scrub brushes

___ Coffee pots

___ Colanders and strainers

___ Cutting boards

___ Dishcloths, towels, and mop

___ Everyday china and glassware

CABINET STORAGE *(Continued)* ✔✔✔✔✔

___ Draining rack

___ Double boiler

___ Juicers

___ Funnels

___ Saucepans

___ Tea kettle, pitchers

___ Garbage can and trash can

Types of Cabinets

There are four basic types of cabinets from which you can select: unfinished wood cabinets, stained wood cabinets, painted wood cabinets, and wood and plastic laminate cabinets.

UNFINISHED WOOD CABINETS

Like any unfinished product, unfinished wood cabinets can be purchased at a substantial savings if you decide to finish them yourself or have the house stainers do the job for you before or after the cabinets are installed. If this method is selected, the cabinets can be finished off to exactly match other woodwork and trim throughout the house.

STAINED WOOD CABINETS

Stained wood cabinets are finished at the shop or factory in a carefully controlled environment that ensures an excellent application and curing of the many finishing coats that are available.

WOOD AND PLASTIC LAMINATE CABINETS

Wood and plastic laminate cabinets are finished either at the factory or at a local shop. They're constructed of wood or a wood product such as particleboard and then covered with a plastic laminate. The plastic laminate offers a wide variety of bright and wood-grain colors and patterns and is easy to clean.

Special Cabinets

Apart from the standard cabinets that are set squarely against a wall, other units are available to fill special storage space needs.

- Pull-out disposable and recyclable bins in the kitchen will permit easy handling of those materials without having to access the garage frequently.

- Two-way cabinets have doors on both their fronts and backs. When suspended from a soffit over a counter peninsula or island, they permit you to put dishes away from the sink side and to take the same dishes out from the dining room side when setting the table. Matching two-way base cabinets also can be purchased.

- Quarter-round cabinets are used at open ends of cabinet rows to give a rounded-off look and to permit items to be stored on the front or side of the cabinet from several angles. Similar half-round cabinets and shelves also can be purchased when needed.

- Mixer cabinets are used for storing large electric mixers. A mixer cabinet is a base unit with a shelf that pulls out and up.

- A bottle cabinet is a base cabinet with pullout trays that are egg-crated to hold bottles.

- When wall and floor cabinets are located on both sides of an interior corner, a revolving round lazy Susan cabinet tray arrangement can make good use of otherwise hard-to-access space.

Cabinet Slide-Out Shelves

Consider having some of your lower shelves as pullout trays that will give greater visibility and ease for reaching their contents. Heavy pots and items can be brought into full view and easy reach simply by pulling a tray forward. Vertical drawers are particularly satisfactory below the sink, where often-used dishpans, strainers, and colanders are kept.

Special drawers are also available with dividers for canned goods if there is no pantry. Bread box and slide-out vegetable bins are good for storing onions and potatoes.

VENTILATION

A poorly ventilated kitchen will suffer from chronic condensation and the odors of your last meal. In addition to strategically placed windows and sliding doors with screens, an overhead lighted hood with a fan that's vented directly to the outdoors is one of the best overall solutions. But a fan built into a countertop range and vented to the outdoors is also very popular and effective. When considering hood exhaust equipment, look for

- At least three fan speeds.

- Multiple light settings.

- Filter cleaning reminder.

- Seamless construction in a metal hood (Otherwise, grease can collect under the edges where joints are welded.)

- Hooded vents vented directly to the outdoors with straight, rigid, smooth, fireproof metal sections to provide practically effortless airflow.

- The terminal (outdoor) vent should be kept as far as possible away from windows so that exhausted air won't draft back into the house when the windows are open.

LIGHTING

The kitchen should have enough illumination, day or night, for cooking, work, or socializing. If possible, locate a window over the sink. Large windows and skylights are always helpful to the family chef.

A kitchen should have task lighting installed under wall cabinets and for the sink, range, and counters. The same goes for all other kitchen work areas and centers.

Consider fluorescent lights underneath cabinets that hang from a soffit over countertops to illuminate counter work surfaces. Plan recessed lights in plain soffits above work counters and ranges (if a light isn't already in a range hood).

There should be separate lighting over the main kitchen area. A light over a table with chairs or over an eating nook should be dimmer-controlled.

KITCHEN WALL FINISHES

The walls of a kitchen, especially the wall surfaces above the work counters, should be finished with an easy-to-clean material. Three popular, functional wall finishes are as follows:

- *Fabric and vinyl wallpapers.* These have excellent surface washability and durability characteristics. They come in a wide variety of colors and patterns.

- *Predecorated wallboards.* These colored and patterned vinyls come in factory-manufactured sheets that are easily cut to fit and applied to the walls.

- *Ceramic tile.* Ceramic tile is durable and attractive, but it requires a little more maintenance and effort to keep clean.

MISCELLANEOUS

1. Make sure that there are enough electrical outlets along the countertops.

2. Consider locating broom and pantry closets in or near the kitchen.

3. Specify on your plans the make, model, color, and style of the sink, refrigerator/freezer, dishwasher, range, oven(s), microwave, garbage disposal, and exhaust system.

4. Consider having a small desk in the kitchen where you can sit down to thumb through cookbooks, make out shopping lists, check bills, and make telephone calls. The desk should be large enough to accommodate a computer, too, for allowing Internet access to cooking information and to enable family members to perform computer work between kitchen tasks.

5. A portable telephone in the kitchen is a must. If the phone rings while you're cooking supper, you can bring it over to the cooktop and keep stirring that sauce or stir frying those potatoes while talking.

6. Every surface in the kitchen should be easy to clean with a damp sponge: countertops, walls, floors, appliances, and cabinets.

7. There should be plenty of receptacles for portable appliances such as coffee makers, blenders, toaster ovens, radios, bread machines, and electric skillets.

8. Ground-fault electrical circuit interrupters (GFCIs) should be supplied in all kitchen and bathroom receptacles.

9. A fire extinguisher should be within an easy reaching distance to the cooktop, and smoke alarm protection should be included near the kitchen.

10. Allow enough space for at least two waste containers: garbage and trash.

REMODELING NOTES

If you're on a tight budget, and unless there's something wrong with the old countertops, it's probably best not to spend a lot of money upgrading. Solid composite materials cut to fit can be an expensive proposition, and so can stone, and your payback may not be worth it. Unless you are remodeling with the sole intention of selling, that could be a different reason. If you're going to live there a while, it's better to invest in energy efficiencies instead of simply replacing serviceable materials with greener components. If there is something wrong with your countertop—can it be repaired or resurfaced? See the section on new countertops if it must be replaced.

Faucets can have aerators installed to reduce flows—faucets in the kitchen should be water efficient, with no more than 2 gallons per minute maximum flow.

Some faucet aerators have small levers that allow you to temporarily reduce the water flow while soaping up, and you won't have to readjust the water temperature when you flip the lever back and resume the main flow.

Ask your contractor to recycle. What is his or her plan for the project's waste management? Low-VOCs adhesives, glues, grout, sealants, and underlayments should have no formaldehyde.

Vinyl is tough and fairly inexpensive but can pose issues to health and environmental safety—there's an ongoing debate about its durability versus health and environmental issues. Linoleum is probably a better choice, but also recycled content tile, salvaged stone, laminates, concrete, cork, and bamboo are all good choices. Think twice about carpeting. Concrete floors are becoming popular for good reasons. They're attractive and easy to keep clean. They can be stained, painted, or integrally colored and can be combined with radiant heat—heavily used areas are prime candidates for radiant floor heat. People who eat and walk around in bare feet and socks or slippers love to feel warm in the morning, especially during winter. In addition, if desired at some point, concrete may be covered with tile or composite flooring while still using the same heating system.

Creative opportunities to buy used—some commercial booths/bench combinations can be installed perpendicularly from a wall or suspended over the floor—can be found in classified ads or purchased inexpensively when fast-food restaurants remodel. Used tables, chairs, and benches are often available from restaurant equipment exchanges.

Can your current sink, cabinets, flooring, lighting fixtures, plumbing fixtures, hooks, and hardware be cleaned or refinished and reused? Towel bars and shelves can be made from unique recycled or reclaimed components. As part of your remodeling project, deconstruct the old components and recycle or give them away to people not as well off through Habitat for Humanity or similar organizations. Get creative. Be careful to identify asbestos, lead paint, dangerous electrical fixtures, and other safety and environmental concerns.

Replace old energy-squandering appliances. The refrigerator/freezer should be the first to get upgraded, with the dishwasher next in line. If the disposal has seen better days, avoid replacing it, if possible. Start composting instead. Start recycling your vegetable matter, and don't worry about tossing your other kitchen waste into the municipal trash; it will break down and decompose anyway. It's better not to mix it with potable water and send it for treatment. Not having a garbage disposal might be less convenient than you're used to, but greenwise, a disposal is a no-no. Doing without one is a lot easier on your plumbing, uses less electricity, and is much kinder to your septic system, sewer lines, and municipal treatment center.

Get set up to use smaller appliances more often, and purchase smaller units for a saving of space and energy. Microwave ovens, Crock-Pots, and other slow cookers, portable grills and electric fry pans, and toaster ovens are all easier on energy because they allow you to control the heat in a smaller area—always a boon to energy savings. They heat quicker and cool down quicker. It's all in control—the more you control, the less energy is wasted warming up and cooling down.

Compost nonprotein kitchen scraps, and use space below the counter for a compost bucket or include a chute (with a cover) in the countertop for tossing scraps into under-the-counter storage. Locate a kitchen recycling center in a lower cupboard (there may be room now that you don't have a garbage disposal below the sink), and arrange a system compatible with your municipal collection.

Enlarge the east- and south-facing windows if possible for morning sun.

▶▶▶▶▶ POINTS TO PONDER

1. When designing a kitchen, carefully consider its four major components: dining facilities, countertops, cabinets, and appliances.

2. Of all parts of a kitchen, countertops (or food preparation tops) are used the most. Plan generous amounts of them.

3. Make sure that there are plenty of GFCI electrical outlets along the countertops.

4. Kitchen cabinets always have been the focal point of any kitchen. More than anything else, they set the flavor of the room and make or break its appearance. It's to your advantage to select quality-grade cabinets. They'll look better and wear longer.

5. Consider installing broom and pantry closets in the kitchen if there's enough room. Cookbook shelves and a small computer desk/workstation also have become popular modern kitchen features.

6. If possible, a window should be located behind or to the side of the kitchen sink to provide natural lighting during the day. Because food preparation tasks entail lots of fine handwork, plan enough task lights into the kitchen. Recessed or track lighting units make excellent choices.

7. Remember, when planning the location of appliances, that certain units, such as trash compactors, garbage disposals, blenders, food processors, and stove/cooktops with front-unit controls, should be off-limits to young children.

8. Good ventilation in a kitchen is a must. This can include window/screen units, sliding-glass door/screen units, and cooktop fans.

9. The walls of a kitchen, especially the wall surfaces above the work counters, should be finished with durable, easy-to-clean materials.

10. Consider running two phone lines into the kitchen in case the household cook plans on being on the Internet while preparing meals.

Floor Coverings

The selection of a particular floor covering depends on where it will be used, its appearance (available styles and colors), durability, ease of care and maintenance, price, and the buyer's personal taste. It's an excellent idea to visit a number of large home stores and specialized flooring stores to see available floor coverings and get a feeling for what's new. There are certainly many floor coverings to consider when planning your home, including carpet, laminate, vinyl, linoleum, wood, cork, bamboo, tile, stone, brick, and concrete.

Flooring is an ideal material to start with when first looking for green products for a new home owing to numerous good choices from which to select. Unfortunately, this statement is true because the flooring industry has been creating materials that have been exactly the opposite of green for many years. The industry has been providing massive quantities of wall-to-wall carpeting, pliable vinyl flooring, and underlayments—sheets of plywood and particleboard—made and installed with binders or adhesives relying on formaldehyde and other high–volatile organic compound (VOC) ingredients that tend to off-gas harmful chemicals into the home's inside.

Right away, a huge step toward green flooring is to decide not to accept any product made with harmful underlayments. Plywoods and particleboards made without formaldehyde or high-VOC binders are available, at a somewhat higher cost. However, as demand increases, the costs tend to level out and approach those of their undesirable counterparts.

Manufacturers, of course, realize what's at stake here and are scrambling to produce greener versions of old stand-by materials. Now there is resilient vinyl flooring using postindustrial recycled content. There is carpeting manufactured with nap, backing, and pads made entirely of recycled materials. There are biocomposite and bamboo hard floors. Water-based paints and sealers are rapidly replacing coatings that previously used solvents and high-VOC ingredients.

To throw a monkey wrench into the green flooring selection process, though, you need to first analyze your entire range of options by asking yourself a few questions. After realizing what some of the answers are, deciding on flooring materials may not be such a purely green choice. Although ideally you want each flooring product to be durable, nontoxic, made not too far away to reduce transportation efforts, and manufactured using renewable ingredients and environmentally friendly production methods, those characteristics are sometimes at odds with each other.

FLOORING QUESTIONS TO ASK

Some flooring questions to consider include

- Will the structure or surface support heavy flooring materials? Stone, concrete, brick, and tile can be great green choices. Can they be supported by floor, wall, or roof framing being planned?

- Will the materials be compatible with underlayments and the heating system being installed? For example, carpeting or resilient flooring products are not the best choices for radiant-floor heat.

- Is resistance to sound transfer from floor to floor an issue? A bedroom above a family room or kitchen, for instance, should not allow noise to easily penetrate from below, or vice versa.

- What kind of use is expected? A floor that provides a safe crawling place for toddlers will have different requirements from a roughly used kitchen floor that needs to cope with broken dishes, grease spatters, and constant pressure from people standing in front of the cooktop and sink.

- Will the floor be able to take accidental abuse, such as dropped weights from a fitness bench or machine?

- Is the floor expected to get wet occasionally, from someone stepping from a shower or bathtub? During those times, will the flooring become slippery to bare feet?

- Will the floor be expected to capture solar heat gain as part of a passive-solar space-heating system? Or to give off warmth as part of a radiant flooring system?

- Would a dark- or light-colored floor best fit into the room and floor plan? Should it absorb or reflect heat from the sun?

- How many layers of flooring do you really need? Green construction guidelines suggest that whenever you can use the structural component(s) of a floor for the actual floor surface itself, you're better off because you're completely eliminating a second flooring product. For example, why cover a concrete floor with stone, tile, or composite flooring when you can finish the concrete floor surface itself to resemble any of those other products? Again, with green construction, less continues to be more.

- Is the material locally made? It may not always be possible, but when you can, try to use flooring produced either locally or manufactured to resemble materials made locally. This fits into a long-standing tradition of using products that have a history of use within a certain geographic area. It may be more obviously the case with exterior siding, but stone, tile, and some wood and composite floorings also may look out of place or exotic in the North, whereas the same flooring in the Deep South looks entirely natural.

CARPETING

There's a lot to like about wall-to-wall carpeting (also called *fitted* or *edge-to-edge carpeting*), but greenwise, there's also a lot to dislike. Likes include the look and feel of new carpet and even that new-carpet smell. It's also a warm and comfortable surface that helps to deaden sounds. Carpeting, with its thick underlying padding, can provide a certain safety factor for children, pets, and anyone else who might accidentally take a tumble to the floor. Many of the different carpeting varieties are extremely tough and long-wearing, especially wool and the synthetics.

On the dislike side, carpeting can throw a big monkey wrench into indoor air quality in a variety of ways. Those same new-carpet odors mentioned above are really coming from the harmful VOCs being off-gassed by carpet backing and adhesives. They can continue to be slowly released into the home for many months. Most synthetic carpeting, such as nylon, acrylic, and polyester, is made of petroleum-based products. After they're manufactured, their fibers are relatively stable, but unfortunately, they're often attached to backing made of materials that aren't so stable. Because the carpet backing needs to be flexible for the carpet to be rolled, transported, and handled during installation, backing is often made from materials such as styrene butadiene rubber, which accounts for that "new carpet" odor and considerable off-gassing of VOCs into the home's atmosphere. Historically, the glue used to attach carpeting to floors contained formaldehyde, a particularly harmful carcinogen. Synthetic carpeting is also difficult to dispose of or recycle. Wall-to-wall carpeting is sometimes replaced before the end of its useful life owing to small spots or sections getting stained or damaged, for decorating reasons, not regular wear factors. Carpeting is difficult to repair. A spilled glass of grape juice easily could cause an entire roomful of otherwise serviceable carpeting to be changed out. Dust mites, fleas, ticks, and other insects and dust-eating microbes can thrive in certain warm carpeting conditions, especially when the pad and fiber-attachment layers hold moisture. A large quantity of landfill capacity is currently taken up by worn, old-fashioned, and other carpeting remnants. This likely will be the case for decades into the future, where old pieces of all kinds of carpet resist decomposition while leaching out a steady trickle of harmful chemicals.

The greenest carpeting fibers still can collect moisture, dust, dirt, dander, and numerous particles and pollutants tracked in from outside. Gases from other non-green materials can be absorbed by carpet backing and then off-gassed from the carpet into the home. Even a natural material such as wool, when woven into a carpet, can pose air-quality problems when imported from foreign countries and fumigated with toxic insecticides. Carpeting made with domestic wool should be okay. In attempts to make greener carpeting, manufacturers have been developing environmentally improved products with fibers woven into the backing or rubber used as the adhesive.

Organic carpeting made of natural fibers such as sisal, jute, coir, organic cotton, and wool can be green choices if they are not chemically dyed or treated with pesticides. Except for wool, the rest probably won't be as durable as nylon and other synthetics, nor as stain resistant, but if taken care of, they can be good options and are far easier to recycle once their useful life runs its course. Couple them with backings also made of sustainable materials such as jute, hemp, recycled or natural latex rubber, or wool felt matting, and they provide healthy alternatives. Manufacturers are also starting to use silk, cotton, and vegetable plant fibers such as corn in partial- and full-ingredient carpeting production.

Manufacturers are working on additional green offerings using paper twines, grasses, and canes tightly woven into matlike configurations in natural colors and shades, backed with nonslip surfaces of rubber and synthetic latex. For a distinctive look, some are created with decorative stripes and designs. A clever way to recycle plastic drink bottles and containers of polyethylene terapthalate (PET) plastic has the material being produced using closed-loop production techniques.

Carpet tiles are also being manufactured with lower piles and tighter weaves, often using sustainable materials, recycled-content fibers, and low-environmental-impact production methods, resulting in little or no off-gassing when installed in a home. They come with their own pad, so even their installation is friendlier, accomplished with neat self-adhesive tabs so that individual tiles that become stained or damaged simply can be replaced as needed without the use of petroleum-based or other adhesives. Some of the tiles are so stiff and heavy duty that they can be installed merely by interlocking their tabs without being attached directly to the floor. Their small, regular sizes enable carpet tiles to cover flooring insets and irregular shapes, so large, wasted cutouts—common with wall-to-wall carpeting—don't have to be made.

An option available for individuals interested in carpeting is the use of individual rugs instead of wall-to-wall varieties. Unlike fitted carpet, rugs can be removed and cleaned periodically and moved from one place to another for an easy change in decor. They don't require professional installation, need only a simple pad or underlay for a feeling of softness and luxury, and even can be removed temporarily when activities occur that could stain or damage them—such as painting a room or hosting a child's birthday party.

An almost limitless array of carpeting is manufactured for home owners to choose from. Practically any quality, basic material, texture, color, weave, or price range can be had for the asking. Carpeting is an all-around excellent floor covering that literally can be used anywhere in a home.

Certainly, carpeting is an interior decorator's dream because it can create as many moods as colors can influence. It can stretch small spaces into large and shrink large spaces small. It can supply a rich, modern look to a room or create a statement of cool neutrality. It feels wonderful beneath bare feet and is equally enjoyed by small children, who can tumble and fall on it without injuring themselves. It helps to control sound from echoing through a home by absorbing noises and is relatively simple to replace when worn out.

On the other hand, it's tough to remove a cupful of spilled grape juice from a lily-white shag carpet. Carpeting shows various stains and soils and can pose big cleaning problems if chewing gum, grease, ink, or various foods and drinks become embedded in its yarn tufts. Pet odors also can find refuge in carpeting, and during times of low humidity, static electricity can collect and shock people who touch metal lamps or even one another. Also, when carpeting is installed in the high-traffic areas of a house, no matter what its quality, it eventually will show wear paths, can be marred by dropped cigarettes, and cannot be refinished in any way. When soiled, carpeting needs either time-consuming shampooing or must be cleaned professionally.

There are carpets that are custom tailored to solve a wide variety of problem situations: fibers designed to control the static electricity that draws dust or delivers shocks on cold, dry days; carpets having soil resistance built right into the fibers themselves; industrial-grade carpeting designed to take unbelievable punishment, indoors and out; textured carpets with a mixture of sheared yarns and loops engineered to camouflage stains and look good while doing so; and lustrous sheared velours and velvets that look so plush that people are afraid to step on them.

You can tell quality carpet by its material and nap or yarn density. Wool makes excellent carpet, but it's expensive. Nylon is the most popular, accounting for over 75 percent of all carpeting manufactured today. Acrylics, polyesters, rayon, and polypropylene or olefin are no longer as popular as they once were but are all still used for specific applications, the latter, for instance, in kitchens and wherever indoor-outdoor carpeting is needed.

Carpets used to be woven but are rarely woven anymore. Instead, they're tufted—a process by which yarns are looped through a woven backing and then locked into that backing with an adhesive and then another thin layer of backing. Then the yarn loops are cut or sheared to various lengths. Higher-quality carpet contains a higher density of yarn, or more yarn per square inch. The higher the density of yarn, the greater is the carpet's wearability.

Because so many varieties of carpeting exist, here are some guidelines to help you plan the carpeting for your house:

1. The first decision to make is one of style. By area, do you want a plush, a shag, or some other style better suited for each application. After you narrow down the style, begin comparing fibers available in each of the style groups you've selected. A general rule is to seek deeper and denser piles (the configurations of the fibers) than you think you'll need. Remember that shag carpeting is intentionally manufactured with low-density yarn to achieve the shag look.

   Two of the most popular styles of surface texture for carpeting are the sculptured and the plush. The sculptured style is composed of designs created by alternate areas with and without heavy pile. The plush type has a constant pile thickness and is more likely to show footprint indentations. Another texture is the level-loop pile, which wears well and hides footprints nicely. A fourth style is the frieze or twist type, which also thwarts footprints and hides dirt and dust fairly well. Like the level-loop pile, the frieze or twist carpet stands up to rough use. And if it has a level surface, it's easy to keep clean. Frieze is ideal for installations where multiple small seams must be matched—for wrapping carpet around and between handrail supports on a stairway, for example.

2. When checking for carpet density, watch out for *crimp*. Crimp is exactly what it sounds like: mechanically induced zigs and zags in the individual carpet fibers that add bulk and fullness. A given amount of crimped fiber will fill more space than can otherwise be filled with the same quantity of regular, straight fibers. The actual crimping of the fibers is on such a tiny scale; it can't be seen at a casual glance. When crimped fiber is spun into yarn, air is captured between the zigzags, the yarn then looks straight and solid, but at the same time it has a fuller, fluffier look than the noncrimped versions.

   This crimping technique is used to make high-bulk yarns that are fluffed or tufted into some very stylish, elegant carpeting. It's one way to obtain a plusher-looking carpet without encountering a higher expense in the process. Crimped-fiber carpeting might look good at first. It might feel and even sound good, but all a consumer really gets is the same amount of fiber that's available in more "honest" versions with thinner piles—plus a lot of air.

3. When choosing carpet styles and types, consider the wear that they're likely to receive. You'll probably want the most beautiful carpet in your living room, but if the room will see heavy family traffic instead of being just a visitor's parlor, then you might be further ahead to avoid light-toned solid colors and favor an antisoiling plush or textured carpet instead. In general, when it comes to the busier areas in a home—the living room, family room, halls, and stairways, for instance—you'll do better with carpeting that will stand up to the traffic it receives. Bedroom carpets receive relatively light duty and thus can be good places to either economize or go luxury.

4. Most carpeting should have a padding of some type laid beneath the entire surface covered. Padding helps to lengthen a carpet's useful life by absorbing much of the footfall pressure that otherwise would grind the carpet backing against the hard and potentially raspy surface of the floor decking. It also makes a carpet seem plusher than the carpet really is by softening the impact of a person's footfalls so that walking on such a surface is more comfortable. Various paddings are available, manufactured from hair, felt, rubber-coated jute, cellular rubber, high-density sponge, latex foam rubber, and urethane foam. All are acceptable when purchased in ¼- to ½-inch-thick layers.

5. Carpeting should be installed only on smooth surfaces that are relatively uniform and ridgeless. Whenever a separate cushion or padding will be used, such undersupport should have all the necessary seams covered with tape.

6. Carpeting should be planned so that the least number of sections and seams will be needed. When possible, the seams should be positioned in low-traffic areas. Carpeting always should be laid in the same direction; that is, a butt end of a fresh roll shouldn't be seamed to the side of a previous roll.

Types of Carpeting

Here are brief introductions to the various types of carpeting materials available.

NYLON CARPETING

Nylon can go by various brand names such as Antron, Anso, Ultron, and Enkalure II. By any name, nylon is the most popular carpet available. It's especially good for entrance halls and stairways where traffic is heaviest. It can be purchased in many bright colors, has excellent resistance to abrasion and overall strength, and is relatively inexpensive.

Advantages

1. Nylon carpeting is fairly inexpensive to produce and purchase.

2. It is available in a huge quantity of styles, textures, and colors.

3. It has good to excellent texture retention.

4. It has good wet cleanability.

5. It has excellent durability.

6. It has good to excellent appearance retention.

7. It is easy to maintain.

8. It has excellent resistance to abrasion.

9. It has good to excellent resistance to alkalis and acids.

10. It has excellent resistance to insects and mildew.

11. It has good resistance to compression and crushing forces.

12. It has good resistance to staining.

13. It has a long life expectancy.

Disadvantages

1. Nylon carpeting in particular needs a good backing material to attain dimensional stability.

2. It tends to pull and fuzz when abused.

3. It can retain oil and soil and "look dirty" easier than several other synthetic fibers can.

4. Some discoloration might result from prolonged exposure to sunlight.

5. Nylon has more sheen than wool and some of the other synthetics.

6. It can develop static buildup.

7. It offers little protection against cigarette burns.

ACRYLIC CARPETING

These synthetic fibers closely resemble wool in texture, appearance, and abrasion resistance. Some acrylic carpeting, though, is very flammable. Given its resistance to staining and soiling and its low maintenance demands, acrylic carpeting works well in kitchens, bathrooms, basements, porches, patios, and poolside areas—wherever dampness could be a problem or spills are likely to occur.

Advantages

1. Acrylic carpeting has good colorfastness and good resistance to sunlight.

2. It resembles wool in appearance and texture.

3. It resists aging well.

4. It has good texture retention.

5. It has good to excellent wet cleanability.

6. It has good resistance to static buildup.

7. It has good to excellent resistance to staining and soiling.

8. It has excellent resistance to insects and mildew.

9. It has good resistance to alkalis and acids.

10. It has good resistance to abrasion.

11. It has good resistance to compression and crushing forces.

Disadvantages

1. Acrylic carpeting offers little protection against cigarette burns. Some acrylics burn very easily.

2. It tends to pull and fuzz when abused.

3. Some loss in textile strength occurs on prolonged exposure to sunlight.

MODACRYLIC CARPETING

Modacrylic carpet fibers are acrylic fibers that are chemically modified to reduce their flammability. They wear and look like acrylic carpeting.

POLYPROPYLENE OLEFIN CARPETING

Polypropylene olefin is synthetic material that has one of the lowest moisture-absorption rates of all carpet fibers. It's easy to clean and very resistant to stains and soils. It can be used instead of acrylics in kitchens, bathrooms, basements, porches, patios, and poolside areas. Be aware, though, that it isn't as resistant to compression or crushing as the acrylics and doesn't retain its texture as well.

Advantages

1. Polypropylene olefin has good appearance retention.

2. It is easy to maintain, with excellent wet cleanability.

3. It has good durability and resistance to aging.

4. It has excellent resistance to staining and soiling.

5. It has excellent resistance to abrasion.

6. It has good to excellent resistance to alkalis and acids.

7. It has excellent resistance to insects and mildew.

8. It can be treated by the factory to give good resistance to direct sunlight.

Disadvantages

1. Polypropylene olefin does not afford much protection against cigarette and other burns.

2. It has only a fair resistance to compression and crushing forces.

3. It has only a fair retention of texture.

POLYESTER CARPETING

Polyester makes an attractive carpet with many fine features, but it's less favored than nylon, acrylics, and polypropylene because of its resiliency deficiencies.

Advantages

1. Polyester carpeting has a soft, luxurious appearance.

2. It has good colorfastness.

3. It has excellent resistance to insects and mildew.

4. It is less static prone than wool.

Disadvantages

1. The resiliency of polyester is somewhat less than that of nylon and some other types, so dense, deeper pile construction is needed for the same performance.

2. It stains easily with oily materials.

3. Prolonged exposure to sunlight will result in some loss of strength.

RAYON CARPETING

Rayon carpeting is not generally recommended over any of the others. It soils easily and gives poor resistance to abrasive wear.

Advantages

1. Rayon carpeting is unaffected by most acids and solvents.

2. It can be an attractive flooring in areas of light usage.

Disadvantages

1. Rayon carpeting has poor resistance to abrasion.

2. It soils rapidly.

3. Fuzzy types are very flammable.

WOOL CARPETING

When it comes to beautiful, durable, top-of-the-line carpeting, there's no doubt that natural wool fiber leads the pack. It's an ideal green material because it's renewable and biodegradable. It resists mildew, lays flat, and feels soft and warm. Wool is a wonderfully durable fiber that has yet to be surpassed for its excellent appearance retention and resilience. Carpet wools are as varied as the different types of sheep across the globe, with fibers that range from fine and lustrous to coarse and springy. It has a natural supply of lanolin oil that helps to prevent water absorption and stains and does not need to be treated with fire retardants—it resists flaming on its own.

Advantages

1. Wool carpeting has excellent appearance and texture retention.
2. It has excellent durability.
3. It has good to excellent ease of maintenance.
4. It is warm and comfortable to the touch.
5. It dyes well.
6. It has good resistance to abrasion.
7. It has good protection against cigarette and other burns.
8. It has excellent resistance to compression and crushing forces.
9. It has good resistance to staining and soiling.

Disadvantages

1. Wool carpeting is expensive.
2. It offers only fair resistance to alkalis and acids.
3. It possesses only fair to good wet cleanability (but many other cleaning methods have been developed over the years).

Carpet Protection

Although frequent vacuuming prevents soil and miscellaneous bits of debris from becoming ground into carpeting, it also makes sense to start out with a quality grade of carpet that already has built-in protection engineered into its construction. When reviewing carpet specifications and manufacturers' claims, look for the following:

■ *Stain resistance.* Spills should bead up on the carpet's surface, allowing easy blotting for quick removal.

- *Soil resistance.* Soil resistance helps to repel dirt and prevents it from becoming embedded and damaging to the carpet's backing. It also helps to prevent dust and tiny bits of debris from sticking to individual carpet fibers, making vacuum cleaning and other soil-removal methods far more efficient.

- *Static resistance.* Static electricity can build up to startling levels and may pose serious problems for youngsters, senior citizens, or anyone who happens to receive an unexpected sharp shock after touching a piece of metal such as a lamp base while going about routine activities at home.

- *Wear resistance.* This quality typically is reflected in the length and breadth of the carpet's warranty.

- *Color/fading resistance.* This feature is especially important in sunny climates and in contemporary homes that use plenty of exterior glass.

Carpet Warranties

Any carpet you purchase should be covered by a warranty against manufacturing defects. The warranty comes directly from the manufacturer and is an assurance that the carpeting wasn't made in a slipshod manner (or if it *was*, by accident, the company will replace the damaged carpet or reimburse the owner). It's the consumer's protection against defects such as the tufts pulling out of the carpet, the face of the carpet coming apart from the backing, or the dye bleaching out during shampooing.

Carpet warranties are very important, so important that you should never even consider buying a carpet that's not guaranteed against manufacturing defects. As important as such warranties are, though, remember that they don't guarantee performance over the long haul.

LAMINATES

Laminate floorings have found favor recently with builders, home buyers, and remodelers and for good reason. Various patterns and styles can supply the look of wood, tile, and stone—without the accompanying care and maintenance hassles. Laminates typically are composed of four layers (if you count the printed photograph of the wood, stone, or tile finish as a layer). The top layer, also called the *wear layer*, is usually made of an extremely durable material called *aluminum oxide*. The thickness of the aluminum oxide is often what sets the price and warranty length of the particular laminate in question. The thicker the layer of aluminum oxide, the more durable is the product surface. Beneath the clear surface layer is the decorative finish layer (the wood plank or stone or tile appearance). Supporting the top layer is the middle, or core, layer, which is often a sturdy

BUILT-IN CENTRAL VACUUM SYSTEMS

Central vacuum cleaning systems have come a long way since their introduction decades ago. They're now more powerful and more convenient. Main vacuum power units can be located in a well-vented utility room, basement, or garage—away from daily living activities, providing quiet operation (Fig. 29.1). Tubing that runs beneath the floors or in the attic from one end of the house to the other connects hose inlets (Fig. 29.2) throughout the house. On many systems, when a portable hose attachment is inserted into an inlet, the vacuum starts automatically. The long hose attachment enables the vacuuming of stairs, walls, ceilings, and furnishings. The vacuum power plant typically is vented to the outdoors—but not onto or near a patio, deck, breezeway, window, or entrance.

Central vacuum systems are convenient for cleaning multistory homes, where you'd otherwise have to lug a portable unit up and down; they're also good for keeping basements, garages, and automobiles vacuumed. Plus, overall, the convenience and ease of using a central vacuum system helps to encourage household members to clean more frequently than they otherwise might. Numerous cleaning attachments also make specific vacuuming tasks easy.

There are even vacuum dust pans built into a cabinet toekick or baseboard that accept dirt swept off vinyl, wood, concrete, and other hard floorings. These are great for kitchens, baths, laundry

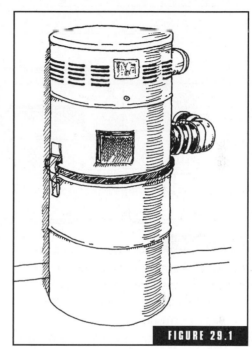

FIGURE 29.1

Central vacuum power unit.

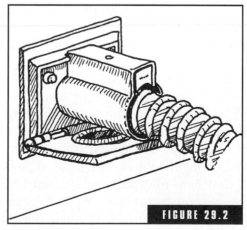

FIGURE 29.2

Hose inlets.

rooms, mud rooms—with smooth flooring; they eliminate the need for dustpans or stooping. The vacuum system automatically activates with the flip of a toe switch (Fig. 29.3).

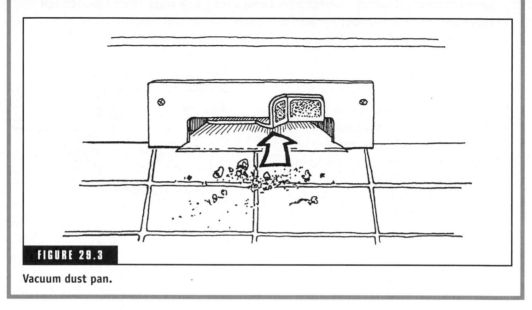

FIGURE 29.3

Vacuum dust pan.

fiberboard or particleboard. The bottom layer can be made of laminated products that sometimes include plastics and melamine. Together, the layers are fused by pressure and heat into a user-friendly flooring. The wear layer enables laminate flooring to withstand stains (even from notorious staining agents such as mustards, red wine, bleach, and some felt-tipped markers), impacts, and abuse that would damage most other types of floorings.

It's a good surface for high-traffic areas such as kitchens, recreation rooms, or exercise rooms. It's simple to care for and maintain, requiring little more than routine vacuuming and an occasional sponge mopping. It comes in a wide variety of styles, colors, and patterns that imitate wood (narrow or wide boards), tile, and stone. The better models even have realistic textured grains or surfaces that match the wood, tile, or stone appearance. Most laminates come in individual boards having tongue-and-groove edges. The boards are installed most often as a "floating floor" over a thin layer of foam without nails, screws, or glue. Although wet areas such as bathrooms and laundry rooms potentially can be a problem for laminates (water may leak through the tongue-and-groove seams), the problem is sometimes solved by using low- or no-VOC glue or sealants between each board. Check with your contractor if you plan a wet-location installation.

VINYL FLOORING

Polyvinyl chloride (PVC) is a commonly used synthetic material found in numerous building products. Better known as *vinyl*, various forms of this petroleum-based plastic help to make up a diverse range of items that include plumbing drain pipe, electrical wire sheathing, roofing membranes, housewrap, siding, gutters, windows, shower curtains, wall coverings, and resilient flooring. It's a relatively inexpensive ingredient that is easy to form and extremely durable. Practically anything made from vinyl is usually advertised as maintenance-free. Although manufacturers concur that the methods used to make vinyl are not all that green—because it's made from crude oil and typically uses large amounts of energy and chlorine in the process and sometimes harmful plasticizers—its durability and long useful life prevent its products from having to be replaced with the regularity of less durable items. A major disadvantage of vinyl products, however, is they're difficult to dispose of. When burned, they give off toxic emissions, and they're almost impossible to biodegrade. There's an ongoing argument between proponents and detractors revolving around the amount of chlorine and heavy metals vinyl leaches out while sitting in landfills. From our perspective, vinyl is not a very green material, but sometimes its durability and performance may offset the disadvantages for certain home owner situations.

Vinyl flooring makes a serviceable floor covering for bathrooms, kitchens, recreation rooms, sunrooms, laundry rooms, and any other rooms for that matter. It offers a wide selection of patterns, colors, and even textures and is available at many quality levels and prices. Although it comes in tile and long strips, most vinyl flooring is manufactured in wide rolls so that a room can be laid out with very few seams. Quality vinyl resists grease and other staining materials and is very durable overall. Lower-quality vinyl should be avoided. Some vinyl flooring never needs waxing, whereas other vinyls might need waxing from time to time.

ADVANTAGES

1. Vinyl flooring is wear resistant and lasts a long time.
2. It is stain resistant.
3. It is scuff resistant.
4. It is tear, gouge, and rip-resistant and practically maintenance-free.
5. It should not discolor from mold, mildew, or alkalis.
6. When installed properly, its seams should not curl.

DISADVANTAGES

1. Vinyl flooring is a petroleum-based product.

2. It often uses chlorine in its manufacture.

3. It requires large amounts of energy to make.

4. It can off-gas harmful chemicals inside a home.

5. It can leach harmful chemicals into the ground.

6. It emits toxic gas when burned.

7. It is almost impossible to biodegrade.

VINYL FLOOR CONSIDERATIONS

- Seams should minimized and protected by seam coats.

- Vinyl flooring with greater percentages of vinyl makeup are tougher and more cushioned than models having less vinyl makeup.

- Thicker vinyl floorings are more comfortable and tend to be more resistant to tears and punctures.

- Ask if the vinyl flooring you're considering comes in 12-foot widths to minimize seams.

LINOLEUM

Before vinyl appeared decades ago, linoleum ruled the kichens, bathrooms, recreation rooms, and laundry rooms throughout the country. *Linum* in Latin refers to flax, which the base is woven from, and *oleum* points to the oils used—resins of linseed and pine, which together are combined with cork and wood waste fiber under high temperatures. Simply put, the linseed oil is dried out and made into a cement powder that bonds ground wood, cork, resins, and other natural materials into an extremely durable material that's backed with a jute fiber or similar layer. Linoleum, in improved versions, is once again available. Don't avoid considering it because you think it's old-fashioned. It's a natural, modern product that's entirely recyclable, a flooring that's recommended for individuals who suffer from allergies or asthma because it's hypoallergenic. Manufacturers also claim that linoleum does not emit gases, is a natural deterrent to bacteria, and resists the transfer of static electricity. Linoleum is used in many of the 12-inch square (and larger) commercial tiles you see in hospitals, stores, and other high-traffic businesses. More recently, this "green alternative to vinyl flooring" has been manufactured in more modern colors, patterns, and shades. Its green characteristics definitely make linoleum a flooring to be considered. It wears well, adds a feel of softness to the floor, is easy to keep clean, and resists staining well.

WOOD

Wood floor covering has been used for centuries and is one of the original and oldest green products. Today it comes in many types and styles and can be used in about every part of a home. Although all wood flooring is no longer green, it can be purchased in a huge variety of products, including *imitation* wood flooring. The most common types include the following:

Dimensional Wood Flooring

Consisting of solid-wood planks, boards, and timbers, this is available in a wide variety of hardwoods and softwoods. U.S., European, and Asian hardwoods have excellent wearing qualities and are readily available from forests responsibly managed and certified by the nonprofit international Forest Stewardship Council (FSC). Tropical hardwoods such as teak, mahogany, iroko, aformosia, and ipe, protected species that the rain forests depend on to keep their delicate ecological systems in balance, are also available through the same certification program. There are other certification systems claiming to reflect sustainable forestry practices, but some are "greenwashing" at its worst, in place only for marketing reasons. Overall, the most popular North American species are white and red oak, maple, ash, sycamore, and cherry. Standard hardwood flooring boards come in widths of 2¼ inches and random lengths. To achieve a more custom look, oak flooring also can be supplied in random widths with or without a distinct V-groove between the lengthwise side edges of each plank. Avoid purchasing floorings that could be from unregulated harvesting. It's best to stick with FSC certification for all new wood flooring. The amount of certified timber is, pardon the green construction pun, "growing" as landowners across the world are joining the sustainable-resources global network dedicated to preserving forestry levels in their home countries, and additional hardwood species are becoming available for flooring use. Other places to look for flooring planks are local lumberyards that are occasionally called on to thin small patches of local forests or clearcut them for road, commercial, or residential construction. Obtaining wind-blown logs after a hurricane or wind storm is also a possibility.

In short, solid wood makes extremely handsome and serviceable floors. When harvested under the right conditions and from the right places, it's a renewable resource, doesn't require much energy or resources to produce, is safe for the home environment, and is easily biodegradable. Although plank-wood floors used to be finished with solvent-based, high-VOC coatings, manufacturers have been developing much healthier alternatives in recent times—including water-based varnishes and polyurethanes and natural penetrating oils such as tung and linseed oils.

Softwood

Softwood floors really mostly mean pine wood planks and some larch, spruce, and European redwood. Softwoods grow quite a bit faster than hardwood trees—between 18 and 24 years to harvest. They come in standard and random widths and lengths. Pine is a lot less expensive than oak and will show wear more quickly than oak. On the plus side, pine has a beautiful grain and takes staining very well.

Reclaimed or Salvaged Wood

Flooring made from reclaimed or salvaged wood is an excellent way to obtain beautiful old-growth wood flooring that may not be available new today. Wood has this advantage over other flooring—it's difficult or unreasonable to expect to reuse worn carpeting or resilient flooring. They get dirty, stained, ripped, and gouged. But wood can be resurfaced to look new or even better than new depending on the refinisher's skills. In addition, wood can be refinished again and again. Back in the times when commercial and industrial buildings were being erected decades ago, millions and millions of board feet of valuable hardwood went into their floors and ceilings. More went into bridges, warehouses, office buildings, elaborate churches, schools, and homes. Now that many of these structures are approaching the end of their useful lives—owing to neighborhood blight, inefficient heating and cooling systems, outdated electric and plumbing systems, and numerous other causes—the old flooring material—perhaps worn and dirty—is waiting to be removed, cleaned, refinished, and reinstalled in upscale residential and commercial projects of all kinds. It's an excellent source of recycled green flooring.

Wood flooring will not wear appreciably if its surface pores are filled in and the entire top is sanded, sealed, and periodically resealed with a protective finish of either layers of wax, varnish, shellac, lacquer, or hard polyurethane. If desired, wood stain can be applied before the polyurethane. Polyurethane is available in a matte (soft gloss) or a hard shiny finish. The choice is one of personal taste. In addition to giving wood flooring a pleasant appearance, polyurethane requires no waxing. Eventually, though, even polyurethane will have to be reapplied.

Wood floors have good grease and other stain resistance and are fairly simple to maintain. While linoleum and carpeting must be torn out and replaced when worn, wood flooring can be resurfaced. It's the only floor that actually can improve with age and successive refinishings.

On the negative side, the periodic refinishings, with their laborious sanding, can be expensive and time-consuming. Hardwood floors also can be very noisy. You can soften up their effects by placing large area rugs in the living spaces and by hanging substantial draperies in the same room to absorb sound. And lastly, wood flooring not securely nailed will squeak when walked on.

Veneers

Veneers of less desirable wood boards or particleboards can have thin layers of more valuable solid timber glued to one or more sides. Veneers can be green products if the glues and bonding glues use no formaldehyde or high-VOC ingredients and if the top protective finish coatings are also water-based. Some manufacturers finish their flooring with coats of clear vinyl, a substance not particularly green or healthy.

Parquet Tiles

Square or rectangular parquet flooring tiles consist of small pieces of wood pressed and held together with an adhesive binder and a finished surface. Parquet floors get great marks for their beauty and how they can easily be the focal points of whatever room they're in, but they can be laborious to maintain and keep looking so nice.

Bamboo

To many individuals, bamboo belongs on this list, even though, technically, it's a grass rather than wood. For all practical purposes, its manufactured result does closely resemble that of flooring made from hardwood.

Composite or Engineered Flooring

Composite flooring consisting of wood and nonwood materials and fibers is bound together with adhesives and made to look and act like real wood. It usually is constructed around a strong core of plywood or middle composite layer sandwiched by a thin hardwood veneer—from which the flooring gets its good looks. This manufacturing process uses smaller wood pieces and wood waste and is an excellent substitute for large-timber forestry use. It's a great way to stretch the good trees into additional flooring coverage. Depending on the thickness of the veneer or wear layer, engineered wood even can be refinished a number of times. In short, engineered wood can look exactly like very expensive, high-quality solid-wood flooring. If the core and surface-layer ingredients include FSC-certified products and adhesives and finishes with low-VOC characteristics, all the better.

Particleboard

This includes flooring make of particleboards and less valuable wood boards printed with a photo of the wood grain of a more desirable species.

Imitation Wood

Imitation wood flooring is made of plastic and printed with the photo of wood grain.

CORK

No, this is not the champagne bottle stopper but rather a surprisingly durable flooring or underlayment made of the replenishable bark of cork oak trees grown around the Mediterranean Sea and in North Africa, Spain, and Portugal. Cork is renewable, but not *that* renewable. The raw cork bark is harvested from cork oak trees—about half the dead bark layer can be removed at a time without hurting the tree—when they reach about 25 years old and thereafter every 10 years or so during the tree's 200-year-long lifespan. When used as an underlayment beneath laminate, hardwood, and other floorings, cork greatly reduces the sound transfer below and above the walking surface. The greenest cork floorings are put together with high-quality low-VOC adhesives and are top-coated with solvent-free finishes. Manufacturers stress that cork flooring, with appropriate finishes, is tough enough to install in living rooms, kitchens, family rooms, hallways, and practically anywhere except places likely to get doused with water every so often, such as bathrooms and laundry rooms. Home hobby areas and hobby craft spaces are good candidates for cork because users may spend a lot of time there on their feet and can benefit from such a cushioned surface. As with any flooring products, stick with the upper-end varieties, and avoid purchasing inexpensive no-name brands. The performances of different cork floorings can range from excellent to poor.

ADVANTAGES

1. Cork flooring is flexible and comfortable to walk on.
2. It has good sound absorbency and is quiet to walk on.
3. It can be recycled easily and is biodegradable.
4. It resists occasional water and other liquid spills.
5. It has natural antibacterial properties.
6. It is available in tiles or sheets.
7. It has high insulating values.

DISADVANTAGES

1. It can be damaged easily if abused.
2. Excessive demand could stress relatively small world cork supplies.
3. Cork is not a rapidly replenishable material.
4. It can be stained if permeated by persistent water contact.
5. It needs a durable wear coat in order to last without gradual deterioration.

BAMBOO

Like cork, bamboo is a replenishable material that has been finding its way into flooring. Similar in strength to oak, bamboo is really a grass that takes only about 3 to 5 years to grow into canes large enough for flooring use (imagine what you could get from an oak or cherry tree in 3 or 5 years). Bamboo also can be harvested from the same plant section a number of times because new stalks grow from previously cut shoots. It grows on poor-quality land and does not need fertilizers or pesticides. Of hundreds and hundreds of bamboo varieties, though, only a few can supply floor-quality material, and even those usable varieties differ from one another for specific applications. When pressed and formed into boards, bamboo flooring is beautiful, superhard, durable, scratch resistant and gouge resistant, and will easily repel moisture. It's produced in a variety of horizontal- and vertical-grain types, colors, and board sizes, manufactured by either pressing shredded bamboo stalks together with a resin binder or pressing solid strips together in a similar fashion. Solid bamboo products are installed in the same way that solid hardwood pieces are. They can be sanded, sawed, drilled, and glued in place. In engineered forms, bamboo can be formed like engineered hardwood products into thick boards with tongue-and-groove edges or onto laminated composite sheets or boards that can be installed with floating, nailing, or gluing techniques. But not all bamboo flooring products are equal. Some of the low-end products rely on bamboo varieties that will practically fall apart after being put in use. Their fibers will warp or delaminate, or they'll likely off-gas pollutants owing to being manufactured with formaldehyde preservatives or installed with high-VOC adhesives. Instead, try to find bamboo made with a boric acid preservative, installed with a low-VOC adhesive, and then finished with a water-based polyurethane sealer. These greener, high-quality varieties will be available from bamboo manufacturers who have a history of providing products to established, quality builders. Expect to pay a fair price, and avoid bamboo flooring offered at cut-rate prices.

TILE

Tile flooring—individual square or other multisided tiles—come in a full range of colors, finishes, and sizes in two popular types: ceramic and quarry. Ceramic tiles generally are glazed in bright, shiny colors and are used to create custom floor designs or mosaics that set or follow a room's decorating scheme. Many ceramic tiles are made in Italy and Portugal.

The term *quarry tile* is misleading. It isn't actually tile that comes from a quarry. Rather, it's made from a mixture of clay, shale, and grit that's baked at high temperatures. Quarry tiles feature muted earthen tones that are not glazed or shiny. Their dull surfaces help to create a natural look inside homes that are planned with unsurfaced or natural building materials and decor. The term *quarry* really hails from the old-fashioned word quarrel, which means a four-sided stone.

Tile makes a floor covering that possesses a lot of character and is often used in hard-service areas such as entrance foyers and patios, and it is equally at home in bathrooms, kitchens, and sunrooms. Tile is ideal to use on floors that will be on the receiving end of passive-solar heating designs. During the day, the tiles will soak up heat that will, in turn, be released gradually during the evening.

Although tile is very durable and will withstand wear and tear well, it has many seams and joints that are susceptible to cracking and staining. These seams and joints should be recoated periodically with an impervious surface sealer. Aside from the grout or other joint cement, the tile itself requires little maintenance. For best results, with the exception of bathrooms, tile should be laid in cement mortar over a dropped or sunken subfloor.

Tile flooring has been around for many, many years, and lots of different types and grades of tile and substrates (material that tile is laid in or set on) exist. Some tile is selected for its resistance to water absorption. Others for slip resistance, stain resistance, or (for outdoors use) frost resistance. Final selections should be made only after consulting contractors and manufacturers with considerable tile expertise.

With all the attention recycling has been getting, tile has jumped into the fray with the addition and combination of recycled glass, ground mussel shells, and other hard-wearing additives used to make strong, durable tiles with unique stain-resistant colors and surfaces. Pieces of old tile are also used to make new concrete-bed mosaics or can be ground up into stone mixtures or sand used for stabilizing beds instead of or in addition to gravel. Whenever possible, select recycled material tiles as your greenest option, and insist they be installed with low-VOC adhesive and mastics. If those tiles are manufactured from locally dug clay or even made within a reasonable distance of your construction, so much the better. This is easier said than done in some parts of the country, but ask at your local building supply stores, and you may be surprised.

STONE

Stone is by and large a green flooring choice. And if you elect to specify a natural stone floor in a foyer or room, there's no doubt that such a floor will be one of a kind. There are dozens of colors and sizes of natural stones, from purple, red, and black slate to multitoned granites, colorful quartzites, and the softer polished marbles.

Practically speaking, most stone used in today's homes is either slate or bluestone. Slate is a smooth gray, red, blue, or black sedimentary stone that splits easily and evenly into convenient slabs. Bluestone is a sandstone that can be gray, green, blue, or buff-colored. Their most popular applications are foyers, hallways, kitchens, and sunrooms.

Although marble is the most luxurious stone that's widely available, it's a soft stone that tends (especially in the darker colors) to scratch easily and to absorb stains readily unless covered with a few coats of a good stone sealer. It's also slippery when wet.

What all well cared-for stone offers is natural beauty and durability, plus ease of maintenance. The seams and joints, however, will need the same treatment as they receive with tile flooring—an impervious surface sealer.

Because natural stone is very heavy, depending on the thickness of stones selected, floor joists should be installed 12 inches on center for additional strength.

ADVANTAGES

1. Stone flooring is durable and resists stains fairly well.

2. It's a natural product that has no adverse effect on indoor air quality.

3. It's ideal for underfloor heating systems.

4. It's awfully dense and heavy and provides an effective way to capture solar heat.

5. There's plenty of it in the world; we won't be running out.

6. It's recyclable and can be discarded without causing pollution.

DISADVANTAGES

1. Stone flooring can crack.

2. It doesn't absorb sound well.

3. It's awfully hard, especially when fallen on.

4. It can be slippery when wet.

5. It can feel cold in bare feet.

6. A lot of energy can be spent quarrying, cutting, polishing, and transporting it.

7. It may need additional flooring support.

BRICK

If you're considering tile and stone or even concrete, you might as well look at brick, too. It also comes in many colors, textures, and types. Brick is installed and cared for in a similar manner to tile, stone, and concrete pavers and other flooring blocks. Any of those four materials can add a lot of character to selected areas in your home.

CONCRETE

As mentioned previously, one more masonry flooring possibility is concrete—not blocks, but larger pours that can have many different appearances. If you've never seen a stained and finished concrete floor, imagine that you're looking at a floor that resembles buckskin suede, or a soft blue aged Italian marble, or terra cotta in soft brown hues punctuated with bits of rust.

A great feature of concrete is that it can do double duty as both the floor structure and walking surface. Especially when the plan calls for a slab-on-grade first floor with no additional floors on top of the first level. This amounts to a savings on materials and labor, plus the home will end up with a truly unique finished concrete floor. Poured concrete can be tinted, inset with stone chips or tiles and polished into a glossy terrazzo finish, or used as a mosaic canvas and as a sturdy bed for in-floor heat-delivery systems. There are individuals specializing in creating work-of-art concrete floors that use industrial fly-ash waste products as binders that not only save land-filling the fly ash but also create a stronger concrete that's less likely to crack and requires less energy-intensive and carbon-dioxide-generating portland cement for a greener product. On the other hand, ask about which surface stains, tints, or sealants will be used and what they consist of because some contain exceptionally strong chemicals that can release high levels of VOCs and other pollutants. Afterward, the cured and tinted concrete should be sealed to reduce staining and maintenance issues. Insist on water-based sealants and treatments whenever possible.

Circular saws can be used to cut the concrete surface to give the effect of tile or cut stone flooring. Stained concrete can be used indoors and outdoors. More and more independent contractors are learning how to stain, etch, and seal thin and thick concrete slabs, which results in competitive pricing. In addition, matching concrete furniture and countertops can be cast and finished—on site—to give a home a one-of-a-kind decorative look.

RUBBER

Because of its tendency to off-gas (its telltale rubber odor is a constant reminder), this material is largely used in areas that have plenty of ventilation and where the home's occupants probably do not spend large amounts of time, such as a garage, basement, exercise area, outdoor walkways, picnic area, and beneath a child's swing set or other outdoor play equipment. It comes in the form of inter-locking tiles, sheets, rolls, and ethylene propylene diene monomer (EPDM) syn-thetic rubber granules commonly found on running tracks and sports fields. Rubber products generally are durable, stain resistant, able to stand wet areas, and yet are soft enough to absorb impacts. They're more pliable and resilient than other sheet floorings; are available in a fair range of colors, textures, and designs; and have companion products such as matching edging and wall protector sheets.

Unlike vinyl and many plastics, rubber-based products are biodegradable over time. Some rubber flooring products use recycled rubber in their manufacture, such as rubber floor tiles partially made from discarded vehicle tires. Other flooring tiles and sheets are made from a combination of natural tree rubber and synthetic rubber and fillers produced from petrochemicals. Most rubber flooring ultimately can be recycled into other products such as welcome mats and safety mats for home, commercial, or industrial use.

FLOORING INSTALLATION CARE

1. The contractor should wait until the latter stages of construction before the home's flooring is installed—to prevent excessive wear and tear.

2. No matter which floorings you select, make sure that when heavy appliances are delivered, the flooring is protected by a thin sheet of plywood or similar material.

3. Remind the contractor that no smoking is allowed. Brand-new floors can be badly marred by burn marks from dropped cigarettes or cigars.

4. Make a point to look closely at the flooring before releasing the contractor's final payment.

REMODELING NOTES

Whenever the need to remodel a home's flooring presents itself, the opportunity can be used to add more green features to the dwelling. Few other remodeling projects can make such an immediate and lasting effect for so little effort. Flooring is one of the most often noticed and greatest used features of any dwelling. When floor coverings draw near the end of their useful life, they can be replaced easily, a room at a time. Larger and odd-shaped rooms can be matched with hard-surfaced, durable materials such as finished concrete or softer and more resilient linoleums, which are relatively easy to cut, fit, and lay. More expensive floorings, such as stone and tile can be economically planned for bathrooms, kitchen work areas, foyers, or other small-floor spaces. Bamboo, hardwood, and composites may be a good fit for bedrooms, hallways, family rooms, and dining rooms. Wherever it is used, bamboo should be treated with a boric acid preservative, laid with a formaldehyde-free adhesive, and finished with water-based polyurethane. Although some flooring materials are better in areas where moisture is present, there are really no strict guidelines; it largely depends on a room's use, available funds, and the occupants' behavior habits.

From an environmental perspective, think twice about including wall-to-wall carpeting in your remodeling plans unless there are particular reasons, such as for a child's playroom; for stairways, hallways, or little-used bedrooms; for resale value to cover up unsightly yet serviceable plywood floors; or for cost reasons—it's a quick way to quickly change a home's appearance and feel. If anything, pay attention to the brand and make of carpet, and try to find a type that's been made to greener standards. Natural-fiber carpet tiles are a green choice in wool with non-toxic backers; the tiles can be replaced in sections and repaired, so smaller amounts are discarded. Vegetable- and natural-fiber carpets, when discarded, can be buried in the garden and will not last in landfills for all eternity. Carpeting tiles also can be made from other environmentally friendly materials such as silk, cotton, jute, and sisal. In all cases, try to find carpets that don't require adhesives and conventional pliable backing made of styrene butadiene rubber, which emits VOCs.

Vinyl is not a very green material, but life-cycle analysis sometimes can justify its use owing to its ability to stand up to hard wear. Linoleum typically is a greener choice, which is also available now in tile form. Always replace plywood and underlayments made with formaldehyde with those made without. Because plywood can expand when damp, it is not a good choice for ceramic tiles as is cement or backer board. Resilient floor coverings can be installed over old vinyl or linoleum flooring in sound condition or over underlayment-grade plywood made from fir or pine. Wood parquet flooring can be laid over old vinyl or linoleum flooring in good condition, underlayment-grade plywood, or hardboard. Laminate flooring will be able to cover almost any surface without cracks and sharply uneven sections that otherwise may permit the laminate to "give" or flex. Solid-wood flooring is best laid over sturdy underlayment-grade plywood. Ceramic tile or stone can be set with no-VOC mastics, adhesives, and grout over sound layers of old ceramic tiles but is best installed over a concrete slab, cement board, or sound layers of underlayment-grade plywood.

▷▷▷▷▷ POINTS TO PONDER

1. Don't skimp on the padding when it comes to carpet. A thick, resilient padding makes a carpet feel much plusher than it would with a marginal, thin pad. Even though you can't see it, padding contributes greatly to lengthening a carpet's useful life by absorbing much of the footfall pressure that otherwise would grind the carpet backing against the hard, raspy surface of the floor decking.

2. Through selective choice of colors and shades, carpeting can create desired "moods" or "feelings" in rooms. It can be used to liven up a simple floor plan or tone down a starkly modern room or dwelling. It can make a room or area look smaller or larger. It can help to separate one part of a room from another.

3. Consider the type of use a carpet will receive before selecting carpeting type, style, and color. Review your needs with several trusted carpeting distributors for suggestions and information on the latest offerings.

4. Become acquainted with the benefits available from laminate flooring. If planning tile, stone, brick, or hardwood flooring, investigate those looks in laminates, and then compare cost, care, and warranties.

5. Vinyl and linoleum floorings offer great appearance and wear at relatively low cost. Some so closely resemble stone, brick, or wood that you can hardly tell the difference. Slip-resistant finishes are available for entrance foyers, kitchens, bathrooms, or wherever flooring is likely to get wet. The better grades of these floorings are virtually maintenance-free.

6. Major advancements have been made to all sorts of wood flooring products, coatings, and maintenance aids. Wood, when installed and cared for properly, has excellent wear qualities, but so do alternative flooring products such as cork and bamboo.

7. Selective use of tile flooring (sometimes with matching or contrasting wall tile) can add beautiful utilitarian, one-of-a-kind floors to a home. The array of ceramic and quarry tile available is mind boggling. Tile is also very durable.

8. Proper installation of tile flooring is critical to the long-term life of the tile. Although the tile itself is rarely a problem, the grout or joint cement can crack or loosen. The stability of the base or underlayment on which the tiles rest is also important. Make sure that the installing contractors are experienced or specialize in laying tile.

9. Stone makes attractive, unique floors. Stones are also heavy and hard and need professional installation techniques in addition to extrasturdy floor framing to support the weight. Brick is installed and cared for in a manner similar to that of stone and tile. Keep an open mind when it comes to the unique, cost-effective looks of stained and sealed concrete.

10. Try to consider your entire flooring picture at the same time instead of going from room to room. Too many different types, styles, and colors of flooring materials can result in a busy look that you may quickly tire of. Real estate brokers and flooring distributors can advise you on decorating traps to avoid.

Home Environmental Issues

A host of materials, building products, and systems all contribute to the overall quality of a home's interior environment. Plumbing and heating, ventilation, and air-conditioning (HVAC) systems rank toward the top of the list, and so do wall, floor, and ceiling wear surfaces, finishes, and furnishings. The furnishings, together with wear surfaces and decorating materials, can be considered the interior "skin" of a house, making up what the occupants come in direct contact with from day to day. Even though they consist of only a very small total proportion of building materials, they encompass almost all the surface areas individuals living in the home encounter while inside the house. It's no surprise, then, that these furnishings, wear surfaces, and decorating materials may have considerable influence on indoor air quality. And since about 9 of every 10 hours at home are spent inside, indoor air quality can have positive or negative effects on occupant health.

Unfortunately, statistics point to the indoor air quality of many traditionally built modern homes as being dangerous to the health of their occupants. Although leaky exterior house shells may have inadvertently resulted in adequate ventilation, the home plumbing and heating systems often produced unacceptable levels of fumes and moisture. Interior floor and wall coverings had relatively high levels of volatile organic compounds (VOCs) slowly off-gassing as days, months, and years elapsed. A common statement by building engineers contended that typical home indoor air was far more polluted than air outside, even in places where outdoors pollution was acknowledged as hazardous. The advent of recent tightly built homes only made matters worse because before the realization (after about 20 years passed) came about that better ventilation was required for tight homes, the same high-VOC materials and products that had been included for decades were still being used. Fortunately, this situation is not true with green-built homes. Instead, green systems, materials, and products are designed to

- Be as inert as possible, with little or no off-gassing of potentially harmful chemicals, odors, and fumes
- Prevent the collection or intrusion of carbon monoxide, radon, mold, excessive moisture, and noise
- Provide steady supplies of fresh, clean air and water

CARBON MONOXIDE, NITROGEN DIOXIDE, AND SULFUR DIOXIDE

Carbon monoxide can be a quick and insidious killer—if you can call sudden death insidious. It's a colorless, odorless gas caused by incomplete combustion that can come from various sources in a home, including exhaust from a vehicle idling in a garage, fumes from poorly maintained furnace or water-heater combustion, or gases from biomass-burning units such as stoves and fireplaces. It also can come from small gasoline engines, lanterns, and even burning charcoal in a barbecue. Carbon monoxide from any of those sources can build up in enclosed or semienclosed spaces. Carbon monoxide prevention is way beyond just a green issue—it's a critical health and safety factor that must be planned into every home. One of the most important preventive measures in order to avoid carbon monoxide poisoning is to install sealed combustion heating appliances. Furnaces, water heaters, fireplaces, and stoves directly vented to the outside that also draw fresh or makeup air from the outside greatly reduce the likelihood of carbon monoxide poisoning in the home. Sealed combustion units and effective installation, workmanship, and materials, followed by periodic inspections and regular maintenance, will go a long way toward preventing carbon monoxide exposure. Other dangerous gases include nitrogen dioxide and sulfur dioxide, which also can be produced by partially combusted biomass fuels from the operation of a wide variety of common heaters and appliances.

Even if you will be installing sealed combustion appliances and fixtures, it still makes sense to arrange for hard-wired carbon monoxide sensors where malfunctions and possible exposures could occur. Also consider plug-in units or battery-powered sensors that display digital readouts of actual carbon monoxide levels. In this way, it's unlikely that a dangerous exposure level will take you by surprise. With the advances in sensing technology, such units are good insurance to prevent a possible tragedy and are reasonably priced, even though they need to be replaced every few years. If fuel-burning fixtures or appliances are other than sealed combustion units, they too will need professional installation and venting, as well as routine inspections and maintenance.

Detached garages are preferred to attached garages when it comes to maximizing indoor air quality. They can be constructed and operated with more self-ventilating features than can garages that are attached to a home's living spaces. Attached garages require weather stripping, gaskets, and even exhaust fans to automatically run for a certain period of time after the garage roll-up door has been opened or closed.

RADON

Radon is a radioactive gas known to be the second leading cause of lung cancer. It is a gas that you cannot see, taste, or even smell. It occurs naturally in the ground in certain areas, often where base rock consists of granite. It comes from the natural breakdown or radioactive decay of uranium. This gas naturally works its way up to the ground's surface and slowly seeps harmlessly into the atmosphere, neutralized by large amounts of fresh air. Trouble occurs, though, when the radon gas rises to otherwise sealed home areas beneath basements, crawl spaces, or slabs. In any of those cases, the gas may leak through cracks in the foundation, walls, and joints or migrate directly through uncracked walls and floors to collect inside the home. Because it is a single-atom gas, it can easily penetrate common building materials such as concrete blocks, mortar, tar paper, and other sheathing; most paints and insulations; drywall; and other materials. A national map on the Environmental Protection Agency's (EPA's) Web site at www.epa.gov/radon shows the United States divided into small sections, with the likelihood of radon's potentially dangerous presence indicated by three separate zones, the darker of which is zone 1, found mostly in the northern and central parts of the country. The map does not exclude the possibility of radon gas from any particular location but only indicates where it can expect to be present in higher concentrations. Individual homes with elevated levels have been found in all three zones. Elevated radon levels have been found in every state, and the EPA has estimated that as many as 8 million homes throughout the country have high levels of radon to contend with.

Because there are no immediate symptoms to alert someone, and because it usually takes years for typical home-level exposures from radon gas before any problems or illnesses develop, testing is the only way to know a home's radon level. How, then, do you estimate the likelihood of radon concentrations before a home is built? There are often local environmental testing and service companies that can predict with fairly good probability where radon gas can be expected. They also know how to prevent or limit exposure.

To prevent possible exposure, the gas must be either prevented from entering in the first place or quickly exhausted before it has a chance to collect inside. The EPA notes that all homes constructed in radon zone 1 should include radon-prevention construction features. These features (estimated at between $200 and $1,000), when planned and done during the initial construction as a preventive measure, include the creation of a sealed gas-permeable area beneath the home

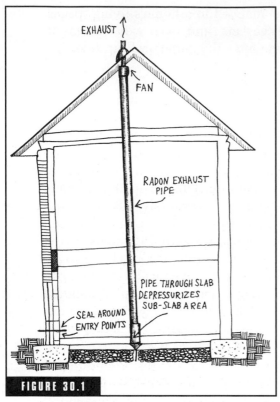

EXHAUST

FAN

RADON EXHAUST
PIPE

PIPE THROUGH SLAB
DEPRESSURIZES
SUB-SLAB AREA

SEAL AROUND
ENTRY POINTS

FIGURE 30.1

Radon prevention.

and outside the foundation walls—any-where in contact with the soil—so that radon gas can be exhausted up a vent pipe from the sealed area and sent up and away from the house, with a fan if necessary (Fig. 30.1). Most systems consist of a layer of coarse gravel below the foundation to allow the soil gases, including radon, to move freely beneath the house in an *air-flow layer* or *permeable layer* that allows the gases to circulate. Alternatives to gravel sometimes include perforated pipes or collection mats. A heavy plastic poly-ethylene sheeting or similar vapor retarder then is placed over the gravel to keep the soil gases from entering the house, and it also keeps the gravel clean when the con-crete floor is poured. The 3- or 4-inch solid polyvinyl chloride (PVC) Schedule 40 pipe then is run up from the gravel through the house and roof and clearly labeled "Radon System." Then all open-ings, cracks, and crevices in the concrete foundation floor and walls should be sealed with polyurethane caulk to prevent radon and other soil gases from entering the home. And lastly, an electrical junc-tion box could be added in the attic, just in case a fan is eventually needed to help pull radon gas through the vent pipe.

If the aforementioned work is not done during construction, and the home is later found to have high levels of radon, similar radon-prevention measures would need to be completed retroactively at much greater inconvenience and cost. Some areas, owing to problems from high radon levels already experienced, include minimum radon-reduction standards in their building codes. It's defi-nitely an issue home builders and home buyers should resolve safely.

BIOLOGICAL CONTAMINANTS: MOLD, MILDEW, AND BACTERIA

Biological contaminants include molds, mildew, bacteria, and pollutants such as viruses, dust, pollen, and other animal- and plant-borne organisms. Our concerns lie mostly with mold, mildew, and bacteria. These three usually can be prevented or minimized by controlling the relative humidity inside a home. The home design must consider construction details that address moisture penetration and reduction processes. Unwanted water and moisture within the home's walls and building materials and components and at undesirable levels in the home's air supply can cause big problems. If your home will be in a humid climate, an air conditioner or dehumidification system may be needed to reduce everyday humidity levels.

The moisture can come from outside in, such as rain that collects behind roofing shingles or wall siding or groundwater that seeps into basement walls, or from inside, with condensation from unvented bathrooms or kitchens or dripping appliance cooling coils, condensate pans, and humidifiers. Proper building techniques and craftsmanship, as well as quality materials and components, should prevent moisture and rain from getting past exterior roofing, siding, and foundations.

Some excessive moisture generated from within the home can be prevented by selecting Energy Star heating, air-conditioning, and ventilation systems, fixtures, and appliances and keeping them in good operating condition. For moisture that comes from everyday activities such as cooking, bathing, and clothes washing and drying, exhaust fans can alleviate much of the problem. Ventilation of attics and basements or crawl spaces also may help (unless the outside air is more humid that the indoor air).

One recommendation from various green guideline programs is to exclude or minimize the amount of wall-to-wall carpeting in a home. This carpeting can affect air quality in several ways. It often contains backing or adhesives with high levels of VOCs, plus carpeting tufts, backing, and pad materials can attract and hold moisture, dust, dust mites, pet dander, and other biological pests and critters. Smooth flooring surfaces such as concrete, tile, hardwood, or bamboo products are much easier to keep dry and clean and are far less likely to turn into habitat for dust mites and other biological contaminants.

VOLATILE ORGANIC COMPOUNDS (VOCS)

VOCs are just what they say they are: organic compounds, often solvent-based petroleum chemicals that are very volatile—they are unstable and tend to evaporate, vaporize, or slowly off-gas into the surrounding air and are at higher concentrations indoors, where they cannot be diluted with large quantities of fresh air. Some chemicals off-gas from the material itself, whereas others emit from chemicals in the product that are left over from the manufacturing processes. Commonly emitted from literally thousands of materials, from fuels to paints and lacquers, varnishes, adhesives, waxes, and sealers, VOCs tend to help these products penetrate and adhere to the surfaces they're supposed to cover and protect. They have always done an effective job at that. The common "new paint smell" or "new carpet smell" can be attributed to organic chemicals or VOCs. Unfortunately, these volatile chemicals pose a danger to human and pet health. Their effects can vary greatly from person to person but include eye and respiratory tract irritation, headaches, dizziness, visual disorders, and memory lapses. Many organic compounds are known to cause cancer in animals, and some are suspected of causing or are known to cause cancer in humans.

All products containing VOCs can release organic compounds when they are being used and after application. The best defense against VOCs is to avoid them in the first place. Most products today come in low- or no-VOC versions, largely owing to recent manufacturer efforts to satisfy healthier indoor air quality requirements. If products with higher levels of VOCs are chosen because of better performance and greater durability, they should be used with plenty of ventilation, and ventilation levels should stay elevated until the products are fully set or dried and the initial high off-gassing levels are reduced.

Formaldehyde and Other VOCs

Formaldehyde is one of the best-known VOCs. Numerous materials, furnishings, and building products contain formaldehyde that slowly emits or off-gases into the surrounding air, some during their application and some that will continue to off-gas long afterward. Pressed-wood products such as particleboard, hardwood paneling, and especially medium density fiberboard (MDF) used in drawer fronts, cabinets, shelves, and furniture tops are often made with adhesives or bonding agents that contain urea-formaldehyde resins. These adhesives and resins are inherently unstable. In addition to formaldehyde, other bad VOCs include products containing methylene chloride, benzene, and perchloroethylene (emitted from newly dry-cleaned materials such as drapes and curtains).

VENTILATION SYSTEMS, MOISTURE, AND FRESH AIR SUPPLY

Homes that are tightly constructed to eliminate cracks, crevices, holes, and other unintended openings in the thermal envelope must have a way to ventilate (Fig. 30.2). "Lived in" air will become oxygen-depleted and moist, and it also may become polluted with fumes, smoke, and VOCs from cooking, cleaning, hobby and work activities, and off-gassing from various building materials and products. There has to be a way to expel the used air and replace it with fresh air.

Specific rooms are fairly simple to ventilate, and this can be done with small ventilation fans designed to expel moist, stale air or cooking smoke, odors, fumes, steam, and other by-products—such as in bathrooms, laundry rooms, and kitchens. These fans can be operated manually or can be installed with semiautomatic or automatic controls linked to humidity controls or the operation of lights or faucets or even motion controls. They can be set to run for specific time periods.

In essence, there are three major types of HVAC systems: supply-only systems, exhaust-only systems, and balanced systems. Some of these systems are planned as separate installations, apart from heating and cooling systems; others are designed into the heating and cooling systems.

Supply-only systems simply bring outside air into the house for conditioning. They don't alter the temperature of it one way or another with already-conditioned exhaust air as the new air is brought in. This raw air from outside must be cooled during summer and warmed during winter from the time it enters the house until it gets distributed through the system's ductwork. This can be quite a large temperature spread, especially when bringing in subzero January night air and heating it for use in your bedroom.

Exhaust-only systems, often applicable in tightly built houses heated with baseboard hot-water or radiant electric systems, use the principle of depressurization of the house. "Used" or stale air is drawn out from inside the home with either individual fans located in bathrooms, kitchens, and anywhere else moisture, smoke, or fumes can be generated or by a centrally located fan having ducts installed to individual rooms. The stale or moist air is replaced with fresh makeup

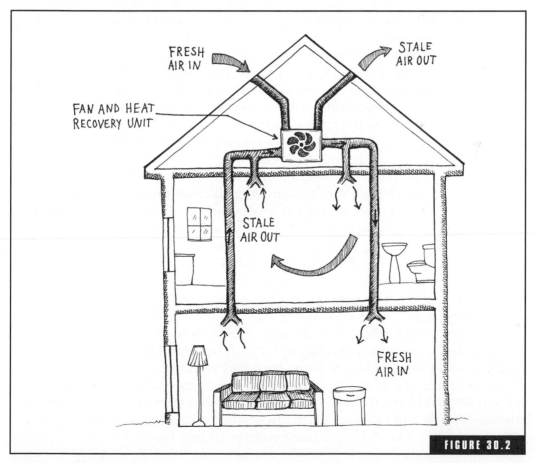

FIGURE 30.2

A simple ventilation system.

air supplied through passive inlets or ports installed in outside walls to bedrooms, family rooms, work rooms, and other living areas. The use of fans, though, can be tricky. First of all, they must be heavy duty, quiet, and energy efficient, designed to run continuously. If they're not sized correctly, they can prevent appliance and furnace fumes and smoke from leaving the house through dedicated exhaust ductwork and cause backdrafting—which is the creation of negative pressure inside the house that literally stops stale air or fumes from incomplete combustion from leaving the house as desired. This is one of the problems when a furnace, fireplace, stove, or other heating apparatus can comingle intake air with exhaust air—and one of the reasons why sealed combustion appliances, where air-intake piping is supplied separately from the exhaust system—is so important for occupant safety.

Air also should be allowed to circulate freely throughout each floor plan. Simple ways to encourage this are to design doors that have wide bottom gaps above the floors and by planning open room transitions and even architecturally pleasing latticework, grillwork, or open-screen room dividers, especially where soundproofing is not an issue.

A more expensive but also more efficient arrangement is a balanced system that—while stale air is being exchanged for fresh air—uses a heat-exchanging pipe or ductwork arrangement to transfer heat energy from outgoing conditioned stale air to incoming, unconditioned fresh air. Why waste warm or cooled air in the exhaust? Effective heat exchanging can be accomplished when two pipes or ducts that each convey a separate airflow—sometimes assisted by fans, one carrying exhaust, and the other, fresh air—share a pipe or duct wall. Two fans—often in the same housing in order to match or balance the airflows—operate simultaneously and draw or push air through two dedicated piping or ductwork conveyance lines. Unless they are in a consistently hot climate location, the larger fans with their heat exchangers will be able to extract the heat from stale air to help warm the incoming fresh air. Again, wherever the pipes or ducts share a wall, the temperature of whichever air is warmer will influence the cooler air by warming it, transferring much of the heat before the target air is either exhausted or brought in with a fresh supply. This process saves energy two ways—by recapturing the warmed or cooled conditioning in exhaust air and by not having to use as much new energy to heat or cool the fresh makeup air as it is drawn inside. Balanced systems must be sized carefully for each home and need to be installed by experienced professionals who know what they're doing.

The addition of a more sophisticated heat-recovery ventilator—for heat transfer only—should be considered in cold climates, whereas an energy-recovery ventilator—for heat and moisture recapture—could be more appropriate in climates where makeup air is desired to bring moister air into home interiors that suffer from low humidity during cold winter temperatures. An analysis of HVAC conditions and needs should be performed by a qualified HVAC specialist. A number of factors must be considered, such as the overall house size, configuration, types of heating and cooling units and delivery systems, and number of people expected to be living in the home.

Few things can ruin a home and its components faster than unwanted moisture. Moisture can come from without or within. If it gets inside or comes from inside, there must be ways to get rid of it. Those ways include mechanical and natural ventilation systems, dehumidifiers, air-conditioning, and stand-alone wall and appliance fans in bathrooms, kitchens, hobby areas, garages, and other areas. If moisture gets behind impermeable wall coverings such as vinyl wallpaper, there may be no way for it to leave—so the wall deteriorates or develops mold from inside. Permeable natural wall coverings that let the wall breathe from inside and ventilated structural gaps beneath exterior sidings and roofing materials help to dry out moisture that may infiltrate those outer layers.

WALL COVERINGS AND FURNISHINGS

As mentioned earlier, surface coverings and furnishings are the most often encountered materials in a home. Horizontal and vertical planes—floorings, ceilings, countertops, and walls, cabinets, cupboards, drawers, open shelves, and furniture—are usually covered with thin coatings or finishing layers of paint, varnish, sealant, wallpaper, fabric, composites, or thicker layers of paneling, composites, wood, tile, stone, concrete, carpeting, and other materials. In the past, that "new home smell" people bragged about was, in reality, the potentially harmful VOCs and new-product odors that were emitted from flooring and wall covering adhesives and binders and formaldehyde-laden flooring, countertop, and furniture substrates. As a rule, rely on sustainable green materials that are inert and don't off-gas (instead of oil-based paints and varnishes) or trap moisture (instead of vinyl wallpaper) or contaminants (instead of wall-to-wall carpeting). Those materials are discussed in the chapters on wall and floor coverings.

Another strategy is to go minimal with the coatings and coverings and let structural materials suffice without additional surfacing as much as possible. This can include structural insulated panels (SIPs); concrete flooring and countertops; tile, stone, bamboo, and cork flooring; natural plasters; and various recycled and reclaimed products. Products resulting from fewer manufacturing processes and ingredients, locally produced, are preferred by green design.

WATER QUALITY

The quality of your drinking or potable water can depend on a number of factors. If you receive it through a municipal utility—a local water department—it's likely to be tested for pollutants and dangerous chemicals, bacteria, and other microorganisms on a regular basis. It may include small amounts of preventive or "healthy" additives such as traces of chlorine or fluoride. But there also may be traces of chemicals from prescription medicines or from dissolved metals present in the water's source and not completely filtered out before it gets to your supply line.

Well water is another story. If you've got a dug or drilled well, it's a good idea to have your water tested every so often by a reputable environmental lab. Another place to get the lowdown on local wells and well water is through the top one or two well-drilling companies in your area. They're usually knowledgeable on how various wells are producing and if there are any issues home owners should watch out for in specific areas. Real estate agents and brokers familiar with places serviced by individual water wells also know where problems have cropped up in the past. In either case, it's important to know what you're drinking, and if the quality is not up to par, find out how to take corrective action. Refer to Chapter 21 on plumbing for additional information about water systems.

OTHER ENVIRONMENTAL CONCERNS

Electromagnetic Fields

Power-line towers and transmission lines have long been suspected of having possible health implications for living creatures, including families living near them. As population densities increase, more of these electrical installations are being constructed near suburban neighborhoods, within urban communities, and often along rural transportation routes. Some researchers suspect that electromagnetic fields generated by these facilities have an influence on and may interrupt the body's delicate, highly tuned natural electrochemical functions, some at a cellular level.

Noise

Visitors to homes constructed near strong intermittent noises such as train traffic, the banging truck tailgates of landfill deliveries, loud manufacturing sounds, highway noises, air traffic, and the like often find the sounds very distracting, whereas occupants may have grown to accept the noises as "natural" and barely notice them anymore owing to repetitiveness and familiarity. The presence of loud noises nearby can influence sleeping habits and can have negative influences on daily living patterns depending on how sensitive the home's occupants are. The sounds also can limit a home's resale value.

Odors

Apart from odors from certain VOCs, other smells can come from a variety of building materials, furnishings, and belongings, as well as from materials and processes near the home site. Most odors are fairly site-specific.

REMODELING NOTES

Any project that improves a home's interior environment qualifies as a worthwhile undertaking and likely will increase both the salability and value of the home. High on the list is the replacement of inefficient combustion space heaters and appliances, wherever possible, with sealed combustion units. Environmental testing services and individual radon and other testing kits will point out what features or systems need to be improved. Just sealing cracks and gaps in basement floors and foundations can make a world of difference in radon intrusions, as before and after testing can attest to. Pay special attention to the dividing walls between attached garages and living areas. The quality of a home's water is also critical to occupant health. Proper humidity levels ensure respiratory comfort, mold prevention, and a moisture-balanced atmosphere supportive of mechanical components. Employ moisture-resistant materials and surfaces in rooms where water and moisture exposure is expected, such as bathrooms, kitchens, and laundry rooms. Old wall-to-wall carpeting with moisture-absorbing pads should be replaced. The use of balanced ventilation systems and fans—including whole-house, ceiling, and kitchen and bathroom models—can be effective and comforting. Identify any "land locked" rooms that do not receive enough air changes, and establish a way to pull in fresh air. Whenever possible, plan as many passive methods of ventilation and cooling as possible.

Where to Build It

Where you decide to live is largely a combination of personal preference and practical choice. City, suburbia, and country all have their good points and bad. Plus, within each of those areas, you'll find potential building sites that each should be evaluated according to the lay of the land in relation to available community services, the sun's orientation, the prevailing winds, and the natural or engineered features of the surrounding territory.

Every trip in all but the greenest of vehicles has a negative effect on the environment. According to the Environmental Protection Agency (EPA), a third of the air pollution in the United States is caused by tailpipe emissions from cars and trucks that spew carbon monoxide, hydrocarbons, nitrogen oxide, particulate matter, and greenhouse gases such as carbon dioxide.

The Leadership in Energy and Environmental Design (LEED) for Homes guidelines would prefer that you find and build in a LEED for Neighborhood Development home on a parcel specifically prepared and certified as meeting strict LEED for Homes green home building requirements. If this is out of the question for you, either because there's no such development in the area where you plan to live or because you elect to settle elsewhere, the next best LEED for Homes guideline says to carefully select a site first by *excluding* building lots that have the following characteristics:

- Land at or below elevations within 100-year floodplains
- Land designated as habitat for any threatened or endangered species

- Land that previously was public parkland (unless you swap an equal amount of equivalent-type terrain)
- Land containing unusually unique or valuable soils, as identified in state conservation soil surveys

Then look for a building site within or adjacent to an established community in order to prevent new "satellite" disturbances to rural landscapes. LEED for Homes awards points for choosing sites situated on the edges of existing developments or on a previously developed lot. The ability to tap into existing sewer and water systems and to use other existing utilities is also encouraged and rewarded with points. In addition, if the site is close enough to satisfy basic transportation needs by walking, bicycling, or public transit—eliminating some reliance on atmosphere-polluting vehicles—all the better, and here come some more LEED for Homes points. Points may be secured simply by locating a half- or quarter-mile from utilities or public transit. Another point is available if the site is within a short distance from open public land that encourages outdoors activities. All these variations have details that must be understood and followed when going after points toward LEED for Homes certification levels. Scrutiny of the latest version of LEED for Homes is a must. Chapter 31—on consideration of city, suburbia, or country—can be reviewed with the LEED for Homes guidelines in mind and can help you, together with your preferences and requirements, narrow down the type and location of a site to suit your plans.

In short, the general location of where you decide to look for and choose your specific building site should be considered with care. Chapter 31 reviews some pros and cons of city, suburban, and rural living.

City, Suburbia, or Country?

Some city dwellers, it seems, have always longed to move to the country or at least to a wide-open suburb where they can stretch out from the small, crowded lot they've grown up on. Other city residents shudder at the very thought of such isolation and opt to remain where they are. The determination boils down to a combination of work and social activities, practical and financial aspects, and personal preference. A country dweller can long to shed the drafty old farmhouse and 40 acres for a tiny ranch full of modern conveniences on an easy-to-maintain 60- by 120-foot lot. Or maybe not.

THE CITY

Before nations came into existence, there were cities. Living in cities is nothing new. At first, they were places where primitive men and women congregated for convenience sake—places where they could farm or gather. During medieval times, the cities had walls around them to provide protection for the inhabitants. Then cities developed into much more sophisticated settlements, and before long, the city existed as a central unifying influence on large groups of people.

Cities and towns are still the most important gathering places for people. The term for city in Latin is *civitas*, from which the English words *citizen* and *civilization* derive. In cities, we manufacture, receive, and provide goods and services. We do research, teach, and learn. We encounter slums and crime and corruption. We wrestle with inadequate public services and enjoy the efficiently run ones.

A city is really a community in which everything is drawn together in hopes of creating a desirable way of life for its inhabitants. In a city, you have—or should have—rapid and inexpensive transit systems, effective law enforcement, proper disposal of sewage and garbage, fire protection, provisions for good housing, jobs for the people, education for children and adults, plenty of libraries and museums, theaters, and places for concerts, plays, and public events. There should be recreational sport facilities, adequate care for the sick and poor, and a government that's not overly corrupt.

We avoid isolation in cities, we take in a full range of enriching cultural activities, and we enter a vibrant nightlife. To some extent, it's a "fast" existence, where the action is and where the greatest number of opportunities in the business world are. It's where big-time radio and television stations are based and where major newspapers and other publications keep track of society's pulse.

All of this highlights the main advantage of city life—convenience. Everything is close, including schools, churches, medical services, supermarkets, restaurants, and corner bars. Plus, within a city it's even possible to find a location that *seems* like a piece of country—an isolated lot bordered by rows of mature pines, for instance.

Why, then, do people move out of cities or elect to build elsewhere? One reason is because city land, with its high real estate taxes, is scarce and expensive, especially in major metropolitan areas. Another reason is that cities tend to have physical atmospheres that are more polluted by vehicle exhaust and industrial emissions than other locations. Some say that cities are too fast paced and too noisy. Other people shy away from city life because of high crime rates. Some make a deliberate choice to live somewhere else to be near people who are closer to their own social status or income level.

Cities have changed substantially since the days before World War II, when the rich, the poor, and the developing middle class all lived relatively close together in the same or adjacent neighborhoods. Back then, there was a sense of social strength in cities that largely has been lost since the masses of middle and upper class people migrated to suburbia.

SUBURBIA

Suburbia is a relatively recent phenomenon that has been studied from every angle by planners, sociologists, and psychologists. In fact, entire books have been written about the suburbanite and his or her environment.

It's true that suburbs were created by a wide variety of technological advances. Automobiles, delivery trucks, rapid transit systems, miles and miles of concrete and asphalt paving, and sundry inventions such as septic tanks, sewer mains, telephone lines, and miscellaneous energy delivery systems all have contributed to the establishment of satellite neighborhoods located "so many minutes or hours away" from the nearest city.

And what's more, suburbanites have developed certain characteristics that tend to bind them together and particular habits that distinguish them from city and country dwellers. The main difference is their mobility: Suburbanites are primarily commuters who tend to own their homes in areas that are on or near open spaces, away from crowded urban locations.

When you think of suburbia, you're likely to think of large yards, modern houses, swimming pools, two-car garages, incoming and outgoing transferred executives, couples jogging along the streets in color-coordinated jogging outfits, and long drives to work.

On the surface, the suburbs sound like fine, clean places to live, and many of them are. On the other hand, quite a few suburbs consist of subdivisions having residents of roughly the same age group, social strata, and even income level. At one time, neighborhoods were differentiated from each other by race or national origin, and within those neighborhoods, you had a healthy cross section of the classes—from rich to poor. Suburbia changed all that. Suburbanites have demanded zoning controls that now completely rule the modern economics of suburban land development and make it impossible for the less affluent to join. Whenever such middle- to upper-class members of the same age group and income level band together, the healthy diversity found in a neighborhood of large and small houses, young and old residents, and rich and poor families cannot flourish.

In some ways, contemporary subdivisions lack the kind of all-aroundness that's characteristic of older communities, and in doing so, they perhaps sacrifice the good of the overall community in order to guarantee that the subdivision itself consists of essentially the same types of occupants, all with similar ages, incomes, and interests.

In subdivisions in the suburbs you're likely to have people more interested in maintaining their own property values, at times through political and zoning maneuvers, than being overly concerned about problems of the entire community or the success of community-wide programs developed for charitable causes, cultural enrichment, or the public good. While the older communities could be described as possessing a beneficial diversity within an overall unity, modern subdivisions are much more homogeneous and self-centered. Ironically, all this tends to reflect on the bottom line of suburban housing values in a positive way. Well-planned subdivisions have been a financial boon for the home owners who live in them. They have been and continue to be places where housing appreciates considerably, unlike the many changing neighborhoods that feature nothing but housing units that are steadily depreciating and losing their owners' life savings at the same time.

Suburbia also has been called the "instant-living environment," so named after the people who simultaneously move into a newly developed area. When this happens, the area has no tradition to rely on and no familiar patterns of living for the residents to follow.

Now that the drawbacks of many suburban subdivisions have been touched on, it's still safe to say that many *other* suburban subdivisions are exceptionally well-rounded places to live and don't fit into the sociologist's definition of suburbia. It's just another case of many exceptions to a rule.

THE COUNTRY

Country living means many things to many people. To some, it means wide-open acreage. It means fields and forests, ponds, meandering streams, corn and wheat and alfalfa, odors of sweet-smelling hay and manure, red barns sporting advertisements for chewing tobacco, snakelike tar-and-chip roads, dug or drilled water wells, spectacular thunderstorms and full moons, tractors, farm machinery and animals, plenty of fair-weather weekend visitors (especially when vegetable and fruit crops mature), and long drives to practically anywhere—to shopping, to school, to church, to work, to visit relatives. It means children do not have many playmates nearby. Although there's peace and quiet most of the time, there are also hunters in the fall and winter and maybe in parts of spring and summer as well.

To others, the country offers little but boredom. Some people feel comfortable cohabiting with nature, whereas others need the fast pace of city life. To novice country dwellers, weeding a garden or feeding a flock of chickens can quickly become tiresome, and routine chores inevitably lose the novelty they possessed at first.

In the country, people generally have time to think, to contemplate. They're likely to have more leisure hours than they would elsewhere because, for some reason, country people tend to get up earlier despite going to bed with a healthy kind of tiredness.

There's freedom in the country for pets to run loose, and there are plenty of birds and other wildlife for naturalists to feed, study, and even manage. There's room to blast a stereo without aggravating neighbors, and there are places to ride horses and to gather wild mushrooms and blackberries.

AREA CHECKLISTS

City Living

- Benefits of community life
- Feelings of security from living close to neighbors
- Fast-moving environment
- A center of media attention
- Nightlife and entertainment

- Less feelings of isolation
- It's where the jobs are
- Provisions for all types of housing
- Heterogeneous neighborhoods
- Good fire protection
- Good police protection
- Hospitals nearby
- Close to schools and churches
- Close to shopping
- Convenient utilities and public services
- Rapid and inexpensive transit systems
- Libraries and museums
- Noisy environments
- Slums and crime
- Polluted air
- Pockets of declining property values
- Occupants ranging from very poor to very rich, all ages and income levels
- Children having friends to play with

Suburban Living

- Security of neighbors with less crowding
- A quieter place than a city
- Stable and appreciating property values
- Less crime and fewer slums
- Cleaner air
- More privacy
- Larger lots
- Modern houses similar in size and type
- Open playgrounds and parks
- Modern utility systems
- Mostly middle- and upper-class occupants of similar age and income level

- High property taxes
- A preoccupation with houses and household items
- Not much nightlife nearby or cultural activities
- Farther away from jobs, shopping, medical services, fire and police protection
- Friends for children to play with

Country Living

- Lots of isolation and quiet
- Good for pets and communing with nature
- Good for farming and raising gardens
- Good for thinking and contemplating
- Low real estate taxes
- Clean air
- Outdoors activities: hiking, horseback riding, hunting, fishing, gathering berries
- Not much crime
- Opportunities to study and manage wildlife and land
- Freedom from prying eyes of neighbors
- More time required for grounds maintenance chores
- More equipment needed for grounds maintenance
- Long drives to practically anything: school, church, libraries, hospitals, shopping, recreation, and work
- Private water and septic systems
- Lack of stringent zoning regulations
- Not many children nearby for youngsters to play with
- Possibility of unwanted lengthy visits (often unannounced) from friends and relatives

▷▷▷▷▷ POINTS TO PONDER

1. Before making a "radical" or major lifestyle change such as moving from city to country or country to city or even to or from suburbia, research the change thoroughly. Determine home-location features most important to

your lifestyle and pocketbook before choosing a rural, suburban, or urban site.

2. City living can mean very close neighbors; friends for children to play with; good transportation systems; convenience to shopping and services; heterogeneous populations; good police, fire, and emergency response capabilities; nightlife and entertainment; and educational and career opportunities.

3. Because so many people have been moving out of cities in recent decades, there are some real bargains—and often direct financial incentives such as real estate tax exemptions, home energy grants, and low-cost loans—for individuals building new homes within city limits.

4. City living also can mean traffic, pollution, slums, high crime levels, noisy environments, declining property values, and small, cramped building lots.

5. Suburban living can mean not-too-far-away neighbors, some public transportation, mostly middle- and upper-class occupants of similar age and income level, open parks and playgrounds, and nearby friends for children.

6. Suburban living also can mean a lack of nightlife or cultural activity; high property taxes; distance from jobs, shopping, medical services, fire, police, and emergency response; and a preoccupation with homes and household items.

7. Country or rural living can mean lots of isolation and quiet; a haven for nature, pets, and gardening; low real estate taxes; clean air; privacy; and outdoor activities.

8. If you're considering a move to the country, and you're still skeptical about being isolated in your new surroundings, see if anyone else is interested in building at the same time (a close friend or relative), and then research the possibility of subdividing a larger parcel into two neighboring sites—each of which can be built on.

9. Country or rural living also can mean septic tanks; water wells; feelings of isolation and loneliness; long drives to almost every sort of need, including shopping, services, medical facilities, schools, and jobs; more time required for grounds maintenance chores; and not many friends for children to play with.

10. If you insist on making a major lifestyle/home change and build a dwelling someplace where it eventually does not work out for your family, you can always sell it and move. But that possibility is another reason why, when planning your new home, it pays to preview your building ideas with a real estate broker who one day may have to put the place on the open market. This may or may not be a concern of yours. If it is—say, if you plan on moving within a relatively short time period—the real estate agent will tell

you why (or why not) to include that third or fourth bedroom, that extra large garage, that bathroom in the basement, or that fireplace in the family room so that the home will be easier to sell if need be. Although green home construction might gravitate to smaller size or avoiding wood-burning stoves and fireplaces, there is no telling exactly what effect such features might have on resale values in rural communities, where residents have learned to build large and where plentiful timber supplies traditionally have been a cheap source of fuel.

Selecting a Building Site

If you know the general kind of area in which you want to live—country, suburbia, or city—then you've already made several of the most important decisions along the way toward selecting a suitable building site. Now it's time to narrow things down further. A number of considerations should weigh heavily in your search for the best individual site for your house.

If you're limited to a certain area because of finances, closeness to work, school system, or any similar reason, then make the best of it. You can follow green construction guidelines on the best lot available. If you're restricted to a particular lot, you still can best arrange the insides to take advantage of sunlight and orientation. You have at the very least a certain control over what rooms you put where. Think positive. Choices you make still can play a major role in energy efficiency no matter what the location. You might want to modify your home's configuration—consider a ranch-style house instead of a two-story house if you can't get the building lot you originally had in mind.

The Leadership in Energy and Environmental Design (LEED) for Homes guidelines would prefer that you select a site that has already been used for development and construction, is already serviced by existing utilities, and is close to public transportation and urban features such as shopping, medical services, and the like. Plus, you receive a certain number of points for building on this kind of site. This type of development enables virgin, undeveloped land to remain that way. Beyond this, there are ways to methodically review the benefits and drawbacks to potential building sites in order to arrive at the best site for your own project.

The first factor to look at is a site's zoning and whether any special building restrictions or rules are in place. You wouldn't want to purchase a site, only to find out later that what you plan will not be allowed.

ZONING

Zoning is one of the most elementary considerations to be made when viewing a potential homesite. Local zoning codes are ordinances that divide all the property in a city, town, or rural area into a number of land-use classifications such as single-family residential, multifamily residential, agricultural, business, commercial, and industrial. In other words, zoning codes state what can and can't be done with all the property within the code's boundaries.

How would you like to invest your life savings into a dream house only to have neighbors move a trailer in across the street, start raising chickens and minks out back, erect big "Eggs for Sale" signs along the road, and have their four sons run a small-engine repair shop in summer and hold snowmobile races during winter? Zoning helps to prevent unhealthy mixes of properties and owners having conflicting interests.

Of course, you can take a chance that even though the property across the street is zoned to permit a trailer park, Old Man Peters has owned the land for years, and he'll probably never move. Suppose that when he dies, his daughter sells out to someone who would leap at the chance of putting in a 200-unit mobile home park.

One way to guarantee that nearby land won't be used for something that bothers you is to purchase enough of it behind, in front, and to the side of your location. This can be costly, however, and there probably won't be that much property available anyway. Even if you do protect your location, you can't be sure that a few hundred yards down the road—if it's a wide-open zoned area—a trailer park won't still be started up. Those are the chances you take when settling in a loosely regulated location.

When considering such a site, you can, of course, use your best judgment and the opinions of real estate professionals. For instance, if nice houses—the kind you're planning—already dominate such a loosely zoned area, chances are that they'll have a positive, inflationary effect on the remaining parcels, and consequently, only nice houses likely will be added to the area because that's the highest and most practical use for the land.

Pay particular attention when considering property that's on the borderline of a residential area or is zoned "transitional." Transitional areas are often dominated by residential dwellings, but they permit some business or commercial uses as well. It's a simple task to check any property by consulting the latest version of the zoning code. Just call the applicable city, town, or county zoning officer. By reviewing a zoning map, the zoning officer can tell what classification the parcel falls under and the classifications of the surrounding properties.

Zoning and building codes have powerful influences over what kinds of renewable-energy systems (if any) can be constructed. Since active solar photovoltaic (PV) systems and wind turbines are still relatively new installations—especially systems that tie into the electrical grid—there may be numerous expensive and onerous hurdles to be navigated before a system can be installed, and the financial details may not save you anything over a long time—if costs are what's being looked at mainly. There may be regulations or restrictions or extensive duplicate safeguards and testing and engineering permits to apply for. Wind turbine heights may not be high enough to be practical, and large setbacks may make such an installation prohibitive. There may be restrictions on where solar panels can be located—only on roofs, for instance, with no stand-alone ground installations allowed. If you must build in an area that permits no major renewable installations, the times and technology are rapidly changing, and a few relatively inexpensive steps can be taken with wiring and structure that will enable you to add systems as they become more efficient (thus smaller installations may become commonplace) and as, by necessity, the building codes become more tolerant of these systems. As mentioned earlier, you don't need on-site electricity generation to have an incredibly energy-efficient home, and you most likely can arrange to purchase renewable energy over the grid at perhaps a slight premium if you desire. The main point here is that if you plan to install wind or solar power generation, make sure that you know that it will be allowed by the regulatory agencies you must go through. Check to see if any other installations have already taken place, and visit them; they'll likely share their stories and may even comment on what they would do differently if building again. Also make sure that if you plan on tying into the grid, you know what the utility requires.

If the lot you are looking at falls under a zoning code and, say, a wind turbine is not included in the building code or is specifically restricted by the code, you may be able to apply for a variance. If this is the case, and township or planning committee members are unfamiliar with what you're designing, you've got to educate them and convince them that your plans are being carried out elsewhere and show them the benefits of putting accepted guidelines in place for sustainable-energy systems in the near future.

THE NEIGHBORHOOD

Ask any realtor what the three most important components of real estate value are, and he or she will likely counter with, "Location, location, location." In a very real sense, the location of a house can set the dollar range of its market value, both the minimum and the maximum. This means that you should seek a neighborhood that lends itself to the kind of house you are planning if you want to ensure the highest possible market value for your home. To attain this maximum value and resale potential, your house should not be the largest and most expensive dwelling on the block. If it is, you will be doing your neighbors a good deed and yourself a disservice. Your house will tend to buoy up the resale value of the less expensive dwellings that surround it, whereas those less expensive, smaller houses will pull the market value of your house down closer to their level.

On the other hand, if you're willing to totally ignore the ideas of market value and resale potential—say, you're planning to live in the house forever and your children and theirs will one day take it over—and if you genuinely like the neighborhood and know it's not in a declining area, it could be a different story. In this case, by "overbuilding," by matching a larger-than-average, more expensive house to a lot in a less expensive area, you probably could obtain a relatively low-cost building site compared with other lots where larger, more-expensive houses are being built. Also, if you'll consider lots with odd locations, near busy streets, perhaps even next to a ramshackle *Tobacco Road* house that sticks out in the neighborhood like a sore thumb and looks ready to fall over in the slightest breeze, you're likely to find bargain building sites.

Regarding the *Tobacco Road* house (and there are many of them out there), you *hope* that it falls to the ground because as soon as it does, the value of your house and lot will skyrocket immediately, especially if something nice is erected in the old shack's place.

The location of the entire neighborhood in relation to modern necessities and conveniences is also important. You'll have to carefully consider the pros and cons. An advantage to a newly married couple might be to be very close to grade schools. To a couple not planning to have children or having children long grown up and gone, that same point could well be a disadvantage.

Is the neighborhood reached by a hilly road that will be difficult to negotiate in winter? Is the potential site far west of town, whereas your workplace is to the east? If so, remember that you'll not only have to drive twice through the entire city everyday, but you'll have to head into the blinding sun each morning—and then into it again at the end of each day on the return trip. Will you be close to a favorite golf course, tennis club, library, or other high-frequency activity location? Will you be uncomfortably far away from good friends and relatives you like to visit frequently?

Is the location in a high-crime area? Be careful when new to an entire city or area. A brief phone call to a local law enforcement agency will be to your advantage. Responsible real estate professionals can be helpful, too, for revealing neighborhood information and for estimating resale potential.

Remember that one main factor will be the location of your workplace in relation to your new home. How will you get there and back every day? If you plan to drive, exactly how far away is it, and how is the traffic along the way? Are you driving into the sun in the morning, and into that same sun at quitting time? Compare that commute, and think about the eventual gasoline, vehicle wear and tear, time in the driver's seat, rush-hour traffic patterns, and the like.

Once you select a building site, if it involves acreage or is a fairly large and diverse lot, try to do a methodical site assessment for yourself as a final data check, evaluation, and preparation for construction by examining:

- *Topography.* What elevations does the site have? Is it flat, gently sloped, multisloped, steep, or consisting of backfilled sections? Will these factors heavily influence where the house should go and where the driveway should be? If a well and septic system are needed, where would they be placed? How would the water drainage be handled during construction to prevent erosion?

- *Surface water.* Are there any wetlands, ponds, streams, or natural springs on the land? In many locations, such waters are protected and may not be disturbed—even by the landowner. Depending on what season you do your evaluation, you may not even be able to tell that there's a wetland present— it may have to be determined through the vegetation or soil makeup on the lot, and you might need professional evaluation to make that determination.

- *Groundwater.* This is a huge factor if no municipal or private water systems are available. How are the wells in surrounding homes? Is there enough water year round? And what is its quality? You can find out by collecting data and opinions from neighbors, well drillers, the county health department, and other organizations—especially those having no conflicting interest in the answers you seek.

- *Soils.* Your local agricultural extension office likely will be able to tell you what soil types are present on the property. You need to know if it's mainly clay (bad for septic systems) or if someone has graded up and removed the valuable topsoil (bad for landscaping and growing gardens and crops). You also need to know the soil makeup to prepare for excavating and backfilling the foundation. The depth or height of the water table is also important to know. Earlier editions of this book advised building on virgin soil whenever possible. Even Chapter 11 of this edition says that conventional construction methods are best carried out on undisturbed ground. Although undisturbed ground provides superior support for a dwelling's foundation, when alternate or recycled sites are available to safely satisfy the new home's requirements, constructing a home on virgin *unused* soil may not be the greenest option. Indeed, filled, compacted, and graded building sites can be acceptable as long as appropriate engineering is used to determine and build to existing soil load-bearing capacities. Using filled-in or reclaimed sites allow virgin real estate to remain undisturbed.

- *Agricultural activities.* Can any parts of the site be used for agricultural activities, for planting orchards, fruit, grapes, vegetables, grain, or other crops? Will the yard be able to accept and absorb all the rain runoff from the home's roof, walkways, and driveway? Has the fertile topsoil been removed by the developer, making it difficult to establish landscaping and vegetation?

■ *Vegetation.* What kinds of trees and vegetation come with the property? Are there any species of plant or tree that you don't recognize? If there are, it's probably unlikely, but someone should check to make sure that no threatened species are within your boundary lines.

■ *Wildlife.* For large building sites situated in acreage, be aware of and considerate to any prime wildlife habitat and any wild game or protected species regulated by state or federal laws, such as wild turkeys, deer, or bald eagles. Also consider the presence of not-so-regulated pests such as ticks, mosquitoes, termites, and carpenter ants.

■ *Weather.* Understand weather patterns to expect. What are the average monthly temperatures? What are the average prevailing winds? If you're thinking of wind energy, are there any obstructions close to your site? For solar energy—passive and active systems for both water and space heating—does your building site afford enough access to southern sunshine? Find out what the latitude is. What's the sun's angle from the horizon on June 21 and December 21 (Fig. 32.1). Make sure that there's no obvious or latent solar obstructions, such as a tightly planted row of evergreen trees planted between your lot and the sun that could block your sunshine access

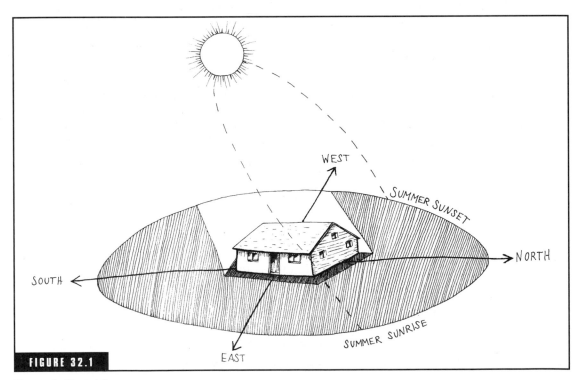

FIGURE 32.1

The sun's "travel."

within 10 or 15 years? Historically, what's the greatest depth of ground frost you should plan for? How many average heating days are there per year? How many cooling days? What about humidity levels—very low year round? Or extremely high? Both will greatly influence your heating, ventilation, and air-conditioning (HVAC) systems and building-envelope construction. Does rain, hail, snow, or the possibility of hurricanes, tornadoes, and earthquakes come into play? Is your site within the possible reach of a Mt. St. Helens or dormant volcano somewhere in Hawaii? What about forest fires? Flooding? Or extreme draughts? Unlikely as these factors may sound, look at recent North American and world weather history.

- *Views.* What views will you have when the project is finished? Will any of them affect how you orient the house or how you plan the interior spaces?

In addition to the site analysis, consider doing what is always recommended to individuals deciding on a particular home or building site: Frequent the place different times on different days. It can only help to observe what goes on there on a week night or early Saturday and Sunday morning. Note who is in the area at those times. Ask neighbors questions about the neighborhood and area in general. How does the place "feel" to you? Do you feel uncomfortable at an urban site? Lonely out there in the boondocks? How does the sun travel over the site? A lot of dogs barking? Young children riding bikes and skateboards everywhere you look?

LOT CONFIGURATION

While shopping for a building site, keep in mind the type of house you're planning. Where is the sun and prevailing winds relative to the site. As discussed in Chapter 6, building sites with certain configurations naturally lend themselves to specific house types and are impractical for others. When you throw in the orientation to the sun's daily travel, it further complicates things. Of course, in some situations, you can alter the lot contours to suit your house, but usually at substantial cost. In many cases, given the lay of the land, it's not possible to change the site's topography successfully.

In a nutshell, here again are the matches and mismatches between lots and house types:

- Single-story ranches are ideally suited to flat building sites or lots that slope gently to the sides or rear, particularly if the plans call for a walkout from a basement or lower living area.

- One-and-one-half-story houses are best matched with relatively flat lots or sites sloping slightly to the rear.

- Two-story houses can be efficiently situated on small, flat lots and sites having slight grades.

- Split-foyer houses are good on sites with front-to-back or back-to-front medium to steep slopes. They're totally incompatible with flat lots.

- Multilevel houses are ideally suited to side-sloping lots on hilly terrain where the bottom level of the house faces and opens toward the downhill side and the upstairs level opens toward the uphill side. A flat lot won't work for a multilevel house.

LOT SIZE

You begin to establish your building site's order of magnitude when selecting either country property (large building site), suburban property (medium building site), or city property (relatively small lot), and then you further limit the possibilities by choosing one or several neighborhoods or areas from which to make your decision. Finally, it's a combination of what's available, what's suitable, what's affordable, and your personal preference. For green construction, rank the possible choices to what you want to build.

Do you like to garden or grow fruit trees? Will you be putting in elaborate swing sets and play areas for children? What about an in- or aboveground swimming pool? Will you be doing a lot of outdoor entertaining, with parties and picnics? Do you prefer to maintain your own landscaping in a big way? Or you could hate the idea of cutting grass and tending bushes, shrubs, and trees. You might want the privacy afforded by a large lot, or you might be nervous not having a neighbor within calling distance. Maybe you don't want to be bothered with a long driveway that has to be shoveled or plowed during winter. Or you might want to be set back from the road to distance yourself from traffic noise.

Some people like to spread out on a roomy parcel or acreage. Others who spend most of their time away from the house on work or recreational activities might find a large lot superfluous and a bother to maintain. A larger lot also can mean higher real estate taxes.

HOUSE ORIENTATION

The orientation or positioning of your house and driveway on any particular lot depends on how the lot is situated along the street, what the topography of the lot and surrounding land is, which direction it faces (north, south, east, or west), local building property line setbacks and regulations, and the house's floor plan. When a choice of lots exists, orientation potential can become a major factor in the decision on which site to purchase. Window selection and positioning are closely related to orientation theories.

Remember, too, that a well-planned house can be constructed with any orientation as long as the dwelling fits the lot. This might mean that you will want to use more or less glass than you would have otherwise, or you'll beef up the insulation or plan extrawide overhangs. You must weigh the pros and cons of each particular site to come up with the best orientation possible.

Your plans for such a house positioning should address which rooms you want to receive maximum exposure to the sun and protection from the cold winter winds and driving rains. In some cases, it might be better to use the mirror copy of your original plans. By flip-flopping the floor plan in certain situations, you can place the garage on the side of the house that shields the living areas from winter storms and subzero chill factors.

SPECIAL LOCATIONS

Some people dream of living on a scenic ocean or lake bluff or out on their own island in a picturesque bay. The trouble is, once they try such locations, they might not like them. The weather can be brutal, house maintenance frequent, and even the views—intense as they are—can become tiresome. Be careful of locations frequented by sightseers, sports enthusiasts, photography buffs, or any special-interest groups. Houses close to steep cliffs or ridges can be hazardous to children. Be aware of long-distance travel time required to reach many special out-of-the-way locations.

BUYING THE LOT

If the zoning is correct, the lot configuration fits your house plan, the orientation is satisfactory, the area meets all your personal qualifications, and you like the site more than anything else you've seen, then go ahead and buy it. But when you do, take care of the following points:

1. *Get a clear title.* If you're purchasing the house with a mortgage, the lending institution will require you to have the property's deed searched. An attorney (or someone representing an attorney or title company) will go to the county clerk's office and look through the records, checking for any possible claims, liens, judgments, or clouds on the deed that would prevent you from receiving a free and clear title. You should have the records searched even if you pay cash for the property and there's no mortgage involved to protect your own interests. Attorneys or title guarantee companies that perform the same services are insured in the unlikely event that they make a mistake.

2. If necessary, *obtain a septic permit.* The ability to secure a septic permit if there is no public or private sanitary system is a must. The site will be worthless if you can't have a septic system on it. If there's any doubt at all, you

should specify in the property's purchase agreement that the transaction be contingent on the ability to obtain a permit for the type of septic system that you want—perhaps a below-ground system instead of a more expensive and unwieldy aboveground "mound" arrangement.

A percolation test will be made when you apply for a permit. It determines how fast sewage liquids can seep into the ground. If the soil is primarily clay, a septic system might not be approved for below ground because the sewage liquids will not readily pass through the impermeable clay for proper disposal. Even when building on a large site, the size of which (10 acres, for example) exempts you from the necessity of securing a septic permit, you still should test the soil permeability to determine which type of septic system will be the most efficient and safest for you.

3. If needed, *procure a water well.* If no public or private water supply systems are available, you'll need to provide your own well. If there's any doubt about the prospect of digging or drilling an adequate well, you can include such a contingency in the property's purchase agreement. The well should provide good, drinkable water in quantities (expressed in gallons per minute) that satisfy local and Federal Housing Administration standards. The well must be dug or drilled a safe distance away from any septic system leaching field.

4. *Find out about any subdivision restrictions.* If you select a building site in a new or established subdivision, make sure that you find out if any building restrictions are in effect. Building restrictions are rules of a subdivision governing various construction and maintenance aspects to make certain that the houses in the subdivision will all be of relatively equal size, condition, and value. They regulate such things as how soon construction must begin and be completed after the lot's deed is transferred to the buyer, how the dwellings must be positioned on each site, what can be stored on the properties and what can't, how the yards must be maintained, and what will happen if those rules and others are disregarded.

In essence, building restrictions are designed to protect the integrity and value of each individual dwelling in a subdivision by prohibiting any house's improper or unusual construction or lack of maintenance that could have derogatory effects on the rest. The theory is that with strict building restrictions, you won't end up with *Tobacco Road* type houses ruining the neighborhood.

What follows are sample subdivision restrictions that are representative (written in the same kind of jargon) of what you'll find in thousands of similar sets of restrictions throughout the country. They address most of the major concerns you'll encounter anywhere. Keep in mind, though, that each set of subdivision restrictions is slightly different, custom-tailored by the people who began and later lived in the subdivision in question.

Declaration of Restrictions for Oakland Hills Subdivision

(A plat of which is recorded in Smith County Map Book 8, page 21)

The following restrictions on property in subdivision to be known as Oakland Hills Subdivision, which is a part of Index No. 202-490-23, located in Crosscreek Township, Smith County, Pennsylvania, and part of Index 7344-700 and 7346-700, located in the City of Dalemont, Pennsylvania, shall govern all lots in said subdivision and they are covenants running with the land and binding upon all owners and their grantees, heirs, legal representatives, successors, and assigns:

1. The property shall be used for private residence purposes only and shall be used only for single one-family residences, together with customary garage with space for not less than two or more than three cars, for sole use of owner or occupant of lot upon which said building is located.

2. No buildings shall be erected nearer to the front line nor nearer to the side street line than the building setback lines of 30 feet shown on the recorded plot, except that where topographical features make it desirable an attached garage on Lots 22 through 37 may, with the approval of the designated Architectural Consultants designated by Realto Corporation, be located no closer than 20 feet from the front property line.

3. Homes built on lots fronting on Ash Street shall have at least the following areas: one-story—shall have at least 2,000 square feet; one-and-one-half-story—shall have at least 2,000 square feet at ground level and at least 700 square feet upstairs; two-story—shall have at least 2,000 square feet at ground level and at least 1,200 square feet upstairs; split-level—shall have at least 2,000 square feet at ground level and at least 600 square feet total on other levels. Homes built on lots fronting on Douglas Street shall have at least the following areas: one-story—shall have at least 1,800 square feet; one-and-one-half-story—shall have at least 1,800 square feet at ground level and at least 600 square feet upstairs; two-story—shall have at least 1,800 square feet at ground level and at least 1,000 square feet upstairs; split-level—shall have at least 1,800 square feet at ground level and at least 500 square feet total on other levels.

4. No building, wall, fence, hedge, or other structure shall be erected or maintained unless plans including all floor plans, elevation, plot plan showing proposed grading, location of buildings, fences, hedges, lampposts, outdoor fireplaces or major planting, such plans and elevations to show clearly the design, height, materials, color scheme,

shall be submitted to, and approved by the Consulting Architectural Firm designated, at the time of lot purchase, by Realto Corporation. The fee for this consulting service, established at the time of purchase, shall be paid by the Purchaser.

5. No weeds, underbrush, or other unsightly growth shall be permitted to grow or remain anywhere upon this property nor upon adjoining right of way between property and street. Until property is actually occupied through construction of a building, permission is given to Realto Corporation to mow the grass and remove the weeds or unsightly growth.

6. Property is subject to an annual charge or assessment of 60¢ per front foot adjusted annually to reflect cost-of-living change, to be paid by the owner of the property into a fund administered by Realto Corporation, its successors or assigns, such charges or assessments to be applied toward payment of the cost of maintaining right-of-ways, planting, or beautifying and caring for parks, plots, and other open spaces owned by the Corporation and maintained for the general use of owners of the property, caring for vacant and improved lots, removing grass and weeds there from and other things necessary or desirable to keep the property neat and in good order.

7. No billboards or advertising signs of any character whatever shall be erected, placed, permitted, or maintained on such property. This shall not be construed, however, to prevent Realto Corporation from maintaining upon the property, at such locations as it may choose, billboards, signs, or sales office on an unsold lot during the initial sale of lots, nor from maintaining attractive signs of moderate size at the entrances to the subdivision identifying it.

8. Any building started on any lot in the subdivision shall be completed within six months.

9. The keeping of any animals or poultry other than ordinary domestic pet animals is prohibited.

10. A house and garage shall be commenced on a lot within one year after the delivery of the Deed to the lot. If the purchaser shall fail to construct the house and garage within this time, Realto Corporation shall have the option of extending the period for construction for six months or repurchasing the lot at the same price it was sold to the purchaser, and the purchaser shall give a good and merchantable deed free and clear of all encumbrances to Realto Corporation or its nominee. Resale of the lot by the purchaser shall not change the

requirements for construction expressed herein in any way, and such resale must be made subject to the initial or optionally extended date.

11. Areas designated as Private Parks in the subdivision plan are the property of Realto Corporation, and use of such park areas by the residents of Oakland Hills or its extension is a privilege extended by the corporation, subject to its reasonable and proper regulations to maintain the charactor of the subdivision, and subject to withdrawal of the right of access and use by any individual(s), at any time for violation of said regulations.

12. No noxious or offensive activity shall be carried on upon any lot, nor shall anything be done, placed or stored thereon which may be or become an annoyance or nuisance to the neighborhood, or occasion any noise or order which will or might disturb the peace, comfort or serenity of the occupants of neighboring properties. Nothing shall be permitted or maintained on the premises or adjoining street or streets unless specifically approved by Realto Corporation, or its successors or assigns. During construction trucks shall use Old State Road exclusively for access in Crosscreek Township.

13. All provisions, conditions, restrictions, and covenants herein shall be binding on all lots and parcels or real estate and the owners thereof, regardless of the source of title of such owners, and any breach thereof, if continued for a period of 30 days from and after the date that the owner or other property owner shall have notified in writing the owner or lessee in possession of the lot upon which such breach has been committed to refrain from a continuance of such action and to correct such breach, shall warrant the undersigned or other lot owner to apply to any court of law or equity having jurisdiction thereof for an injunction or other proper relief, and if such relief be granted, the plaintiff in such action shall be entitled to receive his reasonable expenses in prosecuting such suit, including attorney's fees, as part of the Decree, Order of Court, or Judgment.

    Provided, that any violation of the foregoing provisions, conditions, restrictions, or covenants shall not defeat or render invalid the lien of any mortgage or deed of trust made in good faith for value as to any portion of said property, but such provisions, conditions, restrictions, and covenants shall be enforceable, against any portion of said property acquired by any person through foreclosure or by deed in lieu of foreclosure, for any violation of the provisions, conditions, restrictions, and covenants herein contained occurring after the acquisition of said property through foreclosure or deed in lieu of foreclosure.

14. In the event that any one or more of the provisions, conditions, restrictions, and covenants herein set forth shall be held by any court of competent jurisdiction to be null and void, all remaining provisions, conditions, restrictions, and covenants herein set forth shall continue unimpaired and in full force and effect.

15. Any and all of the rights and powers herein of Oakland Corporation may be assigned to any Corporation, Authority, or Association, and such Corporation, Authority, or Association shall to the extent of such assignment have the same rights and powers assumed and retained by the owner herein.

16. The aforesaid provisions, conditions, restrictions, and covenants and each and all thereof, shall run with the land and continue and remain in full force and effect at all times and against all persons until the following January 1, at which time they shall be automatically extended for a period of 10 years and thereafter for successive 10-year periods unless on or before the end of one of such extension periods the owners of 70 percent of the lots in said subdivision shall by written instrument, duly recorded, declare a termination or modification of the same. The aforesaid provisions, conditions, restrictions, and covenants and each and all thereof may at any time be amended or modified by the owners of 70 percent of the lots in said subdivision by written instrument duly recorded.

17. No delay or omission on the part of the owner or the owners of any lot or lots in said property in exercising any right, power, or remedy herein provided for in the event of any breach of any of the provisions, conditions, restrictions, and covenants herein contained shall be construed as a waiver thereof or acquiescence therein; and no right of action shall accrue nor shall any action be brought or maintained by anyone whomsoever against the undersigned owner or an account of the failure or neglect of the undersigned owner to exercise any right, power, or remedy herein provided for in the event of any such breach of any said provisions, conditions, restrictions, or covenants which may be unenforceable.

18. The "Owner" herein referred to shall include the present owner of the land in Oakland Hills Subdivision and any extensions thereof, their successors in interest and authorized agents. "Oakland Hills Subdivision" as referred to shall include its successors and assigns.

BUILDING SITE CHECKLIST ✔✔✔✔✔

___ Is the site properly zoned? How are the properties surrounding the site zoned?

___ Is it close enough to

- Work
- Schools
- Shopping
- Neighbors
- Friends
- Family
- Church
- Entertainment centers
- Medical services

___ What's the reputation of the school system?

___ Are there any parks or playgrounds for children?

___ How do the real estate taxes compare with those in other areas?

___ Are there any home association dues?

___ Are there other houses similar to yours in size and type and value in the neighborhood?

___ Have you inquired about the crime rate compared with crime rates in other locations?

___ Is the site in an area that is declining, remaining stable, or improving?

___ Are there any potentially irritating factories, dragstrips, or seasonal attractions nearby?

___ Is the location private enough for you? Is there rear and side privacy?

___ Is the site on a hill? Are there loud sounds of trucks and buses shifting gears as they pass by? In winter, could you have trouble making the incline from your driveway?

___ Is the lot at a road intersection where stop signs have the traffic constantly stopping and starting?

___ Is the lot steep where lawn mowing will be required? What about snow removal?

___ Where must the mailbox be placed?

___ Are there any ditches, swampy terrain, right-of-ways, or easements that restrict certain parts of the site from a desired use? Is there a creek or gully that cuts through near the center?

(Continued)

✔✔✔✔✔ **BUILDING SITE CHECKLIST** *(Continued)*

___ Is there an open ditch or culvert across the front, parallel to the road, that will need special attention for driveway access and lawn maintenance?

___ Which utilities, such as natural gas, electricity, water, sewer/septic, phone, and cable TV, are available? Does a utility company have any utility boxes set up or easements for eventual setups?

___ Is the soil sandy—which could require special foundation work?

___ How are the garbage collection services?

___ What kind of fire protection is there?

___ What kind of police protection?

___ What kind of emergency transport system?

___ Does the lot suit the type of house you are planning?

___ Does any portion of the site consist of fill dirt?

___ Is there or will there be good drainage on the site? Is the lot in a floodplain?

___ Is the lot large enough for your house and your activities?

___ Is the lot small enough for your house and your activities?

___ Did you see a plot plan of the site?

___ Has a recent property survey been completed? Are the lot's boundaries staked out so that you can see them?

___ Do you know at what level or height the sewer line will connect the house plumbing?

___ Will the site provide your house with a good orientation? Any special views available?

___ Are the views available from the location good or bad?

___ Can you get a free and clear title to the land?

___ Will you need a septic permit? Can you get one?

___ Do you need a water well? Can you obtain one?

___ How are the water wells nearby?

___ Do any subdivision or other restrictions apply? And if so, do you understand them?

___ Have you inquired into the probable resale value of your house and property in case you must unexpectedly move in the near future?

___ Where's the nearest fire protection? Police protection? Emergency medical service?

BUILDING SITE CHECKLIST

___ Is there good access to major highways?

___ Is the lot close to an airport (noise), set of railroad tracks (noise and crossing hazards), landfill (traffic, dust, trucking and tailgate slamming noise, possible water contamination), exposed power facility (noise), cliff, swamp (mosquitoes), or commercial or industrial property?

___ Will your completed home be the most expensive dwelling in the neighborhood (least desirable), or average, or least expensive (more desirable)?

▶▶▶▶▶ POINTS TO PONDER

1. Unless you're building in an established residential subdivision, make sure that you know the zoning of your site and the sites around you—on the sides of, across the street from, and behind your property. A call to the local zoning officer usually can be a big help toward understanding zoning patterns that exist around the site in question.

2. Any real estate broker, when asked what the most important components of real estate value are, invariably will answer, "Location, location, location."

3. If you're new to an area, secure assistance from individuals you trust (and who have no stake in what or where you buy), such as coworkers, relatives, members of the local police department, and municipal zoning officials or planners.

4. Keep in mind the type of house you want as you look at building sites. For example, if your heart is set on a split-level home, you can pretty much eliminate very flat building sites. If you're thinking of an L-shaped sprawling ranch, that back-to-front sloped ravine site overlooking Higgly Creek probably won't work either.

5. Single-story ranches are ideally suited to flat building sites or lots that slope gently to the sides or rear, particularly if the plans call for a walkout from a basement or lower living area. One-and-one-half-story and two-story houses are also best matched with relatively flat lots or sites that slope slightly to the rear.

6. Split-foyer houses are good on building sites with front-to-back or back-to-front medium to steep slopes. They're totally incompatible with flat lots.

7. Multilevel houses are ideally suited to side-sloping lots or hilly terrain where the bottom level of the house faces and opens toward the downhill side and upstairs levels open toward the uphill side. A flat site won't work for multilevel construction.

8. Does any portion of the site—especially where you plan to excavate—consist of filled material that could interfere with the construction of solid footers and foundations?

9. Don't automatically figure that the front of your new home *must* face the street on which the house is located. Sure, in a traditional subdivision, it doesn't make sense to buck the "front-faces-the-street" rule, but on sites away from close neighbors, you can orient the front of the house to take advantage of interesting views toward the back or sides.

10. Before purchasing a building site, make sure that you will end up with a clear title, utility hookups, a septic permit if required, a successful water well if applicable, and a complete copy of all easements and building restrictions applicable to your site.

Orientation, Positioning, and Landscaping

The way you orient and position your home on a building site and how you landscape its surroundings will greatly affect the benefits or drawbacks your home will receive from local weather conditions, will affect the home's market value and salability, and even will affect the livability of the dwelling in many subtle ways.

ORIENTATION

Four factors play important roles in determining the best orientation for your house:

- The location of the building site in relation to surrounding typographic features, other houses, and the street
- The sun
- The wind
- The available views

Location

If you purchase a building site that's the last one available in a subdivision or is positioned between two existing dwellings or anywhere within a subdivision having strict building restrictions, there's nothing dramatic you can do with the orientation; you already know where the house has to sit, which way it has to face, and even where it must be positioned at the front and sides on any one particular lot.

However, if you have a wide choice of building sites with several different orientations possible, or if you're planning to build in the country, where few restrictions are in force, it's another story. If so, consider how the following three factors might influence your selection.

The Sun

There's nothing in life quite as regular and dependable as the rising and setting of the sun (clouds are the capricious variables of weather). You can take advantage of the sun's free heat and light by planning and facing the side of your house with the most glass toward the south. In this way, low-angled sun rays will penetrate into the rooms during winter, bringing warmth and illumination. Then, in summer, your roof overhangs will block out high-angled rays that otherwise will make your air-conditioning work overtime.

In general, south-facing areas will be warm, north-facing areas will be cold, east-facing areas will get the pleasant early-morning sun, and west-facing rooms will bear the brunt of hot afternoon rays.

Since one of the most important considerations is the orientation and positioning of the house in relation to sunshine access, in a perfect home world, the longer dimension or axis of the house runs east and west so that the greatest percentage of walls and floor plan interior space has sunshine exposure through windows and glass doors on the south side of the house. This also leaves the east and west "ends" of the house the narrower of the outside walls so that they'll absorb proportionally less unwanted solar heat during the summer months, which will lighten air-conditioning or natural ventilation demands. Passive-solar design— essentially major southern window exposure, masonry or other thermal mass to absorb daytime heat from sunshine, plus overhangs, awnings, or other shade mechanisms to restrict solar gain when it's not needed—helps to make a comfortable, energy-efficient home.

On one hand, a single-story L-shaped or other ranch-style home is probably best suited to passive-solar heating and natural daylighting and outdoor living porch and patio design. On the other hand, such a sprawling house will require a larger footprint, with a greater percentage of building-site ground lost to construction. Of course, there may be legitimate reasons why the home's length must be positioned a different way. Maybe the building site is not wide enough to accommodate the length facing south. Maybe building restrictions specify a certain setback or another positioning configuration. Usually, unless the dwelling backs to a huge vertical cliff, there's some kind of southern exposure. It's up to you to figure out how to take advantage of it. This should not automatically eliminate other types of dwellings from your consideration. Two-story houses, Cape Cod houses, and contemporary split-foyer and split-level houses all can benefit from passive-solar design. But other factors can be equally important, such as the site's configuration: Is it flat or sloping or next to a dramatic view?

No matter what type of house you decide on, devising the best floor plan to take advantage of the sun's "travel" can effectively reduce the need for electric lights. If possible, plan where various rooms should be depending on where the sun shines throughout the day. Expert home designers favor the kitchen location at the southeast corner of the home, where breakfast can be had and the newspaper can be read by the morning sun. The family room, typically used more in late afternoon, is best suited for the southwest portion of the house because that's where the sun is then. The bedrooms are places where morning and afternoon sunshine either isn't wanted or doesn't matter much—they're often best placed at or close to the northwest part of the house. To save on electric lighting, first determine exactly where natural daylighting can be designed into the floor plan. Remember that sun tubes, skylights, and clerestory windows often can reach in to naturally light bathrooms, hallways, and closets that are otherwise lacking regular windows. After the daylighting plans are made, then use electric fixtures to balance out the rest of the lighting system. Tracking the sun through the floor plan also will help the home to keep warm and will reduce heating loads—you can reduce heat in the northern rooms of the home during the day and also can use less purchased heat on the south side of the house, where most of the daytime activities are, by allowing the sun to enter for free.

Of course, remember where you will live. If you plan to build in a zone where cooling costs are far more important than heating costs, then orient a narrow side of the home toward the south, and build wide overhangs and covered porches on the south and west outside walls. In short, wherever you build, you need to consider the sun's daily paths, and adjust your planning appropriately

The Wind

Depending on the circumstances, wind can be a help or hindrance. It can rob you of heat during the winter with its icy chill factors. Or it can just as easily get rid of unwanted heat during stifling hot summer days. Ironically, the wind, too, is a protégé of the sun. The winds are caused primarily by sunlight as it heats portions of the atmosphere that shift and move about the planet.

In North America, the prevailing winds blow from west to east, although seasonal and regional variations frequently find warm, moist breezes lofting up from the south and cold, dry winds howling out of the north. Summer breezes usually are desirable for natural ventilation, but remember that they can turn into icy winds during other seasons. This is why fewer and smaller windows typically are placed on the north side of the house. In cases where the summer breezes are just not cooperating, direction-wise, then you might have to plant vegetation and trees and construct building extensions such as an L-shaped wing or covered porch that can divert the breezes to where you want them. In this case, you'll need to analyze historical weather and wind patterns to understand how the plantings and building extensions will best help natural ventilation.

Because of the predictable nature of large weather patterns, whenever possible, you should minimize the number of windows you place on the north and north-west sections of your house because they'll be the hardest hit by the most unfavorable winds. Try to locate your garage there instead to absorb most of the wind's punch before it reaches the rest of your home.

There are several ways that you can modify how the wind affects your home if you want to. One way is to plan building extensions such as L-shapes, covered porches, and garages to block or divert prevailing winds. Another is to plant a windbreak of evergreen trees or shrubs a certain distance between the house and the main direction of wind travel. A windbreak placed a certain distance from the home can reduce the wind effect on the house by between 50 and 75 percent depending how high the trees grow and how close they're planted together. They usually work best when planted along the north and west sides.

On the other hand, if you plan to eventually install a wind turbine to generate your own electricity, you'll want to locate where wind speeds will be maximized. See the section on wind turbines in Chapter 22 on electricity.

Land Topography

When possible, select the site for excavation where major grading changes will not need to be made. If your foundation can be placed on ground that will not need major cutting, grading, and filling, a more stable base will be available for the home.

The Views

To some people, available views will take precedence over anything else. If your lot is on the south side of a lake and you want to face the water, you can't help but face some of your living quarters toward the north. If so, compensate for such a handicapped orientation by paying more attention to selective landscaping, privacy walls, thermal glass, and similar features.

Be aware of the land or water that surrounds you and how a nice view can be changed overnight by neighbors who cut down or plant trees, pile up garbage cans, or park a junk car in their backyard. Although you want to maximize the number of positive views available, you need to consider whether those views may be affected by future development.

POSITIONING

Again, the house that's matched to a regular subdivision lot has few options as to its positioning—the only choice might be to construct the house either the actual way the plans are drawn versus the way a mirror image of those plans would appear. For example, a two-story house might have the garage on the left-hand side of the original set of plans. The same house could be "mirrored" so that the garage would be positioned to the right and could block undesirable views and sounds, such as those from a busy highway.

Keep in mind that any mistake or poor choice on your part could create a house that's obviously mismatched with its lot. Ideally, your home will blend into the site as if it "grew" in place. Several factors determining the best positioning potential follow, although your ultimate choice may be limited by zoning regulations; building code restrictions; home-owner association rules; locations of natural gas, electric, sewer, water, or other utilities; and environmental permitting. These points all should be included in the original site assessment.

Setback from the Street

If there are already houses on both sides of your lot, you don't have much room to maneuver here. The same applies if your building site is part of a strictly regulated subdivision.

On the other hand, if you're building where there's no one else around, consider keeping the house a reasonable distance away from the road to reduce the amount of dust and noise generated from passing traffic. If you drive through the country, you'll notice that some people build very close to the road, whereas others build quite far from it. In cold-climate areas, if you elect to go way back from the road, be prepared to handle the snow removal in some fashion. The larger and longer the driveway, the more snow you'll have to contend with. When a choice exists, weigh the advantages and disadvantages of privacy versus convenience, and arrive at a happy medium.

Utility Connections

A dwelling's corner or side where the utilities need to be connected should be accommodating. A lengthy concrete patio in this area would add difficulty to the hookups and would mean extra length and costs for making those connections. Connections should be planned so that no large trees that otherwise are being saved will be affected by excavation lines or boundaries.

Vehicle Access

You want a practical exit/entrance to your garage from the street. This is especially important in cold-climate locations where snow and ice make driving and walking a chore. Be careful of how steep the driveway's fall will be because it could add to the difficulty of getting in and out. At the same time, watch out for driveways that slope toward the garage. Rainwater could run into the garage, and ice coatings will make such a sloped driveway a definite safety hazard.

The amount of space to allow on the two sides of the house should be considered. Most homes are simply situated at the center of regular city and subdivision lots—sometimes to satisfy subdivision restrictions or to provide minimum clearances from the property lines, as dictated by township or other applicable municipalities. If there is an option, it might be best for you to put the house toward one or the other side of the lot. What if someday a large dump truck or backhoe needs to drive into your backyard? What if you decide that your backyard is sloped too much and you want to level it off with clean fill dirt?

Remember to leave ample space on the side that is most passable for trucks—preferably the garage side of the house. In this way, heavy equipment also will be able to reach your backyard in case you someday decide to install an in-ground swimming pool or put up an addition there.

Pedestrian Use

A second point to remember is one that, if ignored, can become detrimental to the house's value and salability. Depending on how your house is oriented, try to minimize the difficulty of having to climb numerous steps when entering or exiting the home.

Outdoor Functions

Some exclusive subdivisions feature houses that have practically no backyards. Instead, the homes and their front yards are situated to give visitors a showcase effect—beautiful front lawns, stunning flowers, and well-cared-for trees, all surrounding homes that look architecturally designed for each individual building site.

Other houses and lots are planned to permit a variety of practical outdoor activities. Review your interests and those of your family and friends. Do you like to

- *Grow your own food?* Then what about small "kitchen" gardens or large family gardens? What about fruit trees and berry bushes? Do you want to grow your own Christmas trees?

- *Keep pets or farm animals?* Is there enough room somewhere for a dog to run and a cat to prowl? If permitted, do you plan to provide spaces and buildings for farm animals?

- *Participate in recreational activities?* Do you have the space to accommodate badminton, croquet, tennis, horseshoes, swimming, basketball, swing sets for children, a canoe storage shed, rope swings and hammocks, sandboxes, raising roses and tulips, or other interests?

- *Plan large outdoor parties and picnics?*

- *Work at your main business or a part-time business?* What about home workshops behind the garage or those white boxes for beekeeping?

LANDSCAPING

Any realtor will tell you: Take two identical houses, put one on a nicely landscaped lot and the other on a landscape that has weeds erupting everywhere, dying trees, overgrown shrubs, and ankle-length grass. Can you guess which property would be easier to sell? And which one would bring a higher market price? And also, which one would be more pleasant to live in?

Landscaping is important, no doubt. It can help you to reduce energy costs. It can make your home a more comfortable place to live. It can eliminate the need for manufactured fences or privacy screens. It can help to reduce your grocery bills. It can attract interesting wild birds and animals within sight. It can define a play area for children or a picnic area for adults. It can block off an unsightly view or frame a pleasant pastoral scene. Landscaping is certainly one of the finishing touches required to make a new house an attractive property.

Clearing the Part of the Site Reserved for Excavation

After an inventory of features is taken and the smallest possible house footprint is arrived at, the least attractive part of the building site should be excavated in the most minimal way. The goal is to protect as much of the site's integrity as possible while maintaining or establishing proper contours for surface water management and landscaping. This, of course, can be as simple as grading a small treeless building lot in a subdivision or as complex as placing a home on 10 acres with a stream and wetlands so that the house does not intrude on existing habitat. It may involve reserving and reusing topsoil, protecting natural vegetation and wildlife habitat, and even replacing invasive plant species or water-thirsty lawn with native grasses, trees, and vegetation.

To some contractors, clearing a building site is a necessary evil—a time-consuming activity at best, and one that is best done from their perspective by clearcutting and all-out grading. This is exactly what you don't want to happen. Think of developments you've seen, how practically every yard looks the same, treeless except for a single small maple or decorative crabapple tree planted directly in the center of the front yard, a few shrubs around the house, and the rest lawn.

Whenever possible, work with what's there by not disturbing things. Leave as much property alone as you can, untouched by backhoes, front-end loaders, dozers, and graders. Save mature trees. Unless there is a reason for grade changes—smoothing out or altering the site's contours—don't, because grade changes can damage soil structures and tree roots. If major grade changes are necessary, consider landscaping features such as terracing and the use of retaining walls and earthen berms.

If you're lucky enough to have a wooded or partly wooded building site, remove only those trees necessary to permit construction—unless you already have definite landscaping plans for the entire parcel. It takes only a short time to remove a full-grown tree but years and years to replace it. Before even a single tree is removed, you should determine the boundaries needed for construction of the house, driveway, and septic system if one must be installed. Then you can selectively remove and save trees in a calculated manner.

Trees provide numerous benefits when in the right places. Large trees literally can add thousands of dollars in value to a home. Later, the cost of planting new trees and then waiting for them to grow can be a huge expense in both dollars and time. The trouble it takes to work around trees during construction is well worth the effort. It might mean yellow-taping them off limits to heavy equipment that could otherwise sideswipe them, break branches, or compact their roots. It's important to agree in advance with the contractor on what trees are to be left untouched and how that will happen. Who is going to direct the excavators and inform the subcontractors? Speak with the individuals doing the digging—the heavy equipment operators—so that you can personally reinforce what you expect them to do to protect existing trees and vegetation.

Conversely, arrange to have trees that do not fit into the landscaping plan taken down. They might be in the way of passive-solar design on the south side of the house, for example. Those trees—depending on what they are—can be either rendered into mulch and reserved for landscaping finishing touches or even sawn into planks and lumber, kiln dried, and used for flooring, mantles, hand rails, trim, door or window framing, or furnishings. This is going the extra length to reclaim and recycle. Additional vegetation that must be cut also should be mulched and reused on the property, if possible.

Soil

Again, if the contractor simply clearcuts and flat grades the entire site, in addition to tree and vegetation losses, organic-rich, fertile topsoil that took hundreds of years to produce is likely to be lost or mixed in with sterile clay or other subsoils that will not result in a good landscaping growing medium. More than likely, erosion will take place, and hardy invasive weeds and other undesirable vegetation will take root quickly. Instead, have the contractor remove and save the upper 6 inches of topsoil from the areas excavated and graded to plan. The saved topsoil can be placed temporarily behind the back of the driveway, for instance, or in another place where compacting is unlikely to occur. The topsoil may be covered with permeable geotextile fabric or temporarily seeded with fast-growing native grass so that the soil won't compact, dry out, or erode from rain or wind. Before covering, it also would be an excellent time to add more organic materials to the scraped and saved topsoil if a soil analysis performed by the original site assessment found the soil lacking in nutrients and characteristics required to establish healthy plantings. Maybe the topsoil had already been removed years before you acquired the property. For final grading, redistribute the topsoil where vegetation, plantings, flower beds, gardens, trees, and lawn will be planted.

Plantings

Your lot's final grade should be established and stabilized as soon as possible through the planting of native vegetation, grass, or other ground covers to protect the soil from water and wind erosion. A thin layer of straw spread over the seeded areas will minimize harmful water and wind action until the vegetation or ground cover has grown enough to do the job.

Try to arrange for overall, well-balanced plantings—combinations of shrubs, trees, flowers, gardens, or other sections that will alternately bloom or flourish throughout the growing seasons and not burst into magnificent "peacock" displays for 2 weeks and then disappear.

Remember that landscaping, and especially plantings, can be a gradual process. There's no need to rush things. Don't let professional landscapers pressure you into an all-or-nothing strategy. You can first put in a small section of lawn and a few shrubs. Next year you can add a hardwood tree and some ground cover. And the next year you can plant a row of flowering hedges.

Trees and Shrubs

Evergreen trees and shrubs retain their leaves during winter. They can block wind and provide shade year round. When laying out a wind break, evergreens ideally should be placed between the house and the prevailing northern winds to minimize wind-chill factors. (Fig. 33.1).

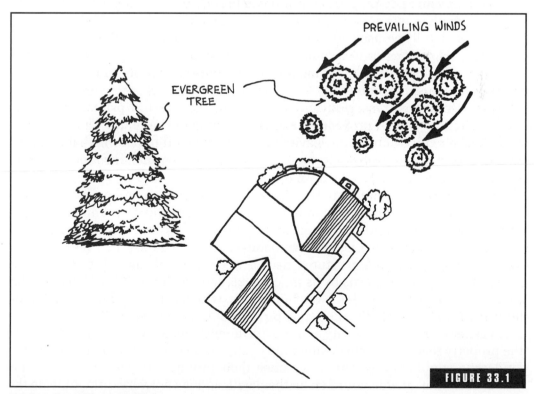

Landscaping with evergreens.

Deciduous trees drop their leaves for the winter. They'll let sunlight filter through in the coldest months when it's sorely needed. They're most advantageously placed to the south and west, where they'll also—because their leaves are full during summer and fall—block out the sun during the warmest part of the year. A small gap, however, should be arranged to the southwest to allow for refreshing breezes during summer. Remember that overall shading of a home located in a warm southern locale can reduce the overall exterior temperature by 10 to 15 degrees. This will save considerable amounts of energy that otherwise would be used for cooling. But consider how close those trees are planted to the house because large tree trunks and limbs can also block sunlight year round—even after deciduous leaves fall. This becomes more important in colder climates where sunshine is counted on as part of a passive-solar heat-gain system.

By shading the house, the walls, shingles, and curtains will all stay cooler, keeping overall temperatures down and enabling those same components to last longer from reduced exposure levels to harmful ultraviolet rays. Occupants also will feel more comfortable sitting indoors near a shaded wall.

Shading the walls is particularly important if they are brick or other masonry materials. Masonry slowly absorbs the sun's heat in the afternoon and radiates it indoors all evening, forcing air-conditioning to run deep into the night. And most ordinary insulation is not so effective at blocking radiant heat. In addition, deciduous trees should be used to help shade outside air-conditioning units. Shade from trees also makes it more comfortable on an outdoor deck or patio, allowing a family to spend less time operating the kitchen range and more time cooking and grilling outdoors in comfort.

With deciduous trees, you may think of shading as the primary means of cooling. While they do provide an excellent source of shade, they also function as natural air conditioners. As leaves on the tree give off moisture, that moisture changes from a liquid phase to a gas, pulling heat from the surrounding air. In addition to blocking the sun's rays, trees also "sweat" by transpiring water from their leaves. This, too, helps to cool their surrounding area and helps to prevent a nearby home from gaining too much more heat. The process is known as *evapotranspiration* and can be counted on to help with cooling effects. With properly placed deciduous trees, air temperatures near a house can be nearly 10 degrees cooler than temperatures near a treeless dwelling. This can reduce home air-conditioning costs by as much as 25 percent. Trees with high canopies will effectively cool and shade roof and walls, whereas lower plantings near the house will help to cool through transpiration and evaporation.

In general, trees offer beauty and provide homes for songbirds. Large trees lend the property that "established community" appearance. Be aware that some of the landscape suppliers might not guarantee their products if you plant the items yourself. On the other hand, many of them will, and it's not very difficult to do the plantings yourself. Just follow the nursery's instructions to the letter.

Native Plants and Trees

In North America, plants and trees are considered "native" if they were already growing here before the days of Christopher Columbus and other Europeans. They had hundreds of thousands of years to adapt to local growing conditions—soil types, climates, rainfall levels, insect pests, and diseases—and also have been supporting local wildlife by providing food and shelter for successful ecocommunities for centuries. As such, they don't need much extra watering, fertilizers, or pesticides. Find out what native plants should work with your landscaping plan by inquiring at your local nurseries or consulting the Internet.

If there's not much topsoil to start out with, you might want to consider grass sod. The advantage of sod is that you'll have an instant lawn that comes with some of its own topsoil. Naturally, sod costs more than a seeded lawn.

Xeriscaping

Xeriscaping is a term from the Greek *xeri*, meaning dry, and *scape*, meaning a visual view or scene. In this case, it means a landscape that needs very little water. The plants used are often native to the area, but others can be planted as well. In these times when entire regions have incurred serious droughts and drinking water is at a premium, landscapes that require either no or very little additional watering, fertilizers, or pesticides can be a huge asset to a new or existing home. Certainly, anything that conserves water and requires no maintenance chemicals lines up as a desirable green feature.

Edible Landscaping

Individuals "from the old country" have been doing it for years, sometimes planting, grafting, and growing fruit trees, shrubs, and bushes—usually perennials—that bear grapes, berries, nuts, apples, plums, peaches, oranges, lemons, and all sorts of other edibles, to the point that sometimes their entire yards resemble impassable jungles of vegetation. In more moderate proportions, edible landscaping has its place on practically any home site.

More conventional gardens also may be considered, and they may be worth a little watering or irrigating. Or you could just plant them here and there and let them fend for themselves.

Mulch and Compost

As an alternative to landfilling or other ways of disposal, weeds, vegetation clippings, leaves, seeds, and pieces of vegetable and fruit organic waste can be recycled in a well-positioned outdoors compost bin. Your local county agricultural department likely has bins or plans for bins available, as well as detailed instructions of how to make and use them. Mulch as compost can be spread around plantings and in soil to hold moisture.

Lawn

A uniform, green, well-manicured lawn does have its good points. It can supply a look of luxury, evoking old-time European royalty or modern-day mansions on exclusive drives. It provides a place on which to place a picnic table or to play croquet, lawn darts, or badminton. On the other hand, a lawn also can require endless watering, fertilizers, and pesticides. Huge amounts of water and chemicals are absorbed by lawns every year. Lawns must be mowed regularly, using air-polluting gasoline or diesel fuels or electricity. And not much wildlife can live in or survive on the short tufts of grass of a mowed lawn.

There are places for lawns in green home sites, but not for large amounts of traditional high-maintenance nonnative grasses that may look good but do not make much practical sense in today's water-starved urban and suburban world. Instead of grass, use landscaping features such as rock gardens with native ground covers and low-clinging shrubs. Clovers and native grasses are options, as are a huger variety of wildflowers and herbs. Depending on the climate, cacti, ferns, mosses, and vines can be considered, as can tall prairie grasses be used for visual barriers and borders. Slow-growing lawn varieties have been developed for years, with deep roots that reach way down for water and do not have to be irrigated at a moment's notice.

Reducing Siding, Sidewalk, Driveway, and Patio Heat

Foliage plantings can help to divert or reduce the amount of heat absorbed by and radiated by sidings, driveways, sidewalks, and patios.

- Tall trees and plants can prevent direct sunlight from striking siding or a sidewalk, driveway, or patio, which reduces heat buildup during the warmest part of the day.

- Medium-height plants can block heat that's reradiating from a warm or hot driveway toward your home's walls and windows. A solar-heated driveway continues to radiate heat well into the evening. The medium-height plants cool off surrounding air at the same time.

- Ground cover in pleasantly planned beds can create a cool buffer zone immediately next to the house. This is where the plant transpiration-evaporation process is very effective. At the same time, ground cover will help to prevent sunlight from reflecting against the home's exterior walls, thus keeping the siding materials cooler (Fig. 33.2). Often, the most effective plantings include a multipurpose combination of different-height species (Fig. 33.3).

When selecting ground cover, consider what grows best in your location as well as the eventual adult plant height, spread, and texture and whether a particular species is deciduous or evergreen. In winter, you'll likely welcome any extra radiant heat, so try to choose ground cover that will not block it from your dwelling. Depending on what level of landscaping your contractor is responsible for, be aware that for him or her (or for you, at some later date) to establish dense, healthy ground cover, a thorough preparation of the planting bed is necessary before actual plants are set.

Cooling effect of ground cover.

This means consider insisting on arranging for at least 2 inches of extra organic matter such as peat moss to lighten clay soils and increase the water-holding capacity of light sandy soils. The soil then should be worked to a depth of at least 6 or 8 inches. Weed seeds and weed plants should be cleaned out so that they won't compete with the new plants during the stress-filled weeks and months when the ground cover is trying to establish itself.

A multipurpose planting.

Then carefully follow instructions provided by the nursery experts who have supplied the plants.

Remember, when choosing tall, medium, and low plants, keep in mind that deciduous plants accomplish quite a lot the year round. Their leaves provide summertime heat protection, but when they shrivel and drop from their branches in late fall, the sun's rays can reach through and warm that concrete driveway and allow the heat to reflect up toward the home for heat gain, and even on cold winter nights, some of this stored heat will slowly radiate upward to create a warm thermal buffer area against the home, which ultimately reduces the rate of indoor heat loss through the walls and windows.

Earthen Berms

Building a landscaping berm or mound of soil, often by using a masonry or treated-wood retaining wall, into the northwestern corner of the lot adjacent to the dwelling in colder-climate locations or into the southwestern corner for hot-climate areas, can save a lot of energy. Essentially a raised area of ground against the home, it can cut energy bills and increase comfort levels by providing an insulating barrier, by reducing air leakage into the home, and by providing a thermal mass to moderate rapid temperature changes.

The comfort improvement from the heavy thermal mass of the ground and retaining wall will be most noticeable in the summer, with the moderation of typical afternoon temperature rises. Then, during cold months of winter, the berm will help to shelter part of the home from freezing temperatures and strong winds.

Drainage

The landscaping should slope away from the home's foundation and drain all the water from the gutters, downspouts, and sump pump out to the street or to some other harmless place. Make sure that the first 10 feet surrounding the house perimeter tapers away from the foundation with at least a 6-inch drop all the way around. Overall, there should be a minimum of 1 to 2 feet of fall from the house to the street, and this includes the driveway. The slope for drainage away from the house is important. Water must be drained away from the home to help minimize the need for sump pump and dehumidifier run times, each of which use a lot of energy.

Some lots need a culvert pipe beneath the end of the driveway for proper drainage along the street. Check with the appropriate government office for the right size and method of installation. In some communities, the highway department will install the culvert pipe at no cost to the owner. If not, see that its installation is included in the site work contract. The best ways to drain a property, though, is to encourage rainwater and snowmelt simply to percolate straight down into the ground, where it avoids storm sewers and instead is filtered and cleaned by the ground as it heads back into the water table. For this, select permeable driveways and walks, decks, and patios.

Erosion

To control minor problems with surface erosion on a bank, plant earth-holding shrubbery or ground cover. If an embankment is going to be steep owing to the lay of the land, consider building a retaining wall out of railroad ties, rocks, or solid masonry. This will control erosion and simplify your lawn maintenance. If you employ solid masonry retaining walls, make sure that they have weep holes to drain groundwater and release hydrostatic pressure that builds up on the earthen side of the wall.

Landscape Irrigation

Some individuals take a lot of pride in their well-landscaped property. Others don't really worry about their trees, shrubs, and lawns being maintained in peak condition. One thing that is for sure, though, is that plants need water to thrive. If your location is in an area where extended periods of drought can occur or if you want to maintain your living landscape in top condition, consider the purchase and installation of high-quality irrigation sprinklers and sprinkler systems. Top-quality sprinkling equipment lasts a long time and will provide excellent watering patterns while operating at desirable lower pressures and flows.

You also can research automatic watering components featured in drip or sprinkler versions. The heart of either type of system is the automatic electronic controller. It can be preset to control several zones to water different areas at various intervals with varying amounts of water. Some units even have automatic rain sensors to skip a watering cycle when it rains. Electronic water timers are great for getting the most out of the watering that takes place. At least one manu-facturer offers a unit that works on a 9-volt battery with low-pressure drip and soaker hoses, as well with standard garden hoses. Sometimes, even with drought-resistant native vegetation, plants need extra water. That water ideally can come from rainwater harvested and stored by a simple system. See the Chapter 21 on plumbing. Whatever the method for watering plants, the least efficient is to sprinkle with a hose. This is so because much of the water simply evaporates into the air from the hose spray and from plant leaves.

FIGURE 33.4

A decorative landscaping accent.

Decorative and Finishing Touches

Browse through any of the numerous mail-order catalogs for an idea of how

FIGURE 33.5

Landscaping decorations.

many unusual, exotic, practical, and frivolous plants and trees are available. See if any decorative items such as fountains, bird baths, trellises, pots, garden fences, ornaments, and automatic sprinklers catch your fancy (Figs. 33.4 and 33.5). The selection of landscaping options practically defies description. Items such as benches, chairs, and tables, as well as decking and fencing products, are available in recycled-plastic versions.

Final Landscaping Payment

If you happen to move into your newly constructed house before the grading is done and the lawn is planted (perhaps owing to inclement weather or the season in which the house was completed), make sure that some of the builder's funds are held back in escrow to be released to the builder after what was promised in the contract is completed. The contract should clearly state whose responsibility it is to provide a final grading with topsoil and a lawn.

▷▷▷▷▷▷ POINTS TO PONDER

1. Consider how the sun, wind, lay of the land, positions of surrounding homes, and available views can affect the home you plan to build.

2. Try to plan and face the side of the house with the most window and door glass toward the south.

3. When possible, minimize the number of windows you place on the north and northwest sides of the home; locate the garage there instead.

4. If pleasant or dramatic views are possible, consider going for the views, and compensate for less-than-ideal orientation with heavier thermal glass, privacy walls, selective landscaping, and similar features.

5. If you have a choice, carefully consider the home's setback distance from the street. The further back you go, the more privacy you'll have, along with less dust and noise from passing traffic. On the other hand, the longer your driveway (and your walk to the mailbox) will have to be. Plus, be prepared to handle snow removal in cold-climate areas.

6. Remove only those mature trees necessary to permit construction, unless you already have definite landscaping plans for the entire parcel. You may have to forcefully express yourself on this point because builders often belong to slash-and-burn, bulldoze-the-whole-lot-clean schools. Consider asking a local agronomist or nursery owner to advise you on which trees should and could be saved and how to protect them during the construction process. Some individuals have integrated their home/deck plans with existing, majestic trees with great success.

7. Landscaping, and especially plantings, can be a gradual process. Don't rush things. Adding a little at a time will help to avoid a frequent problem of overloading a landscape with small plants that—surprise—eventually will encroach on each other and create a tangle of foliage resembling a jungle.

8. Remember to keep the valuable nutrient-rich topsoil from the initial foundation excavation segregated for reuse as final landscaping cover.

9. The landscaping should slope away from the home's foundation and drain all the water from the gutters, downspouts, and sump pump out to the street or to some other harmless place.

10. Solid masonry retaining walls, in the absence of a comprehensive drainage system, at least need weep holes to drain groundwater and release hydrostatic pressure that can build up on the earthen side of the wall.

Driveways, Sidewalks, and Patios

DRIVEWAYS

Driveways are usually a necessity—a way of safely pulling off the street and traveling to the garage or home. Traditional concrete and asphalt driveways, however, are not kindly viewed by green construction guidelines. Since the early days of concrete, through the use of roofing shingle strips that bonded together under the hot sun in a smelly, sticky mess, to black, hot, soft asphalt surfaces, those traditional driveways were not very kind to the environment. At one time, most driveways were green, consisting of either paving bricks or crushed stone or gravel. The earth base below had been compacted by cars and trucks repeatedly driving over it, and then a stone or gravel layer was similarly compacted and used as the driving surface. Unfortunately, ruts and muddy spots usually developed, and weeds often sprouted through the gravel's edges. Such driveways became unsightly and were associated with poor construction. Occasionally, the stone or gravel needed refreshing with another full or partial truckload. While gravel driveways began to be seen as poor substitutes for asphalt and concrete, they're making more sense now during these times of green construction.

The issue of "disappearing gravel or stone" in a driveway can be easily solved by lining the excavated driveway with a few inches of sand and then adding a permeable geotextile fabric to prevent the top six or so inches of stone or gravel from migrating down into the sand layer and ground from the driveway. Pressurized wood or other heavy-duty rails can prevent the stone or gravel from being squeezed out the sides. Rainwater and snowmelt on the driveway surface then can simply percolate directly through the driveway into the ground below. Thus crushed-stone and gravel driveways certainly are a green alternative. To some home owners, though, their irregular surfaces still leave much to be desired. Similar results can be had with paving bricks, stones, adobe blocks, and even rubber blocks that are laid out on a base similar to that prepared for crushed stone or gravel. Even though the bricks, blocks, or stones are impermeable, if they are placed over ¼ inch apart, with those openings filled with coarse sand or compactable fine gravel, the rainwater and snowmelt still will percolate through the driveway and subbase into the ground.

The problem with traditional asphalt and concrete driveways is that of nonpermeability. Their composition prevents rainwater and snowmelt on their surfaces from percolating straight down into the ground, where it otherwise would reenter the groundwater table. Water that moves through the ground is naturally filtered and cleaned of impurities by a host of microbes in the soil en route to the aquifer below, where it becomes a natural resource that can be used again for drinking and other potable uses. Water that cannot reach or be absorbed into the ground becomes *runoff*. Typically, the runoff heads into gutters along the street and then into municipal storm sewers that carry the water into local rivers or lakes. During major rainstorms or snowmelts, this water can easily overpower storm sewer systems and cause flooding or sometimes find its way into sewage treatment plants, where it further burdens municipal treatment capacities. In times of regular weather, the runoff picks up pollutants such as oil, lubricants, fertilizers, pesticides, salts, and antifreeze from driveways, lawns, and roads and carries them directly into local waterways.

As an alternative to regular asphalt and concrete driveways, driveways constructed with either permeable asphalt or concrete mixes or permeable concrete paver blocks or blocks formed into open-grid patterns are greener solutions. The asphalt is rolled with rougher materials, mostly binder, and has no very smooth wear or seal surface, so water simply can drain right through the asphalt's thickness into the ground. An interesting alternative to a traditional concrete driveway is a driveway constructed of either permeable concrete or concrete grid pavers, also called *turf-blocks*. These strong, prefabricated paving blocks have a gridlike structure that enables water to seep through grid holes that can be filled with soil and planted with grass or other ground cover after the blocks are installed (Fig. 34-1). Some contractors will form a few sections of concrete just outside the garage to establish a clear drainage grade away from the garage entrance and in case a steady, smooth support is needed for vehicle maintenance or repairs. Then the rest of the driveway is laid with grid pavers or blocks on a prepared bed similar to that prepared for crushed stone, gravel, brick, and solid-concrete pavers. The grid holes or open cavities also can be filled with small stones, gravel, or similar loose, permeable materials. This "partly open" concrete also can be used for walkways and patios, although it does not offer as smooth a surface for walking—high-heeled shoes may be a tripping hazard on them. With a permeable driveway, walk, or patio, rainwater and snowmelt simply will travel right through to the ground, where natural filtering occurs.

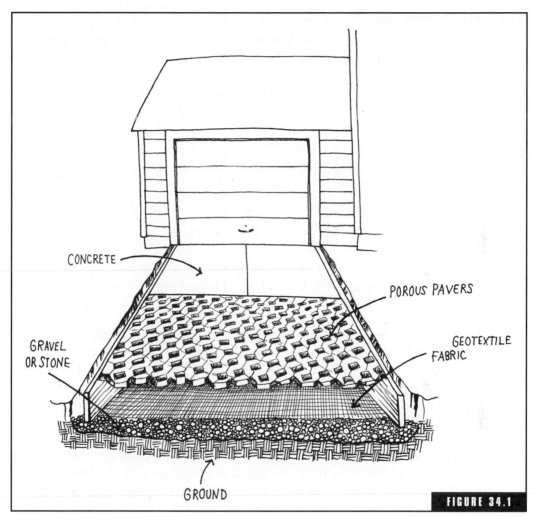

CONCRETE

POROUS PAVERS

GEOTEXTILE FABRIC

GRAVEL OR STONE

GROUND

FIGURE 34.1

Permeable concrete block driveway.

Asphalt Driveways

Asphalt driveways are fairly durable. They can look attractive, and they're generally less expensive than concrete versions. Drawbacks are that they need periodic resealing or they'll deteriorate substantially faster than concrete. Asphalt also softens up during hot temperatures and can be pressed out of shape or indented by heavy vehicles or objects such as the legs of a camper/trailer. Although the black color of asphalt can look very attractive with certain homes, it generally clashes with concrete sidewalks when sidewalks are specified at the front of the property by local building codes.

Concrete Driveways

A concrete driveway is the most permanent and trouble-free driveway you can have. It's durable and strong and can be poured in any configuration desired. It matches concrete sidewalks, steps, and patios nicely. Again, the trouble with traditional concrete driveways is that they're not permeable. However, depending on where they're located, they may not need to be—if their runoff simply goes into a field or large lawn surfaces and not into street gutters and municipal drain lines. In this case, regular concrete installations—with a high percentage of fly ash replacing the regular portland cement—will result in a much greener drive than driveways often just automatically installed with today's new homes.

Driveway Configuration and Location

To a certain extent, these characteristics are determined by the house type, orientation, and position on the building site. Hopefully, you're reading this material *before* you've completed your house and garage so that you can still make any adjustments that are appropriate. Consider the following points when planning your driveway:

1. Make sure that the driveway will be wide enough. This is a safety concern—not a green concern. Naturally, the less driveway, the better. But everyone may not be as safe or as skilled a driver as you are. Measure driveways at other houses to get an idea of what you want. A single-car generously wide drive is usually a minimum of 11 feet wide, with its width at the street (the curb entrance) not less than 17 feet to permit cars to easily turn into and back out of it (Fig. 34.2). If you elect to go with a narrower drive, it might be sufficient to drive a car on, but when visitors have to park on the driveway, they'll have to step out of their vehicles into grass or a planting area. A double driveway should be at least 22 feet wide with an entrance at the street of 28 feet. Where any curvature is involved, a few extra feet of width is desirable to prevent drivers, especially visitors, from driving onto the lawn. Remember, these are suggested guidelines, not rules.

2. Your driveway's length will be determined by your house's setback from the street and by the shape of your driveway's approach: straight, curved, or half-circle. In cold-climate areas, consider that long driveways will have to be plowed out by someone: by you or by a hired plow jockey. Whoever plows will need somewhere to put the snow, too.

3. If your lot is large enough, consider having an automobile turnaround (Fig. 34.3). It takes extra surfacing but offers real convenience. It's difficult to realize how often you come and go by car until you have to back out of a driveway onto a busy street every time. When laid out properly, a turnaround also can serve as a handy parking area for visitors and provide a good spot for car

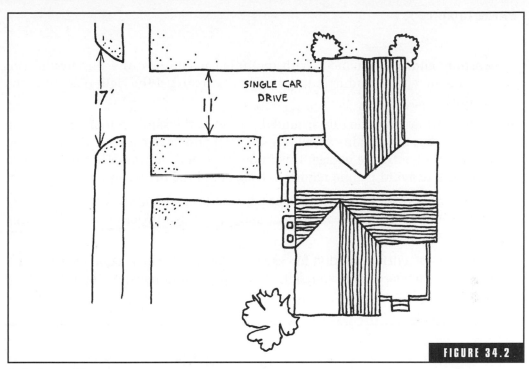

A single-car driveway.

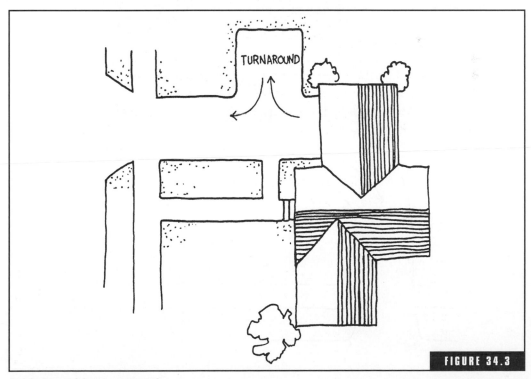

A driveway with a turnaround.

washing and maintenance. With multiple-car families, the turnaround can ease the inevitable and irritating shuffle of cars to get the right one out of the rotation.

4. A step further than the turnaround driveway is the semicircular drive having two accesses to the same street (Fig. 34.4). If you have enough space and you have a front-entrance garage, this in-one-way and out-the-other pattern also can work to avoid people having to back out of the driveway.

5. Garages that open toward a side of a lot are best served by a wide driveway that extends beyond the garage entrance to furnish turnaround and parking space to the rear.

6. Don't accept a driveway that forces you to back out onto a blind curve or hill. It's far too dangerous for yourself, your family, and unsuspecting visitors.

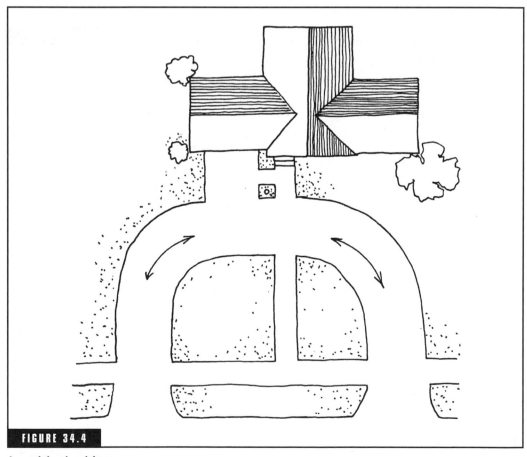

FIGURE 34.4

A semicircular driveway.

7. Should you plan a straight or curved approach to your garage? If you have the option, a curved approach often results in a better appearance. It adds flavor and character to a property.

8. Make sure that the driveway isn't too steep to negotiate safely. This is important in all climates. It's dangerous to constantly keep cars parked on a steep grade—especially when children are in the neighborhood. In addition, it's inconvenient. People can slip on wet or icy sloped pavement. At the same time, don't plan a driveway that slopes down into the garage. It'll provide a runway for rainwater and snowmelt and will be tough to drive up during the winter. If need be, adjust the garage up or down a few blocks.

Regular Driveway Construction Specifications

1. Driveways shouldn't be dug, graveled, and then poured or paved overnight. Rather, it's a two-stage process. First comes the excavation of the ground to permit placement of a base layer of 6 to 10 inches of crushed stone. Next comes the pouring of concrete or laying of blacktop (asphalt) surface layers *after* the base stage has had 8 to 12 months to settle and compact. This waiting period while cars and trucks are compacting the gravel base will result in a more stable concrete or asphalt surface that will show considerably less minor cracking and almost no pavement break-off areas caused by base settling. The waiting period also provides enough time for trouble spots to appear in the base so that they can be repaired before the paving occurs.

2. Have the crushed stone or fill material placed about a foot wider on each side of the driveway than the pavement's eventual width. This prevents undercutting of the slab and subsequent breakage by surface water draining off the driveway.

3. To ensure proper drainage, the driveway must slope away from the garage toward a desired drainage field or the street about 2 or 3 inches downhill for every 10 linear feet of driveway (Fig. 34.5). Of course, this applies only to a typical driveway; for a long, winding driveway, this applies only where it nears the house. If you can't arrange for this much slope on a regular driveway, before the driveway is surfaced, have some fine stone added to the base so that the gravel layer is crowned in the center. An 11-foot-wide drive should have a crowned or raised center that is 2 to 2½ inches high, and a 22-foot-wide drive should have a crown reaching 4 to 5 inches in the center so that water will drain off to the sides. Again, green construction principles pay particular attention to rainwater handling, with the main goal that none of it ever leaves your property, certainly not to enter storm runoff drains.

4. Check out any unusual street problems, such as a fireplug, utility pole, or tree that might be in the way of your driveway. Consider that there could be a city ordinance covering the number, size, and placement of driveway approaches.

FIGURE 34.5

Driveway slope.

5. Where water causes problems around driveways, a length of plastic pipe might help to improve drainage at low spots or water collection points. For instance, if rainwater tends to collect along one side of a driveway, it might cause trouble in the form of surface ice and frost heaving during winter. A length of pipe installed underground, running from a small rock basin at the lowest collection point on one side of the driveway to a screen-covered outlet leading to a natural drainage area on the property on the other side of the driveway, is one way to alleviate the situation (Fig. 34.6).

6. A driveway should be at least 5 inches thick. The builder typically will use 2 × 6s or 1 × 6s to obtain the 5-inch depth, keeping the bottom edges slightly below grade (Fig. 34.7). If permeable concrete will not be used, specify that the contractor use a regular concrete mix containing the concrete producer's recommended highest available fly-ash content for your driveway. This should total up to about a minimum of five and one-half bags of cement/fly-ash mix per cubic yard of concrete.

7. The concrete should have either steel rod or wire mesh running through it for strength. Approximately every 11 feet, a groove should be cut into the concrete to allow the pads room to react to temperature changes and other stressful conditions. Spacer felt—thin strips of felt—should be placed between the individual concrete pads or blocks to allow for contraction and expansion owing to temperature changes.

8. The finish on a concrete drive can be either a swirl or a broomed effect. It's a matter of personal preference.

9. Freshly poured concrete driveways should be barricaded until they cure and have a chance to be coated with a good concrete sealer. As mentioned in Chapter 20 on garages, concrete sealer will prevent the penetration of any oil or grease into the concrete and will make the surface easier to clean.

10. Regular asphalt ideally should be applied in two layers over the stone base. Roughly two-thirds (or 3½ inches) of the total thickness should be laid down as a binder course containing larger stone or aggregate, and then the other third (1½ inches) can be laid on top. The wearing course contains finer material so that it can

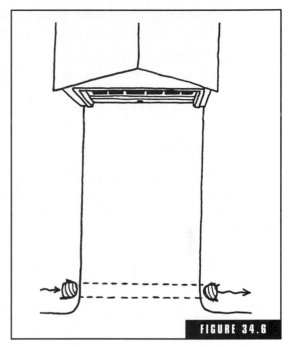

FIGURE 34.6

Driveway drainage.

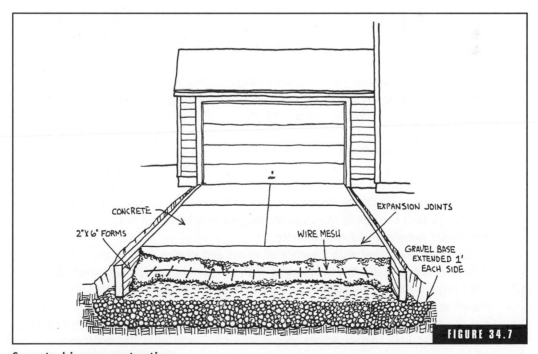

CONCRETE

2"X 6" FORMS

WIRE MESH

EXPANSION JOINTS

GRAVEL BASE EXTENDED 1' EACH SIDE

FIGURE 34.7

Concrete driveway construction.

be tamped and rolled into a smooth, watertight surface. An asphalt driveway also must be sloped so that the rainwater will run where you want it to.

11. Permeable asphalt installations are now available from paving contractors who have been keeping up with green construction guidelines. Although this asphalt is still a heat-attracting black color, at least it allows rainwater and snowmelt to percolate directly through its width to enter the ground below.

SIDEWALKS

Sidewalks are another necessity. You have to get from the driveway to the front, side, and rear entrances somehow. Sidewalks are the accepted, civilized way so that you and your visitors won't have to walk through wet grass or over dusty ground.

Sidewalk Planning

Here are some considerations to help you plan your sidewalks:

CONCRETE INSTALLATION

The following considerations should be reviewed for pouring concrete diveways, sidewalks, patios, mailbox bases, and similar components:

- There should be no presence of groundwater, mud, or soft spots where the pour is being made.
- Half-inch-wide expansion joints must be placed level with the top of the concrete surface. They should be installed between driveway and sidewalk, foundation and driveway/sidewalk, garage and driveway/sidewalk, and individual sections of driveway and sidewalk.
- Unless special precautions are understood and taken by the masonry contractor, try to avoid having concrete poured when temperatures are below 40°F.
- Hot-weather concrete pouring must be managed carefully for rapid drying to prevent cracking that will lessen the strength of the completed job. It makes sense to arrange for pourings in the early morning or very late afternoon, when shade and cooler temperatures are available.
- Concrete can be tinted with a variety of colors and shades such as gray, black, brown, or red to blend in or harmonize with the home's natural surroundings. Ask the contractor to review your options. Numerous textures and patterns also can be achieved with concrete pours—lending the impression of tile or stone without the accompanying installation or maintenance costs of either. Rough-pattern surfaces also help to give driveways and walkways additional slip resistance.

1. Make the lead sidewalk from your driveway to the front entrance steps at least 4 feet wide. Traditional 36-inch-wide sidewalks are fine for side or rear doors, where only one person at a time must be accommodated. Front entrances should be able to be approached by two visitors walking side by side instead of single file.

2. Following the rationale used with driveways, a curved sidewalk adds a certain character and flavor to the appearance of a home (Fig. 34.8).

3. Have adequate lighting along sidewalks, especially where steps are located.

4. Many people are tempted to opt for sidewalks, entrance steps, and patios made of brick, flagstone, masonry, or patio blocks. These materials might sound like a good idea, but they're often more trouble than they're worth. If you go with anything other than concrete, be prepared to do a considerable amount of maintenance work every 2 or 3 years to correct surface deterioration that may occur. If you desire something that looks more unique than concrete, consider some of the results available through concrete finishers—contractors who specialize in staining, etching, scoring, and sealing concrete so that it resembles stone such as marble, slate, tile, or even burnished leather. Also consider, in the long run, how such an unusual finish could influence potential buyers if and when you decide to sell. It's also possible to construct

FIGURE 34.8

A curved sidewalk.

sidewalks out of asphalt, but it's not advisable unless the walk is extremely long and winding, such as a bike path through a wooded area.

Sidewalk Construction

The first step in sidewalk construction (Fig. 34.9) is to excavate the walkway and spread 4 or 5 inches of crushed stone in the excavation, which is to be used as a base layer. The stone base then should be either compacted with a handheld tamping machine or left alone for 6 to 8 months for the ground and gravel to settle naturally. If the ground and stone base are not allowed enough time or compacting effort to settle, the base beneath the sidewalk will sink and move, causing voids that will no longer support the sidewalk in those areas, and cracks or heaved concrete will result. Follow these guidelines:

1. At least 2- by 4-foot lumber should be used to form the sidewalks to provide a 3-inch-thick walk. Permeable concrete or permeable block, brick, or stone constructions similar to those described under the driveway section also will work here.

2. The sidewalk forms should give walks a slight side slope or length slope that falls away from the house for proper rainwater and snowmelt surface drainage (Fig. 34.10).

3. The finish on concrete sidewalks can be either the swirl or the broomed type.

4. As with the garage floor and driveway, make sure that a clear protective sealer is applied over the freshly dried concrete sidewalks.

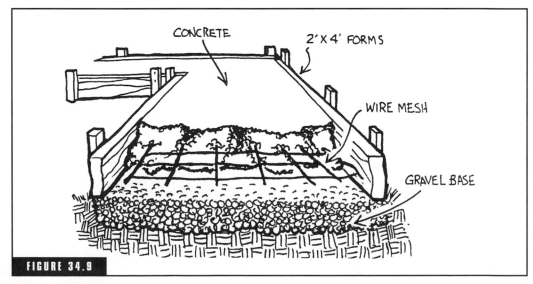

FIGURE 34.9

Sidewalk construction.

FIGURE 34.10

Sidewalk slope.

5. Keep sidewalks above ground level. Don't let weeds and grass sod encroach over sidewalk edges. The surrounding lawn roots should be several inches below the sidewalk surface for easy lawn mowing and a neat appearance.

PATIOS

There are few strict rules when it comes to the size, type, and location of a patio. Some people will find a small concrete patio or wood deck to their liking, positioned off the dining room. Others plan huge, sprawling wood decks that completely encircle their dwelling. Some people like to have roofed-over patios or prefer to close the sides in, too. Certain individuals count on using covered patios year round and will heat them in cold-climate locations.

Patio Planning

Here are some points to consider when planning a patio:

1. The patio is similar to the garage in that it's one of the least expensive parts of a house per square foot of usable area. If you're going to have one, it might as well be a nice roomy one.

2. It's best to construct patios with below-ground footers and foundations so that if you decide to cover it someday, you're sure to have sufficient support and you won't have to worry about it heaving in response to freezing temperatures.

3. Whatever your outdoor patio construction materials are, provide some height to the patio by keeping the patio floor surface at least 4 to 6 inches above the surrounding ground. This will make cleaning much simpler.

4. Consider building in some above-the-floor, raised planter areas, walls, dividers, or other permanent features that will provide horizontal or flat surfaces wide enough for people to sit on comfortably (Fig. 34.11).

FIGURE 34.11

An outdoor patio deck.

5. If a patio is more than a few steps above the ground level, it's advisable that step handrails be installed for safety (Fig. 34.12).

6. Make sure that your patio is positioned properly for privacy and easy access to the living areas of the house, especially the kitchen.

7. Arrange adequate lighting for patio evening use and enjoyment.

8. Unless you plan a year-round enclosed patio, consider what storage facilities you'll be able to use for storing patio furniture, planters, and other seasonal items. If you have the space, one alternative is to construct an outdoor weatherproof closet or storage enclosure adjacent to the patio or near the garage or rear of the house.

FIGURE 34.12

A patio deck with steps and handrails.

Patio Construction

Some green builders are using products made with recycled plastics. Many of these require no stain or sealer and can last 25 years or longer but cannot be recycled and degrade very slowly. Wood composite decking is the most popular alternative to solid wood. It's made with recycled plastic and recycled or virgin wood fibers. The plastic gives the decking rot resistance, whereas the wood gives it strength, ultraviolet protection, and a pleasing texture and appearance. Consider using composite materials in place of all finish (but not structural) elements of a standard deck, and you'll never have to pollute the area with toxins from cleaning agents, stains, or sealants. Some decking products are made with vinyl and offer similar durability to other plastic decking, but the potential risks of polyvinyl chloride (PVC) make it undesirable as a decking material.

If you use cedar or redwood decking or imported hardwoods such as ipe, the only green options are materials from Forest Stewardship Council (FSC)–certified sources or reclaimed lumber. Still, the trouble with any wood is its maintenance and its relatively short useful life—even the most durable wood products cannot match the lengthy life cycles of composite or recycled plastic decking.

There are two primary types of patio foundation constructions: concrete and pressure-treated lumber. A concrete patio employs the idea of a concrete footer below the frost line with a concrete block foundation built up from there. The inside is backfilled and brought up to the top of the foundation with a 12-inch-thick layer of bank gravel. Then a concrete pad reinforced with wire mesh or rod is poured over the top. Once cured, the concrete patio floor should be coated with a good concrete sealant. As with sidewalks, unique finishes are available for patios via concrete staining, etching, scoring, and sealing.

Wood patios or decks have certain attractions to people who like the warm, soft feel and rustic look of wood. Wood also can be stained or painted to match existing color schemes. All wood decks should be constructed with lumber that can withstand the rigors of constant exposure to the weather. This generally means pressure-treated lumber, especially for the structural, load-bearing component such as main posts and deck joists. Before 2004, most pressure-treated lumber was processed with a chemical compound called chromate copper arsenic (CCA) to prevent mold, rot, and insect infestation. By the end of 2003, the Environmental Protection Agency (EPA), following studies that indicated possible leaching of arsenic from the CCA treatment chemicals, banned further use of CCA-treated lumber for most residential uses. This left lumber such as pine, fir, spruce, and larch to be pressure-treated with fairly innocuous chemicals as alternatives. Naturally tough redwood, cypress, and cedar are rather expensive; they're frequently used in many of the more up-scale homes but typically are not quite as durable as the pressure-treated varieties. Treated southern yellow pine is another wood used for outdoor decks, fences, and other landscaping uses. It's a durable type of wood at a bargain price. Always order aboveground grades for lumber that will be used above ground level and belowground grades if it will be used on grade or below. If you're pursuing recycled or reclaimed timbers and happen to come upon some pressure-treated lumber, be aware that it could be CCA-treated and probably is if it's older than 5 or 6 years.

If your patio will be enclosed with treated wood, follow the suggestions given in the preceding paragraph. If it's going to be enclosed as part of the house and covered the same way, then follow the specifications outlined in earlier chapters on interior framing and exterior coverings.

If you plan to go with a treated-lumber deck or enclosure, check into the hardware and fastening devices on the market that are manufactured with rust-resistant metals. They include both galvanized steel and aluminum nails.

The probability of warping will be reduced if spans of railing are kept at or less than 8 feet in length. Built-in benches also will add to the stability.

WOOD DECK CONSIDERATIONS

- To avoid poor matches of deck to ground, wait until the grading and landscaping are complete before wood decks are framed and installed.

- Use premium top-grade lumber. Redwood is strong, with natural oils that help to keep the wood moist so that it doesn't decay quickly. Cedar is also strong and has similar natural oils that maintain moisture and retard decay. Pressure-treated pine, fir, and Douglas fir are less expensive and, if protected against water, will last many years. (Again, if you have located and plan to use older pressurized wood, remember that it may contain arsenic, so it definitely should not be used in areas where it could come into contact with food or where children or pets are left unsupervised to chew on it.) Pressure-treated wood products are available that do not use arsenic yet still resist mold, fungi, and insects. The color is saturated throughout the wood, so periodic staining is not required.

- Galvanized or coated deck screws should be used instead of nails. Screws have greater gripping power; they can pull warped boards into alignment. Screws can be removed easily in the event that individual boards warp or split and need to be replaced.

- Deck boards should have a narrow (⅛-inch) space between each board to allow for ventilation and drainage.

- Posts that support wood decks should not come in contact with saturated soil or standing water. The connections between the posts and deck beams should be covered with flashing to prevent rain or snowmelt from soaking into the end grain of the posts. The tops of concrete support piers should be about 6 inches above ground level to keep the bases of posts dry. Embed post anchors into the piers before the pier concrete dries. The footings for the support posts need to extend below the frost line so that the deck won't heave or move during freezing weather.

■ Strap anchors should be used to fasten the deck beam to the deck's foundation to keep the beam from shifting or sliding and to keep the beam from contacting moist ground. Joist hangers should be the exterior type, galvanized to prevent rusting. Use lag bolts screwed directly into the foundation or floor frame to secure the deck to the house.

■ The seam between the deck and house should be covered with flashing to prevent water from settling into the crack and rotting the side of the home.

■ Rain, melting snow, and other moisture can penetrate untreated wood fibers so that the wood expands and warps, and mold, mildew, and algae can grow. Then some of the wood can start rotting, and as moisture evaporates, some of the wood can dry out, contract, or shrink and may develop long splits and cracks. To prevent this from happening, wood should be treated with preservatives to penetrate the wood and help to make it resistant to biological damage. Good water repellents also will help to keep wood sound by keeping water contraction and expansion cycles at bay. For best results, the wood should be completely dry before preservatives and penetrating water-repellent treatments are applied so that those materials will soak into the wood. Once the boards air dry, they should be further coated with two treatments of a water-resistant coating, the second treatment to be applied after the first dries.

■ After the initial waterproofing and preserving treatments are applied, waterproofing stains or sealers with ultraviolet light absorbers can be reapplied yearly.

■ If a permanent gas grill will be installed near the finished deck, arrange for a gas grill line in advance.

▷▷▷▷▷▷ POINTS TO PONDER

1. Avoid planning a driveway that forces you to back out on a highway, blind curve, or hill.

2. Whenever possible, have a gradual slope on a driveway—not a steep slope.

3. Wait 8 to 12 months after a driveway has been stoned, used, and compacted before laying down the permanent driveway construction material, be it stone, gravel, brick, asphalt, or concrete.

4. Keep driveway and sidewalk surfaces above ground level; make sure that there is a slight runoff slope (away from the home) to rid driveways and walks of water.

5. Make sure that ½-inch expansion joints are strategically located in concrete drives, walks, and patios.

6. Front lead sidewalks should be at least 4 feet wide, and side or rear walks, 3 feet wide.

7. Generally, curved driveways and sidewalks tend to be more interesting and attractive than straight accesses.

8. If you're going to have a patio or deck, consider making it even larger than you first thought it should be.

9. Patios and decks need to be supported below the frost line to remain level and solid and so that freeze/thaw cycles won't cause them to heave.

10. Use only the best grades of deck lumber, fasteners (galvanized or other non-rusting deck screws), and hardware.

Who Should Build It?

Depending on your strategy, either you've jumped ahead to this chapter after reading earlier chapters and you've decided that the builder—or team you're putting together—should be enlisted early in the design phase, which should be the case, especially with green construction, or you're comfortable enough with the rest of the process, including matching the dwelling to a site, orienting the home on the site, and overseeing, with perhaps some help from green planners, the entire design and contractor selection. In any case, this chapter comments on the selection of a general contractor or the main builder of your home. Previously, this chapter introduced a number of builder types when green meant an entirely different thing—a builder new to the general contractor trade.

Therefore, if you already know which house you want, and you have a fair idea of how it should be put together, and you think you know where you want it built, it's time to find a contractor. Finding the right contractor is a task to be taken seriously. To make the entire house-building process a pleasant and rewarding experience, it's paramount to select only an established, skilled, reliable builder who knows what he or she is doing and who's satisfied many previous clients. It also would be helpful if the builder is familiar with or has worked building Energy Star–rated homes or with other good programs such as the National Association of Home Builders (NAHB) *Model Green Home Building Guidelines* or the Leadership in Energy and Environmental Design (LEED) for Homes (LEED-H) standard developed by the U.S. Green Building Council and is up on green construction features and equipment and has employed subcontractors who have done the same. If a contractor has not become familiar with or associated with those or similar programs, this doesn't mean that he or she cannot build a successful green home. Once found, there are ways to work along with a builder that will virtually ensure that a helpful and trusting give-and-take relationship develops.

Selecting a Contractor

By now you should relax and pat yourself on the back. Surely you are miles ahead of most people who will, regretfully, *begin* by selecting a contractor as their initial step toward acquiring a new house. Consider that these trusting souls choose a contractor without really knowing which house would be best, without understanding building jargon, and without realizing the degree to which they can and should participate in the planning of their new home. Also, they have little knowledge of which questions to ask the builder and often spend time and energy worrying about practically meaningless—at least to the overall worth and enjoyment of the house—details. Rather, they are likely to be led by the nose into purchasing a house that is merely convenient and cost-efficient for the contractor to build instead of a customized compatible house that will provide them with more living enjoyment and value for their money.

But you, by now, understand what houses are all about. You have the knowledge to be able to make the correct choices between the various types of homes that will best suit your needs. You know their advantages and disadvantages and how each will affect your own situation. Such information is clearly required to arrive at an intelligent decision. It's a personal thing, the planning and erecting of a house, and to do it right, you needed to consider the pros and cons of traffic patterns, floor plans, and even certain building materials. You needed to understand, at least in a fun, general way, how and even why a house is constructed the way it is. You needed to know the importance of the drawings and prints and about low-grade or minimum-spec materials and construction methods that are being pushed at the unwary by a certain percentage of contractors. And you need to understand why quality materials and methods should be insisted on at contract time.

Thus, in a sense, you've already completed your most critical homework. You know what you want to build. Now you have to determine *who* you want to build it. Select a minimum of four potential contractors from whom you will solicit competitive bids, and then narrow those builders down to one. Of course, at this point, you still might not have located a suitable building site, but that can come later.

Be aware that you are on the verge of entering into a unique relationship that should be mutually rewarding with an individual or a large company or corporation in business to build houses. The contractor thus will be a pivotal figure around which the success or failure of your house-building project can occur. Anyone who thinks about the possible consequences—good or bad—will agree that it's a relationship that must be entered into carefully, not formed on the basis of skimpy information or a casual referral. Ask any real estate agent, housing inspector, or mortgage lending officer what the overriding reasons for bad houses are, and you'll likely as not receive an answer blaming inept or dishonest builders.

Naturally, builders vary in quality, just like individuals in any profession. You have good doctors and bad, capable attorneys and incompetent ones, and you have skilled, sincere builders and shysters. Be aware that although the proportion of good, skillful, and reliable builders is high—just as in the rest of the professions—there seem to be a disproportionally large number of shoddy houses or marginal-quality homes being built by a relatively few inept or dishonest builders who lend their calling a bad name and draw a lot of harmful publicity to their field.

BUILDER TYPES

Because it's so important to make a correct choice when selecting a builder—you certainly don't want to change builders in midstream—here are the major types of builders you're likely to encounter while searching through the marketplace.

Established, Skilled, Reputable Builders

First and foremost are the established, skilled, and reputable builders. This can mean a large company, a middle-size company, a small company, or a partnership. It also can mean a one-person operation. The larger established, reputable builders are "old faithful" contractors who are often associated with prestigious, well-planned subdivisions and also might have built rental complexes along the way. These contractors have been building houses for years, and they tend to specialize in certain types, styles, and price ranges, leaning toward middle to most expensive houses in an area. These builders are so well respected that real estate agents even use the contractors' names in advertising, as a "Bebell Ranch" or a "Luciano Two-Story."

Other highly respected builders specialize in low- to midpriced houses. They've learned how to build as much quality as possible into their dwellings for the lowest possible cost. They purchase large quantities of similar materials at a discount and use the same items in all their homes. They build on less expensive lots. Their floor plans tend to be smaller and simpler. These builders are exceptionally good at the range of homes they're working in, and the need for their product is great. Builders of inexpensive houses frequently work with customers who cannot afford much but who can take advantage of government assistance and financing programs; consequently, these contractors can be very good at creative financing.

All these builders are proven pros. They have the building skills, the business acumen, and the people skills needed to survive in their cutthroat, vicious, tumultuous trade. The established builders have seen it all. They're aware of mortgage financing options, of decorating styles, of landscaping solutions, and of energy-saving ideas. And if they don't build a good, solid house and back it up with professional service, the word will get around. It spreads through the business community like wildfire. Real estate agents will "talk up" for resale the houses built by reputable contractors, boasting so much that they will even raise the market value of such houses in the same way that name-brand recognition will bring more for a supermarket product.

This established, skilled, and reputable builder category also includes those "semiretired" individuals who build only a few quality houses per year, methodically walking around with burnished cherry pipes, slowly and surely, with few wasted motions, constructing most of the house themselves, stick by stick, often with the home buyer helping as a laborer to reduce costs. This type of builder can take a long time to complete a house, but it's worth it if the home buyer can wait. The most specialized parts, such as the foundation, roof, plumbing, and electrical systems, are often subcontracted out. The rest of the house is frequently charged in a cost-plus arrangement, with the builder receiving an hourly wage and the cost of all materials used. It's a good alternative for people who like a lot of individual attention and contact with their builder and who most definitely aren't in a big hurry.

New Skilled Builders

Next come the relatively new skilled builders with good intentions who have recently begun building houses on their own. These are individuals trying to make a name for themselves who have probably "paid their dues" while working for the builders just described—the ones who already have become established and reputable. In fact, these newer skilled contractors are where the established and reputable builders come from.

At first, the new skilled builders are happy to build a handful of dwellings per year and might well build them as soundly as their previous employer. What many of the new skilled builders lack, however, in addition to a proven, solid reputation, are the financial reserves to weather bad times and costly errors, not to mention the ability to run the business end of construction as the artistic science it is. They can be likened to flamboyant baseball rookies coming up through the farm system. Some of them who might be productive initially will fail to weather the distance. These builders often construct their own houses and those of relatives and close friends to get a start and to have finished houses to show potential clients.

Marginal New Builders

The third major type of contractor is the marginal new builder. Note that you won't find any marginal *established* builders around because the very definition defies longevity. These are builders who begin by remodeling their own kitchens or helping someone else do theirs. They might have worked a summer or two on a framing crew or putting up roofs for a good builder before one day deciding to paint their name on a truck, get an answering machine, and run an ad in the classifieds. They could enlist the support of a relative who happens to work for a real estate agency.

These are the "contractors" who aren't all that concerned with erecting a quality house. They keep a disheveled building site and hire the kinds of workers who drink beer on the job and casually toss empty cans and bottles into the foundation excavation. They'd never dream of parting with the dues to join a local builder's organization or chapter of the National Association of Home Builders. They can afford to keep their prices competitive, though, because they tend to build on inexpensive lots, purchase marginal-quality materials, employ construction method shortcuts, and build simple, no-frills floor plans. These are builders who are more interested in making a profit than ensuring customer satisfaction. They might not be dishonest (or they don't mean to be), but they don't have the necessary skills, business sense, and reputation as the first or even the second type of builder. A new company formed specifically to develop a large piece of raw land into a subdivision could fall into this category. These individuals, although they might believe that they are skilled builders and can talk a good game, should not be relied on to come through with a quality house.

Inept, Dishonest Builders

The fourth and last major builder category is that of the inept, dishonest builders. A. M. Watkins, author of a number of fine books on house buying, house planning, and home maintenance, refers to these, the worst kind of contractors, as "vanishing builders." "Vanishing" is an appropriate monicker because even shortly after these builders erect a house, no matter if small or large problems arise, they simply disappear from the scene.

The vanishing builders are the ones you *must* guard against. They might seem completely trustworthy when first approached, and even when a house is completed, everything might look in order—but just try to get them back to take care of a downspout that comes loose from a gutter or, heaven forbid, a major problem such as a leaky roof or basement. Vanishing builders live up to their name and allow their customers no recourse, no means of exacting repair or retribution.

The reasons for these builders' disappearances are legion and their excuses many. They might have simply pulled up stakes and departed for a more favorable climate. They might have disbanded and gone back to work for someone else because they couldn't take the headaches that come with self-employment. Their phone numbers are likely to be disconnected or changed and unlisted. Or they might declare bankruptcy.

In any event, these builders have neither the skills nor the intentions needed to become established, reputable contractors. They chase the fast dollar. Even the best scenarios will find the vanishing builders starting out as subcontractor helpers who understand the basics of how houses are constructed, observe that successful builders earn a good living, and long for a piece of the action. Several form a partnership and paint their names on their trucks and boom-build a house or two for unsuspecting friends (who don't remain friends for long) and later for gullible relatives. At first, the vanishing builders take care in their initial few houses so that they have something they think is nice to show potential customers, and then, when competitively quoting, they give low bids, get several jobs, and begin building the houses. They select subcontractors they have been friends with and aren't firm enough to make them do a good job, so the subcontractors make mistakes that don't show up until later—such as a cellar wall that collapses inward because it isn't properly supported. Meanwhile, the vanishing builders, after running into irate customers, zoning problems, unreliable subcontractors, slow building periods owing to the economy, weather delays, and expert competition from the skilled established and new contractors, cannot last.

In fact, few vanishing builders even know how much money they will make on a particular house. They might actually bid—without fully realizing their expenses—less than it costs them to construct the dwelling. No company, no matter how skilled at building houses, can last or exist unless it generates a fair profit.

Sometimes vanishing builders find backers who put up front money for land they hope to develop. Together the vanishing builders and their representatives can be flashy individuals with persuasive sales skills and wildly inaccurate promises. These people don't care about the satisfaction and security gained by developing a good reputation in the community. Chances are that they won't be around long. This can be exceptionally irritating to the home buyers who invest in the first few houses in a promised subdivision that never quite gets off the ground and is saddled with unfinished roads, inadequate utilities, and surroundings scarred by bulldozers—all from poor overall planning.

Now that you know what kinds of contractors are out there, you should be able to decide on which ones you'll consider. If possible, discount the latter two: the new marginal builder and the inept dishonest builder. This leaves the established, skilled, and reputable builder and the skilled new builder. The first one is a sure thing. Go with one of them, and you'll be guaranteed (or just about) a satisfying, well-constructed dwelling that the builder will stand behind. Go with the newer builder, and you're running a risk, however calculated, that something *could* happen to put that builder out of business in the near future.

Certain factors could influence you to go with a newer builder despite the increased risk. Perhaps you know one personally. Or perhaps you prefer to work with someone closer to your own age. Maybe the builder has bid substantially lower than the established builders on the exact same specifications. All good builders were new contractors when they started, and if you believe one such builder is a rising star on the local scene, fine.

On the other hand, consider that relatively few builders starting out will have the staying power to make a long-range success in the business. Competition is tough, and the home marketplace is not very forgiving. It certainly takes a while to develop the depth of resources, the tricks of the trade, the knowledge of how to handle customers, the required contacts with subcontractors and housing inspectors, and the convenient credit lines at building-material supply houses.

On yet another hand, if you happen to hear that any builder you are considering is being sued for something, it doesn't necessarily mean that the builder is dishonest or incompetent. At one point or another, even the best, most trustworthy, most reliable builders are likely to become involved with some kind of legal actions brought on by unreasonable customers or conditions beyond their control.

THE GREEN FACTOR

Now, to those four groups of builders just discussed, add the current green construction movement as another factor to consider, as another set of skills in the toolkits. You really need to sort through the contractor groups to look for a combination of both sets of skills—the traditional experience of the many facets of home construction and the new green sets of guidelines that have been working their way to the forefront of home building. Because you know that your home will involve green construction, you might as well sort for that factor first—and then decide on which green home contractor would best fit your situation. After you narrow your list down to builders with the proven potential to build green, you can go about using the traditional methods of deciding on which of those would be best for you. How do you screen for green? Through questions and research.

If you've gone through this book and other publications that review main guidelines on green construction, you'll be versed enough to quickly realize—from listening to answers to key green construction questions—whether a contractor is truly knowledgeable and experienced in building green homes. There are lots of questions that can be asked. Here are some you can use in your initial discussions. Ask them verbatim, or paraphrase certain ones in your own words. Remember, you're paying the bill here. You've got the right ultimately to look for not only a skilled, reliable builder but also one who knows how (and wants) to build green into a project. Some of the following questions may stump even the greenest builder because they may be better answered to the degree of detail you're looking for by subcontractor green specialists the builder uses. As long as the builder readily comes up with pertinent scenarios about subcontractors and related green work he or she has contributed to in past projects, that should suffice.

Green Questions for Potential Builders (or Designers or Architects)

- What does green building mean to you?

- What separates a green project from a similar project that is not green?

- Are you active in the green building movement?

- Where do you get your information for green construction?

- When and where was the last green construction training session or function you attended?

- Can you tell me about any green homes you've completed?

- Do you follow the guidelines of a specific green program? Which one, and why?

- Are you a recognized Energy Star contractor?

- Do you use subcontractors who have worked on green projects and can you supply examples?

- What do you think of advanced framing techniques, structural insulated panels, insulated concrete forms, knee trusses, and other similar green building components?

- Do you avoid the use of building products with high volatile organic compounds (VOCs) and formaldehyde?

- Do you insist on using only certified, engineered, or composite and alternate woods such as bamboo?

- What kinds of windows do you recommend?

- Who have you worked with in the past? Green designers? Architects? Building teams?

- What can you tell me about the importance of house orientation?

- How do you approach reducing construction waste on site?

- What steps do you take to minimize the site disturbance during construction?

- How do you supervise and make sure that your subcontractors do what they're supposed to?

- How do you plan to protect the site's groundwater during and after construction?

- Have you employed the three R's on previous projects: reduce, reuse, and recycle?

- Are there any green features that you particularly specialize in providing?

- What passive-solar features have you constructed?

- Do you include any features to conserve water, such as reduced-flow faucets and showerheads, low-flush toilets, rain capturing, graywater systems, or landscaping with native plants?

- Have any of your homes contained sustainable-energy generation components or systems?

- Do you verify indoor air quality, ventilation, and air infiltration efficiency after construction? What kind of performance tests do you complete?

- How will you set me up for the use of my home and its components? Will I get a binder with all the related contacts and information I'll need to contact manufacturers and installers?

SELECTING YOUR BIDDING CONTRACTORS

When approaching contractors for bids on your house, three contractors with passing green résumés—if you can find them in your area—are a good number of builders to insist on. If you would choose only two, they *could* be two of the highest bidders available. With three, at least one of them is likely to be significantly lower. And builders, no matter what they say, are influenced by particulars such as the amount of work they already have waiting for them, if they're familiar with and prefer to build the floor plan in question, the time of year, and a host of idiosyncratic reasons too varied to list. In any event, let at least three contractors submit bids: the three you feel are the cream of the crop. This doesn't mean that you can't go to more than three. Go ahead if you have the inclination, time, and energy. On the whole, however, three will give you a good representation.

While deciding which contractors to select as your bidders, find out what you can about the likely candidates by investigating them in the following manner:

1. *Ask real estate brokers and associates.* However, be careful to ask only established real estate people. They know who builds the best houses and who gives the best service. They'll give you excellent leads that you can follow up on beforehand in terms of what type of house you're looking to build, what price range, and if possible, potential setting (rural or city).

2. *Ask bankers and lending officers.* They know which contractors to avoid and also can refer you to reputable builders. Financial people tend to be slightly more objective than real estate agents, but they also can have slightly less knowledge about current construction particulars in the community.

3. *Ask building-material suppliers and subcontractors*, especially plumbers, electricians, roofers, and siding contractors. If they hedge, tell them you'll keep the information confidential. These individuals know which builders are erecting a lot of homes and which builders are floundering (not paying or unable to pay their bills). They know which builders go with quality materials and which keep coming back for marginal or poor-quality supplies.

4. *Inquire at local chapters of the National Association of Home Builders (NAHB), the Chamber of Commerce, and the Better Business Bureau.* The NAHB is a good place to start. It's a sharp organization that encourages builders to keep up with the latest designs and technology. More often than not, if you describe the type of house you're planning and the approximate cost, the representative (probably a local builder) will shuffle his or her feet and in a low voice suggest a few possibilities—but not officially, of course. The representative probably will give you a membership listing and speak "off the record" in order not to ignore and slight other members by making a publicized referral. For a builder, being a member of an organization such as the NAHB is a plus, but it needn't be mandatory for your purposes.

5. *Follow up your leads and meet the builders.* Select the first candidate, call him or her at his or her place of business, and identify yourself as a potential customer who would like to meet him or her for a few minutes (it's important to stress a few minutes because as you'll quickly find out, builders are extremely busy people). Preferably, meet at his or her office so that you can see firsthand how he or she takes care of the business end of the work. Find out how long he or she has been a contractor, how he or she prefers to work with customers, and what warranties and guarantees he or she makes. What responsibility does the builder assume for subcontractors he or she will hire? Ask for a list of previous houses he or she built from five years ago to the present. Naturally, he or she is not going to steer you to any trouble spots, but any example will be helpful to gauge the quality of the work.

At this point, don't supply a lot of detailed information about the house you want to build. Tell the builder the type, the size, and perhaps a general idea of the floor plan. It's a bad sign if a builder has jumped in and out of several construction companies during the past year or two, if he or she has changed the company's name several times, or if he or she went from a one-person operation to a partnership to a corporation and then back to a one-person show again. A frequent indicator of pride in workmanship (but not 100 percent accurate) is that most good, reputable builders use their names in their company's title.

Ask the builder to tell you what makes his or her houses unique. Don't just listen for green details. How are the builder's homes constructed? What are their selling features? Is one of them attention to detail? The quality of workmanship? Is it energy efficiency using the latest technological advances? Let the builder prove to you why you should consider his or her organization. If the builder is close-mouthed, irritated, and short of patience with you, it could mean one of two things: That's just his or her basic personality, or he or she is not thrilled about receiving the work. If it's the former, remember that if your personality doesn't mesh with the builder's, the relationship probably will be an uncomfortable one. If the latter, maybe he or she has got all the work he or she can handle already, and if so, the bid likely will be high anyway. You're usually better off considering only contractors with whom you can develop an open, friendly rapport and who also seem to really want the work.

6. Now it's time to start looking at some of the houses the builders have erected recently. Attend any of their open houses you can find, and tour some of the examples you've been given as references. It's also a good idea to visit a few open houses constructed by builders you've been told to steer clear of in order to get a firsthand look at marginal or poor construction. Using the information you've learned so far, you can rate the houses you visit and see how they stack up against one another.

7. Contact some of each contractor's past customers. Building a house is a big deal. You want to select someone who will listen to any problems that crop up later, *after* the house is finished and the builder has been paid. Ask the owners of several of his or her houses how the builder followed up on problems that might have occurred. Did the builder act promptly and courteously on anything that needed to be replaced or repaired? Were the owners satisfied with the construction results and after-sale services? Even total strangers like to talk about their houses when approached in a low-key kind of way. From them, you can receive lengthy outpourings of information.

   Don't discuss the houses with the owners while a contractor is present or you'll get clouded information. Owners won't speak freely for fear of insulting or making the contractor angry. If you have to, go back at another time, alone.

8. Have the contractor take you through one of his or her brand-new or under-construction houses. This is only after scoring him or her high on the referrals, the personal interview, and the quality of the construction. If possible, have the builder take you through a house that is similar to the one you are planning. Let him or her do most of the talking. Let him or her demonstrate why you would be better off going with his or her services instead of somebody else.

   Visiting the contractor's job site also will tell you much about his or her construction habits. If the place is messy and disorganized, it's reasonable to wonder whether he or she should be trusted to handle your house.

9. Find out if any of the potential contractors possess traits that would give them advantages over other builders. Do any of them own lumber-supply stores or any other building-supply companies? If this is the case, you might be able to obtain lumber, windows, insulation, fixtures, siding, and roofing at or very close to cost. Do any of the builders own land that you'd consider ideal for your building site? Or will any of them provide their own financing at below-open-market rates and terms?

SOLICITING THE BIDS

Now it's time to take the three or more contractors you select and go to them with your drawings, sketches, specifications, and ideas, and ask them to figure out prices for you. Don't go to your bid meetings unprepared. Instead, make up a copy of what specifications you'd like, and have one for yourself and one for each builder. Give a copy to each of the three or more builders who are in the bidding process for your house so that they're all bidding on the same job.

At the end of this chapter is a sample listing of individual specifications for a 2,400-square-foot two-story house with an attached two-car garage. It contains references to the kinds of specifications with which you should be concerned. You can make up a similar set of your own before you approach your builders for bids and later revise it with input from the builder or design team to be used in the final building agreement.

Now all you do is wait for the bids to come back for evaluation. Chances are that at least two of them will be significantly lower than the other and will warrant your closest inspection. Are they talking apples to apples? Review their quotes with the contractors in person to clarify any points that are confusing or too general.

When your evaluations are through, just pick one, the contractor who you think you should go with based on his or her bid, reputation, construction examples, and any other factors you're considering. If you've done your homework already, any of the builders you asked to bid would be a safe choice.

Choosing a good contractor will save you money, make you money, and ensure peace of mind and a comfortable, well-built home. It will make the entire house-building experience fun. Selecting a wrong contractor definitely will cost you more money and even could destroy your sanity and faith in humankind.

Before we're off the subject, here are a few additional dos and don'ts to remember when dealing with the selection of your contractor:

1. Hire someone who is based out of town as a last resort.

2. Don't hire a contractor based on price alone.

3. Do be suspicious of extremely low bids. A bid that is miles away from the rest could mean that the builder doesn't know the business costs or that a fraudulent

builder is counting on breaking the contract midway through construction by enticing you to change some small detail—consequently rendering the agreement null and void. Once that happens, the builder will renegotiate, charging you additional costs and blackmailing you into accepting either more house or more costs than you originally bargained for.

4. Don't accept oral agreements. Get specifications in writing.

5. Don't believe that you're going to get excellent construction at discount prices. The best you should hope for is sound value at a fair price.

6. Do avoid the marginal and vanishing builders like the plague.

7. Lastly, you need not eliminate a builder solely because he or she does not have much green construction experience. Every builder has to start building green somewhere. If everything else about the builder sounds right, including his or her homework, written plan, past references, and supporting cast of designers and subcontractors, you may be able to get a great house at a reduced "let me use it to show others" price.

AFTER YOU'VE SELECTED YOUR CONTRACTOR

After you've selected your contractor, it's smart to call the unsuccessful bidders and tell them they didn't get the job. Not many people have the courage or consideration to do so, but the contractors will appreciate your honesty and straightforwardness.

On the following pages you'll find a sample checklist of frequently chosen specifications. Your final specification checklist should cover as many details as possible and can include greener specifications that you and your planning team decide on. Giving a detailed specification sheet to the contractor will allow for more complete and accurate bid comparisons.

REMODELING NOTES

Selecting a contractor for a remodeling project can be a difficult job. During times of prosperity, often the better contractors fill their schedules with new construction and higher-end building tasks and don't like to spend time on smaller jobs. Remodeling projects consequently may have to be done by "handyman" types owing to the all-inclusive nature of small remodeling activities that require a variety of relatively minor (but important) plumbing, electrical, carpentry, and finishing tasks, as well as the gathering of numerous parts and materials when prework time requirements are added in, such as on-site meetings for the job, the measuring, the verification of mechanical parts needed (Will components be large enough? Will they fit?). Automatically using home-repair and supply-store repre-

SPECIFICATION CHECKLIST

FOUNDATION:

1. Footers

____ 12- by 24-inch footer; concrete mix
Specification strength of 3,500 psi

2. Foundation wall

____ 10-inch concrete blocks
11 blocks high
Reinforced with ⅝-inch steel rods and cement
filled in holes every other block
Specify number of pilasters

3. Basement floor

____ Concrete slab
____ 8 inches of gravel under slab
____ 4-inch-thick concrete slab

4. Footer drains

____ 4-inch plastic pipe in gravel

5. Supports

____ Specify size of steel I beam
____ Specify size of steel columns

6. Windows

____ Steel (2); specify size

7. Sills

____ 2 by 10 inches
____ ¼-inch foam under sill plate
____ Specify size of bolts for anchors

FLOORING:

1. Floor framing

____ SPF 2 by 10 inches
____ Bridging 1 by 3 inches

2. Subflooring

____ Plywood 4- by 8-foot ½-inch CDX
First and second floor
Right angles
Glued and screwed to floor joists

3. Finish flooring

First floor

____ ⅝-inch particleboard (screwed), all rooms
15-pound felt between layers

Second floor

____ ⅝-inch particleboard (screwed), all rooms
15-pound felt between layers

4. Ceiling framing

____ SPF 2 by 10 feet, second floor bridging 1 by
3 inches

(Continued)

✔✔✔✔✔ **SPECIFICATION CHECKLIST** (*Continued*)

EXTERIOR WALLS:

1. Wood frame
   - ___ No. 2 BTR SPF 2 by 6 inches (16 inches on center)
   - ___ Plywood (½ inch thick)
   - ___ House wrap covering
   - ___ Vinyl or aluminum siding (color), grade A, bevel type, double 4 (8 inches), woodgrain-finish
   - ___ Aluminum nails
   - ___ 6-inch fiberglass insulation
   - ___ Outside cellwood shutters, front only color: smoke
   - ___ 12-inch overhangs

INSIDE WALLS:
   - ___ SPF 2 by 4 feet (16 inches on center)
   - ___ ⅝-inch drywall walls
   - ___ Oak trim throughout (stain, sealer, varnish)

ROOF FRAMING:
   - ___ Engineered wood I-beam roof rafter, joists (16 inches on center)

ROOFING:
   - ___ Solid plywood 4 by 8 feet by ¾ inch CDX
   - ___ Asphalt shingles, 250-pound
   - ___ 15-pound waterproof felt under shingles
   - ___ Tin flashing
   - ___ Ridge and soffit vents

GUTTERS AND DOWNSPOUTS:

1. Gutters
   - ___ Aluminum, 0.025 gauge, 4-inch size, shape style k

2. Downspouts
   - ___ Aluminum, 0.025 gauge, 4-inch size
     Shape—square corrugated, rectangular
     Four drops total

INSULATION:
   - ___ Ceilings: 10-inch fiberglass; walls: 6-inch fiberglass

MISCELLANEOUS:

1. Closets
   - ___ 2 rods/2 shelves per closet

2. Other on-site improvements
   - ___ Rough grading only

3. Landscaping and finish grading
   - ___ By owner

SPECIFICATION CHECKLIST *(Continued)*

4. Walks and driveway ____ Quote separate price for this, 6-inch-thick with mesh and rod reinforcement

5. Hardware (doors) ____ Brass

INTERIOR DOORS AND TRIM:

1. Doors ____ Flush
Oak
1⅜ inches thick with 3 hinges

2. Door trim ____ Modern
Oak

3. Base ____ Modern
Oak
3-inch size

4. Finish ____ Doors and trim, stain, sealer, varnish

5. Dining room: ____ Chair rail

WINDOWS:

1. Double-hung and casement ____ Fiberglass
____ Sash thickness 1⅜ inches
____ Insulated grade with glazed low-e glass
____ Head flashing (vinyl)
____ Weather stripping (vinyl)
____ Triple-track storm windows on the outside
____ Oak trim (stain, sealer, varnish)

ENTRANCES AND EXTERIOR DETAIL:

1. Main entrance door ____ Steel
____ 36 inches wide
____ 1¾ inches thick with 3 hinges
____ White pine for frame

2. Garage overhead doors ____ Steel insulated, two 9- by 7-foot doors with weather stripping

3. Garage entrance door ____ Steel
____ 36 inches wide
____ 1¾ inches thick with 3 hinges
____ White pine for frame
____ Head flashing (aluminum)

(Continued)

✔✔✔✔✔ SPECIFICATION CHECKLIST (*Continued*)

	___ Weather stripping (vinyl)
4. Family room door	___ Double French door
	___ Center-hinged door with screen
EXTERIOR MILLWORK:	___ Aluminum (vented) roof louvers
ELECTRICAL WIRING:	
1. General:	___ Circuit breaker
	___ Specify amp capacity
	___ 24 circuits
	___ All copper cable
	___ Air-conditioning connection
	___ Washer and dryer hookup in laundry room
	___ Provisions for a sump pump hookup
	___ Provisions for garage door openers
	___ Provisions for an overhead fan in the family room
	___ Doorbell (front door and side garage door)
	___ 3 exterior outlets (2 front and 1 back)
	___ Dimmer switch for dining room, family room, and eating area
	___ Humidifier hookup on furnace
	___ Freezer outlet in basement
2. Bathroom no. 1	___ Light over vanity
	___ Exhaust fan
	___ Ground-fault circuit interrupter outlet
3. Bathroom no. 2	___ Light over vanity
	___ Light/exhaust/heat fan
	___ Ground-fault circuit interrupter outlet
4. Bathroom no. 3:	___ Light over vanity
	___ Light/exhaust fan
	___ Ground-fault circuit interrupter outlet
5. Outside lighting	___ 1 at side garage door
	___ 2 at sides of large garage door
	___ 2 at front door
	___ 2 at back sliding doors
6. Inside lighting	___ 3 recessed lights over fireplace
	___ 1 in eating area

SPECIFICATION CHECKLIST (*Continued*) ✔✔✔✔✔

	___ 1 in kitchen
	___ 1 over kitchen sink
	___ 1 in entrance foyer
	___ 2 inside garage
	___ 2 in second-floor hallway
	___ 3 (one in each bedroom)
	___ 1 in dining room
	___ 1 over countertop
	___ 1 inside each clothes closet
7. Kitchen	___ Exhaust fan and light (hood over range)

PLUMBING:

1. General:	___ All copper water pipes
	___ PVC drain pipes
	___ Cast-iron piping below cellar
	___ Washer hookup with sink in laundry room
	___ 3 exterior faucets (back of house, front of house, and in garage)
	___ Provisions for a complete bath in basement (sink, shower, toilet)
	___ Gas line and electric power for laundry room dryer
	___ Glass-lined gas water heater (50 gallons)
	___ Gas hookup for stove in kitchen
	___ Gas starter in fireplace
	___ Gas line for furnace
	___ Dishwasher hookup in kitchen
	___ Water hookup for humidifier on furnace
2. Kitchen	___ Stainless steel double sink
	___ Single-lever faucet with spray
3. Bathroom no. 1	___ Sink and toilet with insuliner (first-floor half bath) (specify color of sink and toilet)
	___ Faucet
4. Bathroom no. 2	___ Sink and toilet with insuliner (second-floor full bath) (specify color of sink and toilet)
	___ Fiberglass tub/shower combo (5 feet) (color)
	___ Faucet
	___ Showerhead to have pressure-balancing safety valve

(*Continued*)

✔✔✔✔✔ SPECIFICATION CHECKLIST (*Continued*)

5. Bathroom no. 3
___ Sink and toilet with insuliner (master bedroom full bath) (specify color of sink and toilet)
___ Faucet
___ Fiberglass shower stall with door (4 feet) (color)
___ Showerhead to have pressure-balancing safety valve

HEATING:
___ Natural gas
___ Fan-forced, two-stage, variable-speed blower
___ Perimeter system
___ Galvanized steel ducts, supply and return furnace ducts to have 2-inch-thick insulation
___ Minimum of 2,400 square feet heating capacity
___ Electric start with pilotless ignition

COOLING:
___ Multilevel cooling, variable-speed indoor blower

PORCHES:
___ Concrete front porch, 1 pillar

GARAGE:
___ Framed as house
4-inch concrete floor, with slope to floor drain

FLOOR COVERING:
___ Carpet to be responsibility of buyer
Kitchen and eating area; foyer; baths 1, 2, 3: inlaid linoleum

BATHROOM ACCESSORIES:
___ Recessed/chrome
___ Attached/chrome

CABINETS AND INTERIOR DETAIL:
___ Cabinets (oak)
___ Countertops
___ Medicine cabinets (2)
___ Vanity (all baths)
___ Mirrors (2)

STAIRS:
___ Oak handrail
___ Oak balustrade

FIREPLACE:
___ Ash dump and cleanout
___ Brick facing
___ Firebrick lining
___ Brick hearth
___ Wood mantel (solid)
___ Gas starter

SPECIFICATION CHECKLIST *(Continued)* ✔✔✔✔✔

CHIMNEY:
- ___ Brick facing
- ___ Block construction
- ___ Tile flue lining
- ___ Heater flue size
- ___ Gas furnace vent size
- ___ Water heater vent size

sentatives may leave much to be desired. They're generally a mixed bag. The more reputable the store, the more likely that better service will be available, but it's still not guaranteed. There can be a considerable turnover of installers for the larger stores because as skilled trade persons get more steady work, many tend to leave the part-time positions for better jobs.

Review the discussions in the beginning of this chapter for selecting a contractor or handyperson. Although you can scale back the amount of investigation proportionally to the magnitude of the work being done, if it's a job that must be even partially undertaken while no family member is home, it's generally a safer and sounder practice to already know, screen, or have references on contractors involved. When this is not possible, arrange to be (or have a trusted observer) home during the entire job, no matter the length.

▶▶▶▶▶ POINTS TO PONDER

1. Inquire. Ask real estate brokers, lending officers, building-material suppliers, and subcontractors, especially plumbers, electricians, roofers, and siding contractors, to point out the most reputable home builders they know.

2. Continue asking. Inquire at local chapters of the NAHB, the Chamber of Commerce, and the Better Business Bureau. You may not get "official" specific recommendations, but you'll likely come away with a number of builder names based on the size and type of home you're planning to build.

3. Decide on a "field" of builders, and then make it a point to meet them, if only briefly. Take a look at homes constructed by the builders you are considering: Tour their open houses, and/or ask them to show you one of their brand-new or under-construction houses.

4. With the builders high on your potential list, contact several past customers of each to find out if any of the builders have distinct advantages over the others (e.g., perhaps one owns a builder's supply company, too).

5. Select the top three or four builders, and supply them with your home specifications. Tell them exactly what you want.

6. Don't be afraid to entertain suggestions from any of the bidding contractors. Just make allowances for those suggestions when comparing the submitted bids.

7. Chances are that at least two of the contractors will bid significantly lower than the other(s) and will warrant your closest inspection. Be suspicious, however, of any extremely low bids. Don't expect excellent construction at a discount price. Instead, be happy with a sound value at a fair price.

8. When your evaluations are through, make your best pick of the contractor you think you should go with based on his or her bid, reputation, construction examples, and any other factors you're considering.

9. Don't accept an oral agreement. Put everything that's agreeable to both you and the contractor in writing.

10. After your decision is made, inform all the contractors—not just the one you selected.

CHAPTER

36

Working with Your Contractor

After selecting the contractor you want, the next step is to draw up an agreement or contract. This agreement, along with the final plans, drawings, and specifications, will act as a guideline for your relationship with the builder. It has to be signed by all parties before the first shovelful of earth is turned. Many builders will have such an agreement already prepared, with specification blanks to be filled in.

On pages 840 to 841 is a sample contract agreement between a general contractor and a party who is arranging the construction of a new house. It's a good example, and covers most of the concerns either party could have, yet it still can be amended, its sections changed, added to, or deleted with the approval of both parties. As another example of how the building materials are described, pages 842 to 846 show a sample specifications form filled out for the same two-story house and called a "Description of Materials."

The sample contract addresses the scope of work involved and expected time for completion and lists reasons for legitimate delays. It also states the inability of the builder to assign his or her responsibilities to others, describes the contract documents, explains insurance particulars, presents procedures for making alterations or extra work, and discusses housekeeping and trash removal from the building site. It covers compliance with ordinances and statutes, arbitration in the event of any disputes, and what constitutes the acceptance and occupancy by the owner. It further provides a schedule by which the builder is paid and describes contractor warranties.

Although you've probably already discussed this—reemphasize the overall site excavation plan so that the site is disturbed as little as possible. Make sure that the topsoil gets reserved, that trees you want to save are roped off, and that

CONTRACT AGREEMENT
By and Between

Mr. <u>Richard C. Jones</u>

Mrs. <u>Jennifer H. Jones</u>

Address <u>2014 Warsaw Avenue</u>

<u>Erie, Pennsylvania</u>

AND

Realto Construction Company
1435 East 12th Street
Erie, Pennsylvania

Building Site <u>Lot #35, Oakland Hills</u>

THIS AGREEMENT MADE THIS _____ day of _____,
20 _____ by and between <u>Richard C. Jones and Jennifer H. Jones</u> of the City of Erie, County
of Erie, and State of Pennsylvania, hereinafter called "Owners"

AND

Realto Construction Company, a corporation with principle offices in the City of Erie, County of
Erie, and State of Pennsylvania, hereinafter called "Contractor."

<u>WITNESSETH</u>   The Owners and Contractor for and in consideration of the mutual covenants of
each other, and for and in consideration of the work to be done by the Contractor and the money
to be paid by the Owners, as hereinafter set forth, it is agreed between the parties as follows:

1. <u>SCOPE OF WORK</u>   The Contractor covenants and agrees to furnish all the labor, perform all
the work that shall be required for the erection of a 2 story frame dwelling which is more fully
set forth in plans, attached hereto and marked Exhibit "A", and specifications attached hereto and
marked Exhibit "B", both of which documents have been initialed by the parties. Said dwelling
house to be built on the property of the Owners, <u>Lot #35 Oakland Hills Subdivision.</u>

The Contractor covenants and agrees to do and complete all the work set forth in said plans
and specifications for the erection of said dwelling house, in a good and workmanlike manner, and
within a reasonable time after the construction job has been started. The Contractor specifically
covenants and agrees to pursue the work diligently without delay after the construction of said dwelling
house has been started by them. All work shall be new and all workmanship done and performed
under this Contract, by the Contractor, shall be of good quality and shall be performed in a good
and workmanlike manner. The Contractor shall protect all the parts of the work from damage by
cold or other elements. The Contractor shall also be responsible for temporary electrical service.
All the work and materials furnished by the Contractor shall meet or exceed the minimum FHA
requirements. The Contractor shall be responsible for the building permit, gas permit, and sewer
permit and for the expense entailed in obtaining said permits. The Contractor further covenants
and agrees to sign a Release of Mechanic's Lien before any work is started.

2. <u>TIME OF COMPLETION</u>   The work shall be started as soon as possible, weather permitting,
and shall be completed as soon as possible, Acts of God, strikes, material shortages, government
regulations, or catastrophes excepted. The Contractor covenants and agrees to pursue the work of
erecting said dwelling house in a diligent manner after the same has been started.

3. <u>DELAY OF COMPLETION</u>   If after the dwelling house has been substantially completed and
livable, full completion thereof is materially delayed through no fault of the Contractor, the Owners
shall, and without terminating the Contract, make payment for the balance due the Contractor for
that part of the work fully completed and accepted by the Owners.

4. <u>ASSIGNMENTS</u>   The Contractor shall not assign this Contract to others. However, this shall
not prohibit the sub-contracting of parts of the work to others by the Contractor.

5. <u>CONTRACT DOCUMENTS</u>   The Contract documents shall consist of the Contract Agreement,
the Specifications, and the Plans and they are all as fully a part of the Contract Agreement as if
attached hereto and herein repeated. The Parties herewith covenant and agree that upon execution
of this agreement they shall, each of them, initial the specifications and the plans.

6. <u>INSURANCE</u> The Contractor shall insure himself against all claims under Workman's Compensation Acts and all other claims for damage for personal injuries, including death, which may arise from operations under this Contract, whether such operations be by themselves, or by anyone directly or indirectly employed by him. The Contractor shall save the Owners of this protection. The Owners shall maintain fire insurance and vandalism insurance on the structure as soon as the sub-floor is completed, and the Contractor shall be reimbursed from said insurance from any and all loss due to fire.

7. <u>EXTRA WORK OR ALTERATIONS</u> The Owners shall have the right to make changes or alterations, but any order for change or alterations shall be in writing and signed by the Owners and the Contractor; said amount shall be stated in the written order, and to be paid to the Contractor (or Owner if it shall be a saving) before final payment is made. The extra charges, if any, shall be considered a part of the contract cost.

8. <u>CLEANING UP</u> The Contractor shall, at all times, keep the premises free from all unnecessary accumulation of waste material or rubbish caused by his employees or the work and at the completion of the work he shall remove all rubbish from and about the building, and all tools, scaffolding, surplus material, and shall leave the work ''broom clean.''

9. <u>ORDINANCE AND STATUTES COMPLIANCE</u> The Contractor shall conform in all respects to the provisions and regulations of any general or local building acts or ordinances, or any authority pertinent to the area. The Contractor covenants and agrees that he has examined the land, plans and specifications, and understands any and all difficulties that may arise in the execution of this Contract. The Contractor specifically covenants and agrees that in laying out the house, he shall observe the building line required in the sub-division. The Owners, however, shall be responsible for providing an exact survey of the building site.

10. <u>ARBITRATION CLAUSE</u> In the event any dispute arises between the parties hereto which cannot be amicably settled between the parties, it is hereby agreed that each party shall appoint an arbitrator within three days after receipt of written request from the other, that the two arbitrators so appointed shall select a third arbitrator within three days after notice of their appointment, and that the arbitrators shall hear the dispute and, by majority decision, make a decision or award. It is agreed that any compensation required by the arbitrators shall be shared equally by the parties thereto regardless of the decision or award made.

11. <u>ACCEPTANCE BY OWNERS AND OCCUPANCY</u> It is agreed that upon completion, said dwelling shall be inspected by the Owners and the Contractor, and that any repairs or adjustments which are necessary shall be made by the Contractor. It is further agreed that the Owners shall not be permitted to occupy said dwelling until the Contractor is paid the full amount of the Contract. Occupancy of said dwelling by the Owners in violation of the foregoing provisions shall constitute unconditional acceptance of the dwelling house and a waiver of any defects or uncompleted work.

12. <u>TIME OF PAYMENTS</u>
    1st Stage—Platform: 10%
    2nd Stage—Under roof: 35%
    3rd Stage—Plastered: 25%
    4th Stage—Trim completed: 20%
    5th Stage—Completion: 10%
    (Or according to bank regulations that closely resemble the above schedule.)

13. <u>WARRANTY</u> The final payment shall not relieve the Contractor of responsibility for faulty materials or workmanship; and he shall remedy any defects due thereto within a period of one year, material free with minimum service charge. This warranty is only valid when the Contractor is paid contract cost in full.

This contract shall be binding upon parties, their heirs, executors and assigns. And by this agreement, the parties intend to be legally bound in witness whereof, the parties have hereunto set their hands and seals the day and year first written above.

VETERANS ADMINISTRATION, U.S.D.A. FARMERS HOME ADMINISTRATION, AND
U.S. DEPARTMENT OF HOUSING AND URBAN DEVELOPMENT
HOUSING – FEDERAL HOUSING COMMISSIONER

*(For accurate register of carbon copies, form may be separated along above fold.
Staple completed sheets together in original order.)*

Form Approved
OMB No. 2502-0192

☐ Proposed Construction

☐ Under Construction

DESCRIPTION OF MATERIALS

No. _____
(To be inserted by FHA, VA or FmHA)

Property address _____ City _____ State _____

Mortgagor or Sponsor _____ _____
(Name) (Address)

Contractor or Builder _____ _____
(Name) (Address)

INSTRUCTIONS

1. For additional information on how this form is to be submitted, number of copies, etc., see the instructions applicable to the HUD Application for Mortgage Insurance, VA Request for Determination of Reasonable Value, or FmHA Property Information and Appraisal Report, as the case may be.

2. Describe all materials and equipment to be used, whether or not shown on the drawings, by marking an X in each appropriate check-box and entering the information called for each space. If space is inadequate, enter "See misc." and describe under Item 27 or on an attached sheet. THE USE OF PAINT CONTAINING MORE THAN THE PERCENTAGE OF LEAD BY WEIGHT PERMITTED BY LAW IS PROHIBITED.

3. Work not specifically described or shown will not be considered unless required, then the minimum acceptable will be assumed. Work exceeding minimum requirements cannot be considered unless specifically described.

4. Include no alternates, "or equal" phrases, or contradictory items. (Consideration of a request for acceptance of substitute materials or equipment is not thereby precluded.)

5. Include signatures required at the end of this form.

6. The construction shall be completed in compliance with the related drawings and specifications, as amended during processing. The specifications include this Description of Materials and the applicable Minimum Property Standards.

1. EXCAVATION:
Bearing soil, type ___Gravel, Clay___

2. FOUNDATIONS:
Footings: concrete mix ___Specify Mix___; strength psi ___3500#___ Reinforcing _____
Foundation wall: material ___10" Concrete Block___ Reinforcing ___Rods & Cement in Core___
Interior foundation wall: material _____ Party foundation wall _____
Columns: material and sizes ___Steel, Specify Size___ Piers: material and reinforcing _____
Girders: material and sizes ___Steel, Specify Size___ Sills: material ___2 x 10___
Basement entrance areaway _____ Window areaways ___Galvanized Steel___
Waterproofing ___Sprayed Asphalt Coating___ Footing drains ___4" Plastic Pipe in Gravel___
Termite protection _____
Basementless space: ground cover _____; insulation _____; foundation vents _____
Special foundations _____
Additional information: ___Sill Sealer Insulation___

3. CHIMNEYS:
Material ___Stone & Block___ Prefabricated (make and size) _____
Flue lining: material ___Tile___ Heater flue size ___Specify Size___ Fireplace flue size ___Specify Size___
Vents (material and size): gas or oil heater ___Specify Size___; water heater ___Specify Size___
Additional information _____

4. FIREPLACES:
Type: ☒ solid fuel; ☐ gas-burning; ☐ circulator (make and size) _____ Ash dump and clean-out ___1 Each___
Fireplace: facing ___Stone___; lining ___Firebrick___; hearth ___Brick___; mantel _____
Additional information: ___Include Gas Starter___

5. EXTERIOR WALLS:
Wood frame: wood grade, and species ___#2 BTR SPF (2x6)___ ☐ Corner bracing. Building paper or felt ___Building Paper Covering___
Sheathing ___Plywood___; thickness ___1/2"___; width ___4' x 8'___; ☒ solid; ☐ spaced _____" o. c.; ☐ diagonal; _____
Siding ___Aluminum___; grade ___A___; type ___Bevel___; size ___DBL-4___; exposure ___8___"; fastening ___Alum. Nails___
Shingles _____; grade _____; type _____; size _____; exposure _____"; fastening _____
Stucco _____; thickness _____"; Lath _____; weight _____ lb.

Masonry veneer __Stone__ Sills __Stone__ Lintels _____ Base flashing _____

Masonry: ☐ solid ☐ faced ☐ stuccoed; total-wall thickness _____"; facing thickness _____"; facing material _____

Backup material _____; thickness _____"; bonding _____

Door sills _____ Window sills _____ Lintels _____ Base flashing _____

Interior surfaces: dampproofing, _____ coats of _____; furring _____

Additional information: _____

Exterior painting: material __Specify brand__ ; number of coats __2__

Gable wall construction ☒ same as main walls, ☐ other construction _____

6. FLOOR FRAMING:

Joists: wood, grade, and species __SPF 2×10__ other _____; bridging __1×3__; anchors __Specify__

Concrete slab: ☒ basement floor, ☐ first floor, ☒ ground supported; ☐ self-supporting; mix __Specify Mix__; thickness __4__";

reinforcing _____; insulation _____; membrane _____

Fill under slab: material __Gravel__; thickness __8__". Additional information: _____

7. SUBFLOORING: (Describe underflooring for special floors under item 21.)

Material: grade and species __Plywood__; size __4×8-½__; type __CDX__

Laid ☒ first floor, ☒ second floor; ☐ attic _____ sq. ft.; ☐ diagonal; ☒ right angles. Additional information: _____

8. FINISH FLOORING: (Wood only. Describe other finish flooring under item 21.)

Location	Rooms	Grade	Species	Thickness	Width	Bldg. Paper	Finish
First floor	All Rooms	5/8"	Particle Board			#15 Felt	
Second floor	All Rooms	5/8"	Particle Board			#15 Felt	
Attic floor		sq. ft					

Additional information: _____

9. PARTITION FRAMING:

Studs: wood, grade, and species __SPF 2×4-Inside__ 2×6-outside size and spacing __2×4 - 16"o.c.__ Other _____

Additional information: _____

10. CEILING FRAMING:

Joists: wood, grade, and species __2×10 - 2nd Floor__ Other _____ Bridging __1×3__

Additional information: _____

11. ROOF FRAMING:

Rafters: wood, grade, and species __I-Beam Roof Rafters__ Engineered Wood Roof trusses (see detail): grade and species __16" o.c.__

Additional information: _____

12. ROOFING:

Sheathing: wood, grade, and species __Plywood__; ☒ solid; ☐ spaced _____" o.c.

Roofing __Asphalt Shingles__; grade __C__; size __4×8-½__; type __CDX__

Underlay __#15 Felt__; weight or thickness _____; size _____; fastening _____

Built-up roofing _____; number of plies _____; surfacing material _____

Flashing: material __Tin__; gage or weight _____; ☐ gravel stops; ☐ snow guards

Additional information: _____

13. GUTTERS AND DOWNSPOUTS:

Gutters: material __Aluminum__; gage or weight __.025__; size __4"__; shape __Style K__

Downspouts: material __Aluminum__; gage or weight __.025__; size __4"__; shape __Rectangular__; number __4__

Downspouts connected to: ☐ storm sewer; ☐ sanitary sewer; ☐ dry-well. ☐ Splash blocks: material and size _____

Additional information: _____

14. LATH AND PLASTER

Lath ☒ walls, ☒ ceilings: material _____; weight or thickness __5/8"__. Plaster: coats __1__; finish _____

Dry-wall ☐ walls, ☐ ceilings: material _____; thickness _____; finish _____;

Joint treatment _____

15. DECORATING: (Paint, wallpaper, etc.)

Rooms	Wall Finish Material and Application	Ceiling Finish Material and Application
Kitchen		
Bath	BY OWNER	
Other		

Additional information: _____

16. INTERIOR DOORS AND TRIM:

Doors: type __Flush__; material __Oak__; thickness __1-3/8"__

Door trim: type __Modern__; material __Oak__ Base: type __Modern__; material __Oak__; size __3"__

Finish: doors __Stain - Sealer - Varnish__; trim __Stain - Sealer - Varnish__

Other trim (item, type and location) _____

Additional information: __3 Hinges Per Door__

17. WINDOWS:
Windows: type _DBL-Hung + Cas_; make _____; material _Vinyl_; sash thickness _1-3/8"_
Glass: grade _Insulated_; ☐ sash weights; ☒ balances, type _____; head flashing _Vinyl_
Trim: type _Modern_; material _Oak_ Paint _Stain-Sealer-Varnish_ number coats _____
Weatherstripping: type _____; material _Vinyl_ Storm sash, number _____
Screens: ☒ full; ☐ half; type _____; number _13_; screen cloth material _Aluminum_
Basement windows: type _Hopper_; material _Steel_; screens, number _____; Storm sash, number _____
Special windows _____
Additional information _6' Aluminum Glass Sliding Door_

18. ENTRANCES AND EXTERIOR DETAIL:
Main entrance door: material _Steel_; width _36"_; thickness _1-3/4"_. Frame: material _W.Pine_, thickness _5/4"_
Other entrance doors: material _Steel_; width _36"_; thickness _1-3/4"_. Frame: material _W.Pine_, thickness _5/4"_
Head flashing _Aluminum_ Weatherstripping: type _Vinyl_; saddles _____
Screen doors: thickness ___"; number ___; screen cloth material ___ Storm doors: thickness ___"; number ___
Combination storm and screen doors: thickness ___"; number ___; screen cloth material ___
Shutters: ☐ hinged; ☒ fixed. Railings _Aluminum (vented)_, Attic louvers _____
Exterior millwork: grade and species _____ Paint _____; number coats _____
Additional information _Roof Louvers_

19. CABINETS AND INTERIOR DETAIL:
Kitchen cabinets, wall units: material _____; lineal feet of shelves _70_; shelf width _12_
Base units: material _____, counter top _____; edging _____
Back and end splash _Formica_ Finish of cabinets _Factory_; number coats _____
Medicine cabinets: make _14 x 18 Bath 2_; model _Mirror - Bath 1 + Lav 1 + 2_
Other cabinets and built-in furniture _Vanity - Bath 1 + Lav 1 + 2_
Additional information _____

20. STAIRS:

Stair	Treads		Risers		Stringers		Handrail		Balusters	
	Material	Thickness	Material	Thickness	Material	Size	Material	Size	Material	Size
Basement	SPF	1-1/2	W.Pine	3/4	SPF	2x10	W.Pine	2"		
Main	Oak	1-1/2	W.Pine	3/4	W.Pine	2x12	W.Iron			
Attic										

Disappearing: make and model number _____
Additional information _____

21. SPECIAL FLOORS AND WAINSCOT: *(Describe Carpet as listed in Certified Products Directory)*

	Location	Material, Color, Border, Sizes, Gage, Etc.	Threshold Material	Wall Base Material	Underfloor Material
FLOORS	Kitchen + Eating Area	Inlaid Lino (# - Sq yd Allowance)		Oak	Particle Brd.
	Bath 1 + 2	" " " " " "		"	" " "
	Lav 1 + 2	" " " " " "		"	" " "
	Foyer	" " " " " "		"	" " "

	Location	Material, Color, Border, Cap. Sizes, Gage, Etc.	Height	Height Over Tub	Height In Showers (From Floor)
WAINSCOT	Bath				

Bathroom accessories: ☒ Recessed; material _Chrome_; number _5_; ☒ Attached; material _Chrome_; number _5_
Additional information _____

22. PLUMBING:

Fixture	Number	Location	Make	Mfr's Fixture Identification No.	Size	Color
Sink	1	Kitchen	or Equal		32 x 21	St. Steel
Lavatory	4	Baths - Lavs	or Equal		18"	White
Water closet	4	" "	" "		Cadet	White
Bathtub	1	Bath 1	Fiberglass		5'	White
Shower over tub ▲	1	Bath 1				
Stall shower △	1	Bath 2	Fiberglass		4'	White
Laundry trays						

▲ ☒ Curtain rod   △ ☒ Door   ☐ Shower pan: material _Fiberglass_
Water supply: ☒ public; ☐ community system; ☐ individual (private) system. ★
Sewage disposal: ☒ public; ☐ community system; ☐ individual (private) system. ★

★ *Show and describe individual system in complete detail in separate drawings and specifications according to requirements.*

House drain (inside): ☒ cast iron; ☐ tile; ☐ other _____ House sewer (outside): ☒ cast iron; ☐ tile; ☐ other _____
Water piping ☐ galvanized steel, ☒ copper tubing; ☐ other _____ Sill cocks, number __3__
Domestic water heater: type __Gas__ ; make and model _____ ; heating capacity __40__
_____ gph. 100° rise. Storage tank: material __Glass Lined__ ; capacity __40__ gallons.
Gas service ☐ utility company, ☐ liq. pet. gas, ☐ other _____ Gas piping: ☐ cooking; ☐ house heating.
Footing drains connected to ☐ storm sewer; ☒ sanitary sewer; ☐ dry well. Sump pump; make and model _____
_____ capacity _____ ; discharges into _____

23. HEATING:
☐ Hot water ☐ Steam ☐ Vapor. ☐ One-pipe system. ☐ Two-pipe system.
   ☐ Radiators. ☐ Convectors. ☐ Baseboard radiation. Make and model _____
   Radiant panel ☐ floor; ☐ wall; ☐ ceiling. Panel coil: material _____
   ☐ Circulator. ☐ Return pump. Make and model _____ ; capacity _____ gpm.
   Boiler: make and model _____ Output _____ Btuh.; net rating _____ Btuh.
Additional information _____
Warm air ☐ Gravity ☒ Forced. Type of system __Natural Gas, 2-Stage, Variable Speed__
   Duct material supply __Galv. Steel__ ; return __Galv. Steel__ Insulation __Fiberglass__, thickness _____ ☐ Outside air intake.
   Furnace: make and model __Brand, Model__ Input __130,000__ Btuh.; output _____ Btuh.
   Additional information: _____
☐ Space heater; ☐ floor furnace; ☐ wall heater. Input _____ Btuh.; output _____ Btuh.; number units _____
   Make, model _____ Additional information: _____
Controls: make and types _____
Additional information _____
Fuel: ☐ Coal; ☐ oil; ☒ gas; ☐ liq. pet. gas; ☐ electric; ☐ other _____ ; storage capacity _____
   Additional information: _____
Firing equipment furnished separately: ☐ Gas burner, conversion type. ☐ Stoker: hopper feed ☐; bin feed ☐
   Oil burner: ☐ pressure atomizing; ☐ vaporizing _____
   Make and model _____ Control _____
   Additional information: _____
Electric heating system: type _____ Input _____ watts; @ _____ volts; output _____ Btuh.
   Additional information: _____
Ventilating equipment: attic fan, make and model _____ ; capacity _____ cfm.
   kitchen exhaust fan, make and model _____
Other heating, ventilating or cooling equipment __Vent Fan   L2v 1 + 2__

24. ELECTRIC WIRING: Specify
Service ☒ overhead; ☐ underground   Panel: ☐ fuse box; ☒ circuit-breaker; make __GLS__ AMP's __Amps__ No. circuits __20__
Wiring ☐ conduit; ☐ armored cable; ☒ nonmetallic cable; ☐ knob and tube; ☐ other _____
Special outlets ☒ range; ☐ water heater; ☐ other __Dryer__
☐ Doorbell. ☒ Chimes. Push-button locations __Front Door__   Additional information: _____

25. LIGHTING FIXTURES:
Total number of fixtures __22__   Total allowance for fixtures, typical installation, $ ___ __Retail__
Nontypical installation _____
Additional information: _____

26. INSULATION:

LOCATION	THICKNESS	MATERIAL, TYPE, AND METHOD OF INSTALLATION	VAPOR BARRIER
Roof			
Ceiling	10"	Fiberglass	Included
Wall	6"	Fiberglass	Included
Floor			

27. MISCELLANEOUS: (*Describe any main dwelling materials, equipment, or construction items not shown elsewhere; or use to provide additional information where the space provided was inadequate. Always reference by item number to correspond to numbering used on this form.*)
__Shelf + Rod in Closet__

HARDWARE: (make, material, and finish.) _Brass (Quickset or Equal)_

SPECIAL EQUIPMENT: (State material or make, model and quantity. Include only equipment and appliances which are acceptable by local law, custom and applicable FHA standards. Do not include items which, by established custom, are supplied by occupant and removed when he vacates premises or chattles prohibited by law from becoming realty.)

    JKP27 Double Oven

    GSD551W Dishwasher

    GFC310 Disposal

    C221 Range

PORCHES: Concrete Front Porch

TERRACES:
    By Owner

GARAGES:
    Framed as house, 4" concrete floor, 2-9'x7' Overhead Doors

WALKS AND DRIVEWAYS: By Owner
Driveway: width _____ ; base material _____ ; thickness _____"; surfacing material _____ ; thickness _____"
Front walk: width _____ ; material _____ ; thickness _____". Service walk: width _____ ; material _____ ; thickness _____"
Steps: material _____ ; treads _____"; risers _____". Cheek walls _____

OTHER ONSITE IMPROVEMENTS:
(Specify all exterior onsite improvements not described elsewhere, including items such as unusual grading, drainage structures, retaining walls, fences, railings, and accessory structures.)
    Rough Grading Only

LANDSCAPING, PLANTING, AND FINISH GRADING: By Owner
Topsoil _____" thick: ☐ front yard; ☐ side yards; ☐ rear yard to _____ feet behind main building.
Lawns (seeded, sodded, or sprigged): ☐ front yard _____ ; ☐ side yards _____ ; ☐ rear yard_____
Planting: ☐ as specified and shown on drawings; ☐ as follows:
_____ Shade trees, deciduous, _____" caliper.   _____ Evergreen trees. _____' to _____', B & B.
_____ Low flowering trees, deciduous, _____' to _____'   _____ Evergreen shrubs. _____' to _____', B & B.
_____ High-growing shrubs, deciduous, _____' to _____'   _____ Vines, 2-year _____
_____ Medium-growing shrubs, deciduous, _____' to _____'   _____
_____ Low-growing shrubs, deciduous, _____' to _____'   _____

IDENTIFICATION.—This exhibit shall be identified by the signature of the builder, or sponsor, and/or the proposed mortgagor if the latter is known at the time of application.

Date_____   Signature _____

                                   Signature_____

DESCRIPTION OF MATERIALS
HUD-92005 (6-79)
VA Form 26-1852, Form FmHA 424-2

excavation lines are clearly indicated. Discuss where lumber and components will be stored, where heavy equipment will park, and where tool trailers and deliveries to the site will occur. Make sure that you know where the driveway will be. Again, try to keep the affected area as small as possible.

When it comes to your contract, you should slowly review each section with the builder and question anything that isn't crystal clear.

INSURANCE AND WARRANTIES

The contractor probably carries general liability and completed operations insurance. Certainly, if you're working with a relatively new contractor, ask to see his or her insurance certificates to be safe.

Your contractor also may claim that he or she will take care of the insurance—all of it—during the early stages of construction. Even if he or she means well, consider that the contractor's insurance is purchased specifically with the contractor's best interest in mind, not that of the home owner.

It's a good idea to obtain your own home owner's policy before the ground is broken. This will make for an overall combination of the contractor's insurance and yours. The contractor's policy may only cover mistakes that he or she and subcontractors make plus general liability—but not accidental damage that could occur to the house at any stage of construction. Conversely, your home owner's policy probably will not cover any contractor errors. The contractor's insurance will enable him or her to make repairs if they're needed because his or her workers or a subcontractor he or she hires make errors resulting in a sunken footer, a collapsed basement wall, or a faulty roof. Your home owner's policy likely will cover only hazards and accidents.

For the relatively inexpensive cost of protection, it's best to watch out for your own interests from the very start.

Warranties are another important consideration. Few houses are constructed perfectly. No matter how good or conscientious the builder is, small problems will inevitably occur, such as sticking doors, a defective appliance, a crack in the basement floor or driveway, or even a minor settling of a wall. Many builders will fix practically anything, no questions asked, some within time periods far beyond that outlined in the original warranty. Others will make the owner work (from repeated phone calls to begging) for the repairs, yet still do them begrudgingly. Some contractors turn around and blame the owner for any problems and refuse to honor the warranty on those grounds—when they can get away with it. Of course, the vanishing builder is nowhere to be found to be made aware of his or her mistakes.

All new houses carry an "implied warranty of habitability," which forces builders to repair major construction defects such as a caved-in basement. Smaller problems, however, especially after the standard warranty period of one

INSURANCE

Insurance is something people hate to buy but can't do without. Ideally, you want as much as you need but as little as possible. How do you determine which coverage and how much coverage are best?

Many people go for years and years paying for home owner's insurance they know practically nothing about. Plus, they rarely, if ever, collect on it.

The best way to inspect a potential home owner's policy is to simply read the entire proposal, including the fine print. In this day and age, it's foolish not to protect yourself against a major loss. The amount of protection you have on your home owner's policy in addition to the basics—theft, fire, and liability—depends on the type of policy you elect. Some policies are more comprehensive than others. Some may cover items such as damage from frozen pipes, electrical surges, lightning, and wind-blown trees. Keep in mind that the higher the deductible—the amount you have to pay on each claim or accident before the insurance company begins payment—the lower is the cost of the premiums.

■ **Home owner's policy.** A home owner's policy is a package of theft, fire, and liability coverages. It should be reviewed annually because inflation, rising property values, and additional possessions you may have purchased will gradually add to your property's total value. Unless your policy has a built-in factor for inflation, you should consider raising your coverage to keep pace with the value of your property and possessions.

Here are a number of ways you can cut home owner's insurance expenses:

— If your home is protected by approved fire or burglar alarm systems you may be eligible for a 5 to 10 percent discount depending on whether the system automatically notifies the fire or police department.

— Newer homes sometimes qualify for discounts of up to 16 percent of the total home owner's insurance cost. Make sure that your agent gives you the company's new-home rate.

— Using the same insurance company for auto, life, and home owner's insurance may save between 2 and 15 percent of the total cost.

— Consider going with a higher deductible. Again, as a rule of thumb, the higher the deductible, the lower is the premium.

■ **Fire insurance.** Fire insurance is just that. But besides covering full damage from fire and lightning, it also should cover miscellaneous related hazards such as water damage and vandalism.

■ **Liability insurance.** The ice cream vendor slips on a patch of ice on your porch and decides to sue you. Under personal liability insurance, you are insured for up to a set amount of dollars if a visitor such as the ice cream vendor falls down your front steps, slips on your sidewalk, or is bitten by your dog. It also covers certain medical expenses if you or a member of your family accidentally injures someone or damages someone else's property.

■ **Property insurance.** Property insurance is generally extended coverage against loss or damage to your property. It doesn't include personal liability. Property insurance can cover some of a home's contents, including furniture, clothing, appliances, books, and electronics. Additional supplements, floaters, or riders can be purchased to cover artwork, cameras, furs, jewelry, musical instruments, silverware, sports equipment, stamp and coin collections, and other valuable possessions. Keep in mind when applying for a floater policy to establish how much it would cost to replace the items you are having insured, not simply how much you originally paid for them.

It's a good idea to make a list of your possessions. Take an inventory of all appliances, pieces of furniture, and other items of value. Photographs are an excellent way to catalog your home's contents. Once you've made an inventory, put it in a safe place such as a bank deposit box or a fireproof container. Revise the inventory whenever you make significant changes. Most insurance companies have checklists or booklets to help prepare your inventory.

■ **Burglary and theft insurance.** This insures property against theft. Some policies include an off-premises clause that's active against theft of your possessions that may occur anywhere in the world.

---

year, can leave home owners with no alternative but to make repairs themselves and eat the costs. Although an owner has little recourse for the small problems after the first year is up, there is an alternative for major defects.

See if your builder can subscribe to any home warranty programs initiated by a home builders association in your area. If so, new home warranties can be extended to up to 10 years of protection. The builder typically pays a single one-time premium that's passed along to the home buyer in the dwelling's cost. But the major house structure, the potentially dehabilitating plumbing, heating, cooling, and electrical systems, plus the general workmanship and materials are protected.

If for some reason the builder can't or doesn't follow through on repairs, the home warranty will cover their cost after a relatively small deductible is paid by the owner. Warranties available from your builder or other individuals and institutions should be thoroughly researched and considered before the contract is completed.

AFTER THE CONTRACT IS SIGNED

After the contract is signed, it's time for the house construction to begin. Between that time and the date of completion, you'll be locked into a unique and, you hope, satisfying relationship with the general contractor or, if it's a large construction company, with whichever individual is responsible for supervising the construction.

Naturally, in this relationship, like any, there are things you should do and things you shouldn't. While you want to become involved enough to let the contractor know that you understand the building process and are aware of the progress he or she is making, you don't want to become an impediment to that progress. You don't want to irritate the contractor by making unreasonable demands or by asking too much of his or her time. Certainly, you don't want to make the contractor angry with you.

To keep the relationship on the up and up, here are a few suggestions that have worked for other home buyers in the past and are likely to work for you as well.

Keep Communications Honest, Open, and Current

The most critical part of your relationship is to keep the lines of communication honest, open, and current. Yes, the builder should return your calls . . . eventually. To say "promptly" is probably asking too much. On the other hand, you shouldn't have to trap him or her to get his or her attention. Builders, however, are notoriously hard to pin down. They *are* busy, especially during times when construction is booming, and especially if they're any good. In fact, if they call you right back, something's probably amiss. Maybe it's written somewhere, in a secret oath, that one irritating characteristic of a master builder is his or her delinquency in getting back to you. But, and here is how he or she differs from the vanishing or marginal builder who never calls back, once the good builder does return your call, he or she gives you his or her full attention (undoubtedly irritating some other customer who is waiting for a callback) and usually will go way beyond what could be expected as a normal response to your concerns, or he or she will explain to you in depth just why it is that you're wrong.

You want the builder to treat you honestly and fairly. If he or she makes a mistake, he or she should tell you about it and then stand by his or her work until the error is corrected. And a good contractor expects the same from you. Sure, it's kind of a biblical attitude—Treat others as you would have them treat you—but it works. So be honest and aboveboard. Don't sandbag. If something looks wrong, don't wait until the entire house is completed before bringing it to the builder's attention. If you do, more complications invariably will result because the builder didn't repair the error shortly after it occurred. In fact, bring up concerns as soon as you have them. This also shows the builder that you've prepared yourself to intelligently discuss the ongoing construction with him or her. You don't want to relinquish all control.

Try not to be at the site just anytime. Instead, time your visits to coincide with important steps of the building process that you'd like to watch to make sure that no skimping is done and so you'll understand fully what was done for future reference. For example, good times to be there are when the foundation is being poured over the reinforcement rods, when some of the wall insulation is going up, and when the first layer of roofing is being laid.

If you have a complaint, don't stand on the job site and argue with the builder in front of the crew. Motion him or her off to the side or call him or her by phone later and explain why you have misgivings, and then give the builder a reasonable amount of time to correct the situation if he or she was wrong.

Contractors almost always take care of minor, irritating problems, at the very least because they'd rather have a satisfied customer than a person bad-mouthing them throughout the neighborhood. Satisfied home owners can be used as references to develop more business.

Don't Try to Get Extras from the Contractor

You should decide exactly what you want *before* the contractor begins construction. But if you must make a change along the way—and a *few* minor changes are often made with little fuss by the contractor—tell the contractor as soon as possible. For some people, the temptation to make one change after another becomes an obsession. Could the builder make the family room a few feet longer? Maybe. Maybe not. Perhaps there isn't enough room at the side of the house to extend any closer to an adjacent lot. Perhaps the house then would require different roof trusses than the ones already delivered. Could the builder install a bay window in the living room, now that you've just received a surprise income tax refund? Or, since the contract, you have decided not to have any more children and would the builder make the original four bedrooms into three? Can a shower stall be put in the basement? It would only take a few more lengths of pipe and a floor drain, right?

These kinds of changes, when insisted on, especially when requested at a middle or last stage of construction, and especially when one change is piled atop another, have ruined many a healthy relationship between builder and owner. To avoid such conflicts of interest, try to make all your changes before the construction starts, or at least keep the changes to a bare minimum and make them as early as possible after the construction begins—plus, be prepared to reimburse the contractor for any additional costs incurred because of those changes.

Empathize with the Builder

The builder has his or her own problems: People not showing up for work, the weather, suppliers running out of materials or sending the wrong things, and subcontractors making mistakes that the builder takes the blame for. Try to see things from his or her point of view, too.

Keep a Friendly Eye on the Work

Don't do it in a hypercritical way. While on the site, jot down questions or concerns for later discussion with the builder. The construction of a house is an interesting process, and you should watch a good deal of it simply to understand how it's put together in case you ever want to modify any part of it or effect major repairs. If you know what went into the house, no one can buffalo you later on as to what's there and where.

Your main reason for keeping tabs on the construction shouldn't be as watchdog—although you can't help appearing a little like one—but as a student, because you've already guaranteed yourself a good builder and good workmanship by virtue of your initial contractor selection.

One thing to consider—and this gives you a reason for being on the site and carefully watching the major steps—is to keep a photographic record of the house as it is put together. Perhaps the builder would agree to do it in some fashion. With digital photography and digital cameras with high-powered optical zooms and storage cards that can hold hundreds of images, it's relatively simple to prepare a comprehensive record. Start with the excavation and proceed through the foundation, walls, framing, and shell, and keep a record of where the electrical wiring, plumbing, heating system, framing members, and other components are before the drywall covers them up. It might come in handy some day if you need to rearrange interior walls or expand or modify parts of the home. You'll have a record of what's in the walls, floors, and roof. Try to take some overall views that will line up with the construction plans and drawings. It makes a great record while you're living there and to pass along whenever the place is put up for sale.

Be Friendly and Tactful, Yet Firm

You want to foster an amiable relationship so that you wouldn't be afraid to use the same contractor to build another house, should you ever want one. To this effect, you should treat the contractor with the same courtesy you'd treat a good friend or relative. However, do remember that you're picking up the tab; you're paying for everything—the supplies, the labor, the contractor's overhead, and a fair profit all come out of your pocket. Be friendly and tactful, yet firm, and the contractor will respect you for it.

These pointers should help you to develop a solid working relationship with your builder. But remember, your builder has seen a lot of customers, a lot of problems, and a lot of crazy situations while in the business. As a group, builders know customer psychology, having seen many more customers than you've seen builders. Many contractors who probably follow a list of their *own* pointers (e.g., listen to whatever the customer says, and then build it your own way) are experts at convincing you to see things their way.

An example of this occurred when one particularly taciturn builder, a man of few words yet a master at his craft, was called on by an owner who was considering knocking out a bedroom wall to expand the sleeping space into an adjacent living room. The builder knew from past dealings with the owners that the husband would be continuously wondering if such a modification would be the right thing to do.

After listening to what the couple wanted done and agreeing that it was a smart move to make, the builder slowly got up and sidled over to the plaster wall in question. He leaned against the wall near a framed oil painting and asked the seated owners if they were sure they wanted the job done. The owner looked at his wife and uttered a tenuous yes. Then the builder, in fluid motion, lifted his steel claw hammer from his belt and smashed a hole in the wall the size of his fist, right then and there, in front of the startled owners.

After the shock wore off, the owners realized why he had done it. The builder's action left little room for them to change their minds overnight and also took some of the worry out of the very decision itself. They *had* to do something to fix the hole.

REMODELING NOTES

The main difference between a remodeling project and new construction is that typically, during a remodeling project, the contractor will be working at your home while everyone is living there, including pets. A few guidelines: Try to arrange schedules so that family members won't need the rooms being worked on when the contractor is present. Keep the cat or dog in the basement or garage. It's usually best not to give out house keys. If a trusted contractor must be in the home alone to work, arrange to let him or her inside at a certain time in the morning, with perhaps you coming home for lunch in case a supply run must be made during the day. Or have someone the contractor could call, a relative or trusted neighbor, if something is needed sooner. Refrain from going into a lot of conversation with the contractor while he or she is there or from having anything else around to distract him or her, such as a television that's on all the time or a running computer with open Internet access. Make sure that you know what the contractor should be doing, but don't micromanage the job. Obviously, keep money, bills, other unresolved mail, and any personal information or records out of sight.

As long as things are going according to plan, be observant but not overbearing and omnipresent. Some contractors become self-conscious when watched, and it will cause them to work slower, even if they do not consciously try to do so. Arrange for a waste-disposal strategy with the contractor. Have a plan for recycling unused parts and scrap or for reclaiming and donating components that still work but are simply being upgraded for more efficient models.

▶▶▶▶▶ **POINTS TO PONDER**

1. Have a written agreement, contract, or "blueprint" for the expected work agreed on by you and your contractor before any actual work takes place.

2. Read and understand all sections and items in the agreement before signing it.

3. Make sure that your contractor's insurance covers mistakes the contractor and his or her subcontractors might make.

4. Obtain your own home owner's policy to cover accidental damage that could occur to the house at any stage of construction.

5. Keep lines of communications with the contractor honest, open, and current.

6. Don't expect or try to get extras or freebies from the contractor.

7. Empathize with your builder. Don't jump to conclusions if there are problems; get the whole story before making judgment calls. Be reasonable. Recognize problems that may not be within the contractor's control, and participate in a positive manner in their resolution.

8. Keep a friendly eye on the work; don't smother the contractor with your presence, and refrain from nagging.

9. Try to arrange for a photographic record of the major building steps; especially document what goes into the walls before they're sealed.

10. On the other hand, be friendly and tactful, yet firm. Insist that you get what was agreed upon. Nothing less.

11. Once the home is completed, don't be a stranger. If you're satisfied, let the builder know that you appreciate his or her efforts. It pays to keep in touch.

Understanding How Everything Works and Setting Up Your Maintenance Program

This is where you make sure that you know how everything works and how to make it keep working and how you set up your maintenance program. The Leadership in Energy and Environmental Design (LEED) for Homes guidelines award certification points for operations and awareness training on how the key green components work, how they should be operated, and how best they should be maintained. It's best to set up a maintenance program before the contractors leave and before the final inspection. After all, why wait until all the contractors are gone? In this way, the house and its components are still fresh in the builders' and subcontractors' minds, and you can readily get all the information you need to customize a schedule and checklists for your particular house and equipment.

What better time to record the serial numbers and to file away the instruction manuals, purchase receipts, and pertinent information such as the installers' phone numbers and manufacturers' spare parts lists? And after you plan your maintenance program, while in the first part of the final inspection with your builder, pretend that it's your first maintenance inspection and draw what feedback you can from him or her about what you're inspecting for.

If your entire project is being run as LEED for Homes certified, then the builder should do much of the preparation work for you. You should receive an operations and maintenance binder that lists all the LEED for Homes features, including manufacturers' manuals for space-heating and -cooling equipment, mechanical ventilation equipment, water-heating equipment and captured-water systems, renewable-energy systems, and safety equipment such as radon, smoke, and fire-protection/alarm systems. The supporting manuals and information, including warranty certificates for major appliances and other components having usage and care instructions, also should be included. The builder also should provide some direction on energy-efficient appliance selection, lighting choices, and care of landscaping by using water-efficient irrigation methods and avoidance of harmful pesticides and chemical fertilizers. Some words are also expected on biodegradable and user-friendly cleaning supplies and methods. Special care should be taken to include language that can easily be understood (versus highly technical data) for components you may never have encountered before, such as the renewable-energy system, tankless water heater, or any of a variety of heat-recovery systems. Ideally, the book can be prepared and given to you so that you have a chance to review it before your final inspection with the builder takes place.

RECORD KEEPING

Part of any good maintenance program is accurate record keeping. Keeping records will tell when inspections were last done and when they're due again. Records include pertinent backup such as appliance operating manuals, parts lists, servicing and repair histories, warranty and cost information, and vendor names, phone numbers, and addresses.

Some problems will occur so infrequently that you'll need to jog your memory as to a solution. What did you do the last time the flame in your clothes dryer went out? Was that 3 years ago when you installed that new water heater or 5? Is it still covered by the warranty? And where is the warranty? Did you throw it out with your old high school papers? Or was it in with the boxful of papers you kept in the garage—the boxful of papers the field mice chewed to smithereens when they constructed their nest last winter.

Reasons to develop good record-keeping habits are many. The most important are as follows:

1. *For your convenience.* It's much more convenient to keep everything together in a house file or binder. With your new home, this means all the documents you obtain from the builder, plus all the written information you accumulate after taking over. Exactly how you organize the material is nowhere near as important as the fact that all house construction-, ownership-, and maintenance-related materials can be found in the same place.

2. *For your income taxes.* You never know when your home could turn into investment property. What if you decide to sell, but nobody wants to buy? So you rent your home for a summer, and make other living arrangements for yourself. A year passes. The renters renew their lease, and suddenly you drop the idea of

selling and plan instead to handle it as a long-term rental income property. Once this happens, you need to track capital or long-range improvements you make in the property. And maintenance expenditures become tax deductible. Even if you never rent your home, it's still a sound idea to keep track of all home-related costs. It will help you to budget for future expenses, and you can better plan repair jobs when needed.

3. *To save money.* If your builder or contractor needs to be approached about warranty work, it's important to have organized information to fall back on. Most problems are usually taken care of by reputable construction or repair companies. If a nonroutine situation comes up, you should follow certain procedures to have something corrected:

- Check whether the problem is covered under the builder or contractor warranty.
- Identify the exact nature of the problem in a letter to the builder or contractor. Include your name, address, and work phone number. Type the letter, if possible. Typed letters are considered to be more official. They get faster and more serious results. Make the letter brief and to the point, but include all relevant details. State exactly what you want done and how soon you expect the problem to be resolved. Be reasonable. Don't ask for anything beyond what's in the warranty. Include copies of all documents regarding the problem. Keep a copy of the letter for your records. If you have an insured warranty, send a copy of your letter to the warranty company as well as to the builder or contractor.

Having readily accessible home documents and records can make life much easier. If you already have a house file, a cold February day is the time to update it.

Years ago, there wasn't the common expectation of maintenance-free houses as there is today. Sure, it has a lot to do with modern materials and improved manufacturing processes, but also, people today want to spend less time being caretakers to their belongings, houses included, and more time pursuing career and leisure activities. People no longer want to spend a month of their summer scraping and painting a house from foundation to weathervane. They don't want to varnish a porch every year. Or to reseal and caulk windows every fall. Instead, everyone wants trouble-free houses, and for the most part, we have them. In fact, compare a drive down a new subdivision street with another ride down a block of older dwellings. There, many of the 60- and 70-year-old houses stand, grouped together on narrow lots, with narrow driveways, tiny front yards, and big porches that are chipped and peeling.

Nowadays, fiber/cement, factory-coated steel, composite, aluminum, vinyl, and a host of other weather- and time-beating materials are standard fare. However, even though you go to great lengths to obtain the most advanced, efficient, green maintenance-free components available for your new home, it doesn't mean that you can just live there trouble-free without caring for the place. While there aren't as many ways for a house to deteriorate as there were in previous years, some maintenance inspections and fine-tuning are in order to prevent long-range problems from developing.

Several valid reasons for preventive maintenance exist. Just as people should schedule themselves a physical examination every so often to detect and take care of potential health problems before they can turn into serious conditions with catastrophic results, so should the major components of a house be inspected to identify and take care of conditions that could lead to serious failures. More specifically, here are the main reasons for preventive maintenance:

1. To prevent failures at inopportune times that could result in safety hazards, such as improper wiring, a malfunctioning furnace or water heater, or a plugged fireplace flue.

2. To allow you to make repairs at your convenience instead of on an emergency basis.

3. To prevent minor failures that are inexpensive and simple to correct from becoming complex, expensive repairs.

4. To make sure that your house is a safe and comfortable place to live in.

5. To keep the energy-efficient systems "tuned up" and running at their maximum efficiency to continue to use as little energy as possible.

6. To maintain your house's value and ensure your pride of ownership.

7. To avoid the expense of a breakdown and repair on a holiday or weekend.

Components in a house seldom fail suddenly. There are usually warning signs. If you know what to watch for and act when you see danger, life on the home front will be easier and much less expensive. The smart home owner is the one who knows his or her house intimately and who routinely follows a checklist of inspections to make sure that no problems are developing. To do this, you should understand the construction and the operation of all appliances and major pieces of equipment. You should know where things are, even hidden items such as septic tanks, wells, sewer lines, and other underground utilities. You should know what the builder and manufacturer guarantees and warranties cover and what your home owner's insurance is all about.

Preventive maintenance is the idea that you lessen the likelihood of major damage by repairing minor problems. But to repair or even prevent the minor problems, you need to be aware of what they are and where to look for them.

It's a known fact that most breakdowns you're going to encounter will be small ones—many of which you probably can repair or learn to repair yourself. You won't have to worry about replacing washers in a washerless faucet, but you still must contend with such items as plugged drains, cracking asphalt or concrete driveways, sticky windows, and worn-out blower belts on furnaces. Preventive maintenance can't guarantee that breakdowns will never occur, and it won't even prevent surprise failures, but it *will* minimize the time, effort, and money you'll spend on major repairs.

Yes, there's something nice about knowing that your house is in top shape. It instills a feeling of confidence. The proof is reflected in a house's condition. Find a rundown, shoddy-looking house that's not too old, and chances are that it got that way through a lack of maintenance—a cumulative deterioration that starts out slowly, almost imperceptibly, but gains momentum once it negotiates past the "maintenance-free" characteristics of new materials as the seasons roll by and each tiny problem mushrooms into others.

SAVING MONEY ON SERVICE CALLS

Planning preventive maintenance in advance gives you time to anticipate what's needed to perform the tasks and lets you make the best schedule possible for your time and pocketbook. Many home owners will do this hit or miss, counting that their everyday movements throughout the house will reveal anything that's obviously failing or failed without having to go out of their way to perform specific inspections.

When something does need attention, there's always the question, "Who should do the work?" The days of old-fashioned handymen who could fix anything for a song are disappearing. Instead, we have armies of specialists: plumbers for plumbing, roofers for roofing, electricians for electrical repairs, and septic people for sewage systems. Naturally, home owners must pay not only for their time but also for their training and expertise as well; the same person who comes to your house to fix a leaking pipe can easily be an individual qualified to lay out the plumbing for an entire high-rise apartment building. There's no doubt about it: Service calls are expensive.

Whenever possible, you can save money by learning how to do the most basic maintenance and repairs. Even if you never want to lay a finger on a furnace or hot-water tank, it's worth it just to learn about their operations. Then, when you must call a professional, you can accurately describe the problem so that the serviceperson can bring the right tools and materials and won't waste any time once arriving at your house. In fact, a serviceperson might even be able to tell you what to do over the phone.

The largest part of the typical service call bill usually consists of labor. And in most cases, the time spent just getting to and from your house makes up the lion's

FINDING A GOOD HANDYPERSON

Notice the difference in terminology here? In previous chapters we *selected* contractors from individuals and companies known to the open market. In this case we're *looking* for someone special, someone who most likely is already part of an underground network of "informal" or unofficial contractors. We're trying to find a jack-of-many-trades who can tackle a wide variety of jobs around the house: replacing a screen door, painting and caulking the bathrooms, painting the inside of your garage, and so on.

Such a person should be

- Even-tempered
- Reliable
- Qualified for what he or she does and will accept only work that he or she can complete safely and correctly
- Able to do or arrange for the entire job
- Able to get help when needed
- Doing it not only for additional or supplemental income but also for the love of the work (Be wary of "informal" contractors or handypersons who are trying to support a family solely through their moonlighting efforts.)

Where can such a person be found? You've got to ask around. Inquire of friends, coworkers, and casual acquaintances. Who do they use? Finding a good handyperson is part luck and part persistence. It's not easy, but the effort will pay off if successful.

You'll save a great deal of money, time, and aggravation over the years if you find a good handyperson who will help you with routine and emergency jobs. Often he or she, though not able to tackle a particular task, will come up with options and provide help deciding which avenue is best.

Unfortunately, good handypersons are a dying breed. Most maintenance people these days are specialists: plumbing, electrical, concrete, roofs, and framing.

If you find a good general, all-seasons handyperson, a person who's available at practically any time, who does quality work at reasonable cost, who cleans up after every job, who has a way of suggesting the best of all possible solutions, and who has a wealth of household repair knowledge, treat him or her well. In return, you'll get peace of mind, slimmer repair outlays, and an ongoing friendship that's frequently lacking with many home owner/contractor relationships.

When more specialized help is needed—for putting in a new driveway or a patio, for example—an alternative to hiring a large concrete or paving contractor is to ask a person who works in a plant or organization that frequently uses the services of paving contractors if any paving contractor employees do driveways or patios on the side. Often the same skilled labor available through higher-priced companies can be obtained at considerably less cost on weekends and during evening hours for anyone who learns how to make the contacts and arrangements.

Are there disadvantages to having "unofficial" contractors and handypersons do work for you? There could be. Handypersons are typically not insured as legitimate contractor businesses, so if damage or injuries occur as a result of their work, major problems could result. Will your home owner's insurance policy be adequate if an injury occurs? Like anything, you've got to weigh the risks. There are excellent handypersons who have been moonlighting their services for years—with nary a problem. But this is why homework on finding a safe, reliable, knowledgeable, and skilled handyperson is so important. As a general guideline, avoid "handyperson contracting" for electrical, plumbing, roofing, and structural work.

Also, make sure that you work within the maintenance and repair guidelines given by manufacturers' warranties. If you have a handyperson perform "unauthorized" services, even if the services are correct, they could void the remaining portion of a warranty.

share of that. The trick is to get as much efficiency out of a call as possible. Do that by finding several other jobs that can be done by the same serviceperson on the same service call. This is why it's important for you to know what kind of shape your equipment is in and what can be inspected, adjusted, and serviced. Then, when you call a plumber to fix a leaky pipe, he or she also can service the sump pump and inspect the hot-water tank.

If your preventive maintenance is good enough, you should be able to keep the servicepersons away from weekends, late-evening hours, and holidays—all time for which you must pay premiums.

Line up qualified servicepersons *before* you need them so that you'll know who to call without blindly paging through the phone book. Keep away from repairpersons who have the same characteristics as vanishing builders.

POTENTIAL TROUBLE SPOTS

For the record, here are most of the items in a typical house that need preventive maintenance inspections and attention.

Heating and Cooling Systems

Poorly maintained, defective heating and cooling units produce less warmth and coolness for the money and cost substantially more to operate. A more important consideration for the heating unit is that one not working properly can be extremely hazardous, with fire and asphyxiation two possibilities.

Many home owners take both heating and cooling systems for granted until the systems quit working, the former most likely at the front end of a New Year 3-day holiday weekend and the latter in the middle of a Death Valley–like heatwave.

FUEL BURNERS

Have igniters and burners cleaned and adjusted for safety and efficiency by qualified servicepersons. Oil burners need more frequent attention than gas burners because oil does not burn as cleanly, but even the most modern gas models still can benefit from yearly inspections and adjustments.

FURNACES

Forced-air furnaces are reliable workhorses that need to have their filters cleaned or changed at least once per month when in use. Otherwise, a dirty, clogged filter can reduce the efficiency of heat output by as much as 70 percent and will cause the entire heating unit to overexert itself trying to reach a 68-degree thermostat setting when outside temperatures plummet below freezing. The air that passes through the filter is cool air drawn from outside (sometimes pre-warmed) or inside of the house. After being filtered clean, it gets warmed by the fuel burner flame and then blown back into the house through ducts and registers. Naturally, if you live in a dusty environment or own a long-haired pet, you'll have to clean or replace air filters more frequently than if you live in a cleaner area and don't own a pet.

Most furnaces now are direct drive. If your furnace is belt driven, check the condition of the belt (adjust/replace if needed).

A qualified serviceperson should inspect the furnace yearly.

Some of the blower motor and fan assemblies have permanently lubricated bearings, whereas other bearings should be oiled before each heating season begins and periodically throughout the fall and winter months.

HUMIDIFIERS

If your furnace has a humidifier, it should be checked annually. Change the water panel; make sure that the unit is receiving water through its system and discharging excess water out the drain line.

BOILERS

Boilers are expensive and somewhat temperamental heating units, especially if their operating conditions are allowed to vary from those suggested by the manufacturer. Read the instructions and maintenance literature carefully, and have the boiler inspected by a professional before each heating season, and then do it by yourself at least once per month during the rest of the cold months while the boiler is in use. There should be a low-water emergency cutoff that will prevent the boiler from operating in case not enough water gets into the boiler for it to run safely. The low-water cutoff should have water drained through it—to expel any rust or corrosion that might settle there and plug the line (follow the manufacturer's instructions).

If pockets of air form in the pipes, radiators, and baseboards of hot-water systems, they must be bled or released so that the hot water can circulate freely.

OTHERS

Although electric heating systems traditionally have been some of the most expensive to operate because of the cost of "heating" electricity when compared with the cost of heating with natural gas or oil, they're practically maintenance-free. About all that's needed is to periodically vacuum dust and dirt from the heater and heating coils.

Solar, wind, and other renewable heating and cooling systems should be inspected and maintained as recommended by the manufacturers. With all equipment, be aware of where emergency shutoff valves and switches are and how to restart a system if needed. Ask the serviceperson what maintenance you should be doing between service calls and how you can confirm that everything is working safely and efficiently.

Plumbing

Naturally, the most obvious conditions to inspect plumbing for are leaky pipes and fixtures. You should know quickly if a leak develops by observing a puddle nearby or water dripping from ceilings or stained walls. For the most part, plumbing systems are reliable, with only a few points to keep in mind.

If outside temperatures approach freezing, shut off valves to outside connections and faucets. These shutoff valves should be located inside the house, close to where the pipe goes through the outside wall. When the inside shutoffs are closed, then open the outside fixtures to let any standing water drain from those outside pipes and fixtures.

Every few months remove a gallon or so of water from the drain valve at the bottom of your hot-water tank. Along with this expelled water will be any rust, sediments, and mineral deposits that settle on the tank bottom and hinder the efficiency of heat transfer.

Septic tanks should be examined professionally once a year to determine if pumping and cleaning are needed. If services are in order, you won't want to undertake them yourself. They're for specialists with equipment designed to handle such unpleasant tasks.

Sump pumps and well pumps also should be serviced as noted in their instruction manuals. If they're rarely used, put them into service several times per year to make sure that they'll work when needed.

Floor drains in the garage and basement should be tested at least twice per year to make sure that they'll work in case they are needed during an emergency. Just lift their covers and stick a running hose down them. If mud or debris has accumulated beneath the grate cover, shovel it out first.

Fireplaces and Stoves

In this modern age, it isn't surprising that most people who use wood-burning equipment have had little, if any, practical experience heating with wood. Consequently, a sizable number of fires occur each year owing to faulty installation, misuse, and lack of proper maintenance of fireplaces and stoves. Most fires are caused by one or more of heat radiation from the stove, stovepipe, or chimney igniting adjacent combustible materials; sparks escaping into the house; sparks from the chimney top; and flames catching on creosote accumulation in the chimney flue. (Creosote is a dark, sticky, resin-like material formed by unburned chemicals that are borne by smoke up the chimney flue. They coat the inside of the flue and create the danger of chimney or flue fires.)

Before each heating season, make sure that the chimney flue is not partially obstructed with bird or squirrel nests, beehives, a fallen branch, or a child's softball. And see that the dampers are in good working order. Remove any ashes and debris from the ash pit, and if the flue is thick with creosote and ash, have it cleaned.

Central Air-Conditioning

With air-conditioning it's filters, filters, filters. Dirty filters really can block the output of cool air and will greatly increase the effort and length of time needed to cool a house. If air-conditioning filters are too dirty or clogged to see the beam from a flashlight through, it's time to clean or replace them.

It's also necessary to check the air conditioner's outside condenser. Keep condenser vents free of vines, leaves, mud, grass, and any other encroaching materials that hinder air circulation. Keep drainage tubes clear.

When it's time to stop using air-conditioning for the year, remove dust and dirt from each unit with a vacuum cleaner, and securely cover the exterior housing until the next cooling season begins.

Electrical Systems

The wiring installed in most modern homes is largely trouble-free. Circuit breaker boxes are included as safety valves. If a circuit breaker trips because too much demand is placed on that part of the wiring from too many appliances plugged in at once or from operating a defective appliance, just follow the resetting instructions on the panel—usually you flip the circuit breaker switch back on. Of course, the cause of a tripped circuit should be identified and corrected.

Even if your breakers never trip for any reason, it's a good idea to manually trip them a few times per year to make sure that they're operable and that the contacts are in working order.

Also, whenever power is lost to the entire house, such as during a lightning or ice storm, there can be high-voltage surges that burst through the house wiring that can damage plugged-in appliances and equipment such as stereos and personal computers. During violent storms, it's best to unplug as many appliances as possible.

Roofs

As mentioned earlier, roofs take a beating—from rain, sleet, hail, wind, sun, and alternate freezing and thawing temperatures. Even if no inside water marks or leaks are noticed, you still should take a pair of binoculars periodically, and depending on the roof's pitch, inspect the entire surface from either the ground nearby or from the second-story windows of neighbor's homes. Look for bent, ripped, or missing shingles and for metal flashing that's warped, torn loose by the wind, or rusting and corroding.

If a leak does develop, consider that the actual damage might be a substantial distance away from where the water is dripping. If you decide to take care of your own minor repairs, fine. But be careful. Never venture out on a roof when it's wet or during winter when the shingles are frozen and ice-laden. If ice dams occur on the roof owing to constant melting snow running to the roof edges where it keeps freezing and accumulating, and water eventually backs up under the shingles and seeps through the roof into the house, this is a sign that too much heat is escaping near the roof's peak. The outer surface of the roof, even near the peak, should be kept cold during winter by the use of proper insulation above ceilings and by the installation of adequate roof ventilation.

Gutters and Downspouts

Gutters and downspouts absorb much of the same abuse as roofs do, mostly from the elements. Periodically remove collected debris such as twigs, leaves, acorns, and dirt from gutters and downspouts, and then flush them clean with water. Observe the gutter system while it's raining, and check for blockages, leaks, and places where it might be coming loose from the house. Check to see that the water running through the downspouts is flowing away from the house foundation. During winter, don't let large icicles build up and hang on the gutters and downspouts.

Siding and Trim

Few people are aware of just how dirty their siding and trim can get in a year. Weather, dust, soil, and corrosion all conspire to destroy that "new house look" and insidiously damage outer surfaces, causing these materials to wear out far sooner than expected. It's hard to tell, however, because everything gets dirty at the same rate.

To keep your siding and trim in good shape, choose a nice summer day, hop into your bathing suit, get your garden hose and a soft brush attached to an extension handle, fill a pail with mild detergent and water (as specified by the siding manufacturer), and go to town.

Doors and Windows

Here, as with many parts of a modern house, maintenance has changed radically for the better from what it was years ago—an unending scenario of scraping, painting, varnishing, dewarping, unsticking wooden doors and window sashes, sills, and frames, and playing with rotten ropes and pulleys from heavy window weights. Today's doors and windows barely need wiping with a damp cloth.

Basement windows are the most notable exceptions. You still have to keep their outside wells or excavations free of leaves, weeds, and rotting grass, and make sure that water doesn't collect and rise above the window bottoms. In areas where heavy snowfalls occur, consider using plastic covers designed for protecting basement window wells. Periodically inspect these window frames and sills for rust if metal and decay if wood.

Wood Porches and Decks

If you used high-quality, pressure-treated wood, you're practically home free. It's a good idea to reseal it once per year, and beyond that, just watch out for and correct cracked boards or boards that have come loose from walls, foundations, or steps. If you haven't used pressure-treated wood, stock up on paint brushes and lots of low–volatile organic compound (VOC) paint or sealant. And keep some funds available to replace rotting boards as needed.

Mildew

Mildew is simply a mold, and mold is a fungus of some type. Mold spores are practically everywhere, borne in the air, and need only a cool or warm, moist environment to flourish. Mildew is not only irritating, but it's also harmful. It can ruin furniture, furnishings, walls, and ceilings and even can present a health problem to occupants. It's especially persistent in leaky, damp basements but will occur readily during periods of high humidity, when the water vapor present in warm air condenses on the cool surfaces of walls, floors, pipes, and other items that can provide perfect breeding grounds for fungi.

To combat mildew, merely increase the air circulation. Don't place rubber-backed carpets on basement floors. Keep furniture away from walls where air circulation could be blocked, and operate dehumidifiers around the clock during humid summer months. Small fans will help in cramped locations. Mildew in an attic is a sure sign that ventilation there should be improved.

Asphalt

This material might seem tough, and it is … kind of. It'll support your car nicely and even a large boat and trailer, but it can be ruined gradually by a combination of frost damage, oil and gasoline residues, and road-salt drippings.

Whenever asphalt loses its original dark-black sheen and begins to dry out, developing small cracks and fissures, and starts absorbing oil and gasoline that spills onto its surface, it's time for maintenance. To be safe, inspect blacktop every year during warm weather. Any cracks, holes, or broken edges should be repaired with blacktop patching compound. This will prevent water from running beneath the pavement and undermining the asphalt. This is particularly critical in cold-climate areas where freezing water can "frost wedge," lift, and crack blacktop to bits.

After the patching is complete, a coat of blacktop sealer should be brushed or broomed over the surface to form a protective coating that will repel water, oil, and gasoline. The sealer also fills cracks that are too small to be repaired with the patching material.

Concrete and Masonry

Concrete and masonry surfaces are substantially more durable than asphalt *if* cracks are repaired when they occur and are not allowed to go untouched through periods of freezing and thawing temperatures. With concrete driveways and walks, to prevent water penetration and frost wedging, large cracks should be filled with concrete patching material that you can mix yourself. Small cracks can be caulked.

If a flaking problem exists, it may be due to poor-quality concrete or the harsh effects of rock salt or other chemical snow and ice melters. Brush and clean the surface, preferably with a solution of muriatic acid (be sure to read the directions and safety precautions), and then apply a plastic cement surface material available at hardware and building-supply stores.

Oil and grease stains on concrete can be removed with a degreaser. A number of spray degreasers can be found in auto-supply stores. Simply spray the material on the stains, wait 15 minutes or so, and then hose it off. If you're wondering why all the fuss over a black stain here and there—it's for safety, because an oil stain can cause slips and falls, especially when it gets wet. And it's also for aesthetics, for looks. The nicer the appearance, the greater is the value, and the easier it is to keep concrete clean and well maintained.

To prepare for the finishing touch, after all the stains are taken out and the cracks and flaking areas are fixed, the concrete can be cleaned with another diluted solution of muriatic acid. Once this is completed, you can put down a protective coating of clear cure-and-seal to get your concrete safely through winter.

Mortar joints in brickwork likewise are susceptible to the elements, and they should be inspected closely, especially any bricks in direct contact with the ground.

Mortar joints between foundation concrete blocks are the weakest part of foundation walls. These joints should be firm and should not crumble when poked with a sharp tool. If the mortar does crumble easily, or if some has cracked and fallen out, the damage should be repaired to prevent water or termite intrusion. If the foundation is made of solid poured concrete, all cracks should be patched or caulked for the same reasons.

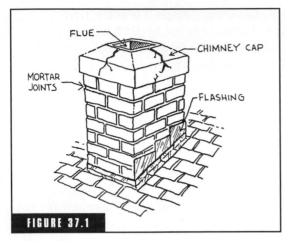

FIGURE 37.1

A chimney cap.

Chimney maintenance usually comes under concrete and masonry. The chimney cap is the part of the chimney that extends above the roof. It takes a terrible beating from the elements and deserves annual inspections. The concrete cap at the very top protects the inside of the chimney from water and downdrafts. If this cap cracks (Fig. 37.1), water can seep into the mortar joints along and between the bricks. All cracks should be patched or caulked.

The mortar between the chimney bricks or stones below the concrete top cap also should be inspected and caulked if necessary. The same goes for the flashing where the roof meets the base of the chimney cap.

After all areas are patched or caulked as needed, a coat of clear chimney water-repellent sealer should be brushed over the chimney to protect the whole works from water penetration.

A MAINTENANCE CHECKLIST

Remember that a well-maintained house does not come naturally to most of us. It might be a pain, but it's the best defense against the toll otherwise taken by the elements, nature, and time. Prepare a year-long maintenance schedule based on where you live, the type of house you have, and the equipment that is in it; then try to follow it. Concentrate on exterior repairs and maintenance during the nice weather, and then go inside during the colder months. Naturally, a new house won't require much attention, especially at first. And you can keep it that way with regular preventive maintenance schedules and by following through with repairs.

REMODELING NOTES

Just because you never had a maintenance binder on your current residence doesn't mean that you wouldn't benefit from creating one yourself. You could start it along with your first remodeling project. In a binder, create a section on the project, including date completed, contractor and manufacturer contacts, warranty information, operating manual or instructions, and costs of installation. Then gradually, whenever other improvement or maintenance tasks are undertaken, add related information to the binder. This is a way of collecting important household maintenance and operating data and organizing it in one place. Not only will you find it helpful to your household management, but you'll also be able to present a prospective buyer or new owner with the binder some time in the future.

THE FINAL INSPECTION

A completed house is the complex result of thousands of separate pieces and parts put together by many craftspeople—craftspeople who have their good days and bad. The materials, too, are not always perfect. Consequently, with this or any effort resulting from sundry components and multiple construction steps (an automobile is another example), there are likely to be errors and imperfections in the final product—"bugs" that must be discovered and taken care of. In addition, a house will go through an initial settling and shrinking period, and as it does, plaster can crack, windows can stick, wood steps can start squeaking, or the plumbing can spring a leak.

Before everyone gets together at your closing—when the attorneys, the contractor, and you all sign the final papers so that you can receive the deed and house keys and the contractor any remaining payments—it's a good idea that you schedule what will be the first step of the final inspection of the property. The first step is a meeting at the site between you and the contractor or crew chief in charge of the construction. Schedule the meeting at least a week in advance (and don't forget to *remind* the builder a day or two in advance) and ask him or her to bring along any warranties for major appliances or materials such as a water heater, refrigerator, range, or garage door opener. You should bring any warranties you've already received and the maintenance file you've been putting together.

At this meeting, resolve any questions you have already jotted down on previous visits, and determine as best you can that what was specified in the contract actually was performed. At the same time, inspect the property for obvious flaws. Ask the contractor what imperfections you can reasonably expect, and get his or her advice on what to do about them if they actually occur. To whom do you report the problems? How would the most likely problems be solved?

The initial and continuing parts of the final inspection are important because *you* are expected to be the moving force in finding, reporting, and making sure that steps are taken to correct any imperfections that develop. The lender won't be worried about minor, irritating defects. All the lender expects is to receive your monthly mortgage check—usually by mail. And even if something major does go wrong, your payments can't be stopped. Rather, they continue like clockwork. The builder, too, can't fix what he or she doesn't know about. And you can't tell him or her about problems you don't recognize.

Fortunately, if you've followed the advice presented in the chapters on selecting and working with your contractor, problems that arise likely will be handled quickly and professionally. This is not so likely if you have elected or have been unsuspectingly duped into going with an inept or vanishing builder.

Before the meeting is over, review the warranties that were supplied at the time the building contract was signed, and check to make sure that you have copies of all the other applicable warranties. Be certain that you know who all the subcontractors were and exactly who you should call for maintenance and repairs at a later date. Go through your maintenance file with the contractor. Ask him or her if there's anything else he or she would add to it, or if he or she sees any part of it that doesn't look quite right. Find out if there's anything special you should do to "break in" certain components of the house.

Maybe during the initial inspection you'll discover that the builder has forgotten to include something promised. It happens. Or maybe the builder is planning to finish a few items that were not completed in time because of scheduling or weather delays. You want to make sure that you'll receive what you contracted for—nothing less. If anything has not been completed, find out what the completion schedule is, and for all but the most minor detail, have the attorneys keep a portion of the builder's final payment in escrow—to be released when the remaining work has been completed.

Make sure that you know how to operate all the appliances, including heating and cooling units, sump pumps, and well pumps. Know also where a septic tank is located or where the sewer connects to the house.

So you take an hour or two to go through the house with the builder. That's the first step of the final inspection. The rest of the steps are inspections that you'll be making alone, especially during the first year that you live in the place or until the builder's warranty period is up, whether it's a single year or longer.

During that year, keep a sharp eye and ear out for the development of small flaws that could become serious problems if not taken care of. Don't be afraid to contact the builder later on either. Remember, the builder wants you to be satisfied. It's in his or her best interest to have you say nice things about him or her so that you can be counted on as a future business reference.

But really, if you've followed a good portion of the proven specifications and ideas in this book, there shouldn't be much need for the builder to come back and redo things. You're likely to have a high-quality home, one that will suit your needs, will hold its value, will require a minimum of upkeep, and will provide you with maximum living comfort, convenience, safety, and privacy.

It's more likely that after the final checkout period of 1 year, you can spend most of your free time enjoying your home, knowing that you've received the most value for your dollars and efforts and that you're far ahead of the average person who will just take what's available or what marginal or vanishing builders offer in floor plan, construction quality, and value (Fig. 37.2).

As a parting note, after your home is checked out fully, about a year after the day you move in, send to the builder—as long as he or she has taken care of you—a brief note, letter, or call expressing your appreciation and telling him or her how much you are enjoying the house, if that's the case.

FIGURE 37.2

Enjoying the home.

You might even want to send him or her a case of beer, a fruit basket, a dinner for two at a classy restaurant, or something you know would be appropriate and safe. You'd be surprised at how few people will *ever* call a builder with something nice to say. Instead, builders, even the best builders, hear mostly brickbats and complaints.

Surprise your contractor with a token of appreciation. People in the service industries don't usually get them, no matter how good their services are (especially after the services have been transacted). Such a gesture will keep you in that builder's mind for a long, long time and will likely cement a friendship, and anyway, if he or she has done a good job for you, it's the right thing to do. It's just another way for you to lift up the entire house-building process from the routine and cap off the entire experience with style.

INDEX

Note: **Bold** page numbers indicate illustrations; *t* indicates a table.

ABS (acrylonitrile butadiene styrene plastic), 655–656
accent lighting, 521, **521**
accessibility, planning for, 52, 94
acrylic carpeting, 713, 715, 718–719
active-solar design, 125–126, 473, 564–565
Adobe homes, 95
advanced wall framing, 242–244
air cleaners, 592, 594
air conditioning, 584–586, 864. *See also* heating and cooling systems
Air Conditioning Contractors of America (ACCA), 540
air-infiltration barriers, exterior wall finishing and, 321–324. *See also* house wrap; vapor barriers
air leakage around windows, 347, 370
air-source heat pumps, **552**, 552–554, **553**
airtight drywall approach (ADA), 634
alarm systems, 504
alternate housing, 116–129
aluminum flashing, 293
aluminum garage doors, 433
aluminum screening, 381
aluminum shingles, 289
aluminum siding, 306–308, **308**, **309**, 324
American Forest and Paper Association, 175
American National Standards Institute (ANSI), 21
American Plywood Association. *See* Engineered Wood Association
anchor bolts
    foundation, 123, **124**, 193, **194**, 211, **211**, 212
    steel-frame construction, 123, **124**
annual fuel utilization efficiency (AFUE) rating, 539
appliances, 686–699, **687**. *See also individual appliances*
    checklists, 496–498, 690
    cost, 178
    electrical wiring, 496–498
    Energy Star program (USDOE), 18
    in garage, 87–88
    product evaluations, 688
    service contracts or extended warranties, 688–690, 869
arches, brick, **313**, **314**
architects, in preparing prints and drawings, 165
architectural style, 95. *See also* house styles and types
area surveys, 5
asbestos, 177
ash pits, fireplace, 58–59, 88, 580
asphalt driveways, 798, 799, 805–806, 866–867

asphalt shingles, 284–286, **285**, 290, 297
attic fans, **279**, 279–280, **280**, 594
attics, 89–90, 262
    electrical service to, 89, 442
    Energy Star program (USDOE), 17
    finishing for living space in, 152–154, **153**
    folding and extension-type stairways for, 89–90, **339**, 339–340, **441**, 441–442
    gable vents in, **276**, **277**, 277–278, **291**
    garage, 89, 441–442
    house style and type, 105, 108
    insulation and, 617–621
    lighting, 442
    ridge vents in, **276**, 277
    roof fans in, **279**, 279–280, **280**
    roof turbines in, 278, **278**
    roof vents in, **276**, 278
    soffit vents in, **276**, **278**, 278–279, 290–292, **291**, 619–620
    stairways and, 89, 90, **339**, 339–340, **441**, 441–442
    in truss-built construction, 272
    ventilation, 89, 275–280, **276**, **277**, **278**, 442
    window fans in, 279
autoclaved aerated concrete (AAC) blocks, 245
automatic garage door openers, 435–438, 439, 440
automatic on/off switches, lighting, 503, 518, 525
automatic timer switches, bathroom fan, **671**, 671–673
automatic ventilation fans, 673, **673**
awnings
    for doors, 402–404
    for windows, 327–328, 384, **384**
awning-type windows, **351**, 351–352, 377

backfilling, foundation, 217, 221–222
background lighting, 516
backsplash
    bathroom, 654
    kitchen, 682
baffles, 280, 290–292, 619–620, **620**
balloon wall framing, 240, **242**
bamboo, 179, 182
bamboo flooring, 729, 731, 735
base/baseboard trim, 643–646, **644**
baseboard heating systems, **551**, 551–552, 590, 596–597
base cap trim, **644**, 646
basements, 88–89. *See also* foundations
    bathrooms in, 154
    doors, 404–405